# Poetry
## for Students

# Poetry for Students

**Presenting Analysis, Context and Criticism on Commonly Studied Poetry**

*Volume 5*

*Mary K. Ruby, Editor*

*Foreword by David Kelly, College of Lake County*

## The Gale Group

DETROIT • SAN FRANCISCO • LONDON • BOSTON • WOODBRIDGE, CT

# Poetry for Students

## Staff

**Series Editor:** Mary Ruby.

**Contributing Editor:** Lynn Koch.

**Managing Editor:** Drew Kalasky.

**Research:** Victoria B. Cariappa, *Research Team Manager.* Andy Malonis, *Research Specialist.* Tamara C. Nott, Tracie A. Richardson, and Cheryl L. Warnock, *Research Associates.*

**Permissions:** Maria Franklin, *Permissions Manager.* Kimberly F. Smilay, *Permissions Specialist.*

**Production:** Mary Beth Trimper, *Production Director.* Evi Seoud, *Assistant Production Manager.* Cindy Range, *Production Assistant.*

**Graphic Services:** Randy Bassett, *Image Database Supervisor.* Robert Duncan and Michael Logusz, *Imaging Specialists.* Pamela A. Reed, *Photography Coordinator.* Gary Leach, *Macintosh Artist.*

**Product Design:** Cynthia Baldwin, *Product Design Manager.* Cover Design: Michelle DiMercurio, *Art Director.* Page Design: Pamela A. E. Galbreath, *Senior Art Director.*

## Copyright Notice

This book is printed on acid-free paper that meets the minimum requirements of American National Standard for Information Sciences—Permanence Paper for Printed Library Materials, ANSI Z39.48-1984.

ISBN 0-7876-3566-9
ISSN 1094-7019
Printed in the United States of America.

10  9  8  7  6  5  4  3  2

# National Advisory Board

# Table of Contents

# *Just a Few Lines on a Page*

I have often thought that poets have the easiest job in the world. A poem, after all, is just a few lines on a page, usually not even extending margin to margin—how long would that take to write, about five minutes? Maybe ten at the most, if you wanted it to rhyme or have a repeating meter. Why, I could start in the morning and produce a book of poetry by dinnertime. But we all know that it isn't that easy. Anyone can come up with enough words, but the poet's job is about writing the *right* ones. The right words will change lives, making people see the world somewhat differently than they saw it just a few minutes earlier. The right words can make a reader who relies on the dictionary for meanings take a greater responsibility for his or her own personal understanding. A poem that is put on the page correctly can bear any amount of analysis, probing, defining, explaining, and interrogating, and something about it will still feel new the next time you read it.

It would be fine with me if I could talk about poetry without using the word "magical," because that word is overused these days to imply "a really good time," often with a certain sweetness about it, and a lot of poetry is neither of these. But if you stop and think about magic—whether it brings to mind sorcery, witchcraft, or bunnies pulled from top hats—it always seems to involve stretching reality to produce a result greater than the sum of its parts and pulling unexpected results out of thin air. This book provides ample cases where a few simple words conjure up whole worlds. We do not ac-

tually travel to different times and different cultures, but the poems get into our minds, they find what little we know about the places they are talking about, and then they make that little bit blossom into a bouquet of someone else's life. Poets make us think we are following simple, specific events, but then they leave ideas in our heads that cannot be found on the printed page. Abracadabra.

Sometimes when you finish a poem it doesn't feel as if it has left any supernatural effect on you, like it did not have any more to say beyond the actual words that it used. This happens to everybody, but most often to inexperienced readers: regardless of what is often said about young people's infinite capacity to be amazed, you have to understand what usually does happen, and what could have happened instead, if you are going to be moved by what someone has accomplished. In those cases in which you finish a poem with a "So what?" attitude, the information provided in *Poetry for Students* comes in handy. Readers can feel assured that the poems included here actually are potent magic, not just because a few (or a hundred or ten thousand) professors of literature say they are: they're significant because they can withstand close inspection and still amaze the very same people who have just finished taking them apart and seeing how they work. Turn them inside out, and they will still be able to come alive, again and again. *Poetry for Students* gives readers of any age good practice in feeling the ways poems relate to both the reality of the time and place the poet lived in and the reality of our emotions. Practice is just another word for being a student. The information given here helps you understand the way to read poetry; what to look for, what to expect.

With all of this in mind, I really don't think I would actually like to have a poet's job at all. There are too many skills involved, including precision, honesty, taste, courage, linguistics, passion, compassion, and the ability to keep all sorts of people entertained at once. And that is just what they do with one hand, while the other hand pulls some sort of trick that most of us will never fully understand. I can't even pack all that I need for a weekend into one suitcase, so what would be my chances of stuffing so much life into a few lines? With all that *Poetry for Students* tells us about each poem, I am impressed that any poet can finish three or four poems a year. Read the inside stories of these poems, and you won't be able to approach any poem in the same way you did before.

David J. Kelly
College of Lake County

# Introduction

## Purpose of the Book

The purpose of *Poetry for Students* (*PfS*) is to provide readers with a guide to understanding, enjoying, and studying poems by giving them easy access to information about the work. Part of Gale's "For Students" Literature line, *PfS* is specifically designed to meet the curricular needs of high school and undergraduate college students and their teachers, as well as the interests of general readers and researchers considering specific poems. While each volume contains entries on "classic" poems frequently studied in classrooms, there are also entries containing hard-to-find information on contemporary poems, including works by multicultural, international, and women poets.

The information covered in each entry includes an introduction to the poem and the poem's author; the actual poem text; a poem summary, to help readers unravel and understand the meaning of the poem; analysis of important themes in the poem; and an explanation of important literary techniques and movements as they are demonstrated in the poem.

In addition to this material, which helps the readers analyze the poem itself, students are also provided with important information on the literary and historical background informing each work. This includes a historical context essay, a box comparing the time or place the poem was written to modern Western culture, a critical overview essay, and excerpts from critical essays on the poem, when available. A unique feature of *PfS* is a specially commissioned overview essay on each poem by an academic expert, targeted toward the student reader.

To further aid the student in studying and enjoying each poem, information on media adaptations is provided when available, as well as reading suggestions for works of fiction and nonfiction on similar themes and topics. Classroom aids include ideas for research papers and lists of critical sources that provide additional material on the poem.

## Selection Criteria

The titles for each volume of *PfS* were selected by surveying numerous sources on teaching literature and analyzing course curricula for various school districts. Some of the sources surveyed included: literature anthologies; *Reading Lists for College-Bound Students: The Books Most Recommended by America's Top Colleges;* textbooks on teaching the poem; a College Board survey of poems commonly studied in high schools; and a National Council of Teachers of English (NCTE) survey of poems commonly studied in high schools.

Input was also solicited from our expert advisory board, as well as educators from various areas. From these discussions, it was determined that each volume should have a mix of "classic" poems (those works commonly taught in literature classes) and contemporary poems for which information is often hard to find. Because of the interest in expanding the canon of literature, an emphasis was also placed on including works by international, multicultural, and women authors. Our advisory board members—current high school and college teachers—helped pare down the list for each volume. If a work was not selected for the present volume, it was often noted as a possibility for a future volume. As always, the editor welcomes suggestions for titles to be included in future volumes.

## How Each Entry Is Organized

Each entry, or chapter, in *PfS* focuses on one poem. Each entry heading lists the full name of the poem, the author's name, and the date of the poem's publication. The following elements are contained in each entry:

- **Introduction:** a brief overview of the poem which provides information about its first appearance, its literary standing, any controversies surrounding the work, and major conflicts or themes within the work.

- **Author Biography:** this section includes basic facts about the poet's life, and focuses on events and times in the author's life that inspired the poem in question.

- **Poem Text:** when permission has been granted, the poem is reprinted, allowing for quick reference when reading the explication of the following section.

- **Poem Summary:** a description of the major events in the poem, with interpretation of how these events help articulate the poem's themes. Summaries are broken down with subheads that indicate the lines being discussed.

- **Themes:** a thorough overview of how the major topics, themes, and issues are addressed within the poem. Each theme discussed appears in a separate subhead and is easily accessed through the boldface entries in the Subject/Theme Index.

- **Style:** this section addresses important style elements of the poem, such as form, meter, and rhyme scheme; important literary devices used, such as imagery, foreshadowing, and symbolism; and, if applicable, genres to which the work might have belonged, such as Gothicism or Romanticism. Literary terms are explained within the entry, but can also be found in the Glossary.

- **Historical and Cultural Context:** This section outlines the social, political, and cultural climate *in which the author lived and the poem was created.* This section may include descriptions of related historical events, pertinent aspects of daily life in the culture, and the artistic and literary sensibilities of the time in which the work was written. If the poem is a historical work, information regarding the time in which the poem is set is also included. Each section is broken down with helpful subheads. (Works written after the late 1970s may not have this section.)

- **Critical Overview:** this section provides background on the critical reputation of the poem, including bannings or any other public controversies surrounding the work. For older works, this section includes a history of how poem was first received and how perceptions of it may have changed over the years; for more recent poems, direct quotes from early reviews may also be included.

- **Sources:** an alphabetical list of critical material quoted in the entry, with full bibliographical information.

- **For Further Study:** an alphabetical list of other critical sources which may prove useful for the student. Includes full bibliographical information and a brief annotation.

- **Criticism:** at least one essay commissioned by *PfS* which specifically deals with the poem and is written specifically for the student audience, as well as excerpts from previously published criticism on the work, when available.

In addition, most entries contains the following highlighted sections, set separately from the main text:

- **Media Adaptations:** a list of audio recordings as well as any film or television adaptations of the poem, including source information.

- **Compare and Contrast Box:** an "at-a-glance" comparison of the cultural and historical differences between the author's time and culture and late twentieth-century Western culture. This box includes pertinent parallels between the major scientific, political, and cultural movements of the time or place the poem was written, the time or place the poem was set (if a historical work), and modern Western culture. Works written after the mid-1970s may not have this box.

- **What Do I Read Next?:** a list of works that might complement the featured poem or serve as a contrast to it. This includes works by the same author and others, works of fiction and nonfiction, and works from various genres, cultures, and eras.

- **Study Questions:** a list of potential study questions or research topics dealing with the poem. This section includes questions related to other disciplines the student may be studying, such as American history, world history, science, math, government, business, geography, economics, psychology, etc.

## *Other Features*

*PfS* includes a foreword by David J. Kelly, an instructor and cofounder of the creative writing periodical of Oakton Community College. This essay provides a straightforward, unpretentious explanation of why poetry should be marveled at and how *Poetry for Students* can help teachers show students how to enrich their own reading experiences.

A Cumulative Author/Title Index lists the authors and titles covered in each volume of the *PfS* series.

A Cumulative Nationality/Ethnicity Index breaks down the authors and titles covered in each volume of the *PfS* series by nationality and ethnicity.

A Subject/Theme Index, specific to each volume, provides easy reference for users who may be studying a particular subject or theme rather than a single work. Significant subjects from events to broad themes are included, and the entries pointing to the specific theme discussions in each entry are indicated in **boldface.**

Illustrations are included with entries when available, including photos of the author and other graphics related to the poem.

## *Citing* Poetry for Students

When writing papers, students who quote directly from any volume of *Poetry for Students* may use the following general forms. These examples are based on MLA style; teachers may request that students adhere to a different style, so the following examples may be adapted as needed.

When citing text from *PfS* that is not attributed to a particular author (i.e., the Themes, Style,

Historical Context sections, etc.), the following format should be used in the bibliography section:

"Angle of Geese." *Poetry for Students.* Eds. Marie Napierkowski and Mary Ruby. Vol. 1. Detroit: Gale, 1997. 8–9.

When quoting the specially commissioned essay from *PfS* (usually the first piece under the "Criticism" subhead), the following format should be used:

Velie, Alan. Essay on "Angle of Geese."*Poetry for Students.* Eds. Marie Napierkowski and Mary Ruby. Vol. 1. Detroit: Gale, 1997. 8–9.

When quoting a journal or newspaper essay that is reprinted in a volume of *PfS,* the following form may be used:

Luscher, Robert M. "An Emersonian Context of Dickinson's 'The Soul Selects Her Own Society.'" *ESQ: A Journal of American Renaissance* 30, No. 2 (Second Quarterl, 1984), 111–16; excerpted and reprinted in *Poetry for Students,* Vol. 2, eds. Marie Napierkowski and Mary Ruby (Detroit: Gale, 1997), pp. 120–34.

When quoting material reprinted from a book that appears in a volume of *PfS,* the following form may be used:

Mootry, Maria K. "'Tell It Slant': Disguise and Discovery as Revisionist Poetic Discourse in 'The Bean Eaters,'" in *A Life Distilled: Gwendolyn Brroks, Her Poetry and Fiction,* edited by Maria K. Mootry and Gary Smith (University of Illinois Press, 1987, 177–80; excerpted and reprinted in *Poetry for Students,* Vol. 1, Eds. Marie Napierkowski and Mary Ruby (Detroit: Gale, 1997), pp. 59–61.

## *We Welcome Your Suggestions*

The editors of *Poetry for Students* welcome your comments and ideas. Readers who wish to suggest poems to appear in future volumes, or who have other suggestions, are cordially invited to contact the editor. You may write to the editor at:

Editor, *Poetry for Students*
Gale Research
27500 Drake Rd.
Farmington Hills, MI 48331–3535

# Literary Chronology

**ca. 700:** *Beowulf* is composed at about this time.

**1300–1699:** Humanism as a philosophical view of the world is prevalent in this period.

**1300–1699:** The Renaissance begins in the 14th century and continues for the next 300 years.

**1558–1603:** The Elizabethan Age begins with the coronation in 1558 of Elizabeth I as Queen of England and continues until her death in 1603. Elizabethan literature is recognized as some of the finest in the English language.

**1564:** William Shakespeare is born in Stratford-upon-Avon.

**1575–1799:** The literary style known as Baroque arises in the late 16th century and remains influential until the early 18th century.

**1600–1625:** The Tribe of Ben, followers of Ben Jonson, were active in the early part of the 17th century.

**1600–1799:** The Enlightenment period in European social and cultural history begins in the 17th century and continues into the 18th century.

**1600–1650:** Metaphysical poetry becomes a prominent style of verse in the first half of the 17th century.

**1603–1625:** The Jacobean Age begins with the coronation in 1603 of James I of England and continues until his death in 1625.

**1609:** William Shakespeare's "Sonnet 55" is published in *Shake-speare's Sonnets*.

**1616:** William Shakespeare dies in Stratford and is buried in the chancel of Trinity Church.

**1621:** Andrew Marvell is born in Winestead-in-Holderness, Yorkshire, England.

**1625–1649:** The Cavalier Poets, a group of writers that includes Robert Herrick, Richard Lovelace, and John Suckling, are active during the reign of Charles I of England (1625–1649).

**1660–1688:** The Restoration Period begins when Charles II regains the throne of England, and it continues through the reign of his successor, James II (1685–1688). Restoration literature includes the first well-developed English-language works in several forms of writing that would become widespread in the modern world, including the novel, biography, and travel literature.

**1675–1799:** Neoclassicism as the prevailing approach to literature begins late in the 17th century and continues through much of the 18th century.

**ca. 1678:** Andrew Marvell's writes his poem "To His Coy Mistress" which is published posthumously in 1681 in *Miscellaneous Poems*.

**1700–1799:** The English Augustan Age (the name is borrowed from a brilliant period of literary creativity in ancient Rome) flourishes throughout much of the 18th century.

**1700–1725:** The Scottish Enlightenment, a period of great literary and philosophical activity, occurs in the early part of the 18th century.

**1740s–1775:** Pre-Romanticism, a transitional literary movement between Neoclassicism and Romanticism, takes place in the middle part of the 18th century.

**1740s–1750s:** The Graveyard School, referring to poetry that focuses on death and grieving, emerges as a significant genre in the middle of the 18th century.

**1750–1899:** The Welsh Literary Renaissance, an effort to revive interest in Welsh language and literature, begins in the middle of the 18th century and continues into the following century.

**1772:** Samuel Taylor Coleridge is born in the village of Ottery Saint Mary, Devonshire, England.

**1775–1850:** Romanticism as a literary movement arises in the latter part of the 18th century and continues until the middle of the 19th century.

**1798:** Samuel Taylor Coleridge's poem "Kubla Khan" is published in his collection *Lyrical Ballads*.

**1800–1899:** The Gaelic Revival, a renewal of interest in Irish literature and language, takes place throughout much of the 19th century.

**1809–1865:** The Knickerbocker School, a group of American writers determined to establish New York as a literary center, flourishes between 1809 and 1865.

**1830s–1860s:** The flowering of American literature known as the American Renaissance begins in the 1830s and continues through the Civil War period.

**1830–1855:** Transcendentalism, an American philosophical and literary movement, is at its height during this period.

**1830:** Emily Dickinson is born in Amherst, Massachusetts.

**1834:** Samuel Taylor Coleridge dies from complications stemming from his opium addiction.

**1837–1901:** The Victorian Age begins with the coronation of Victoria as Queen of England, and continues until her death in 1901. Victorian literature is recognized for its magnificent achievements in a variety of genre s.

**1848–1858:** The Pre-Raphaelites, an influential group of English painters, forms in 1848 and remains together for about ten years, during which time it has a significant impact on literature as well as the visual arts.

**1850s:** The poets of the so-called Spasmodic School are active in the 1850s.

**ca. 1862:** Emily Dickinson's poem "I Heard a Fly Buzz—When I Died—" is published in *The Poems of Emily Dickinson*.

**1863:** Ernest Lawrence Thayer is born in Lawrence, Massachusetts.

**1865:** William Butler Yeats is born in Dublin, Ireland.

**1872:** John McCrae is born in Guelph, Ontario, Canada.

**1874:** Robert Frost is born in San Francisco, California.

**1875–1899:** Aestheticism becomes a significant artistic and literary philosophy in the latter part of the 19th century.

**1875–1899:** Decadence becomes an important poetic force late in the 19th century.

**1875–1925:** Expressionism is a significant artistic and literary influence through the late 19th century and the early 20th century.

**1875–1925:** The Irish Literary Renaissance begins late in the 19th century and continues for the next several decades.

**1875–1925:** The Symbolist Movement flourishes in the closing decades of the 19th century and the opening years of the 20th century.

**1875–1950:** Realism as an approach to literature gains importance in the 19th century and remains influential well into the 20th century.

**1878:** John Masefield is born in Ledbury, Herefordshire, England.

**1886:** Emily Dickinson dies.

**1888:** Ernest Lawrence Thayer's poem "Casey at the Bat" is first published in the June 3, *San Francisco Daily Examiner*.

**1890–1899:** The decade of the 1890s, noted for the mood of weariness and pessimism in its art and literature, is known as the Fin de Siècle ("end of the century") period.

**1892:** Archibald MacLeish is born in Glencoe, Illinois.

**1900–1999:** The philosophy of Existentialism and the literature it inspires are highly influential throughout much of the 20th century.

**1900–1950:** Modernism remains a dominant literary force from the early part to the middle years of the 20th century.

**1902:** John Masefield's poem "Cargoes" is published in his collection entitled *Poems*.

**1907–ca. 1930:** The Bloomsbury Group, a circle of English writers and artists, gathers regularly in the period from 1907 to around 1930.

**1910s–1920s:** Georgian poetry becomes a popular style of lyric verse during the reign of King George V of England.

**1910s–1930s:** New Humanism, a philosophy of literature, is influential for several decades, beginning around 1910.

**1912–1925:** The Chicago Literary Renaissance, a time of great literary activity, takes place from about 1912 to 1925.

**1912–1922:** Imagism as a philosophy of poetry is defined in 1912 and remains influential for the next decade.

**1914:** Dudley Randall is born in Washington, D. C.

**1914:** Robert Frost's poem "Mending Wall" is published in his collection *North of Boston*.

**ca. 1919–ca. 1960:** The Scottish Renaissance in literature begins around 1919 and continues for about forty years.

**1918:** John McCrae dies of pneumonia in Boulogne, France.

**1918:** Al Purdy is born in Wooller, Ontario, Canada.

**1919:** John McCrae's poem "In Flanders Fields" is published posthumously in *In Flanders Fields, and Other Poems*.

**1920s:** The Harlem Renaissance, a flowering of African American literary activity, takes place.

**1920s–1930s:** The label Lost Generation is applied to a generation of American writers working in the decades following World War I.

**1920s–1930s:** The Montreal Group, a circle of Canadian poets interested in dealing with complex metaphysical issues, begins in the late 1920s and flourishes for the next decade.

**1920s–1970s:** New Criticism as a philosophy of literature arises in the 1920s and continues to be a significant approach to writing for over fifty years.

**1920s–1960s:** Surrealism, an artistic and literary technique, arises in the 1920s and remains influential for the next half century.

**1920:** William Butler Yeats's poem "Easter 1916" is published in an issue of *The Dial*.

**1923:** William Butler Yeats is awarded the Nobel Prize for Literature.

**1924:** Robert Frost is awarded the Pulitzer Prize in poetry for his collection *New Hampshire*.

**1926:** Allen Ginsberg is born in Newark, New Jersey.

**1927:** W. S. Merwin is born in New York City.

**1928:** Archibald MacLeish's poem "Ars Poetica" is published in his collection *Streets in the Moon*.

**1930–1967:** John Masefield is Poet Laureate of England.

**1930s–1965:** Negritude emerges as a literary movement in the 1930s and continues until the early 1960s.

**1930s–1970s:** The New York Intellectuals, a group of literary critics, are active from the 1930s to the 1970s.

**1931:** Carter Revard is born in Pawhuska, Oklahoma.

**1931:** Robert Frost is awarded the Pulitzer Prize in poetry for his *Collected Poems*.

**1933:** Archibald MacLeish is awarded the Pulitzer Prize in poetry for his collection *Conquistador*.

**1935–1943:** The Works Progress Administration (WPA) Federal Writers' Project provides federally funded jobs for unemployed writers during the Great Depression.

**1937:** Robert Frost is awarded the Pulitzer Prize in poetry for his collection *A Further Range*.

**1939–1944:** Archibald MacLeish serves as the United States' Librarian of Congress.

**1939:** William Butler Yeats dies in Cap Martin, France.

**1940s:** The New Apocalypse Movement, founded by J. F. Hendry and Henry Treece, takes place in England in the 1940s.

**1940s:** Postmodernism, referring to the various philosophies and practices of literature that challenge the dominance of Modernism, begins in the 1940s.

**1940:** Ernest Lawrence Thayer dies of a brain hemorrhage in Santa Barbara, California.

**1943:** Louise Glück is born in New York City.

**1943:** Robert Frost is awarded the Pulitzer Prize in poetry for his collection *A Witness Tree*.

**1947:** Yusef Komunyakaa is born in Bogalusa, Louisiana.

**1950s:** The so-called Beat Movement writers begin publishing their work in the 1950s.

**1950s:** The Black Mountain Poets, emphasizing the creative process, become an influential force in American literature in the 1950s.

**1950–1975:** Structuralism emerges as an important movement in literary criticism in the middle of the 20th century.

**1953:** Archibald MacLeish is awarded the Pulitzer Prize in poetry for his *Collected Poems 1917–1952.*

**1955:** Cathy Song is born in Honolulu, Hawaii.

**1956:** Allen Ginsburg writes his poem "A Supermarket in California" which has been published in *Collected Poems 1947–1980.*

**1956:** W. S. Merwin's poem "Leviathan" is published in his collection *Green with Beasts.*

**1958–1959:** Robert Frost serves as Consultant in Poetry to the Library of Congress.

**1960s–1970s:** The Black Aesthetic Movement, also known as the Black Arts Movement, takes place from the 1960s into the 1970s.

**1960s–1999:** Poststructuralism arises as a theory of literary criticism in the 1960s.

**1963:** Robert Frost dies in Boston.

**1966:** Dudley Randall's poem "Ballad of Birmingham" is published in his collection *Cities Burning.*

**1966:** Seamus Heaney's "Digging" is published in his collection *Death of a Naturalist.*

**1967:** John Masefield dies of gangrene and is buried in Poet's Corner of Westminster Abbey.

**1968:** Al Purdy's poem "Lament for the Dorsets" is published in his collection *Being Alive.*

**1970s–1999:** New Historicism, a school of literary analysis, originates in the 1970s.

**1971:** W. S. Merwin is awarded the Pulitzer Prize for poetry for his collection *The Carrier of Ladders.*

**1982:** Archibald MacLeish dies in Conway, Massachusetts.

**1983:** Cathy Song's poem "Lost Sister" is published in his collection *Picture Bride.*

**1988:** Yusef Komunyakaa's poem "Facing It" is published in his collection *Dien Kai Dau.*

**1992:** Carter Revard's poem "Birch Canoe" is published in his collection *Cowboys and Indians Christmas Shopping.*

**1992:** Louise Glück's poem "The Gold Lily" is published in her collection *The Wild Iris.*

**1993:** Louise Glück is awarded the Pulitzer Prize in poetry for *The Wild Iris.*

**1994:** Yusef Komunyakaa is awarded the Pulitzer Prize in poetry for his collection *Neon Vernacular: New and Selected Poems.*

**1996:** Jorie Graham is awarded the Pulitzer Prize in poetry for the collection *The Dream of the Unified Field.*

**1997:** Lisel Mueller is awarded the Pulitzer Prize in poetry for her collection *Alive Together: New and Selected Poems.*

**1997:** Robert Pinsky serves as Poet Laureate of the United States.

**1997:** Allen Ginsberg dies.

**1998:** Charles Wright is awarded the Pulitzer Prize in poetry for his collection *Black Zodiac.*

# *Acknowledgments*

The editors wish to thank the copyright holders of the excerpted criticism included in this volume and the permissions managers of many book and magazine publishing companies for assisting us in securing reproduction rights. We are also grateful to the staffs of the Detroit Public Library, the Library of Congress, the University of Detroit Mercy Library, Wayne State University Purdy/ Kresge Library Complex, and the University of Michigan Libraries for making their resources available to us. Following is a list of the copyright holders who have granted us permission to reproduce material in this volume of *PFS*. Every effort has been made to trace copyright, but if omissions have been made, please let us know.

**COPYRIGHTED EXCERPTS IN *PFS*, VOLUME 5, WERE REPRODUCED FROM THE FOLLOWING PERIODICALS:**

*The CEA Critic*, v. 34, May, 1972. Copyright © 1972 by the College English Association, Inc. Reproduced by permission.—*English Language Notes,*, v. 26, December, 1988. © copyrighted 1988, Regents of the University of Colorado. Reproduced by permission.—*Journal of Popular Culture,* v. 31, Summer, 1997. Copyright © 1997 by Ray B. Browne. Reproduced by permission.— *The New Republic,* May 24, 1993. © 1993 The New Republic, Inc. Reproduced by permission of *The New Republic.*—*Papers on Language and Literature,* v. 4, 1968. Copyright © 1968 by The Board of Trustees, Southern Illinois University at Edwardsville. Reproduced by permission.—

*Waves,* v. 15, Fall, 1986 for "From Isandhlwawa to Flanders Fields: With John McCrae" by Milton Acorn. Reproduced by permission of the Literary Estate of Milton Acorn.

**COPYRIGHTED EXCERPTS IN *PFS*, VOLUME 5, WERE REPRODUCED FROM THE FOLLOWING BOOKS:**

Duncan-Jones, Katherine. From an introduction to *Shake-speares Sonnets and A Lover's Complaint.* Folio Society, 1989. © The Folio Society Limited 1989. Reproduced by permission.—Ginsberg, Allen. From *Collected Poems: 1947-1980.* Harper & Row, 1984. Copyright © 1955 by Allen Ginsberg. Copyright renewed. Reproduced by permission of HarperCollins Publishers, Inc.—Glück, Louise. From *The Wild Iris.* Ecco Press, 1992. Copyright © 1992 by Louise Glück. Reproduced by permission of the publisher. In the British Commonwealth by Carcanet Press Ltd.— Heaney, Seamus. From *Death of a Naturalist.* Faber and Faber, 1966. Reproduced by permission of Faber & Faber Ltd.—Hill, John Spencer. From *A Coleridge Companion: An Introduction to the Major Poems and the Biographical Literaria.* Macmillan, 1983. © John Spencer Hill. Reproduced by permission of Macmillan, London and Basingstoke.—Komunyakaa, Yusef. From *Dien Kai Dau.* Wesleyan University Press, 1988. Copyright 1988 by Yusef Komunyakaa. Reproduced by permission of University Press of New England.— MacLeish, Archibald. From *Streets in the Moon.* Houghton Mifflin Company, 1926. Copyright

1926, renewed 1954 by Archibald MacLeish. Reproduced by permission of Houghton Mifflin Company.—Molino, Michael R. From *Questioning Tradition, Language, and Myth: The Poetry of Seamus Heaney.* The Catholic University of America Press, 1994. Copyright © 1994 The Catholic University Press of America. All rights reserved. Reproduced by permission.—Prescott, John F. From *In Flanders Fields: The Story of John McCrae.* The Boston Mills Press, 1985. Reproduced by permission.—Purdy, Al. From "Lament for the Dorsets" in *Rooms for Rent in the Outer Planets.* Harbour Publishing, 1996. Reproduced by permission.—Revard, Carter. From *Cowboys and Indians Christmas Shopping.* Point Riders Press, 1992. Reproduced by permission of the author.—Ringnalda, Don. From *Fighting and Writing the Vietnam War.* University Press of Mississippi, 1994. Reproduced by permission.—Song, Cathy. From *Picture Bride.* Yale University Press, 1983. Copyright © 1983 by Cathy Song. All rights reserved. Reproduced by permission.

**PHOTOGRAPHS AND ILLUSTRATIONS APPEARING IN *PFS,* VOLUME 5, WERE RECEIVED FROM THE FOLLOWING SOURCES:**

Coleridge, Samuel Taylor, drawing by J. Kayser.

Dickinson, Emily, photograph of a painting. The Library of Congress.

Frost, Robert, photograph. The Library of Congress.

Ginsberg, Allen, photograph. The Library of Congress.

Glück, Louise, photograph. AP/Wide World Photos, Inc. Reproduced by permission.

Macleish, Archibald, photograph. The Library of Congress.

Marvell, Andrew, engraving. Archive Photos, Inc. Reproduced by permission.

Masefield, John, photograph. The Library of Congress.

Merwin, W. S., photograph. AP/Wide World Photos, Inc. Reproduced by permission.

Purdy, Al, photograph. Harbourfront Reading Series, Toronto. Reproduced by permission.

Randall, Dudley, photograph by Yancey Hughes. Reproduced by permission.

Revard, Carter, photograph by Herbert Weitman. Reproduced by permission.

Shakespeare, William, drawing. The Library of Congress.

Yeats, William Butler, photograph. The Library of Congress.

Heaney, Seamus, photograph. Jerry Bauer. Reproduced by permission.

Song, Cathy, photograph by John Eddy. Reproduced by permission of Cathy Song.

# Contributors

**Emily Archer:** Emily Archer holds a Ph.D. in English from Georgia State University, has taught literature and poetry at several colleges, and has published essays, reviews, interviews, and poetry in numerous literary journals. Entry on *Lost Sister.*

**Betsy Beacom:** Betsy Beacom holds an M.A. in English from the University of Virginia, Charlottesville, and has also undertaken doctoral studies in English. She has taught literature and writing courses at Albertus Magnus College in New Haven, Connecticut, and has published articles in various periodicals. Entry on *Mending Wall.*

**Jennifer Brostrom:** Jennifer Brostrom has taught writing at American University in Washington D.C. and has published poetry in several journals. One of her essays has been anthologized in *Commodify Your Dissent: The Business of Culture in the New Guilded Age* (Norton, 1997). Entry on *Sonnet 55.*

**Craig Dworkin:** Craig Dworkin is a poet and assistant professor of English at Princeton University. Original essay on *Mending Wall.*

**Jhan Hochman:** Jhan Hochman holds a Ph.D. in English and an M.A. in Cinema Studies. His articles have appeared in *Democracy and Nature, Genre, ISLE,* and *Mosaic.* Entries and original essays on *Cargoes, Easter 1916, The Gold Lily, Lament for the Dorsets,* and *Leviathan.* Origi-

nal essays on *Ballad of Birmingham, Birch Canoe, I Heard a Fly Buzz—When I Died—,* and *Sonnet 55.*

**Jeannine Johnson:** Jeannine Johnson received her Ph.D. from Yale University and is currently visiting assistant professor of English at Wake Forest University. Original essays on *Casey at the Bat* and *Facing It.*

**David Kelly:** David Kelly is an instructor of creative writing at several community colleges in Illinois, as well as a fiction writer and playwright. Entries and original essays on *Ars Poetica, Birch Canoe, Casey at the Bat, In Flanders Fields,* and *To His Coy Mistress.*

**Sharon Kraus:** Sharon Kraus is a poet who teaches creative writing, literature, and poetry at Queens College, City University of New York. She holds an M.A. in creative writing from New York University and is pursuing doctoral studies at City University of New York. Kraus is the recipient of an Editor's Choice Award from *Columbia: A Journal of Literature and Art,* a MacDowell fellowship, and other awards for her poetry. Her book of poetry is *Generation* (1997); she also publishes reviews of contemporary poetry and essays on medieval literature. Original essays on *Facing It* and *The Gold Lily.*

**Michael Lake:** Michael Lake earned an M.A. in English from Eastern Illinois University and is a published poet who has also taught composition and literature courses at the collegiate level. Entry on *Kubla Khan*. Original essay on *I Heard a Fly Buzz—When I Died—*.

**Mary Mahony:** Mary Mahony earned an M.A. in English from the University of Detroit and a M.L.S. from Wayne State University. She is an instructor of English at Wayne County Community College in Detroit, Michigan. Original essay on *Kubla Khan*.

**Bruce Meyer:** Bruce Meyer is director of the creative writing program at the University of Toronto's School of Continuing Studies. He is the author of 14 books, including the poetry collections *The Open Room, Radio Silence*, and *The Presence*. Original essays on *Cargoes, Casey at the Bat, In Flanders Fields, Lament for the Dorsets, Mending Wall,* and *To His Coy Mistress*.

**Carolyn Meyer:** Carolyn Meyer holds a Ph.D. in modern British and Irish literature and has taught contemporary literature at McMaster University, Mt. Allison University, and, most recently, the University of Toronto. She has presented papers internationally on the poetry of Seamus Heaney and John Montague. Her article "Orthodoxy, Independence, and Influence in Seamus Heaney's *Station Island*" has been reprinted in *Critical Essays on Seamus Heaney*, edited by Robert F. Garratt (1995). She is the coeditor of *Separate Islands: Contemporary Irish and British Poetry* and of a forthcoming college reader. Original essays on *Digging* and *Easter 1916*.

**Tyrus Miller:** Tyrus Miller is an assistant professor of comparative literature and English at Yale University, where he teaches twentieth-century literature and visual culture. His book *Late Modernism: Politics, Fiction, and the Arts Between the World Wars* is forthcoming. Original essays on *Digging* and *A Supermarket in California*.

**Marisa Anne Pagnattaro:** Marisa Anne Pagnattaro is a writer and teaching assistant at the University of Georgia in Athens. She is the book review editor and editorial board member of the *Georgia Bar Journal*. Pagnattaro is currently writing a dissertation on women, justice, and American literature. Original essays on *Ars Poetica* and *A Supermarket in California*.

**Morton Rich:** Morton Rich holds a Ph.D. from New York University and is a professor of contemporary American literature. He currently teaches at Montclair State University in New Jersey and publishes poetry and critical articles. Original essay on *Digging*.

**Sean K. Robisch:** Sean K. Robisch teaches composition and literature at Purdue University and holds a Ph.D. in American literature. His fiction has appeared in *Hopewell Review* and *Puerto del Sol*. Original essays on *Lost Sister* and *Sonnet 55*.

**Chris Semansky:** Chris Semansky holds a Ph.D. in English from Stony Brook University and teaches writing and literature at Portland Community College in Portland, Oregon. His collection of poems *Death, But at a Good Price* received the Nicholas Roerich Poetry Prize for 1991 and was published by Sotry Line Press and the Nicholas Roerich Museum. Semansky's most recent collection, *Blindsided*, has been published by 26 Books of Portland, Oregon. Entries and original essays on *Ballad of Birmingham, Facing It,* and *A Supermarket in California*. Original essays on *Leviathan* and *Lost Sister*.

**Kristina Zarlengo:** Kristina Zarlengo earned both an M.A. and Ph.D. in English and comparative literature from Columbia University. She taught writing and literature at Columbia University and has most recently worked as a freelance book reviewer and feature writer. Entry and original essay on *I Heard a Fly Buzz—When I Died—*.

# Ars Poetica

## Archibald MacLeish
## 1928

"Ars Poetica" is one of the most famous and most quoted poems of twentieth-century American literature, possibly because it addresses a subject that all poets and poetry teachers hold dear—poetry itself. The title is Latin and can be translated as "The Art of Poetry." In addition, the life of the poem's author, Archibald MacLeish, showed the sort of commitment and received the sort of recognition that supporters of the art like to think of when examining the artist.

MacLeish was born into a well-to-do, but not extremely wealthy, family in 1892, in Glencoe, Illinois. He went to private school, prep school, and then Yale University, where he was active in writing and had work published in *The Yale Review*. After his graduation, he married, and then served in France during World War I. Like many who were to become that generation's greatest literary figures, MacLeish had his belief in the world's basic goodness and logic smashed by the inhuman scale of destruction that modern warfare reached. Upon returning to the United States, he earned his law degree and successfully practiced law for four years.

In 1923 MacLeish gave up his law career to write poetry, moving with his wife and two children to Paris, where he associated with some of the most innovative writers America has ever produced, including Ernest Hemingway, F. Scott Fitzgerald, and John Dos Passos, as well as artists from other countries and disciplines. He later said that, like practicing law, the poet's job was to

*Archibald MacLeish*

"make sense of our lives. To create an order which a bewildered, angry heart can recognize. To imagine man." It was in Paris that he wrote "Ars Poetica," published in the 1928 volume *Streets in the Moon.*

## Author Biography

MacLeish was born in 1892 in Glencoe, Illinois, a wealthy suburb of Chicago. He attended Yale University, where he was a successful scholar and athlete. In his junior year, he was elected to the Phi Beta Kappa Society. At Yale MacLeish began writing poetry and short stories for the *Yale Literary Magazine,* and he won the Yale University Prize for Poetry in 1915. After graduation, MacLeish entered Harvard Law School, where, he claimed, his education really began. MacLeish temporarily suspended his studies to serve as an ambulance driver in France during World War I; he transferred to active duty shortly thereafter and rose to the rank of field artillery captain. MacLeish's first full-length volume of poetry was published by one of his English instructors at Yale while MacLeish was in the army. In 1918 the poet's younger brother Kenneth, a Navy flyer, died when his plane was shot down. This event inspired several of MacLeish's poems. Following the war, MacLeish returned to Yale and completed his law degree as class valedictorian. After teaching constitutional and international law at Harvard for a year, MacLeish worked with a New England law firm until 1923, when he decided to pursue a full-time career as a poet.

Moving to Paris with his wife, Ada, and their two sons, MacLeish associated with many of the writers who were to revolutionize twentieth-century literature, including Ernest Hemingway, James Joyce, and Ezra Pound, whose poetry greatly influenced MacLeish. Devoting himself to perfecting his writing, MacLeish published several volumes that distinguished him as one of his generation's most promising poets. MacLeish received his first Pulitzer Prize in 1932, four years after he and his family had returned to the United States. After briefly attempting a turkey–farming venture in Conway, Massachusetts, MacLeish accepted an editorial position with Henry R. Luce's *Fortune* magazine, where he wrote essays on a wide variety of topics and developed his political and social consciousness. During the 1930s MacLeish chaired the League of American Writers, an anti-fascist organization that also included Hemingway and John Dos Passos. In 1939 President Franklin Roosevelt appointed MacLeish to the position of Librarian of the Congress, an office he held until 1944, when he became Assistant Secretary of State. While in office, MacLeish was a member of the committee that drafted the constitution for the United Nations Educational, Scientific, and Cultural Organization (UNESCO). After retiring from public life in 1945, he taught literature and creative writing at Harvard from 1949 to 1962. MacLeish received two additional Pulitzer Prizes as well as such honors as the National Book Award, a Tony Award, and the Bollingen Prize for Poetry; he also won an Acadamy Award for one of his screenplays. After his retirement from Harvard, MacLeish returned to his farm in Conway, where he continued to write poetry, essays, and verse plays until his death in 1982.

## Poem Text

A poem should be palpable and mute
As a globed fruit,
Dumb
As old medallions to the thumb,
Silent as the sleeve-worn stone                    5
Of casement ledges where the moss has grown—
A poem should be wordless

As the flight of birds.
A poem should be motionless in time
As the moon climbs,                                                          10
Leaving, as the moon releases
Twig by twig the night-entangled trees,
Leaving, as the moon behind the winter leaves,
Memory by memory the mind—
A poem should be motionless in time                          15
As the moon climbs.
A poem should be equal to:
Not true.
For all the history of grief
An empty doorway and a maple leaf.                           20
For love
The leaning grasses and two lights above the sea—
A poem should not mean
But be.

## Media Adaptations

- *Archibald MacLeish Reads His Poetry* was released on audio cassette in 1972 by Caedmon.

- A web page featuring three of MacLeish's poems and a brief overview of his career can be found at http://www.geocities.com/Athens/Delphi/7086/0508.htm.

## Poem Summary

### Lines 1-2:

The first four stanzas of "Ars Poetica" say that a poem should communicate with its reader without words, nonverbally, a concept that contradicts reality, since poems are made of nothing but words. Instead of expressing ideas, this section says that a poem should give its reader actual, tangible items that can be experienced with the senses. Since words are themselves marks on paper or, if spoken, patterns of vibration and not the actual objects and actions they represent, this description appears to ask poetry to do the impossible. Contradicting our normal expectations about the scope of its subject is what "Ars Poetica" is all about.

The word "palpable" in the first line means that a poem should be tangible—something that can be touched—, but the word also refers to something that is obvious or immediately evident. Students who have spent hours in English classes laboring to determine what a poem "means" may be surprised to find it said that a poem should be understood at first glance. MacLeish uses "mute" in the same line to contradict the traditional idea that a poem "speaks" to its reader with a unique, identifiable "voice." Writers concentrating on these aspects are too self-conscious. He says instead that a poem should be like a piece of fruit, suggesting qualities that a piece of fruit has: it is recognized across cultures, is alive, sweet, and grown to ripeness. The adjective "globed" emphasizes this idea without making the reader look for a meaning that is separate from the imagery used: a globe, or sphere, is a universal shape that is constant, regardless of what angle it is viewed from, and it therefore holds no secrets.

### Lines 3-4:

Having made the point in the first stanza that the words of a poem should have direct, not abstract, influence on the reader, MacLeish uses onomatopoeia to support this point. Onomatopoeia is the use of words that mimic their meaning in their sound. In this case, "dumb" and "thumb" both have blunt, dull sounds, and they are used to discuss words that have no secrets below the surface.

Line 4 uses the phrase "to the thumb" where it could have said "to the touch," precisely because the point of this piece is that poetry should be a physical, not an intellectual, experience, and one way to accomplish this is to use a solid object ("thumb") in place of a concept ("touch"). Medallions are generally given to people for their symbolic meaning—to recognize bravery, achievements, etc.—and not for the actual monetary value of the metal of which they are made. In using the image of a thumb reading old medallions, MacLeish implies that the poet cannot count on readers to understand abstract significance because meanings fade, just like an imprint pressed into metal wears down, and readers are often as insensitive as a thumb. This, he says, is how it "should be" (line 1).

### Lines 5-6:

The image given in these two lines is of a window frame, or casement, that has overgrown with moss but has been buffed, even "worn," by the sleeves of someone looking in and leaning on the ledge. This implies that someone, presumably the poet, has been looking in for a long time at a situation that has been there for an even longer time (which is, in fact, how poets do involve themselves in life). MacLeish's suggestion that poems be silent is good advice to any outside observer.

### Lines 7-8:

The first section of the poem ends with an image from nature in line 8. As mentioned before, a poem cannot be "wordless" because it is made of words: a person might just as easily try to be "cell-less." A poem can, however, not concentrate on its own words, in the same way that a bird can accomplish something as miraculous as flight without being aware of the individual actions that make it possible.

### Lines 9-10:

The second section of the poem, from line 9 to line 16, starts and ends with the same couplet, and the two stanzas in the middle begin with the same four words. The main image in this section is the moon, which, like the globed fruit of line 2, is a universal figure familiar to all people at all times in the world's history. Central to this section is the idea that a poem should be "leaving"—not carrying new ideas to the reader, but displaying ideas that the reader already knows.

Line 9 says that a poem should be motionless, but then line 10 explains this point by comparing it to the climbing of the moon, which actually does move, but imperceptibly so to the naked eye. It is redundant for MacLeish to say "motionless in time," since motion takes place in time and could not take place without it, but putting it this way allows him to stress two ideas: that a poem does not need to build up from one stanza to the next (an idea based on poems as concepts, not images), and that poetry should have the same meaning to all generations of mankind.

### Lines 11-16:

The syntax of these lines is confusing. By arranging his words in the way he has, the poet is able to imply that "behind the winter" is the location of the moon, while at the same time retaining the idea that the moon leaves the winter behind. Either of these readings is right: the moon is behind the winter if the winter is embodied by the trees that it shone through in line 12, and it leaves the winter behind by climbing up into the sky. Line 14 is even more problematic because the poet does not use a verb in this clause. It is impossible to know whether it is the memories or the mind that is leaving.

By repeating lines 9 and 10 in lines 15 and 16, MacLeish reiterates his idea of a poem motionless

in time in several ways. Most obvious is the emphasis given to anything that is said twice. Also, by having these lines return, he shows defiance against the passage of time, as the poem ends up back at the same place again, as if it had never left. Having put the reader through the twisted logic of lines 11 through 14 makes the contradiction of "motionless" with "climbing" seem less strange when encountered a second time.

### Lines 17-18:

"Beauty is truth, truth beauty." John Keats wrote these words in "Ode On a Grecian Urn," which, like "Ars Poetica," is a meditation on the timelessness and mystery of art. In that poem, the figures painted on an urn in ancient Greece are considered to be models of truth and beauty because they will not change, so they can never be untrue. Since the second section of "Ars Poetica" declared that a poem should be motionless, it would be natural for a reader familiar with the Keats poem to assume that this is MacLeish's way, like Keats, of showing how a poem can be truer. But "truth" is exactly the sort of intangible concept that MacLeish says poems should not concern themselves with. He does not say that a poem should not be true, just that poems should "be equal to: / not true." Seekers of abstract truth—philosophers, for example—too often fail to make their writing have an effect on their readers.

### Lines 19-20:

"Grief" is a huge subject, combining two basic concepts that are the core ideas behind a majority of poems: love and death. MacLeish expands the subject of grief to include "all" of history, including practically everybody who ever lived. The way to convey this idea, he suggests, is with "An empty doorway and a maple leaf." These images cannot be intellectualized—this is the point of the poem. We can say that the empty doorway symbolizes emptiness, opportunities lost, or a gaping hole, or that the maple leaf is strength, coursing veins, or a reminder of autumnal death and rebirth, but the images do not clearly fit any of these ideas with a one-to-one correspondence. These are personal images, and the best that a reader can do is to know approximately how the poet relates them to grief.

### Lines 21-22:

These lines offer the same type of evasive images that were offered for grief in the preceding couplet. There is something about blades of grass, being touched by the wind and bowing to it, that is like the experience of love, just as the two parties in love are like lights, and the sea is like the world that reflects their love, but these relationships between the concepts and the objects are inexact. "Ars Poetica" explains to the poet and to the reader that the principle that poems cannot convey both experience and ideas is not to be regretted, but is the nature of things. If poems can only cover one of these tasks, MacLeish says it should be experience, and let the ideas, which are the abstract functions of words, "remain mute" (line 1).

### Lines 23-24:

By cutting these two lines short and by offering no direct object after "mean" and "be," MacLeish draws the vast distinction between the two verbs more clearly than even if he had said "should not mean anything" and "be anything," because the specific object provided by the reader to fill in these lines will be more striking than the general concept of "anything." Specificity is the goal of this poem.

## Themes

### Language and Meaning

In "Ars Poetica" MacLeish suggests that readers should not analyze a poem to determine its meaning, because, ideally, a poem should not have hidden meanings beneath its surface. However, this suggestion introduces a dilemma that concerns the interaction between poets, their text, and readers. On one hand, it is easy for the poet to write with the faith that "A poem should not mean / But be," because the poet is free then to write in a rush of instinct or inspiration, ignoring the obligation to careful language and form, which serve to convey meaning. The reader, however, has come to expect meaning in a poem, for it is often thought of as the poem's purpose of existence. Any written work can be considered as just a collection of words on a page until a reader is able to determine its meaning. In "Ars Poetica" MacLeish may be asserting that a poet should not construct his poem to be a vehicle for conveying an already-decided meaning. Outdated standards, such as ones that demand that a poem should be "about beauty" or that it should be for the benefit of humanity, can be debated by artists, and "Ars Poetica" is MacLeish's countering of those who would impose such generalized rules. It is possible, however, that he states his case

## Topics for Further Study

- Write a poem that expresses what you think a poem should not be. Use specific imagery, the way MacLeish uses "globed fruit" and "an empty doorway and a maple leaf," to get your point across.

- Many people have said that poetry should express the writer's feelings. Is it possible to express feelings and at the same time be mute and dumb and motionless? Explain why you think it is or is not.

- Do you think poets in general follow MacLeish's advice? Do you think they should?

a little too strongly: poets who concern themselves *only* with writing that is "not true" are more likely to produce gibberish than art.

Any language must have figures with meanings assigned to them. For instance, the letter "c" attached to the letters "a" and "t" indicate to English-speakers a small, carnivorous mammal. In this poem, MacLeish seems to propose a type of language that uses birds, trees, the moon, doorways, and so on, in place of letters and punctuation. These objects have meaning in a poem, he tells us, while abstract ideas such as "meaning" and "truth" do not. On the one hand, he rejects language as we know it, saying that a poem should be "wordless," but at the same time, he suggests a new set of natural objects that would communicate to readers as a language would. The irony here is that MacLeish must necessarily use words to represent his natural objects.

### Search for Self

In this poem's rejection of intellectual concepts and its embrace of actual, physical things, readers can see a hint of what MacLeish thinks the search for self should be. After covering the methods that a poem should use, the work's final four couplets get down to replacing the ideas that we use to express our feelings with images that MacLeish believes will be more effective than words. For example, the poet proposes that mankind does not need the word "love," as long as we have leaning grasses and lights above the sea. Likewise, it is not only the current dictionary definition of "grief," but all grief felt throughout all of history, that can be replaced by "an empty doorway and a maple leaf." In spite of the popular notion that poetry is a very intellectual matter, in "Ars Poetica" MacLeish wants to show that poetry is actually very physical. He tells readers that self-recognition takes place in the world at large—in doorways, in fields, in tree branches, and in the sky, not in the mind. The three concepts that he looks at—truth, grief, and love—can be seen as covering just about all questions humans have about their identities: a person who understands these three mysteries would have a thorough understanding of herself or himself. MacLeish, however, suggests that there can be no understanding of them, just experience of them. If poetry speaks about life, then anything that is said about how a poem should work also applies to how life should work, and understanding the true nature of a poem can lead to understanding oneself.

### Art and Experience

The world that we experience is what art represents with paint on a canvas or music or words. "Ars Poetica" calls a poem "wordless," which makes as little sense as calling a song "soundless." Traditionally, the thing that distinguishes one's experience of a poem from one's experience of reality is that a poem represents a shared reality *plus* a poet's own ideas. Taking the ideas expressed in "Ars Poetica" too literally would completely eliminate the job of the poet: when the poem's intention is only to reflect reality without expressing a poet's perception of it, then who needs the poet to come between reality and the reader? This question about the purpose of art is increasingly relevant today, as technological advances in the fields of sound and graphics can create virtual realities that are becoming increasingly successful in replicating actual experience.

Readers would better benefit by looking for MacLeish's intentions for writing "Ars Poetica." He proposes that poets should refrain from preaching, or adapting a superior moral pose, and that they are more likely to touch readers' emotions with specific, tangible images than with vague concepts. MacLeish implies that poets should rein in their ambitions to keep poetry in touch with reality. Writers who learn these lessons from "Ars Poetica" are more likely to create meaning than those who deliberately try to create something "meaningful."

## Style

"Ars Poetica" is written in twelve stanzas, which are the poetic equivalent to paragraphs in prose. Each stanza consists of a rhyming couplet. While the two lines in couplets usually match in length and meter, MacLeish very specifically varies the lengths of the lines here: although he is willing to follow traditional poetic form by rhyming the ends of the lines of each pair, it would be contrary to the idea that he is expressing about poetry if his poem were trapped in a constricting pattern, rather than being free to explore its subject through imagery. Imagery is the poet's use of tangible, describable things to evoke the feeling he or she has in mind.

The stanzas in this poem divide into three equal sections. The first section asserts that a poem should be "mute," "dumb," "wordless"—unusual concepts, given that poems are made up of words and have always been used by poets to "speak" of their subjects. The second four stanzas say that a poem should be "motionless," which again contradicts the average reader's training that a poem should be "moving" and that poems should be active, as well as incite action. In the final third, the poem tells us that a poem should be meaningless or not true.

## Historical Context

### World War I

While international conflicts before World War I (1914-1918) destroyed lands and property and devastated populations, World War I brought destruction to a new level. The technological advances of the early part of the twentieth century brought terrible new methods of warfare. Long-range artillery sent bombs across greater distances, while airplanes, which were first widely used during the First World War, let a small flight crew rain explosives down on thousands of unsuspecting people. Chemical weapons, most notably mustard gas, caused their victims to die miserable, convulsive, choking deaths. The war was waged by the Triple Entente of Great Britain, France, and Russia against the Triple Alliance of Germany, Austria-Hungary, and Italy. As it continued, however, it involved most of Europe. Upon their return home, veterans who fought in this war had an even more difficult time than the veterans of previous wars in reconciling the horrors they had witnessed. The effects

# *Compare & Contrast*

- **1928:** Television station WGY, in Schenectady, New York, airs the country's first regularly scheduled television broadcasts.

  **1948:** One million homes in the United States have televisions, up from five thousand just three years earlier.

  **1952:** Nearly 17 million homes in the United States had television sets.

  **1962:** Ninety-eight percent of the households in the United States have at least one television.

  **Today:** Television screens are seen frequently in public places, including grocery stores, airport terminals, stadiums, and classrooms.

- **1928:** A year after the first commercial talking movie, *The Jazz Singer,* Disney releases the first cartoon with a voice track. Named *Steamboat Willie,* the cartoon introduces the popular character Mickey Mouse.

  **1938:** Disney releases the world's first full-length animated film, *Snow White and the Seven Dwarfs.*

  **1961:** *The Flintstones* becomes the first animated television series to be broadcast during the prime-time evening hours.

  **Today:** Computer artists use graphic simulations to design impressive visual effects for movies and television.

- **1928:** Penicillin is first proven to have bacteria-fighting properties. In following years a number of antibiotics are developed, changing the face of medicine.

  **Today:** Researchers are finding antibiotics to be less successful than they were a generation ago. Because of the extensive use of antibiotics, tougher bacteria strains that are resistant to antibiotics have evolved.

---

of World War I on Western society helped bring about the general atmosphere of change in the 1920s. Some of the new attitudes that emerged during this era formed the tenets of what became known as "Modernism." Formerly accepted rules of art and society were no longer suitable. The past was viewed with irony, and conventions that had been accepted by previous generations were challenged or ignored.

In the United States, the younger generation's alienation from their elders was intensified by the prosperity that the country enjoyed throughout the 1920s. World War I elevated the United States to the status of an economic superpower. Most of the European economies had suffered from the aftermath of four years of fighting and the destruction of their manufacturing abilities. America, safely across the Atlantic from the bombing, had entered the war late, participating only from April of 1917 to the war's end in November of 1918. Before that, American factories had prospered by making products that European plants, busy making weapons and war supplies, could not produce. As one of the few world economies left intact after the war, the United States was prosperous throughout the 1920s, until the stock market crashed in November of 1929, starting the Great Depression.

## *The Jazz Age*

Financially comfortable, America in the 1920s turned its attention toward less serious concerns. Luxury, recreation, and the pursuit of pleasures mark the memories we have of the decade. The relatively new presence of the automobile, which became common after Henry Ford developed assembly-line construction in 1914, helped make this recreational lifestyle viable and changed the American way of life. People were freed from their immediate surroundings, able to associate with others who shared common interests with them, and no longer restricted to their families and neighbors. Attendance at sporting events skyrocketed, giving rise to the sports hero, including people with whom we are familiar today, such as Babe Ruth, Knute Rockne, Bill Tilden, and Jack Dempsey. Those who lived too far from cities or colleges to attend sporting events could listen to them on radio broadcasts, which started in 1920.

The 1920s are referred to as "The Jazz Age" because jazz music, an original American musical form, was received enthusiastically by the nation's young people. The music was part of the lifestyle that differentiated them from the older generations. They dressed in flashy new clothing styles and attended wild dances. In the wake of the war, many old customs were dead. Americans were more interested in having a good time and spending money than they were in tradition. In the 1920s millions of Americans, who otherwise would have been law-abiding citizens, associated with criminals to get liquor, because the sale and possession of alcohol was illegal from 1919 to 1933.

### The Expatriates

The word "expatriate" generally refers to a citizen of one country living in another, but often it pertains to the community of artists, mostly American, who lived in Paris during the 1920s. While many people in the United States enjoyed the flourishing economy, many artists went to reside in Paris, finding the attitudes of the French more in line with their artistic sensibilities. The French were more jaded about their political expectations, more casual about sex, and more serious about art—in short, they supported the values that might make an expatriate artist subject to criticism in her or his native country. Books that were banned in the United States, such as James Joyce's *Ulysses* and D. H. Lawrence's *Women in Love,* were celebrated in France. Another factor that was very important, because many artists considered creating art their full-time profession, was that an American could live cheaply in France with American currency. In 1919, one American dollar could buy eight French francs; by 1923 a dollar bought 16 francs; and in 1923 the dollar was worth 25 francs—a 300 percent growth in seven years.

A partial list of the expatriates living in Paris in the 1920s includes Ernest Hemingway, F. Scott Fitzgerald, Gertrude Stein, T. S. Eliot, Ezra Pound, John Dos Passos, Sherwood Anderson, and, of course, Archibald MacLeish, who moved there in 1923 and returned to the United States in 1928, the year "Ars Poetica" was published. These people all associated with each other and gathered to converse about weighty issues such as art, poetry, and responsibility. Many great artists alive at the time spent some time in Paris and joined in the discussion.

## Critical Overview

Although "Ars Poetica" is regarded as one of MacLeish's finest accomplishments, he himself is remembered as only a minor poet, with few truly impressive artistic accomplishments in his long and prominent career. Some critics consider the post-World War I period, when MacLeish lived as an expatriate in France along with hundreds of other aspiring artists, to be the only period of his life when he produced poems worth critical analysis, even though he continued to write for more than forty years after returning to America. "Ars Poetica" was produced during his French period, and, in its narrow focus and philosophical rumination on how man can (and cannot) turn ideals into reality, it is thought to contain what is best in MacLeish's work. Grover Smith, in a short book on MacLeish, lists these features as "conscious symbolism; witty, almost metaphorical strategies of argument; compressed and intense implications," and these elements are all certainly present in "Ars Poetica." While reviewing a play written late in the poet's life, John Wain took time to give an overview of the works of MacLeish—the essays, books, dramas, and poems long and short—and observed that "the evidence of his shorter poems is there to remind us that he is, or has been, a poet of true sensibility and originality. One of these, 'Ars Poetica,' must be one of the most often quoted of all modern poems, partly no doubt because it has provided a slogan for the modern criticism of poetry, but also because it is genuinely impressive."

Some critics have found fault with some of MacLeish's poems, especially publicly responsible pieces that brought out the poet's worst qualities. "The voice of civic rectitude in his verse is pious, stentorian, false, … a poor surrogate for action or impotent rage," noted critic Hilton Kramer. He goes on to note that MacLeish's best-known poems, including "Ars Poetica," "are eloquent warnings against precisely this sort of tendentious sermonizing." Though he is much respected for a few sterling accomplishments such as "Ars Poetica," Archibald MacLeish is not considered to be a poet of the first order.

## *What Do I Read Next?*

- The accomplishments of MacLeish's long career are beautifully presented in *Archibald MacLeish: Collected Poems, 1917-1982,* published by Houghton Mifflin in 1985.

- Ernest Hemingway's *A Moveable Feast* (1964), is one of the best-known books about Paris in the 1920s. Hemingway does not have anything to say directly about MacLeish, but his discussions of his own life at the time, and the lives of other prominent writers he and MacLeish associated with, give a good sense how serious this crowd was about art.

- In 1962, after almost forty years as a public figure, MacLeish sat down for several long, uninterrupted conversations with Mark Van Doren, who was a friend and an equally famous poet.

Their discussions were filmed, and a small portion was put together and broadcast on CBS in 1962. A longer transcript was compiled into a book titled *The Dialogues of Archibald MacLeish and Mark Van Doren* that was published in 1964. Although the conversations had no set topics, almost every subject mentioned reaches back to poetry in one way or another.

- The same spirit of reform that is present in "Ars Poetica" can be found throughout *A Time To Act,* a collection of Archibald MacLeish's essays written in the late 1930s and early 1940s. The focus of the collection is politics, not poetry, but this book reveals the same attitude toward civic responsibility that the poem shows toward artistic responsibility.

## Criticism

### David Kelly

*David Kelly is an instructor of creative writing at several community colleges in Illinois, as well as a fiction writer and playwright. In the following essay, Kelly explores the idea of age—as both a personal and societal concept—and its influence on "Ars Poetica" and the later events in MacLeish's life.*

Late in his life, Archibald MacLeish became very political, but you would not guess it from reading his poem "Ars Poetica." Political thought involves more than parties and campaigns; it is about how human beings interact with one another and how groups relate. It is about who will cooperate and who will take orders from the ones holding power over them. The poem purposefully and forcefully ignores human interaction. It does not want to deal with communication as we generally think of it, preferring to imagine a world where words can be "dumb" and "mute." What accounts for the change in values during the course of the poet's life? Age, I would guess, in both senses of

the word: the poem reflects a young man's thinking that he later outgrew, and it also reflects the sensibilities of the age, or period, in which he was writing.

The ideas expressed in "Ars Poetica" are ideas that appeal to young people. It is in youth's interest to be anti-intellectual. This is not meant as an insult to young people, but it just describes life's structure, on a basic level of comfort and fulfillment of immediate needs. Brain work is an acquired skill. Young people can think as well as older people, but it takes years of accumulated experience to stockpile a battery of ideas—both good and bad—with which the thinking mind can play. Since young people lack the inventory of experience to catch cultural references and points of common memory, this leaves them just a few options when dealing with a subject, such as poetry, that stresses a full background of one's culture. Where do youth fit in, then?

The first option is to submit. Believing that it does take a certain amount of experience to fuel a worthwhile mind, youth *could* simply toss their hands up and admit that they will be second-class

> *... the most obvious problem with connecting 'Ars Poetica' with youthful sensibilities is that the poem's author was in his mid-thirties when he wrote it."*

thinkers until they have lived a little longer, been around the block a few more times. Doing this would mean sitting back, keeping quiet, and letting older folks run things, with the faith that they know best. But this goes against the principles of democracy, which respects each person's opinions and gives no preference to any group. I know that I myself wouldn't relinquish authority to some other group simply because of something as inconclusive as age, height, wealth or ethnic origin, so I can't find fault with young poets who are not willing to say of their elders, "They're probably right, and I'm probably wrong." In some societies age is revered, and Americans sometimes look jealously at such systems, but humility is not something that we can force—at least, we do not want to become the sort of society that would force intellectual humility.

A second way for youth to cope with the disadvantage inherent in intellectual pursuits would be to reverse the culture's priorities, so that intellectualism becomes less important. Young people may lack experience, but older people lack the speed and strength and stamina that they had when they were young. To secure their own self-respect, young people could claim that knowledge is overrated by older people to justify their waning physical prowess. This attitude seems to work well for school bullies, who may not be able to keep up with assignments and so do their best to belittle intelligence. Muscle and beauty, the tools of youth (certainly not the tools of the aged), get a lot of attention in popular culture, especially in television and movies and the advertisements that support them. That should not be taken, however, to mean muscle and beauty ensure power. A culture that celebrates youth is run, at the top, by people who are clever, whether they are strong and good-looking

or ugly weaklings. Societies that have only valued the things that youth have to offer have always been brief.

No, the best way for youth to level the playing field against people with more experience is to embrace values that stress the importance of instinct. Suppose the issue at hand is a bridge. If the important thing is the design of the bridge, then the experienced ones in a group hold the important tools, because they can draw off of knowledge of all the bridges they've seen and all the laws of physics they may know. If the important thing is its construction, then the healthier (generally younger) people have the advantage, because they're better able to hoist I-beams and move sacks of concrete without sprains or ruptures. *But* ... if we forget about function and agree that the important thing is to experience the bridge, then all can approach it with equal status, and no one has an advantage over anyone else. Meaning is irrelevant: all we want of the bridge is what MacLeish wants of a poem, which is, "to be."

There are quite a few existing systems of thought, including Zen and Existentialism, that shift the emphasis of life away from the stored-up knowledge of humankind and the arts to the experience of the here and now. At the heart of them all is a distrust of intellectualism, a suspicion that anything, even lies, can be proved with enough fancy words. While the intellectual tradition scoffs at anti-intellectuals as having a primitive fear of what they cannot understand, the anti-intellectual trusts her or his own instinct over claims that, "This might not seem to make sense, but it does. Trust me." Our culture produces a good deal of intellectual youths and an equal share of adults who reject the artificial limits of "meaning," but the majority of youths will always be anti-intellectual, because doing otherwise confirms their own lack of complexity.

As some readers no doubt have already figured out, the most obvious problem with connecting "Ars Poetica" with youthful sensibilities is that the poem's author was in his mid-thirties when he wrote it. Here is where the rise of Modernism in the postwar world of the 1920s comes in. At the time, tradition was rushed out, and almost everyone discussing art was talking from the fresh perspective that we associate with youth. The war destroyed a lot more than buildings and families; it destroyed the old way of seeing things, as wars always do. Every outbreak of violence shatters faith and leaves affected populations open to the ques-

tion of whether or not we can handle things a little better in the future. When no new ideas arise,
the old ones slip like sand back into the hole they
left. When there are new ideas, as there were after
the French Revolution, the First World War and
Vietnam, the disruption caused by the war provides
them with an opportunity. It is as if an old, established company—the literary establishment—lost
its entire board of directors in a tragic elevator ac-
cident, and a new board had to be appointed from
the company's junior executives. They may not exactly be kids, but their new ideas, appearing so
abruptly, would surely seem either childishly im-
mature or youthfully innovative.

It helped that the writers of the 1920s had a
place where they could congregate and assure each
other that their devotion and their artistic theories
were not only revolutionary, but also smart and inspired. In general, that gathering place was Paris,
where living was cheap and where the culture apparently appreciated art—at least when compared
to the crass commercialism of the United States
(where the national government was run by the
crooks in Harding's administration and local politics were ruled by bootleggers). In particular, the
young artists' clubhouses were the apartment of
Gertrude Stein and Alice Toklas and Sylvia
Beach's bookstore, *Shakespeare and Co.* The writers who passed through both of these places—
MacLeish, James Joyce, Ezra Pound, John Dos
Passos, T. S. Eliot, Ernest Hemingway, and Andre
Gide, to name a few—were able to stretch the understanding of what literature is by trying new
forms, by inventing different things that art could
be. With so many innovators around, it became a
struggle to be unique. Following Pound's precept,
"Make it new!"— which was one of the few rules
of Modern art—these writers had the comfort of
being with a group of others who shared their goals.
They also had the strain of making art that was
newer than the ideas that were new yesterday and
had already been made newer that morning.

This young person's way of seeing the world,
one that favors living for the present moment and
gives no advantage to experience, is present in "Ars
Poetica." What could be newer than experiencing
the natural world raw, with no intellectual inter-
ference from the poet? As an artistic stance, though,
the immediacy called for in this poem is too limited to continue throughout a writing career. Saying that words should be "dumb" and "mute" is like
saying that telephone lines should not be bothered
with carrying current. What would they be good

for, then? How could we admire or appreciate a
phone line if we did not know whether it was doing
its job well? Apparently, we would have to admire
it for its own sake, and this is what "Ars Poetica"
tells us we should do with poetry. Art for art's sake.
After a while, though, readers or viewers or listen-
ers grow tired of experiencing or encountering artistic pieces, whether they are stone casements,
telephone lines, or poems. After nodding and saying "uh-huh" a few times, the mind starts wandering, and in doing so, it starts kicking around the kinds
of ideas the poem tells us not to burden poetry with.

In MacLeish's case, he finished saying all he
had to say about not saying things, and he started
saying things about things. He started using art to
address the concerns of people, not just art itself.
After the stock market crash in 1929, like many
artists of his time, he became concerned with the
plight of the poor in America, having returned to
his native land the year before. Unlike many artists,
however, he joined the government and worked enthusiastically for Franklin Roosevelt. For the rest
of his life, throughout the great changes that affected America—isolationism, World War II, the
Communist scare, and the Civil Rights movement—MacLeish continued to inspect society in
poems, essays, and that most social artistic form—
dramas. The more MacLeish aged, the less he used
art for its own sake, and the more he concentrated
on the political world around him.

**Source:** David Kelly, in an essay for *Poetry for Students,*
Gale, 1999.

### *Marisa Anne Pagnattaro*

*Marisa Anne Pagnattaro, who holds a J.D. and
Ph.D. in English, is a freelance writer and a Robert
E. West Teaching Fellow in the English Department at the University of Georgia. In the following
essay, Pagnattaro explores MacLeish's philosophy
that poetry should use concrete images to capture
a moment of personal experience and the richness
of being.*

Archibald MacLeish was a man of great
courage who dedicated himself to his art: on the
very day that he was offered the coveted position
of partner at the prestigious Boston law firm of
Choate, Hall and Stewart, he announced "I'm giving up the law." In his biography of MacLeish titled *Archibald MacLeish: An American Life,* Scott
Donaldson detailed how this successful attorney
decided to leave behind a lucrative law career to
join American expatriates on the Left Bank in Paris
in the early 1920s. MacLeish studied the poetic

> **" ... *MacLeish maintains that poetry should capture a moment of human experience — for example grief or love — through concrete images.* "**

philosophies of his contemporaries and was a frequent visitor to Sylvia Beach's bookstore, Shakespeare and Company. Among other writers, he was fascinated by T. S. Eliot's intellectualized verse and Ezra Pound's dedication to "make it new."

It was Pound's work that led MacLeish to Ernest Fenollosa's essay on Chinese written characters. Fenollosa used the example of Chinese characters to argue that the "more concretely and vividly we express the interactions of things the better the poetry." Fenollosa added that the best poetry must "appeal to emotions with the charm of direct impression, flashing through regions where the intellect can only grope"—it is not enough for poetry "to furnish a meaning to philosophers." MacLeish described in a notebook in February of 1924 that he was quite taken with Fenollosa's theory, which insisted on the concrete nature of images. MacLeish wrote, "This is one of the most important pieces of writing I have happened upon."

Fenollosa's ideas, thus, form an important aesthetic underpinning for MacLeish's poem "Ars Poetica." MacLeish began to look at the world anew. Just before writing his most famous poem, he commented in a letter, "To write one must take the world apart and reconstruct it." Then, on March 14, 1925, MacLeish composed "Ars Poetica" in his notebook. This important poem reworked Eliot's theory of the "objective correlative," that the "only way of expressing emotion in the form of art is by finding an 'objective correlative' ... a situation, a chain of events which shall be the formula of that *particular* emotion." In espousing a critically different formulation, MacLeish acted upon Fenollosa's observation that metaphor was "the very essence of poetry" and, accordingly, wrote in his notebooks that "Metaphor *itself* was experience."

The title, "Ars Poetica," is Latin for "Art of Poetry." As in Horace's *Ars Poetica* (19-18 B.C.), MacLeish expresses principles of poetic composition with great authority. Using twelve rhyming two-line stanzas, MacLeish works in a formal style, yet by varying the line length, he also refuses the constraints of symmetry. The poem is further divided into three eight-line sections. Contrary to most poetic theory, the first section asserts that a poem should be "silent." Continuing in this same vein of thought, the second section asserts that a poem be "motionless." In the final section, MacLeish insists that a poem should just "be." Unlike some of his poetic predecessors, MacLeish did not believe that a poem should speak to readers and urge them to action by revealing "truth." Instead, MacLeish maintains that poetry should capture a moment of human experience—for example grief or love—through concrete images.

The first lines of "Ars Poetica" are designed to prompt readers to rethink their expectations about poetry. They should not look to poems to "speak" to them, but rather should be able to experience a poem as they as they do objects in the world. To this end, MacLeish maintains that "A poem should be palpable and mute / as a globed fruit." The words should have a direct effect on the reader; they should be able to feel the images in the poem. Moreover, it shall be "Dumb / As old medallions to the thumb, / Silent as the sleeve-worn stone / Of casement ledges where moss has grown." These metaphors suggest that the poem should be imbued with great experience, of having lived in the world and seen much in life. Medallions are generally associated with commemorating an event, recognizing achievement, or rewarding merit. As such, this image is infused with greatness in life. Yet, inasmuch as the relief on the medal is worn, there is just a subtle lingering sense of the triumph that once was acknowledged. Likewise, the mossy ledge where someone spent much time looking out the window, wearing down the casement with his or her sleeves, suggests a contemplating place where there has been a good bit of history. These first six lines of the poem are an appeal to universality, the passage of time and knowledge that cuts across the barriers of language. The final couplet in this section sets the poem free from the heavy weight of artifice:

A poem should be wordless
As the flight of birds.

Obviously, a poem cannot literally be "wordless," but it can have the appearance of great fluid spontaneity and the ease of the natural world. MacLeish is suggesting that the art of poetry should present itself with *sprezzatura,* or subtle ease of manner, unfettered by the individual words that create the whole.

According to MacLeish's philosophy, a poem should not only be silent; it should be "motionless in time." The second section of the poem develops his notion that an effective poem is timeless. Such a poem is not rooted in any time or place. To express this concept, MacLeish uses the image of the moon:

> A poem should be motionless in time
> As the moon climbs,
>
> Leaving as the moon releases
> Twig by twig the night-entangled trees,
>
> Leaving, as the moon behind the winter leaves,
> Memory by memory the mind—
>
> A poem should be motionless in time
> As the moon climbs.

Like the imperceptible, incremental movement of the rising moon, so should a poem move readers. There have been several different interpretations of this section. The first, presented by Donald Stauffer in *The Nature of Poetry,* is consistent with the above reading that a good poem has the ability to transcend time. Stauffer, however, also presented a second reading in which he contends that this section asserts "that a poem wakens in the reader's consciousness memory after memory, complex, minute, and exact, just as moonlight, against the motionless, durable, illimitable night, etches out twigs and leaves and innumerable silhouettes." This less widely held reading has been advanced by Thomas E. Sanders in his critical anthology *The Discovery of Poetry.* A third interpretation by Edwin St. Vincent in *The Explicator* contends that these "lines set forth the doctrine that a good poem makes a lasting impression on the mind, suffering loss in the memory but only in imperceptibly slow degree." In reaching this conclusion, St. Vincent "untangles" the syntax of the lines and construes the word "leaves" as a verb (instead of a noun). While he admits that the construction of the word is inherently ambiguous, St. Vincent advances his reading based on two factors: "first, because the poet in his recording of the poem in *An Album of Modern Poetry* ... clearly reads it as a verb; and second, because the idea of the moon (in contrast to its anthesis the diurnal sun) slowly measuring off seasonal change further enriches the effect of imperceptible release."

The final section of "Ars Poetica" summons the poetics of Romantic poet John Keats only to dismiss this predecessor's ideal for poetry. In the well-known last lines of "Ode On a Grecian Urn," Keats states, "'Beauty is truth, truth beauty,'—that is all / Ye know on earth, and all ye need to know." Interpretations of these much-debated lines vary, but they are often cited as reflecting the search for truth in art. Disputing this function of art, MacLeish states:

> A poem should be equal to:
> Not true.

In other words, a poem should not concern itself with the abstract, unknowable concept of truth. The role of the poet is to present images from which readers can reexperience emotion. For example, MacLeish offers the image of an "empty doorway and a maple leaf" as metaphors for grief. The first image evokes a sense of emptiness or uncertainty and the second the changes that come with autumn. Both, however, have the ability to evoke a highly personal resonance of loss. Similarly, "For love," MacLeish uses "leaning grasses and two lights above the sea." The Whitmanesque grass and the harmony of two lights suspended together summon readers to a place where they can grasp a moment of devotion. Neither example is intended to produce a neat correspondence to the emotion. Instead, each has multiple and different layers of meaning for all readers.

The last couplet of the poem provides a concluding statement about MacLeish's poetics:

> A poem should not mean
> But be.

These deliberately short lines underscore MacLeish's belief that poetry should use concrete images to capture and evoke a moment of personal experience. Poetry should not endeavor to take on great, unanswerable philosophical questions; it should merely be a means of taking in the richness of being. To that end, "Ars Poetica" echoes Fenollosa's belief that "Metaphor, the revealer of nature, is the very substance of poetry."

In 1961, nearly forty years after writing "Ars Poetica," MacLeish's insights about poetry were published in *Poetry and Experience.* In this collection, MacLeish reiterates his belief that "It is true enough that a poet, an artist, serves his art and not a cause. He goes his own way with his own will beside him and his own truth to find. But on the great issue, on the issue of man, his truth and the truth of history are one." In other words, as paraphrased by MacLeish biographer Scott Donaldson, the "business of poetry was to communicate such truth, not the rational scientific knowledge of science but the intuited knowledge derived from one person's particular experience, yet universally resonant."

**Source:** Marisa Anne Pagnattaro, in an essay for *Poetry for Students,* Gale, 1999.

## Sources

Beach, Sylvia, *Shakespeare and Company,* New York: Harcourt Brace and Co., 1956.

Donaldson, Scott, *Archibald MacLeish: An American Life,* Boston: Houghton Mifflin Company, 1992.

Eliot, T. S., "Hamlet and His Problems," *The Sacred Wood,* London: Methuen & Co., Ltd., 1932.

Fenollosa, Ernest, "The Chinese Written Character as a Medium for Poetry," reprinted in *Instigations by Ezra Pound,* Freeport, NY: Books for Libraries Press, 1967.

Forma, Warren, *They Were Ragtime,* New York: Grosset and Dunlap, 1976.

Kramer, Hilton, *New York Times Book Review* October 3, 1976, p. 28.

MacLeish, Archibald, *Poetry and Experience,* Boston: Houghton Mifflin Company, 1961.

Perrett, Geoffrey, *America In the Twenties: A History,* New York: Simon and Schuster, 1982.

Smith, Grover, *Archibald MacLeish,* University of Minnesota Pamphlets on American Writers Series, No. 99, Minneapolis: University of Minnesota Press, 1971.

St. Vincent, Edwin, "MacLeish's Ars Poetica, 9-16," *The Explicator,* Vol. 37, No. 3, Spring 1979, pp. 13-15.

Sanders, Thomas E., *The Discovery of Poetry,* Glenview, IL: Scott, Foresman and Co., 1967.

Staffer, Donald, *The Nature of Poetry,* New York: W.W. Norton & Co., 1946.

Stein, Gertrude, *Writings: 1903-1932,* New York: Library of America/Penguin Putnam Inc., 1998.

Wain, John, "Mr. MacLeish's New Play," *New Republic,* July 22, 1967, p. 25.

## For Further Study

Eberhart, Richard, "The Pattern of MacLeish's Poetry," *New York Times Book Review,* November 23, 1952.
   Eberhart, himself an acclaimed poet of recent times, gives serious examination of and explanation about MacLeish's works.

Faulk, Signi Lenea, *Archibald MacLeish,* New York: Twayne Publishers, 1965.
   The poet's career was far from over when this scholarly study was published, but he had been published enough for Faulk to get a sense of his influences. This book has plenty of comparisons of MacLeish's works to those of great authors who came before him such as Wordsworth, Keats, and Yeats.

MacLeish, Archibald, *A Continuing Journey,* Boston: Houghton Mifflin Co., 1967.
   This book is a collection of MacLeish's personal essays. The focus of the pieces shifts between his three main concerns, which he identifies in the introduction as "politics, poetry, and teaching."

Miller, Linda Patterson, ed., *Letters from the Lost Generation: Gerald and Sara Murphy and Friends,* New Brunswick, NJ: Rutgers University Press, 1991.
   Centered on the couple in the title who were involved with the Paris expatriate scene of the 1920s Paris, this book features dozens of MacLeish's letters and a great amount of background information about MacLeish and his family during that time.

# Ballad of Birmingham

## Dudley Randall
## 1965

Published in 1965, "Ballad of Birmingham" is significant both as an example of Dudley Randall's use of traditional poetic form to talk about political events and as the first broadside—a large, single-sheet publication—to appear in the Broadside Series from his extremely influential Broadside Press. Randall holds an important place in America's literary history, not only as an accomplished poet, but also as an editor and promoter of African-American poetry, publishing African-American writers at a time—the early and mid-1960s—when the civil rights movement had just begun to galvanize and unite previously unrecognized artists of color.

Throughout 1963, Americans had watched as civil rights demonstrators and racist city and government officials clashed in Birmingham, Alabama. On September 15, 1963, the tragic culmination of those events occurred when a bomb ripped through the basement of the Sixteenth Street Baptist Church and killed four girls as they prepared for church. Randall personalizes this event in "Ballad of Birmingham" by recounting an imagined conversation between one of those girls and her mother. The child wants to participate in the children's freedom marches led by Reverend Martin Luther King, Jr., but the mother is afraid to let her daughter be part of something she views as dangerous. But, as the poem points out, in a racist society, no place—no matter how sacred—can possibly be safe; the mother tells her daughter to go to church rather than march, but in the poem, it

*Dudley Randall*

is, ironically, the church that is the site of greatest danger for the child. The ballad form of the poem and the conversational quality of its language all make it very accessible to a range of readers—a quality Randall prizes in poetry. "Ballad of Birmingham" shows the potent voice poetry can have in the struggle for social justice and political change.

## Author Biography

Randall was born in Washington, D.C., on January 14, 1914. His interest in poetry began when he was just a child and he published his first poem—a sonnet for which he won the prize of a dollar—in the *Detroit Free Press* on its "Young Poets' Page." His father was a minister who took him to see such influential speakers as W. E. B. Du Bois and James Weldon Johnson, and his mother was a teacher. Randall worked for the Ford Motor Company in Dearborn, Michigan, from 1932 to 1937, an experience that sharpened his awareness of the feelings and lives of working people and affected his later writing. He was employed at the U.S. Post Office in Detroit while working on his bachelor's degree in English at Wayne State University, and he served in the Army Air Corps before finishing his degree in 1949. He received a master's degree in Library Science from the University of Michigan in 1951 and went on to work as a librarian in Detroit. His interest in Russia led him to study and become fluent in the Russian language (from which he has frequently translated the work of other writers), and he established Broadside Press in 1965. He has won a number of awards for his literary contributions and was named the first Poet Laureate of Detroit in 1981.

In 1969, Paul Breman characterized Randall as "quietly dedicated to the revolution and quietly doing something about it." Indeed, Randall's work as Broadside's editor has often been cited as his most important contribution to American letters. Beginning with "Ballad of Birmingham" in 1965 and his mythic, poetic rendering of Kennedy's assassination in "Dressed All in Pink," Randall's own poems constituted the first two broadsides in his Broadside Series that published almost one hundred titles by 1982. *For Malcolm: Poems on the Life and Death of Malcolm X,* coedited with Margaret G. Burroughs, appeared as the press's first collection, and Randall went on to publish what would be the first anthology of African-American poetry published by an African-American publisher—*Black Poetry: A Supplement to Anthologies Which Exclude Black Poets*—in 1969. Under Randall's leadership, Broadside Press first published or gained the publishing loyalty of such key African-American writers as Gwendolyn Brooks, Nikki Giovanni, Etheridge Knight, Haki R. Madhubuti, and Sonia Sanchez.

Randall's own collections of poetry include *Poem Counterpoem* (1966) with Margaret Danner, a collection that juxtaposed his and Danner's thematically linked poems; *Cities Burning* (1968), published following the Detroit riot of 1967; *Love You* (1970), a collection of fourteen love poems; *More to Remember: Poems of Four Decades* (1971); *After the Killing* (1973), which considers racism and nationalism; *Broadside Memories: Poets I Have Known* (1975), which includes selections of Randall's memoirs; *A Litany of Friends: New and Selected Poems* (1981), the collection most closely following Randall's experience of suicidal depression: and *Homage to Hoyt Fuller* (1984). He has edited a number of other collections, including the 1971 Bantam anthology *The Black Poets,* and he has published essays and collections of nonfiction as well.

## Poem Text

### (On the Bombing of a Church in Birmingham, Alabama, 1963)

"Mother dear, may I go downtown
Instead of out to play,
And march the streets of Birmingham
In a Freedom March today?"

"No, baby, no you may not go,                                   5
For the dogs are fierce and wild,
And clubs and hoses, guns and jail
Ain't good for a little child."

"But, mother, I won't be alone.
Other children will go with me,                              10
And march the streets of Birmingham
To make our country free."

"No, baby, no, you may not go,
For I fear those guns will fire.
But you may go to church instead                            15
And sing in the children's choir."

She has combed and brushed her night-dark hair,
And bathed rose petal sweet,
And drawn white gloves on her small brown hands,
And white shoes on her feet.                                   20

The mother smiled to know her child
Was in the sacred place,
But that smile was the last smile
To come upon her face.

For when she heard the explosion,                              35
Her eyes grew wet and wild.
She raced through the streets of Birmingham
Calling for her child.

She clawed through bits of glass and brick,
Then lifted out a shoe.                                        30
"O here's the shoe my baby wore,
But, baby, where are you?"

## Poem Summary

### Title:

Randall's title—"Ballad of Birmingham"—immediately creates specific expectations in the mind of the reader about what kind of poem this will be. By calling the poem a ballad, Randall places it within an ancient, and initially oral, folk tradition. Typically stories about events or people that were already known to a general audience, ballads often narrate the lives of social outcasts—outlaws such as Robin Hood—or those alienated from the main centers of power in society—like the poor folk for whom Robin Hood stole. Ballads are always stories, often with tragic endings, and they frequently rely on dialogue to tell their tales. They were originally sung, so we can expect that the poem will be strong, musically. Finally, by noting that it is a ballad about Birmingham, Randall signals to his readers what story he will probably be telling: some aspect of the civil rights struggle in Alabama and the events that took place there.

### Lines 1-4:

The very first stanza places the reader directly in the mind and voice of one of the characters of this story. Obviously, a child speaks here, because the speaker asks permission to go "downtown" to join those marching with the demonstrators for "freedom" rather than merely going "out to play." Randall introduces a kind of gentle irony at this point by turning our expectations as to what a child would usually ask permission to do—go outside and play—upside down; we get the feeling that this child's childhood is very different from what we imagine or tell ourselves childhood is or should be about. The child asks the question with affection—she calls her mother "dear"—so that we understand the relationship between them to be warm and loving.

### Lines 5-8:

In the next four lines, Randall introduces the second speaker in the poem: the mother. She tells her child—her "baby" as she says—that she can't go with the marchers because it is too dangerous. Here, Randall incorporates what had become the central televised and photographed images in the American public's mind of the civil rights struggle in Birmingham; the mother mentions the "fierce and wild" police dogs that were set upon the demonstrators, as well as the billy clubs, fire hoses, guns, and jails that were used to intimidate the marchers. Randall is not concerned here with introducing readers to the actual events that took place in Birmingham; he counts on a general recognition on the part of his readers to understand that when he says "hoses," he means the tremendously powerful fire hoses that knocked demonstrators down to the streets of the city. He also plays on a strange expectation here; while we generally think of the police and the law—the highest kind of civilized body—as protective of citizens and their rights, the dogs that are extensions of police power are portrayed as savage and linked to whatever lies beyond the borders of law, order, and civilization. Randall also uses the word "ain't" here to give us a sense that the mother is a less-educated woman, probably a member of the working class, and all the more a realistic and believable figure for that ungrammaticality.

# Media Adaptations

- A cassette titled *Broadside on Broadway: Seven Poets Read* was released in 1970 by Broadside Voices. Dudley Randall, Jerry Whittington, Frenchy Hodges, Sonia Sanchez, Don L. Lee, Margaret Walker, and Gwendolyn Brooks read.

## Lines 9-12:

The child responds here and tries to persuade her mother to let her go by pointing out that other children will be marching. She likewise explains why they're marching—"to make our country free." The speaker in these lines uses a typical ploy to convince her mother to let her do what she wants to; everyone else is doing it, she suggests. But again, because of what she's asking to do, something so solemn and seemingly unchildlike as promote freedom in America, we are reminded of how this child's life simply does not fit the myth of innocence we usually associate with childhood. By this point, too, it is apparent that Randall wants us to feel the intimacy and reality of this conversation as well as its immediacy by letting us overhear it as if we were present in the room. Again, Randall counts on his reader's awareness of the happenings in Birmingham when he refers specifically to the way in which civil rights leaders Reverend Martin Luther King, Jr., and Reverend Fred Shuttlesworth organized demonstrations composed specifically of younger people.

## Lines 13-16:

In this stanza, the mother still refuses to let her child go, telling her that she is afraid of the violence that may occur. It is here, in lines 15 and 16, that the poem's central irony is introduced: while the mother won't allow her child to march with the demonstrators because she's afraid of how dangerous it might be, she encourages her to go to "sing in the children's choir" and "go to church instead," trusting that the church will be a protected, safe place.

## Lines 17-20:

In this fifth stanza, Randall offers us narrative description, rather than dialogue, to continue the story. In itself, such a shift sets up some kind of change in the poem's line of action. The activity described in these lines is all preparatory; the daughter combs her hair, washes herself "rose petal sweet," and puts on white gloves and white shoes. The action is all lovingly described and, because the "she" of the stanza lacks a clear referent and only ambiguously refers to the daughter rather than the mother, the action described in this section echoes the washing and dressing of the dead that traditionally was a familial and communal pre-burial ritual, a dressing as tenderly undertaken as is this preparatory washing. Randall's use of the color white for the little girl's gloves and shoes has multiple and possibly opposing connotations. On one hand, white is the traditional color of purity and innocence, surely everything we would associate with the kind of sweet child described in this poem. But white also symbolizes an oppressive power for this girl and her mother, and it may be symbolic that both her hands and feet—those limbs with which we write, make things, and literally move in the world—are, in fact, encased in that color, reminding us of the control it has over them.

## Lines 21-24:

These four lines feel somewhat abrupt and, in fact, act as a kind of warning to the reader that something wrong is now certain to occur. While the mother is comforted by the thought that her child is in "the sacred place," Randall tells us in no uncertain terms that she will not smile again. The "sacred place" referred to here may also suggest a more expansive sacred place such as heaven; this allows the poem to imagistically foreshadow what will happen at the end of the poem—the child will be killed.

## Lines 25-28:

The event the poem has had us anticipating finally occurs here in stanza 7. The mother hears "the explosion" that Randall would have expected his reader to understand as a reference to the bombing of the Sixteenth Street Baptist Church in Birmingham. Obviously, the mother is afraid and, even before she even knows for certain what has happened to her daughter, fears the worst, her eyes "wet and wild." She runs through the city, calling for her.

### Lines 29-32:

In this final stanza, what we have feared would come to pass indeed does. The mother digs through the debris at the bombed church and finds only a shoe belonging to her daughter. The poem's last two lines are a brief and painful return to dialogue as the mother plaintively and helplessly exclaims that the shoe she holds is indeed her daughter's, but asks, "baby, where are you?" Randall elaborates on the mother's fear and grief that he introduced in the previous stanza by using the word "clawed" to indicate the desperate scramble the mother makes at the bomb site to find her child and by addressing the last line of the poem directly to the child, who we now understand is dead. The painful futility of the mother's actions is apparent in this line. Likewise, Randall skillfully avoids describing a grotesque scene of mangled human remains while hinting at such when he depicts the mother going through the "bits of glass and brick"—small chunks of sturdy building materials that are all that remain of that section of the church—and when the mother finds only the shoe. The shoe, in and of itself, is a powerful image with which to end the poem. It is evocative of the tiny shoes parents bronze as mementoes of their children's childhoods, but it also reminds us of what the daughter initially asked permission to do—to march in the streets for freedom, an activity that was, sadly and ironically, not the most dangerous thing she could have done that day. The poem leaves us with the understanding that the most dangerous threat to this child's life was not the demonstrations staged by the freedom marchers, but, instead, the racism those demonstrations nonviolently opposed.

## Themes

### Civil Rights

The scene Randall describes in "Ballad of Birmingham" provides the reader with a personalized view of the struggle against racism fought by the demonstrators and activists of the civil rights movement of the 1950s and 1960s. Relying on his readers' awareness of the events in Birmingham, Randall dramatizes what happened there from a unique, intimate perspective in order to bring the situation into the sharpest possible focus for his reader. The mother and daughter who converse throughout the first four stanzas of the poem provide a very human, sympathetic portrait of how the struggle against racism affected real people. In fact,

by downplaying the presence of race in this poem, Randall even more effectively battles against the consequence of thinking about the value of people as determined by the color of their skin. Randall never makes direct reference to the African-American identity of these speakers, and by not doing so, he highlights the unimportance of such a detail for any reader's understanding of what this mother must have felt like when she realized her child had been killed by a bomb while at church.

The poem also illustrates the fact that it is racism—not the struggle against it—that threatens the safety of individuals in society. The mother in this poem makes an understandable mistake by judging Birmingham's civil rights demonstrations as too dangerous for a child to participate in. Yet the central and poignant irony of Randall's ballad is precisely this: that racism endangers the little girl's life at least as powerfully, if not far more, than any action she may take against it. By arguing that others will be marching with her as she does in lines 9 and 10, the child expresses a central tenet of any struggle for social and political equality—namely, united we stand, but divided we fall. Randall's ballad, then, effectively argues against passivity on the parts of those treated unjustly in our society, giving hard evidence of the danger implicit in such fear of action or in apathy. He also clarifies the way in which racism turns all of our realities inside out and upside down, so that a child could be more courageous than an adult in the struggle against this oppression, and a church could be more dangerous than a street filled with vicious dogs, violent policemen, and high-pressure fire hoses.

### Victims and Victimization

Typical of the ballad form that leaves its audience to flesh out the details of its story given its heavy emphasis on character rather than development of plot, "Ballad of Birmingham" demands a reader's knowledge of the 1963 bombing of Birmingham's Sixteenth Street Baptist Church to fully appreciate the nuances of the story it tells. But without that knowledge, Randall's poem tells a more simple story, if just as tragic. A woman tries to protect her daughter from a threatening world and learns that no place is necessarily safe from the violence occurring around her. At its most basic level, "Ballad of Birmingham" pulls us through the heartbreaking experience of a tragic loss and exposes us to the senselessness of such a victimization. Both the murdered child and the mother are victims, and no reader can miss the agony in the mother's voice—in lines 31 and 32—when she finds her

# *Topics for Further Study*

- Write a ballad of your own about some contemporary event or story that your peers would recognize. Use the traditional ballad stanza form and make your own decorated, single sheet broadside of the piece.

- Find all of the words that are stressed in "Ballad of Birmingham" and make a list of them, keeping in mind the stress pattern of the traditional ballad stanza. Why do you think these words receive special emphasis in the poem? Are there others you were surprised to find were not accented? What part would you say meter plays in the meaning of "Ballad of Birmingham?"

daughter's shoe and asks the most difficult question posed in the poem: "O, here's the shoe my baby wore, / but, baby, where are you?" Death has claimed her daughter and whatever myths we embrace regarding what that means, none of them, Randall seems to suggest, can finally provide real comfort in the shape of a clear meaning or significance for the brutally final form it takes here. By ending the poem in such an open fashion, though, Randall seems to present the question of how we deal with death when it comes in such a violent, raging form; how can victims like this mother respond in such a way as to give her child's death appropriate significance? By making her child's shoe the evidence the mother finds, Randall may be encouraging the reader to see this as an invitation for the mother to join the march her daughter now cannot and to move out of the space of passive victimization and into one of peaceful, but determined action.

## *Style*

"Ballad of Birmingham" follows the metrical structure of a traditional folk ballad. Ballads utilize the ballad stanza which consists of four lines that rhyme in an *abcb* rhyme scheme. In other words, in each stanza, the second and fourth lines rhyme, while the first and third lines do not. The metrical, rhythmical pattern of the ballad decides how many syllables will be stressed in each of those four lines; the first and third lines of each stanza will contain four emphasized syllabic stresses, while the second and fourth will each contain three. When working with metrical forms (something Randall was particularly fond of), the challenge for the poet becomes how to vary the format ever so slightly so as to add rhythmic tension to the piece or, in Randall's case, a heightened sense of music. In "Ballad of Birmingham," Randall generally maintains the three- and four-stress line pattern of the traditional folk ballad stanza, but he does vary the total number of syllables from line to line. Reading the poem aloud makes it clear that there is a fairly regulated pattern of stresses at work in the poem, but extra unstressed syllables before and between the more clearly accented ones can allow for a sound not unlike a musical trill. For instance, the first two syllables in line 6 trip over the tongue to get us to the most important syllables and words in that line: "for the" are both unstressed syllables, while "dogs," "fierce," and "wild" carry the three central stresses of the line. By using accented syllables in this way, Randall underlines the importance of select words in the poem by rhythmically directing the reader to give them extra emphasis when the poem is read aloud. But, by altering the number of overall beats per line, Randall actually gives "Ballad of Birmingham" a fuller musical tone.

Repeating lines or refrains also appear as stock features in ballads, and "Ballad of Birmingham" offers such repetition in two forms. First of all, the stanzas that document the mother and daughter's question-and-answer session quickly construct a formula to be followed, so that we can predict what is likely to come next in this conversation between the two; we know that the daughter will ask to go march, give a reason why she should be allowed, and that the mother will say no. The form that "no" will take appears as the poem's only real refrain and is its second instance of repetition: "No, baby, no, you may not go," the mother says each time her daughter poses the question. The poem's closing line recalls this refrain, echoing the mother's command in her own confused final question as she, who has told her child she can't go to march and place herself in danger, now hopelessly wonders where indeed her child has gone.

## Historical Context

If you were an African American in the 1950s and early 1960s in the southern United States, you lived under a separate code of behavior than your white counterparts. You only drank from water fountains labelled "Colored," you went to "Colored Only" movie theaters, you went to schools that taught only other African-American children and received only a fraction of the funding white schools did, you rode in the rear "Colored" section of the bus, and understood that it was in some states illegal for you to even play checkers in public with white people. This was segregation, and it was the result of a series of "Jim Crow laws" that white, southern lawmakers had established after the Civil War (Jim Crow was a stock comic character in black-face minstrel shows first introduced in the nineteenth century). Southern planters were angry over the emancipation of the African Americans who had been previously enslaved by them and who had provided the unpaid labor on which their economic system and wealth were founded prior to the Civil War. Segregation was the social and legal result of the social inequity created by that system, and other forms of more violent intimidation accompanied it—actions including the public harassment, lynching, bombing, and murder of random African Americans by groups such as the Ku Klux Klan (KKK). Usually, local southern officials did not trace such actions to any particular figure, and even if they did, the stronghold powerful racists exerted on the legal system in the South insured that few of these perpetrators would ever actually be prosecuted for their crimes.

It was in the 1950s that more and more people—both African American and white—began to question and confront this system of inequity, creating the civil rights movement. African Americans themselves had been resisting the limits of their position in American society since the time the first Africans were kidnapped and brought to America as slaves. But the civil rights movement was a composite of actions and events that led to the most substantial change in the legal and political status of nonwhite persons in America since the nationwide abolition of slavery following the Civil War. The civil rights movement consisted of organized and sustained public protests and demonstrations like the Montgomery bus boycott and other nonviolent displays of civil disobedience promoted and led by groups such as the National Association for the Advancement of Colored People (NAACP), the Southern Christian Leadership Conference (SCLC), the Congress of Racial Equality (CORE), and the Student Nonviolent Coordinating Committee (SNCC). The movement also consisted of specific legal cases, such as the Supreme Court judgment that decided that educational segregation was unconstitutional, and therefore illegal, in the 1954 case, *Brown v. Board of Education of Topeka.* The movement both affected and was affected by specific political events, including the election of John F. Kennedy as president of the United States in 1960. And it also, sadly, was shaped by acts of violence, such as the 1955 murder of fourteen-year-old Emmett Till, who enraged a group of white men in Mississippi when he spoke to a white woman in a store on a dare from his friends. His body was found three days later, a bullet in his head, an eye missing, and barbed wire wrapping the fan from a cotton gin to his neck. Events and actions like this created the civil rights movement and gave it the momentum, purpose, and shape to address one of the most enduring systems of social injustice ever to be seen in this country.

Birmingham, Alabama, played a key role in the civil rights movement in America. The largest city in Alabama at the beginning of the 1960s, Birmingham was, according to SCLC leader Reverend Martin Luther King, Jr., "the most thoroughly segregated city in the United States." On Mother's Day in 1961, a mob had attacked Freedom Riders (black and white demonstrators riding buses from Washington, D.C., to New Orleans in defiance of segregation policies pertaining to interstate travel) as they entered Birmingham; the Birmingham police did nothing to stop the attack. The incident had drawn national attention to Birmingham, and the local leader of the Alabama Christian Movement for Human Rights (ACMHR), Reverend Fred Shuttlesworth, convinced King to take the city on as his next site for nonviolent action against segregation. Birmingham had been nicknamed "Bombingham" because of the eighteen unsolved bombings that had occurred there between 1957 and 1963 (Shuttlesworth's own home had been completely destroyed by a bomb in 1956). It was time for Birmingham to move forward, civil rights leaders decided, and 1963 would be the year of concentrated demonstrations and protest marches all geared to force city officials to negotiate with black leaders in the attempt to end segregation in the downtown and financial sectors of the city. Using the Sixteenth Street Baptist Church as their headquarters, the civil rights leaders developed "Project C" and began the protests in March.

# Compare & Contrast

- **1957-63:** Eighteen unsolved bombings in primarily African-American neighborhoods and locales earn Birmingham, Alabama, the nickname "Bombingham."

  **1995-96:** More than thirty African-American churches in the South—Alabama, Georgia, Louisiana, Mississippi, North Carolina, South Carolina, Tennessee, and Virginia—are burned in what are feared to be racially motivated crimes.

  **1998:** A bomb explodes outside of a women's clinic in Birmingham, Alabama, that performs abortions; an off-duty police officer is killed and a nurse is severely wounded.

- **1960:** The median annual income for African Americans is $3,000, less than half of what it is for white households.

  **1990:** In Selma, Alabama—one of the poorest sections of the country—the median household income for white households is $25,580 and, for African-American households, $9,615. Nationally, African Americans make about $63 for each $100 made by whites.

- **1970:** Five times as many African-American workers between the ages of 24 and 44 are high school dropouts, as opposed to college graduates. Among all young professionals, only one in twenty is African American.

  **1990:** Almost as many African-American workers between the ages of 24 and 44 are college graduates as high school dropouts. Among all young professionals, one in twelve is African American.

- **1963:** On August 28, more than 250,000 marchers descend on Washington, D.C., in the largest public demonstration held in this country, to protest the poverty, segregation, and lack of civil rights for African Americans.

  **1989:** On April 10, more than 500,000 people march in Washington, D.C., to show their support of the 1973 *Roe vs. Wade* decision that made abortion legal in the United States.

  **1995:** On October 17, approximately 400,000 African-American men participate in the Million Man March in Washington, D.C., to reinvorgate public interest in the problems of racial division and injustice in America.

- **1965:** On March 7, later dubbed "Bloody Sunday," mounted police use tear gas and billy clubs to stop some six hundred demonstrators marching across the Edmund Pettus Bridge in Selma, Alabama, in support of voting rights and protected registration for African Americans. The Selma March helped galvanize federal support for the Voting Rights Act of 1965.

  **1995:** On March 10, civil rights leaders and workers march in Selma to commemorate the 1965 demonstration; former Alabama governor George Wallace, staunch segregationist of the 1960s turned apologist, joins the group, holding hands with those his policies and actions had at times brutally opposed thirty years before.

---

The events that took place in Birmingham quickly made the city a national symbol of the struggle and difficulty incurred by opponents of segregation. Police under the authority of the Birmingham Commissioner of Public Safety, T. Eugene "Bull" Connor, used police dogs and fire hoses—powerful enough to tear the bark off trees—to disperse demonstrators that King, Shuttlesworth, and others organized and led. Although specifically forbidden to do so by a court injunction, King—and 132 other civil rights leaders—led another march downtown on April 12, Good Friday, and was subsequently arrested. Four days later, he completed his famous "Letter from a Birmingham Jail" that explained to local white clergymen (who had publicly denounced King's actions) why this was indeed the time to act against segregation. Finally, movement leaders took an unprecedented approach when they recruited children—ranging in age from 6 to 18—for special Freedom Marches; many people were concerned about the risk involved in such a move, but the media coverage that resulted from those marches helped galvanize national support for what the demonstrators were attempting to do. On the first day of these marches, Connor and his men arrested 959 children, using school buses to carry them to jail. The next day, more than a thousand children stayed out of school to march, and Connor called out the dogs and fire hoses. The African-American community, enraged by Connor's attack on their children, came out in even greater numbers to demonstrate. The American public at large watched the nightly news in horror as children were attacked by dogs and washed down the streets of the torn city.

More than two thousand demonstrators had been sent to jail by May 6, and, concerned by the image of America such media coverage was sending to the rest of the world, President Kennedy sent a federal aide to work with King and local business leaders on negotiations. The day after an initial agreement was announced, bombs went off at the home of King's brother and the hotel where the movement leaders had been staying. Riots ensued, and Kennedy sent federal troops to nearby Fort McClellan to ward off further disturbances to the fragile peace already established. In part a response to the events in Birmingham, Kennedy sent a civil rights bill to Congress in June, and, in support of this bill's passage, civil rights groups and leaders from around the country held in August what was then the largest public demonstration in American history—more than 250,000 people—in Washington, D.C., where King delivered his famous "I Have A Dream" oration.

Despite the success of the march on Washington, just weeks later, on a Sunday morning before church, a bomb went off in the Sixteenth Street Baptist Church. Eleven-year-old Denise McNair and fourteen-year-old Addie Mae Collins, Carole Robertson, and Cynthia Wesley were all killed in the blast on September 15. Much later, in 1977, the state's key witness, the defendant's niece, named her Klan-affiliated uncle, Robert Chambliss, as the man centrally responsible for the action. Fourteen years after the bombing, Chambliss was convicted and sentenced to life imprisonment.

The struggle for human civil rights continues, and in 1992, the Birmingham Civil Rights Institute opened—its mission to educate visitors about the civil rights struggle of the 1950s and 1960s and to further their understanding of how people all over the world continue to struggle for equality. In 1998 Spike Lee received an Academy Award nomination for his documentary *4 Little Girls,* in which he retells the story of the bombing of the Sixteenth Street Baptist Church through interviews with friends and family members of the four murdered girls. While still a largely segregated city with weighty problems of black poverty and crime, Birmingham has begun to address its history as the rest of the country remembers those who died as a result of it.

## Critical Overview

Randall receives mention and praise in historical accounts of African-American literature most often as an editor, founder, and head of Broadside Press. In his contribution to *The Black American Writer* series, Paul Breman writes almost exclusively about Randall's work as a publisher, and Richard Barksdale and Kenneth Kinnamon, in their volume *Black Writers in America,* claim that "undoubtedly, Randall's most notable contribution is not his poetry but the arrangements he has made to facilitate the publication of the poetry of young men and women who, without his aid and counsel, would have remained 'Black and Unknown Bards' just as their early forefathers did." These scholars note that Randall serves as a kind of "bridge connecting an older generation of poets with a younger generation," and they highlight Randall's work as a translator of Russian and French as well as noting the range of styles he utilized in his poetry.

When "Ballad of Birmingham" is specifically mentioned by Randall's critics, it receives most attention as the first broadside to be published by the press. But it also reflects Randall's "firm sense of the lyric," according to Ron Welburn, so powerfully as to have been a natural choice for the musical adaptation it was given by New York folk singer Jerry Moore. Other critics highlight Randall's sense of formalism, particularly R. Baxter Miller and D. H. Melhem. In an essay titled "'Endowing the World and Time': The Life and Work of Dudley Randall," Miller argues that Randall's poetry, "so accomplished technically and profoundly concerned with the history and racial identity of Blacks, benefits from the ideas and literary forms of the Harlem Renaissance as well as from the critical awareness of the earlier Western Renaissance." In an article in *Black American Literature Forum,* D. H. Melhem mixes his own critical readings of selected poems by Randall with Randall's own reflections on his work, culled from a personal interview with the poet. Preceding his discussion of "Ballad of Birmingham," Melhem claims that Randall's strongest poems in *Cities Burning,* (one collection in which "Ballad of Birmingham" appears) "employ the lyrical understatement of black folk poetry and the terseness of blues, 'ballards,' spirituals, and seculars, and of old English ballads … in which deep feeling compresses into rhythm, rime, and the tragic frame." He describes "Ballad of Birmingham" as "complementing both subject and genre [the ballad form itself]" with a "spare dignity." Melhem and others also indicate that Randall's use of the broadside format to distribute this and other poems on similar themes of social injustice is appropriate given the broadside's historic use as a tool for political provocation. Prior to and during the American Revolution, for instance, Thomas Paine used the broadside format to distribute writings he composed to stir up support among his fellow colonists for American independence. But, as Melhem also adds, despite his political interest, Randall's "deep concern was always for the best poetry."

Randall's work has also been hailed in poetry by other writers. In his "For Dudley Randall," Lenard D. Moore describes a reading by Randall in which his poems "… stretch eyes wide / make lips hang / pierce eardrums deep / and send brothers & sisters sliding / to the edge of their seats." For Moore, Randall's words are "gems" and a "reminiscence of Blackness."

## Criticism

### Jhan Hochman

*Jhan Hochman's articles appear in* Democracy and Nature, Genre, ISLE, *and* Mosaic. *He is the author of* Green Cultural Studies: Nature in Film, Novel, and Theory *(1998), and he holds a Ph.D in English and an M.A. in Cinema Studies. In the following essay, Hochman provides the background concerning the bombing of the Sixteenth Street Baptist Church.*

On September 15, 1963, at 10:25 a.m. on a Sunday morning, an African-American church in Birmingham, Alabama, the Sixteenth Baptist Church, blew apart. When the rubble settled, fourteen people were injured, and four girls were found dead—buried under pieces of the building. They were Denise McNair, age 11; Cynthia Wesley, 14; Carol Robertson, 14; and Addie Mae Collins, 14. The four girls killed in the blast had just, moments before, heard their teacher, Mrs. Ella C. Demand complete the Sunday-school lesson for the day, "The Love That Forgives."

While African-American leaders in the city did not counsel forgiveness, they did plead with the black community to contain their anger. This, understandably, was only partially successful. According to a *New York Times* article on September 16, 1963, "hundreds" of blacks took to the streets. While the report of the aftermath is, at best, sketchy, five whites were reported injured and two black youths were dead. One of these youths, Johnny (or James) Robinson, age 16, was shot in the back by police as he ran from them. A second, Virgil Wade, age 13, was attacked and killed by a group whites while riding his bike. As three buildings burned and people fought in the streets, the police poured into the streets to contain the explosion of black rage and white hate.

The church had blown apart as a result of at least fifteen sticks of dynamite, probably lobbed into a window by a passing car. Just five days after three, all-white schools were forcibly desegregated, the church, which had been used for civil rights organizing as well as religious activities, became the site of the fourth bombing incident in less than a month, the twenty-first in eight years, and the forty-first in sixteen years. Birmingham came to be known as "Bombingham," and a black section of the city, "Dynamite Hill." The targets of all of the bombings were either the homes of African Americans moving into previously white neighborhoods, the homes of civil rights leaders, or African-American churches. Though white supremacist groups such as the Ku Klux Klan (KKK) openly preached hate and local white officials publicly supported segregation, not one of these bombings was ever solved. Perhaps it was incredible that the explosion of September 15, 1963, marked the first time anyone had been killed in these racist bombings.

The subtitle of "Ballad of Birmingham" reads "(On the Bombing of a Church in Birmingham, Alabama, 1963)." But in Dudley Randall's anthology *The Black Poets* (1988), in which "Ballad of Birmingham" is included, Randall's subtitle has been left out. Why? My hypothesis is that this poem is

## *What Do I Read Next?*

- Randall's first book publication from Broadside Press was the collection of poems he coedited with Margaret G. Burroughs commemorating the life and work of assassinated African-American activist Malcolm X called *For Malcolm: Poems on the Life and Death of Malcolm X* (1969). Learn more about Malcolm X from Alex Haley's *Autobiography of Malcolm X* (1965).

- Other poets have also written poems about the Birmingham church bombing. Raymond Patterson's "Birmingham nineteen sixty three" appears in *Celebrations: A New Anthology of Black American Poetry* (1977) and Langston Hughes's "Four Little Girls" can be found in the collection he edited with Arna Bontemps, *The Poetry of the Negro, 1746-1970* (revised edition, 1970).

- Pulitzer Prize winner Gwendolyn Brooks was one of Randall's Broadside poets and someone he esteemed highly for his ability to deeply connect and communicate with others. She published her autobiography, *Report from Part One*

(1972), with Broadside, and her *Selected Poems* (1982) provides a good overview of the progression of her writing over several decades.

- Randall wrote a dialogue in poetic form in which African-American leaders Booker T. Washington and W. E. B. Du Bois express their views on racial development and progress in America; you can find it reprinted in Richard Barksdale and Kenneth Kinnamon's *Black Writers of America* (1972). Find out more about Washington's ideas in his autobiography, *Up From Slavery* (1901) and more about Du Bois's ideas in his *The Souls of Black Folk* (1903).

- The civil rights movement has been the topic of numerous novels as well as poems. Alabama writer Vicki Covington's *The Last Hotel for Women* (1996) tells the story of Dinah Fraley and the struggles that occur in her household when she takes an injured freedom rider into her care, against the wishes of the belligerent "Bull" Connor who was once in love with Dinah's mother.

---

not simply about the bombing of September 15, 1963, but is more generally about Birmingham during the civil rights years and, specifically, about a strategy used by civil rights leaders several months prior to September 15, 1963. It is Randall's juxtaposition of these two historically separated events—the incidents of several months prior and the September 15 bombing—that is the real creative genius of this poem.

Let us back up about five months from September 15, 1963, to April 20. Martin Luther King, Jr., and Ralph Abernathy accepted release on bail from the jail cell where King had been held after being arrested during a demonstration and where he wrote his 6,500-word "Letter from a Birmingham Jail." Immediately after leaving jail, both King and Abernathy went to the nearby Gaston Motel to plan the next phase of "Project C"—their plan for

desegregating Birmingham. There they met James Bevel, a veteran of the student sit-ins in Nashville. Bevel had a provocative plan: to use children in protests and demonstrations. Bevel's argument was that while many African-American adults were reluctant to march for the very real fear of losing their jobs, children had no such fear. Furthermore, the spectacle of children being hauled off to jail would hopefully unsettle the white public. As Bevel said, "Most adults have bills to pay—house notes, rents, car notes, utility bills, but the young people ... are not hooked with all those responsibilities. A boy from high school has the same effect in terms of being in jail, in terms of putting pressure on the city, as his father, and yet there's no economic threat to the family, because the father is still on the job." While King was back in the clutches of the law to stand trial, civil rights leaders recruited

> *Birmingham came to be known as 'Bombingham,' and a black section of the city, 'Dynamite Hill.'"*

black schoolchildren from all over the city. Before any demonstrations, the children were instructed to first see a film, *The Nashville Story,* about a student sit-in. On Thursday, May 2, Martin Luther King, free from jail pending appeal, addressed a gathering of the children—ranging in age from six to eighteen—at the site of the future bombing, the Sixteenth Street Baptist Church. Then the children marched downtown in a demonstration where they sang freedom songs. By the end of the day, the police jailed more than 959 children. Despite a request to King from President Kennedy to stop using children, more than 1,000 African-American children stayed away from school the next day and gathered at the Sixteenth Street Church to march. This time, the police moved in with attack dogs, and firemen marshalled high-pressure water hoses. With German shepherds attacking and 100 pounds of water pressure per square inch being sprayed at them, children were sent running and rolling through the streets. Angered, blacks now consolidated behind King, but the next day, as James Bevel attempted to calm them, African Americans brandished guns and knives. The marches grew, and by Monday, May 6, more than 2,000 demonstrators had been jailed, either in Birmingham or at the temporary site at the Alabama state fairgrounds. On Tuesday, police again met protesters with hoses and dogs, while journalists shot it all for newspapers and television. Governor George Wallace, an ardent segregationist, called out 500 state troopers. Angry at the whole affair, Kennedy sent in Burke Marshall to try and settle the conflict. After a KKK rally denouncing the agreement between business and civil rights leaders, two bombs went off at Martin Luther King's brother's home and at the Gaston Motel where King was staying. Violence erupted again and thirty-five blacks and five whites were injured as police pummeled blacks with clubs and rifles. President Kennedy, on the urging of his brother Robert, readied the National Guard just out-

side of Birmingham and threatened to send them into the city. This and other tactics finally ended the immediate violence in the streets. But on June 11, Governor Wallace would stand in the doorway of the University of Alabama, blocking entrance to two black students who had been admitted. Stepping aside because of threats from the federalized National Guard, the university became integrated for the first time in its history. Kennedy was so angered by events in Birmingham that he sent a new Civil Rights Bill to Congress on June 19, calling for the outlawing of all public segregation, allowing the attorney general to initiate suits for school integration, and granting the right to cut off funds to any federal program violating the new laws against segregation. To urge the passing of the bill, civil rights leaders marched on Washington on August 28, 1963, a march in which more than 250,000 people heard Martin Luther King's "I Have a Dream" speech. The Civil Rights Bill was signed into law by President Johnson on July 2, 1964. And so the story that began with marching school children in Birmingham ended by having a major impact on the nation.

In "Ballad of Birmingham," the little girl has a choice of either going to out to play, to a protest march, or to the Sixteenth Street Baptist Church for Sunday services. But unlike the little girl in the poem, none of the four girls killed in the church blast on September 15 had such a choice. No freedom march was planned for that Sunday, a day of the week more often than not reserved for recuperation and religious worship. Randall brought into proximity two sets of events separated by a space of six months into one Sunday morning to make a key point: that though the church is usually the place of community, safety, salvation, and God—and the civil rights march often a locale of danger, death, and white attackers—the African-American church had become an even more dangerous place than the freedom march. Attacked in their homes and churches, with even their children being murdered, African Americans had no place of security—nowhere they could escape the ugliness of white America. With no acceptable place to turn, it became clearer and clearer that renewed and united confrontation with whites was black America's only hope for deliverance. To gain any salvation in the world of the living, African Americans would have to keep up the pressure on whites by letting freedom sing—not just from choirs in the church, but from congregations in the streets.

**Source:** Jhan Hochman, in an essay for *Poetry for Students,* Gale, 1999.

## Chris Semansky

*A widely published poet and fiction writer, Chris Semansky teaches literature at Portland Community College in Portland, Oregon. In the following essay, Semansky discusses the significance of Randall's use of the ballad form in "Ballad of Birmingham."*

In the twentieth century, poetry has had the reputation of being difficult to read. This holds true even for those who read often and widely. Poetry has "won" this reputation because of its frequent use of obscure allusions (think of Ezra Pound and T. S. Eliot), its often difficult metaphors (think of Wallace Stevens), and its heightened self-reflexivity. It has not won a large audience outside of academia because readers do not see how it relates to their own lives. This has not been the case with Dudley Randall's poetry, much of which was written in a direct, accessible style with clear references to the world outside of the poem. His "Ballad of Birmingham" is one such poem. Written to memorialize the bombing of a Birmingham, Alabama, church that killed four young girls, Randall's poem uses a conventional poetic form (the ballad) that incorporates dialogue, understandable historical allusions, and—though the poem tells the story of a historical event with real people—stock characters to evoke sympathy, shock, and outrage from the reader.

Because many later twentieth-century poets were interested in probing the limits of language and stretching the "readability" of their poems, the ballad—one of the most traditional and highly readable verse forms—has not been used much. Instead, poets with widely diverse styles—such as Elizabeth Bishop, Amiri Baraka, Allen Ginsberg, and John Ashbery—probed organic forms, which arose from the subject matter itself, rather than fitting their words into a prescribed format. By using the ballad form, Randall signals that he wants to reach as wide an audience as possible. Historically defined, ballads were songs passed on orally that told a story with action and dialogue, most often without reference to the narrator's personal feelings or attitudes toward the subject matter. Using the third-person point of view is effective, because the audience is free to focus on the story itself, rather than having to think about the relationship between the speaker and the story or emotion expressed. In using the ballad to commemorate a tragic incident in the civil rights movement of the early 1960s, Randall helped the story of the Birmingham bombing reach almost mythic proportions.

> *This identification on the part of the reader with the characters gives the poem the kind of emotional punch Randall intended . . . . "*

Focusing on the relationship between a mother and her child allows Randall to evoke as much horror and pathos as possible from the story. Represented as an obedient, dutiful child who not only does what her mother tells her but who also does what is morally right (desiring to take part in a freedom march), the little girl embodies the virtues and ideals of the civil rights movement. Randall's description of her preparation for church emphasizes her innocence and vulnerability:

> She has combed and brushed her night dark hair,
> And bathed rose petal sweet,
> And drawn white gloves on her small brown hands,
> And white shoes on her feet.

Although these lines help us visualize the girl's appearance, we are unsure of whether the girl is dressing herself or if the mother is dressing her. If she is dressing herself, we see the image of a young child dutifully doing what she has no doubt done many times before: preparing for participation (singing in the children's choir) in a ritual supposedly far from the ongoing demonstrations in the streets. If the mother is dressing her, we see the image of a possibly recalcitrant child being put in her place by her mother. The distinction is important, because reading it the latter way highlights the very real generational tensions inherent in the civil rights movement. Younger African Americans (and many whites) were more likely to publicly demonstrate for equal rights, while many older African Americans often chose the relative safety of social institutions such as the church to voice their grievances and pray for better days. Juxtaposing the girl's "night dark hair" and "small brown hands" with her white gloves and shoes echoes the "black and white" issues of the civil rights movement itself.

The mother in Randall's poem is both the mother of one of the four girls killed in the bombing and a universal mother figure who desires to shield her child from potential danger. Using these characters—who were directly involved in the bombing—rather than, say, an eyewitness to the carnage, allows Randall to extract as much emotional capital as possible from his readers. Because we can visualize what the little girl looked like, we are all the more shocked in the final stanza, when we discover the daughter has been buried in the rubble of the bomb. We can see the mother holding up her daughter's little white shoe and crying out for her, just as we've seen mothers and fathers and children digging in the rubble of an explosion or natural catastrophe crying out for their loved ones in numerous television news reports. This familiar, late-twentieth-century image doesn't diminish the impact of the tragedy; it heightens it, as it personalizes what has become a more-or-less generic image of horror and loss in our time. Such stock personalization also functions to sentimentalize the image. Sentimentalism isn't necessarily a pejorative term, but one defined by history. Eighteenth-century novels of sensibility, for example, relied on sentimental plots and descriptions to elicit strong emotional responses from their readers. What were considered humane and original representations two hundred years ago, however, are now often laughed at by experienced readers. But Randall's use of sentimentalism and his poem aren't aimed at an elite readership of literature but, instead, are geared to the general public—many of whom don't read poetry or fiction regularly, so they wouldn't see the poem as using overtly manipulative rhetorical devices.

The imagined dialogue between the mother and the daughter also serves to sentimentalize the story and to underscore the ironically tragic fate of the daughter. The daughter asks her mother if she can take part in a freedom march instead of going out to play. Freedom marches, though intended to be peaceful protests for African Americans in the 1960s, often turned violent, as local police—ignoring the very civil rights the marchers were fighting for—used force to break up the demonstrations. By voicing her desire to march instead of play, the daughter appears as a martyr figure in the very first stanza of the poem. Randall emphasizes the irony of the mother's refusal to allow her daughter to march by having the mother spell out her reasons:

> "No, baby, you may not go,
> For the dogs are fierce and wild,
> And clubs and hoses, guns and jail
> Aren't good for a little child."

Attack dogs, truncheons, and rubber hoses were tools police chief Eugene "Bull" Connor's men routinely employed to disperse demonstrators and break the will of the marchers. The mother, by understating (vastly, almost comically) the obvious in saying that these things aren't "good for a little child," foreshadows the irony of what will later befall her child in the assumed safety of the church (the "sacred place"). This imagined conversation captures the precise tone a mother would use in explaining a complicated subject to her child and, hence, allows us, as readers, to identify both with the mother's concern and the daughter's desire. This identification on the part of the reader with the characters gives the poem the kind of emotional punch Randall intended, as we are all the more shocked when we discover the little girl has been killed in a bomb blast at her church. Rather than telling us directly that the girl has been killed, Randall lets us infer from the final image what occurred.

Randall initially published "Ballad of Birmingham" a few years after the bombing as a broadside ballad. Broadside ballads deal with current events and tell stories that are often polemical or didactic in nature; they take a position and have an explicit point to make. "Ballad of Birmingham" remains a successful example of such a ballad, because it fuses the universal and the particular, and it takes a stand against racial injustice—a stand as valid today as it was more than thirty years ago when it was written.

**Source:** Chris Semansky, in an essay for *Poetry for Students,* Gale, 1999.

## Sources

Barksdale, Richard, and Kenneth Kinnamon, eds., *Black Writers of America: A Comprehensive Anthology,* New York: Macmillan, 1972.

Breman, Paul, "Poetry into the Sixties," in *The Black American Writer,* Vol. II, edited by C. W. E. Bigsby, Deland, FL: Everett/Edwards, 1969, pp. 99-109.

Cobbs, Elizabeth H., and Petric J. Smith, *Long Time Coming: An Insider's Story of the Birmingham Church Bombing that Rocked the World,* Birmingham, AL: Crane Hill, 1994.

Garrow, David J., ed., *Birmingham, Alabama, 1956-1963: The Black Struggle for Civil Rights,* Brooklyn, NY: Carlson Publishing, 1989.

Melhem, D. H., "Dudley Randall: A Humanist View," in *Black American Literature Forum,* Vol. 17, No. 4, Winter 1983, pp. 157-67.

Miller, R. Baxter, "'Endowing the World and Time': The Life and Work of Dudley Randall," in *Black American Poets between Worlds, 1940-1960,* edited by R. Baxter Miller, Knoxville, TN: University of Tennessee Press, 1986, pp. 77-92.

Moore, Lenard D., "For Dudley Randall," in *Black American Literature Forum,* Vol. 21, No. 3, Fall 1987, p. 242.

Mootry, Maria K., "'Chocolate Mabbie' and 'Pearl May Lee': Gwendolyn Brooks and the Ballad Tradition," in *CLA Journal,* Vol. 30, No. 3, March 1987, pp. 278-93.

*The New York Times,* September 16, 1963; September 17, 1963.

Randall, Dudley, ed., *The Black Poets,* New York: Bantam, 1971, 1998.

Riley, C., ed., *Contemporary Literary Criticism,* Vol. I, Detroit: Gale Research Co., 1973, p. 283.

Williams, Juan, *Eyes on the Prize: America's Civil Rights Years, 1954-1965,* New York: Penguin, 1987.

## *For Further Study*

Cobbs, Elizabeth H., and Petric J. Smith, *Long Time Coming: An Insider's Story of the Birmingham Church Bombing that Rocked the World,* Birmingham, AL: Crane Hill, 1994.

This is a firsthand account of the bombing of the Sixteenth Street Baptist Church written by the state's witness and niece of the convicted bomber, Robert Chambliss.

King, Woodie, Jr., ed., *The Forerunners: Black Poets in America,* Washington, DC: Howard University Press, 1975.

King's collection includes selections of poetry and personal statements from a range of poets from the 1960s and 1970s, including Dudley Randall who also wrote the collection's preface. Many of the writers included here published their work with Broadside Press.

Randall, Dudley, *Broadside Memories: Poets I Have Known,* Detroit, MI: Broadside Press, 1975.

Randall includes both poetry and nonfiction in this collection celebrating the writers and history of Randall's Broadside Press.

Thompson, Julius, *Dudley Randall, Broadside Press, and the Black Arts Movement in Detroit, 1960-1995,* New York: McFarland, 1998.

This is the most recent critical study of Randall's and Broadside Press's influence on the African-American literary scene in Detroit.

Williams, Juan, *Eyes on the Prize: America's Civil Rights Years, 1954-1965,* New York: Penguin, 1987.

In this companion volume to the PBS television series of the same name, Williams clearly and vividly recounts the history of the civil rights movement in America. As well as being a very readable, straightforward historical account, this book is full of photographs, in-depth interviews with individual members of the movement, and reprints of important texts, such as Martin Luther King's "I Have A Dream" speech.

# Birch Canoe

## Carter Revard

## 1992

Carter Revard's "Birch Canoe," published in 1992, speaks in the persona of the canoe, carved out of white birch wood by American Indians. In doing so, it examines the relationship between the way of thought of white Americans and that of the people who lived in North America before the Europeans arrived. Revard is part Osage Indian, and he was raised on the Osage reservation in Oklahoma, but readers should not believe from this that he is more familiar with Native-American ways than traditional European culture: he was educated in the European tradition, including time spent studying at Oxford University in England and Yale University, and for almost forty years he has taught Medieval English literature. Although the author's field of specialty is Western history, including the European and white American tradition, this poem indicates an appreciation gained from discovering the traditions that come from his Indian heritage. With recent expansions of information and communication products—global television systems, the internet, videos, etc.—and especially since the fall of the Soviet Union in 1990, the influence of the Western way of thinking has become dominant around the globe. Native Americans, who had their indigenous ways of life limited practically to the point of extinction by Western culture, could certainly find liberation in learning or relearning Indian traditions, as the poem indicates. When the poem speaks of "my body's whiteness" and the way that it is transformed by Indians into something that travels freely, readers can sense an au-

tobiographical element, although it is not necessary to know much about Carter Revard to appreciate "Birch Canoe."

## Author Biography

Carter Revard was born in 1931 in Pawhuska, Oklahoma, on the Osage Indian Reservation. He attended a one-room schoolhouse in nearby Buck Creek Valley for the first eight years of his education and, after gradating from Bartlesville College High, he won a scholarship from a radio show, "Quiz Kids," to attend the University of Tulsa. He attended Oxford University in England on a Rhodes Scholarship in 1952 and received his Ph.D. from Yale University in 1959. After graduation, he taught briefly at Amherst College. In 1961 he began teaching at Washington University in St. Louis, Missouri, where he teaches to this day. He has also been a visiting professor at University of Tulsa and University of Oklahoma. His scholarly work has concentrated on linguistics, American Indian literature, and Medieval English literature, with special concentration on the social context surrounding particular pieces. Collections of Carter Revard's poetry include *Ponca War Dances* (1980), *Cowboys and Indians, Christmas Shopping* (1992), and *An Eagle Nation* (1993). *Family Matters, Tribal Affairs* is a recent collection of essays with a strong focus on autobiographical details.

In 1952, the year that he received the Rhodes Scholarship, Revard was given his Osage name, Nom-Pa-Wa-The, which means "Fear-Inspiring." His early poetry shows a strong influence of Western tradition, but as the years have passed, he has become more successful using the language and themes that he grew up with on the Osage reservation. While his Indian heritage has been an influence on his work, Revard makes it clear that readers should not take him as a representative of the Osage, that being Indian is just one part of his genealogy and it is also a limited percentage of the influences that have formed his worldview. He warns readers to not confuse his narrow experience of Osage tradition with the vast knowledge of tribal elders, who have studied the songs, legends and ceremonies that make up the tribe's history.

## Poem Text

Red men embraced     my body's whiteness,
cutting into me     carved it free,
sewed it tight     with sinews taken

*Carter Revard*

from lightfoot deer     who leaped this stream—
now in my ghost-skin     they glide over clouds     5
at home in the fish's     fallen heaven.

## Poem Summary

### Line 1:

Throughout this poem, there is a contrast between the first part of each line and the second part, which is separated from it by a space (the space is called a caesura and the half-line on either side of it is called a "hemistich"). In Line 1 there is contradiction in both idea and tone. The first hemistich has a sharp, punchy quality to it, with three of the four syllables stressed, hammering away with a staccato rhythm: "red," "man," and "-braced" all hit the reader with force, while the soft syllable "em-" softens the effect just slightly. The irony here is that the idea being put forth, an embrace, is warm and pleasant, the opposite of the violent percussive tone. While the first three words are all bound together with the "e" sound that is common to each, the three words that finish the line share the common "i" sound. This section of the line has a cool smoothness that sets it apart as much as does the wide, blank space in the middle. In addition to sens-

## Media Adaptations

- *More than Bows and Arrows,* narrated by N. Scott Momaday, was released by Camera One Productions in 1992.

- Finley-Holiday Film Corp. released *The Indian And His Homeland: American Images, 1590-1876* in 1990.

- *Indians Among Us,* directed and produced by Jonathan Donald, was released by Discover Communications in 1992.

ing the contrast of styles, most readers come to this poem aware of the tradition of conflict between native Americans and European Americans, which is implied here: until the next line, there is no reason to think that the body mentioned is anything other than a human body. By presenting a situation that defies expectations—history leads us to expect Indians and Europeans to be at odds, not embracing—the poem piques the reader's curiosity and works to undo the assumptions that stereotypes have established.

### Line 2:

Since line 1 spoke of a human-sounding body and an embrace, it comes as a shock to find the phrase "cutting into me." It is at this point in the poem that the reader first receives evidence that the speaker of the poem is the birch tree referred to in the title. The benign, emotionless tone used in these three words conveys nature's attitude of acceptance: the tree is matter-of-fact about being cut open and bears no animosity about it. The second hemistich, in fact, finds a positive aspect in the freedom that the uprooted tree finds. Throughout this poem, the joy of freedom prevails. Motion is emphasized. Stylistically, the second half of this line mirrors the first, in the repetition of the "c" sound in "cutting" and "carved," the similarity of "into" and "it," and the rhyme of "me" with "free."

### Line 3:

"It," in this line, still refers to "my body" from the first line, evoking the gruesome image of an emptied body being sewn together like Frankenstein's monster at the same time that it describes the ordinary business of putting a canoe together. The allusion is appropriate because in this poem the birch tree is receiving new life. The fact that the canoe is being put together with "sinews"—taken from the insides of once-living animals—makes the idea of raising a new life out of the old dead even more prominent to the reader. Of all of the activities required in making a canoe, this poem singles out sewing—possibly because sewing evokes the notion of careful craftsmanship, rather than the simple violence of cutting and carving, and possibly because, as mentioned, sewing seems to allude to skin. This line, too, uses alliteration, the repetition of sounds at the beginning of words, to unite the two sides of the line, in contrast to the middle space that separates them. In this case, not only is the "s" repeated in "sewed" and "sinews" and the "t" in "tight" and "taken," but the "ew" sound from "sewed" is also repeated.

### Line 4:

The focus of the poem changes in this line, away from the birch canoe and its process of becoming and onto the deer and its activity. Of course, both are related to the canoe—the deer's sinews hold the canoe together so that it can float in the stream—but this line takes a break from the canoe, in order to establish for the reader what the outdoor setting is like on its own, untouched by the influence of red or white people. In the simple action of a deer leaping a stream, much is given: the deer's strength is implied, even though the ingenuity of humans eventually overcomes the deer to take its muscles, and we also learn that the stream the canoe is to ride cannot be all that wide if an animal is able to jump over it. At the end of line 4, the dash provides the poem with its longest pause, which is even longer than the spaces within the lines because it is an end-stop that combines punctuation with the natural halt of the line's end. In this case, the pause signifies a change of the time frame, from the past, when the birch tree was cut down and fashioned into a canoe and when the deer ran freely through the forest, to the canoe's present state.

## Line 5:

The "ghost-skin" here is a dual reference, indicating both the whiteness of the birch that was referred to in the first line (since ghosts are often pictured as white) and also the fact that the hollowed-out tree has lost its life to become the canoe of the present tense. While "ghost" is a reminder of death, "skin" is a reference, like "body" in the first line, to the relationship that the poem makes between birch trees and white people. This new allusion to whites is balanced on the other side of the gap that splits the line with "they," a new reference to the red men. The end of line 5 indulges in a little visual imagery that sounds mysterious because of the way it is worded, but actually presents a common sight. The surface of the stream would naturally mirror the images of the clouds above it, so that the canoe floating on the surface would look like it is gliding over the clouds. The poem presents this action in metaphor, relating the clouds to their reflection on the water without saying that it "looks like" the canoe is above the clouds. The reader is slightly disoriented, forced to deal with a dream-like reality in which the impossible can happen.

## Line 6:

It is in the last four words of this poem that the culture clash that is implied in all that came before is made open and obvious. "Fallen heaven" is an obvious reference to the biblical story of humanity's expulsion from the Garden of Eden. The biblical fall from grace is central to much of Western theology, a basis for Judeo-Christian world-views, and is therefore crucial to how members of white culture think of themselves. The seriousness of being thrown out of heaven is gently mocked here, because it is the fish, a lower order of animal, whose heaven has fallen. If white culture is based on the idea of "original sin," making everyone guilty at birth, then even the natural world would be a sad place for white culture. By contrast, the Indians referred to in this poem are "at home" in the natural setting where white men assume guilt. Unlike other literary works that see white culture as nothing but an intrusion into the wilderness, "Birch Canoe" presents whites as being as much a part of the natural setting as anything else around. The poem does not claim that white people are intruders, only that the sense of guilt inherent in European culture makes white people feel uncomfortable. Once again, alliteration is used to connect the line's two halves, with the "h" in "home" and "heaven" and the "f" in "fish" and "fallen."

## Themes

### Return to Nature

The white body of the birch tree is presented in this poem as being somehow distanced from nature, as if the stiff tree, rooted to one patch of ground, is on its own, no matter how busy or crowded its surroundings might be. There is more to nature as represented in this poem than the objects that occur in a natural setting (even though plenty of these are squeezed into six short lines, including the birch tree itself, deer, clouds, and fish). The significance of these natural objects is impressive, and the poem makes the most of the things of nature by putting them into motion with action verbs. Readers are not simply allowed to view nature existing, but are invited to enter a busy, living world, swirling with activity.

The red men mentioned in "Birch Canoe" are not clearly defined as being either a part of nature, as they are in many other poems, or just as men with a clear understanding of nature. Their actions in the first two lines—embracing, cutting, carving and sewing—are presented as being in harmony with nature, not as actions that occur outside of nature, as human actions often are in pieces that divide humans and nature. Whether the red men's actions are natural or not is irrelevant in the poem's second half, which takes the speaker, the birch-tree-turned-canoe, into the domain of nature, among deer and fish. The fact that the canoe glides without disturbing its surroundings suggests that it is accepted as a natural element itself, as are its passengers. The birch, of course, represents white people, as indicated by personifying the tree in the phrase "my body's whiteness." This is appropriate because it is white culture, European culture, that most often places itself in opposition with nature. In this poem it is the red men, with the help of the deer, who help bridge the gap between nature and white culture.

### Freedom

Readers find it discomforting to find a positive idea such as "freedom" associated with the violent acts of cutting and carving—as if mutilation leads to liberation and freedom requires destruction. In terms of this poem's central metaphor, it is clear that the birch tree cannot be free of the ground it is rooted to until someone cuts it free. The bonds that hold human beings together socially may be seen as holding us with similarly strong attachment, affixing people to one place or one situation until some turn of events occurs to sever the connection.

## *Topics for Further Study*

- "Birch Canoe" only mentions that the canoe is carved and sewn: research what other skills are needed to make canoes by hand. Use diagrams to report on traditional canoe designs and ornamentation.

- This poem alludes to the lives of Native Americans, but it is written in a traditional European form that is mostly forgotten today. Research more about the history of Anglo-Saxon verse and find specific similarities between Anglo-Saxon culture and American Indian culture.

- What objects in the contemporary world are made of "ghost-skin"? Find an object that is made of a once-living material—fur or leather or wood or bone, for instance—and write a poem that speaks for the object, saying how it was changed.

Still, it would be wrong to oversimplify and interpret the poem as saying that freedom can only be attained with a hatchet. The implications of "Birch Canoe" are far more complex than that. For instance, there is the prominence of the word "embraced" in the first segment of the first line, which indicates that the red men did not approach the birch tree with only destruction in mind. With this embrace shining over the whole poem, the cutting, carving and sewing are not presented as acts of hostility or wanton destruction, but as necessary acts of love. The relationship that freedom has with breaking bonds is readily accepted when those bonds are chains, but the relationship does not look as appealing when the bonds are presented as being natural, like the birch tree that is carved hollow or the deer separated from its muscles. What this poem reminds its readers of is that freedom is gained only at a price.

### Identity

It is almost impossible to fully appreciate this poem without understanding how it reflects the life of Carter Revard. The author grew up surrounded by his Indian heritage in Oklahoma, but the strongest influence on him was white culture, in part because he was only part Indian. "I think I have Indianness in me, but I am only a small part Osage," he told Alan R. Velie in a letter. "When I jumped into my genes they were mostly white, but the red ones spelled OSAGE." Although the poem can be read and understood without any biographical background, it helps readers to know that the interaction it shows between red men and the speaker's whiteness is an exchange from the speaker's firsthand experience.

While the speaker of this poem, a birch tree, is open to the experience of Indian ways, even at personal cost, we are not supposed to feel that this speaker is finding a completely new identity, but instead experiences a shift from its earlier identity. The white birch does not consider itself to be a different thing than what it was. It does not identify itself as a canoe hull, but instead it refers to the canoe as its "ghost skin," retaining its link to the tree it was before. The human implication here is that the speaker identifies with neither red nor white culture, which may explain the final allusion to being "at home" in a "fallen heaven": if there is any identity in this poem, it is that of a human consciousness identifying with nature. This idea can be seen as either definitive, if one assumes that "nature" encompasses all things in this world, including humans, or as impossible, if one thinks of human consciousness as being the opposite of nature.

## Style

"Birch Canoe" is structured in a traditional, arcane poetic style called Anglo-Saxon verse, which was the prevailing poetic style during the Anglo-Saxon period of English history, from the fifth century to the twelfth century. It is seldom used today. There are three characteristics associated with Anglo-Saxon verse. The first, and most noticeable to even a casual reader, is that each line of the poem has a medial caesura, which means that there is a blank space in the middle of each line that divides it in two. The second characteristic is that each line has four stressed syllables. Readers who are not aware that this poem fits an established form will tend to read the first line as having five stressed syllables—"RED MEN em-BRACED / my BOD-ys WHITE-ness"—but the poem can be made to fit the form easily enough if "whiteness" is read with no stress at all. The third characteristic of Anglo-Saxon verse is alliteration, the use of the same initial sound, between one word in the first half of each line and one in the conclusion. This can be seen in the pairs "men/my," "cutting/carved," "sewed/sinews," "lightfooted/leaped," "ghost-skinned/glide," and "fish's/fallen." For readers who are aware that this poem uses a centuries-old form, it has the added presence of European tradition to counterbalance the Indian tradition of canoe making that it describes.

## Historical Context

On his Internet site, Carter Revard cautions readers to avoid making too much of his Osage background, reminding us that as a poet he mixes his cultural heritage with personal experiences, opinions, and family stories. His warning is meant to keep readers from assuming that the viewpoints of his poems represent a worldview that is somehow typical Osage. Even with this in mind, there is no question that Revard's upbringing in the Native American tradition had some influence on "Birch Canoe." The last image of the poem, for instance, that of the fish's "fallen heaven," reflects an early myth about the Osage people's origin. According to the legend, the great life force of the universe, *Wah' Kon,* The Mystic Force, sent the Osage's ancestors down from the stars to live on earth. Archeological information suggests that since ancient times these people lived as far east as the Piedmont region of Virginia, and that they traveled from there along the Ohio River. By 1673, when European settlements were established along the eastern seaboard, the tribe had settled in the area known today as western Missouri, along a branch of the Missouri River near where it splits from the Mississippi River. Today, that branch is called the Osage River. The tribe was then called the Children of the Middle Waters.

European influence into this area of the country began in 1673, when Father Jacques Marquette and Louis Joliet, on a mission for the French government, explored the Wisconsin, Mississippi, and Illinois rivers. At the mouth of the Missouri, the Illinois Indians they had acquainted themselves with pointed to the southwest and said that was the land of the *Wa-Sha-She.* To the French, this was pronounced "Ouzhagi," and when English speakers pronounced the French word it came out "Osage." Soon an influx of French fur traders and trappers came to the area, and the Osage became close allies with them, trading furs for such manufactured goods as rifles and cookware. They sided with the French against other Indians, and they sold Indians captured from other tribes into slavery. They helped the French against the British in the French and Indian War, from 1754 to 1763. When it ended and the French had lost, the area west of the Mississippi River fell under Spain's control: though there was hostility between the Osage and Spain and some battles were fought, the fighting was minimal. In 1800 the area was returned to France, and in 1803 France sold it to the United States as part of the Louisiana Purchase. The property deals between the non-Indians had only slight influence on the tribe's activities, as they adjusted to work with each new trading partner.

The way the American Indians were treated by the United States government is one of the country's darkest legacies. The treatment the Osage received by the westwardly expanding country is fairly typical. First, Eastern tribes that were displaced during the country's growth, including the Cherokee, Choctaw, Creek, and Chickasaw, were pushed into Missouri, where they joined forces with the Osage's traditional enemies, the Potawatomi, the Sac, and the Fox. Then a series of new treaties were presented by the government in 1808, 1818, and 1825, pushing the Osage further and further west and onto smaller and smaller parcels of land. Crowded onto a tiny reservation in what is now Kansas and barraged by government programs designed to make them give up their "barbaric" traditions and become "civilized," the Osage resisted and held on to their own identity. When America grew more, and the reservation in Kansas was found to be in the way, the land was sold to settlers, and in 1871 the Osage were moved to a new reservation in Indian Territory, in Oklahoma. This is where Carter Revard grew up, and it is the home of the Osage tribe today.

Fate was much kinder to the Osage in their new location than it was to most of the tribes who had been displaced. In 1894, oil was discovered under their reservation, and soon the Osage were among the richest people in the world. By 1904 there were 155 oil-producing wells and 18 natural gas wells on the reservation. The revenues gained by leasing land to oil companies became the property of the whole tribe and were divided among everyone who was a tribe member by July 1, 1907: after that date the number of shares, called headrights, could not increase or decrease, only their value. Thus, a family of five in 1925, the year the headrights reached

# *Compare & Contrast*

- **1992:** After a videotape of white Los Angeles police officers beating black motorist Rodney King was broadcast frequently on television, a jury with no black members found the four policemen innocent of any wrongdoing. As a result, a wave of rioting, looting, and arson erupted in several urban areas of America, most notably South Central Los Angeles, where 52 people died.

  **Today:** Although flare-ups of violence over racial issues are rare, more Americans are aware, from the King case, of the different views of justice held by members of different races.

- **1992:** Bill Clinton, the former Governor of Arkansas, won the presidency from George W. Bush. The year before, Bush had enjoyed record-setting popularity with the American people because of his decisive action taken during the military action against Iraq.

  **Today:** Despite a seven-year investigation into his finances and widespread reportage of sexual affairs he conducted in the White House, President Clinton has managed to retain public support.

their peak at $13,200 each, would have an income of $66,000 just for being tribe members, at a time when a good annual salary was $2,000 to $3,000. In the 1920s the extravagant spending sprees of Osage members were covered in newspapers across the globe, with photos of Indians who had found themselves suddenly rich wearing mink coats and silk tuxedos with top hats and standing in front of expensive luxury automobiles that they bought, even though they did not know how to drive. The value of the Osage oil shares dropped during the Depression of the 1930s, but the Osage were still better off than most tribes: the Depression was particularly hard on reservations. Osage descendents still live comfortably on oil revenues, but as the years pass, the ownership of the official headrights has fallen into the hands of fewer and fewer tribe members, making for resentment from the full-blooded Osage who do not receive any benefits.

## Criticism

### *Jhan Hochman*

*Jhan Hochman's articles appear in* Democracy and Nature, Genre, ISLE, *and* Mosaic. *He is the author of* Green Cultural Studies: Nature in Film, Novel, and Theory *(1998), and he holds a Ph.D in English and an M.A. in Cinema Studies. In the following essay, Hochman focuses on the symbolism pertaining to the canoe.*

Carter Revard's "Birch Canoe" revisits the tradition of the canoe as a vehicle of both life and death. Just as boats are vehicles of transport in life, they have long been vehicles to, or of, the land of the dead. According to Mircea Eliade in *The Encyclopedia of Religion,* this especially pertains to the canoe, homologue of a hearse and bearing a vague likeness to a coffin:

> Among certain North American Indians burial customs involving boats and a journey to the land of the dead have been documented. For instance, the typical grave of the Twana and other Coast Salish Indians consists of a canoe suspended on poles or on an elevated platform .... According to a Twana tale, the inhabitants of the realm of the dead come in a canoe to claim the newly deceased. Late at night it is said that one can hear their paddles in the water as they come to carry away their new companion.

Virtually all boats and ships were once made of wood and became, at least in Germany, so associated with death that early medieval German usage of the words *naufus* or *naucus* ("ship") alongside *trunkus* ("trunk") formerly denoted a coffin. Moreover, the tree is often likened to the human body, with its branches and leaves (arms, head, and hair), trunk (body, spine), and roots (feet): "The

## What Do I Read Next?

- Carter Revard's life, and his reflections on life, are on display in his recent collection of essays, *Family Matters, Tribal Affairs,* published by the University of Arizona Press in 1998.

- Like most of the entries in its "Portable" series, Viking Press' 1973 anthology *The Portable North American Indian Reader,* edited by esteemed author Frederick W. Turner III, gives a scholarly and insightful tour through historic and modern readings. A large part of the book is myths and tales that comprise the Indian traditions.

- The University of Oklahoma Press has stronger ties to the Native American culture than other publishers, and this shows in the selections included in the 1991 anthology *American Indian Literature.* Despite its unassuming title, this collection includes a fascinating variety of authors, from anonymous writers of legends up to Carter Revard himself.

- Since many of the great ideas of Native American history are lost because they were oral, and not written, cultures, it is fascinating to read a collection of the spoken words of Indians, such as those compiled by Virginia Irving Armstrong in the 1971 collection *I Have Spoken: American History Through the Voices of the Indians,* published by Swallow Press in Chicago. The introduction, by famed Indian scholar Frederick W. Turner III, is itself a brief but powerful summation of the situation faced by the indigenous people of North America.

- John Bierhorst's *The Mythology of North America,* published in 1985 by William Morrow and Co., does a very entertaining job with a poten-

tially dry subject, anthropology. This book is extremely well supported with documentation and written at a level that most students can appreciate.

- Other than Carter Revard, the most prominent writer among the Osage is clearly John Joseph Mathews, a noted intellectual whose career spanned the middle of the twentieth century. In his 1961 book *The Osages: Children of the Middle Waters,* he applied his talent to explaining his own tribe, resulting in a comprehensive 800 pages about Osage history and customs. The third printing of this book was in 1981, by University of Oklahoma Press. Also of interest by Matthews is *Wah'Kon-Tah: The Osage and the White Man's Road,* although, first published in 1932, it is of course limited in information.

- The benefit of Margot Edmonds and Ella E. Clark's 1981 collection *Voices of the Wind: Native American Legends* is that it contains nearly a hundred pages of myths of tribes from the central region and the Great Plains states: one major shortcoming is that none of these is from Revard's tribe, the Osage. Still, reading many legends helps put one in a frame of mind to appreciate "Birch Canoe" more.

- By far, the most prominent international figure to come out of the Osage tribe is Maria Tallchief, one of the century's great ballerinas and a principle dancer in the New York Ballet under her husband, George Balanchine. The story of her rise from the reservation to international attention is covered in her autobiography, *Maria Tallchief: America's Prima Ballerina,* written with Larry Kaplan and published in 1997 by Henry Holt.

---

Lakota on the upper Missouri River say that the first man and woman were two trees and that a snake chewed their roots off in order to allow the couple to walk away," according to Eliade. As a human body, the tree might make an appropriate

receptacle for the soul, but the canoe, as the moving corpse of a tree, is especially suited for a soon-to-be-liberated human soul. In perception, the tree corpse is so changed by formation into a canoe (its horizontality, placement on water, and new shape)

> *... [T]he canoe not only means life, but a means to near-divinity, since the canoe made by humans then transforms them into birds of flight, even gods, in the way they are able to 'glide over clouds / at home ... in heaven.'"*

and so overpowered by metonymic association with the human dead it transports, that its identity as a tree corpse—the body of a once living being—is absent. Just as standing trees are perceived as not quite alive (at least not as alive as humans), the horizontal log does not really seem as if it was ever alive. Trees and logs deprived of the fuller meaning of life and death relegate them to the realm of nature's inanimate elements, represented primarily by rocks and minerals.

This, however, is not the case in "Birch Canoe." The birch tree in Revard's poem speaks English, not only speaks, but narrates its observations in a poem. This renders the living tree as "fully alive" as a person is thought to be fully alive. Even when the birch tree is felled to construct a canoe, the boat is not an inert object but becomes a ghost, a floating member of the living-dead. In this way, Revard renders tree and canoe as animated with a kind of haunting presence that most Western peoples do not usually attribute to either trees or canoes.

It is this matter of life and death I want to examine in "Birch Canoe." To do this, I demarcate four kinds of characters—deer, fish, humans, and trees—to show each of their relationships to the life and death embodied in canoes. "Lightfoot deer," as this poem indicates, are killed by humans for food and for materials out of which objects are made. In the case of the canoe, the deer's sinews—its tendons—are used to sew parts of the canoe together. To deer then, the rather innocent-seeming canoe

might represent deer's subservience to humanity, its identity as the prey of human predators. Native Americans, on the other hand, possibly did and do not think of deer as fully dead since the animals continue to "lend" their once-living power and strength to the canoe. Somewhat in the way that a deer might easily and gracefully leap across a stream, canoes refigure streams from obstacles into vehicles, from streams impeding mobility into "canals" enhancing it. Through such conceptions, people might convince themselves they have not killed the deer, or come to believe that deer have allowed themselves to be "killed," to "live on" as part of a canoe and be of service to humans. Revard's birch narrator does not really take a stand on this matter of life and death but does seem to relate to deer who once "leaped the stream" but cannot do so any longer.

The canoe itself may be perceived as a weapon. With canoes, people can more extensively kill fish than if they were standing on a bank. Because of canoes, fish, as the birch says, might see the stream as a "fallen heaven," because they are yanked upward by fishermen into death. If fish articulated their religious conceptions, heaven would likely be below, and the land of death, above just opposite of the human conceptions of water as the place of death and drowning and air as the place of life and breathing.

Unlike what might be the conceptions of deer and fish, people usually conceive of the canoe as life, not only to living persons using it to travel and get food, but for the dead souls who, as I wrote previously, are thought to be transported by means of canoe to the eternal "life" of the dead. If the canoe is ever thought by people to represent death, it is only by way of empathy with the animals killed because of the canoe, the tree felled to make it, or because the canoe holds the human dead. Otherwise the canoe not only means life, but a means to near-divinity, since the canoe made by humans then transforms them into birds of flight, even gods, in the way they are able to "glide over clouds / at home ... in heaven." The canoe enables mastery of nature: of animals, plants, and streams; allows men to magically sit on water and move upon it while remaining still. Native Americans were especially attached to birch canoes, because they were so strong and flexible that they survived most natural disasters, lasting an average of ten years. Birch canoes shot rapids, travelled the ocean, and, with the French, crossed three thousand miles of Canadian waterways to establish trade routes to the far northwest. Canoes were fashioned from the barks of other trees, but they eventually would become waterlogged. Not so with the slick, waterproof bark of the birch tree. Perhaps it was the red man's attachment to the birch, with its striking whiteness, that partially allowed Indians to "embrace" white men. Initially, at least.

The birch-tree narrator's feelings about the canoe seem torn or ambivalent. On one hand, the tree appears appreciative of the Indians' embrace, that use of the birch allows Native Americans to gain some mastery over nature. On the other hand, the narrating tree seems solemn, grave that its white birchbark, its "skin," has been transformed into a ghost-canoe and an incubus that in turn brings death to other denizens of nature.

Having discussed deer, fish, humans, and trees in relation to canoes, only one thing seems left out: the stream. Just as a stream divides banks of land on either side—mimicked in the look of Revard's poem with the continuity of Anglo-Saxon line breaks forming a meandering "stream" between hemistiches (stream banks) down the middle of the poem—the stream also divides above from below, heights from depths, heaven from hell, or, in the case of fish, hell from heaven. This is the dividing line, or stream, that canoes ride—streams that make the difference between land and heavens as canoes make a difference between the life and death of deer, fish, humans, and trees.

**Source:** Jhan Hochman, in an essay for *Poetry for Students,* Gale, 1999.

### David Kelly

*David Kelly is an instructor of creative writing at several community colleges in Illinois, as well as a fiction writer and playwright. In the following essay, Kelly argues that "Birch Canoe" can be read as a shaped poem, with the caesura up the middle representing a river.*

We have tamed the world with tools and machines, so that the course of nature hardly matters any more beyond what's said on the morning's weather report. Imagine, though, what a river meant to pre-industrial civilizations. It provided food, and it fed the crops. It was the express mode of transportation. Dams siphoned power from the rivers' flow long before humanity drew its energy from burning fossil fuels. Having a river nearby is quite a handy thing, and that is why the great cities are on rivers, usually at the point where the river meets the sea, where goods from other lands can be fed up into the interior, through the river's mouth. The

> *Human activity dominates within this poem, and that is why it is important to see the poem itself dominated by an image that is even more powerful and enduring than men with hatchets or paddles ...."*

huge rivers of the world, with really astounding reach—the Nile, the Amazon, the Mississippi—have exerted more influence on who lives where than puny humans, with their wars and changing laws, could ever hope to control. The story of civilization is a history of people trying to accommodate rivers.

Rivers are the lines that nature has drawn across the topography of the land. We see them on maps, jagged and blue, dividing countries, states, provinces, and cities. They mark the border between the land we walk on and the "fallen heaven" of fish. Like any lines, though, they could mean one thing, or they could mean its opposite. A river could be seen as the line where two sides are separated, but it could just as likely be considered the place where those with differences come together.

There is a jagged line running up the middle of Carter Revard's poem "Birch Canoe." In its uneven bending, it resembles the twists of a river. It could also look like a fault line or a cracked glass, but then, this is not a poem about an earthquake or an opera singer hitting double-high C. It's about a canoe, a river-faring vessel.

Shaped poems—poems that are laid out on paper to resemble some visual image—have always been fascinating, and sometimes they can be meaningful, although they always raise suspicions that a poem too concerned with visual design is just playing a clever but meaningless trick. Almost every semester I ask a new batch of college students to respond to John Hollander's "Swan and Shadow," which looks on the page exactly like what the title calls it, a swan and its shadow. The most discouraging, and frequent, reaction that they come up with is unsupported approval: many say they "like" it, even though they cannot tell you what the poem says. They like the fact that letters have been arranged on a page into a recognizable picture. There's not really a whole lot of talent to accomplishing such a thing, especially not with recent widespread availability of computer programs that manipulate visual images.

"Swan and Shadow" is a good poem because it has something to say about beauty and light and darkness and death, a message that would be worth hearing even if it poem were printed in one long column with one word per line. The same holds true for all other successful shaped poems. Of course, the way the words appear on the page is important to any poetry, or else poems would be printed in blocks of text, margin-to-margin, the way all other written material is. The poet has to do something with the words on the page to make the visual effect serve and support the point being made. It's not cheating if the pattern that emerges once the words have been chosen and the line breaks fixed actually looks like something: the only unfair thing is when the shape of the poem is treated as the most important thing, when the meanings of the words are only considered briefly, if at all. Meaning can't be sacrificed to fit the words into a shape, but the shape of a poem can be used to add a richer level to the poem's meaning.

Is this uneven gap up the middle of "Birch Canoe" really a river? I think it is. The uneven lines on either side of the blank space remind me of the uneven banks of a river, the way that the banks follow no firm order and only vaguely recognize each other. I do not know the poet, and so I can't ask what he had in mind when he started writing "Birch Canoe," but my guess is that he did not set out to build a river. It probably was not in his mind at the beginning, although, since I believe greatly in the process of revision as "re-seeing," and not just as "fixing-up," I would speculate that he found the river there, the way a reader might come across it. The style of the poem clearly is patterned on a long established poetic form called Anglo-Saxon verse, which requires a caesura, or gap, in the middle of each line; in theory, every poem written in Anglo-Saxon verse over the centuries would look like it is trying to imply a river. My guess is that Revard, whose academic work is focused on medieval English literature, would have known and liked the form, and in using it, he may or may not have seen this river thing. If the form he wrote in offered up

something else that is useful to readers and germane to the message, then the author is obliged to embrace it, just as the red men embrace the speaker's whiteness in the poem's first line.

Regardless of how it got there, the significance of finding a river running up the middle of this poem is that it marks all that is said with the spirit of "something greater." There has always been a tendency in Western thought to romanticize cultures that are closer to nature and to look at human social life as corruption. The term "noble savage" was introduced back in 1688, in Aphra Behn's novel *Oroonoko,* and was popularized a hundred years later in the writings of French philosopher Jean-Jacques Rousseau: it's the term applied to those who live closer to the land, with fewer social rules, who are seen as being purer in spirit. Unfortunately, this idea is often applied by people who just refuse to acknowledge the complexity of other societies. In America, this spiritual correctness is projected onto Native Americans, who are often considered noble people because their lives seem simpler. An entire industry has formed around selling paintings and greeting cards with idealized images of Indians, using the faces of anonymous people to represent courage and spirituality and pathos in the same way that a pie manufacturer might use a picture of an old woman to represent the idea of "just-baked freshness." Because Indians are romanticized this way and assumptions are made about Indian spiritual beliefs and freedom from social constraints, it would be easy for readers to think "Birch Canoe" is about Indian heritage rescuing white culture from itself and setting it free to rejoin the natural world, using traditional Indian customs. When I look at this poem and see a river, though, I don't think of the relative virtues of different cultures. I am reminded that there is something bigger here than either white or red culture.

The text of the poem gives us the natural world being acted upon and manipulated for the use of humans (in the poem they are red Indian humans, but that may only be because white culture's abuses of nature are so obvious that they are not worth examining). The tree is carved, the guts of the deer are taken and used for twine, and the fish have their heaven superceded by the manufactured canoe. Human activity dominates within this poem, and that is why it is important to see the poem itself dominated by an image that is even more powerful and enduring than men with hatchets or paddles: seeing a freely twisting river here is like putting today's concerns, or this week's or this month's, into perspective by looking at photos of Earth from space, to remind us that, for all of our running about, we are just a small part of the larger system.

**Source:** David Kelly, in an essay for *Poetry for Students,* Gale, 1999.

## Sources

Baird, W. David, *The Osage People,* Phoenix, AZ: Indian Tribal Series, 1972.

Bruchac, Joseph, *Survival This Way* Tucson: University of Arizona Press, 1987.

Eliade, Mircea, *The Encyclopedia of Religion,* New York: Macmillan, 1987.

Reviere, Bill, *The Open Canoe,* drawings by L. Randell Boyd, Boston: Little, Brown and Co., 1985.

Rupp, Rebecca, *Red Oaks and Black Birches: The Science and Lore of Trees,* Pownal, Vermont: Garden Way Publishing, 1990.

Velie, Alan R., *American Indian Literature: An Anthology,* Norman, OK: University of Oklahoma Press, 1991.

Waldman, Carl, *Encyclopedia of Native American Tribes,* New York: Facts File Publications, 1988.

Williams, Miller, *Patterns of Poetry: An Encyclopedia of Forms,* Baton Rouge: Louisiana State University Press, 1986.

Wilson, Terry P., *The Osage,* New York: Chelsea House Publishers, 1988.

## For Further Study

Gaddis, Vincent H., *American Indian Myths and Mysteries,* Radnor, PA: Chilton Book Co., 1977.
Gaddis divides the myths in this book into two sections: "The Historical Mysteries" and "The Mystical Mysteries." The ancient stories included here cover the rich tradition of most North American peoples.

Owen, C. Roger, James J. F. Deetz, and Anthony D. Fisher, eds., *The North American Indians: A Sourcebook,* New York: The MacMillan Company, 1967.
Although slightly outdated, this anthology of essays about Native American cultures and practices provides curious readers with explorations of various nations, grouped by geographical location.

Rollings, Willard H., *The Osage: An Ethnohistorical Study of Hegemony on the Prairie-Plains,* Columbia: University of Missouri Press, 1992.
This serious scientific exploration of the Indians of the central United States is difficult for students not majoring in sociology, but it has some fascinating information for the casual, patient reader.

Weatherford, Jack, *Native Roots: How the Indians Enriched America,* New York: Crown Publishers Inc., 1991.
Rather than approaching relationship of Europeans and Native Americans as a conflict, Weatherford, a noted anthropologist, takes the broader perspective and looks at how both cultures together have created the society that we know today.

Wright, Ronald, *Stolen Continent: The Americas Through Indian Eyes Since 1492,* Boston: Houghton Mifflin, 1992.
This book divides the indigenous population up into five major groups—Aztec, Maya, Inca, Cherokee and Iroquois—and examines the reaction of each to the major challenges presented to them in the five hundred years since Columbus.

# Cargoes

*John Masefield*

*1902*

"Cargoes" is perhaps the most well-respected of John Masefield's shorter poems and, like a great many of his poems and prose works, pertains to ships. Masefield began a love-hate relationship with ships and the sea when he took his first and only overseas voyage as a teenager. This trip left indelible marks—some of them scars—on his character and work. "Cargoes" was included in Masefield's second volume of verse, *Ballads,* published in 1903. At this time, the British Empire was still the most powerful in the world, vesting in ships and the cargo they could carry. Turn-of-the-century England, then, was an ideal time and place to reflect back on the history of shipping, cargoes, and, most important, on power and empire.

In "Cargoes," one ship sails through each of three stanzas. The first ship rows around the lands of the Old Testament, the second sails across the Atlantic Ocean sometime between the fifteenth and eighteenth century, and the third motors through the English Channel, probably at the turn of the twentieth century, the time the poem was written. The poem is thus a concise history of ships, shipping, consumption, and empire. For Masefield, much has changed, apparently for the worse. Once, Masefield's story goes, ships had exotic names and sailed through idyllic climes to and from faraway destinations with strange and marvelous cargoes. But by the turn of the century, dirty, polluting ships motored their way through the bad weather of the confining English Channel. The cargo these ships carry is not only produced in the same country it is shipped to, but it is cheap and plentiful—a cargo destined for the masses instead of the kings and queens of yesterday. These three snapshots of three ships might be quick, but they are also somewhat complex. In contemplating "Cargoes," we might understand that what Masefield has given us is not only the lushness of poetry, but also the austerity of photography.

## Author Biography

John Masefield was Poet Laureate of England for thirty-seven years. He was honored with numerous awards and received honorary degrees from the most prestigious universities in England and the United States. He published a huge body of plays, poems, criticism, and works of fiction, some of which sold very well. Now, however, he is a rather obscure poet, much criticized and infrequently anthologized. Perhaps it was Masefield's preoccupation with poetic conventions such as meter and rhyme, or his romance with sea and ships, or perhaps it was a limited education that would have likely subdued his rather dreamy, expressive voice—one mostly unencumbered by hardened analysis, political anger, or nagging self-doubt. In a phrase, Masefield was more a poet of emotion than thought.

Masefield's childhood was, in his own words, like "living in Paradise." Born June 1, 1878, in a Victorian house with vistas of fields and woodlands, and grounds with garden and orchard, Masefield was the third of six children. When he was a child, his mother recited poems to him. Loss of paradise came with the death of his mother when he was six and the death of his grandparents a year later, which put a financial strain on the family and slowly drove his father into insanity. Until he went to boarding school at age ten, he and his siblings were looked after by a governess they despised (John going so far as once stabbing her with a fork). Masefield also hated boarding school but, instead, took the violence out on himself: he attempted suicide by eating laurel leaves. By the time he began to like school—the place he began writing verse— his father became so ill that Masefield was forced to return home. His father died when Masefield was thirteen, and he fell under the guardianship of his father's brother and his wife, both of whom tried to keep him from reading. Fed up, they resorted to sending Masefield to a school to learn seamanship aboard the H.M.S. *Conway.* Here, he continued

*John Masefield*

reading, and showed ineptitude with mathematics and an aptitude for writing. After graduation, Masefield apprenticed on the H.M.S. *Gilcruix* and in April of 1894 began his first and only voyage as a sailor, an experience that furnished the material for his long, narrative poem *Dauber* (1913). The stormy and emotionally difficult thirteen-week voyage resulted in sunstroke and a nervous breakdown that landed Masefield in a Chilean hospital. Although he was sent back to England to recover, his unsympathetic aunt soon forced him to enlist in the service of another ship, which he was supposed to meet in New York. He never met it: "I deserted my ship and cut myself adrift from her and from my home. I was going to be a writer, come what might." Masefield would stay in New York as a tramp, doing odd jobs and wandering about to evade detectives employed by his uncle to find him. In New York City he worked as a barboy in Greenwich Village and then at a carpet mill in Yonkers for two years, all the time reading and writing. When Masefield quit the factory and sailed back to England, he was barely nineteen years old. His assessment of this period in his life was that it was "a seclusion … among the looms of Yonkers, a seclusion due to my hatred of Americans." Seclusion though it was, it resulted in his first two collections of verse that were never published. Back in England, Masefield found steady employment, first with a business firm and then at a bank, which provided a stable enough income for him to recover from his ill health. In 1899 his first poem was published in *Outlook,* a literary and political journal. By 1900, Masefield had become a literary man, visiting W. B. Yeats's Monday evenings of liquor and literature and meeting people such as Irish playwright John Millington Synge and the scholar-poet Lawrence Binyon. In 1901, at the age of 23, Masefield left the bank and began life as a free-lance writer. His first book, *Salt Water Ballads* (1902), sold out its initial run of 500 copies in six months. In 1903 Masefield married Constance Crommelin and later fathered two children with her. After the wedding, Masefield worked as a book reviewer, an editor, and even organized an art exhibit. By 1910 Masefield had published one book of poetry, three plays, four novels, and six volumes of prose. During his wife's second pregnancy, Masefield developed a deep infatuation for a woman, Elizabeth Robins, who was old enough to be his mother. (Indeed, he called her "mother," she called him "son.") After several months, she broke off the relationship that had been conducted mostly through intense letter writing—he once wrote her nine letters in one day. From 1915 to 1918, during World War I, Masefield made four trips to France, one to the Middle East, and two to the United States. On his first trip to France, Masefield nursed soldiers for the Red Cross. During the next trip, he surveyed the hospital area in the city of Tours for the purpose of setting up a fresh-air hospital, a plan that never materialized. The third trip was under the auspices of British Intelligence. It was to gather knowledge of American aid for French medical units, the report of which, it was hoped, would enlist more support from America for the war effort. The last trip to France was to chronicle the battle of the Somme. Masefield also went to Gallipoli, in Turkey, to nurse the wounded for the Red Cross in 1915. In 1916, before the United States entered the war, he was sent to America, ostensibly to deliver lectures, but also to assess the attitudes of Americans toward the Allies. Masefield's second trip to America in 1918—the United States had already entered the war—was made to strengthen ties between Britain and America. Masefield visited training camps to give lectures to the soldiers. In America, Masefield met and befriended Florence Lamont, the wife of a wealthy financier in the House of Morgan. The Lamonts would, on occasion, help Masefield out with money for theater projects. In his letters to Florence Lamont, Mase-

field frequently expressed his love of the common man and the simpler life of the countryside and his aversion to ugly cities and rampant commercialism. In 1922 Masefield help set up a theatrical company called The Hill Street Players, which produced plays by Shakespeare, Moliere, and himself.

When Poet Laureate Robert Bridges died in 1930, Masefield assumed the post and served until his own death in 1967. As Poet Laureate, Masefield generated awards for younger poets, held verse recitations, and generally stimulated literary activity. Masefield believed that verse was an oral art: "I am all for a stringed lyre and speech: the printing press is a mistake; one of the many mistakes that the Renaissance made." Masefield lost his son in combat in World War II and his wife in 1960. With his sister, Judith, at his bedside, Masefield succumbed to gangrene—rather than have his leg amputated—at the age of 89 in 1967.

## Poem Text

Quinquireme of Nineveh from distant Ophir,
Rowing home to haven in sunny Palestine,
With a cargo of ivory,
And apes and peacocks,
Sandalwood, cedarwood, and sweet white wine.          5

Stately Spanish galleon coming from the Isthmus,
Dipping through the Tropics by the palm-green
          shores,
With a cargo of diamonds,
Emeralds, amethysts,
Topazes, and cinnamon, and gold moidores.          10

Dirty British coaster with a salt-caked smoke stack,
Butting through the Channel in the mad March
          days,
With a cargo of Tyne coal,
Road-rails, pig-lead,
Firewood, iron-ware, and cheap tin trays.          15

## Poem Summary

### Lines 1-5:

A quinquireme is an ancient ship with five banks of oars. Nineveh is the ancient capital of Assyria (now Iraq), whose ruins are opposite Mosul (Al Mawsil) on the Tigris River. This area is considered one of the cradles of civilization, a source for some of the earliest written and built histories of ancient human communities. Ophir is an ancient country of uncertain location mentioned in the Old Testament. From Ophir, gold was brought to

Solomon, King of ancient Israel in the tenth century B.C. Presumably, this particular quinquireme is bringing its cargo to Solomon. The Nineveh reference is unclear. Perhaps the ship was built in Nineveh, rowed to Ophir, then on to its destination in Palestine. The traditional cargo of Ophirian gold is replaced by an exotic catalog of luxury items from Nineveh or from other places along the route. It is uncertain whether Masefield is referring here to a particular historical voyage or even a particular period of ancient biblical history. It seems just as likely that these words laden with history have been collected for their ability to create the desired sound and meter as well as the desired image.

### Lines 6-10:

The Spanish ship of stanza two, a large sailing vessel, is likely sailing from the Isthmus of Panama back to Spain through the North Atlantic approximately 2,500 years later. This is the period of the Spanish Empire—beginning in the 1500s—when Spain controlled the commerce from much of the Americas. Again the cargo is of luxury goods, especially precious stones, bound for Spanish royalty and nobility. The gold moidores, or coins, are of Portuguese origin and are likely from Brazil, Portugal's only Western colony. Stanzas one and two have several things in common. First, their valuable cargo is destined for the only ones who can afford it: those in power, namely, King Solomon the ruler of the biblical "empire" of Israel, and, in stanza two, for Spanish royalty in Spain's much later and larger empire. Second, the items are nonessential, extravagant luxuries. Third, the climates are sunny and beautiful. In these two stanzas, then, impressive ships on exotic voyages carry exotic cargo to exotic and extravagant rulers. The overall impression is of beauty.

### Lines 11-15:

The ship of the third stanza stands in for the somewhat later empire of Britain. With its colonization of North America, Britain began its empire building approximately a hundred years after Spain and Portugal; these two countries already controlled a great many of the world's newly explored areas. This dirty British coaster, a ship engaged in coastal trading, sounds like a vessel of Masefield's own time. This particular ship is different than the two others, not just because it is unimpressive, but because it is not travelling to or from abroad. Instead it carries materials from one part of Britain to another through the English Channel. The coaster's material is also different than that

of the quinquireme or the galleon. No longer luxury items, this cargo is not beautiful, but purely practical and, one might assert, ugly as the coaster is dirty and salt-caked. The material is not bound for royalty and nobility, but for the captains of industry to process. Finally, the setting the ship sails in is quite different: the first two ships sail through sunny weather and tropical climes, while the last sails through the channel during the "mad March days." Masefield juxtaposes these three ships to show that while trade was once a romantic business of beautiful goods for beautiful people, it has become a dirty business of processing nature into drab products for the masses; through years and empires, trade has been transformed into mere commercialism. Through almost picture-like images of three ships representing three successive empires, Masefield economically sums up and negatively comments upon the history of capitalism and trade.

## Themes

### Romance and Reality

The first two stanzas of "Cargoes" fall under the heading of "romance" and the last stanza under "reality." Even without any understanding of the words "quinquireme," "Nineveh," and "Ophir," their unfamiliarity and the repetition of sounds in the first two words make them seem magical—the stuff of witches' curses and wizards' incantations. The first stanza describes an ancient ship, placed by Masefield in the time of Solomon, the son of David who ruled Israel from 961 to 922 B.C. From Ophir (an unknown locale that might have been located in what is now Saudi Arabia), and from other locales, Solomon received the expensive and exotic products of gold, cedar, and sandalwood (called "almug" in the Old Testament) for vast building projects, especially a temple and his palace. Also imported were ivory for his throne, and the other cargo mentioned, except for "sweet white wine," which Masefield seems to have invented. Solomon had a glorious kingdom that magically combined the virtues of incredible wealth, deep wisdom, and devoted religiosity; that is, until he began worshipping other gods and his kingdom fell apart. The second ship belongs to the Spain of the sixteenth and seventeenth centuries that imported products from its empire in South America. This glittering cargo is for an empire that once ruled half of the world (Portugal controlled the other half). By the time of the third stanza, how-

# Topics for Further Study

- In the first two stanzas of "Cargoes," transporting products from one country to another sounds beautiful and exotic. One might say that these stanzas are written from the perspective of the country receiving these goods. To gain another perspective, research the effects on a people and area that has supplied or still supplies the labor and such materials as are described in "Cargoes." Some examples from the present day might be copper from Indonesia and oil from Nigeria.

- Research the history of trade to see how it has changed through the centuries. If a more specific topic is desired, one could research how ships and navigation have changed and the effect this had on trade. Or, one could investigate different means—military, diplomatic, etc.—that countries have used to get other countries to trade with them.

- List reasons why road rails, pig-lead, firewood, ironware, and cheap tin trays are apparently less desirable than topazes, cinnamon, diamonds, ivory, and exotic animals. Try to be precise in your answer.

- On a map, draw out the trading routes in this poem. Map out some present-day trading routes. For example, how does Egyptian cotton reach the United States?

- What are the reasons for having an empire, for imperialism?

ever, these days had vanished. What Masefield's England was left with was the British version of empire: one that began with the conquest of foreign lands and the importation of exotica, but one that had become a grubby country of factories and machinery churning out massive amounts of materials for masses of people forced into cities when their land was taken from them. Succinctly put, the world of trade had been transformed from glamorous to grimy.

## Growth and Development

From the first to the third stanzas there is growth and development. The first stanza's Palestine was an area that included the Kingdom of Israel, a rather small "empire" by later standards such as Portuguese and British. Still, Israel was made rich by conquering areas around it and enslaving its peoples. Solomon employed these slaves, according to Kings I of the Bible, to build his cities. By the time Spain was an imperial power, enabled by the Pope who gave it rights to the Western world, Spain controlled a large part of North and South America. The later British Empire was even larger, penetrating into America, the Middle East, Asia, and Africa. But as empires grew and developed, they also fell. By the time of the British coaster in stanza three, Britain had become a large factory, processing not only materials from the rest of the globe, but also from those it cut down and mined in its own country. Instead of just importing goods from other climes to make itself wealthy as Israel and Spain had, Britain was destroying itself—through procuring and processing—in order to make itself rich. With the Industrial Revolution, Britain had turned itself into a noisy, grimy machine that turned development into a dirty word.

## Wealth and Poverty

As to wealth and poverty, there is again a difference between the first two stanzas and the last. In the first stanza, the cargo on the quinquireme is wealth meant for King Solomon, his family, and those lucky enough to move within his orbit. The "stately Spanish galleon" carries a shipment of goods thought even more to belong to the province of kings and queens—those jewels meant for royal robes and diadems, that cinnamon meant for feasts, and those gold moidores, Portuguese coins, meant for Spain's royal coffers. The wealth shipped on the quinquireme and the galleon, then, is wealth destined for the very few, to be distributed to just a few more. Not so with the British coaster. This is wealth of another kind that only a captain of industry, not a king or queen of state, could love. The coaster's cargo will not be confined to palaces and manor houses; it will be distributed throughout the country to factories for energy and for reprocessing, furnishing jobs to the urban masses dispossessed of any link to lands they once farmed. While this material will be distributed to the masses in the form of wages and some services, such as railroads, these masses will arguably be poorer and more dependent on someone else than ever before. This time the people, however, are not dependent upon the reach of a central royal family, but on the grip of capitalists in every town and hamlet across Britain. As Jorge Luis Borges has written, "Yesterday's poverty was less poor than the poverty handed down to us today by industrialism." Masefield championed the poor and the common man: he too had worked at low-paying jobs at a bar, a farm, a factory, and on a ship. It appears Masefield longed, despite the drawbacks, for the glory days of the ruling monarchy. For then, even when the very few got richer, the poor did not necessarily get poorer.

## Style

From a formal viewpoint, "Cargoes" is a fascinating poem. Its three, five-line stanzas follow an unusual *abcdb* rhyme scheme. The first, second, and fifth lines of every stanza are best read with three feet to a line (trimeter), though some lines, such as the first line, are comfortably read with four feet (tetrameter). All of the stanzas' third and fourth lines have two feet (dimeter). The poem's rhythm at the beginning of the first, third, and fifth lines of each stanza mostly follows a form called the paeon, which is a foot with one accented syllable followed by three unaccented syllables: "QUIN qui reme of / NI ne veh from." In actuality, the accents, in stair-step or wave-like fashion, gradually fall or descend in the words "quinquireme" and "Nineveh," then slightly rise with the preposition before rising still higher with the beginning of the next foot. The rhythm is thus a gradual movement from unaccented to accented syllables and vice-versa, much like the repetitiously gentle dipping and rising of peaceful ships at sea. Things change, however, at the third foot of most of the first, second, and fifth lines of each stanza. Here, we usually come upon what is called a mollossus, a foot with three consecutive strong beats as in lines 1, 7, and 15:

> / **distant Oph**ir /
> / **palm–green shores** /
> / **cheap tin trays**

Lines with two feet follow different variations of iambs, anapests, trochees, and dactyls. In the following line there are two feet of dactyls, a first accented syllable followed by two unaccented syllables:

> **Em**eralds, / **Am**ethysts

But in the following line there are two trochaic feet:

> **Road**–rails/ **pig**-lead

Finally, there is the repetition of sounds. For instance, in lines 6 and 11, an "s" sound dominates. In line 5 a "w" sound repeats. Throughout the poem, there are instances of repeated vowel sounds, called assonance (firewood, iron-ware); repeated consonant sounds, called consonance (salt-caked smoke stacks); and repeated sounds at the beginning of words, called alliteration (salt-caked smoke stacks). The repetition of these sounds not only feel good in the mouth, but along with regularities of stanzas and lines, it pulls disparate parts of the poem together into different unities. One might think of the poem itself as a ship carrying and storing different kinds of poetic cargo in similar places.

## Historical Context

"Cargoes" was published in 1903 during what has come to be known as the Edwardian Age or Edwardian Decade. Spanning the period from 1901-1910, The Edwardian Age began with the death of Queen Victoria, who had reigned from 1837 over the most successful imperialist country in history—one that, at its height, controlled more than one quarter of the earth's surface. Perhaps the most important domestic result of Victorian expansionism was the forced and almost complete transition from a rural economy of people attached to land to an urban economy of people toiling in trade and manufacturing. London became the center of the West, increasing its population from two million to six and a half million in just sixty years. With the increase of imports and of manufactured exports such as cotton and wool through cheap labor working under harsh conditions, the invention of new machinery that increased production and cut down on labor costs, and due to having the world's best fleet of ships, England became the world's workshop, its dominant and wealthiest nation, and its largest banker. The result was a Britain of overweening pride, nagging guilt, and obsessive propriety.

Other countries besides Britain were now experiencing their imperial rites of passage. In 1898 Spain and the United States, a new imperial power, came to blows over Spanish-controlled Cuba and the Philippines. The United States won the Spanish-American War easily, partially because the Spanish colonies were far from Spain and close to the United States. At the war's end, the United States took control of the Philippines, Puerto Rico, and Cuba.

Meanwhile, various nations were also fighting over China. Japan was the first to make inroads,

# *Compare & Contrast*

- **1900:** The Chinese Boxers (a.k.a., The Society of Harmonious Fists), supported by former empress Tz'u Hsi, seized Peking, murdering Western diplomats and Chinese who had converted to Christianity. The Western imperialist powers with interests in China, including Great Britain, band together and put down the Boxer Rebellion. The Emperor Kuang Tsu is forced to resign.

  **1998:** In the spring, students revolt for several days in Jakarta, Indonesia. The rioting and looting is a response to skyrocketing prices brought about by austerity measures, themselves caused by a $40 billion loan from the International Monetary Fund. Millions of dollars worth of property is destroyed and hundreds are killed. Under local and international demands, President Suharto resigns.

- **1901:** H. G. Wells publishes *The First Men on the Moon.*

  **1966:** U. S. spacecraft *Surveyor I* makes a soft landing on the moon and transmits more than 11,000 television images. Edwin Aldrin steps out of the Gemini spacecraft for 129 minutes.

  **1997:** The Pathfinder Probe lands on Mars. The Soujourner vehicle moves about the surface of Mars taking pictures.

- **1898:** In a blow to the once world-dominating Spanish Empire, Spain loses the Spanish-American War to a newly emerging imperial power, the United States. As part of the treaty, Spain must cede the colonies of Cuba, Puerto Rico, and the Philippines to the United States.

  **1991:** The Russian Empire breaks up from the mounting costs of competition and the cost of maintaining its empire. The Soviet Union and its satellites are replaced by the independent nations of Eastern Europe, Czechoslovakia, and Yugoslavia to name two, and the Commonwealth of Independent States, comprised of Russia, Ukraine, Belarus, Armenia, Azerbaijan, Kazakhstan, Kyrgystan, Moldova, Tajikistan, Turkmenistan, and Uzbekistan.

---

but at such a cost that it was weakened. The European countries, beginning with Russia, seized their chance and ousted Japan from the Chinese peninsula. Britain added two naval bases to its other possessions. China, however, survived partition; France, Germany, Britain, and Russia were too much at odds to agree to any arrangement. In 1900, China made a violent attempt to kick out the Western powers with its anti-Christian Boxer Rebellion. The attempt failed and Europe, especially Russia, clung more tightly to China, especially that part known as Manchuria. This bothered both Britain and Japan, so in 1902, these two countries signed the Anglo-Japanese treaty. Among other things, the treaty stated that should Japan go to war with Russia over Korea and eastern parts of China, Britain would do its best to prevent any other imperial power from aiding Russia. The Russo-Japanese War broke out in 1904, and by 1905, Japan would win the Liaotung Peninsula and Korea. Britain's move had paid dividends.

When Edward VII assumed the throne in 1901, Britain was an unpopular country fighting an expansionist war. The Boer War began in 1899 when Britain annexed the Boer-controlled provinces of Transvaal and the Orange Free State in South Africa. The Boers were descended from Dutch settlers who had invaded South Africa before the British and had coexisted, though uneasily, with the British for decades. The discovery of diamonds and gold, however, and the increasing desire of the British to create a corridor of possession over the whole East-African coast to monopolize access to the Indian Ocean and their prized possession, India, changed British plans. The British government—fueled largely by mining corporations, especially De Beer whose head, Cecil Rhodes, was also the Prime Minister of England—began a war to take the Transvaal and the Orange Free State. The war took three years to win and resulted in a terrible loss of humanity. Boer farms were burned to the ground, and women and children were rounded up into "concentration camps," a brand-new, British invention. Disease and lack of food were so prevalent in the camps that out of 117,000 people imprisoned, 20,000 died. The war and the decision, in 1903, to import forced Chinese laborers to work the British mines deeply divided Britain and soured the world about imperialism, especially the British version, even if some of Britain's most radical thinkers—Karl Marx included—could look on the bright side of British colonial rule: British rule, it was said, had its advantages; and besides, the rule of the other imperialist countries was far worse. Nonetheless, it might be said that while Britain won the Boer War, it began to lose the Imperialist battle. English guilt was surpassing English hubris.

## Critical Overview

As early as 1922, in the first book-length study of Masefield's poetry, the fault-finding begins. Though generally an advocate of Masefield, especially his "realism" and characterization, W. H. Hamilton's assessment, in *John Masefield: A Critical Study,* of the poet's first two books of poetry is dismissive: "Indeed it must be confessed that the best things in the book—the nearest to perfect—are the merest trifles; the pretty jingles of rime and curiosities of design like the well-known 'Cargoes,' which cannot boast one finite verb. Such verses, were they never so perfect, must of need be minor—mere exercises in word colouring." Not only is the poetry of *Ballads* trivial, says Hamilton, but imitative, especially of Yeats: "The poems quoted and referred to show verse more restrained [than in *Salt-Water Ballads*] ... but still, at best, only a very skilful discipleship of other older cunning artists." Hamilton believes that while poets must admire and study other poets, they should never imitate them, at least not in published work. By 1973, in his *John Masefield's England: A Study of the National Themes in His Work,* critic Fraser Drew would steer away from all assessment of "Cargoes," only saying that it is a "favorite anthology piece." This, by the way, is no longer true: neither the comprehensive *Harper Anthology of Poetry* (1981), the *Norton Anthology of English Literature* (1986), nor the *Norton Anthology of Modern Poetry* (1988) in-

cludes any of Masefield's work, let alone "Cargoes." Drew's only remarks about the content of the poem is his observation that the three ships signify three civilizations, and that while the British coaster of "Cargoes" is Masefield's icon of disdain, the stately clipper ship is elsewhere in Masefield an index of that Britain called "Great." In might be noticed that, in both Hamilton and Drew, there is a near absence of interpretation, perhaps signalling that the poem is too simple to need it. In 1985, however, Neil Corcoran expresses admiration for "Cargoes" because it has "clearly imposed a self-denying ordinance on itself: it has made a canny judgment about the point at which delight, if pursued, is likely to become indulgence." But this admiration of "Cargoes" serves primarily to set off Corcoran's more general disdain: "... much of Masefield's poetry is cripplingly disabled by unselfconsciousness about language." It appears that Hamilton's dismissiveness of Masefield's early work has now spread to a dislike of most of Masefield's oeuvre. Finally there is the brief comment of June Dwyer, in her work *John Masefield,* that, like the comment of Drew, interprets only what is most obvious, and, like Corcoran, cites "Cargoes" as a contrast to Masefield's poorer verse: "Avoiding both the vagueness and the regularity of his weaker verse, Masefield comments on the passing of time through the description of three cargo-laden ships from three different periods of history. The beauty and romance of the past founder against the grimy industrial present in the last stanza." What all these critics say without quite saying it is that while "Cargoes" has value, it does so largely in contrast to most, much, or some of Masefield's weaker work. "Cargoes," then, appears like a tiny diamond in the rougher body of Masefield's work—a body of work thought, unfortunately, by many critics to resemble the rougher and cheaper freight of a dirty British coaster.

## Criticism

### Jhan Hochman

*Jhan Hochman's articles appear in* Democracy and Nature, Genre, ISLE, *and* Mosaic. *He is the author of* Green Cultural Studies: Nature in Film, Novel, and Theory *(1998), and he holds a Ph.D in English and an M.A. in Cinema Studies. In the following essay, Hochman describes and interprets the meaning of the cargo from the three ships in Masefield's poem.*

# What Do I Read Next?

- David Cooperman and E. V. Walter's *Power and Civilization: Political Thought in the Twentieth Century,* published in 1962, is an anthology of writings by some of the most important figures of the twentieth century—George Santayana, Karl Kautski, Adolph Hitler, Joseph Stalin, and Herbert Marcuse, to name just a few. Its 600 pages are divided into the modern (1918-39) and the postmodern world, from World War II to the present day.

- David Harvey's 1990 work, *The Condition of Postmodernity,* investigates the relationship of space and time to flexible modes of capitalist accumulation in the last third of the twentieth century.

- George Lukacs's 1968 influential work, *History and Class Consciousness: Studies in Marxist Dialectics,* is a collection of writings during a period that Lukacs's calls his "apprenticeship in Marxism." He is especially effective at showing how the capitalist system influences all aspects of life.

- John Masefield's long narrative poem from 1913, *Dauber: a Poem* is not only a completely different example of Masefield's poetic talents, but it is drawn from his only sea voyage—an odyssey that developed into an obsession with ships and poems about ships.

- Masefield's *On the Spanish Main* (1906) is a factual history—in a storytelling mode—of the looting expeditions of Drake and other sixteenth-century pirates operating in the West Indies.

---

"Cargoes" would appear to be saying little more than this: whereas the products of empire were once glorious, they are no longer. But why say it? This will be the question I will try to answer. In order to do so, I will have to force these three cargoes to speak—to tell where they came from, how they were got, who got them, and what they were used for. Only then might we understand what these cargoes represent.

The first ship rows right from the Bible's Old Testament, Kings I. In that book, there is no mention of Nineveh, an ancient town on the Tigris River in ancient Assyria whose ruins are in what is now present-day Iraq. Nineveh was likely selected for its general historical relevance and, most important, for its contribution to the poem's metrics. Just as there is no mention of Nineveh, the word "quinquireme" is also absent in Kings I, but quinquireme is the name of an ancient ship with five banks of oars, which could have been similar to the kind used by Solomon, King of Israel, in the tenth century B.C. Solomon sent a fleet of ships, perhaps quinquiremes, to get gold from Ophir. No one quite knows where Ophir was located, but it is thought to have been in what is now southern Saudi Arabia. The ships from Ophir brought back a bit more than gold. For one thing, they carried Ophirian almug wood, now called sandalwood. Sandalwood was used to build not only the supports of Solomon's extraordinarily lavish temple, but also to make lyres for his singers. Ivory was also brought back from Ophir. With it, Solomon made his throne, which he also overlaid with gold. But this was not enough: "The throne had six steps, and at the back of the throne was a calf's head, and on each side of the seat were arm rests and two lions standing beside the arm rests, while twelve lions stood there, one on each end of a step on the six steps." Apes and peacocks were also shipped in, but there is no mention of precisely what Solomon did with these. Two materials in the poem do not come from Ophir. Cedar came from Lebanon, not from Ophir. Solomon used a great deal of cedar to build his palace and temple. And sweet white wine seems to make no appearance at all in this section about Solomon. We might safely assume that the three "w"'s and the three consecutive accented syllables of "sweet white wine" seduced Masefield into using the words for his poem. As I briefly mentioned, much of this cargo was used for two building projects: Solomon's temple and palace. Who built these immoderate structures? The forced labor of 183,300 men who saw their labor as a yoke, one which earned such resentment that it would later cause disruption in Israel under Solomon's son, Rehoboam. To summarize: valuable cargo from a distant land was shipped to the Kingdom of Israel, heaped upon the backs of men under the yoke of a king who used wealth and labor to glorify himself through a god he claimed had spoken to him. But even after Solomon's death, his deeds acted on the living: Solomon's use of forced labor to build his temple and palace later caused trouble for his son.

In the second stanza, readers find themselves on a Spanish galleon, a sailing ship used for commerce and warfare. The ship is sailing from Central America, specifically from the Isthmus of Panama—now the locale of the Panama Canal. Generally the ship is coming from the Tropics, the Caribbean, the Gulf of Mexico, the West Indies—the major outposts of what would become the largest empire the earth had thus seen, the Spanish Empire. This title was due to the conquests of Hernan Cortes, conqueror of Aztec Mexico in 1521, and Francisco Pizarro, who left from the Isthmus of Darien (now the Isthmus of Panama) and conquered Incan Peru in 1532. From Mexico and Peru came fabulous wealth: gold, silver, and the precious gems mentioned in "Cargoes." Worth noting is that, while gold was the major booty in both Ophir and the Americas, Masefield hardly mentions it in "Cargoes," except when it is processed into moidores, or Portuguese coins. An explanation might be that gold has only one syllable and it does not sound as exotic as the rest of the booty. Here is one description of the treasure found by Cortes in Tenochtitlan, then capital of Mexico: "The Spaniards ... saw mounds of golden ornaments and jewels and stacks of gold bars." On one occasion, it was reported that Montezuma, Tenochtitlan's ruler, sent green stones, probably emeralds, to Cortes as a gift. And on Cortes's first shipment of Aztec gifts back to Charles V of Spain, was "a gold necklace set with both green and red stones and pearls and hung with gold bells, a gold bracelet; a wand or scepter girdled with gold and pearls: a wood headdress decorated with gems and golden bells...." There was reputed to be even more wealth from the Incas. When Pizarro took the Incan King Atahualpa hostage, he demanded the ransom of a room's

> *Overall, what distinguishes the coaster from the quinquireme and the galleon is that the coaster does not hide what it is: a dirty ship carrying on a dreary commerce that reflects the tawdry society that produced the ship and its 'goods.'"*

worth of gold and jewels, some of which were emeralds like those that studded the King's robes. The loot from the Americas meant unbelievable wealth for Spain: "The precious metals arriving in Spain had by the end of [Charles V's] reign increased ten-fold: from a yearly average of 200,000 pesos between 1516 and 1520, to 1,975,000 pesos between 1551 and 1555." And what happened to the Indians of the Americas from the Spanish invasions? They were made into slaves or treated to near genocide from war and disease. The Indians also got Christianity. Charles V spent at least some of Cortes's first shipment of booty on an expensive coronation in Germany where he would succeed his grandfather, Maximilian I. As in the Kingdom of Israel, the Empire of Spain grew rich off of the misery and decimation of lands and peoples: Israel enslaved its men at home (no mention is made of the Ophirians), and Spain enslaved and killed the native peoples of the Americas.

The last ship in Masefield's brief history of civilization is a coaster, a ship of commerce operating along the coast of Britain. This motorized ship is dirty and is neither exotic like the quinquireme, nor stately like the galleon. The coal-driven ship is likely soiled because of its own smoke, the pollution from the ports at which it docked, and the rough weather—indicated by "mad March days" and "salt-caked"—through the English Channel. It might be said that while the coaster is dirty, the other ships are, in comparison, clean. Finally, the ship is operating within one country, not coming from distant lands like Ophir or the Americas. Not only are ship, weather, and route different, but so is the cargo. The British cargo is distinct in several ways. First it is bound not for kings, but for industrialists who will process it and sell it—directly or indirectly—to masses of people forced into cities because they had been formerly dispossessed of land and because they are needed to stoke the furnace of industry. The British cargo is also different from the cargoes of the past because, in and of itself, it is not valuable. It only becomes valuable through being processed and sold to many people. The cargo is not so much dirty, but the result of dirty processes involving the burning of coal and wood. Another difference is that the cargo is a combination of imported goods (tin from Nigeria and Malaya) and "home-grown" goods such as coal and iron. Lastly, the coaster's cargo is mostly named by thudding words of two syllables, whereas most of the cargo of the other ships is composed of a mellifluous three syllables.

Overall, what distinguishes the coaster from the quinquireme and the galleon is that the coaster does not hide what it is: a dirty ship carrying on a dreary commerce that reflects the tawdry society that produced the ship and its "goods." Victorian and Edwardian England (1837 to 1910) is the setting of "Cargoes," a time when Britain produced—for internal use and for export—more coal, iron, and steel than any other country. Yet one third of its people lived a ghastly existence: "Conditions were so bad that it was believed they were producing degenerate physical types, anaemic mothers of rickety children, young men incapable of defending the Motherland and the Empire." Among the hard hit were dockers, those who loaded and unloaded British coasters. Workers toiled twelve or more hours a day for subsistent wages. Miners worked dangerous jobs in isolated, dirty towns and tramps abounded, probably having come to the conclusion that they could no longer work so long and so hard for so little. The government did not help. It showed itself hostile to labor unionism, especially in the Taff-Vale Case of 1901. Laborers had little recourse but to accept their lot and do the best they could. One reason for such abjection was an entrenched class-consciousness that produced England's version of a caste system. It was thought by the upper classes, said J. B. Priestly, that if the working masses were given more money and leisure time, there was no telling what they might do with it. Besides, the upper classes would say, workers had chosen these conditions since, if they wanted to, they could work harder and climb out of poverty. It was plain that England would have

to wait until after the writing of "Cargoes" for improved social programs and working conditions for the working classes. Poor regard and miserable conditions for the people who helped produce the wealth of the British empire contributed to the early-twentieth-century decline of a dirty, hyperrational empire. The British empire was so rife with injustice that it deeply divided the people between those who wanted capital spent on more production that would produce more riches, supposedly for more people, and those who wanted some of the wealth immediately diverted to decent wages and working conditions. English society was also divided about its empire overseas, especially when it came to the Boer War (1899-1902), fought largely for the possession of diamond and gold mines that had been discovered in South Africa. The South-African countryside was decimated, concentration camps to house Boer women and children were invented (20,000 died), and, altogether, 5,774 British and 4,000 Boers were killed in the conflict. Notice here that while the British won this capitalist war of conquest, they lost more lives than the Boers.

Through the experience of England, the largest imperial power the world has ever seen, the desire for empire was now tainted. Before the British, empire had seemed a glorious undertaking—worth killing, enslavement, and the risking of one's own countrymen. After all, there was money and glory to be had as well as souls to be saved. After Britain, however, the cost of directly maintaining an empire became too great, both in money and lives. The British coaster is the most ignominious ship in "Cargoes," but it is also the most important: the British empire destroyed not only distant peoples and distant lands, as in the case of Spain, but its own people and land, as in the case of ancient Israel.

**Source:** Jhan Hochman, in an essay for *Poetry for Students,* Gale, 1999.

### Bruce Meyer

*Bruce Meyer is the director of the creative writing program at the University of Toronto. He has taught at several Canadian universities and is the author of three collections of poetry. In the following essay, Meyer characterizes Masefield's poem as "a political examination of human development as seen through artifacts."*

John Masefield's "Cargoes" is a unique poem that implements meter and language to convey a gradual sense of diminution through time. The world, as the poem suggests, is a victim of progress, of a reductio ad absurdum where values are shrinking. For Masefield, a passionate observer of maritime experiences and traditions, an age is weighed and measured in the scope of human history by what its participants choose to convey over great distances. The major question that the poem raises is why Masefield is so fascinated with the manifests of these ships? Are we to perceive the cargoes as metaphors for worth, importance and values? The poem examines three different epochs—the Ancient, the Modern and the contemporary-and, by process of comparison, exposes progress and human development as a question of values. At first glance, what was once stately, opulent, and rich is bathetically shrinking, lowered and diminished so that the poem is not only a commentary on history but an indictment of progress. But the ultimate picture that the poem paints, a political examination of human development as seen through artifacts, suggests a much different reading to the poem.

Structurally, Masefield has divided the poem into three very distinct—both in terms of content and meter—sections. The first section deals with the ancient world, the second with what can be loosely termed the "modern" world (the term modern here applied to anything after the Medieval era), and the last with the contemporary world. By dividing the poem into these three period units, Masefield is very subtly hinting at a much broader literary theme: the debates between the ancients and the moderns—a line of argument that was used by such writers as Machiavelli in *The Prince* and Swift in *The Battle of the Books* to measure the changes and development in human knowledge over the centuries. In the battle of the ancients versus the moderns, the question is always who is better and who is wiser. The stanzas, each self-contained and with their only segues and connections based on the theme of "cargoes," are meant to raise comparisons simply through the juxtaposing of periods. The addition of a third stanza about the contemporary world underscores the twentieth-century ideal to reinvent all ideas and to question all aspects of the past, whether ancient or modern. The relationship between the third stanza and the first two highlights the discrepancies between the twentieth century and all previous eras; the result is a world that is absurdly far different from anything that has gone before. The implication of this structure underlying the poem, at first glance, is that time is a bathetic, reductive process and that things are heading downhill at a very rapid and unstoppable pace.

Within the poem, the process of thematic reduction is expressed by Masefield through the use of three metrical variations. The stanzas, each one representing a journey that defines one of the three eras, literally become faster and faster sounding as time progresses and riches fade. For Masefield, who throughout his poetry echoes the themes of preservation and even repugnance at the impositions and devaluations that modern times impose on the world, "Cargoes" is both an evocation and a demonstration of his poetic thesis.

The first ancient, leisurely journey is set approximately in classical times and is undertaken on a "Quinquireme" or Roman galley "with five files of oarsmen on each side" between "Ophir" in North Africa to "Nineveh" in the Middle East. The opening line of this first journey evokes a feeling of slowness. The slowness of the opening line is achieved sonically through the use of ionic (major) feet—metrical measures in which each foot is composed of two heavy stresses followed by two light stresses. The ionic (major), as a measure, is graceful, archaic, and leisurely, with the two leading, heavy stresses echoing the solemnity of a spondee, but without the unrelieved gravity that the funereal and drumlike spondee implies. As meters go, it is almost ritualistic in the tonal connotations it carries. By establishing the ionic (major) as the initial and shaping measure of the opening stanza of "Cargoes," Masefield is setting the reader up for the gradual rise in the tempo of the stanzas and for the surprising metrical shifts and variations that hallmark each succeeding stanza.

The second stanza, in contrast, opens with a line composed of iambic feet. The iamb is the rhythm of poetic speech and moves with an elegant pacing that is usually in equated in poetry with stateliness, eloquence, persuasion, address, and precision. The iambic foot is also the measure of the Renaissance—the meter of Shakespeare's plays and sonnets—and it is no coincidence that Masefield chooses to frame his Renaissance journey of a "Spanish galleon ... / Dipping through the Tropics" in the iambic foot. In a subtle play between meter and image, the reader is reminded that the iambic foot "dips" from measure to measure with the light stress followed succinctly by a heavy stress. The sonic movement in the second stanza is faster, but it is far from the heady and breathtaking pace set by the third and final stanza of the poem.

The third stanza opens with a line that sets a tone of mindlessness and hurriedness established

> " ... *more than simply a clever play with meters and sound, 'Cargoes' is a very specific satire, perhaps even an invective, against Masefield's own society.*"

through the use of ionic (minor) meter, a reversal of the opening stanza. The ionic (minor) foot is composed of two light stresses followed by two heavy stresses. It is giddy, quick, and almost frivolous in its tone, and it conveys a character of inconsequential lightness and flimsiness. The ionic (minor) foot contains the image of the "Dirty British coaster with a salt-caked smoke stack," a tramp steamer that hurriedly plows "the Channel" in the "mad March days." The suggestion here is that speed is burning everything up, and that the world is a place not of precious preservation, but of mass consumption reliant on coal from the Tyne region in northern England. The overall impression is that of a world that is frenzied, sooty, and ugly. The meter in this final stanza supports the bathetic notion that the cargoes of the modern world are not gold or spices or jewels but are "pig-lead" (essentially ingots that are going to be melted into other metals to debase the stronger base metals into alloys for mass production), iron-ware (a kind of all-purpose pottery for rough, daily use) and "cheap tin trays."

But more than simply a clever play with meters and sound, "Cargoes" is a very specific satire, perhaps even an invective, against Masefield's own society. In these three portraits that examine the values and the valuables of humanity through the ages, Masefield is questioning the nature of progress as it relates to humanity and the shifting perspectives of what is deemed important. Here, the key to understanding the underlying statement of the poem, all metrical pyrotechnics aside, is in an examination of the ships that he chooses as the focus for each stanza. Each ship is a metaphor that masks a very different truth from the surface reality and the sonic implications that the poem presents on first reading. Through a powerful sense of allusion through very controlled and subtle understatement, the cargoes of the poem operate almost as miniature allegories on the nature of materialism and its relation to human beings.

The "Quinquireme," or Roman galley, was powered by five tiers, or rows, of slaves. The ship is slow and the meter is almost ritualistic. However, the reality is that the cargo is not simply the exotic items of the manifest observed by the lines of the opening stanza. The "cargo" is also the slaves who are driving the vessel. The suggestion here is that beneath the splendor and preciousness of material goods and exotic items such as the "sandalwood, cedarwood, and sweet white wine," there is a far darker reality where human beings are valued less than inanimate items. Politically, man, in the opening stanza, is a slave to materialism. Masefield is making a wry and subtle comment on the nature of materialism—that material beauty is often built upon ignoble principles—through an image that is at once deceiving and elliptical, yet he makes no outward statement of the issue. A reading public reared on naval terminology and history, however, would easily see through the image and establish it as an allegory on tyranny.

The "Stately Spanish galleon coming from the Isthmus" is a pleasant-enough image at first glance. The underlying truth, however, is far different. As an Englishman and a seafarer, Masefield's unspoken reality of the galleon is that it is a target for plunder, a vessel of the Spanish Main that is laden with "diamonds, / Emeralds, amethysts, / Topazes, and cinnamon, and gold moidores." This cargo manifest of gemstones, spices, and precious metals is essentially the stuff of plunder, perhaps goods that are themselves about to be plundered. Here the allegorical aspect is that material goods are the result of plunder and that the world operates on the "dog-eat-dog" principle of one group taking from another.

In the final stanza, Masefield is locating his action and his ship in the world of democratic consumerism. No longer are human beings pulling on the oars or plundering each other; they are the masters of their own destiny, "butting" ahead as if stepping out of line or pushing against their own limitations. There is a wonderful undertone in the final stanza of liberation, of heady excitement and unlimited potential. The use of the month of "March," coupled with the adjective "mad," suggests that the notion of progress, which binds up so much of the industrial world's consciousness, is actually a "mad march" toward some indefinite, chaotic goal. The material goods are now shared by all. The cargo is no longer exotic, but it is utilitarian and of mass appeal. The liberation into this world of "cheap" consumer goods masquerading as items of either beauty or artistic worth is bought at the price of the materials that make for the fabric of wealth, power, and civilization. This shift in values and the value of valuables signals a new "mass" era that, on the surface, is "cheap" but that underneath is of consummate reward to human kind.

So, the question that emerges for the reader when confronting Masefield's cargoes is a simple one: should we establish value in material items or in ideals? The poem is a political statement that does not make an open statement. It is an allegory in which the reader must penetrate the purpose of the poem and examine its contents and weigh the value of those contents as if looking inside a ship, peering down into the hold, and wondering why the vessel is transporting what it carries and where it is going. By leaving the poem open-ended, by not commenting upon the reason for writing about the cargoes or the destiny and use of such materials, Masefield is being more than merely descriptive. He is offering an allegory. What should be remembered about allegories is that they leave their completion in the hands of the reader, and it is the reader who captains the extended metaphor to its inevitable destination or conclusion.

**Source:** Bruce Meyer, in an essay for *Poetry for Students,* Gale, 1999.

## Sources

Alvarez, Manuel Fernandez, *Charles V: Elected Emperor and Hereditary Ruler,* London: Thames and Hudson, 1975.

Dwyer, June, *John Masefield,* New York: Ungar, 1987.

Hamilton, W. H., *John Masefield: A Critical Study,* Port Washington, NY: Kennikat Press, 1969.

Johnson, William Weber, *Cortes,* Boston: Little Brown, 1975.

Masefield, John, *Poems,* New York: Macmillan, 1947.

Priestly, J. B., *The Edwardians,* New York: Harper and Row, 1970.

Read, Donald, *Edwardian England 1901-15: Society and Politics,* London: Harrap, 1972.

Smith, Constance Babbington, *John Masefield: A Life,* Oxford: Oxford University Press, 1978.

Spark, Muriel, *John Masefield,* London: Hutchinson, 1992.

von Habsburg, Otto, *Charles V,* New York: Praeger, 1967.

## For Further Study

Drew, Fraser, *John Masefield's England: A Study of the National Themes in His Work,* Cranbury, NJ: Associated University Presses, 1973.
> Some of the national themes explored in Masefield's extensive oeuvre are England's heritage, countryside, people, games and pastimes, ships, sailors, and soldiers. There is also an extensive bibliography divided into categories.

Hearnshaw, F. J. C., ed., *Edwardian England: A.D. 1901-1910,* Freeport, NY: Books for Libraries Press, 1968.
> This anthology contains an overview of the period, an entry about King Edward VII, and essays on the politics, religion, literature, and science of the period. There is also an interesting essay on empires.

Marx, Karl, *Capital: Volume One,* New York: Vintage, 1976.
> Marx's first of three volumes from 1867 is itself over a thousand pages. This volume studies capitalism through commodities and money, the transformation of money into capital, the production and accumulation of surplus value, and wages.

O'Day, Alan, ed., *The Edwardian Age: Conflict and Stability 1900-1914,* London: Macmillan, 1979.
> O'Day's anthology contains exclusively political and social essays on such topics as the period's standard of living, the Labour Party, the family, and the role of women. An especially relevant article is on the coming of World War I.

Smith, Adam, *(An Inquiry into the Nature and Causes of) The Wealth of Nations,* Chicago, IL: University of Chicago Press, 1976.
> Smith's work of one thousand plus pages from 1976 rests on a solid belief that humanity is moved most effectively by self-interest. Such topics include land, labor, stocks, and the progress of opulence in different nations.

# Casey at the Bat

*Ernest Lawrence Thayer*

*1888*

There are certain works of art that have gained the status as true pieces of Americana, such as Mark Twain's novel *Huckleberry Finn,* Thomas Hopper's painting *Nighthawks,* Tennessee William's play *A Streetcar Named Desire,* and Ernest Thayer's ballad "Casey at the Bat." Thayer was a newspaperman for William Randolph Hearst's *San Francisco Daily Examiner* during the last part of the nineteenth century and the beginning of the twentieth century. He was assigned to write editorials and ballads for the newspaper, and "Casey at the Bat" was published in the *Examiner* on June 3, 1888, under his pseudonym "Phin." Although Thayer wrote many other ballads besides "Casey at the Bat," they all passed into obscurity. "Casey at the Bat" gained its fame through a novelist, Archibald Gunter, who gave a newspaper clipping of the ballad to an actor friend named DeWolf Hopper. Hopper recited the ballad in August of 1888, in between acts of a play he was performing in New York, and the audience gave him a riotous standing ovation. Thus, DeWolf Hopper launched his own career and immortalized "Casey at the Bat." Hopper later wrote that he had recited baseball's most famous poem more than ten thousand times during the following forty-seven years.

## Author Biography

Thayer was born in Lawrence, Massachusetts, on August 14, 1863. He was the son of Edward Davis (a manufacturer of woolen goods) and Ellen Darling Thayer. While a philosophy major at Harvard, Thayer met future newspaper tycoon William Randolph Hearst when the two worked together on the Harvard *Lampoon.* Following his graduation in 1885, Thayer was offered a job by Hearst, who had just taken over the *San Francisco Examiner.* For the next year and a half, until his health failed, Thayer worked for the *Examiner,* turning out editorials, obituaries, and ballad poems, often under the pen name "Phin," for five dollars a column. "Casey at the Bat" was written in May of 1888 and first appeared in the *Examiner* on June 3rd of that year.

The poem might have been forgotten except for its reading by renowned actor De Wolf Hopper in New York City during the late 1880s. Hopper was performing at Wallack's Theatre, which was featuring a baseball theme night, with members of the Chicago White Sox and New York Giants in the audience. The reading was a hit and gained wide popular acceptance. It also created a kind of mini-industry for Hopper, who estimated that he recited the poem more than 10,000 times during his career.

Thayer wrote only a few poems after that, all of which appeared in newspapers and were quickly forgotten. During these years, Thayer worked in his family's textile mills and traveled abroad until his retirement in 1912. The following year he married Rosalind Buel Hammett. He died of a brain hemorrhage at his home in Santa Barbara, California, on August 21, 1940.

## Poem Text

It looked extremely rocky for the Mudville nine
   that day,
The score stood four to six with but an inning left
   to play.
And so, when Cooney died at first, and Burrows
   did the same,
A pallor wreathed the features of the patrons of the
   game.
A straggling few got up to go, leaving there the    5
   rest,
With that hope which springs eternal within the
   human breast.
For they thought if only Casey could get a whack
   at that,
They'd put up even money with Casey at the bat.
But Flynn preceded Casey, and likewise so did
   Blake,
And the former was a pudding and the latter was a    10
   fake;
So on that stricken multitude a death-like silence
   sat,

For there seemed but little chance of Casey's
   getting to the bat.
But Flynn let drive a single to the wonderment of
   all,
And the much despised Blakey tore the cover off
   the ball,
And when the dust had lifted and they saw what    15
   had occurred,
There was Blakey safe on second, and Flynn a-
   hugging third.
Then from the gladdened multitude went up a
   joyous yell,
It bounded from the mountain top and rattled in the
   dell,
It struck upon the hillside, and rebounded on the
   flat,
For Casey, mighty Casey, was advancing to the    20
   bat.
There was ease in Casey's manner as he stepped
   into his place,
There was pride in Casey's bearing and a smile on
   Casey's face,
And when responding to the cheers he lightly
   doffed his hat,
No stranger in the crowd could doubt, 'twas Casey
   at the bat.
Ten thousand eyes were on him as he rubbed his    25
   hands with dirt,
Five thousand tongues applauded as he wiped them
   on his shirt;
And while the writhing pitcher ground the ball into
   his hip—
Defiance gleamed from Casey's eye—a sneer
   curled Casey's lip.
And now the leather-covered sphere came hurtling
   through the air,
And Casey stood a-watching it in haughty grandeur    30
   there;
Close by the sturdy batsman the ball unheeded
   sped—
"That hain't my style," said Casey—"Strike one,"
   the Umpire said.
From the bleachers black with people there rose a
   sullen roar,
Like the beating of the storm waves on a stern and
   distant shore,
"Kill him! kill the Umpire!" shouted some one    35
   from the stand—
And it's likely they'd have done it had not Casey
   raised his hand.
With a smile of Christian charity great Casey's
   visage shone,
He stilled the rising tumult and he bade the game
   go on;
He signalled to the pitcher and again the spheroid
   flew,
But Casey still ignored it and the Umpire said    40
   "Strike two."
"Fraud!" yelled the maddened thousands, and the
   echo answered "Fraud,"
But one scornful look from Casey and the audience
   was awed;
They saw his face grow stern and cold; they saw
   his muscles strain,

And they knew that Casey would not let that ball
    go by again.
The sneer is gone from Casey's lip; his teeth are    45
    clenched with hate,
He pounds with cruel violence his bat upon the
    plate;
And now the pitcher holds the ball, and now he
    lets it go,
And now the air is shattered by the force of
    Casey's blow.

Oh! somewhere in this favored land the sun is
    shining bright,
The band is playing somewhere, and somewhere    50
    hearts are light,
And somewhere men are laughing, and somewhere
    children shout;
But there is no joy in Mudville—mighty Casey has
    "Struck Out."

## Poem Summary

### Lines 1-6:

The poem begins with a gloomy situation: the game is almost over and the home team is losing. There are three references to death: Cooney and Burrows have "died," and the crowd in the stands is "wreathed"—as in a funeral wreath—in a "pallor," or an absence of color, especially in the face, as in a corpse.

### Line 7:

This is the first mention of Casey, when the exposition of the poem begins. Casey's power in batting is obviously well known by everyone watching.

### Lines 8-10:

Casey's teammates are well beneath his power. The first two players mentioned are less than adequate: Flynn is a "pudding" and Blake is a "fake." Clearly, these two are not expected to get on base.

### Lines 11-12:

The fourth mention of death comes in line 11. All hope seems to be gone for any redemption by the hero. The speaker of the poem suggests that the only chance the team has rests with Casey. And only Casey, in a heroic way, can breathe life into the crowd, can help them escape "death."

### Lines 13-16:

When Flynn and Blakey both get hits, it seems as though a miracle has taken place, lending the moment an almost religious feeling.

### Lines 17-20:

The crowd is delirious: a reason to hope has been brought to the multitude by Casey. They look to him for their deliverance. The two players who went before him, Flynn and Blakey, struggle just to get on base, a stark comparison to what is expected of "mighty Casey." By the time Casey comes to bat, the poet has prepared the reader to anticipate his Herculean powers.

### Lines 21-24:

Casey is not only superhuman, but also a confident gentleman, tipping his hat to the crowd.

### Lines 25-26:

Although wiping dirty hands on a shirt is usually considered bad manners, it seems in Casey's case a heroic gesture worthy of applause.

### Lines 27-32:

Casey is in complete control of the situation. Cocky, unflustered, Casey lets an inside pitch fly by without any attempt at hitting it.

### Lines 33-35:

The masses rise up as one to angrily defend their hero from the unjust official.

### Lines 36-38:

With a reference to Christ, Casey's might is established. He is not only in charge of the duel between him and the pitcher, but he is also able to control five thousand people in the bleachers, simply with a smile and by raising his hand.

### Lines 39-41:

The crowd in the stands continues to act like a mob, uncontrolled and prone to violence. Note how Thayer uses the rhythms of the game of baseball, with its successive pitches and judgments by the umpire (and the crowd's increasing anger), to increase the tension of the situation step by step.

### Lines 42-44:

Casey's smile has turned to a "scornful look." His cocky confidence has begun to evaporate, and he begins to take the situation seriously. The tension is mounting for him, too.

### Line 45:

The poem now shifts from past tense to present tense, giving the situation at hand even more of a dramatic tone, as if we are in the stands watching the baseball game as it unfolds in front of us.

### Line 46:

The "Christian charity" mentioned in line 37 is now gone. Now there is violence in Casey's actions, just like the violent feelings of the unruly mob in the stands. Casey is no longer above the common man's emotions—he has become one of them.

### Lines 47-48:

Casey has finally swung his bat, for the first time, but we are left hanging by the speaker: is it a foul ball, a strike, a home run? This is the climax of the poem, and we aren't told what has happened.

### Lines 49-51:

The suspense is greatly heightened by the poet describing events outside of the baseball field, still leaving untold the outcome of Casey's swing. Thayer seems to be deliberately telling us everything but what we want to know most.

### Line 52:

This last line is one of the most famous in American poetry. With the buildup of the all-powerful Casey coming to bat to save the day, then finally shattering the air with his mighty blow, we hope and pray for the ball to be knocked out of the park. But Casey doesn't hit the ball foul, or hit the ball for a single or double. He misses the ball completely, striking out. Lines 49-51, describing scenes of happiness, are in stark, bittersweet contrast to the failure of Casey the hero and the effects of that failure on the crowd.

## Themes

### Success and Failure

In the last line of this poem, the unthinkable happens. Not only has the Mudville team lost—that has been anticipated from the very first line—and not only has Casey failed to score, but the thing that really drains all the joy from the town of Mudville is that Casey is the cause of his own failure. Fans learn to accept loss from their team; that is just part of the way the game is played. The game described in the poem is a turbulent ride for the fans' emotions, swinging from the gloom of the first twelve lines to ensuing hope and then ultimate loss. They could still walk away with the consolation that it is only a game, that nobody was permanently injured, that there is always next week, or next season, for Mudville to win. A team's loss

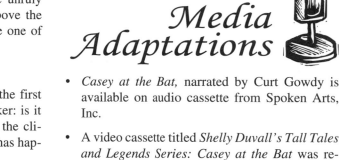

## Media Adaptations

- *Casey at the Bat,* narrated by Curt Gowdy is available on audio cassette from Spoken Arts, Inc.

- A video cassette titled *Shelly Duvall's Tall Tales and Legends Series: Casey at the Bat* was released by Playhouse Videos in 1994.

- *Casey at the Bat,* a record album, was released by Raintree Publishers in 1985.

is not really a failure on the scale that a man's loss is.

The successes of Casey's teammates do not make much of an impression on the fans. They expect nothing of Flynn, the "pudding," so his base hit could be looked at as something of a miracle, but not much is made of it. Blakey's hit is so solid that it tears the cover off the ball. He is so despised, however, that this achievement only quiets them, but it does not win their admiration. It is only Casey who can succeed or fail in the mob's eyes. The great thing about hero worship is that one person's success can spread to all who empathize, as is the case with the five thousand Mudville fans, who would feel personally triumphant if Casey had won the game. The terrible thing about hero worship, as we see here, is that the reverse is also possible; the failure of one man spreads out to encompass the whole town.

### Ubermensch ("Superman")

When German philosopher Fredrich Wilhelm Nietzsche (1844-1900) developed the idea of the *ubermensch* (which is most often translated into English as "superman," but could also be "overman" or "beyondman"), he certainly did not have in mind a baseball player, not even one as talented as readers are led to believe Casey is. Nietzsche used the word to mean the highly developed individual who could see beyond the bonds of conventional morality, with the assumption that morality holds most people back from the heights of the fullest human potential. Nietzsche did not

## Topics for Further Study

- Compose a ballad to a moment that is not really a life-and-death situation, but appears to be because of the way you tell it. Add numerous details to prolong the suspense.

- Research myths or tall tales of other world cultures and compare them to "Casey at the Bat." Report on what a myth tells you about aspects of the culture in the modern world.

- Explain how the slang that is used in this poem heightens the tension of the drama.

think that the superman he had envisioned even existed yet, but was to be the future of human evolution. Although his theory is based on moral growth, so that the superman of his dreams is one who would be, in the words of one of his book titles, "beyond good and evil," the word has come to refer to someone who has attained physical powers beyond those of ordinary humans.

Much of the common understanding of the word comes from the comic book character named Superman, which was created during the Great Depression in 1938 and is still widely popular today. This character was created to be all things that ordinary humans are not: he can fly, bend steel, see through objects with his X-ray vision, and in the popular 1978 movie incarnation, he even reversed time. These are the sort of unimaginable accomplishments readers associate with Casey from the poem. We associate them with Casey, but we do not know what incredible feats Casey is capable of because the poem's source of humor is precisely that he never does anything extraordinary. The crowd does expect greatness of him, though. He is presented as their savior, a godlike being who can accomplish things that mere mortals cannot. Though the baseball game is hardly important by real-world standards, it is presented as a life-or-death situation for the Mudville fans, with the thought of defeat "wreathing" a "pallor" around them and causing a "death-like" silence. They represent the ordinary things about humanity—with the emphasis on mud and death and failure—and they rely on Casey to show them mankind's greatness.

### Pride

This poem would tell a terribly unhappy, even tragic, story if it were simply a matter of Casey being unable to ease his fans' feelings of inadequacy. While that element is present, the poem is at the same time humorous because of Casey's own overestimation of himself. Anyone can strike out in baseball. Failure is expected more often than not: the best batters in the game have base hits only one out of three times at bat. But Casey has no idea that he can fail. If he kept his confidence to himself, he might have been remembered as a man who gave his best. It is a tradition in American humor, though, that what a character thinks of a situation is broadly different than what the situation actually is. A person in Casey's position needs to have more than the usual amount of pride in order to put up with the pressure of his fans' expectations and still be able to play decently. Casey's problem is that, even as he overcomes the odds that are against him to have a chance in a hopeless situation, his own pride is the cause of his downfall.

Any player can swing at the baseball and miss at any time, and Casey should not bear blame for that, but what about first two pitches, which he allows to pass him by? "That hain't my style," is a claim of a man who feels confident that he will be able to hit any pitch he feels *is* his style. In this case, that confidence is misplaced. The pride he feels in his hitting ability is not in sync with reality. True pride reflects approval of something that one has done, and readers can assume from the expectations of his fans that Casey has done many things in his career for which to be proud. The false pride shown here comes from Casey enjoying the pleasure of what he thinks he will accomplish without his having even accomplished anything yet.

## Style

"Casey at the Bat" is considered a ballad. Its subtitle when it was originally published was *A Ballad of the Republic, Sung in the Year 1888*. The poem lends itself well to being spoken aloud. With its four-line style, the rhythm has a singsong quality to it. "Casey at the Bat" can also be categorized as a "narrative poem." It follows the general narrative pattern: a fear of impending tragedy, the last-minute appearance of a hero (Casey) who is seen as a deliverer, and finally, the achievements of the hero (or in this case, lack of achievements). "Casey at the Bat" focuses on the relationship between society and the hero. There is also a mock-heroic quality to the ballad, elevating a baseball player to the position of savior.

## Historical Context

The history of baseball that is commonly discussed was made up in 1905, when a committee appointed to study the game's origin accepted a myth, rather than seeking the truth, and they crowned this myth the official version. According to the committee, which was appointed by sporting goods magnate Albert G. Spalding, baseball was invented in Cooperstown, New York, in 1839, by Abner Doubleday. No serious historians believe this story: there are too many documented references to baseball well before that date, and too many similarities exist between baseball and the traditional English game "rounders" for credit to be handed out this way. There are several possible explanations for why they might have committed such a glaring, obvious error. The first is simply a matter of bad research: although the commission was composed of famous, esteemed men, including two U.S. senators, they were too lazy to find and examine old historical records, instead putting out advertisements for anyone who might have knowledge about the matter. This method netted Abner Graves, a resident of Cooperstown who supposedly remembered Doubleday inventing the game seventy years earlier. The committee was inclined to believe Graves's story because it supported—in what was a hot controversy of the time—the patriotic theory that America's national pastime owed nothing to England, that it had sprung entirely from the mind of one American. If there was going to be one lone mythical inventor of the game, Abner Doubleday was a good candidate for the position: later in life he was a Civil War hero, a general for the Union Army who had ordered the Northern troops to return the South's fire when the war started at Fort Sumter.

In fact, baseball probably has no such clear-cut time and place of origin and likely, historians agree, evolved out of games that came before it. Children's games played with bats and balls, such as "old-cat" and "one-old-cat" and "barnball" were played around America for decades before Doubleday was alleged to have been touched by inspiration. More evidence that baseball preceded Doubleday came in 1991, when the librarian at the Baseball Hall of Fame, Tom Heitz, came across a July 12, 1825 account of nine men from Delaware County, New York, challenging any team to a game. The most distinct changes in the game's evolution into baseball as we know it came from the New York Knickerbockers, a sporting organization started by clerks, professional men, and shopkeepers who used to play the game in 1842 and 1843 at 27th Street and Fifth Avenue in Manhattan. Tired of battling horse-drawn carriage traffic, the Knickerbockers rented a section of Elysian Fields in Hoboken, New Jersey, and in 1845 they wrote up rules, including the measurements of the field and the foul lines, the number of strikes a batter was allowed, outs per inning, and innings per game. Under the Knickerbockers' rules, the game's only umpire sat at a table along the third base line, sometimes in a top hat and tails. This was acceptable for the way they played, with the pitcher throwing soft underhand pitches that a batter was expected to hit. In the following decades, as pitchers tried to purposely make batters swing at impossible pitches, the umpire was required to move up behind the catcher and rule on good pitches and bad ones.

By the mid-1850s, the craze for baseball had spread across the country. People were already calling the game America's national sport, and at least one song, "The Baseball Fever" (1857), had been written about it. The Civil War and a 1862 tour by the New York Excelsiors helped the New York rules devised by the Knickerbockers spread across the country. In 1862, William H. Connmeyer of New York took a big step toward changing the game from an athletic competition to a show for spectators when he enclosed a field, constructed seating for 1500 people, and charged admission: as an act of patriotism, he started the performance with a band playing "The Star Spangled Banner," a tradition carried on to this day.

The sport changed once it was discovered that money could be made off of it. Players became professional, with the best pulling in enormous salaries. In the 1870s, newspaper sportswriters built certain players up in the public's imagination to the status of legends, describing superhuman, Herculean feats with the sort of inflated language that Thayer, a newspaperman himself, parodies in "Casey at the Bat." With more and more money invested, team owners organized themselves—first

# *Compare & Contrast*

- **1888:** The National Geographic Society was founded by Gardiner Greene Hubbard, the father-in-law of Alexander Graham Bell, and the first issue of the society's magazine was published.

  **Today:** *National Geographic* magazine is published monthly and is one of the most popular periodicals in the entire world. The company's television programs are staples of educational broadcasting.

- **1888:** Americans feared Chinese immigrants: anti-Chinese riots swept Seattle, and the Chinese Exclusion Act—which forbid Chinese workers who had left the United States to return—was passed by Congress.

  **Today:** Although many American citizens disagree with China's policies on human rights, the country's huge population makes it too economically important for the government to break off diplomatic ties.

- **1888:** Hype from sportswriters invented the first generation of baseball heroes, including Michael J. ("King") Kelly, the inspiration for one of the most popular songs of the day, "Slide, Kelly, Slide."

  **1920:** The popularity of major league baseball dropped dramatically with news of the "Black Sox Scandal," a conspiracy by members of the Chicago White Sox to throw the 1919 World Series

  **1994:** Bad publicity from a strike by major league players left many fans disgusted with the players' astronomical salaries and the team owners who proved to be just as greedy. Attendance at games plummeted after the strike.

  **1998:** The race between St. Louis' Mark McGwire and Chicago's Sammy Sosa to beat Roger Maris's home-run record inflamed national attention.

---

into the National Association of Base Ball Players in 1858 and then into the stronger, more dominant National Association of Professional Base Ball Players in 1871. The change of name was slight, but the new organization made sweeping changes. Among these, they cut the number of professional teams from around two dozen to seven, located in the country's largest cities, and they initiated the notorious "Reserve Clause," which prohibited players from negotiating the best deals they could find and instead allowed team owners to "trade" players like property with each other. The struggle between players and owners mirrored labor struggles all over America during the late 1800s, the period of urban growth known as the Industrial Revolution. Cities grew crowded, noisy, and polluted by factories during the 1880s, which is certainly one reason why people were attracted to the large open fields of grass at ballparks and the mythic struggles of heroes, such as the one presented in "Casey at the Bat."

## *Critical Overview*

In *Something about the Author,* it is noted that by the time of Thayer's death, "Casey at the Bat" had been established as an authentic masterpiece. William Lyon Phelps of Yale commented, "The psychology of the hero and the psychology of the crowd leave nothing to be desired. There is more knowledge of human nature displayed in this poem than in many of the works of the psychiatrist." And yet, Thayer himself was not overly impressed with his particular work. He is quoted in *Something about the Author* as saying, "During my brief connection with the *Examiner,* I put out large quantities of nonsense, both prose and verse…. In general quality 'Casey' (at least in my judgment) is neither better nor worse than much of the other stuff." Jim Moore and Natalie Vermilyea noted in their *Ernest Thayer's "Casey at the Bat,"* that when Thayer had a request in 1896 for a handwritten copy of "Casey at the Bat" for the Worcester Free Library, he made changes that he felt improved his poem, although some of these alterations have since been disregarded. "The changes he made in this poem were mostly cosmetic," Moore and Vermilyea write. The authors go on to describe the "curious change" that Thayer made to the poem's final line. Instead of "mighty Casey has struck out"—as it was originally written—Thayer changed the line to read "great Casey has struck out." Moore and Vermilyea note that the original phrase "is one of the most famous in the poem.... The original sounds better and most reprintings over the years use 'mighty Casey' despite Thayer's change." As far as poetic inspiration for "Casey at the Bat," Thayer answered that question himself in a letter to *The Sporting News* in 1905, reprinted by Moore and Vermilyea: "You ask me what special incentive that I had for writing Casey. It was the same incentive that I had for writing a thousand other things. It was my business to write, and I needed the money."

## Criticism

### Jeannine Johnson

*Jeannine Johnson received her Ph.D. from Yale University and is currently a visiting assistant professor of English at Wake Forest University. In the following essay, Johnson explains the elements of the mock-heroic form in "Casey at the Bat."*

"Casey at the Bat" by Ernest Lawrence Thayer was first published in 1888 in the *San Francisco Examiner*. It was common at that time for daily newspapers to publish poems of all kinds, from the serious and scholarly to the comic and popular. "Casey at the Bat" fits in this latter category, and it has always been cherished more for its entertainment and cultural value than for its literary merit. Thayer was a reporter and humor columnist for the *Examiner,* and he never imagined that his light piece would be embraced as ardently as it was. Immediately after publication, the poem achieved tremendous popularity, and its last line—"But there is no joy in Mudville—mighty Casey has 'Struck Out'"—still sounds familiar to contemporary ears.

The poem records one brief, dramatic moment in the history of the Mudville baseball team. It is the bottom of the ninth inning and the home team is trailing by two runs. There are two outs, with two men on base, and the great slugger Casey is coming to bat. The poet uses five stanzas to establish the situation prior to the hero's first appearance. He prolongs his description and delays

> " *'Casey at the Bat' ... has always been cherished more for its entertainment and cultural value than for its literary merit.* "

introducing Casey, thereby using the poem's form to replicate the anticipation and the agony felt by the crowd as they await their deliverer. The poem's first line makes it clear that the state of affairs is quite dire: "It looked extremely rocky for the Mudville nine that day." The circumstances worsen when the first two outs of the inning are recorded, at which point "a pallor wreathed the features" of the spectators. The poet stresses the seriousness of their plight, suggesting that even "that hope which springs eternal within the human breast" is an insufficient comfort. He then reiterates just how grave their condition is: "on that stricken multitude a death-like silence sat."

Thayer magnifies the enormity of Mudville's predicament. However, the team's situation quickly changes from ominous to favorable. After two consecutive hitters reach base, the speaker triumphantly announces, "from the gladdened multitude went up a joyous yell, / It bounded from the mountain top and rattled in the dell; / It struck upon the hillside, and rebounded on the flat, / For Casey, mighty Casey, was advancing to the bat." The cry of the crowd acts as a herald or trumpet call for the hero's imminent conquests. And Thayer amplifies the spectators' shout by pursuing it from the ballpark to the wide expanse of the fictional surrounding country.

By this point, we recognize the poet's overstatements as a mark of the mock-heroic genre. The poem's solemn tone and elevated language are undercut by its commonplace subject matter: a single at bat by a minor-league baseball player. "Casey at the Bat" imitates the grand style and regular, intricate form of epic, or heroic, poetry. The poem is written entirely in quatrains that are each made up of two rhyming couplets. Each line contains fourteen syllables and is therefore called a "fourteener." In English, epic poetry has traditionally been writ-

# What Do I Read Next?

- *The Annotated "Casey at the Bat": A Collection of Ballads About Mighty Casey* is a fun anthology containing three versions of the poem by Thayer and a collection of spin-offs, imitations, and parodies. Some tell what became of Casey later in life, such as Clarence P. MacDonald's "Casey: Twenty Years Later" and Neil McConlogue's "Casey: Forty Years Later." Quite a number carry the theme of Thayer's poem over to other people, such as "Mrs. Casey at the Bat," "Casey's Son," "Casey's Sister at the Bat" and "Casey's Daughter at the Bat." One of the most interesting is famed science-fiction author Ray Bradbury's combination of the Casey and *Moby Dick* legends in "Ahab at the Helm." The second edition, edited by Martin Gardner, was published by the University of Chicago in 1984.

- Baseball players are a notoriously superstitious bunch, for some reason. Many of their legends and beliefs were assembled by Kevin Kerrane and Richard Grossinger in *Baseball Diamonds: Tales, Traces Visions and Voodoo from a Native American Rite,* published in 1980. Included here are poems, stories, interviews, drawings photographs and other materials.

- *Baseball's Best Short Stories* is a recent publication from 1995, edited by Paul D. Staudohar. The first one in the collection is Frank DeFord's 1988 story spun off of Thayer's poem and also named "Casey at the Bat," and Chet Williamson's "Ghandi at the Bat." Those stories that do not mention "Casey" certainly carry the poem's spirit.

- One of the best fiction writers to ever write about the game of baseball was Ring Lardner (1885-1933), who wrote at a time considered the golden age of the game and who applied a light, humorous touch to his subjects. All of his short stories about baseball are collected in *Ring Around the Bases,* an anthology published in 1992.

- None of the baseball players interviewed in Lawrence S. Ritter's 1966 collection *The Glory of Their Times: The Early Days of Baseball By The Men Who Played It* was active at the time Thayer wrote "Casey at the Bat," but most of them played during the first and second decades of the twentieth century. The yarns that ball players spin are a unique literary form full of lies, bragging, and exaggeration that reflects the idea captured in the poem.

---

ten in heroic couplets, or rhymed pairs of ten-syllable (usually iambic pentameter) lines. The paired fourteeners look a bit like long heroic couplets, and indeed they are meant to recall this form. However, the four extra syllables seem unnecessary or gratuitous, and they exaggerate the poetic structure, just as the poet exaggerates his portrayal of the hero. The lines also have something in common with the verse ballad, which consists of four-line stanzas in which each line usually contains seven syllables. The second and fourth lines of a ballad stanza rhyme, like many hymns and songs. Fourteeners combine two lines of ballad meter into one, creating extended, rambling phrases that further aggrandize the poem's subject.

Though the poem's form contributes to the satire, it is the theme of the poem that is most important in Thayer's parody of heroic verse. Epic poetry conventionally celebrates the marvelous deeds of men (and it is almost always men) who are in some way larger than life. The classical poems the *Odyssey* and the *Iliad* by Homer exalt ancient Greek warriors and gods who battle against powerful foes and against impervious fate. In the English epic tradition, John Milton's *Paradise Lost* both laments and rejoices in the biblical story of Adam and Eve, presenting a formidable antihero in Satan. Thayer describes his twentieth-century, American hero as "the mighty Casey." He characterizes "great Casey's visage" as stern, scornful, and sneering. He is self-assured and revered, dignified and feared. When the umpire calls the first strike, a fan insists on killing him until his hero intervenes: "it's likely they'd have done it had not Casey raised his hand." Casey's authority is so great that it takes only a simple gesture to command his subjects. When strike two is called, again the belligerent crowd objects and again Casey quiets them with "one scornful look."

In his poem, Thayer both confirms and satirizes the tendency to make heroes of professional athletes. Baseball in the 1880s and 1890s was already thoroughly embedded in American culture. By that time, it was already a heavily commercialized spectator sport: several professional baseball associations had been formed before and during the 1870s, including today's National League. In addition, amateur and semiprofessional teams, in large and small towns, were widespread and beloved by their communities. By the late 1800s, sports reporting had become a staple of daily newspapers, and there was an extraordinary proliferation of magazine articles, novels, histories, and instruction manuals all dedicated to baseball.

One of the reasons for the exceptional popularity of Thayer's own baseball poem can be traced to an actor and comedian named DeWolf Hopper. Writer and editor George Plimpton explained why in *The Norton Book of Sports:*

> In 1889 [Hopper] was performing in the comic opera *Prince Methusalem.* Hearing one afternoon that members of the New York Giants and Chicago White Stockings baseball teams would be in attendance that night, he hoped to do something specifically for them. A friend of his recommended the Thayer ballad—a frayed clipping of which he was carrying around in his wallet. Hopper memorized it and in the middle of the second act stopped the performance and dedicated the poem to the ballplayers to their astonishment and delight, as well as the audience's. Hopper added the piece to his repertoire and estimated at the end of his career that he had performed it over 10,000 times.

Of course, Hopper's continued recitation of the poem did not alone create its success, but it did testify to the wide renown of the poem, independent of his own performances. Somewhat ironically, within about a year of its publication, Thayer became exasperated with his poem's celebrity and he ultimately distanced himself from it.

Thayer's disdain for this unwanted attention perhaps derived from a distaste for the kind of simple-minded adoration that he satirizes in "Casey at the Bat." But even if the poet mocks a tendency toward hero worship in professional athletics, there

is affection in Thayer's parody. In Casey, the poet creates a figure who seems invincible, and yet the poem ends in the hero's failure. In the last two stanzas, as Casey faces the last pitch, the poem shifts in verb tense, from the past to the present: "And now the pitcher holds the ball, and now he lets it go, / And now the air is shattered by the force of Casey's blow." The narrator repeats "and now" three times to expand this climactic moment and compound the sense of urgency shared by Casey and the crowd. The repetition also indicates the speaker's reluctance to admit that the seemingly impossible has occurred: Casey has struck out. The narrator wants to maintain the present—the "now" in which victory is still possible.

Knowing such denial is unreasonable, the speaker exclaims in despair, "Oh! somewhere in this favored land the sun is shining bright, / The band is playing somewhere, and somewhere hearts are light, / And somewhere men are laughing, and somewhere children shout; / But there is no joy in Mudville—mighty Casey has 'Struck Out.'" The speaker uses the vocative "Oh" to declare his agony and to reinforce the poem's connection to the elevated form of heroic poetry. And here, again, the poet uses repetition to underscore the importance of his statements. The word "somewhere" is repeated four times, as if the speaker were trying to convince himself that somewhere in the world there yet exists happiness and satisfaction, even if there is no joy in Mudville. But this insistent repetition proves to be no consolation, and the poem ends by explicitly confirming what has been, in the preceding lines, only indirectly conveyed: that the mighty Casey has indeed failed. The speaker has been forced not only to witness but to broadcast what was previously unthinkable, and once having done so, he is left with disbelief, distress, and nothing more to say.

**Source:** Jeannine Johnson, in an essay for *Poetry for Students,* Gale, 1999.

### Bruce Meyer

*Bruce Meyer is the director of the creative writing program at the University of Toronto. He has taught at several Canadian universities and is the author of three collections of poetry. In the following essay, Meyer points out the irony of the concluding message of "Casey at the Bat," given that the work is a celebration of the popularity and heroic quality of the game of baseball*

Ernest Lawrence Thayer's narrative ballad "Casey at the Bat," written in 1888, characterized a moment in American baseball when the game rose from being a sporting activity to a national pastime. At the time Thayer wrote "Casey at the Bat," baseball was becoming a matter of life and death to many of its fans. The rising enthusiasm for the game, as Thayer seems to point out in the poem, was presenting some difficulties for an American public that was hungry for the spectacle and mythological satisfaction that sporting events can provide. The promoters of the sport, chiefly major-league team owners and sporting-good manufacturers, did little to diminish the notion that baseball was a matter of life and death played by champions or heroes for the honor of a town or a city.

Coincidentally, during the same year, 1888, Albert Goodwill Spalding, the St. Paul of the game, launched his famous world tour of the Chicago White Sox and a team of All-Stars drawn from the fledgling National League. In a famous photograph from their international excursion, the touring teams stand atop the shoulders and arms of Egypt's famous Sphinx—a moment that crystallizes, for many, the rise of baseball to the cohesive role that it continues to play in the American consciousness.

Thayer's ballad, which is both a celebration of the game and an artifact of the era, is not about the modern show biz of the major leagues, but about the importance of how a small game in a small town—a place synonymous with almost every small town in America—symbolizes the life-and-death aspirations of those who hang their hopes on their heroes. As a mock tragedy, it says almost as much about the literary structure of tragedy as it does about baseball.

As many narrative ballads often do, "Casey at the Bat" hyperbolizes the game to the point that every gesture and every play take on a universal significance. The question that continually strikes readers of the poem is whether it is or is not a parody of the game. As a verbal structure, the poem gleans its language of hyperbole from baseball writing from the period—the purple prose of game reports that exploded successful players and events with partisan enthusiasm and dismissed losers with equal verbal zeal. To readers of the poem in 1888, the description of the game details and the players would not have seemed as uncharacteristically large and verbose as they appear today. Therefore Thayer, with tongue-in-cheek, is actually mimicking, rather than parodying, the language of the sport. The line "Then from the gladdened multitude went up a joyous yell," sounds almost exactly like a description from Toronto's *The Globe* news-

paper about Ned "Cannonball" Crane's home run in the top of a Saturday double-header in 1887 that clinched the American Association championship: "And then the mighty audience arose and cheered and stamped and whistled and smashed hats ... the frantic fans rushed onto the field and carried Crane aloft ... it was a great day for sports in Toronto." (Crane, coincidentally, was a member of the All-Star team on Spalding's 1888 World Tour).

What baseball chose to celebrate in 1888, whether in poems or newspaper accounts, was the heroic quality of the game. In its fledgling years, heroes were the substance behind the public-awareness campaigns of Spalding and his competitors in the sporting-goods industry that spread baseball throughout America. In "Casey at the Bat," however, Thayer exaggerates the nature of heroes to hilarious proportions and, in the process, echoes the motif of the champion—the questing knight of Medieval and Celtic legend or the failed attackers of Thebes in classical Greek drama. Like the heroes of Irish legends, such as Cuchulain or Fergus, the characters of "Casey at the Bat" are portrayed as a pantheon of classical champions, each with a particular gift to contribute to victory or a foible that could contribute to disaster in the game. Thayer's use of Irish names—a subtle reminder that the majority of ballplayers in the 1880s were of Irish background—adds to the mythical quality of the ballad and calls to mind the characters of Irish legend. "Cooney," who dies at first, is the lost warrior. Little is expected of "Flynn," who bats before Casey in the line-up. He is described as a "pudding," an nineteenth-century equivalent of a .098 hitter. "Blake," who with "Flynn" succeeds in getting a hit and setting the stage for Casey's unexpected, tragic and mindless at bat, is considered a "fake," the type of player who only puts on a show when he thinks he can grab the spotlight. Little is expected of these players, yet they both succeed in getting base hits. But this gathering of Iliadic failed or partially successful champions serves only as a precursor to the focus of the poem, "mighty Casey." Like the heroes of legend or epic, much is expected of Casey.

The failure of Casey as a dramatic character is self-explanatory in the poem. He is a showoff who has bought into his own legend and who destroys the hopes of his team and his town through his antics of letting strikes go by. Casey is more than a failed hero: he is a Lancelot type figure drawn almost directly from Arthurian romance—a character who, through his failures, triggers or causes a wasteland situation to develop. Not only does

Mudville lose the game, it appears to lose its sunlight ("somewhere in this favored land the sun is shining bright"), its musical appreciation or power to generate communal interface ("The band is playing somewhere, and somewhere hearts are light,"), and its power of regenerative and vital joy ("somewhere men are laughing, somewhere children shout"). "But there is no joy in Mudville," Thayer concludes. "Mighty Casey has 'Struck Out.'" The roster of heroes—Flynn, Blake, Burrows, Cooney and Casey—, like the seven champions who throw themselves against Thebes and die in the process, are doomed to failure through the sin of one player's pride. The consequence, in absurdly hilarious terms, is a fall from nature. Such is the impact of loss.

Compared to today's players, pampered millionaires who are supported by a cast of trainers and physiotherapists, the players of 1888 were heroic because the game they played was much more physical, dangerous, and dirty. The pitcher's mound was about eight feet closer to home plate. Only the catchers wore catching mitts and most grabs were made barehanded. The fast ball would not be invented until 1896, but the pitches were mostly a selection of what today would be termed junk balls—inside curves, high stuff aimed at the head and the body—and the balls themselves were rough and unpredictable in their trajectories. Scruffing the ball, as Thayer indicates ("the writhing pitcher ground the ball into his hip"), was part of the pitcher's routine and made standing in the batter's box an iffy proposition. Fans often stood on the field itself and interfered with the play, and dirty tricks, such as spiking and spitting in the face of runners, were the order of the day. Through the use of game details, the "violence" and the "cruel" aspects of the game are conveyed by Thayer and make the story that he tells more real and his heroes more heroic for the dangers that they face.

To further support this hyperbolized drama and its delightful absurdity and mock profundity, Thayer mixes a few well-chosen terms of baseball ("Cooney died at first") with several essentially dramatic poetic devices. The lines of the poem are eight feet long and sound like two, four-foot lines that have been fused. The couplet end rhymes, therefore, make the reader wait with anticipation to catch the sonic resonances and connections—a delaying tactic that parallels the excitement and breathless anticipation of a successful climax, a climax that Thayer thwarts through Casey's antics at the plate.

What further supports the sense of drama is a tense shift between stanzas eleven and twelve, where the poem suddenly departs from the past tense and slips into the present, as if to transport the reader from the perspective of legendary memory to the actual moment of the game. This shift, and the transport which it effects, further serves to draw the reader into the action and build the sense of tension that is dashed by the letdown of the ending. The suffering, the dramatic "spectacle" as Aristotle terms it in his work *The Poetics,* is an essential aspect of tragedy. "Casey at the Bat" is a mock tragic poem—after all, it is only a game—that utilizes the key elements of classical tragedy.

Nothing popularizes a concept such as tragedy, because tragedy in its truest sense is a shared experience of the group. Tragedy is about the loss of hope on a mass scale, the defiance of the spectator's desire for poetic justice and victory. Thayer aptly notes the expectations of the fans who share "that hope which springs eternal within the human breast." As a drama, "Casey at the Bat" bears all of the basic, six elements that Aristotle claims are the key ingredients in tragic drama: plot, character, diction, thought, spectacle, and song. The plot aspect is simple enough. The home team wants to win and it does not. There is the protagonist, Casey, on whom the hopes of the group are pinned. He fails. The language of the poem, even in a mocking sense, is poetic—elevated and elegiac with its references to the cheers "bound[ing] from the mountain top" and rattling "in the dell." The long lines, with their marching rhythms, are reminiscent of *The Iliad* and of epic poetry, even though the poem is a dramatic narrative ballad that has acquired the reading of a folk tale because of its inseparable connection with the commonplace, idyllic passion of baseball. In Casey's pompous pride at the plate, the reader is allowed a glimpse of "thought," a look inside the mind of a hero who has acquired a distinct sense of hubris bordering on Sophoclean blindness—a tragic flaw. The fans are the chorus. They comment on the action and witness the spectacle. The loss of the game and suffering of the fans, a mass suffering that is portrayed throughout the poem by a faceless, chorus-like group ("bleachers black with people"), causes an enormous tragic catharsis that is felt, in an elegiac way, not only by the audience but by nature itself. And the entire poem, with its ballad structure, long lines, rhyming couplets, and marching rhythms, presents the drama in verse that is "song."

Thayer's "Casey at the Bat," as a tragic structure, however, conveys a very important message to readers, players, and fans of baseball: it is only a game. As St. Augustine argues so vehemently in *The Confessions,* the problem with spectator activities such as sports or the theater is that people expend real emotions on illusions. Tragedy, St. Augustine notes, is the worst offender of the theater, because it evokes such extremes of emotion that people lose perspective on life and reality. The underlying statement of "Casey at the Bat" is that baseball is a game, not a matter of life and death. It is ironic that the poem most synonymous with the sport and a foundation of so much mythology associated with baseball (the flawed champion of Malamud's *The Natural* or the bathetic knights of *Eight Men Out*) is also an effort to keep the pastime in perspective and a humorous warning that the "perfect game" is something to be enjoyed rather than suffered.

**Source:** Bruce Meyer, in an essay for *Poetry for Students,* Gale, 1999.

## Sources

Burk, Robert F., *Never Just A Game: Players, Owners, and American Baseball to 1920,* Chapel Hill: The University of North Carolina Press, 1994.

Moore, Jim, and Natalie Vermilyea, *Ernest Thayer's "Casey at the Bat,"* McFarland & Company, 1994.

Plimpton, George, ed., *The Norton Book of Sports,* Norton, 1992.

Rader, Benjamin G., *Baseball: A History of America's Game,* Chicago: University of Illinois Press, 1992.

*Something about the Author,* Volume 60, Gale, 1990.

Thayer, Ernest Lawrence, *Casey at the Bat: A Centennial Edition,* afterword by Donald Hall, Boston: David R. Godine, 1988.

## For Further Study

"Beginnings: Hooray for Captain Spalding!" *A Baseball Century: The First 100 Years of the National League,* edited by Sally Andrews, et. al., New York: Rutledge Books/ MacMillian Publishing Co., 1978, pp. 23-40.
    This opening chapter of a commemorative picture book gives the early history of the game concisely and includes rare pictures of players, parks, paintings, etc.

Heyleer, John, *Lords of the Realm: The Real History of Baseball,* New York: Villard Books, 1994.
    The author, a reporter for *The Wall Street Journal,* mentions the way that baseball developed in the 1800s, but his main focus in this book is the business of the game in recent decades.

Honig, Donald, *Baseball When The Grass Was Real,* New York: Coward, McCann and Geoghegan, 1975.
    This book contains interviews with major-league players who played from the 1920s to the 1940s. Many of the attitudes, the pride, and the exaggeration that are seen in the poem can be seen in their stories.

Voigt, David Quentin, *American Baseball: From Gentleman's Sport to Commissioner System,* Norman, OK: University of Oklahoma Press, 1966.
    This well-researched and annotated book is mostly concerned with baseball's evolution in the 1800s and gives an excellent description of the tensions between the venture capitalists who owned the teams and the players who were the country's first generation of sports heroes.

# Digging

## Seamus Heaney
## 1964

Written in the summer of 1964, "Digging" is the first poem of Seamus Heaney's debut collection, *Death of a Naturalist.* In it, the speaker tries to reconcile his poetic vocation with the Irish, rural tradition from which he comes, a tradition embodied initially by the poet's father, who is heard digging outside the window as the poet writes. The sight of his father stooped over his spade triggers in the poet childhood memories of his father digging potatoes and his grandfather cutting peat. The poet describes both activities with great care and admiration, focusing not only on the earthy smells, sounds, and rhythms of digging, but also on the refined technique with which both men practiced their occupation. "By God," the poet reflects, "the old man could handle a spade. / Just like his old man."

In a romantic fashion, then, digging represents both an art form and a means of identification with his native people and land—his own "living roots." And though he feels briefly alienated from his forebears' tradition ("I've not spade to follow men like them"), he quickly realizes that poetry itself is a form of digging, of "going down and down" into memory to express the experience of his father and grandfather. Thus, while his poetic career is in one way an emancipation from the rustic Irish past—Heaney is, after all, writing in English, a language once foreign to rural Ireland—it is also a way in which he, too, can help carry on his family's tradition.

*Seamus Heaney*

## Author Biography

Heaney is generally regarded as one of Ireland's preeminent poets of the late twentieth century. His verse frequently centers on the role poets play in society, with poems addressing issues of politics and culture, as well as inner-directed themes of self-discovery and spiritual growth. These topics are unified by Heaney's Irish sensibilities and his interest in preserving his country's history. Using language that ranges from, and often mixes, sexual metaphor and natural imagery, Heaney examines Irish life as it relates to the past and, also, as it ties into the larger context of human existence. He was awarded the Nobel Prize for literature in 1995 for, as the Swedish Academy noted in its press release, "works of lyrical beauty and ethical depth, which exalt everyday miracles and the living past."

Heaney was born in 1939 in Mossbawn, County Derry, Ireland. The eldest of nine children, he was raised as a Roman Catholic and grew up in the rural environment of his father's farm. Upon receipt of a scholarship, he began studies at Saint Columb's College in Northern Ireland and subsequently attended Queen's University in Belfast. It was at Queen's University that he became familiar with various forms of Irish, English, and American literature, most notably the work of poets such as Ted Hughes, Patrick Kavanagh, and Robert Frost. Like these poets, Heaney would draw upon childhood memories and past experience in his works. Using the pseudonym Incertus, Heaney began contributing poetry to university literary magazines. Upon graduating, he directed his energies toward both his writing and a career in education. He assumed a post at a secondary school and later served as a lecturer at Queen's University. As a poet, he published his first collection, *Death of a Naturalist*, in 1966; the volume quickly established him as a writer of significance.

As Heaney's stature increased, he was able to use his literary works to give voice to his social conscience. Of particular concern to him was the 1969 conflict between Catholic and Protestant factions over religion and national autonomy. Living in Belfast, the epicenter of the fighting, Heaney had a front-row seat for much of the ensuing violence, and his poetry of this period reflects his feelings on the causes and effects of the upheaval. Although he moved out of Belfast in 1972, his work continued to address themes directly relevant to the conflict. After a brief period in the early 1970s during which he wrote full-time, Heaney returned to teaching in 1975 as head of the English department at Caryfort College in Dublin. Throughout the 1980s and early 1990s, he divided his time between writing, teaching, and reading tours. His subsequent academic posts have included professor of poetry at Oxford University and Boylston Professor of Rhetoric and Oratory at Harvard University.

## Poem Text

Between my finger and my thumb
The squat pen rests; snug as a gun.

Under my window, a clean rasping sound
When the spade sinks into gravelly ground:
My father, digging. I look down                5

Till his straining rump among the flowerbeds
Bends low, comes up twenty years away
Stooping in rhythm through potato drills
Where he was digging.

The coarse boot nestled on the lug, the shaft   10
Against the inside knee was levered firmly.
He rooted out tall tops, buried the bright edge deep
To scatter new potatoes that we picked
Loving their cool hardness in our hands.

By God, the old man could handle a spade.       15
Just like his old man.

My grandfather cut more turf in a day
Than any other man on Toner's bog.
Once I carried him milk in a bottle
Corked sloppily with paper. He straightened up          20
To drink it, then fell to right away

Nicking and slicing neatly, heaving sods
Over his shoulder, going down and down
For the good turf. Digging.

The cold smell of potato mould, the squelch and          25
          slap
Of soggy peat, the curt cuts of an edge
Through living roots awaken in my head.
But I've not spade to follow men like them.

Between my finger and thumb
The squat pen rests.                                      30
I'll dig with it.

## Poem Summary

### Lines 1-2:

The first stanza may be read as a rhymed couplet, or a pair of lines set in end rhyme. This is true even though the words "thumb" and "gun" are not exact rhymes as, for instance, "thumb" and "dumb" would be. Instead, they are an example of assonance, words whose vowel sounds agree but whose consonants do not. Heaney uses this technique often throughout the poem to stress certain words. Sometimes examples of assonance occur at the ends of lines, as here or in lines 4 and 5. At other times, they occur within lines. Two instances of internal assonance can be seen in line 2: "pen" and "rests," and "snug and gun."

The effect of setting these two lines together in such a way is important to the poem's central concern: the poet's isolation from his family's way of life. Here, the speaker discusses the act of writing. The poem's structure, however, sets this act apart from the subject he is writing about—the "digging" described in stanzas 2 through 7. Further, while writing poetry might normally seem to be a beautiful endeavor, here it is portrayed in clumsy terms. The pen is a blunt, "squat" tool and is described mechanically, resting "between [the speaker's] finger and thumb." In keeping with the speaker's uncomfortable feeling about writing, there is a halting sound to the lines. This is created in line 2 by the string of stressed monosyllables ("squat pen rests") as well as by the line's caesura, or the strong grammatical pause represented by the semicolon. The caesura gives way to the most uncomfortable feature of the couplet, the comparison between the speaker's pen and a gun. This simile suggests that the speaker feels poetry to be a forceful, even a violent, activity: an attempt to hammer subject into form and to derive poetic meaning from a world—in this case, the world of rural Ireland—in which things exist and relate to one another naturally.

### Lines 3-9:

In these lines, writing is contrasted with "digging" in two ways. First, while the poet's occupation is described in its incipient state—the "pen rests"; it is like a "gun" that is aimed but has not yet been fired—the father's digging is work in progress. In other words, the poet contrasts the inaction of writing with the action of digging. A certain amount of guilt arises from this contrast. The speaker's father, though older, exerts himself as the poet does not: he "bends low"; he is "stooping," his "straining rump among the flowerbeds." The second contrast stems from the first. While writing is a silent activity, digging is portrayed mostly through aural sensations: the "clean rasping sound" as the "spade sinks into the gravelly ground." Thus, the poet becomes aware of the essential division between himself and his father. This separation is represented by the window. While the digger's job is physical, the poet's task is observational. With perception, however, comes a certain amount of condescension: the poet looks, but he also "looks down." In this way, the speaker suggests a progression from his father to himself: that as a poet rather than a digger, the speaker has risen to a level his father could not attain.

### Lines 10-14:

If the speaker feels a degree of superiority over his father, he also senses the abstractedness and the futility of the poet's occupation in comparison with the digger's. In the memories triggered in stanza 2 and described in stanza 3, digging is described as an activity requiring great precision, even artistry. The details the speaker remembers are as precise as the digger's work: "nestled on the lug," "against the inside knee," "levered firmly," the "bright, deep edge." Through these we understand that the poet respects his father's craft. Though it is "coarse," it is also elegant. Further, its product is one that gives the kind of tactile satisfaction that a poem cannot. While a poem is merely a reflection of the natural world, potatoes are to be held and felt: The speaker recalls "loving their cool hardness in our hands."

### Lines 15-18:

Memories of the speaker's father lead to memories of his grandfather. Digging, then, is more than

## *Media Adaptations*

- Audio recordings of Heaney's *Stepping Stones,* released in 1996, and *The Spirit Level,* released in 1997, are available on cassette by Penguin Audiobooks.

- Audio recordings of Heaney's poems, along with other resources, are available online at http://sunsite.unc.edu/dykki/poetry/heaney.

- *Seamus Heaney at Harvard,* which includes Heaney reading his own poems as well as those of many other renowned poets, is available from Harvard Reading Room on two cassettes.

- *Poet's Night: Eleven Leading Poets Celebrate Fifty Years of Poetry at Farrar, Straus, & Giroux* includes readings by Heaney and other poets including Derek Walcott and Robert Pinsky. It is available on cassette by Penguin Audiobooks.

- *Seamus Heaney,* a video recording, features Heaney reading selected poems and speaking with interviewer Michael Silverblatt. The video was released in 1991 and is available from the Lannan Literary Videos series.

- *Seamus Heaney: Poet in Limboland / London Weekend Television,* is a video recording that presents Heaney at work amidst the turmoil in his native Northern Ireland. Released in 1988, it is available from Films for the Humanities.

---

an occupation: it is a tradition passed over generations of the speaker's family. While the father farmed potatoes, the grandfather cut turf, or peat—a dank, dense substance formed from vegetable matter and used as fuel. Turf is cut in brick-shaped slabs from bogs, and the speaker recalls a specific bog as the site of his grandfather's heroic work. The reader, of course, is supposed to have no knowledge of "Toner's bog" other than what the speaker reveals. It is an example of local lore, and by naming the bog and noting that his "grandfather cut more turf in one day" there than any other man, the speaker authenticates this parochial experience, elevating it to the level of myth. This attempt to find the mythic in the mundane is an important element in much of Heaney's work.

### *Lines 19-24:*

The speaker's recollections contrast his own childish ineptitude with his grandfather's firmness and vigor. The bottle is "corked sloppily." The grandfather "straightened up / Nicking and slicing neatly," his attention focused on the work at hand. This work comes to life here and elsewhere in the poem through a number of poetic devices. One is onomatopoeia, or the verbal imitation of the sounds represented. Some examples of this are "sloppily," "nicking and slicing," "heaving," and, in line 25, "squelch and slap." Another device the poet employs is enjambment, a French term meaning "straddling." This is when a description overruns the end of its line, enhancing its effect. In lines 22 and 23, the grandfather is described "heaving sods / Over his shoulder." The line break interrupts the action of "heaving," conveying the physical sense of a suspended moment when the sods are "over his shoulder."

### *Lines 25-31:*

In the final lines, the poet realizes that by reflecting on his family's tradition, the "living roots"—that is, the speaker's own connection with his past—"awaken in [his] head." This feeling is brought on not by intellectual contemplation but by the force of sounds and images: by the experience of digging, the "cold smell of potato mould," the "soggy peat" and "curt cuts of an edge." Though the speaker is not himself a actual digger like his father and grandfather, he knows that poetry is a kind of digging, a way of cutting through surfaces to find "the good turf." Thus, the skill and technique that apply to digging could also be applied to poetry. The speaker reflects again on the "squat pen," which is no longer a gun but a spade. "I'll dig with it," he resolves, and thus an identity continuous with that of his father and grandfather becomes clear.

## Themes

### Customs and Tradition

Referred to implicitly in "Digging" is the idea that young men are often expected to assume the same occupation as their fathers or "follow in his footsteps." At the poem's beginning, however, the speaker appears very removed from his father's lifestyle, a concept that is reinforced by the stanza break between descriptions of the two. Heaney's task, then, is to explain how he will carry on the tradition of digging maintained by his father and grandfather. To this end, he creates a metaphor that extends throughout the poem comparing the writing of poetry to digging and, furthermore, equating a digger's tool—a spade—with the poet's pen. The poem opens with an image of the poet's hand, in which a "squat pen rests; snug as a gun." The scene suggests the period of reflection prior to writing, and this idea is supported by the manifestation of his memories of his father and grandfather in the following stanzas. Heaney describes both men with reverence, portraying their movements as deliberate and efficient: of his father he exclaims, "By God, the old man could handle a spade," and he regards his grandfather as a local legend who "cut more turf in a day / Than any other man on Toner's bog." But, for himself, the speaker has a less-admirable characterization; he is associated with the bottle of milk delivered to his working grandfather that is "corked sloppily with paper." The unfavorable comparison entails sloppiness, the flimsiness of the paper, and the runny milk, which contrasts sharply with the efficiency and no-nonsense attitude of his grandfather, who "straightened up / To drink it. Then fell to right away." Heaney realizes he does not measure up to his father and grandfather—whose strong physicalities he admires—when he writes, "But I've not spade to follow men like them." His accomplishment is letting go of the guilt associated with leaving behind—and perhaps looking down upon—the manual labor that was "good enough" for his father. The speaker's labor is mental—reflection—and, in this way, he unearths his connection to his relatives and his past. But in the last stanza, when Heaney writes of his pen, "I'll dig with it," he decides that he can indeed carry on the tradition of his fathers by writing poetry.

### Search for Self

In an essay written ten years after "Digging," Heaney stated that implicit in his poems are the notions of "poetry as revelation of the self to the self, ... poetry as a dig, a dig for finds that end up being plants." Heaney's "Digging" illustrates these ideas about the function of poetry with its central metaphors. For instance, the pen is related to the spade—a tool that brings things buried to the surface—, and the process of writing is compared to the act of digging. One occurrence of this metaphor lies in stanza 7, in which Heaney describes his grandfather's digging as "Nicking and slicing neatly," which through sound—the tight internal rhyme, along with the alliterative "n" and harsher consonants, "k" and "t"—and meaning connote exacting and precise methods. The writing of poetry is similarly accomplished because a successful poem is economical; a poet selects words that most effectively communicate the image, emotion, or idea the poet would like the reader to experience. Meanwhile, the poet rejects many imprecise words that would clutter the poem and obscure the thing the poet would like to express, thus the poet-digger is "slicing neatly" or "heaving sods / Over his shoulder, going down and down / for the good turf." The "good turf" correlates to what Heaney referred to as the "finds that end up being plants." They are true-to-life and genuine things worthy of being evoked in a poem. Heaney suggests that genuine experiences and emotions are often buried by "facts and surfaces," or they are often eclipsed or hidden by everyday conventionalism and trivialities and they must be re-discovered through digging. Of "Digging," itself, Heaney wrote that it "was the first place where I felt I had let down a shaft into real life." This poem demonstrates how he sees "poetry as a dig"; in it Heaney draws upon personal memories to help him decide his career choice, or what will be his identity as an adult.

### Memory and Reminiscence

Often the sight, smell, or sound of something familiar has the power to evoke memories. In "Digging," when Heaney hears a "clean rasping sound" and sees his father working in the garden, it awakens memories, or takes him back to his childhood. This transition back in time is depicted by his father "bend[ing] low" and "com[ing] up twenty years away." His father stoops "in rhythm through potato drills." "Rhythm" and "drills" imply repetitiveness that Heaney saw this sight often when he was younger. Although his father's life work was repetitive, and Heaney suggests that he scorned

## Topics for Further Study

- Write a poem comparing the act of writing a poem with a profession practiced by someone in your family. Give your poem a title that draws attention to the connection.

- How does Heaney use this poem to tell you about what a writer does? Why does he compare his pen to a gun?

this—he looks down on his father from the window and describes him comically, "his straining rump among the flowerbeds"—he also remembers the appeal of it. He describes his working father and grandfather admiringly and they are portrayed as strong and adept. He admits to enjoying helping out by picking up the potatoes his father uncovered, remembering "loving their cool hardness in [his] hands." These memories are vivid with sensations—"the cold smell of potato mould, the squelch and slap / of soggy peat"—and remind him of his family ties, or his "living roots."

## Style

Many of Heaney's poems, including his early ones, are recognized for their conventional constructions, often demonstrating set stanza forms and rhyme schemes. For an example of this, the reader might consider " Follower," another poem from *Death of a Naturalist*. In that poem, Heaney constructs a series of four-line stanzas in order to convey the symmetry and regularity of the father's plowing. In "Digging," however, the speaker's main concern necessitates a different kind of structure. While the poem's images describe the graceful and fine-honed technique of digging, it is the art of poetry that is called into question. Compare, for instance, the way the speaker compares the implement of the poet's trade ("the squat pen … snug as a gun") with his grandfather's orderly approach to cutting turf ("nicking and slicing neatly"). While digging seems to the speaker an organic form, adapted to the con-

ditions of nature, poetry seems a man-made artifice, one external to the subject and requiring a kind of blunt force to push images together. Thus, we see an irregular pattern of line and stanza lengths that suggest the randomness of memory more than the diggers' occupation. Rhymes occur inconsistently and often internally, conveying a groping sense of order. By the final stanza, however, the speaker has gained the confidence that poetry itself is a kind of digging and, we assume, that poetry's art must come from natural experience rather than forced artifice. Thus, though the last words echo the poem's first, a sense of greater order has been resolved. The gun has become a tool of digging, and a second line break shows that the technique of poetry must come from the rhythms of its subject.

## Historical Context

At the time Heaney wrote "Digging" in 1964, he lived in Belfast, the largest city in Northern Ireland. Since its institution as a nation, Northern Ireland has endured violence caused by the conflicts between Unionists (who are generally Protestant and want Northern Ireland to remain a part of Great Britain) and Republicans (who are mostly Catholic and believe that there should be only one Ireland). In the early 1960s, though, there was a rising interest among Catholics to abandon the border dispute and focus, rather, on the closer-to-home issues concerning their civil rights. Their main focus was the disparity in the quality of life between Northern Ireland's Protestant and Catholic communities due to discrimination by the Protestant majority against Catholics. Determined to resolve this situation without violence, the Catholic community began a civil rights movement modeled after the one led by African Americans in the United States. Activists and supporters of the movement made specific complaints about the inequality of treatment suffered by the Catholic population. This inequality had been institutionalized at the creation of the Northern Ireland state, although discrimination against Irish Catholics had existed for centuries before the partition.

### The Roots of the Troubles in Northern Ireland

In 1912 when the British government introduced the Irish Home Rule Bill, which was to grant Ireland self-government, Irish Catholics and Protestants were already forming segregated communities. Although the introduction of the Home Rule Bill can be seen as the start of the violence and turmoil in twentieth-century Ireland, its introduction was the culmination of centuries of civil unrest caused by the approaches by which Britain had practiced its rule over Ireland. Since the 1200s Ireland had been under loose British rule, but in 1607 the British began to "plant" Protestant settlers from Scotland and England in order to spread Protestantism in Catholic Ireland's northern regions during what was dubbed the Plantation of Ulster. Eventually, Ulster became a mostly Protestant and industrialized settlement, while predominantly agricultural Catholic communities resided in the rest of Ireland. Catholics, both in the Ulster and the southern regions of Ireland, became a subordinate class under Protestant British rule; they were subject to unfair laws, one of which prohibited them from owning the land upon which they lived. Subsequently, at the end of the nineteenth century tolerance about the unfair treatment dissipated. Irish nationalism began to grow and demands were made on the British government for Irish independence.

Although there were several unsuccessful uprisings against the British rule in Ireland, there was not a widespread rise in Irish nationalism until the early 1800s. The movement divided Ireland along lines of religious affiliations—Protestants, fearing "Rome Rule," or Catholic dominance in government, preferred for Ireland to remain under British rule, while Catholics wanted independence. The British government at Westminster conceded to demands made by the nationalist Catholics and introduced the Irish Home Rule Bill. The Protestant community responded by building up a military force in retaliation, while the Catholic population countered with the formation of the Irish Republican Army (IRA). Violent conflict ensued throughout the 1910s. In 1921, in an attempt to end the violence, the partition between northern and southern Ireland was established. Since the partition there has been bloodshed in both Irelands over the existence of the border. Terrorist groups and police forces on both sides of the conflict have raided arsenals, bombed buildings and transportation, and have killed many partisan military personnel as well as innocent civilians.

## Civil Rights Campaigns

In 1962 the IRA announced the end of its six-year "border campaign," which was a series of bombings and attacks on government and military institutions and assassinations of security-force personnel. The IRA campaign was unsuccessful;

by the end of the campaign, many members were either dead or imprisoned, and their violent practices eroded much of the Catholic community's support. The end of the IRA campaign was concurrent with the emergence of the civil rights movement which aimed to reform rather than rebel. The conflict over the border dissipated as groups such as the Campaign for Social Justice and the Campaign for Democracy in Ulster were formed, in 1964 and 1965, respectively. These groups successfully raised consciousness of and gave voice to the unfair treatment of the Catholic minority in Northern Ireland, and they later gave rise to an organization called the Northern Ireland Civil Rights Association (NICRA) in 1967. With the birth of NICRA, the civil rights campaign went into the streets, as thousands of citizens became involved in marches and rallies, protesting a number of inequalities, including suspect electoral procedures and discrimination in public-housing allocation, against the Catholic community that had existed since the creation of Northern Ireland.

Another goal of NICRA was to see the abolition of a menacing and powerful police force called the B-Specials and the Special Powers Act, which gave military and police forces in Northern Ireland a wide range of power. The B-Specials force was formed in 1920 during a violent civil war—between British loyalists and Irish nationalists—that resulted in the partition of Ireland. The B-Specials gained notoriety for using undue force and for being blatantly sectarian. Although it was to represent Northern Ireland's population proportionately, by 1969, there was not one Catholic among the nearly 9,000-member B-Specials. In addition, the group was backed by the Special Powers Act, which had also been established—allegedly for only one year—in the violent period of the early 1920s. The Act allowed security forces like the B-Specials a sweeping range of power; according to *Northern Ireland: The Divided Province,* edited by Keith Jeffery, police officers were allowed to arrest without a warrant "anyone 'on suspicion of acting, having acted, or being able to act' in a manner contrary to the peace." The Special Powers Act also provided that police did not need warrants to search or seize property and that even without charge, those arrested could be interned indefinitely. Ironically, although NICRA and protesters called for its abolition, in 1968 the Special Powers Act was invoked to side-track a large march through the city of Londonderry and, several months later, club-wielding off-duty B-Specials who were among a Protestant mob that attacked protesting marchers.

# *Compare & Contrast*

- **1964:** After the rejection of more than 4,000 designs, a new design for the Canadian flag is chosen to replace the Canadian Red Ensign, a red flag featuring the British Union Jack and the Arms of Canada shield. The new composition is a red maple leaf centered over a white square which is over a red background.

  **1976:** In the Canadian province of Québec, the provincial flag, a blue flag with a white cross, and four fleur-de-lis, symbolizes the French-Canadian nationalist movement. Québecers vote the Parti Québecois, a political party that wished to achieve Québec independence from Canada, into power.

  **1995:** Québec citizens vote in a referendum on whether or not Québec can secede from Canada. The proposition is voted down by only a one-percent margin.

  **Today:** The Canadian flag is banned from the Canada's Parliament to end disruptions caused by its presence. Representatives of the Canadian Reform Party had waved Canadian flags and wore maple-leaf ties in Parliament to antagonize Québecois members who complained that there were too many Canadian flags at the 1998 Winter Olympics in Nagano, Japan.

- **1964:** Nelson Mandela, an activist and leader of the movement against apartheid, segregation, and the repression of the black majority in South Africa, is sentenced to life in prison after being charged with sabotage and treason.

  **1973:** The United Nations votes to ban and punish apartheid. Many countries later take economic sanctions against South Africa to punish the government's repression of nonwhite citizens. The sanctions result in economic troubles for South Africa.

  **1990:** Mandela is released from prison under the orders of F. W. DeKlerk, then president of South Africa. His release came after DeKlerk's successful effort to ban apartheid.

  **Today:** Since being elected in 1994, Mandela has served as president of South Africa, which now is ruled by a much more democratic government.

- **1964:** In Yugoslavia communist rule under President Josip Broz Tito keeps relative peace by repressing expressions of nationalism among the country's numerous ethnic groups.

  **1988:** Yugoslav unity begins to fall apart as its economy declines. New President Slobodan Milosevic riles up nationalism among Serbs, one of Yugoslavia's largest ethnic groups, and hatred between ethnic groups resurfaces.

  **Today:** Wars between ethnic groups continue in Yugoslavia, most recently between Serbs and Albanian Kosovars. Many suspect Milosevic had planned to drive out the Albanian majority of the Kosovo region of Serbia. Leaders of the international community have repeatedly issued threats of military intervention to Milosevic, and they have been reluctant to let this course of action materialize.

---

NICRA had looked to the African-American Civil Rights movement on which to model their own and organized demonstrations, sit-ins, and petitions. As many as 4,000 people would gather to march through Northern Ireland's cities and towns, carrying picket signs and singing or cheering. The Protestant/Unionist responses to the demonstrations were greatly varied; while some Protestants believed in reform and agreed with the moderate demands of the Catholics, many others resisted it and refused to acknowledge any institutionalized discrimination against Catholics. In 1968, the Prime Minister of Northern Ireland, Terence O'Neill introduced legislation that was to meet some of the demands made by the campaigners, but heavy resistance of right-wing Unionists caused

O'Neill to resign several months later before the follow-through of the legislation. The marches that were intended to be moderate expressions brought extreme backlash from Protestant mobs, and police forces assigned to control the crowds and riots broke out. Conversely counter-marches that were planned by Protestants were attacked by Catholic mobs. August of 1969 seemed to be the end civil rights movement as riots became out of control and mobs of armed Protestants attacked Catholic residential areas. Unable to control the situation, Northern Ireland's government authorities agreed to the deployment of British Army troops to protect Catholic areas under attack. The presence of British troops did not, however, keep the peace for long, as the troops tended to side with the Unionists, and Catholics found increased resistance. In the 1970s the IRA re-emerged and, to call attention to their renewed demands for the withdrawal of British rule, they used terrorist practices for their cause. Presently there has not been a permanent cease-fire in Northern Ireland, but hopes for peace have risen after voters in Northern Ireland overwhelmingly approved a peace accord in May of 1998.

## Critical Overview

In a 1974 essay, "Feelings into Words," published in *The Poet's Work*, Heaney himself offers an insightful assessment of "Digging": "[It was] the first poem I wrote where I thought my feelings got into words, or, to put it more accurately, where I thought my *feel* had got into words. Its rhythms and noises still please me, although there are a couple of lines in it that have the theatricality of the gunslinger rather than the self-absorption of the digger." Heaney's seems an honest evaluation of the gun metaphor. Critic W. S. Di Piero agrees that the first stanza may reveal the poet's insistence more than his subject: "It must be said that [Heaney's] ambition, which is in almost every way admirable and pure, does on occasion lead him to will connections by virtue of overwrought metaphor." Still, Di Piero argues, the overarching metaphor of the poem, that of digging, is successful. " Digging" becomes at once a signal of origins and legacies and a sounding of Heaney's own poetic ambitions," Di Piero writes. It represents, according to Di Piero, both the method by which the poet will work and his departure from family tradition: "Although the fancy may be somewhat strained and self-important, Heaney's intention is clear enough: he wants

connections, continuities, and historical justification for his art." Irish screenwriter and critic Elmer Andrews takes a more esoteric view toward the poem. "Digging," he writes, demonstrates Heaney's occasional wish to break out of the "essentially passive role" of the poet; from the beginning of the poem, "the shadow of a gunman is present, as if to convince us that the pen can be as mighty as the gun. He compensates for his failure to follow men of action by making promises: he'll dig with his pen, he says."

## Criticism

### Carolyn Meyer

*Carolyn Meyer holds a Ph.D. in Modern British and Irish Literature and has taught contemporary literature at several Canadian universities, including the University of Toronto. In the following essay, Meyer notes that "Digging" is a pastoral lyric that commemorates the commonplaces of Heaney's rural childhood, yet, in blurring the distinction between digger and artist, Heaney finds the means to articulate his own artistic goals and to address his dual commitment to his craft and the traditions that are his by birth.*

"Digging," the opening poem of Seamus Heaney's first collection, *Death of a Naturalist*, serves to introduce the Irish Nobel Laureate's abiding preoccupation with poetic identity as well as his continuing endeavor to plumb the depths of soil and selfhood. Part ars poetica, part homage to a waning tradition of rural craftsmanship—a birthright the poet can claim only figuratively—"Digging" explores yet seeks to reconcile the gaps that exist between father and son, between past and present, between agricultural and cultural labor, and between the aspirations of the individual and the expectations of his first community. Yet, as Heaney remarks in his essay "Feeling into Words," "Digging" also stands out as "the first poem where I thought my feelings had got into words, or to put it more accurately, where I thought my *feel* had got into words." For Heaney, writing the poem in a way that would "define his own reality" was something of a breakthrough. As a signal of the poet's coming of age, it is not simply an exercise in what Heaney calls "craft"—the things you can learn from other verse—, but an embodiment of what he terms poetic "technique"—"the whole creative effort of the mind's and body's resources to bring the meaning of experience within the jurisdiction of

## What Do I Read Next?

- Heaney was influenced by the poetry of Patrick Kavanaugh, who is considered to have given an authentic voice to the culture of rural Ireland. Kavanaugh's long poem "The Great Hunger" impressed Heaney as one way to make effective poetry out of the sort of native Irish subject matter familiar to him. The poem is included in Kavanaugh's *Complete Poems.*

- *Preoccupations: Selected Prose 1968-1978* is a collection of essays written by Heaney about his own works, his education, and his initiation into writing, as well his reflections on the works of other writers. Heaney discusses works by poets such as W. B. Yeats, Theodore Roethke, and Stevie Smith.

- *North* is a collection of poems published in 1975, in which Heaney relates to some realities of the Troubles in his native Northern Ireland.

- Heaney has cited the work of British poet Ted Hughes as one of his influences. Hughes's 1960 collection, *Lupercal,* garnered wide acclaim.

---

form." Though not wishing to overstate the importance of this poem, Heaney writes in his essay "Feeling Into Words":

> I now believe that the "Digging" poem had for me the force of an initiation … I wrote it in the summer of 1964, almost two years after I had begun to "dabble in verses." This was the first place where I felt I had done more than make an arrangement of words: I felt that I had let down a shaft into real life. That facts and surfaces of the thing were true, but more important, the excitement that came from naming them gave me a kind of insouciance and a kind of confidence. I didn't care who thought what about it: somehow, it had surprised me by coming out with a stance and an idea that I would stand over…. As I say, I wrote it years ago; yet perhaps I should say that I dug it up, because I have come to realize that it was laid down in me years before that even.

In saying that he "dug up" the poem, Heaney exposes the multiple implications of its title. Digging, in this case, refers not only to the harsh yet

exacting work of Heaney's County Derry forebears, extracting potatoes and peat from the intractable terrain, but to the process of recollecting, delving into, and retrieving experience—of unearthing the past, the "living roots"—by which the poem itself is created. The activity of digging, then, becomes a metaphor for writing, just as it remains integral to Heaney's view of "poetry as divination, poetry as revelation of the self to the self, as restoration of the culture to itself; poems as elements of continuity, with the aura and authenticity of archaeological finds, where the buried shard has an importance that is not diminished by the importance of the buried city; poetry as dig, a dig for finds that end up being plants."

As much as "Digging" is about the gradual displacement of rural life, about a young writer's experience of being torn between the lessons of his upbringing and the dictates of his formal education, it is also a postmodernist poem about writing poetry and about the forging of poetic identity. In the family tradition of rural craftsmanship that Heaney admires and honors, he ultimately discovers an appropriate model and precedent for the comparable literary craftsmanship to which he dedicates himself. To this end, Heaney makes what he calls "the simple heart of the matter": an analogy between the pen and the spade—tools of very different trades but identical function, both bringing to the surface the treasures that lie buried," as he noted in his essay "Feeling into Words." "Digging" celebrates creativity by making a vital connection between what can be derived from the soil and what can be drawn from the fertile ground of memory and imagination.

Calm and factual in its assertions, the poem, according to critic Elmer Andrews in *The Poetry of Seamus Heaney,* "attempts a direct transcription of particular moments dug out of memory." Those moments, in themselves, are simple enough but give rise to a welter of emotions: from beneath his window where he sits and writes, the poet hears the sound of his father digging. As he looks down to watch, the sight brings back proud and vivid childhood memories, first of his father digging up potatoes and then of his grandfather cutting peat. Yet because the poet has opted to live by the pen and not the spade (as improved educational opportunities for Ulster Catholics enabled Heaney to do), those time-honored skills are soon to be regretfully forsaken, though not forgotten. Conscious of the impending loss, but just as determined to reverse it, the poet, in the end, manages to claim kinship with his forefathers and remain faithful to the land they tilled by resolving, with the unshakable force of a manifesto, to dig on—not with a spade but a pen.

Heaney once referred to "Digging" (in "Feeling into Words") as "a big coarse-grained navvy of a poem." What, in part, accounts for its sturdiness is the way its auditory effects heighten the impact of its descriptions. Like the physicality, power, and precision of the diggers, Heaney's heavily stressed monosyllables bristle with a robust, almost muscular energy. Their "curtness" and economy evoke the taciturnity of a country people whose actions speak louder than words. The demanding harshness of a life spent working the land is equally registered in the poem's strong auditory appeal—in the vigor of its verbs, the dissonances of its slant rhymes, and its sporadic outcroppings of hard, sometimes guttural consonants. Altogether, Heaney's management of phonic echo—alliteration, assonance, consonance, internal rhyme, not to mention mis-rhyme—gives the poem a sonic richness that enhances and reinforces its conceptual content. His liking for free verse, seen here in the infrequent rhymes and irregular line and stanza lengths, helps in this case to reproduce the gapped and episodic workings of memory, to provide a visual metaphor for the speaker's independent course in life and to reflect the discontinuities which that freedom brings about. Often it is through the silent pressure of the white spaces between stanzas that the advances in consciousness and understanding take place. Heaney critic and fellow Ulsterman John Wilson Foster, writing in his essay "The Poetry of Seamus Heaney," has even suggested that the poem's "chopped lines and caesurae imitate turf-cutting."

Many of Heaney's early poems are about the use of tools and "Digging" is no exception, owing its origins to the familiar adages "the pen's lighter than the spade" and "learning's easy carried" which taunted him as a schoolboy, according to the poet in "Feeling into Words." The opening stanza finds the poet, pen in hand, in the act of composition, but the burden of his work is by implication anything but light or effortless. Though the pen "rests" snugly between his thumb and finger, its squatness is more akin to the thick round shaft of a Ulster spade than to the elegance of a writing implement. As analogy follows analogy, the pen acquires not only the unwieldiness of a farm tool but the menace of a weapon—"snug as a gun." The combined shock value and macho appeal of this simile has prompted Heaney to comment that "Digging" has to it the "theatricality of the gunslinger." However, it is not alone among the poems of *Death of a Nat-*

> *That restorative return to origins, aided by the poem's retrospective impulse, helps to make 'Digging' singularly important within Heaney's poetic canon, marking a crucial stage in his development as a writer where he learned to trust his own background ...."*

*uralist* in presenting images of violence or detonation (the "pottery bombs" of "Churning Day" being another example) and it is necessarily, by means of indirect reference or subtext, that the threats posed to the Ulster Catholic minority, even before the return of the Troubles in the late 1960s, are made abundantly clear. Cautioning him against outspokenness, Heaney's mother once told him, "whatever you say, say nothing," and for Northern Irish writers as a whole, the effort to confront the barbarities of sectarianism without a disguising metaphorical framework or mode of displacement—that is, to address them directly—has been a relatively recent phenomenon. Beyond the swaggering staginess and political overtones of Heaney's latently violent images, the pen-as-gun is more specifically a symbol of the empowerment to be achieved through writing and, as figurative phallus, of the male power he associates with his father and with which he seeks kinship. The insistent assonantal repetitions of "thumb," "snug," and "gun" further contribute to the forcefulness of this compact opening metaphor.

Sound and subject are equally allied in the next stanza, where the euphonic effect of end rhyme ("sound ... ground") and alliterative triple meters ("gravelly ground") satisfies the ear in a way that hints at the satisfactions to be derived from the work itself. The poem's only rhyming couplet, with its emphatic terminal punctuation, lends climactic importance to the poet's identification of the sounds' origins—"My father, digging." The activity being named likewise gains an immediacy from the participle ending as well as from the simplicity of the statement itself. In looking down to where his father digs, however, the poet reveals a detachment that is not merely spatial but psychological. The distance between the son and his father, between interior and exterior, between observer and observed, between one way of life and another is emphasized by the white space between stanzas that interrupts the syntactic unit: "I look down // Till his straining rump among the flowerbeds / Bends low." Given the undignified, endearingly comical depiction of the father, who past his prime is reduced to no more than a "straining rump," "I look down" strikes a similar note of condescension at the apparent lowliness of manual labor. For a time, it seems, the customary subservience and hero-worship of the parent-child relationship is reversed, much as it is at the end of "Follower," but in this case the natural dynamic of father and son is quickly restored. The poet subsequently recalls how, as a child, he dutifully gathered the potatoes his father cultivated and offered up a bottle of milk to his toiling grandfather who likewise assumed heroic status in his boyish imagination.

Even the somewhat humbling sight of his father struggling with tasks he once performed with ease is enough to trigger the recollection of another scene twenty years earlier—a scene that unfolds with a slow descriptive exactness which imbues the workaday skill with the aspect of ritual. Like a close-up shot from ground-level up, the view is one that lingers to capture the sensuous melding of digger and spade: "The coarse boot nestled on the lug, the shaft / Against the inside knee was levered firmly." The memory of such expertise is enough to elicit a heartfelt expression of filial pride: "By God, the old man could handle a spade. / Just like his old man." The friendly colloquialism "old man," when repeated, comes to signify the idea of permanence fostered by succession within the male line. As the memory of one man merges with that of another, the father, who, according to critic David Lloyd in "'Pap for the Dispossessed' [Heaney and the Postcolonial Moment]," "stands initially for the writer's exclusion from identity with the land and past ... by way of his own father slides across into the position of a figure for continuity."

In the boastful assertion "My grandfather cut more turf in a day / Than any other man on Toner's bog," Heaney not only sounds a note of one-upmanship or familial pride but expresses a profound sense of place or personal geography, a trust in the local and in the sense of identity it provides. Contributing to the detailed evocation of place that follows are phrases such as "the squelch and slap / Of soggy peat" that alliterate the harshness of the terrain at the same time as they rely on onomatopoeic effect to bring that landscape to life. The exacting nature of the work, as Elmer Andrews observes in *The Poetry of Seamus Heaney,* is captured in a corresponding precision of diction, particularly in the short vowels of "nicking and slicing" and in the clipped monosyllables of "curt cuts." An equal sense of its strenuousness emerges through the abundance of hard consonants—the "d" and "g" sounds of "going down and down / For the good turf"—and through the long-vowelled sounds of "neatly, heaving." Even the natural pauses in the digging rhythm are reproduced in the broken syntax of run-on lines such as "heaving sods / Over his shoulder," where stressed syllables give way to unstressed ones as the motion is carried through to completion. The simple one-word sentence—"Digging"—supplies a kind of coda to the stanza, formalizing the activity and, in the process, creating an inescapable sense of distance from it. That distance proves troubling for the poet. On the one hand, he recognizes how the familiar rhythms of those country ways continue to govern his life and nurture his creativity, but on the other hand, he is faced with the sobering fact of his own dispossession and the extent to which that traditional way of life is no longer accessible to him: " ... the curt cuts of an edge / Through living roots awaken in my head. / But I've no spade to follow men like them." "Digging" is the first of many poems centered on the tension between two contradictory commands: to be faithful to the collective experience of family and community or to be true to the recognitions of the emerging self. His dilemma is one of commitment—whether to depart from his heritage or conform.

At a point where the breeching of tradition seems inevitable and old skills are destined to give way to the new, the aesthetic resolution of the final stanza neatly reconciles the poet's craft with the hereditary claims upon him. The guilt he harbors about failing to carry on a family tradition is put to rest with his symbolic appropriation of the spade and metaphorical continuation of his forefathers' work. Not merely consolatory or compensatory, his resolution to "dig" with his pen represents a conscious and willed striving for continuity. Moreover, in making that pen simply "squat" and not menacing like a gun, Heaney seems to have found within the diggers' example and legacy the kind of strength and deftness he wants his writing to have. The partial repetition of the opening lines gives the poem a circularity that reinforces the idea of continuity: the poem comes back to the point from which it began, it returns to origins. That restorative return to origins, aided by the poem's retrospective impulse, helps to make "Digging" singularly important within Heaney's poetic canon, marking a crucial stage in his development as a writer where he learned to trust his own background and "let down a shaft into reality." Ultimately, by making artists of the diggers and a digger of the artist, Heaney minimizes both the corrosive effects of change and the gulf that had existed between agricultural and cultural livelihoods. Reconciliation is achieved, in the best tradition of his family, with a skillful sleight of hand.

**Source:** Carolyn Meyer, in an essay for *Poetry for Students,* Gale, 1999.

## Tyrus Miller

*Tyrus Miller is an assistant professor at Yale University, where he teaches twentieth-century literature and visual arts. In the following essay, Miller presents Heaney's struggle to favorably compare writing poetry with age-old rural labor.*

Seamus Heaney's "Digging," from his first book, *Death of a Naturalist,* seeks to justify his choice of vocation as a poet and sets out the principles by which he will pursue his chosen trade. It presents the poet working at his writing desk and moves through successively deeper levels of memory before returning to the present tense, in which his poem is taking shape. Through this imaginary trip back in time while writing, Heaney meditates on the nature of tradition, the changes that have occurred between previous generations of Irishmen and his own, and the analogies between poetry and other forms of labor characteristic of the Northern Ireland society in which he grew up and came into manhood. Heaney's own poetry, this poem suggests, can become a new link in the seemingly broken chain of tradition that might connect the rural labor of the grandfather and father with the more intellectual and reflective work of the writer. At the same time, poetic meditation, of the sort dramatized by the poem, is self-reflexively shown to be the very instrument by which the poet unearths his connection to the past, "digging" back into his memory in order to connect with his farming ancestors.

Much of emotional impact of "Digging" comes from Heaney's ability to keep in play two opposed feelings of time simultaneously. On the one hand, he registers the irreversible passage of time, in which he has grown up from the boy who once worked alongside his father and grandfather into the man presently writing at his desk. His grandfather, presumably, is long dead; his father, too, is older, perhaps now retired, for we see him now straining among flowerbeds instead of performing hard work like "scattering new potatoes." We sense as readers a kind of melancholy feeling of aging and decline, also subtly evoked by the reversal of the relative physical positions of father and son. If once the son literally looked up to the father as he worked by his side, the son now is working apart from and poised above his father. Equally, however, Heaney also suggests that the lapse of time between then and now might be reversed or canceled through poetic "digging," which tries to bring memory to life again and reconnect past and present. Neither time definitively wins out in the poem, and it is precisely that lack of resolution that sets the task for the poet: he must poetically dig against time, single-mindedly going at it again and again, just as his grandfather once did in cutting "more turf in a day / Than any other man on Toner's bog."

Heaney begins his poem with a tight focus on the instrument of writing and the hand that grips it. Yet the image of the writing hand is unexpectedly heavy, thick, and muscular, seemingly more appropriate to a farmer or gamekeeper than to a poet or scholar: "Between my finger and my thumb / The squat pen rests; snug as a gun." The pen lies "squat" and "snug" in the hand, words which connote tension and compression within the powerful grasp in which the writer's tool lies. The simile of the pen to a "gun," an instrument otherwise outside of the basic agricultural imagery of the poem, also picks up this sense of coiled power: the pen, now at "rest," holds within itself a reserve of force which could even prove explosive if released all at once. "Squat," "snug," and "gun" also anticipate an imitative sound-imagery, used throughout the poem, which is made explicit in the next stanza: "a clean rasping sound / When the spade sinks into gravelly ground: / My father, digging." The repeated uses of hard sounds such as "sp," "gr," and "g" suggests the analogy between the manual labor of digging and turf-cutting in the Irish soil and the poet's "digging" in medium of Northern Irish speech to turn up harsh, hard-edged sounds. The sound of words, as much as their meaning, will help the poet uncover a partly hidden pathway into the rural Irish past.

The first three stanzas are marked by a rapid shift of scenes within the mind and text of the poet at work. We start in stanza one in the poet's room,

> *The poet lends his father's digging—the real physical labor of grubbing in the soil—a kind of magic power to reignite flashes of youth, as if to dig were akin to reciting a spell for conjuring up the lost past."*

his hand poised to begin writing or in a pause from the writing that he has momentarily interrupted. In the second stanza, we are referred outward from the poet's workplace and vantage point ("Under my window") to the garden, in which his father is digging. While he is watching his father and listening to the sounds of the shovel scraping the earth, he drifts into a reverie. In a set of lines akin to a cinematic dissolve and flashback, the present-day father, an aging man now, bends down but comes up again as he was twenty years earlier: "I look down / / Till his straining rump among the flowerbeds / Bends low, comes up twenty years away / Stooping in rhythm through potato drills / Where he was digging." By the fourth stanza, we have shifted to an entirely subjective space of memory, in which the poet reappears as a boy.

This stanza, with its strange translation of the father back in time in the act of digging, is crucial to the thematic development of the poem. Though ultimately it is the poet's own imagination and memory that is bringing about this transformation, he presents it at this point as if it were the *father's* digging in the garden that has allowed him to tap into an earlier time. The poet lends his father's digging—the real physical labor of grubbing in the soil—a kind of magic power to reignite flashes of youth, as if to dig were akin to reciting a spell for conjuring up the lost past. Yet Heaney wants to suggest that for his grandfather and father, digging was indeed a way of connecting with the past, of making contact with age-old customs and rhythms of Irish rural life. For them, tradition was no written history, but rather the elemental smells, textures, and sounds of country labor such as

harvesting potatoes and cutting the peat-moss "turf" for fuel. The poet-son is divided from this tradition by time, education, and his vocation of writing. For him, in contrast to his elders, Irish history has become, at least in part, a body of written texts rather than the feelings and perceptions of a peasant body laboring on the land. But the memory evoked by the sound of his father's digging carries him back to forgotten moments of his childhood and reminds him of a time when he still did have contact with the elemental realities which his father and grandfather experienced in everyday life.

These boyhood experiences, notably, revolve around his participation in the labor of the father and grandfather. Thus, for example, in the fourth stanza, he recalls helping his father gather the potatoes the father's spade had rooted up: "He rooted out tall tops, buried the bright edge deep / To scatter new potatoes that we picked / Loving their cool hardness in our hands." Heaney evokes the pleasure of the scene, subtly mingling the child's love of his father with the sensual texture and scent of a potato dug fresh from the earth. In turn, the mature poet's remembrance of these scents and feelings becomes a covert way of recapturing a closeness to his father possible only for a young child, the unqualified admiration and love of a little boy for his father. Momentarily drawing back from memory into the present, the fifth line dramatizes the mature man's sense of astonishment at recapturing a hint of the boy's utter self-abandonment to the "miracle" of his father at work: "By God, the old man could handle a spade." In turn, this leads him to another link back in the chain of memories: "Just like his old man."

The memory of the grandfather is linked to even more elemental realities, milk and sod. As if transporting the poet mentally back toward infancy, this stanza shifts the sensual character of the images from the "cool hardness" of the round new potatoes to a more formless, liquid set of images. "I carried him milk in a bottle / Corked sloppily with paper": the impression a reader gets from these lines is of milk sloshing over the edge of the glass as the boy trots along, the paper cap becoming soggier with every step. Similarly, the grandfather is digging among the partly decayed, tangled roots of peat in the damp bog, throwing the pieces over his shoulder. If the father is rooting up the hard, round potatoes near the surface with a spade, turning the soil over to expose them for the children to gather, the more distant grandfather is "falling to it" with the turf cutter's blade, slicing deep into the soft tissues of the earth, "going down and down" into the more archaic levels of the soil for the "good turf."

The next stanza confirms this regressive movement back into an infantile, formless world of elemental sounds and smells: "The cold smell of potato mould, the squelch and slap / Of soggy peat." Yet the continuation of that fantasy pulls the poet up short, severing the family roots he has been tracing back into the Irish soil: "the curt cuts of an edge / Through living roots awaken in my head. / But I've no spade to follow men like them." The interruption of the poem's powerful movement into the past seems to render literal the imagined "cutting of roots" of which the image speaks. His father dug potatoes; his grandfather dug turf; but he has no spade with which to dig. He cannot connect himself to the soil like his father and grandfather did; hence the tradition that they formed must remain alien to him.

Not having a spade, the instrument of physical labor, moreover, would also seem to represent a loss of the masculine potency so marked in the men of his line. Heaney's image of his father's "shaft," "firmly levered," his burying "the bright edge deep" in the soil, and the depiction of his grandfather thrusting his sharp blade deep into the damp turf, is strongly shaded with sexual connotations. With a disturbing violence that Heaney seems here to celebrate, these virile male figures tear open and harvest the fruits of the dark, feminized soil. But time, having severed the "living roots" that would connect the poet to these diggers, also emasculates the son. The poet's generation, it is suggested, no longer has the phallic power for such feats as breaking open virgin turf or churning up the new potatoes from their womb of earth.

The poet's pen, however, offers him another way to reconnect himself to this legacy and regain his masculine power. He will "dig with it." His digging, of course, will no longer be the literal labor of turning over the soil, but rather a poetic excavation of the layers of memory in which the real digging of his ancestors, linked to the soil through labor, persists. The "squat pen" of the poet will gain virile strength by imitating in the medium of writing what his fathers and forefathers performed for centuries in the medium of the Irish soil. The mute, manly power that once allowed his grandfather to perform heroic feats of turf cutting will get narrowed and concentrated into the gun-trigger tension of the poet's hand, tightly gripping his pen and writing short, terse, cutting verses. With the same combination of rugged force and violence with

which his ancestors dug, unconsciously connecting with the tradition hidden in the soil, he will consciously pursue a rough, manly, muscular style that will continue the work of rural labor in an analogous language of poetry

**Source:** Tyrus Miller, in an essay for *Poetry for Students,* Gale, 1999.

## Morton D. Rich

*Morton D. Rich is an associate professor of English at Montclair State University who teaches writing and contemporary literature. He is guest editor of the Spring 1999 issue of* Inquiry: Critical Thinking Across the Disciplines. *In the following essay, Rich explores the relationship Heaney presents between digging in the earth and digging for meaning with words.*

"Digging" is a nostalgic poem. In it, Seamus Heaney responds to a question many artists ask: How shall I justify the most important activity of my life—my art—when all of the world seems to be doing something more useful? He wonders if he can abandon the traditions of the family farm and adopt a new way of being in the world. "Digging" celebrates living on the land far more than it offers a tribute to writing poetry, yet it promises that poetry will carry forward a new kind of handwork, thereby honoring his forbears, those who took pride in "Stooping in rhythm through potato drills" and "Nicking and slicing neatly, heaving sods."

The speaker does not claim to have their skill yet, only his tool, presented in surprising language: "Between my finger and my thumb / The squat pen rests; snug as a gun." This couplet offers a plain enough image of the writer holding a pen between finger and thumb, but why is it "squat" and "snug as a gun"? Pens are usually long and sleek, not short and thick. The verb "squat" means to hunker down, a potentially uncomfortable position, perhaps implying how a poet works, were he digging potatoes in a field. The sound of the word is unpleasant and uncomplimentary to the pen and the speaker. Does he judge himself harshly for writing rather than farming? The image is complicated and intensified by the ending phrase "snug as a gun." How is a pen comparable to a gun? Is the speaker under siege and in need of a weapon to defend himself? From what? The four-beat meter of the couplet plus the sound patterns suggest something less than profound, a kind of bluntness not usually found in Heaney's poetry. The repeated "u" of "thumb," "snug," and "gun" in monosyllabic words squeezes the focus of the couplet onto the last syl-

> *. . . ['Digging']*
> *signifies the importance to*
> *Heaney of a statement of his*
> *beliefs about the*
> *fundamental value of*
> *writing poetry in a world of*
> *men laboring in the earth."*

lable of each line in an almost nursery-rhyme mode, and onto the image of the thumb and gun. Critic Roland Mathias writes that the "consonantal mis-rhyme here perhaps suggests the gap between the hand, the symbol of family inheritance, and the newly acquired weapon." The old weapon is the spade, that sharp extension of the farmer's hands. Is the new weapon, the pen, comparable to it in any way? We will see how the poem treats this image later, whether it be expansion or transformation of meaning.

Other questions are raised by the position of "Digging" in Heaney's opus. As the first poem in Heaney's first published collection, *Death of a Naturalist,* as well as the first poem in his *Selected Poems 1966-1987* (1990), it signifies the importance to Heaney of a statement of his beliefs about the fundamental value of writing poetry in a world of men laboring in the earth. He does not disdain their labor—indeed he celebrates it—but he does need to establish the equivalent value of the poet's work. Using digging as a metaphor for writing, Heaney shows the depth of his connection with his early life on the farm and the lives of his father and grandfather. By analogy, he credits them with preparing the way for his kind of digging. Curiously, several critics have quoted Heaney's remark in his essay "Feeling into Words" that "'Digging' is a big coarse-grained navvy of a poem," while ignoring other comments he makes that are more significant. He writes: "'Digging', in fact, was the name of the first poem I wrote where I thought my feelings had got into the words, or to put it more accurately, where I thought my *feel* had got into words.... This was the first place where I felt I had done more than make an arrangement of words: I felt I had let down a shaft into real life. The facts and surfaces of the thing were true, but more im-

portant, the excitement that came from naming them gave me a kind of insouciance and a kind of confidence.... I now believe that the 'Digging' poem had for me the force of an initiation: the confidence I mentioned arose from a sense that perhaps I could do this poetry thing too, and having experienced the excitement and release of it once, I was doomed to look for it again and again." The importance of digging as metaphor is underlined by his comment "I felt I had let down a shaft into real life." Real life, for the poet, is not surface life, the life that poet and critic Stephen Dobyns calls a shell, "the temporal, finite, measurable world." The poet, writes Dobyns, reaches into "another world that we attempt to measure not with our senses but with our emotions." That is the work celebrated by Heaney in "Digging" and in his entire opus.

Examining the diction of "Digging," that part of the whole language that Heaney has chosen for this poem, shows the reader a high proportion of farming words, for example: "digging, spade, gravelly ground, flowerbeds, potato drills, lug and shaft, turf, bog, sods, soggy peat, living roots." These words are part of the everyday language of the farmer and the peat cutter who work the land and pass on their skills from generation to generation. However, the youngest generation of this family does not till the land but works words instead, naming the tools of writing with "fingers, pen, gun." But in order to present and justify writing poetry as a legitimate activity, even if it does not produce turf or potatoes, Heaney uses the language of the land, not the language of the poet or critic. For Heaney, poetry begins in the earth, both literally and metaphorically, and his language reflects that origin beautifully. In his essay "The Sense of Place" he wrote: "And when we look for the history of our sensibilities ... it is to ... the stable element, the land itself, that we must look for continuity."

Thus Heaney expresses in "Digging" a continuity that his forbears could not express in language. If he had become a farmer or sod cutter, he might have continued to work in the "stable element," but his expressive consciousness would have been lost to the world. "Digging" tells us that the time has come for a deeper excavation, the kind that language provides both directly and by surprise.

Like many of Heaney's poems, "Digging" is relatively brief, consisting of thirty-one lines in eight stanzas of irregular length. The pace of the poem is largely determined by the arrangement of sentences within the stanzas, rather than by a regular metrical scheme. The first stanza comprises a single, compact, self-contained sentence, rich with repeated vowels. (A grammarian would argue that "snug as a gun" is a separate elliptical sentence. For this reading, periods are used to define ends of sentences.) The second stanza has a sentence plus the beginning of another—"I look down"—that carries the reader's eye smoothly into the third stanza, which completes the sentence. Twice the word "digging" ends sentences. This present participle as well as others—"rasping, straining, stooping, nicking, slicing"—help create an atmosphere of hard labor in the poem, labor the reader is invited to associate with writing poetry. The fourth stanza continues the narrative with two sentences, then the brief fifth stanza provides a transition to another, related narrative in the longest, four-sentence sixth stanza. The seventh and penultimate stanza brings together the two narratives and returns the speaker to the point of the poem. The last stanza, comprised of two sentences, varies and expands the first stanza.

> Between my finger and my thumb
> The squat pen rests.
> I'll dig with it.

The pen is no longer "snug as a gun," but has become the writer's spade, his tool for unearthing meaning. While critic Thomas Foster complains that the writing-digging connection is forced, the idea couched in the image is powerful enough to overcome its bluntness. The circle of the poem is completed by the transformation of the pen from a destructive gun to a tool for farming words. The poet has announced his intentions for his future writing.

One effect of generating the content of the poem in sentences of varying length, reserving three shorter sentences for the last two stanzas, is an increase in emotional intensity from beginning to end. Longer sentences require more unpacking of syntax—especially the triply embedded "I look down" that begins at the end of the second stanza—thus their impact is less immediate than shorter sentences. Perhaps paradoxically, however, the longer sentences that comprise the middle stanzas—containing rich images of the poet's father and grandfather at work—create a cumulative emotional effect that opens the reader to the direct impact of the final three words. When Heaney writes "I'll dig with it," we are convinced, and ready for his next poem.

**Source:** Morton D. Rich, in an essay for *Poetry for Students,* Gale, 1999.

## Michael R. Molino

*In the following excerpt, Molino asserts that Heaney's poem "Digging" provides an example of how the author's "act of poetic creation ... is permeated with his personal experiences and the tradition of his country and his race."*

Key to the poetry of Heaney is the question of tradition, but that question is tied to two other questions—that of language and that of myth. Collectively, the topics of tradition, language, and myth recur throughout Heaney's poetry. In his early works, though, tradition, language, and myth are examined, at least to some extent, individually as Heaney sorts through his cultural and literary heritage. The fact that each of these issues is explored separately in succeeding volumes of poetry does not make them themes in the traditional sense—that is, unified, coherent, or isolated topics that, poetically rendered, either provide the writer or the reader access to the "Hidden Ireland" as Corkery envisioned it or act as the vehicle for reaching (or creating) a stable identity and origin. Rather, the questions of tradition, language, and myth, as they are explored in Heaney's poetry, lead away from the notion of a Hidden Ireland or a stable origin rooted in a Celtic past and then passed on, broken but still potent, over the centuries. While I shall discuss tradition, language, and myth separately at first, it is important to see these as interrelated elements which constitute the "gapped, discontinuous, polyglot tradition" that [Thomas] Kinsella identifies as the Irish writer's heritage.

In his poetry, Seamus Heaney explores the continuation of the past—manifest in the form of tradition, language, and myth—in the present and evaluates the molding effect that the past has had on himself and his culture. Heaney looks for the past in himself and in the people and places he knows best.... Heaney's relationship with the past is ... complex: he does not poetically create voices whose utterances ascribe a moment in a singular, linear progression of tradition. Moreover, Heaney does not have a narrow political agenda that he wishes voiced through his poetry....

Throughout his career, Heaney has resisted the call to "conserve the past" as well the call to arms. He is neither a gentle yet plaintive pastoralist nor a defiant yet articulate patriot. In his early volumes, Heaney's poetry resonates with voices that assimilate yet subvert these two, often contradictory, facets of his tradition. While tradition may provide a rich resource of experience for exploration, act as a source of continuity, or provide a sense of ready-made identity, it can also act as a deterrent to creative exploration, insist upon a singular or linear perspective on its own development, or repress the possibility of continued self-identification. Working with and through this complex web of tradition is difficult, but it is a necessary first step to understanding the question of tradition....

In Heaney's verse, the influences of tradition are too strong and too much a part of his personal and cultural consciousness to be ignored. Tradition entails the beliefs and practices of the culture as well as the fact that it is not derived from a single, stable origin. Consequently, each time the speaker in one of Heaney's poems forges a new utterance that excavates tradition that speaker both regenerates and subverts tradition in a complex interplay of sameness and difference—what [Jacques] Derrida [in his *Writing and Difference*] calls "originary repetition."

In his first two volumes of poetry, Heaney stands between ... the assertion that the myths which constitute his tradition are "programmed into" his language and the assertion that these myths are always already inscribed by language. For instance, Heaney frequently probes tradition in an attempt to discern whether or how the Irish consciousness has been influenced or infected by its tradition....

Heaney, at least in his first two volumes of poetry, may be characterized as a postmodernist in the making, a writer inclined in the postmodern direction but still not fully immersed in a postmodern perspective of history, tradition, and the practice of writing....

In *Death of a Naturalist* and *Door into the Dark,* though, Heaney is primarily an explorer, charting his ground, then excavating and reinscribing tradition. For instance, in "Digging," the first poem in *Death of a Naturalist,* the speaker in the poem, a writer, creates an analogy between his own work with a pen and the work of his father and grandfather with a spade. The title of the poem, "Digging," is in the form of a nonfinite verbal, which has voice and tense inflection. The word *digging* appears three times in the poem: the first in the present, "My father, digging"; the second in the past, twenty years away, recalled in a memory, "he was digging"; the third in reference to the grandfather, even further in the past, but in reference to a present moment, the single word sentence, "Digging."

The poem begins as a recollection of events in tranquility—the speaker's thoughts of his father and grandfather as farmers, men of the soil. The frame of the poem is the speaker sitting at his desk, pen "snug as a gun" in his hand. The second stanza initiates a sequence that lends itself to contrasting interpretations: the speaker hears the sound of his father digging in the garden below (the son looking down upon the father); the father bends low to thrust his spade into the earth and "comes up twenty years away / Stooping in rhythm through potato drills." The father "twenty years away" could be the speaker remembering a past event that parallels or echoes the present, or the father could be digging (in an archaeological sense) to a time far "away," each spadeful apparently bringing him closer to the past, his origins.

The fact that the father has some kind of "rhythm" implies the naturalness of his actions, although it could be the speaker's perception of the father being in harmony with nature, a trait the speaker feels he does not share. Similarly, the speaker's grandfather spent his days, "going down and down / For the good turf. Digging," as if the depth of the soil holds a special secret.

The second-to-last stanza is significant because it could be either a moment of continuation or a moment of rupture in tradition: "The cold smell of potato mould, the squelch and slap / Of soggy peat, the curt cuts of an edge / Through living roots awaken in my head." The smells and the sounds of digging, as well as the cuts of the spade in the turf, "awaken" in the speaker's head. Are these synaesthetic sensations triggering memories that the speaker recalls in his contemplative state—that is, are the "smell," the "squelch and slap," and the "cuts" memories awakened in the speaker's mind as he looks down upon his father digging? Or, is the act of digging turf also the act of excavating the speaker's personal heritage (his lineage through his father and grandfather) or his mythic/historical heritage (a connection with a tradition of soil and land)?

Both interpretations are invited by the images of the son, the father, and the grandfather—ancestral echoes of men of the soil. With the latter interpretation, though, the words *squelch and slap* resonate not only with experiences of life on the farm, but of political and social repression. The words *smell* and *cuts* evoke not only images of cutting turf, but of battles fought and lives lost throughout a history of violence. The paradox of digging is that it is both an act that bonds the generations as well as an act that severs "living roots." Digging is, then, both a productive and a destructive act. The poem ends as the speaker chooses to continue his digging, not with a spade but with a pen.

Digging, however, does not merely uncover layers of historical violence or take someone, such as the speaker's father, back to a stable origin or past; digging itself is a form of violence, as the image of the gun implies. Digging with a spade or with a pen not only uncovers but also severs the living roots of the past....

The act of digging into the turf—like excavating the peat bogs of Jutland and Ireland in later poems—is not merely commemorated, but performed in the poem, for the poem is a form of digging. Furthermore, digging is more than a simple analogy; it represents a process of writing that recurs throughout Heaney's poetry. Writing entails a conflation or juxtaposition of past events, memories of past events in the present, and the moment of utterance which, because it often resonates with ambivalent or contradictory impulses, can be a disruptive factor in the continuation of the speaker's tradition. The connection between digging—with all its personal, political, historical resonances—and writing is the most important aspect of Heaney's poetic imagination.

The word *digging* signifies an act that occurs always in the present, but that present moment may concern a memory of past events. Thus, in "Digging," the father and the grandfather are captured in a continually present moment as events from the past continue, or echo, in the present. The act of writing, like that of digging, is a consistently present moment that, while inhabited by echoes of the past, truncates and reinscribes those echoes as they occur. In other words, the tradition that has so influenced Heaney and of which he often writes is not evolving in any linear or teleological sense, even though some may read it as such. Each poem has the potential to contribute to that apparent evolution or progression of tradition, but it also has the potential to create a rupture in that tradition. Tradition, like the "self," is a collection of discursive surfaces inscribed by language and open to the free-play of language. No single meaning is possible, and no place of origin exists outside this free-play of language. Thus, one cannot expect to arrive at a form of meaning external to language....

Many critics have noted that Heaney is tentative about the value of poetry in his early volumes, constantly needing to justify the act of writing poetry in relation to more practical pursuits, such as digging potatoes, thatching a roof, or forging a

> *In Heaney's verse, the influences of tradition are too strong and too much a part of his personal and cultural consciousness to be ignored."*

horseshoe. In "Personal Helicon," that lack of assurance lingers, but the speaker realizes that the act of writing locates him within a tradition, just as the memory of his father and grandfather did. And, just as the speaker had to situate himself in relation to his ancestors in order to discern his own continually shifting identity against the discursive surfaces of his tradition, so too the speaker discovers that the poetic utterance is the point at which that tradition and his identity intersect and that the utterance recovers or discovers a discursive plurality and grasps the numerous discursive sequences that constitute his tradition....

"Digging" and "Personal Helicon," respectively the first and last poems in *Death of a Naturalist,* establish a framework that recurs throughout Heaney's other poetry. His poetry is one in which the act of poetic creation or articulation is permeated with his personal experiences and the tradition of his country and his race. As Heaney state[d in Terrence Brown's *Northern Voices: Poets from Ulster*], "Our sense of the past, our sense of the land and perhaps our sense of identity are inextricably interwoven." Even the persona or speaking voice in these two poems, as in many of Heaney's poems, is a poet or writer, a person actively engaged in excavating, examining, interpreting, and reinscribing his own experiences and tradition.

The speaker in Heaney's poems does not wish to blend with the events of the poem, to become one with the objects of his poetic vision, as Keats suggests in his "Ode to a Nightingale." Rather, it is that difference between self and past, of self and tradition, that is all-important.

**Source:** Michael R. Molino, "A Question of Tradition" in *Questioning Tradition, Language, and Myth: The Poetry of Seamus Heaney,* Washington D.C.: The Catholic University of America Press, 1994, pp. 2–15.

## Sources

Andrews, Elmer, *The Poetry of Seamus Heaney: All Realms of Whisper,* Macmillan Press Ltd., 1988, 219 p.

Di Piero, W. S., "Digs," in *The American Scholar,* Vol. 50, No. 4, Autumn 1981, pp. 558-62.

Foster, John Wilson, "The Poetry of Seamus Heaney [On Wintering Out]," in *Critical Essays on Seamus Heaney,* edited by Robert F. Garratt, New York: G. K. Hall, 1995, p. 27; reprint of "The Poetry of Seamus Heaney [On Wintering Out]," *Critical Quarterly,* Spring 1974, pp. 35-48.

Heaney, Seamus, "Feelings into Words," in *The Poet's Work: 29 Masters of 20th Century Poetry on the Origins and Practice of Their Art,* edited by Reginald Gibbons, Houghton Mifflin, 1979, pp. 263-82.

Jeffery, Keith, ed., *Northern Ireland: The Divided Province,* Crescent Books, 1985, 128 p.

Kennedy-Pipe, Caroline, *The Origins of the Present Troubles in Northern Ireland,* Addison Wesley Longman Limited, 1997, 204 p.

Lloyd, David, "'Pap for the Dispossessed' [Heaney and the Postcolonial Moment]" in *Critical Essays on Seamus Heaney,* p. 122; reprint of "'Pap for the Dispossessed' [Heaney and the Post-colonial Moment]" in *Anomalous States: Irish Writing and the Post-colonial Moment,* Dublin: The Lilliput Press, 1993, pp. 20-37.

Tonge, Jonathan, *Northern Ireland: Conflict and Change,* Prentice Hall Europe, 1998, 218 p.

## For Further Study

Buttell, Robert, *Seamus Heaney,* Cranberry, NJ: Associated University Presses, Inc., 1975.
Provides critical analyses of the poems included in Heaney's first three volumes and considers how Heaney's personal experience and literary education have influenced his poetry.

Morrison, Blake, *Seamus Heaney,* New York: Methuen, Inc., 1982.
A biocritical study that also focuses on explaining Heaney's poems concerning the "troubles" in Northern Ireland.

Parker, Michael, *Seamus Heaney: The Making of the Poet,* Iowa City, IA: University of Iowa Press, 1993.
Provides historical contexts and analyzes the biographical, literary, and political influences within Heaney's poetry.

# Easter 1916

**W. B. Yeats**

*1916*

One of the most important political poems of the twentieth century is W. B. Yeats's "Easter 1916." Inspired by events that transpired in Dublin, Ireland, the poem pays tribute to the leaders of the Irish uprising that was timed to coincide with Easter, the religious holiday commemorating Christ's resurrection. During the rebellion, or what came to be known as the Easter Rising, Sinn Feiners—members of a political party whose name means "We Ourselves" in Irish Gaelic and who favored an independent Ireland—overtook key buildings in downtown Dublin on April 24, 1916. They were forced to surrender under heavy British fire six days later. Sixteen Sinn Fein men were subsequently executed and one woman was jailed. Yeats knew many of the participants, some of whom were fellow poets and writers. While Yeats was sympathetic, like many of the Irish, to the cause of an independent Ireland, he was troubled by the violence of the rebellion and its destructive aftermath. With the executions and the public's anger at them, however, he also felt something was accomplished: the executions had inspired the Irish with the conviction that England was a ruthless power that must be forced to leave Ireland. Besides being favorably disposed, Yeats was also troubled by something else: the sensitive Sinn Feiners he had known were hardened by their participation in politics, especially violent political insurrection. While Yeats refrained from condemning the leaders for becoming involved in politics—a realm in which he thought they did not belong—he did, however, regret that

*W. B. Yeats*

they had. The "terrible beauty" serving as the refrain of this poem thus describes a twofold conflict: first, that passion for peace often breaks out in violence, and, two, that thoughtful and sensitive natures are often hardened by a quest for justice. Perhaps one reason this poem is still a vibrant symbol of the movement for Irish independence is that Yeats's double conflict was, and still is, Ireland's—particulary in Northern Ireland. In a country fractured by political and religious divisions, it would not be surprising if every man and woman were divided within themselves—vacillating between the need for restraint and the desire to retaliate.

## Author Biography

It would be difficult to choose a more important twentieth-century poet than W. B. Yeats. In the space of 74 years, Yeats led the Irish Literary Revival; became an Irish senator in the recently independent Irish Free State; influenced and promoted the most prominent figures of twentieth-century literature, such as Ezra Pound, T. S. Eliot and James Joyce; and won literature's most prestigious honor, the Nobel Prize. Born June 13, 1865, Yeats was a fitting Gemini, the sign of the twins:

"I begin to see things double—doubled in history, world history, personal history," he once said. His sensibilities were not only doubled, but split: between literature and politics, the occult and the self-evident, the mythic and the mundane. Born in Dublin, Yeats would spend a great deal of time in both Ireland and England. His father gave up law for painting and abandoned his family for New York in 1907, but not before exercising a profound influence on his oldest son by schooling him at home. Yeats's mother raised four children, inspired in "Willie" his love of Ireland, and eventually suffered a stroke, dying in 1900. Yeats received no formal schooling until age 11, at which time he attended grammar school in England. Later, at a Dublin high school, he was a poor student and poorer athlete. He dropped out, and from 1884 to 1886 attended art schools in Dublin. While there, he cofounded the Dublin Hermetic Society with a schoolmate, poet George Russell ("AE"). This would be only the first of several memberships in occult societies, two others being Madame Blavatsky's Theosophical Society and, later, The Golden Dawn. An interest in the occult was kindled primarily through his maternal uncle, George Pollefexen, and the latter's servant, Mary Battle. Battle would become the largest single inspiration for Yeats's *The Celtic Twilight,* a work of 1893 illustrating the mysticism of the Irish countryside, the population's belief in fairies, ghosts, and spirits. Battle also acted as a surrogate mother figure after the death of Yeats's own mother. By 1937, when Yeats was asked if he believed in the images and structures of his occult system as illustrated in the text *A Vision,* he would only say, "Oh, I draw from it images for my poetry."

Concurrent with and related to Yeats's occult studies was his interest in Irish mythology and nationhood. It was kindled especially by his association with John O'Leary, an Irish ultra-nationalist imprisoned and exiled in France twenty years for his work on an Irish newspaper. O'Leary's talk of the "terrible continuity" in things Irish has been thought by some critics to have inspired the "terrible beauty" of "Easter, 1916." In the group gathered around O'Leary, Yeats met radical Irish nationalist Maud Gonne, fell in love with her, and proposed marriage several times. Yeats would also unsuccessfully propose to Gonne's daughter, Iseult. Finally giving up on the Gonnes, Yeats married Georgina ("George") Hyde-Lees, who captivated Yeats four days after their wedding with her purported expertise in automatic writing. Despite later affairs, Yeats remained married to George until his death, fathering two children. In 1894, Yeats met Lady Gregory, with whom he would develop an Irish Literary Theater and share his long-lasting interest in Irish folk and fairy tales. After the Easter Rising of 1916 and Irish independence, Yeats served as an Irish Senator from 1922-28, and in 1923, won the Nobel Prize for literature. After an amazingly full and influential life doubled and split by literature and politics, Yeats, in a final letter, described what would be his last aphorism of division: "Man can embody truth but he cannot know it." He died on January 28, 1939.

## *Poem Text*

I have met them at close of day
Coming with vivid faces
From counter or desk among grey
Eighteenth-century houses.
I have passed with a nod of the head          5
Or polite meaningless words,
Or have lingered awhile and said
Polite meaningless words,
And thought before I had done
Of a mocking tale or a gibe          10
To please a companion
Around the fire at the club,
Being certain that they and I
But lived where motley is worn:
All changed, changed utterly:          15
A terrible beauty is born.

That woman's days were spent
In ignorant good-will,
Her nights in argument
Until her voice grew shrill.          20
What voice more sweet than hers
When, young and beautiful,
She rode to harriers?
This man had kept a school
And rode our winged horse;          25
This other his helper and friend
Was coming into his force;
He might have won fame in the end,
So sensitive his nature seemed,
So daring and sweet his thought.          30
This other man I had dreamed
A drunken, vainglorious lout.
He had done most bitter wrong
To some who are near my heart,
Yet I number him in the song;          35
He, too, has resigned his part
In the casual comedy;
He, too, has been changed in his turn,
Transformed utterly:
A terrible beauty is born.          40

Hearts with one purpose alone
Through summer and winter seem
Enchanted to a stone

To trouble the living stream.
The horse that comes from the road,          45
The rider, the birds that range
From cloud to tumbling cloud,
Minute by minute they change;
A shadow of cloud on the stream
Changes minute by minute;          50
A horse-hoof slides on the brim,
And a horse plashes within it;
The long-legged moor-hens dive,
And hens to moor-cocks call;
Minute by minute they live:          55
The stone's in the midst of all.

Too long a sacrifice
Can make a stone of the heart.
O when may it suffice?
That is Heaven's part, our part          60
To murmur name upon name,
As a mother names her child
When sleep at last has come
On limbs that had run wild.
What is it but nightfall?          65
No, no, not night but death;
Was it needless death after all?
For England may keep faith
For all that is done and said.
We know their dream; enough          70
To know they dreamed and are dead;
And what if excess of love
Bewildered them till they died?
I write it out in a verse—
MacDonagh and MacBride          75
And Connolly and Pearse
Now and in time to be,
Wherever green is worn,
Are changed, changed utterly:
A terrible beauty is born.          80

## *Poem Summary*

### *Lines 1-8:*

These lines describe the narrator having crossed paths with some of the Dubliners who would become leaders of the Easter Rising. Their vitality is set against a contrasting background of the deadening places where they work—"counter or desk"—that are old and perhaps dirty, indicated by "grey / Eighteenth-century houses." The vital souls Yeats meets occasionally will be those ushering in the modern era of Ireland. But with them, the narrator engages in only small talk.

### *Lines 9-14:*

In describing these future revolutionaries, the speaker emphasizes their commonness, their status as ordinary "good old boys." Or, on the other hand, their commonness might be negative, serving as

*Media Adaptations*

- An audio cassette titled *The Poetry of William Butler Yeats* is available from Audiobooks.

- Three American poets—Philip Levine, Peter Davison, and Richard Wilbur—offer a reading of "Easter 1916" at http://www.theatlantic.com/atlantic/atlweb/poetry/soundings/easter.htm

grounds for mocking in the company of more cultured men at the club. But whether these would-be revolutionaries are merely common or dreadfully common, the backdrop of a drab Ireland sets off the farcical character of its idealistic people and the cynical character of its realists.

**Lines 15-16:**

These two lines jolt, employing a shock cut from a depiction of a mundane and shallow Ireland to one of dead solemnity. If the reader has no knowledge of the Rising, he or she is immediately locked in: What could this "terrible beauty" be, one that completely changed everything? On the other hand, if the reader is in the know, he or she is likely to be intrigued or impressed with the description, which consists of an oxymoron—an especially provocative one at that.

**Lines 17-23:**

This stanza marks a change from the general to the more specific. The first person discussed is Constance, or "Con," Gore-Booth who, upon marrying a count, became Countess Markiewicz. For her role as an assistant commander in the Rising, she was imprisoned, although later released (see Yeats's "On a Political Prisoner"). Yeats had met Markiewicz and her sister Eva at their mansion, Lissadell, while she was doing charity work that the poet refers to as "ignorant good will". Apparently, she could imitate the cries of hares with her young and beautiful voice as she hunted them with her dogs (harriers). It was this voice that became shrill by politics.

**Lines 24-26:**

"This man" was Patrick Pearse, the founder of a boy's school in Dublin and the Commandant-General and President of the provisional government during the Rising. He was a member of the Irish bar and was also a poet. The winged horse is Pegasus, a symbol for poetry or the poet's inspiration. Pearse was a poet and one of the leaders executed.

**Lines 27-31:**

"This other," Thomas MacDonagh, taught English Literature at University College, Dublin, and was a poet, playwright, and critic. Yeats had met him and felt that "within [MacDonagh's] own mind this mechanical thought is crushing as with an iron roller all that is organic." MacDonagh was also executed for his leadership in the Rising.

**Lines 32-37:**

"This other man" refers to Major John MacBride, the man who had married and divorced Maud Gonne, Yeats's longtime passion who refused his requests to marry several times. The "some who are near my heart" are likely Maud and her daughter, Iseult, who Yeats had, also unsuccessfully, asked to marry. While Yeats did not like MacBride, he felt he owed him tribute for his part in the Rising. Like MacDonagh and Pearse, MacBride "resigned his part" (was executed) and no longer had to act in the "casual comedy" of Ireland described in the first stanza. Thus, political events are compared to theatrical events.

**Lines 38-40:**

Because of MacBride's martyrdom, he was changed from a lout to a hero. This is part of the meaning of "terrible beauty": that even a fool could become transformed into a thing of beauty.

**Lines 41-56:**

This stanza is another rapid edit away from specific heroes, even if unnamed, to abstract observations by way of images known as metaphors. Briefly put, this stanza says that those willing to sacrifice themselves and others to principle, ideology, or by another reading, the stone that refers to Ireland herself, are those "enchanted to a stone." They become stony because they are committed, while those around them ("the living stream") react and change with differing circumstances. Or as Yeats puts it, while stones do not change, most everything else does: moving horses suddenly veer off course; riders react to their horses (as poets react to Pegasus's inspiration); birds dive, careen, and call; and clouds and their reflections shift and mutate. The softer beings of animals, clouds, and water change; that hard thing—stone—does not.

### Lines 57-64:

The transition into the last stanza, unlike the previous changes between stanzas, is gradual. From the description of stones as obdurate and perhaps unsympathetic things, Yeats moves on to explain the reason people become like stone: through self-sacrifice. Yeats's explanation makes it easier for readers to sympathize with the insurrectionists. In line 59, Yeats himself turns to sympathy. As if pleading to heaven, the poet asks how long people must sacrifice themselves, must make a stone of their heart, in order to gain what is just. Because the question is unanswerable, Yeats says that all we can do is remember the dead ("To murmur name upon name") as when a mother utters the name of her sleeping child to make sure he awakens and remains with her.

### Lines 65-69:

Almost as soon as Yeats enters into his analogy between recalling the martyrs and "naming" the sleeping child, he exits with the words "not night but death," because, after all, the revolutionaries are not sleeping but dead. The poet wonders whether their deaths were needless since Britain had promised Ireland a great measure of independence as soon as World War I was over. In the meantime, Ireland felt forced to furnish the British with men and food, something that angered Irish dissidents and helped drive them to revolt.

### Lines 70-73:

The revolutionaries dreamed of an independent Ireland, but the reality is that they are dead. Now the question is what to make of them. From the revolutionaries characterized as overly hard in stanza three, to those at the beginning of stanza four who sacrificed themselves to make a stone of their heart, the revolutionaries now become, in lines 72 and 73, those who loved too much and were confused by an "excess of love." Is this a contradiction, or can it be said that the revolutionaries turned to stone because of love?

### Lines 74-80:

The new name in these lines is James Connolly. Under Pearse, Connolly was second in command of the Republican forces and Commandant at the General Post Office, the principal location of the Republican forces. Connolly was perhaps left to the end of the poem because Yeats did not know him well, even though they had been in demonstrations together in the 1890s. Due to their revolutionary action, the four men mentioned in the poem, and presumably the others executed who were not mentioned, will be transformed from the more or less average people they were into heroes—especially "Wherever green is worn," that is, in the Emerald Isle, Ireland. By the end of the poem, even if ignorant of the Rising, readers can venture a pretty sound guess as to what "terrible beauty" at least partially refers: martyrdom.

## Themes

### Public vs. Private Life

For much of his life Yeats struggled with his conviction that public life had an adverse effect on the private person—especially the poet. He thought that mixing with or leading the crowd would coarsen sensitivity due to constant arguing as well as unsettle one's peace and principles from repeated compromise. Yet he was a social and political person, a tireless joiner and fraternizer, even becoming a senator in the newly independent Irish Free State for six years. In "Easter 1916," Yeats's conflict between the public and private spheres is transposed to five of the revolutionaries of the Easter Rising. Where Yeats saw a conflict, it is probable that some of the revolutionaries—especially the writers, Thomas MacDonagh and Patrick Pearse, and the charity worker, Constance Markiewicz—saw the act of revolt as less a conflict with their private sentiments and lives than a necessary continuation of them. While, for Yeats, revolt would have meant troubling self-examination, to the revolutionaries, to *not* revolt would have meant the same. In this poem, and in comments made to others, Yeats expressed regret that peaceful, sensitive souls got involved with the Rising, not only because politics and militarism did not suit some of the revolutionaries—Yeats might even say, coarsened them—but also because it killed them.

The dichotomy between public and private is clear for Yeats when it comes to observing how privately sensitive natures are made shrill in argument and combat; the poet is therefore comfortable with his regretful sentiments. Where the poem becomes more than an elegy, however, is not where the binary between public and private has been tragically and regretfully transgressed by the revolutionaries,

# Topics for Further Study

- What different events or phenomena in the realms of psychology, politics, nature, etc., can you describe with the words "terrible beauty?"

- Consider the advantages and disadvantages of using pictures or textual images, instead of words of explanation to describe ideas such as those in stanza three.

- The Easter Rising was timed to coincide with Christ's rising. Compare and contrast events and figures of the Easter Rising with the story of Christ's life, death, and resurrection.

but, instead, where the polarized difference between public and private is not so clear and where it becomes troublesome. This is the tension that has made this poem endure. The reader might sense that Yeats, fully understanding the transformation that the Rising has brought, is annoyed by the possibility that he himself might have had more effect on Ireland if he had also put down his pen and picked up a gun. Against his more rational or rationalizing side, the poet of "Easter 1916" seems to wonder just under his breath whether the extensive space he once saw between the public and the private appears only from certain angles. From another viewpoint—after the Rising and the quick execution of its leaders—the public and private do not look so far apart, because it can be said that these men and this woman died for something that, before it became extremely public, was passionately private. But as Yeats's lifelong friend Maud Gonne had remarked, perhaps there would have been no public Rising without the publication of Yeats's private passions for Irish tradition—publications that were likely internalized by the likes of Pearse, MacDonagh, and Markiewicz before they would again emerge in the public explosion of 1916.

## Memory

The Easter Rising lasted from April 24 to April 29, 1916. Yeats dated his poem "Easter 1916" on September 25, 1916. Why did it take as long as it did to finish the poem? Even with Yeats's appended date, critics disagree as to when the poem was written. Some say it was a couple of weeks after the executions, which would be the last two weeks in May. Others say the writing took place in July and August. Whatever the case, Yeats reportedly did not know what to make of the event immediately. Additional incidents would have to take their course, people would have to be listened to, and thoughts sifted. Perhaps what is even more surprising is that the poem was not published until 1920. While this is not the place to speculate on exactly why Yeats waited to write and publish, some general remarks may be ventured. After the Rising, most of Ireland was angry at the revolutionaries. But after the executions, anger was directed at Britain. Yeats's sentiments seem as fickle as the public's. Unlike what might have been a public response, Yeats did not direct a poem of hate at Britain but, instead, took a more indirect and arguably a more effective route: he remembered the martyrs with love.

"Easter 1916" is nothing if not a eulogy—one that could have been read at the martyrs' funeral. Yeats, while acknowledging certain failings of the martyrs, always ends on a note of praise, remembering these men for what could have been their finest hour. Yeats's course resembles that of memory itself. With time, memory—unless the self suffers a major blow that provokes revenge—sluffs off its anger and keeps its fondness, usually an easier emotion. "Easter 1916" is a poem of memory and, even if Yeats was unaware of it, about memory. With the passage of time, Yeats could more easily forgive the leaders of the Rising and even praise them.

The recitation of the revolutionaries' names in the last stanza is like so many names upon the walls of war memorials or on AIDS quilts. Names connected with tragedy are forgiven, since it is difficult to hate or remain angry at those who have suffered, even if they have caused others to suffer. Perhaps Yeats waited as long as he did to write the poem, even publish it with changes, until the action of memory softened his tone and until the poem could inspire its readers to identify the insurrectionists as heroes. Perhaps Yeats believed that love, more than anger, was the best emotion to provoke the populace into passion for the liberation of Ireland

## Change

Memory's connection to change has already been discussed—more often than not, bruises and anger are minimized or forgotten, leaving behind what can be praised. This is how the Rising's rash revolutionaries were transformed into heroes. Ireland also changed after the Easter Rising; the "terrible beauty" was born. Before the Easter Rising there were other Risings—in 1798 and 1803—but none lasted as long and resulted in so many martyrs. After the 1916 Rising, a more entrenched nationalism—a hunger for independent nationhood—took hold and took on a militant aspect that continues to this day. The "terrible beauty" of Yeats's time would eventually result in a completely independent Republic of Ireland and may yet result in a united Republic of Ireland: in May, 1998 a Northern Ireland peace agreement was signed, giving more power to Ulster Catholics, many of whom are sympathetic to unification and complete independence. This is probably the most prominent feature of the utter change foreshadowed in Yeats's poem.

There is also another type of change depicted in "Easter 1916." In stanza three—the only part of the poem written in the language of images—Yeats shows himself devoted, almost religiously, to the idea of change. Yeats paints change in the transformations of clouds, reflections, animal movement, and seasons. For the notion of stagnancy, that thing that does not change and that presents an obstacle to those things that do change, there is the image of the stone. Stanza three contains no argumentation, just presentation of the notion that change is good and that which stays the same is bad. The same is true in the first two lines of stanza four. Here, the imagery is transferred to inside the body where the constantly beating, changing heart is transformed into a stone by holding on to unchanging ideas and passions. Yeats is undialectical, change being all good and constancy being all bad. Further, the imagery is ineffective, especially because it is difficult to invest stones with the image of an incorrigible person. True it is that people can take on characteristics attributed to stone: hardness, denseness, deafness, coolness. In this respect Yeats's image of a heart turned to stone is successful. But it is more difficult to turn stones into a certain kind of person, because constancy and stability have their place in the scheme of things, and because stones are rarely invested with threat. While tales of monstrous plants and animals abound, seldom do stones cause fear. More, stones are the product of fear—as in petrified wood and people. On the other hand, Yeats was astute in selecting the word stone rather than rock, in that rock connotes solidness and dependability. Perhaps Yeats even considered transforming the troubling stone of

stanza three into the rock of commitment at the end of "Easter 1916." But this would have clashed with the three refrains describing utter change and transformation, even risked privileging constancy over change. For a man who valued change so highly, this would not have been the best option.

## Style

"Easter 1916" is a four-stanza poem, with the stanzas being composed of an unusual number of lines. The first and third stanzas contain 16 lines, perhaps referring to the last digits of 1916, the year of the Easter Rising. The second and fourth stanzas have 24 lines, pointing to April 24 as the first day of the Rising. In every stanza, the rhyme scheme is *abab* and Yeats employs both full rhyme ("day" and "grey") and near or slant rhyme ("faces" and "houses"), where only the last syllables rhyme. Though Yeats employs primarily end-stopped lines, he sporadically uses enjambment, a technique used to make sense and syntax spill over one line and into the next. As an example, in the following lines, "grey" makes much more sense if read, not as a noun, as would be the case if read with its own line, but as an adjective modifying houses: "From counter or desk among grey / eighteenth-century houses." The poem is in iambic trimeter, with three feet per line composed mostly of one unaccented syllable followed by an accented syllable. This meter was often used by dramatists—which Yeats was—because its rhythm and meter was thought to most faithfully reproduce that of conversation. However, there are variations. Two unaccented syllables which are followed by an accented syllable are called an anapest as are the last two feet in line three:

From **coun**/ ter or **desk** / a mong **grey**

Another variation on the iamb is the first foot of line two:

**Com**ing/ with **vi**/vid **faces**

This line's first foot, with its accented syllable followed by an accented syllable, is called a reversed foot, or trochee.

No rhythm has been used in English verse as much as iambic meter, though five feet per line (pentameter) is more frequent than three feet per line (trimeter). The iamb is thought by many critics to relate to the beat of the heart, the act of breathing, the alternation of feet and arms in movement—all of which repeat thousands of times a day and tend to reinforce the iambic character of language.

## Historical Context

On April 24, 1916, Easter Monday, Dubliners were enjoying a relaxed public holiday. Many were out of town. While an occupying force of 400 British troops stood duty in Dublin, Patrick Pearse and James Connolly led a company of 150 men—part of a total force of 1,500 volunteers from the Irish Citizen's Army and the Irish Volunteers—through downtown Dublin from Liberty Hall to the General Post Office a short distance away. After his group stormed the post office and easily overpowered an unarmed guard of seven, Pearse reappeared on the front steps to read The Proclamation of the Irish Republic whose most important sentence read: "We declare the right of the people of Ireland to the ownership of Ireland, and to the unfettered control of Irish destinies, to be sovereign and indefeasible." While Pearse and Connolly commandeered the forces at the post office, Thomas MacDonagh led those at Jacob's Biscuit Factory, and Michael Mallin and his second-in-command, Countess Constance Markiewicz, occupied St. Stephen's Green. By Sunday of the same week, all would surrender, easily overpowered by a larger, more heavily armed British counterforce. This was expected by the leaders of the Rising, as Connolly was reputed to have said "We're going out to be slaughtered, you know." In the wake of the Easter Rising, portions of Dublin were in ruins, hundreds were homeless, factories and shops were closed down, one third of the population—100,000 people—found themselves on public relief, 2,500 had been wounded, and 400 were dead. As might be imagined, the public turned against the Sinn Fein leaders, that is until the British executed sixteen insurrectionists—Pearse, Connolly, MacDonagh, and MacBride among them.

The larger backdrop of the Easter Rising was World War I. Since the war began in 1914, Ireland had objected to the recruitment of its soldiers by England. In posters, pamphlets, newspapers, and armed demonstrations, dissident Irishmen insisted it was neither Ireland's duty nor business to fight for a British government that had not even granted Ireland its freedom. The British saw it differently, since in 1914 the Irish Home Rule Act (a decree of somewhat limited self-government) was supposed to have become enacted, but was delayed, England said, because of the necessity for Irish exports and volunteers to fight in World War I. Even though Irish dissidents advertised their anger, Britain decided against any systematic suppression. So afraid was the United Kingdom of further inflaming militant demands for home rule and the consequent loss of Irish food exports and volunteers (by the time of the Rising there were more than 150,000), that it excepted Ireland from a January, 1916 decision to draft men into the armed forces from Wales, Scotland, and England. But by April 22, 1916, two days before the Rising, two events provoked Britain into quashing Irish unruliness. First, the British captured a merchant ship carrying munitions from Germany to the Irish rebels. Second, Roger Casement, a retired British diplomat turned Irish revolutionary, was captured when it was discovered he had been recruiting for the Rising by trying to gather a militia of Irish prisoners of war within Germany. Because Germany was Britain's enemy in World War I, a German-Irish conspiracy was intolerable. When Britain rushed to stop the rebellion—discovered as a result of investigating the arms shipment and Casement—it was already too late. The first shots of the Easter Rising had already been fired. While it might have served Germany's interest to get behind the Rising in order to cripple Britain, Germany collaborated only to the extent of sending munitions. Requests from Irish groups for troops and money were apparently denied. In fact, the most outside money for the Rising was sent by an Irish-American group, Clan na Gael, that sided with Germany rather than Britain because of Britain's continued occupation of Ireland.

After the Rising and Britain's quick execution of the sixteen leaders in May, Irish independence demanded resolution if Britain was going to win the war. Especially troublesome was the refusal of United States, with its large Irish population, to get behind Britain until it resolved the troubles in Ireland. But talks between Britain and Ireland proved ineffectual. With the increasing radicalization of Ireland subsequent to the execution of the Rising's martyrs and the imposition of British martial law, Sinn Fein ("we ourselves"), the party led by the rebels of 1916, gained popularity and won elections even though its members, in protest, refused to sit in the British House of Commons. But it was the announcement of conscription in Ireland on March 28, 1918—the result of intense German attacks against the Allies—that really angered Ireland and solidified respect for Sinn Fein. Even with English promises of home rule for Ireland, neither home rule nor, for that matter, conscription, were actually instituted by 1918, the end of the war. After the war, Britain had to fight Ireland on two fronts: the political and the military. Sinn Fein had sweeping victories in local elections in 1920, and by 1919, Michael Collins was leading the Irish Republican Army (IRA) in a successful guerilla war against

# *Compare & Contrast*

- **1916:** For almost one week—April 24 to 29—the Irish Volunteers and the Irish Republican Army held key buildings in downtown Dublin during the Easter Rising. After a fierce battle, the revolutionaries surrendered to a much stronger and larger British force. The following month, sixteen revolutionaries were executed by the British.

  **1998:** Three young, Roman Catholic boys were burned to death in an arson attack in the Protestant village of Ballymoney, Northern Ireland. The flaming gas bomb that killed them is believed to have been thrown by a Protestant angry that a Protestant march through a Catholic neighborhood was banned by the British.

- **1916:** In February, one of the major battles of World War I begins and lasts for ten months. France (Britain's ally) and Germany (Britain's enemy) fight over the French town of Verdun. An estimated 700,000 soldiers lose their lives.

  **1994:** From 500,000 to one million Tutsis are slaughtered by Hutus in a four-month period during the Rwandan Civil War. This war sets a record for the most people killed in the shortest time period outside of the U.S. atomic bomb blasts in Hiroshima and Nagasaki.

- **1916:** The art movement known as Dada is started by Hugo Ball, Tristan Tzara, and others at the Cabaret Voltaire in Zurich. Employing intentional insanity, nihilism, and irony through text, image, and performance, Dada launched an attack against a modernity that led to the insanity and mass destruction of World War I.

  **Today:** Four grants from the National Endowment for the Arts (NEA) are denied in 1990 to performance artists Karen Finley, Holly Hughes, etc. ("The NEA 4") on the basis that their art is lewd. Their grants are restored in 1993. The question of content restrictions and definitions of obscenity regarding NEA funds is still in court.

---

Britain. While the Irish terrain was unfavorable to guerrilla warfare, the Irish populace was not. The British found that the Irish would not betray IRA positions and activities. Casualties on both sides were high and British repression was brutal, an indication that British occupation was beginning to unravel. On December 6, 1921, a treaty was signed effecting semi-independent "dominion" status for Ireland, the retention of two British naval bases in the southern part of Ireland, and a review of the border between Northern Ireland and the now nearly independent Ireland. The Irish pro-treaty forces settled for this comprised state of affairs because the British threatened all-out war if they didn't. But only one of two Irish factions supported the treaty, that of Michael Collins. Eamon de Valera opposed the treaty. By June 28, 1922, the first shots would be fired in the Irish Civil War between pro- and anti-treaty forces. The outnumbered, anti-treaty forces could not win and surrendered on May 24,

1923. Five hundred people had died and 77 were executed, 53 more than the British had executed. The treaty resulted in complete internal control of the new Irish Free State. By 1937, the Irish Free State would become Eire after it dropped its allegiance to the United Kingdom in 1932. In 1938, naval rights were abandoned by Britain. In 1949, Eire became The Republic of Ireland and withdrew from the British Commonwealth. As any follower of international news knows, however, Ireland is still not at peace. The major source of contention remains a non-unified Ireland, with the six counties of mostly Protestant Northern Ireland (Ulster) still separated from a mostly Catholic Republic of Ireland and aligned with Britain. In May of 1998, however, the Northern Ireland Peace Agreement was passed, providing Northern Ireland with a new Assembly to give Catholics more political power. Though the conflict is far from over, an independent Ireland may yet see unification.

## Critical Overview

"Easter 1916" is one of Yeats's most popular and discussed poems, especially in Ireland where it anticipated the birth of that nation. Yeats's other political poems that focused on the Easter Rising are "The Leaders of the Crowd," "Sixteen Dead Men," "The Rose Tree," and "On a Political Prisoner." All can be found, along with "Easter 1916," in *Michael Robartes and the Dancer* (1921).

Richard Ellman, in *The Identity of Yeats*, maintained that Yeats's poem contained both a nationalist and anti-nationalist position, since its assertions were accompanied by qualifications and questions. Ellman believed this indicated Yeats's passionate and fundamental skepticism in circumstances riddled by conflict. Hazard Adams, writing in *The Book of Yeats's Poems*, holds a differing opinion. Adams asserts that Yeats rises to the occasion of glorifying the revolutionaries because he praises the poets who became revolutionaries and appears to criticize himself for once having mocked them behind their back at the club (stanza one). Adams also understands Yeats's imagery of stanza three not so much as critical of people wedded to a singleness of political purpose but as praiseworthy. These "stones" were necessary to trouble the living "stream of Dublin workers" who presumably were too complacent about English occupation and the deculturation of Ireland. In *Yeats and the Poetry of Death*, Jahan Ramazani praises "Easter 1916" for avoiding eulogistic cant. Much like Ellman and Hazard, Ramazani understands the poem to embody an interior quarrel or conflict but goes further to understand Yeats's quarrel as an interiorization of the social and historical forces of revolution. Ramazani also stresses that not only did the revolutionaries utterly change Irish history, but, in the process, they were transformed into Irish heroes. Finally, and perhaps controversially, Ramazani has Yeats not merely questioning or praising what the martyrs accomplished, but instead coming to identify with them: "Yeats sees himself in their revolutionary act." Whatever the case may be, "Easter 1916" is a poem that has sparked far less interpretive controversy than it has nationalist pride.

## Criticism

### Jhan Hochman

*Jhan Hochman holds a Ph.D. in English and has published a book and numerous articles. In the following essay, Hochman explores the "play of twos" found throughout "Easter 1916."*

Throughout the warp and weft of "Easter 1916" is a play of twos. First, there are the pairings. Many critics believe "Easter 1916" to be the sister poem, or palinode (a re-singing or recanting) of Yeats's earlier poem "September 1913." Whereas in "September 1913" Yeats bemoaned the death of Irish culture and its political resolve under the thumb of British oppression, in "Easter 1916" Yeats heralded the birth of a "terrible beauty," a violently vital Irish push for nationhood. In another pairing, the poem unfolds in a two-part structure, each part composed of two stanzas. The first stanzas of each part contain 16 lines, most likely a play on the year, 1916. The second stanzas in each part contains twenty-four lines, reminding the reader of the first day of the Rising: April 24. Not only are stanzas paired, but so are lines: every other line is married through full or canted rhyme. There is also the pairing of revolutionaries: Constance Markiewicz and John MacBride, the first and fourth persons mentioned in stanza two, are portrayed with negative and positive traits. Patrick Pearse and Thomas MacDonagh are characterized as sensitive writers. In the last stanza, minor leaders MacDonagh and MacBride are paired, as are the major leaders, Connolly and Pearse. Finally, there is, even before Yeats's poem, the overall "comparing" of Ireland's Easter Rising with Christ's Easter resurrection and with the spring, a time of newly born green symbolizing both nature and Ireland.

Another play of twos is found in a series of transitions. First, there is the transition from grey to green. The grey of "grey / eighteenth-century houses" suggests withering age, death, dirt, and unclarity. On the other hand, the green of "Wherever green is worn" implies Ireland, the resurrection of spring, and a general vitality. The Easter Rising in the spring of April 1916 and the execution deaths of sixteen revolutionary leaders a short time later mark the transition from an old, dying, politically unmotivated country (grey) to an Ireland reborn through martyrdom (green). The poem's other chromatic transition is that from motley to green. Motley, an outfit of many colors, indicates the fool who, even when wise, speaks but never acts. Before the Easter Rising, the wearing of motley indicates that Yeats's Ireland is a silly, lighthearted place—one that may talk but rarely acts. After the Rising, wearing green will come to indicate something different: that the country has grown

*What Do I Read Next?*

- Elias Canetti's *Crowds and Power,* written in 1962, is an extensive study of different kinds of religious and political crowds and explorations of elements necessary to crowds, such as symbols and commands. Because the table of contents is so detailed, the work only suffers slightly from the absence of an index.

- Seamus Deane's 1986 work, *A Short History of Irish Literature,* commences in the fifth century and ends in the 1980s.

- Eric Hoffer's landmark study of 1951, *The True Believer: Thoughts on the Nature of Mass Movements,* focuses on the characteristics of mass movements be they religious, social, or nationalist.

- The United Irishmen—a group that began in the latter part of the eighteenth century—had a tremendous impact on the popular culture of Ireland. This impact is reviewed in great detail by Mary Helen Thuente in her 1994 text, *The Harp Restrung.*

- Between Thoreau and Martin Luther King, the torch of nonviolent rebellion was carried not only by Gandhi, but by Leo Tolstoy whose essays are collected in *Tolstoy's Writings on Civil Disobedience and Non-Violence,* published in 1967.

- Yeats's 1938 work, *A Vision,* explains from whence Yeats's system of occult visions arose— from the automatic writing and sleep monologues of his wife, George—and describes their nature, structure, and relationships to each other.

---

and matured into an independent nation, one that has acted to gain that independence. Yeats's prediction that a "terrible beauty" had been born was correct: while most of Ireland was critical of its revolutionaries during and just after the Rising, the popular tide turned green after the executions. On this count, Yeats was in agreement with the people of Ireland. If there was a difference between Yeats and his countrymen, it was only that he believed the sensitivity of the revolutionaries made them ill suited for their hardened roles in the Rising.

That the revolutionaries were miscast takes us to another play of two, that of opposition. Yeats believed in the need for a barrier between political and private life, because he thought that politics would coarsen and corrupt the individual. As Yeats wrote, Countess Markiewicz, in her private life, was full of "ignorant good will" and had a young and beautiful voice made shrill by her public role in politics. MacDonagh and Pearse were sensitive writers in their private life but eventually took up arms and publicly revolted. During the Rising, Yeats was staying in England with a friend,

William Rothenstein, who recounted that Yeats had commented on the revolutionaries: "These men, poets and schoolmasters ... are idealists, unfit for practical affairs; they are seers, pointing to what should be, who had been goaded into action against their better judgment." Still, later in life, Yeats would grow firmly against a life of politics, made clear in an unpublished letter from April 7, 1936: "Do not try to make a politician of me, even in Ireland I shall never I think be that again—as my sense of reality deepens, & I think it does with age, my horror at the cruelty of governments grows greater ...." In "Easter 1916" Yeats metaphorizes the opposition between the sensitive souls of private life and those hardened by public politics. It is done in stanza three by means of the opposition between the living stream, signifying life and change through motion, and the stone, indicating hard-heartedness and stubbornness through immobility. Rather than viewing the politician as bending with the breezes of public reaction or soft money donations as we might today, Yeats depicts the politician as an argumentative, unyielding, obdurate

> *Was [Yeats] bitter because no matter how many plays and poems he wrote, or stories he collected, all in the name of promoting a proud and independent Ireland, literature did not, perhaps could not, have the impact of an event like the Easter Rising?"*

ideologue, paradoxically more befitting the marginalized politician of change and revolution than the entrenched politician of business as usual.

The problem with Yeats's metaphorical complex of stone versus stream becomes an all-out contradiction in stanza four. Where, in stanza three, the hearts of the revolutionaries are hardened to changing life, in stanza four the revolutionaries are said to be bewildered by an excess of love. Did Yeats notice this contradiction or was he trying to say what seems extremely unlikely, that an excess of love *hardens* the heart? As this is improbable, the contradiction might not be a contradiction at all, since Yeats could have decided that the martyrs suffered both from an excess of love for Ireland and of hate for Britain. Whatever drove them more—love or hate—is anybody's guess

One might want to argue that the refrain, "terrible beauty," finally emphasizes beauty over terrible since the adjective is subservient to the noun modified. Still, the phrase effectively maintains the tension of an irreconcilable polarity, a kind of vacillation between traditional male and female principles: the sublime "terrible," inspiring fear, and the beautiful, which arouses love. On one hand, a characterization of the sentiments in "Easter 1916" might be resolved contradiction, but another might be its opposite—indecision. Indecision characterized Yeats's father, the family member who perhaps most influenced Yeats, who said, "I am not sure that this absurd 'rising' will not in the end help

home rule and make it more substantial." The elder Yeats uses the word absurd for the Rising because the revolutionaries could not hope to succeed at immediately extricating Britain from Ireland, though they might be influential over the long haul. Yeats shared some of his father's sentiments, as indicated in the lines "Was it needless death after all? / For England may keep faith / For all that is done and said." These indicate indecision, with Yeats wondering whether England would have instituted the postponed Home Rule Act of 1914 at the end of the World War I. If England, as it promised, would have instituted a measure of Irish independence by war's end, then, Yeats thinks, the revolutionaries died in vain—perhaps an "absurd" death, to use his father's word. In 1916, this was an interesting problem, its very unsolvability producing paralytic indecision when it came to whether the martyrs wasted their time and lives in the Rising.

Whether, from the viewpoint of 1916, the martyrs of the Easter Rising died in vain provoked not only indecision, but a more problematic internal conflict: Yeats's suspicion—fear even—that in order to accomplish political change one had to make a stone of the heart:

Too long a sacrifice
Can make a stone of the heart.
O when may it suffice?
That is Heaven's part …

Yeats does not and cannot resolve the question, leaving it to heaven to decide. Apparently he is unwilling or unable, through sacrifice, to make a stone of his own heart. On the other hand, he, in effect, admits the strategy has been productive because it brought about "utter change" and a "terrible beauty." Perhaps Yeats even wonders whether insurrection was more effective than merely murmuring "name upon name … MacDonagh and MacBride / Connolly and Pearse" as he did in "Easter 1916." Why did Yeats not simply praise the heroes of the Rising and accept his inability to do what they did? Was he bitter because no matter how many plays and poems he wrote, or stories he collected, all in the name of promoting a proud and independent Ireland, literature did not, perhaps could not, have the impact of an event like the Easter Rising? That the pen might not be mightier than the sword would have split the dean of Irish cultural nationalism in two. Maud Gonne, Yeats's long–admired and unattainable love, however, would have thought this internal schism groundless. After Yeats's death, Gonne claimed that "Without Yeats there would have been no Literary

Revival in Ireland. Without the inspiration of that Revival and the glorification of beauty and heroic virtue, I doubt if there would have been an Easter Week." At the present time, when literature and politics are seen by so many to have little to do with each other, Gonne shows their pairing as complementary and their relationship reciprocal: without Yeats's work there might not have been an Easter Rising; without an Easter Rising there could be no literature written about it. Perhaps this is a reason why writers and actors are often interested in politics and even run for or serve in office. Ever since its beginnings, literature has glorified and criticized existing military and political figures, inspiring or discouraging those who would learn from their example. Though Yeats did not always seem to think so, his life as a senator and opinion maker not only divided him from his poet-self, but also united him, just as it united the writer-heroes of the Rising and made their thoughts live through action. Perhaps nowhere in his work is it more evident that politics and literature can be closely paired—and paired forcefully—as in "Easter 1916."

**Source:** Jhan Hochman, in an essay for *Poetry for Students,* Gale, 1999.

## Carolyn Meyer

*Carolyn Meyer holds a Ph.D. in Modern British and Irish Literature and has taught contemporary literature at several Canadian universities, including the University of Toronto. In the following essay, Meyer notes that "Easter 1916" negotiates between the extremes of art and politics and, through its ambivalence and ambiguities, renders the complexities of the historical event. Both an elegy and political poem, it finds its creative tension through opposition and paradox.*

The poet Patrick Pearse, one of fifteen militant nationalists jailed and executed for his role in the failed Easter Rising of 1916, believed with a near-messianic fervor, as noted in his *Plays, Stories, Poems,* that only those willing to die "in bloody protest for a glorious thing" could bring Ireland to the brink of independence. Three years before he signed the Proclamation that would effectively seal his fate, bringing about his martyrdom at the hands of the British judicial system, and three years before his deliberate "blood-sacrifice" launched Ireland on its violent course toward nationhood, Pearse wrote in his political tract "The Coming Revolution":

> I do not know if the Messiah has come yet, and I am not sure that there will be any visible and personal

Messiah in this redemption: the people itself will perhaps be its own Messiah, the people labouring, scourged, crowned with thorns, agonising and dying, to rise again immortal and impassable.... [B]loodshed is a cleansing and a satisfying thing, and the nation which regards it as the final horror has lost its manhood. There are many things more horrible than bloodshed; and slavery is one of them.

In what turned out to be a self-fulfilling prophecy, made all the more poignant by its sacrificial language, Pearse outlined the intractable terms of a fanatical republicanism. Yet not all in Ireland were prepared to rally to the cause as he defined it. Among them was W. B. Yeats.

While Yeats had done much to further the cause of cultural nationalism by helping to establish a national theater, the Abbey, and by renewing ancient Irish myths and legends through his poems and plays, he had always prided himself on being an aesthete, dismissive of the vulgarities of politics, and had been genuinely dismayed by the destructive political passions of his friend and would-be lover, Maud Gonne. The political poems that he did write were, as his critic Richard Ellmann has noted in his critical survey *The Identity of Yeats,* "always complicated by his being above politics." At the time of the insurrection in Dublin, Yeats was not even in Ireland but on an estate in England, having long divided his time between the two countries. Yet even at a distance, the events of April and May 1916 had a profound effect on him, leading in part to his renewed commitment to Ireland. Shortly after the Rising, he wrote to his friend and collaborator Lady Augusta Gregory:

> I am trying to write a poem on the men executed— "terrible beauty has been born again." I had no idea that any public event could so deeply move me and I am very despondent about the future. At the moment I feel that all the work of years has been overturned, all the freeing of Irish literature and criticism from politics.

Despite his obvious disapproval, by late September Yeats had completed one of his rare political poems, a meditation that fixes the historical moment at the same time as it transcends mere political fact. Structured around antitheses and embodying a host of contradictions, "Easter 1916" is as paradoxical as the oxymoronic aphorism "terrible beauty" that echoes through its refrains, for it expresses not only Yeats's disapproval but his approval of the activists he had once decried. A revisionist martyrology, it commemorates heroes at the same time it questions, with awakened compassion, the idealism of their cause and recognizes their progressive depersonalization in the face of public idolatry. It is moreover a public poem, oratorical in its rhetoric, yet until 1919 it was published only as a privately printed underground pamphlet intended mainly for the poet's friends. Above all, however, "Easter 1916" is an elegy that, while mourning and eulogizing the dead, offers consolations only to doubt and undermine them.

As politically divided as Yeats and Pearse had been, both were convinced of the decline of civilization and expressed this in their writing through metaphors of violence. For Yeats, the Easter Rising constituted one of several cataclysmic events that signaled the coming of a new, darkly heroic yet violent age—one that would reverse the tide of two millennia and sweep away its systems of belief.

The choice of a title evocative of Christ's passion and resurrection reinforces already pronounced parallels, from their joint persecution and to their seminal roles in reshaping human destiny and the course of civilization. In this case, however, it is national, rather than strictly spiritual, redemption that comes through the shedding of blood. The fallen patriots' transformation from distinct, yet maligned, average citizens to worshiped national demigods is examined over four stanzas of alternating lengths (16 lines, 24 lines, 16 lines, and 24 lines) and alternating rhyme (*ababcdcd*). To dramatize their metamorphosis over the course of the first two sections, Yeats draws his metaphors from the world of drama. Life in prerevolutionary Dublin is said to have resembled a stage comedy in which the business of commerce and petty bureaucracy ("counter and desk") is rounded out by trivial social routine. In two syntactically similar lines ("I have met them at the close of day" and "I have passed with a nod of the head"), the speaker stresses his passing acquaintance with the rebels, almost to convince himself of the fact. Yet his familiarity with them is of the kind that breeds contempt:

> And I thought before I had done
> Of a mocking tale or a gibe
> To please a companion
> Around the fire at the club.

Within the stratified, class-conscious society still dominated by the grey, eighteenth-century houses of the Ascendancy (the English ruling class), those of political conviction are singled out only as a source of humor. Along with the sense of decline ("close of day") and ennui, even language has been reduced to "polite meaningless words," a script seemingly memorized by actors in "motley," a costume that makes fools of them all. Recalling this spiritually enervated period before the Rising, Yeats

wrote in *Autobiographies,* "doubtless because fragments broke into ever smaller fragments, we saw one another in the light of bitter comedy." While comedy, Yeats observed, has a way of magnifying or enhancing traits of characters, tragedy does precisely the opposite, negating or obscuring them: "tragedy must always be a drowning and breaking of the dykes that separate man from man, and ... it is upon these dykes that comedy keeps house," he wrote in *Essays and Introductions.* Having resigned their roles in "the casual comedy," the patriots are no longer themselves—the distinct personalities sketched in the second stanza—but selfless, nameless adherents tragically absorbed in their cause.

Each of the four portraits in Yeats's eulogizing series is readily identifiable—Countess Constance (Gore-Booth) Markiewicz, whose sentence of execution was commuted, Patrick Pearse, Thomas MacDonagh, and Major John MacBride, the latter the estranged husband of Maud Gonne. As Yeats remembers them, they are all too human—idiosyncratic, full of promise, and beset by weaknesses. Yet in withholding their names, Yeats suggests how their individual identities are subordinated and ultimately lost to both the cult of extreme nationalism and the mantle of tragic heroism. Warning of this transformation with the forcefulness of a tragic chorus, the refrains that close the first and second stanzas intermingle the antitheses of death and birth, terror and beauty, and in so doing reflect the complexity and ambiguity of the poet's response. No longer second-stringers in a petty modern comedy, the rebels are beautiful yet terrible—to be admired and feared—for having risen above normal life. Their armed revolt provides the stimulus for the birth of a nation, but it is a birth achieved at the expense of life. The refrains uncannily echo words that Patrick Pearse had spoken only a year before his execution: "life springs from death and from the graves of patriot men and women spring living nations."

The two final stanzas register an abrupt shift in the speaker's way of thinking, since what he feels is remarkable about patriots is not their capacity to change, but their essential changelessness. Their steadfast and single-minded devotion to their cause has made them stone-hearted, immune to the joys of life, just as it has allowed them to transcend the mutable world, the world subject to time ("summer and winter," "minute by minute") and death. The stone becomes a symbol for the rebels' intransigence and a metaphor for what political fanaticism does to people. It is made all the more terrifying by its contrast with the burgeoning beauty and regenerative vitality of the natural world. Yeats conveys this dynamism, this ceaseless flux, not only through the exhaustiveness of his catalogue (which includes horses, riders, birds, clouds, moor-hens, and moor-cocks) but through a single elaborately structured sentence marked by alliteration ("long-legged"), strong consonantal verbs (range, change, slides, plashes, dive, call, and the verb that encompasses all of the preceding, live), as well as galloping triple meters that hasten the movement of the lines and replicate the flow of "the living stream." Through syntax alone, all living things are linked in a single, cohesive whole. All, that is, except the stone, set off by the colon that precedes the stanza's final line. It resists, even impedes, the flow of life. Conspicuous by its stasis, its deadness, and its timeless permanence, the stone is also something of a gravestone, touchstone, and foundation stone—an unassailable reminder of sacrifice, a moral center "in the midst of all," and focal point for the task of nation building.

As the final stanza begins, Yeats once again unites his two opposing symbols—"Too long a sacrifice / Can make a stone of the heart"—resulting in a wry comment on how Maud Gonne's obsessive love of country diminished her ability to love. Though the contemplation of it may be a comfort, the permanence the heroes have achieved has come at a considerable cost. The delusive power of political belief, the efficacy of the actions committed in its name, and the inadequacy of any outsider's response to it are among Yeats's primary concerns as the poem draws to a close. Where, according to convention, the standard elegy seeks to find consolation, an antidote to loss, Yeats makes several tentative and unsuccessful attempts at this, each one fraught with doubt and skepticism. As much as he praises his subjects, he is equally aware of the folly of their actions. The speaker asks more questions than he answers, but in so doing, he reproduces the thought processes by which we attempt to deal with loss. What has "changed, changed utterly" is the speaker's attitude toward the leaders, who are no longer the objects of scorn and mockery, but compassion. It is not even his place to judge—"that is heaven's part." The role left to everyone else is chiefly commemorative: "To murmur name upon name, / As a mother names her child," an acknowledgment of the public masses that elevated the leaders to the status of martyrs within weeks of their death. Beyond this, however, reality intrudes on the search for consolation. Despite the lines that recall Hamlet's self-deluding take on mortality—"To die, to sleep— / To sleep / perchance to dream"

> *"Easter 1916' is a poem that traverses the dangerous ground between art and politics, bringing both into a peaceable accord."*

(*Hamlet* 3.1.64-65)—the deaths of the patriots are unassailable facts. Given the remote possibility that England could still make good on its 1913 promise to grant part of Ireland home rule, their sacrifice might well be in vain. Yeats even speculates that they were led astray and betrayed by their romantic idealism, "bewildered" and "enchanted" by their cause and ideology. In writing of the "excess of love" that led the patriots to the deaths, Yeats borrows directly from Pearse's *Political Writings:* "If I die it will be from the excess of love that I bear the Gael."

Only in the final lines does it become clear that the entire poem enacts the response Yeats prescribes: "I write it out in a verse— / MacDonagh and MacBride / And Connolly and Pearse." Their names made plain for the first time, they belong not to the temporal world, over which they have triumphed, but to a timeless one. That is where their identity lies "now and in time to be." Critic C. K. Stead, in his well-known essay "On 'Easter 1916,'" observes, "the world is, for the moment in which the event is contemplated, 'transformed utterly.'" Language itself has also been transformed as "polite meaningless words" have given way to poetry that has the power to enshrine and celebrate, it too achieving its own victory over time.

"Easter 1916" is a poem that traverses the dangerous ground between art and politics, bringing both into a peaceable accord. Northern Irish poet and critic Tom Paulin, in his introduction to *The Faber Book of Political Verse,* argues that "Yeats's insistence on art's superiority to politics was partly a ruse.... Yeats was an intensely political writer and his frequent sneers at politicians, journalists and other 'groundlings' are part of his consistent deviousness, his influential habit of first affirming that art and politics are hostile opposites and then managing to slip through the barrier, a naked politician disguised as an aesthete." It is this latent enthusiasm combined with the deep unease of Yeats's ambivalence that has helped to make "Easter 1916" one of the best-known and least reductive political poems of this century.

**Source:** Carolyn Meyer, in an essay for *Poetry for Students,* Gale, 1999.

### Marjorie Perloff

*In the following excerpt, Perloff examines the significance of the characters in "Easter 1916," noting that only three of them were actually involved in the uprising.*

Yeats was staying with friends in Gloucestershire when the Easter Rising of 1916 broke out, and, according to his biographers, the news took him with the same surprise as it took the general public in Ireland. The Rising was chiefly promoted by the extreme Nationalists of the Irish Republican Brotherhood, a group of Nationalists of whom Yeats really knew very little because they had come into prominence since the days when he and Maud Gonne were actively engaged in the Gaelic movement. But one of the leaders, Thomas MacDonagh, whose book on Gaelic influences on English prosody Yeats admired, was an old friend, as was Constance Markiewicz, in whose home Yeats had frequently stayed when she was still a Gore-Booth of Lissadell. He was also acquainted with Pearse, Joseph Plunkett, and James Connolly; the latter had worked with Yeats on the '98 Memorial Committee for Wolfe Tone. His English friends noticed that at last Yeats seemed to be moved by a public event. He spoke to them of innocent and patriotic theorists carried away by the belief that they must sacrifice themselves to an abstraction. They would fail and pay the penalty for their failure.

On May 11, Yeats wrote to Lady Gregory that the Dublin tragedy had been a great sorrow and anxiety. "I am trying to write a poem on the men executed—'terrible beauty has been born again.' If the English Conservative party had made a declaration they did not intend to rescind the Home Rule Bill there would have been no Rebellion. I had no idea that any public event could so deeply move me —and I am very despondent about the future.... I do not yet know what she [Maud Gonne] feels about her husband's death. Her letter was written before she heard of it. Her main thought seems to be 'tragic dignity has returned to Ireland.'" And on May 23, he wrote to John Quinn [as reprinted in *The Letters of W.B. Yeats*], "This Irish business has been a great grief. We have lost the ablest and most fine-natured of our young men. A world seems to have been swept away. I keep going over the past in my mind and wondering if I could have done anything to turn those young men in some other direction."

It is no coincidence that the first word of "Easter 1916" is "I" and that the pronoun recurs three times in the first stanza. Yeats is immediately present *in* the poem, "meeting" other men, "passing," "nodding," "lingering," and "mocking." The political event that is the occasion for this poem is not viewed from the outside ...; the center is rather the "I" who must come to terms with the public event. And the important thing to notice is that the speaker does not really understand the Rising until the end of the poem, which charts, to paraphrase Langbaum, the evolution of an observer through his evolving vision of the Irish scene.

... "Easter 1916" begins with a remembered locale: the place is Dublin with its "grey / Eighteenth-century houses," the time the "close of day," the speaker Yeats himself meeting the clerks and shopkeepers, who were to form the hard core of the Irish Republican Army, as they leave their places of business at closing time. The casual reference to "them" in the first line—a reference made before one knows who "they" are—immediately implicates the reader in the speaker's drama; it implies that he shares the speaker's frame of reference, that he knows these persons and places. As the poet recalls his random streetcorner meetings with the future patriots, he is puzzled by the triviality and inconsequence of their former existence. In the days before the Rising, he remembers with a measure of self-reproach, he had paid little attention to these amateur soldiers, exchanging a few "Polite meaningless words" with them and joking about their activities with the Dublin clubmen with whom he dined, "Being certain that they and I / But lived where motley is worn." But the trivial and slightly ridiculous pre-Rising Ireland, of which Yeats himself, as the "and I" testifies, was a part, has been completely transformed: "All changed, changed utterly: / A terrible beauty is born." In the first instance of the refrain, the word "terrible" seems to be used chiefly as an intensive: it means "very great" or "excessive." The observer's initial reaction is one of sympathy and respect for the action that could "change" such aimlessness into something tragic and powerful. Even the image of the opening lines has this implication: the "vivid" faces of the working men are contrasted both to the darkness of the "close of day" and to the greyness of the office buildings from which they emerge.

In the second stanza, four "vivid" faces emerge from the crowd of Stanza I, and the poet characterizes them, one at a time, with a few swift strokes. The choice of characters is extremely odd. Of the seven men who actually signed the Proclamation of the Republic—Padraic Pearse, Thomas Mac-Donagh, James Connolly, Eamonn Ceannt, Joseph Mary Plunkett, Sean MacDermott, and Thomas Clarke—only Pearse and MacDonagh play a part in "Easter 1916," although Connolly is briefly mentioned in the roll-call of the last stanza. Thomas Clarke, usually considered the "chief moving force behind the Rising," [according to Goddard Lieberson in *The Irish Uprising,*] is never named. The point, of course, is that Yeats is not trying to be an objective reporter; he includes only those whose transformation will be relevant to his theme. Thus he begins by pondering the tragic evolution of the beautiful Constance Gore-Booth of Lissadell, the aristocratic horsewoman whom he admired as a young man, into the Con Markiewicz of revolutionary politics, the "shrill" demagogue whose marvelous energy is dissipated in "ignorant good will." The potential of Padraic Pearse, the man who "kept a school / And rode our winged horse," and of Thomas MacDonagh, "his helper and friend," has similarly been dissipated by the Rising. Both men had considerable literary and intellectual gifts which might have done much for the Irish cultural revival. Pearse, the Gaelic enthusiast and timid poet, who, according to Timothy Coogan, could hardly bring himself to handle a knife to cut a loaf, is strangely transformed into the General of the Irish Republican forces, who preaches violence and bloodshed. The transformation of "sweet" and "sensitive" MacDonagh may be glossed by a passage in Yeats's *Autobiography:* "Met MacDonagh yesterday—a man with some literary faculty which will probably come to nothing through lack of culture and encouragement.... In England this man would have become remarkable in some way, here he is being crushed by the mechanical logic and commonplace eloquence which give power to the most empty mind, because, being 'something other than human life,' they have no use for distinguished feeling or individual thought."

But why is MacBride, that "drunken, vainglorious lout," included in the poem and placed in the climactic position at the end of the second stanza? Neither a major figure in the Rising, nor, like Con Markiewicz, Pearse, and MacDonagh, a symbol of tragically wasted potential, MacBride has a significance for Yeats that is purely personal: he was Maud Gonne's estranged husband, the man who "had done most bitter wrong" to the woman Yeats adored. His transformation, in contrast to that of the other leaders mentioned, is one for the better; courage and suffering have given him a brief moment of nobility and grandeur: "He too has resigned his part / In the casual comedy; / He, too, has been changed in his turn, / Transformed utterly: / A terrible beauty is born." In this context, "terrible beauty" continues to have positive connotations for the poet. Although great gifts were sacrificed by the Countess Markiewicz, by Pearse and MacDonagh, their sacrifice is awe-inspiring: it is a sacrifice that can make even the despicable life of MacBride meaningful. In line 35, "Yet I number him in the song," the speaker displays his personal generosity: he can praise even the enemy when praise is deserved.

But the mood of sympathetic admiration is rapidly dissipated. With the imagery of stone and stream in the third stanza, attitudes that are only implicit in the first two stanzas in such references as "Until her voice grew shrill," come into the foreground:

Hearts with one purpose alone
Through summer and winter seem
Enchanted to a stone
To trouble the living stream.

It is sometimes argued that the "stone" here symbolizes the firmness of purpose and strength of mind of the patriots, a strength that "troubles" or rouses the average man from his daily round of blind, aimless living. But such a reading ignores the positive connotations of the "living stream." In the world of nature, "change"—the key word recurs here in a radically altered context—is a steady but gradual process; it is not the radical, abrupt, and overwhelming transformation ("All changed, changed utterly") of the patriots. In the natural world, birds, horses, clouds, and water are in perpetual free movement; there is constant sliding, plashing, and mating: "hens to moorcocks call." But the "Hearts with one purpose alone" of the 1916 leaders have been "enchanted to a stone"—a spell has been cast upon them by their total absorption in a Utopian vision until they become rigid, inflexible, petrified—ultimately beyond change. By the end of the stanza, "The stone's in the midst of all": the joy and spontaneity of natural life have been cramped by the stonelike hardness and rigidity of the rebels. Their inflexible purpose absorbs everything into a system. Here, then, Yeats as dramatized speaker dissociates himself from the political movement. The third stanza is the only one that ends without the refrain "A terrible beauty is born."

> *When the speaker declares in line 74, 'I write it out in verse,' the reader feels that he is actually looking over his shoulder; the poem seems utterly spontaneous, immediate."*

Readers often feel that the sudden introduction of stone and stream imagery in Stanza III is arbitrary and unmotivated: how does one jump from the concrete characterizations of Stanza II to the symbolic image of the third stanza? True, the symbols are marshalled rather abruptly, but the very abruptness is telling. The sharp break after line 40 suggests that the speaker has suddenly been struck by the thought that, contrary to Maud Gonne's view that "tragic dignity has returned to Ireland," he himself could never participate in or condone such a rebellion; it is repugnant to him. Instead of giving elaborate reasons for this outlook, Yeats simply presents the image of the stone troubling the stream as it *now* strikes the speaker. The poem, in other words, imitates the structure of the observer's experience; he "discovers his idea through a dialectical interchange with the external world" [according to Robert Langbaum in *The Poetry of Experience*].

This discovery is brought to a climax in the opening lines of Stanza iv:

Too long a sacrifice
Can make a stone of the heart.

It is easy to mistake this assertive statement for the theme of the poem; in fact, however, the speaker passes beyond it to his final perception or epiphany. His first step is to realize that disparagement of the rebels is no better than excessive admiration. Perhaps impartiality is the answer. It is, after all, "Heaven's part" to judge the rebels, while "our part," the poet bravely declares, is "To murmur name upon name, / As a mother names her child / When sleep at last has come / On limbs that had run wild." But the nightfall of the rebels is not that of the peacefully sleeping child. "No, no, not night but death," the speaker suddenly realizes, and with that thought he finds it impossible to remain aloof and impartial. The crucial question must finally be

asked: "Was it needless death after all? / For England may keep faith / For all that is done and said."

It is a question that history, quite apart from the poem, has never satisfactorily answered. Amy Stock observes [in *W.B. Yeats: His Poetry and Thought*] that "The men who made the rising did so with the clear expectation of defeat. They thought it useless to wait for the consent of England and died deliberately in the belief—justified by the event—that their death would commit the nation to fight on till freedom was won. Their courage could not be questioned: their judgement might, for it was conceivable that after the war the English might have consented to Home Rule. But the rising made that question unanswerable forever."

The ultimate significance of the Easter Rising is similarly ambiguous to the speaker of "Easter 1916." The perception toward which the poem moves is his understanding of its "terrible beauty." It is *beautiful* because of the sublimity of the tragic gesture of the patriots ("We know their dream; enough / To know they dreamed and are dead"), but is is also *terrible*—the word is now used in the sense of *awful* or *frightening*—because the gesture was, in the final analysis, not only misguided but futile: "And what if excess of love / Bewildered them till they died?" The speaker can now "write it out in verse" because he has come to terms with the paradoxical "terrible beauty" of the Rising. For the first time he names the patriots directly: "Mac-Donagh and MacBride / And Connolly and Pearse." It is not only these tragic figures who are "changed, changed utterly"; the speaker, too, has been "changed in his turn"; from initial puzzlement, he has passed through the extremes of admiration and condemnation to a moment of aloofness, immediately followed by a return to engagement, to an active participation tempered by a new awareness of the "terrible beauty" of human life. "The most impressive thing about the whole poem," writes [critic] Donald Davie, is that "the 1916 leaders are mourned most poignantly, and the sublimity of their gesture is celebrated most memorably, not when the poet is abasing himself before them, but when he implies that, all things considered, they were, not just in politic but in human terms, probably wrong."

In "Easter 1916," then, Yeats solves a problem which Arnold attempted but failed to solve in "Haworth Churchyard." Arnold wanted to assimilate the historical and documentary, to absorb the public event into the fabric of the romantic lyric. But the references to persons, places, and events are stated rather than dramatized; the poet himself is not *in* the poem. In "Easter 1916," on the other hand, the reader adopts the poet's extraordinary perspective and shares his experience, an experience that is not fully understood until the poem is over.

That understanding makes clearer why "Easter 1916" is, in Auden's words, a "reflective poem of at once personal and public interest." It avoids being "an official performance of impersonal virtuosity" in that it presents the Rising only in terms of its impact on a particular observer, the poet Yeats. The autobiographical convention dominates the poem; the persona is not the "prophet," the "spokesman for Irish culture," or any other such abstraction; it is the dramatized "I" of Yeats himself, reacting to an actual historical event involving his own friends and acquaintances. When the speaker declares in line 74, "I write it out in verse," the reader feels that he is actually looking over his shoulder; the poem seems utterly spontaneous, immediate. On the other hand, "Easter 1916" rises far above "trivial *vers de societé*" because its analysis of the particular historical event isolates those qualities that are typical of any major political upheaval: the splendor and terror that are the inseparable and inevitable consequences of change. The particular occasion is endowed with universal significance.

**Source:** Perloff, Marjorie, "Yeats and the Occasional Poem: 'Easter 1916,'" in *Papers on Language and Literature,* vol. 4, 1968, pp. 320–27.

## Sources

Adams, Hazard, *The Book of Yeats's Poems,* Tallahassee: Florida State University Press, 1990.

Ellmann, Richard, *The Identity of Yeats,* New York: Oxford University Press, 1964, p. 143.

Ellman, Richard, *Yeats: The Man and the Masks,* New York: Macmillan, 1948.

Paulin, Tom, introduction to *The Faber Book of Political Verse,* London: Faber, 1986, p. 21.

Pearse, Patrick, "The Coming Revolution" in *Political Writings,* Dublin, n.d., pp. 91, 98-99.

———, *Plays, Stories, Poems,* Dublin, 1924, p. 333.

———, *Political Writings,* pp. 25, 136-7.

Pierce, David, *Yeats's Worlds: Ireland, England and the Poetic Imagination,* New Haven: Yale University Press, 1995.

Ramazani, Jahan, *Yeats and the Poetry of Death,* New Haven: Yale University Press, 1990.

Stallworthy, Jonathan, *Between the Lines: Yeats's Poetry in the Making,* Oxford: Clarendon, 1963.

Stead, C. K., "On 'Easter 1916,'" in *Yeats: Poems, 1919-1935,* edited by Elizabeth Cullingford, London: Macmillan, 1984, p. 162.

Timm, Eitel, *W. B. Yeats: A Century of Criticism,* Columbia, SC: Camden House, 1987.

Ward, Allan, J., *The Easter Rising: Revolution and Irish Nationalism,* Arlington Heights, IL: AHM Publishing, 1995.

Yeats, W. B., *Autobiographies,* London, 1955, p. 195.

———, *The Collected Poems of W. B. Yeats,* second edition, edited by Richard Finneran, New York: Scribner, 1996.

———, *Essays and Introductions,* London, 1961, p. 241.

———, *Letters,* edited by Allan Wade, London, 1954, pp. 612-13.

## For Further Study

Allison, Jonathan, ed., *Yeats's Political Identities,* Ann Arbor: University of Michigan Press, 1996.
   This anthology consists of essays on Yeats's relationship to fascism, aristocracy, nationalism, and revolution.

Caulfield, Max, *The Easter Rebellion,* New York: Holt, Rinehart & Winston, 1963.
   Caulfield writes his history like a novel, one filled with lesser characters seldom heard from.

Cullingford, Elizabeth, *Yeats, Ireland and Fascism,* New York: New York University Press, 1981.
   Cullingford explores the more distasteful side of Yeats's sympathies, descending especially from his readings of Nietzsche.

Jones, Francis P., *History of the Sinn Fein Movement and the Irish Rebellion of 1916,* New York: P. J. Kenedy and Sons, 1921.
   This is a history of the Rising from a frankly anti-British viewpoint. Jones traces the Rising back to its roots in 1903 at the First National Council Convention.

Jordan, Carmel, *A Terrible Beauty: The Easter Rebellion and Yeats's Great Tapestry,* London: Associated Universities Press, 1987.
   Jordan's book explains how Druidic and Christian elements influenced Yeats's works related to the Easter Rising.

Loftus, Richard J., *Nationalism in Modern Anglo-Irish Poetry,* Madison: University of Wisconsin Press, 1964.
   Besides Yeats, Irish figures such as A. E., Pearse, MacDonagh, Plunkett, and Padraic Colum are discussed.

Ure, Peter, *Yeats and Anglo-Irish Literature,* Liverpool: Liverpool University Press, 1974.
   Ure discusses Yeats's life and influences as they relate to his work as poet and playwright.

# Facing It

## Yusef Komunyakaa
## 1988

Yusef Komunyakaa's poem "Facing It" describes a Vietnam War veteran's painful experience of visiting the Vietnam Veterans Memorial in Washington, D.C. From interviews and biographical details, we can assume the speaker of the poem is Komunyakaa himself. Komunyakaa served in Vietnam from 1965 to 1967, and his memories of those years haunt him when he visits the memorial, causing him to question his own identity as a black, Vietnam War veteran and the kind of survivor he has become.

Told in the first person, Komunyakaa's poem draws on the physical properties of the memorial sculpture itself to create a symbolic setting. He uses the capacity for the memorial's mirror-like surface to create ghostly reflections of all that surround it to underline his own incapacity to reach emotional resolution concerning his war experience. Ironically, the memorial is popularly referred to as "the wall" because it is shaped like a wall; however, its "nickname" also signifies the emotional dead end many survivors of the war come up against when visiting the site. Throughout the poem, the speaker does double takes, thinking he has seen one thing but then seeing something else. His perceptual "mistakes" are actually memories from the war that get in his way of experiencing present time and space. Though he pledges to himself to be hard as stone, the speaker is overcome by grief as he looks at the more than 58,000 names of soldiers who died in the war or are missing in action.

"Facing It" is included in Komunyakaa's 1988 collection, *Dien Cai Dau,* which tackles other difficult Vietnam-War subjects as well. Written one year after Komunyakaa first visited the memorial, "Facing It" was the second poem of the volume that the poet finished. In an interview with William Baer in *Kenyon Review,* Komunyakaa claimed that "Facing It" became the standard for the rest of the collection. "Tonally, I believe, it informed the other poems," he said. "I wanted to deal with images instead of outright statements. That's pretty much how I remember the war—imagery that we sort of internalized, that was informed by the whole vibrations of the body."

## Author Biography

Though a writer's work should never be reduced to (or explained as) the result of childhood circumstances, Yusef Komunyakaa's own upbringing provided him with more than enough emotional lighter fluid to get his poetic fire roaring. Born on April 29, 1947 in Bogalusa, Louisiana, a small paper–mill town 100 miles north of New Orleans, Komunyakaa was the oldest of six children. He owes his unusual last name to his grandfather, who emigrated to Louisiana from the island of Trinidad. Komunyakaa recounts the story of his grandfather's trip to America in his poem "Mismatched Shoes." Growing up as a black man in the American South in the 1950s meant that you learned about despair and hope in a very particular way, as segregation and racism formed the background of daily life.

Komunyakaa served in Vietnam from 1965 to 1967 as an information specialist and an editor for a military newspaper titled *The Southern Cross;* he also received a Bronze Medal for his tour of duty. Though opposed to the United States' participation in the war, Komunyakaa made the best of his circumstances. About that time, Komunyakaa has said, "The pressures of survival were so woven into who I was, into who we are as humans, that if placed against a war, one reacts to survive." His 1988 volume of poems, *Dien Cai Dau,* which includes the poem "Facing It," tackles the conflicting feelings that the poet had about taking part in the war. Literally translated, "Dien Cai Dau" is Vietnamese for "crazy," which was how locals referred to American soldiers fighting in the war. Komunyakaa began writing the poems in *Dien Cai Dau* in earnest more than fourteen years after his tour in Vietnam ended. He was remodeling his house in New Or-

leans, scraping the paint away on a hot, muggy day, when images and words began coming to him, quite unexpectedly. Komunyakaa partly attributes this sudden explosion of memory to the almost–tropical heat that day that reminded him of Vietnam. It is no coincidence, then, that the dialectic between memory and forgetting, past and present, informs so much of Komunyakaa's writing.

Komunyakaa published his first book, *Dedications and Other Dark Horses* in 1977, and he has maintained a steady output of books ever since. *Lost in the Bonewheel Factory* came out in 1979; *Copacetic* in 1984; *I Apologize for the Eyes in My Head,* which received the San Francisco Poetry Center Award in 1986; *Magic City* in 1992; and *Neon Vernacular: New and Selected Poems,* which received the Pulitzer Prize for 1994 and the $50,000 Kingsley Tufts. He has also coedited *The Jazz Poetry Anthology* (1991) with Sascha Feinstein and cotranslated *The Insomnia of Fire* by Nguyen Quang Thieu with Martha Collins. His poems have also been widely anthologized, appearing in W. D. Ehrhart's groundbreaking collection *Unaccustomed Mercy: Soldier-Poets of the Vietnam War,* among others.

Komunyakaa's working life as a poet has been fortunate. After taking an master's degree in creative writing from Colorado State University and then an master's of fine arts from the University of California at Irvine, Komunyakaa began his teaching career at the University of New Orleans, where he met and then married Mandy Sayer, an Australian fiction writer. He has since taught at a number of universities and colleges, including Indiana University (where he held the Lilly Professorship of Poetry), the University of California at Berkeley, and Washington University. He is currently on the creative writing faculty at Princeton University.

## Poem Text

My black face fades,
hiding inside the black granite.
I said I wouldn't,
dammit: No tears.
I'm stone. I'm flesh.                                          5
My clouded reflection eyes me
like a bird of prey, the profile of night
slanted against morning. I turn
this way—the stone lets me go.
I turn that way—I'm inside                                    10
the Vietnam Veterans Memorial
again, depending on the light
to make a difference.

I go down the 58,022 names,
half-expecting to find                              15
my own in letters like smoke.
I touch the name Andrew Johnson;
I see the booby trap's white flash.
Names shimmer on a woman's blouse
but when she walks away                             20
the names stay on the wall.
Brushstrokes flash, a red bird's
wings cutting across my stare.
The sky. A plane in the sky.
A white vet's image floats                          25
closer to me, then his pale eyes
look through mine. I'm a window.
He's lost his right arm
inside the stone. In the black mirror
a woman's trying to erase names:                    30
No, she's brushing a boy's hair.

## Poem Summary

### Lines 1-2:

In the first two lines of "Facing It," the narrator suggests that one of the poem's themes will be identity. He does this by making his "black face" the first image of the poem. The face is literally both the first thing we show to others and to ourselves. When it hides, as it does here, we know that the speaker has lost not only his self-image in the black granite, but his own sense of who he is. The speaker's reflection is a "doppelganger" or ghostly double of a living person. From this first line we can also infer that the speaker is an African American, like Komunyakaa himself.

### Lines 3-5:

We are introduced to the governing emotion of this poem: (barely) restrained grief and shock. The speaker is being literal and metaphoric when he says that he is both stone and flesh, as he is referring to both his body and its double as reflected in the granite. Being stone also suggests that he is hardening himself against the powerful emotions he feels.

### Lines 6-9:

The poet further develops the image of the split self, as the reflection now is given intention of its own, eyeing the speaker "like a bird of prey." This tells us that the double is an adversary of sorts for the speaker and someone we can expect will haunt the speaker further as the poem continues. The reflection is a "profile of night" because it is on the black granite; but this image also hints that it is a potentially dangerous self being reflected. The re-

flection appears and disappears depending on how the speaker moves in relation to the sun and the granite.

### Lines 10-13:

The speaker locates himself at the Vietnam Veterans Memorial. Originally designed as a student project in 1981 by Maya Ying Lin of Yale University, the memorial is located northeast of the Lincoln Memorial in Washington, D.C. The memorial is a long black granite wall, in the shape of the letter "v," on which the names of the American military dead and missing are inscribed. When the speaker says that he is "inside" the memorial, he means his reflection. But he also suggests that a deeper part of himself is enmeshed with the past that the monument represents. Again, he continues using light as a metaphor for the appearance and disappearance of his two selves.

### Lines 14-16:

The speaker refers to the memorial's list of 58,022 names of the American missing and dead. By "half-expecting" to find his own name among those listed, the speaker underscores just how alienated from himself he feels—how dead he feels. The letters are like smoke because smoke is itself a vague and transitory substance, which is what the speaker himself feels like.

### Lines 17-21:

The narrator experiences a flashback when he touches a name on the monument, reexperiencing the death of a comrade. We can now infer unequivocally that the speaker was a participant in the Vietnam War. Simultaneously, he sees the names on the memorial reflected on a woman's blouse. Such rapid shifts in perception underscore the narrator's dream-like state of mind. While he sinks deeper into the memories of his own painful experiences in the Vietnam War, he is also jarred out of those memories by what is happening in the present. This in-between state of mind and perception is reminiscent of surrealist verse and art, which attempted to show the dream-like quality of existence through its juxtaposition of seemingly disparate, unrelated elements.

### Lines 22-24:

The "brushstrokes" here refer to the narrator's experience of being jolted out of his reverie about the war. The red bird's wings (flying by) are like a brushstroke. That he is lost in his memories is emphasized by the fact that he is staring. Human beings frequently stare when they are daydreaming or obsessed with a particular memory, as they are focused on what is happening inside rather than outside of them. The speaker is now aware of the external world of the present tense, of the sky above him and the plane crossing that sky.

### Lines 25-31:

The narrator sees the reflection of a white veteran, or vet, in the memorial. The fact that the image "floats" and that the narrator refers to himself as a window reminds us of how fragile the speakers feels—how lost in time and how lost to his body he feels. That he represents the vet as seeing through his eyes suggests that the speaker sees himself as transparent, both literally (in his own reflection) and metaphorically (what he feels and what the two of them share is obvious in his expression and eyes). Describing the vet by his race ("white") allows Komunyakaa to underline his own similarity to (they are both survivors) and difference from (the speaker is African American) the man. The blackness and whiteness of appearances also ironically contrasts with the grayness of memory, and of war itself. Komunyakaa continues to play with ideas of appearance and reality when he says, in line 28, that the vet has lost his arm. He could mean that the veteran is literally an amputee. But, given that in the very next line we are told that the arm has been lost "inside the stone," the poet could also mean that the man turned a particular way and the light made his reflection appear as if he had lost an arm. The poet is more clear with the poem's last image when he sees one thing and then corrects himself, seeing something else. That the speaker's initial perception is of a woman attempting to erase the names from the monument highlights the speaker's enormous grief. If only the names weren't there, then the deaths they represent wouldn't have happened. In both cases and throughout the poem, the speaker's perceptions move between the past and the present, the desired and the real, from what he remembers to what is actually there in front of him.

When we finish reading the poem we can finally understand some of the varied meanings of its title. "Facing It" refers quite literally to the speaker looking at his face. However, "facing" something also means to confront it with awareness; and the word "facing" is, of course, a verb form of the noun "face," which refers to that part of ourselves most visible to others and what we visualize when we think of someone. The "it" is also richly ambiguous. "It" refers to the speaker's past

## Media Adaptations

- In association with BBC Television and Time Inc., Planet 24 Production produced a video on the Vietnam Veterans Memorial. Art critic Robert Hughes wrote and directed the documentary titled *The Republic of Virtue*

- In 1990 the Heritage America Group released the video documentary *All the Unsung Heroes: The Story of the Vietnam Veterans Memorial.*

and the tortured emotional legacy it has left him, but also to the Vietnam War itself and the memorial that represents it.

## Themes

### War and Peace

"Facing It" addresses one of the most powerful questions of Vietnam veterans: How do they incorporate their memories of the war into their lives without letting those memories destroy them? Throughout the poem, the speaker attempts to ward off the overwhelming emotions associated with visiting the memorial. He tells us he won't cry: "I said I wouldn't, / dammit: No tears." Soon after that declaration, he sees that the reflection of himself in the memorial is stalking him "like a bird of prey." Regardless of the defenses he puts up, however, the memories flood over him. As he literally loses (the reflection of) himself in the memorial's surface, he experiences a series of flashbacks and perceptual "mistakes." He remembers the explosion that killed one of his comrades; he thinks he sees a vet who's had his arm amputated; and he imagines a woman who is combing her son's hair is actually erasing the names on the memorial. Wherever he turns, he is met with the brute fact of his brutal memories. At one point toward the end of the poem, he says that "I'm a window," underscoring the fact that he has lost a deeper, more coherent, sense of self. Indeed the speaker's unrelenting memories and the grief that accompanies them have shouldered out any other sense of self. In attempting, futilely, to

# *Topics for Further Study*

- Maya Ying Lin, the architect who designed the Vietnam Veterans Memorial, said that the names on the memorial, though "seemingly infinite in number, [would] convey the sense of overwhelming numbers, while unifying these individuals into a whole." Think of an event or idea that involves a number of people that you would like to memorialize and describe a structure you would like seen built to serve that purpose.

- Research the effects of the Vietnam War on the war's veterans and write an essay arguing for whether or not you think the U.S. government has met its moral obligations toward those veterans

- Research the war memorials (for any war) and monuments in your own state or city and, comparing and contrasting them, write an argument for which one most effectively represents the veterans of that war.

ward off these memories, the speaker has, in essence, become a new incarnation of the war he initially thought he had escaped. Seeking peace or some sense of resolution by visiting the memorial has, ironically, resulted in the eruption of a new war—this one with himself. And as with the war in Vietnam, there are no clear winners. What the speaker experiences in confronting himself and his past at the memorial is what hundreds of thousands of Vietnam veterans have also, no doubt, experienced. This fact, though it is not a pleasant one, nevertheless provides at least acknowledgement of the hardships that so many vets have experienced and continue to experience as they try to find peace with the past.

### Death

Since the seventeenth century, an elegy has denoted a lament for the death of a particular person. Often that person would be a loved one, and the poem would be a form of consolation for those who remained. In Yusef Komunyakaa's poem "Facing It," however, the lament is as much for himself as it is for the Vietnam-War dead, with whom he quite literally identifies. The speaker mourns his own loss through representing himself as two people: the observing self, which attempts to ward off any emotional response to his memories, and the reflection in the Vietnam Veterans Memorial. These two selves "fight" each other during the poem, each trying to force its version of reality on the other. Using doppelgangers (a German word meaning "doubled self") to comment on the ways that stable human identity itself is a Western myth has become fairly common in both fiction and poetry. Edgar Allan Poe regularly made use of this motif—most popularly in his short story "William Wilson"—in the nineteenth century, and in the twentieth century, writers such as Jorge Luis Borges and Mark Strand have made their entire careers mining the literary possibilities of the idea. In his own use of the doppelganger, Komunyakaa demonstrates the ways in which certain parts of ourselves mourn the passing of other parts. Throughout the poem, his past self—represented in the memories that erupt whenever he looks at the memorial—insistently intrudes upon his present self, causing the speaker anguish and doubt and to question the physical world in front of him. When the speaker does manage to live in that world (for example, when he becomes aware of a plane flying overhead), he is just as quickly pulled out of it again by the image of a vet whom he thinks has lost his arm. Such relentless battling between his multiple selves causes the speaking self to surrender. Toward the end of the poem he states, "I'm a window," in essence creating yet another self, whose only duty is to witness the inability of his other selves to reach resolution. That the poem ends with yet another misperception and correction suggests that this battling will see no resolution.

### Style

"Facing It" is written in free verse, a form of poetry that does not use meter or rhyme in any conventional or prescribed way; rather, this poem relies on prose rhythms to give it momentum. A catalogue of "I do this" and "I do that" statements of description, "Facing It" asks the reader to see the same things as the speaker. The poem succeeds because the poet has succeeded in letting his images carry the emotional weight of his experience. We are shown, rather than told, what the speaker feels. That Komunyakaa imbues his images with so much resonance makes sense when we understand that two of his other passions are painting and photography.

Komunyakaa accomplishes his aim of showing us his feelings by using an extended metaphor throughout the poem. The speaker's changing capacity to see and not see what is literally in front of him represents his alternating ability to see and not to see what is inside of him: that is, his emotional response to his past, which the memorial symbolizes. Critic I. A. Richards's model of dividing the metaphor into its tenor and vehicle can help us grasp Komunyakaa's technique. The vehicle of the extended metaphor, which refers to the images used to signify meaning, is the speaker's acts of looking; the tenor of the metaphor, which refers to the actual subject of the comparison, is the speaker's acts of understanding the significance of what he sees. However, because we are not explicitly told what he does or does not understand, the tenor is implied. For example, the situational and verbal context of the speaker's first seeing a woman trying to erase the names of the Vietnam War dead, and then correcting himself and seeing the same woman brushing a boy's hair, serves as the vehicle for the implied tenor, which is the speaker's desire to erase or escape the memories of his past.

The kind of metaphoric imagery that Komunyakaa uses is often described as surrealist. Surrealist imagery attempts to evoke an otherworldly state of mind by embodying the logic of dreams. The speaker's experience of the hallucinatory world of war is reenacted in his experience at the memorial, as the past and the present meld into a new reality, a surreality.

## Historical Context

When "Facing It" appeared in *Dien Cai Dau* in 1988, the United States was still grappling with the meaning and the painful legacy of the Vietnam War. Though the Vietnam War had officially ended in 1975, Americans remained as divided over the war's significance as they were during the height of the conflict in the late 1960s. This division was no more apparent than in the controversies surrounding the United States' involvement in the Latin-American conflicts of the 1980s. Upon as-

suming office in 1981, President Ronald Reagan suspended economic aid to Nicaragua, arguing that democratically elected president Daniel Ortega aimed to establish a communist state allied with the Soviet Union; soon after this, Reagan authorized the CIA to support "contra" rebels who fought to overthrow the Ortega government. In 1986 Congress voted to give $100 million to these "freedom fighters" in economic and military aid. In 1983, under the pretext of rescuing more than 1,000 American medical students, the Reagan administration invaded the island of Grenada, whose president had just been murdered by Marxist dissidents. The Reagan administration also stepped up U.S. military assistance to El Salvador, which was in the midst of a bloody civil war pitting the right-wing military-led government against leftist insurgents. Government security agents and death squads targeting rebel groups helped account for the more than 30,000 El Salvadoran deaths between 1980 and 1983. The arguments that the Reagan administration voiced to justify its policies in Central America echoed the arguments the United States had used in support of its policies during the Vietnam War. Sensing that America was repeating the same mistake it made during the Vietnam War, many Vietnam veterans joined protestors demonstrating against increased U.S. involvement in Central America.

During the United States' involvement in Central America, in what many were beginning to term "another Vietnam," the Vietnam Veterans Memorial Fund started to work on a project to honor the men and women who died in that war. While money was being raised for the project, a competition for the memorial's design was held. Maya Ying Lin, a graduate student at Yale University won with a design that focused on the concept of names. She conceived of a structure that would be shaped like the letter "v" and have two walls; the east wall would point toward the Lincoln Memorial and the west wall would point toward the Washington Monument, thus drawing on the historical import of two of America's most prominent monuments. Reactions to the memorial were mixed when it was unveiled in 1982. Some felt that it was inherently conservative and sought to put to rest the memory of the war; others believed that it was unheroic and even impersonal. Some praised its simplicity and understatement. Daniel Abramson, a professor of art history and architecture at Connecticut College, thought the memorial nothing less than inspired genius. Abramson maintained, in a *Critical Inquiry* article, that Lin's use of a time line

# *Compare & Contrast*

- **1964:** As a response to the increased military clashes in the waters off the coast of Vietnam, the House and the Senate unanimously pass The Tonkin Gulf Resolution with only two dissenters. The resolution states that "Congress approves and supports the determination of the President as commander-in-chief to take all necessary measures to repel any attack against the forces of the United States and to prevent further aggression."

  **1965:** American troops begin full-scale offensives against the Vietcong, engaging in search and destroy missions.

  **1968:** By this date President Johnson has ordered approximately half a million troops to Vietnam.

  **1968:** The Vietcong launch their Tet Offensive, a coordinated attack targeting every major South-Vietnamese city. More than 4,000 Americans and 32,000 North Vietnamese are killed.

  **1969:** The United States changes its war strategy and begins to withdraw ground troops while escalating its air attacks.

  **1972:** The United States conducts the most intensive air attack in military history against the Vietcong.

  **1973:** Nixon announces a peace agreement that would provide for the withdrawal of 25,000 American troops in exchange for the repatriation of 587 American prisoners of war.

  **1982:** The Vietnam Veterans Memorial is built.

  **1982:** The first of a series of *Rambo* movies starring and produced by Sylvester Stallone is released. These movies fantasized daring rescue of soldiers missing in action in Hanoi. As showcases for Stallone's own testosterone-driven machismo, these movies deeply influenced young males, encouraging them to romanticize the war.

  **1986-87:** Vietnam War films such as *Platoon, Full Metal Jacket,* and *Hamburger Hill* are released. These movies explored the ethical dilemmas soldiers faced during the war and heightened public awareness of the emotional and moral conflicts many soldiers had to live with.

  **Today:** War movies continue to be a box-office draw, and two acclaimed films are *Saving Private Ryan* and *The Thin Red Line.* The setting for these pictures, however, is not Vietnam, but World War II.

---

"is altogether new in the history of monument design" and claimed that using chronological, rather than alphabetical, order in listing the dead and missing was brilliant because it symbolized closure of the Vietnam war without suggesting that we should ever forget it.

The 1980s also witnessed a flood of films about the Vietnam War and returning Vietnam veterans. Americans were both angry and guilty, and many remained confused as to how to treat veterans. Sylvester Stallone's series of *Rambo* films tended to romanticize the war, representing Vietnam vets as misunderstood and neglected heroes whose mission was incomplete until every last soldier was rescued or accounted for. Stallone's veteran-as-macho-hero has been duplicated in a number of other action adventure films, including Chuck Norris's popular *Missing in Action* series. Aiming for more realistic treatment of the Vietnam War, films such as *Birdy, Jackknife, Gardens of Stone, Distant Thunder,* and *Born on the Fourth of July* showed the ongoing emotional trauma vets suffered from and their painful attempts to put their lives right again. These films picked up themes initially introduced during the 1970s in movies such as *Coming Home* and *The Deer Hunter.*

## Critical Overview

"Facing It" is included in Komunyakaa's collection of poems titled *Dien Cai Dau*, which in Vietnamese means "crazy." Published in 1988, the book investigates the poet's experiences in the Vietnam War and his ongoing attempts to come to terms with his memories of the conflict. In her article "A Poet Who Danced with Death," Susan Baxter argued that the poems in *Dien Cai Dau*, "more than editorials, movies, or documentaries, make us understand the searing, personal pain that lies beneath the rage that came with the Vietnam War. Reading … [Komunyakaa's] work, we accept that physical survival was the order of the day during the war, and understand how serious a challenge it was to remain human afterward." Reviewing *Neon Vernacular: New and Selected Poems,* which includes a selection from *Dien Cai Dau,* Matthew Rothschild assessed, "For Yusef Komunyakaa, the experience that seared him into poetry was serving in Vietnam … Vietnam stalks Komunyakaa." Often this stalking takes the form of haunting memories, which Komunyakaa writes about in "Facing It."

The fact of death permeates *Dien Cai Dau.* In "We Never Know," the speaker discovers a corpse, whose hands clutch a photograph: "When I got to him, / a blue halo / of flies had already claimed him." Toi Derricotte has observantly pointed out that the poems in *Dien Cai Dau* "are held together by the excruciating tension between memory and forgetting…. This is a book about seeing and not seeing," Derricotte writes, "about not being there in order to be there. It presents the paradoxes of a psyche, of an art that is compelled to examine itself, and yet is determined to control reality in a way that makes it able to be endured." The relationship between sight and insight form the central theme of "Facing It," as the speaker struggles to understand his own responses to the past, just as that past intrudes upon what he sees in the present. Kirkland C. Jones claims that the comparative devices Komunyakaa uses in the poem allow him to "make order of a war that has no moral clarity." William Baer writes that "Facing It" "demonstrates that combination of sharp, telling images and dialectic complexity that uniquely marks … [Komunyakaa's] work," and R. S. Gwynn calls the poem "the most poignant elegy that has been written about the Vietnam War."

## Criticism

### Sharon Kraus

*Sharon Kraus is a poet who teaches creative writing, literature, and poetry at Queens College, CUNY. In the following essay, Kraus analyzes "Facing It," praising the effectiveness of the poet's juxtaposition of disparate images in the work.*

Yusef Komunyakaa's poem "Facing It" is the concluding poem of his 1988 book *Dien Cai Dau* (which means both "crazy" and "American soldier" in Vietnamese), a book of poems that deals with Komunyakaa's experience as a black soldier during the Vietnam War. In its dizzying sequence of images that juxtapose violence and beauty, the poem gives us Komunyakaa's central themes: the brutal experience of war, the potential of race-based discrimination to fracture human relationships among Vietnam soldiers and in daily life, and the jarring contrast between external identity and interior emotional life. What makes the poem powerful, though, is not merely the range and importance of these themes, but the poem's emotional use of imagery and its focus on one black soldier who is reporting to us his personal experience.

In fact, that focus gives the poem an apparently simple structure. The speaker of the poem relates to us what he sees while looking at the Vietnam Veterans Memorial Wall. It is important to remember that, throughout the poem, the speaker is looking only at people and things reflected in the monument's glossy surface, not at the actual people and things. The minimalist monument, designed by Maya Lin when she was a twenty-one-year-old architecture student, sparked a great deal of controversy when it was chosen, because, unlike traditional monuments, it has no sculptured representations of soldiers in a battle posture. The Vietnam Veterans Memorial, unveiled in 1982, is extraordinarily unadorned: a V-shaped, 500-foot-long black granite wall, on which is carved the names of soldiers who died or were missing in action. We see through the speaker's eyes that the black surface is so glossy that it functions as a smoke-colored mirror. To look at the inscribed names, one must also look at oneself. Part of the monument's message, therefore, like the poem's message, is that the viewer is "literally" among the fallen; it compels even the civilian viewer to regard him- or herself as part of the war.

Just as the Wall compels viewers to see themselves as they look at it—to perceive the Wall as a dynamic rather than static symbol—the poem also

## What Do I Read Next?

- Norman Poderhetz's *Why We Were in Vietnam* provides a conservative's explanation of the reasons the United States became involved in the Vietnam conflict.

- The Vietnam War was the basis for many protests and demonstrations in the late 1960s. Alexander Kendrick's study *The Wound Within: America in the Vietnam Years, 1945-1974* examines the relationship between the war and the unrest at home.

- Probably the best anthology of poetry about the Vietnam War, W. D. Ehrhart's *Carrying the Darkness: American Indochina: The Poetry of the Vietnam War* includes poems written by sol-

diers, conscientious objectors, draft dodgers, flag burners, and relatives of the men and women involved in the war.

- Todd Gitlin's *The Sixties: Years of Hope, Days of Rage* provides an unapologetically leftist view of the events of that turbulent decade and how they related to the Vietnam War.

- Alan Oskvarek's search engine (www.goodnet .com/thewall/) lets you search the Vietnam Veteran's Memorial by name, hometown, and branch of service. When a name is returned, it tells you at which panel and line the person's name can be found, along with the birthdate, length of service and how the individual died.

---

compels us to do more than read. We must, in fact, watch the poem unfold as though it were a movie. We see the cinematic images through the speaker's eyes. The poem delivers a jolt in its opening lines, the way a suspense movie might open with a close-up: "My black face fades, / hiding inside the black granite." Then, slowly, the poem pans away so that the viewer can gain perspective: The speaker sees his own face and his own blackness, but, with a trick of the eyes, these disconcertingly fade, as though his very identity were mutable and could melt into the polished granite. Moreover, we don't yet know what that granite is: at this point, it could be the granite of a tombstone. We are not told until after that initial image, in line 11, to be exact, that this is the granite of the Vietnam Veterans Memorial. The jolt of seeing one's own face, and then seeing it disappear, has the effect of locating the speaker in his identity as a black man and as a mortal being, and it simultaneously remarks how impossible it would be for a person to lose those identities.

"[W]e cannot crawl out of our skin," Komunyakaa has said in an interview with scholar Muna Asali, "even when we try to lie to ourselves or say that race doesn't matter, that art and artists are color-blind…. And I couldn't escape the prison of my skin, which has also been the source of my

strength." For this poet, identity is about an individual's constellation of experiences in the personal and social worlds. For example, most of the poems in *Dien Cai Dau* deal with the speaker's relationship, as a black soldier serving in Vietnam, with white soldiers and Vietnamese civilians. "Facing It" faces not only the experience of war, which is now in the speaker's past, but also faces the speaker's continuing relationship with white men, as is shown in the poem's penultimate image. As we shall see, the image is ambiguous and indicates the problematic and complex quality of that relationship.

As a whole, the poem's organization mirrors in miniature the book's organization: in short order, we meet the speaker in his public identity ("my black face fades") and then more intimately, as a feeling human being ("dammit: No tears."); we move through a series of disorienting images depicting violence and beauty side by side; we see the speaker encountering a "white vet" who may or may not rightly perceive the speaker in his full ("flesh[ly]") humanity; and we are given a single image of nurture and care that the poem seems to offer as the underlying reason for life.

Most important, though, is that the speaker perceives and misperceives that series of images. Komunyakaa's poem captures the confusion and longing that comprise so much of this speaker's experience of life: "I turn / this way—the stone lets me go. / I turn that way—I'm inside / the Vietnam Veterans Memorial / again." It is important to notice the skillful, elegant line breaks in the poem. Here, they work cumulatively, and each line stands as a single entity, yet gains information and emotionality from the next. For example, the line "I turn that way—I'm inside" depicts the speaker as moving from the outside world to the inside that is the stone of line 2, namely the unspecified black granite that might well be a tombstone. It is not until we proceed to the next line that we find the stone's identity narrowed, or localized in the historical and social moment that was the Vietnam War.

Just as each line has its own integrity, so too does the poem. It does not rely on the rest of the book, which preceded it, to supply its subject, which is, in part, the speaker's relationship to the war. The lines "I go down the 58,022 names, / half-expecting to find / my own" let us know that the speaker also fought in this war and feels somewhat surprised—astonished, with its etymological root of "stone"—to find himself still alive. The "half-expecting" is ironic in multiple ways, playing as it does on the absolutely precise numerical quantity in the line above it, and in its recognition that the speaker, against all odds, has survived the war, when so many of his fellow white and black soldiers died there. The ironic tone is transient, though. Once the speaker has that recognition of his own survival, his attention necessarily snaps back to the terrible fact of mortality: "I see the booby trap's white flash." The poem does not specify whether the speaker knew Andrew Johnson or is surmising that dead soldier's fate; perhaps the ambiguity indicates that such knowledge is, now, immaterial. The speaker knows how easily Andrew Johnson's fate might have been his own—he himself might have stumbled onto that booby trap and been killed in a "white flash" of "smoke." The poem links the two men's fate at the same time that it comments on the startling relief linked with finding oneself alive.

That feeling of relief informs the next image. "The names," which are like and unlike the speaker's own, "shimmer on a woman's blouse." In the midst of a vivid flashback of the war's horrific violence (the murderous "white flash"), the poem gives us a startling, weirdly beautiful image: the names shimmer on the blouse, much like the reflections of dragonflies would shimmer on a still pool of water. The image subtly depends on our re-

> *The poem delivers a jolt in its opening lines, the way a suspense movie might open with a close-up ...."*

alizing that the blouse is itself shimmering, reflected, in the glossy Wall. The poem watches the world through the Wall and thereby sees the world in its historical accuracy; if the poem looked at the world directly it would not gain such insightful "misperceptions."

The "but" of the subsequent line ("but when she walks away / the names stay") mitigates the prior image of beauty, however, as it points out that its very beauty is contingent on a misperception. The woman's departure indeed signals that such beauty is a misperception, relying as it does on a confusion of the outside world with the reflected one, "real life" with symbolic life, past with present. It turns out, the poem cautions us, that such distinctions are not to be ignored. As the speaker's gaze remains fixed on the Wall, the outside world intermittently reflected in it becomes jarring: "Brushstrokes flash," the speaker reports, the "flash" echoing that violent white flash of four lines ago. The speaker is only subsequently able to identify the flash as coming from the outside world: "a red bird's / wings cutting across my stare." That the reflected image of mere feathers is said to be "cutting" suggests how violent present-day experience feels to this veteran of both war and race conflict. As the speaker continues narrating what he sees of the outside world reflected in the Wall ("The sky. A plane in the sky."), he catches sight of a white vet whose face is also reflected there; the speaker's perception of this image, as mentioned above, is ambiguous. Perhaps the poem's greatest skillfulness is its ability to put us in the speaker's position here. We too must attempt to understand this image. Is the white vet feeling himself to be a witness at the Wall, as the speaker is? Does the white vet notice the speaker, or the reflected speaker, and feel confusion? Does the white vet see the speaker as someone with whom he has some shared history? In other words, does the white vet recognize the speaker to be a black vet and an equal? When the speaker reports that the white vet's eyes "look through" the speaker, as though he were a window, we must wonder, as must the speaker, why: has the white vet recognized the speaker as a fellow vet or, even if not, has he learned, as writer Kevin Stein suggests, to look through another person's eyes, in empathy? Alternatively, has the vet even registered the speaker's existence? Is the speaker, a black man, in fact invisible in a white world? Or has the white vet looked away from the speaker, and if so, is that due to discomfort, hostility, or distraction?

These questions are raised, as they must be for the speaker, and not resolved. Instead, the speaker recognizes that the white vet may have been irremediably damaged: "He's lost his right arm / inside the stone," an image of the war's capacity to maim, physically or spiritually. The poem looks elsewhere, with that knowledge, and offers us a final, generous image, of compassion and nurture. Significantly, the speaker initially misperceives this image to be of a woman "trying to erase names"—a gesture of grieving beyond rationality. The most subtle rhetorical touch, "No," allows us to take the closing line as a resolution to that misperception. "She's brushing a boy's hair" points to the next generation, with a hopefulness that the boy will be cared for, rather than damaged.

The poem's strategies, of reporting perceptions in a vivid, unmediated way, and of juxtaposition ("I'm stone. I'm flesh."; "letters like smoke … the booby trap's white flash"; "Brushstrokes flash, a red bird's / wings") point out to us, as critic Vicente Gotera has noticed, that meaning depends on point of view, and that the speaker's experience of "depending on the light" to see the Wall's full significance is our experience, too. In fact, the poem tells us, the significance is a life-or-death one: the speaker could, after all, find himself to be inside the stone—nightmarishly, inside the past that is the war. The outside world is also jarring in its own right: in this world, birds' wings may cut, and another visitor to the Wall may or may not recognize you as a fellow soldier or fellow human being—perhaps because of that other juxtaposition which is race. The poem's ultimate strength is its mastery at depicting the disrupting, surreal, indeed absurd quality of such juxtapositions. Distinctions such as black/caucasian are shown to be strange and possibly frightening, inescapable, and dependent on individual point of view. The human's ability to perceive is constrained and flawed, the poem teaches us, and it is all we have.

**Source:** Sharon Kraus, in an essay for *Poetry for Students,* Gale, 1999.

### Jeannine Johnson

*Jeannine Johnson received her Ph.D. from Yale University and is currently a visiting assistant professor of English at Wake Forest University. In the following essay, Johnson discusses how Komunyakaa, in order to better understand the relationships between art and history, examines the Vietnam Veterans Memorial as a kind of poem.*

Yusef Komunyakaa served as a reporter and editor for a military newspaper during the Vietnam War, and his experiences there have proved a fruitful, if painful, source for poetic material. Writing for the armed forces publication *The Southern Cross* from 1969 to 1970, Komunyakaa chronicled the activities of American soldiers both on and off the battlefield. In "Facing It," he creates another record of the war. In his poem Komunyakaa, a recipient of the Bronze Star, recalls viewing the Vietnam Veterans Memorial in Washington, D.C., and the many conflicting sensations he feels in its presence. This time removed temporally and geographically from Vietnam, Komunyakaa explores possible methods of representing and memorializing the war: in particular, he deals with the conflicts between private and public expressions of mourning and memory. Throughout "Facing It," the poet's identity fuses with the wall and the wall unites with its visitors, a circumstance that for Komunyakaa is at once disturbing and comforting.

The poem dramatizes the ways that art is both a necessary and an inadequate medium through which to disclose the history of war. In the opening lines, Komunyakaa announces, "My black face fades, / hiding inside the black granite." Immediately, the poet demonstrates his personal investment in both his poem and in the other artwork, Maya Lin's granite war memorial. He is pulled into the wall—"I'm stone"—but in the following instant disengages himself from it, reassured that "I'm flesh." The poet's identity becomes uncertain in the presence of the wall. Its polished stone surface acts as a mirror, reflecting the images of those who look at it. This feature establishes a sense of intimacy between the viewer and the art, but it also reinforces a sense of alienation. For Komunyakaa, this alienation is compounded by his race: the repetition of the word "black" in the poem's first two lines subtly underscores the fact that his experiences in Vietnam differed from those of white soldiers. In any case, the poet informs us that his reflection is not clear and illuminating but "clouded" and, furthermore, that it "eyes me / like a bird of prey." His reflection seems to have an existence separate from his own, and its intentions appear quite menacing. The bird of prey symbolizes his memory (and its attendant grief), and its autonomy suggests that Komunyakaa exercises little control over it.

Despite his uneasiness, the poet is not entirely estranged from the wall. He is intrigued as he moves around it, altering his view and manipulating his reflection: "I turn / this way—the stone lets me go. / I turn that way—-I'm inside / ... depending upon the light / to make a difference." Komunyakaa sports with his mirror-image, and in the poem he performs a parallel verbal action by playing with various meanings of "reflection." He is literally describing the visual phenomenon of seeing one's image in a two-dimensional surface, but the poet also invests other meanings of reflection. He invokes the idea of reflection as a thought process, such as contemplation, meditation, or recollection. Komunyakaa reflects on the past and on its present-day significance. However, these kinds of reflections, too, are clouded: the poet's memories of Vietnam are still keen, but his relationship to them are conflicted—complicated by the time that has passed and by his own imperfect powers of recall. Moreover, Komunyakaa is well aware that his experiences are in no way the sum total of the experiences of all Americans—or even of all African Americans—in Vietnam. Likewise, his poem and the wall reflect a part of history, but these reproductions of the past are necessarily incomplete. Neither the poet nor art can ever fully recover or replace what has been lost.

In the next lines, Komunyakaa makes more clear the connection between the wall and poetry: "I go down the 58,002 names, / half-expecting to find / my own in letters like smoke." Etched into the Vietnam Veterans Memorial are the names of the war's dead and missing. The inscriptions comprise more than a simple catalogue of casualties: for many visitors, the act of touching the wall or copying a reverse image of a name on a piece of paper constitutes an important part of their encounter with the monument. Nevertheless, language—whether it be in the poem or on the wall—provides only a tenuous connection between art and people: "Names shimmer on a woman's blouse / but when she walks away / the names stay on the wall." Komunyakaa affirms the power of art to honor sorrow and memorialize sacrifice, and yet

> *The poem dramatizes the ways that art is both a necessary and an inadequate medium through which to disclose the history of war."*

that very promise of permanence or comprehensiveness is undermined when we inevitably turn our attentions elsewhere.

Even when we do attend to the public reminders of history, we must confront their (and our own) imperfections. The figure of incompleteness appears literally in the form of a white veteran who has "lost his right arm / inside the stone." Komunyakaa's vivid and compelling phrase makes the obvious remarkable, as it informs us that the vet's missing arm is not reflected by the wall. The granite will release neither the man's arm nor his arm's reflection, as both are trapped within the space and time that the wall commemorates. This physical, individual injury goes unreflected, symbolizing the limits of representative art. Yet art proves serviceable to society, at least as a lens through which people can view the lives of others and review their own lives. The veteran's reflection intermingles with the poet's, and in the process, the poet becomes a "window" through which the vet looks. This incident unsettles the poet, but it affirms their common bond. It also helps prepare the poet to illustrate the importance of the human imagination and to testify that art's value exceeds its public serviceability.

Like many of Komunyakaa's poems, "Facing It" concludes with a surprising turn. In a 1994 interview, he confirms the value of the unexpected in poetry: "If I don't have surprises, poetry doesn't work for me. What gives my poetry its surprising element is that I have not systematically planned out in a directed way what I am going to say. It is a process of getting back to the unconscious." In "Facing It," Komunyakaa purposefully retreats to the world of the unconscious and surprises us with the abrupt shift in perspective from that of the poet to that of another mourner. The poem ends as he looks away from his own dim reflection in the wall to watch another visitor: "In the black mirror / a woman's trying to erase names: / No, she's brushing a boy's hair." The poet describes the woman's actions in two ways: first from his own conceptual viewpoint and then from hers. His initial description involves a verbal metaphor, comparing the woman's gesture to blotting out letters, something a poet might do. But then Komunyakaa corrects himself, reprimanding his imagination with a simple "No," and in so doing, he transports us into the mind of this woman. Now writing from her perspective, the poet correlates her action with a maternal caress that has little, if anything, to do with artistic production. This woman is not cognizant of her visible movements, nor does she consciously reflect on their meaning. In this way, she stands in stark contrast to the poet who has shown himself to be all too aware of his surroundings. The woman offers an alternative way to confront the past, a way to achieve consolation—and perhaps even temporary compensation—for the sorrows of history.

"Facing It" is the last piece in *Dien Cai Dau,* a collection of poems mostly about Vietnam. This book was published in 1988, nearly twenty years after Komunyakaa's return from the war. "Dien cai dau" means "crazy" in Vietnamese and was very often used by the Vietnamese people to describe American soldiers. Komunyakaa's use of this phrase for the title of his book is in part accusatory, implying that American military efforts in Vietnam were unwise, misguided, or even corrupt. His title also suggests that there is something intellectually and emotionally disconcerting about using poetry to recuperate memories of the war. But ultimately Komunyakaa does not believe it is crazy to use art to understand the Vietnam conflict; instead, he would likely think it crazy for a poet to willfully ignore the past. In fact, Komunyakaa has said that it was not until after he had returned from the war and written "Instructions for Building Straw Huts"—another Vietnam poem—that he felt sure of his poetic calling. Paradoxically, with this external vocational certainty came a need to permit particular instabilities to reside within his poetry. Komunyakaa shows that in composing his poem about the Vietnam Veterans Memorial, his own identity and imagination are composed and discomposed by the wall. But this mutual interdependence between the public world and the private, between history and art, is compulsory and ultimately beneficial to the poet.

**Source:** Jeannine Johnson, in an essay for *Poetry for Students,* Gale, 1999.

## Chris Semansky

*A widely published poet and fiction writer, Chris Semansky teaches literature at Portland Community College in Portland, Oregon. In the following essay, Semansky comments on the role of memory in self-identification in the poem "Facing It" and in the larger category of confessional poetry.*

Philosophers, anthropologists, and cognitive psychologists have long maintained that two of the defining features of human beings are language and memory. Through using language to represent our past (both to ourselves and to others), we are building a coherent identity—a sense of who we are in relation to who we've been. In "Facing It," his poem about a Vietnam veteran's traumatic visit to the Vietnam Veterans Memorial, Yusef Komunyakaa draws attention to how this inescapable relationship between memory and language acts to construct a self-image. When the speaker of the poem attempts to ward off undesired memories, or at least the potential emotional impact those memories might have, he denies a part of himself. This denial results in the splitting of his identity.

> My black face fades,
> hiding inside the black granite.
> I said I wouldn't,
> dammit: No tears.
> I'm stone, I'm flesh.
> My clouded reflection eyes me
> like a bird of prey, the profile of night
> slanted against the morning …

The speaker's dilemma is knowing with which self to side—knowing, literally, to whom he should turn. On the one hand, he wants to remain "stone" against the potential effects of such memories. Yet that very self that he desires becomes represented in his reflection in the black granite as a "bird of prey," turning what he wants against himself. The stone that the speaker wants to be metaphorically (e.g., hardened against memories of the past) when realized literally (e.g., in his reflection in the granite) becomes an enemy whose job it is to destroy the very self who desired it into existence. By describing this now-adversarial reflection as "the profile of night" and his embodied observing self as "morning," the speaker details both how the Memorial physically reflects his image and what his future stance will be in relation to these memories and this self that he could no longer bear. By detailing the ways in which the speaker deceives himself, these opening lines set the tone for the rest of the poem.

This poem about memory and language reminds us of the connection between the sensuous world of things and the power those things have to evoke powerful feelings in us. As might be expected for a poem about seeing, all of the imagery in the poem is related to sight. Just as our feelings are able to fool us so often, so too can the physical world of appearances. The perceptual mistakes that the narrator makes in the poem—seeing things not as they are but as they are affected by his memories and emotional state of mind—are echoed by the narrator's own emotional mistake of thinking that he could remain a "stone" against the onslaught of memories and emotion when at the Memorial.

Perhaps the most telling illustration of the ways that emotions can cloud both memories and sight happens when the speaker is reading the names of the war dead.

> I go down the 58,022 names,
> half-expecting to find
> my own in letters like smoke.
> I touch the name Andrew Johnson;
> I see the booby trap's white flash.

The speaker is so overwhelmed by grief and loss and so alienated from himself that he cannot think rationally. Not only does he expect to see his own name listed among the dead "in letters like smoke," but his flashback of the death of a fellow soldier allows him to vicariously experience his own demise. Johnson was a member of the army infantry from Komunyakaa's hometown of Bogalusa, Louisiana, and was killed in action in Vietnam in 1967. The "booby trap's white flash" that the speaker sees after touching Johnson's name is both a literal memory of a past experience and a metaphor of sorts for the way that that very memory is a "booby trap" for his own life in the present.

Mistakes are not only in the eyes of the beholder of the Vietnam Veterans Memorial, but a part of the Memorial itself. Out of the more than 58,000 names of the Vietnam War dead listed on the Vietnam Veterans Memorial, twenty-five do not belong; they are still among the living. G. Burkett, whose book *Valor* details this fact, says that these living veterans form the wall's "honor guard." When he found out his name was listed among the dead, war veteran Robert Lee Bedker said, "We were so close to being one of the actual victims. It really makes you feel humble."

Survivor's guilt is a common response by veterans who have lived through a war or other catastrophe, and the speaker of "Facing It" illustrates

> *Ultimately, the poet's ability to translate the terror of his wartime experiences into an aesthetic object speaks to the potentially therapeutic function of poetry ...."*

this response in his repeated, though unsuccessful, attempts to stave off the past. Dr. Matthew J. Friedman, a professor of psychiatry at Dartmouth Medical School, says that this guilt is often symptomatic of Post-traumatic Stress Disorder (PTSD), which many war veterans experience. Friedman notes that intrusive recollections often accompany PTSD. "For individuals with PTSD, the traumatic event remains, sometimes for decades or a lifetime, a dominating psychological experience that retains its power to evoke panic, terror, dread, grief, or despair as manifested in daytime fantasies, traumatic nightmares, and psychotic reenactments known as PTSD flashbacks," Friedman says. "Furthermore, traumamimetic stimuli that trigger recollections of the original event have the power to evoke mental images, emotional responses, and psychological reactions associated with the trauma." Though we don't know if Komunyakaa suffered from Post-traumatic Stress Disorder, the responses of the poem's speaker while at the Memorial certainly suggest the possibility.

But because this poem itself is told about an experience the speaker had about other experiences, and because it is told in a coherent well-organized manner, we can assume that the speaker has survived and that his awareness of his own capacity to fool himself is, at least by the end of the poem, well developed. He is battered and emotionally scarred, but he has managed to find a place for those memories—even if just in a poem. Ultimately, the poet's ability to translate the terror of his wartime experiences into an aesthetic object speaks to the potentially therapeutic function of poetry, a role that critics often scorn. Such critics like to separate art from the messiness and drama of human life, even if that very same art remains inextricably entwined with that messiness. They object to confessional poetry because of what they believe to be its inherent "artlessness," that somehow the unadorned utterances of the human heart do not qualify as poetry because they are not sufficiently "aestheticized."

Contemporary confessional poetry itself grew out of psychoanalysis, with Robert Lowell, Allen Ginsberg, Anne Sexton, Sylvia Plath and others—from the 1950s on—using verse as a tool with which to explore their own traumatized lives. Poetry became the means through which to understand experiences deeply locked in memory. For better or worse (and there's plenty of very good and very bad confessional writing), this mode of writing has come to dominate American poetry in the last four or five decades, and Komunyakaa's work represents some of the very best being written today. This is because so many of his poems, including gems such as "Facing It," don't dwell merely on moments of private grief or confusion, the daily surrenders that each of us make every day of our lives (but don't feel compelled to write about); rather, they explore the ways in which public events become the stuff of our private lives. They show how awareness of social history is indispensable for achieving awareness of our present selves.

**Source:** Chris Semansky, in an essay for *Poetry for Students,* Gale, 1999.

### Don Ringnalda

*In the following excerpt, Ringnalda discusses the Vietnam Veteran's Memorial, the centerpiece of Komunyakaa's "Facing It."*

A familiar sight at the Vietnam Veterans Memorial (VVM) in Washington, D.C., is people tracing onto a piece of paper the name of a relative or friend who was killed in Vietnam. Anyone who has visited the memorial has observed this practice. On one hand, this gesture is sadly poignant; likely it's even cathartic. On the other hand, it also seems symptomatic of the perceptions many Americans hold of the Vietnam War, whether in the 1960s or the 1990s: when we have the name of something, we somehow also possess the thing named. Even though there is obviously an enormous semiotic gap between that symbol, etched in stone, and its object, long gone, the symbol nevertheless acquires a powerful ontological status. A traced symbol of a symbol on a symbol becomes reality. Whenever I witness this scene, I can't help asking myself, "just what kind of legacy is this reification of a purely human construction?"

It is difficult to know the thoughts of those people doing the tracing, and coldhearted to denigrate their actions.... [I]t needs to be stated at the outset that these actions, at the very least, seem to run counter to the design and spirit of Maya Lin's troubling and humbling black wall, one of the greatest postmodern "texts" to come out of the war. Because the VVM "begins" and "ends" on dates in 1968—the middle of the war—when the killing and destruction reached the most intense level, the memorial offers viewers who pay attention no entrance or exit. The "circularity" of the wall precludes closure as well as any pretense of "kicking the Vietnam syndrome." Therefore, any catharsis derived from the experience will at best be ambivalent, convoluted, and hard-earned. More likely, however, it will be misappropriated through denial or ignorance of the wall's treatment of space and time....

... Lin's memorial courageously, brilliantly, and literally gathers, faces, and makes new use of more than 58,000 unpleasant facts. The problem Lin had to face is the same one faced by any memorialist of any war: how to commemorate the war without conferring dignity on it, how to elicit thought, rather than goose bumps and sentimental tears....

What makes the VVM a great piece of art, though, is not just what it precludes (or tries to), but the ways in which it provokes the visitor to attain Perry's third stage of interrogative affirmation. The iconography of the memorial is well known to almost everyone; so I will reiterate and interpret only those aspects of its design that are pertinent.... I've already mentioned that the memorial both "begins" and "ends" in 1968, during the heart of the war. This lack of closure makes the interaction of viewer and monument a dynamic event—almost a mobile experience. When we try to make an end to our visit, we are pulled back into the war's insane middle. Further, as we approach the vortex of the two wings, we are whiplashed either forward or backward sixteen years, always moving in a 1959–75 / 1975–59 interface. Regardless of the direction we choose to move in, the flashbacks and flashforwards force us into a much more complex relationship with time and history than our future-oriented, narrative-obsessed sensibilities are used to.

But more needs to be said about the "beginning," "middle," and "end" of this memorial. It is peculiar not only that the beginning and end of our walk represent the middle of the war, but that those representations are at first so small—just inches high. Yet, at the vortex of 1959–75, two seemingly unimportant dates, because almost no killing was taking place, the Wall reaches its greatest height—ten feet. One explanation for this, if I may return to Severo and Milford, is that Lin's "text" is "parenthetical." Like *The Wages of War,* the VVM turns parenthetical material into main clauses. In a sense, 1959 and 1975 *are* the Wall's two most important dates: in 1959 almost no one had started to pay any attention to the dangerously myopic, solipsistic thinking of U.S. military and political leaders; in 1975, heavily into denial, almost everyone stopped paying attention. Drawing our attention to these two dates, the VVM, as Charles L. Griswold reminds us [in 1986 article in *Critical Inquiry*], is a "monument" in the true sense of the word, derived as it is from the Latin *monere,* meaning "to admonish," "warn," "advise," "instruct."

There are other ways in which the VVM is "parenthetical," thereby warning us to pay attention to details. First, its very location seems "bracketed" by the landscape. If one were to approach it from the north, one would almost literally have to fall into it to see it. Even from the standard approach routes, it is so inconspicuous that one can nearly miss it. People often do. By contrast, the Washington Memorial is visible from many miles away. Does this mean the VVM lacks power? Yes and no. When asked by Elizabeth Hess [who wrote "Vietnam: Memorials of Misfortune"] if the memorial has a female sensibility, Lin answered: "In a world of phallic memorials that rise upward, it certainly does. I didn't set out to conquer the earth, or overpower it, the way Western man usually does. I don't think I've made a passive piece, but neither is it a memorial to the idea of war."

Actually, the memorial is anything but passive and powerless. Grant F. Scott comments [in a 1990 *Journal of American Culture* article]: "Whereas the other monuments are eerily self-sufficient, boasting forms that are clearly closed, the VVM necessitates our existence and our gaze for the completion of its aesthetic. Its form is wonderfully open and unfinished." Scott also refers to the monument's "choreography" and to the fact that it "makes us work." Again, we see that sense of the granite's "mobility." This is due in part, as we've seen, to the Wall's nonlinearity and lack of temporal closure. As many people have noted, it also is due to Lin's decision not to arrange the names alphabetically, but instead, according to the date of death. This requires the visitor to search, ask for

> *Because the VVM "begins" and "ends" on dates in 1968—the middle of the war—when the killing and destruction reached the most intense level, the memorial offers viewers who pay attention no entrance or exit.... Therefore, any catharsis derived from the experience will at best be ambivalent, convoluted, and hard-earned."*

help, even get up on a ladder to find a name. Like a postmodern novel, Lin's text doesn't offer a completed plot to entertain the passive reader. Its power thereby resides in what it engenders, not in what it is.

The power also resides in the scope of what it embraces. Its polished black granite reflects its surroundings—visitors, grass, trees, water, clouds, airplanes taking off overhead, and both the Washington and Lincoln memorials. In other words, it integrates the visitor in a complex mobile collage in which the viewer watches himself look as others watch him look at names of the dead, which are conjoined by the landscape and a compression of history stretching from the Revolutionary War to the Civil War to the Vietnam War. In this sense, the VVM is a metamemorial, a metafictional reflexive text compelling us to check out Doc Peret's wires and circuits and filters.

I should add that the Wall is *self*-reflexive as well, particularly at night. It watches itself. Standing at the vortex, one notices that the two wings not only reflect each other but that the footlights along each wing place one in the middle of a lighted runway, an eerie corridor that seems both to rise and descend to those two troubling dates when America didn't pay and stopped paying—stopped paying and didn't pay—attention. The effect is overwhelming. Still standing at the vortex, the viewer's metamemorial experience is further enriched by a slight movement of the head to the left or the right. An inch to the right brings the Lincoln Memorial into view; an inch to the left produces the Washington Monument. The effect transforms linear history into a spatial collage that almost gently reminds us to contextualize and interrogate our history, not to celebrate certain parts in isolation.

There is much debate regarding Lin's intentions in having the Memorial reflect the Washington and the Lincoln....

But to point fingers, to indict, is to impose an exit on the Memorial. It is to rearrange the furniture of stage one. It is to forget our own reflection in the Wall. If Washington and Lincoln are implicated in the march to Vietnam, then so are we. We're all family—an extremely dysfunctional one, to be sure. And, indicting two different old uncles named Sam won't change that fact, unless we indict ourselves along with them....

Only one thing is wrong about the VVM; but it's a big wrong.... Where is any recognition of the millions of dead and maimed Indochinese? Why isn't it even possible to trace the Vietnamese people onto a piece of paper and take that home? Lady Borton, a frequent visitor to Vietnam and the author of *Sensing the Enemy: An American Woman Among the Boat People of Vietnam,* has asked this question many times for many years. In an *Akron Beacon Journal* editorial, she said,

> It was years before I could visit the Wall. In the early '80s, I often read about the Vietnam Wall.... I would read by my living room stove, surrounded by photographs I had taken during the war. The photos were faces of Vietnamese civilians—mostly children— who had lost legs or arms. Surrounded by those photos, I felt angry about the Wall.

The combat veteran Dan Reeves seems instinctively to have recognized that the Vietnamese are missing on the VVM. He both begins and nears the end of his video *Smothering Dreams* (a phrase from Wilfred Owen's poem "Dulce et Decorum Est") being interviewed by Susan Stamberg by the Wall. The film surrealistically replays, over and over, both the games and the rhetoric that send eager boys to war and the actual horrors of a platoon almost wiped out in an ambush. After he replays the ambush for the final time, ending it with an off-camera soldier, desperately trying to stay alive without squares and rectangles, screaming "Which way?" he displays the kind of graphic missing from Maya Lin's memorial: "This work is dedicated to the men of the 2nd Platoon Company A 1st Amtrac Battalion and the North Vietnamese soldiers who died on January 20, 1969 along the Cua Viet River." In a simple yet powerful gesture, Reeves takes the first step in carrying out what Borton called for this nation to do in her editorial: "It seemed to me that stories behind the names etched into that granite must someday press through the earth to Vietnam itself. Perhaps only then, when we reach through with our own wall of sorrow to theirs, can we all be healed."

**Source:** Ringnalda, Don, *Fighting and Writing the Vietnam War,* Jackson: University Press of Mississippi, 1994, pp. 3–4, 233–41.

## Sources

Abramson, Daniel, "Maya Lin and the 1960s: Monuments, Time Lines, and Minimalism," in *Critical Inquiry,* summer 1996.

Anderson, Donald, ed., *Aftermath: An Anthology of Post-Vietnam Fiction,* New York: Henry Holt, 1995.

Asali, Muni, "An Interview with Yusef Komunyakaa," *New England Review,* 1994, pp. 141-47.

Aubert, Alvin, "Stars and Gunbarrels," in *African American Review,* Vol. 28, No. 4, Winter 1994, pp. 671-74.

Baer, William, "Still Negotiating with the Images: An Interview with Yusef Komunyakaa," *Kenyon Review,* Vol. 20, No. 3/4, Summer/Fall 1998, pp. 5-21.

Baxter, Susan, "A Poet Who Danced with Death," *Freedom Review,* Vol. 25, No. 5, September/October 1994, pp. 45-8.

Collins, Michael, "Staying Human," *Parnassus: Poetry in Review,* Vol. 18-19, 1993, pp. 26-51.

Derricotte, Toi, "The Tension Between Memory and Forgetting in the Poetry of Yusef Komunyakaa," *Kenyon Review,* Vol. 15, No. 4, Fall 1993, pp. 217-23.

Ehrhart, W. D., ed., *Carrying the Darkness: The Poetry of the Vietnam War,* Lubbock, TX: Texas Tech University Press, 1989.

Finkelstein, Norman, "Like an Unknown Voice Rising Out of Flesh," *Ohio Review,* No. 52, 1994, pp. 136-40.

Friedman, M. J., "Neurobiological and Clinical Consequences of Stress: From Normal Adaptation to PTSD," Philadelphia: Lippincott-Raven, 1995.

Gotera, Vicent, " 'Depending on the Light': Yusef Komunyakaa's *Dien Cai Dau,*" in *America Rediscovered: Critical Essays on Literature and Film of the Vietnam War,* edited by Owen W. Gilman, Jr., and Lorrie Smith, NY: Garland, 1990.

Hass, Kristin Ann, *Carried to the Wall: American Memory and the Vietnam Veterans Memorial,* University of California Press, 1998.

Moore, Lenard D., "Book Reviews: Arts & Humanities," *Library Journal,,* Vol. 118, No. 5, March 1993, p. 81.

Rollins, Peter C., "The Wall," *World & I,* Vol. 8, No. 11, November 1993, p. 266.

Rothschild, Matthew, "A Feast of Poetry," *Progressive,* Vol. 58, No. 5, May 1994, pp. 48-52.

Sevy, Grace, ed., *The American Experience in Vietnam,* Norman, OK: University of Oklahoma Press, 1991.

Stein, Kevin, "Vietnam and the 'Voice Within': Public and Private History in Yusef Komunyakaa's *Dien Cai Dau,*" *The Massachusetts Review,* 1995-1996, pp. 541-61.

## For Further Study

Palmer, Laura, *Shrapnel in the Heart: Letters and Remembrances from the Vietnam Veterans Memorial,* New York: Random House, 1987.

*Shrapnel in the Heart* is a heart-wrenching collection of more than 100 letters left at the memorial—and the stories of the wives, children, and buddies who wrote them.

Lanning, Michael Lee, and Lee Lanning, *The Only War We Had: A Platoon Leader's Journal of Vietnam,* Ivy Books, 1987.

A platoon leader's diary of his tour of duty, Lanning's experiences are alternately gruesomely fascinating and predictably mundane, just like war itself.

# The Gold Lily

*Louise Glück*

*1992*

Louise Glück's "The Gold Lily" is the penultimate poem in Glück's sixth book of poetry, *The Wild Iris* (1992), a volume for which Glück received the 1993 Pulitzer Prize for poetry. *The Wild Iris* is composed of poems partly inspired by Glück's avocation as a gardener. Most often, there are three voices in *The Wild Iris:* those of flowers speaking to humans, humans speaking to God, and God speaking to humans. In "The Gold Lily," the flower speaks to humans or, possibly, to God. As the gold lily dies, it asks to be saved by the one who raised it, but one who is helpless to fulfill the request.

At the same time the poem gives voice to a voiceless creature, a flower, it also, as an extended metaphor, gives voice to the human subject on the eve of death, a creature unavoidably wasting its voice pleading with a Being who cannot hear, does not listen, cannot help, or is not there at all. As such, the poem speaks to the inevitable in nature and to strength and weakness in the face of perhaps life's greatest fear: death. In its own small way, "The Gold Lily" is a preparation for death, a poem attempting to confront one's mortality and eternal end through tragic words shared with those who can hear and might listen: one's readers and oneself.

## Author Biography

Louise Glück was born April 22, 1943 in New York City, and was raised, along with her sister,

on Long Island. From an essay, "Education of the Poet" in her prose volume *Proofs and Theories* (1994), we know that both of her parents "admired intellectual accomplishment" and nurtured the children's every tendency or talent. Glück's mother went to Wellesley and her father into business, though he wanted to be a writer. As for the poetry she began writing, Glück had to please her mother, a woman who taught her daughter by age three to read and know the Greek myths. In 1962, Glück attended Sarah Lawrence College, and she studied at Columbia University from 1963-66 and from 1967-68, during which time her teacher and mentor was poet Stanley Kunitz, a Pulitzer Prize winner. Twice married with a son (Noah) by her first husband, she is presently married to prose writer and teacher John Dranow. In their spare time, the couple gardens. Since the early 1970s, Glück has taught at numerous universities across the country: Goddard, Columbia, the universities of Virginia, Iowa, Cincinnati, California at Davis, Irvine, Los Angeles, and Berkeley. Presently she teaches at Williams College in Massachusetts and has six books of poetry to her name. *The Wild Iris* (1992), from which "The Gold Lily" was taken, won the prestigious Pulitzer Prize in 1993. This was only the most recent in a long string of fellowships and awards: the Academy of American Poets (1966), the Rockefeller Foundation (1967), the National Endowment of the Arts (1969, 1979, 1988), the Guggenheim Foundation (1975 and 1987), and several others.

*Louise Glück*

## Poem Text

As I perceive
I am dying now, and know
I will not speak again, will not
survive the earth, be summoned
out of it again, not                                   5
a flower yet, a spine only, raw dirt
catching my ribs, I call you
father and master: all around
my companions are failing, thinking
you do not see. How                                   10
can they know you see
unless you save us?
In the summer twilight, are you
close enough to hear
your child's terror? Or                               15
are you not my father,
you who raised me?

## Poem Summary

### Lines 1-7:

It might be easier to read this poem if these lines are understood as one long sentence. The sentence's dependent clause begins at the beginning and ends with the word, "ribs." The main clause then continues the sentence on line seven with the words, "I call you." Also helpful might be understanding that the first word in the poem, "As," can be replaced by "since" or "because" to get virtually the same meaning. The lily is the speaker in this poem, a flower that is "dying" or, more accurately, wilting, since the lily plant is classified as a perennial, one which returns year after year. The lily blossom can be imagined as a kind of mouth uttering this lament, the poem, in the face of imminent death. The flower says that once it wilts and falls to earth it will not survive to bloom again ("be summoned," presumably by god or human). Flowers "die" because they do not sprout—do not become "a spine only" with dirt stuck to its "ribs," do not push themselves out of the ground.

### Lines 7-8:

This line can be written out in prose as "I call you, father and master," with the comma being crucial. Without it, the sentence would designate a naming rather than an address to a specific subject. "Father and master" could refer to either human or deity, although the word "raised" in the final line suggests the flower is calling a human gardener. At any rate, by this point, readers are confronted with a talking, dying blossom calling upon a kind of parental figure.

### Lines 8-10:

In prose, this line would read, "All around, my companions are failing, thinking you do not see." These other companions are probably lily blossoms who also seem to believe in some deity. The word "failing" has at least two interpretations: dying and losing faith in the master/father. Like Job of the Bible's Old Testament, the lilies are being "tested" by death—tried to see if they can retain their faith even in the face of death. The colon that precedes the line has a double function: it not only serves its normal function to direct attention to something, but it serves to break the line in much the same way that a period would.

### Lines 10-12:

"How / can they know you see / unless you save us?" asks the flower, pleading with its maker to prove the maker exists by saving the flower, or to show that the maker understands that the flower is dying by saving it. The flower's logic is similar to that utilized by a human supplicant: if the master does not save them, the flowers will not believe the master can see or understand them, nor will the flowers believe that the master is powerful. We never find out if this logic works on its auditor, but we can imagine.

### Lines 13-15:

This line ends with a question mark. Lilies die in late summer, usually around August, and so "twilight" functions doubly: it signals the end of life and the end of day. "Child" refers to the lily. In these lines, it seems as if the lily is becoming more and more desperate, somewhat excusing the master for silence, thinking he might be too far away to hear.

### Lines 15-17:

The last utterance, "Or / are you not my father, / you who raised me?" signals even graver desperation than the question just before. Whereas previously, the lily thought the father was too far away to hear, the lily now wonders if the master is actually its father at all. The lily thinks it might be mistaken in praying to the master. "The Gold Lily" appears at the end of *The Wild Iris,* a fitting place for a late-summer bloom and a dying plant (the book begins with the early-blooming iris). The "Gold" of the title "The Gold Lily" seems ironic or tragic; gold is the color of immortality and yet the flower is dying. Furthermore, there is tragedy in the state of affairs of the lily calling upon a gardener to save it, since the gardener is impotent to do so. If God is the entity the lily calls, then here, too, we have tragedy, since God does not appear to interfere with the life-and-death cycle in nature.

## Themes

### Death

In "The Gold Lily" a flower pleads with a higher being, human or god, to be saved from dying. The Brahmanas, a series of Hindu prose pieces on ritual, say that gold equals immortality. In other traditions, gold is a symbol of light and, therefore, life, as in the golden appearance of Apollo and, later, the gold emanation, or halo, of Jesus. Lilies symbolize, among other things, purity and surrender to the grace of God. If the symbology of gold and lily are combined, we might come up with the idea that purity and surrender to God's grace is rewarded with immortality. The gold lily of Glück's poem, however, seems destined for anything but immortality; it appears not about to live forever, but to die despite its apparent sinlessness and surrender to the will of its father and master. As the flower approaches death, the realization that it is dying and will not be reborn next spring drives it to ask for rescue. But even this pure, innocent, helpless flower will die, unhelped by gardener or God. This is the inherent cruelty of existence, when life is betrayed by death.

### Natural Law

Natural law states that in order for there to be life, there must also be death. Despite the human symbolism of gold and the lily mentioned above, nature appears to be unaware of purity, innocence, and immortality as relevant factors to the question of what lives or dies. And though the lily plant is a perennial that is often able to reappear year after year thanks to its bulb, a particular blossom appears only once. Specifically, the flower must die so that the fruit can be born and so that the plant, through the fruit's seed, might reproduce and diversify its species. In this way, a variety of plants with an assortment of attributes stand a better chance of surviving when their environment becomes unfavorable. Therefore, an underlying aspect of natural law is that individual flowers must die in order to make way for the fruit that bears seeds that will be dispersed and ensure the adaptation and survival of the species. In sum, then, the blossom not only decays into soil that nourishes plant and animal life in general, but the blossom dies and becomes part of the nutrients on which the parent plant feeds. Glück's lily, however, seems unwilling to be sacrificed for the life of its parent, its kind, or of life in general. The lily can only see death, not the hope of rebirth. While the positive aspect of death can be inferred, it is uncertain whether it is implied.

## Strength and Weakness

Confronted with death and natural law is the individual, a flower whose symbolic meaning residing in the terms "gold" and "lily" cannot save it from the inevitable. The lone individual against the largest forces in life represents the most difficult test of one's strength. The flower's questions become more plaintive as its desperation intensifies. First, it attempts to appeal to the master's vanity: "How / can they know you see / unless you save us?" This characterizes the master as needful of earth's worship of heaven—of a lower life form to flatter a higher one. When the question goes unanswered, the flower poses another: "In the summer twilight, are you / close enough to hear / your child's terror?" Where before the master was considered vain, now it is approached as a creature who pities the suffering of its subjects. When again there is no answer, the supplicant wonders whether it is even directing its pleas to the correct party. Perhaps this is both the height of despair and the beginning of the descent into acceptance of death and helplessness. This slope into courage and strength could be variously characterized as a final agnosticism or deism in which one is inured to the idea that, while there may have been a God of creation, there is no God to prevent death. And if this God is instead construed as a human gardener, the situation will be similar: the gardener can bring about the conditions for life but cannot save the plants it raised. The gardener-god then somewhat ably represents the God of deism who is able to bring about (not create) life, but is powerless in the face of death.

## Topics for Further Study

- Try writing your own flower poem or small prose piece from a religious voice: Buddhist, Christian, Jewish, Islamic, etc. In order to do an effective job you will have to research the religion you choose, and most importantly, how in that religion salvation is attained. A day of in-class readings from a variety of well-known and obscure religions should make for an interesting experience in religion and poetry.

- Gluck uses a talking flower. What might be the concerns of another part of a plant? Attempt to write a poem from the viewpoint of a leaf, a stem, roots, etc., of a specific plant. To do an effective job you should familiarize yourself with the botany specific to your topic.

- Gluck construes the gardener or God of the lily as male. Investigate religious traditions where primary deities are female and then attempt to answer the question: Why is the master of "The Gold Lily" male?

## Style

"The Gold Lily" has little or no alliteration, consonance, or assonance; it has no stanzas, and its lines do not begin with capital letters as in traditional poems. Most important, the poem has no rhyme nor syllabic or accentual meter. The term describing this latter absence is "free verse," a now-common contemporary form, whose "free" means free of meter and free to take a unique or individual form relevant to the poem's content. Modern use of free verse is usually attributed to Ezra Pound (1885-1972) who in 1912 wrote that poetry should be composed "in the sequence of a musical phrase, not in sequence of a metronome." Because there are endless ways to turn a line into a musical phrase, it might be difficult for the reader to hear the line the way the poet does unless the reader attends a reading or listens to a recording. Free verse opened up such a panorama of possibility for the poet that critic Edward Storer went so far as to declare that "every man's free verse is different." While free verse was thought free, it was, according to its adherents, supposed to uniquely serve or form itself around the poems' meaning or content. However, Pound himself said that "Whether or not the phrases followed by the followers [of free verse] are musical must be left to the reader's decision. At times I can find a marked metre in 'vers libres,' [free verse] as stale and hackneyed as any pseudo-Swinburnian, at times the writers seem to follow no musical structure whatever." While it seems that Glück falls into the latter category, she has done something interesting with form in terms of line breaks.

If this poem of seventeen lines were written out in prose, it would be clearer that there are two statements at the beginning of the poem—the first ending with a colon and the second a period—and three questions at the end. But we know that this is a poem and not a prose piece, because Glück has broken the sentences into short segments, the longest being only ten syllables and six accents (line 6). So how has Glück broken these lines? In three ways: two lines are heavily end-stopped (lines 12 and 17), eleven lines are lightly end-stopped (lines 1-4, 6-9, 11, 14, and 16), and four lines are enjambed (lines 5, 10, 13, and 15). To better understand line breaking, it is probably helpful to think of line breaks as not so much one thing or another, but as happening along a continuum: from enjambed to lightly end-stopped to heavily end-stopped. Enjambed lines end with no punctuation so that the meaning continues on the next line; lightly end-stopped lines end with a pause marked by a comma or no punctuation; and heavily end-stopped lines end with a period or question mark. Lightly end-stopped lines, in almost all cases in "The Gold Lily," make sense alone and in conjunction with the next line. In this way, the lightly end-stopped line combines the traits of the heavily end-stopped and enjambed lines. If we are apt to say that "form follows function," then we might explain that the preponderance of lightly end-stopped lines fosters a staccato pace—a motion somewhat unsure about pausing or moving forward, a pace that is mildly confused as to which way to proceed. This, it seems, is an impeccable kind of line to suit the flower's faltering and its questioning about whether to keep asking for help or to stop as it moves inevitably toward its end.

## Historical Context

### Religion

If it is granted that two themes in "The Gold Lily" are death and the hope to be saved/salved by a deity who is unnamed and nondenominational, then it is fitting to begin this history with religious information on Americans. While an overwhelming percentage of the U.S. population in 1990 defined themselves as Christian (46 million alone being Roman Catholic), a substantial 24 million were non-Christian, and the majority of these—13 million—claimed no religion at all. Also comprising the category of non-Christian, 1.1 million people identified themselves as agnostic and 6,000 called themselves "deists." Deism is a belief system vaguely construed as a "natural theology," or a belief that God created the universe but then bowed out from all influence and intervention. The lily of Glück's poem might be characterized as somewhat characteristic of the a-religious attitudes of some 14 million Americans in that the blossom does not seem to believe in life after death, and because under pressure from the onset of death, such a-religionists can be driven to reconsider religion and God.

### International Affairs

August of 1991 marked the beginning of the end of the Soviet Union and heralded the quick declarations of independence by many of the countries of Eastern Europe that where formerly held together by the military might of the Soviet's powerful central government. This was a relief to many Americans for whom it signalled an end to the Cold War, a state of affairs that had led the postwar United States into an anticommunist frenzy resulting in, among other things, the executions of Ethel and Julius Rosenberg as communist spies; the McCarthy hearings staged to publicly root out communists from the American government; the Bay of Pigs invasion of Cuba; the Korean War; and the Vietnam War. But while the end of the Cold War signalled an era of peace to most Americans, it liberated ethnic groups previously held together by the Soviets to fight for control of what they considered their historical territory. This was the year Yugoslavia exploded in ethnic fighting, a complicated civil war that as of 1999 was not wholly stilled.

In addition to the ethnic and political conflicts of Eastern Europe, a battle broke out in the Middle East between Iraq and Kuwait over oil prices and debt. On August 2, 1990, Iraq invaded and be-

# *Compare & Contrast*

- **1992:** Bosnia and Herzegovina secede from Yugoslavia. The siege of Sarajevo begins and "ethnic cleansing" becomes a new phrase for genocide.

  **1999:** The new terrain of battle in the former Yugoslavia is Kosovo where Serbians stage attacks on ethnic Albanians. When NATO threatens with air strikes Serbia gradually, and temporarily, withdraws its forces.

- **1992:** William Jefferson Clinton is elected President of the United States in an electoral college landslide: Clinton earns 380, as compared to President George Bush's 168, votes.

**1999:** President Clinton is impeached and then acquitted for lying to a grand jury about an extramarital affair with Monica Lewinsky, a former White House intern.

- **1992:** Off La Coruña, Spain, the Greek tanker *Aegean Sea* hits rocks in a storm, breaks apart, and catches fire; the resulting oil slick contaminated some sixty miles of coastline.

**1998:** Several American diesel truck companies are together fined a total of one billion dollars for rigging trucks so they cannot be detected spewing unlawful amounts of heavy pollutants into the air.

---

gan annexing Kuwait. While this posed some threat to American dependance on Middle-East oil, an even bigger danger was Saddam Hussein's threats against Saudi Arabia, an even larger oil-producing country. With access to oil jeopardized, the United States, on August 6, began Operation Desert Shield to protect Saudi Arabia, all the while pressuring Iraq to leave Kuwait through sanctions and a multinational military buildup. Iraq continued its threats with its own buildup of troops along the Saudi-Iraqi border to the point that President Bush readied the United States for a possible attack on Iraq. Toward that end, he assembled 750,000 international troops. Many of these forces and weapons, drawn from Western Europe, would not have been available had not the Cold War ended and the Soviet Union been given its high-profile accord to the war plans of its former enemies. On January 15, 1991, Bush won Congressional approval to lead coalition forces into Iraq with the largest air attack in history. By the end of February, with ground troops having finished off what planes had begun, Iraq suffered some 100,000 civilian and military casualties. Humiliated, Iraq took its revenge by releasing large amounts of crude oil into the Persian Gulf that killed plant and animal life on an immense scale. In addition, Iraqis set fire to an estimated 1,000 of Kuwait's oil wells, causing black rain over

an extensive area. These fires were not put out for five months. But Iraq was not the only side responsible for environmental disaster. Coalition bombing of nuclear and chemical plants released toxic substances into air, ground, and water. Perhaps for the first time, people paid serious attention to the impact of war upon nature.

### *Environmental Woes*

Meanwhile, back at home, the environment was becoming increasingly hostile to animal and plant life. The World Wildlife Foundation reported that the conditions of air, water, forests, and wildlife had worsened. The Bush Administration refused to sign a bill calling for a 40-percent increase in vehicular fuel efficiency, and while auto emissions had been cleaned up earlier and a 1990 Clean Air Bill passed, gains were continually being undone by the increase in the number of vehicles on the road. The Great Lakes, the Environmental Protection Agency acknowledged, were being poisoned by toxic wastes and the "stresses" of 425 oil spills and 75 chemical spills every month and needed to be cleaned up. Because, even by 1990, there were still no laws protecting national forests, the northern spotted owl became the focus of forest protection. With the government's declaration of the spotted owl as an endangered species, environmentalists rallied around the bird as a way to protect the forest through the back door of protecting the owl's forest habitat. The Forest Service responded by unveiling a plan to cut its harvest of trees from 12.2 billion board feet to 10.8 billion board feet by 1995. As if the prognosis on the environment were not bad enough, the World Resources Institute ventured the opinion that by 2010, one quarter of the species of all plant and animal life present in 1985 would be extinct.

## Critical Overview

"The Gold Lily" is one of the last poems in Louise Glück's sixth volume of poetry, *The Wild Iris*. The work garnered favorable reviews and, in 1993, received the Pulitzer Prize. While there is an abundance of criticism and reviews on the book, few have singled out "The Gold Lily" for specific discussion. What follows is a survey of some of the criticism that applies to the book, but can also be applied to the poem. Judith Kitchen had this to say in *Georgia Review:* "The poems of *The Wild Iris* are intellectual, wholly realized within the rational mind, and yet they depend not only on an intimate knowledge of nature but also on a respect for (and passionate love of) the natural world." In other words, in the poems about flowers, Glück displays a knowledge of both horticulture and iconography.

In *Poetry,* Henry Taylor remarked on the double voice of the plants throughout Glück's book: "In poems mostly titled by the names of plants, other voices address existence and divinity. On the face of it, the poems are in the voices of plants, but it is somehow unfair to leave it at that: could a poet of Glück's gifts truly expect us to suspend our disbelief so far above the rocks? Say rather that the device is a trope, that the poet's voice imagines assorted vegetable conditions."

Finally, there is veteran critic Helen Vendler who remarked in *The New Republic* on the three different voices employed in Glück's book: "[*The Wild Iris*] is really one long poem framed as a sequence of liturgical rites: the flowers talk to their gardener-poet; the poet, who is mourning the loss of youth, passion and the erotic life, prays to a nameless god … and the god, in a very tart voice, addresses the poet. As the flowers are to their gardener-poet, so is she to her gardener-god; the flowers, in their stoic biological collectivity, and their pathos, speak to her, sometimes reproachfully, as she speaks, imploringly to her god."

## Criticism

### Jhan Hochman

*Jhan Hochman's articles appear in* Democracy and Nature, Genre, ISLE, *and* Mosaic. *He is the author of* Green Cultural Studies: Nature in Film, Novel, and Theory *(1998), and he holds a Ph.D in English and an M.A. in Cinema Studies. In the following essay, Hochman acknowledges the effectiveness of "The Gold Lily" as a work of art, but objects to the metaphor of the flower as human.*

"The Gold Lily" is surely a poignant look at death. Using a flower to represent both itself and the human being, Glück portrays an individual overwhelmed by the process of dying. First, the flower-as-flower, pleading to be saved, is an effective image because Glück carefully keeps out all references to what is strictly cultural, namely, specific religions or gods. The only demarcation accorded to the being with whom the flower pleads are the words "father," "master," and "you who raised me." This is as it should be, for a Christian or Jewish flower, say, would have seemed absurd, Glück already running the risk of absurdity by employing a talking flower, and one talking to its god/God no less. Second, the flower as metaphor for a human works to the extent that both flowers and humans appear once in life and then die. Third, there is a viable parallel between a flower appealing to a human gardener as a person might appeal to a God, especially the God who created the Garden of Eden. And last and least, the image works to the extent that a dying flower is a cultural symbol of loss, one indicating both the mortality of life and love. The dying flower usually represents waning romance, but in "The Gold Lily" there is no representation to the extent that the flower itself suffers from loss because its own "love" appears thrown away on a powerless, pitiless, or nonexistent maker.

Now then, I do not want to spoil the party I have just briefly joined—the one raising a toast to this poem and the book, *The Wild Iris* (1992) from which "The Gold Lily" comes and which won the Pulitzer Prize—because it might make me look the crank. But I feel the need to voice some objections to what, even by my own standards, is an effective work of art. For this reason: an effective work of art is sometimes an ineffective tool for looking at and dealing with the world. In other words, art isn't everything. And so, the upcoming objection is not about the poem's technique, which is impressive, nor about the poem's sentiment, which appears to me properly tragic. My objection entails the nature of the metaphor: flower equals human. First, let me try to understand Glück's metaphor before I proceed to criticize it. Glück's metaphor works because in the Western imagination, a flower is often synonymous with a plant, in other words, flower equals plant. And second, the metaphor works because a flower looks somewhat like an organ of speech in that many flowers have what looks like an opening resembling a mouth as well as petals that look like materialized figurations of uttered or shouted speech. So perhaps Glück should be excused for merely tapping into Western tradition and appearances. But I cannot wholly excuse her because the metaphor is misleading, and for the rest of this essay, I would like to plead my case.

While I do not want to promote strict adherence to the views of science, neither do I want to ignore them. So let me begin by stating that the metaphor, flower equals human, is inaccurate. Flowers are the sexual organs of a plant, most often bisexual because comprised of both pistil (female) and stamens (male). The flower is no more the plant than the vagina and ovaries are the woman or the penis and testicles are the man. Furthermore, the idea of talking sexual organs usually provokes laughter, undoing the poignancy of a flower appealing to a higher power on the eve of death. And if supplicating sexual parts are absurd, the idea of sexual parts that die is misleading. Genitals lose their effectivity, not their life. Flowers are more comparable to other parts of the plant like root, stem, leaf, and fruit than they are a synecdoche for a whole plant that lives or dies. One might say that Western humanity, as far as certain flowers are concerned, is overly fixated on genitals, mistaking the sexual apparatus for the whole plant. On the other hand, mistaking the flower for the plant might also be, unfortunately, understandable. Certain plants are only allowed to flower before they are cut and sometimes killed, as if their life was only useful as a pubescent creature and didn't exist except for the swelling of its sexual organs. There is even an explanation for so many men seeing women as nothing more than the sum total of their sexual parts: visual and textual representation often highlights these parts—wet lipsticked lips and accentuated breasts and pelvic areas—without saying much else about the represented subject. Perhaps, then, there *is* an accurate parallel between human and flower: as society "understands" and reduces some plants to flowers, men "understand" and reduce some women to genitalia. And thus this rule: Beware the man bearing flowers.

## What Do I Read Next?

- *The Ohio Review* put out a special issue (number 49) in the mid-1990s called *Art and Nature: Essays by Contemporary Writers,* a series of wide-ranging essays, some of which are written by poets such as Hayden Carruth, Charles Simic, and Stanley Plumly.

- Susan Griffin's 1978 work, *Woman and Nature,* discusses how certain aspects of nature and culture have come to be gendered either male or female.

- Rudolph Otto's *The Idea of the Holy* (1923) attempts to write about the nonrational or suprarational in the depths of what Otto calls "divine nature." The book has a Christian slant.

- Keith Thomas's *Man and the Natural World: A History of the Modern Sensibility* is a virtuoso study of Britain's regard and treatment of nature, especially as it progresses from a nature that should be exploited to a nature deserving of care and preservation. This study is relevant to conceptions of nature in the United States.

There is one other general objection to the metaphorical complex of flower equals human in the "The Gold Lily," and that is the relationship between the flower and the higher being to whom it appeals. While this being could be a god, it is more likely that the "father and master" is the gardener, since the flower calls him, "you who raised me." As gardeners raise flowers, the gardener best qualifies here as "master" of the flowers. This is a problem because it promotes the age-old analogy that as God is to humans, so are humans to nature: superior to animals, plants, and elements with rights to control and manipulate according to whim and desire. For even if the flower is apt to mistake the gardener for its father-god, are we not authorized to make the same mistake? To Glück's credit, though, the lily, by the end of poem, begins to suspect that the gardener is neither god nor father and cannot save it. In fact, if we understand the usual use to which a garden is put, the gardener is, as of-

> *... [T]he gold lily should have realized it was lucky enough to have reached maturity in the ground, to have survived the keen edge of the shears and the narrow tomb of the vase.*"

ten as not, less a god or father to his plants than a killer or attacker/pest. At least this is so when it comes to harvesting certain parts like leaves, roots, and flowers, and of course, the whole plant (on the other hand, harvesting fruit appears to be doing the plant's will as much as our own). With this in mind, the gold lily should have realized it was lucky enough to have reached maturity in the ground, to have survived the keen edge of the shears and the narrow tomb of the vase.

Finally, we come to what is most curious about the flower's relationship to the higher being in this poem: the fact that the human or god is gendered male ("father and master"). This is most curious, because Glück is both a woman and a gardener. To give Glück credit, the reason for gendering the ascendant figure male might have been to increase its ambiguity and therefore generality; that is, a male figure is more ambiguously or ambivalently both human and God. If Glück had gendered the ascendant figure female, there would have been the ambiguity between human and mother nature or earth mother. While this might seem perfectly acceptable, mother nature, as she is usually imagined, is not petitionable for salvation from death. God is the being selected to do that job. Still, could not Glück have refrained from gendering the gardener at all, merely referred to the gardener with the pronoun "you"? While I cannot explain Glück's choice of a male overseer and therefore run the risk of misreading her poem, her choice would seem to reinforce not only God as male, but humanity as "man." Further, the flower, though bisexual, will more likely than not be read as female, since flowers are traditionally gendered female: there is a woman's flowery clothing and jewelry, a woman's genitalia

represented by a flower, and women themselves metaphorized as flowers—specifically, Mary's association with the rose and the lily.

"The Gold Lily" may not look or read like a conventional nature poem in the Romantic vein, because Glück seems to try to get inside the "mind" of the flower—to empathize with its otherness and the way it might suffer. But, while what the flower says is poignant, it is primarily so in terms of the flower serving as a metaphor for human suffering in the face of death. Otherwise the poem is wholly conventional in what the flower says and how the flower and its "master" are conceived. While the term "conventional" might not be a criticism in and of itself, it is when the term refers to notions promoting continued misunderstanding, or understandings better off abandoned. In this conventional poem, the flower almost disappears under the cultural avalanche of conventional symbolism, of a conventional relationship between nature and culture, and lost or abandoned knowledge of botany. In the end, Glück's flower may talk, but what it says is only too human.

**Source:** Jhan Hochman, in an essay for *Poetry for Students*, Gale, 1999.

### Sharon Kraus

*Sharon Kraus is a poet who teaches creative writing, literature, and poetry at Queens College, CUNY. In the following essay, Kraus examines how "The Gold Lily" achieves its strong, emotional effect.*

"The world is complete without us," Louise Glück has written in her prose discussion of American poetry, and this is an "[i]ntolerable fact." "The Gold Lily" is a poem that, like so many of Glück's poems, attempts to respond to that fact, by uttering a kind of prayer in the midst of heartbreak.

"The Gold Lily" is the penultimate poem in Glück's Pulitzer Prize-winning sixth volume of poetry, *The Wild Iris*. Glück wrote every one of the 54 poems in this book within a ten-week period, and this unusual method of composition may contribute to the book's strikingly cohesive approach (in fact, some readers, among them the eminent critic Helen Vendler, regard the book as "one long poem"). *The Wild Iris* is composed of a series of prayers, spoken by an assortment of characters: domesticated and wild flowers speak to the gardener-poet, the gardener-poet speaks to the god she regards as "her" gardener, and that gardener-god replies with his (this is very much a male, paternal god) version of events.

The implicit motif that organizes "The Gold Lily," and indeed the book as a whole, is the story of Adam and Eve. For Glück, the significant aspects to explore in that story are their fall; their exile from Eden; and their subsequent (postlapsarian) roles as male and female in a fraught relationship with each other and with their god. Yet Glück tells not the story of those first humans but our story: The voices speaking in these poems are contemporary ones, with contemporary concerns. In "The Gold Lily," a poem that serves as a partial ending for this story, we hear a creature conscious of being abandoned to face death alone. The form of the poem seems to be a modern version of a petition (a type of prayer asking God for something we desire, for ourselves, or for others: e.g., Jesus petitioned God in the Garden of Gethsemane that the cup of suffering might pass from him), and it might be argued that the most important element in a petition is the voice. Certainly the voice of this poem is its most distinctive feature.

Glück herself defines voice as "style of thought," as opposed to what she terms "style of speech," which, in its habitual turns of phrase, tics, and refrains, is conventionally regarded as voice. Rather, the voice in this poem reveals its speaker's mind: clipped, terse syntax conveys to us the agonizing effort it costs this speaker to address the "father," and this state of emotional pain is produced by the speaker's discovery, already achieved before the poem's opening, of the father's unavailability.

The opening lines deliver a shock, in their stark statement and unflinching gaze—"As I perceive / I am dying now"—and set the tone that the rest of the poem will unpack. Notice the plainness of the language. There are only two adjectives in the poem ("raw" and "summer"), which is indicative of a remarkable paring down of detail. The poem has no preamble. Instead, we begin at the moment of crisis: the speaker is dying. The situation unfolds: this particular dying is slow enough to allow contemplation of the vast unknown.

There are a few features to this voice that are especially revealing: the diction is extremely blunt and simultaneously precise without being cerebral. And the pauses, marked by line breaks, work as a counterpoint to the syntax of these sentences, to slow the voice's delivery and emulate a thinking process, a verbalized logic.

The syntax of the first sentence, which comprises more than half of the poem's 17 lines, requires that we read it as an abbreviated litany, in order to make sense of it: "As I perceive / I am dying now," "[As I perceive / I] will not survive the earth," "[As I perceive / I will not] be summoned out of it again." This concision is striking, because it demonstrates the speaker's self-denial; the speaker does not allow herself such rhetorical flourishes as an actual litany. The poet could have chosen, after all, to write a series of short declarative sentences but instead left traces of a litany (a sequence of lines each beginning with the same phrase) to suggest the impulse and the speaker's rejection of it. This is a significant feature of the speaker's character and helps us understand the complexity of the speaker's response to being abandoned: there is terse anger, yes, but also self-rejection.

The speaker further emphasizes that self-rejection in the following lines: "not / a flower yet, a spine only, raw dirt / catching my ribs." The description is both unflattering (the poem's title might lead another poet to refer to lavish, fragile petals, for example) and quietly self-compassionate. The speaker has not yet reached her prime yet, has not opened into the fullness of her life yet (notice also the word "raw" hinting retrospectively at the last vestiges of a naive youth), and already knows how evanescent that life will be, and that she will lose it. The lines bear a suggestion of tragedy, which is both painful and terribly ordinary.

Moreover, this initial sentence sets up the speaker's humble position in the cosmic order. The earth is ancient (it will survive, as it always has), and our speaker is small and without power: if she is not "summoned," she must relinquish life. The poet's decision to use the grammatical passive voice reinforces that echo of powerlessness, and the diction balances that echo with a suggestion of courtliness, in the word "summoned," to achieve an effect of simultaneous restraint and grief.

The word "ribs" in this sentence is both strange and sensual, and works to locate more precisely the speaker's situation. Literally, the image recalls the papery surface of the iris bulb's top, breaking through the surface of the soil. Where so much of the language is transparent, "ribs" is unusual and, in its strangeness, suggests with exquisite economy the character of Eve, who was born of Adam's rib. Such a suggestion helps us understand the address that follows: this "father and master" is no mere secular being; he is linked to the Old Testament God, who banished Eve and Adam from Eden and from immortality, and sent them to their difficult, finite lives. In "The Gold Lily," we hear a speaker

> " ... *'The Gold Lily' does not allow itself an easy bid for compassion. The poem's internal logic forces us to think that the wish cannot be fulfilled ...."*

calling on this entity of ultimate power, in the certainty of that entity's ability to wrest her and her companions from death, if only he were willing.

And yet the speaker does not cry out, pleading, to be saved. This voice, not precisely self-effacing, but instead denying herself the opportunity to argue for her own interests, speaks on behalf of her companions, only later including herself among them (in the "us" of line 17). Again, we encounter the speaker's complex thought process: the speaker, in ultimate despair, is struggling to be honorable, to not beg.

The speaker would not beg, in fact, merely to be saved. Instead, the speaker's implicit charge against this father is more layered, intimate, and exact. She wishes to be seen, to be heard, to be noticed. Perhaps also to be cared for and cherished, but the speaker, significantly, denies herself this logical extension. To be seen would be enough. Moreover, she is not even expressing this wish directly. Our speaker pointedly leaves herself out, as noted above. The first of the three questions with which the poem ends does not say "How / can *we* know you see" [emphasis added], it says "How / can they know you see." Her companions might be convinced by the miraculous sign (of being saved from death) that the god indeed sees them, but, the lines suggest, she has no such high expectations—of being seen. Importantly, the syntax of this question accords greater weight to being seen than to being saved. Our speaker's feelings of abandonment hinge on the unsatisfactory relationship with her god, more than with the prospect of imminent death.

The poem gains a tone of bitter irony, perhaps most clearly in this first of the three questions, from the speaker's mix of yearning and self-rejection. If

the father and master being addressed were simply a human being (and not introduced into the poem as, at least on a symbolic level, divine), the speaker's wish to be acknowledged might seem an altogether reasonable one and all the more plaintive for not being fulfilled. But "The Gold Lily" does not allow itself an easy bid for compassion. The poem's internal logic forces us to think that the wish cannot be fulfilled, because the entity being addressed is, after all, a god and necessarily not present in the ways the speaker might desire. By choosing to reveal the gardener's divine identity, the speaker is stern with herself, as well as with this rejecting god, so like a modern-day absent father, who on another level of the poem is indeed a mortal human, the gardener-poet.

The speaker's despair drives her to abandon at last the posture of self-denial. In the final two lines, she moves toward identifying herself more explicitly, by referring to herself, in the second person, as someone with a rightful claim on her god: "your child" (line 15). The transparency of the language has lulled us (e.g., "In the summer twilight"), so the word "terror" is all the more unsettling, while also mellifluous because it is knitted into the line by the consonance of the preceding word, "summer." Despite the despair that drives her to declare herself, the speaker's self-denial falls away in stages: it is not until the "me" of the final line that the "child" of line 15 is grammatically identified. Thus the poem's last word, "me," seems even more naked and daring a self-assertion. Desperate need, the speaker reveals to us, has driven her to put herself forward so boldly. Out of this urgency, she makes her claim, using the possessive pronoun for the first time ("my father") in addressing the one from whom she wishes so much and so little.

The power of "The Gold Lily" derives from the tension of conflicting emotions. The voice utters its petition, not in a pleading tone but in one of harrowing grief mixed with anger, yet as we have seen, this explosive mix is contained by iron self-restraint, even self-denial. The penultimate image, "are you / close enough to hear / your child's terror?" suggests the sound of a small child weeping in terror, a sound that is haunting because the terror is never soothed; the cries continue, reverberating. And the poem's final question, which is a rhetorical one, and thus has a surprisingly hostile edge, intensifies the depiction of the speaker's grief to an unsustainable pitch. The speaker has given up all hope of winning her god's care or recognition, we realize. She has posed a rhetorical question, one that does not have an answer, because she cannot have an answer. In the midst of an unfurling field, she has cried out in her loneliness, and she knows that she will not be answered.

**Source:** Sharon Kraus, in an essay for *Poetry for Students,* Gale, 1999.

### Helen Vendler

*In the following excerpt, Vendler reviews* The Wild Iris, *Glück's volume of poetry that includes "Gold Lily."*

Louise Glück is a poet of strong and haunting presence. Her poems, published in a series of memorable books over the last twenty years, have achieved the unusual distinction of being neither "confessional" nor "intellectual" in the usual senses of those words, which are often thought to represent two camps in the life of poetry. For a long time, Glück refused both the autobiographical and the discursive, in favor of a presentation that some called mythical, some mystical.

The voice in the poems is entirely self-possessed, but it is not possessed by self in a journalistic way. It told tales, rather, of an archetypal man and woman in a garden, of Daphne and Apollo, of mysteriously significant animal visitations. Yet behind those stories there hovered a psychology of the author that lingered, half-seen, in the poems. Glück's language revived the possibilities of high assertion, assertion as from the Delphic tripod. The words of the assertions, though, were often humble, plain, usual; it was their hierarchic and unearthly tone that distinguished them. It was not a voice of social prophecy, but of spiritual prophecy—a tone that not many women had the courage to claim.

It was something of a shock, therefore, when Glück's recent book *Ararat* turned away from symbol to "real life," which was described with a ruthless flatness as though honesty demanded a rock-bottom truth distilled out of years of reflection. In that book Glück restrained her piercing drama of consciousness, and reined in her gift for poetic elaboration. It was clear that some sort of self-chastisement was underway.

Now, reversing course, she has written a very opulent, symbolic book, full—of all things—of talking flowers. The book is really one long poem, framed as a sequence of liturgical rites: the flowers talk to their gardener-poet; the poet, who is mourning the loss of youth, passion and the erotic life, prays to a nameless god (in Matins and Vespers, many times repeated); and the god, in a very tart voice, addresses the poet. As the flowers are to

> *Louise Glück is a poet of strong and haunting presence."*

their gardener-poet, so is she to her gardener-god; the flowers, in their stoic biological collectivity, and their pathos, speak to her, sometimes reproachfully, as she speaks, imploringly, to her god. The god has a viewpoint both lofty and ironic, and repeatedly attacks the self-pity or self-centeredness of the poet. These are dangerous risks for a late twentieth-century poem to take, but Glück wins the wager of her premises. The human reader, too, is placed in "this isthmus of a middle state" (Pope) between the vegetatively animate world and the severe spiritual world, and shares the poet's predicament.

She is here returning to an earlier sequence of hers called "The Garden," which rewrote the myth of Eden. As *The Wild Iris* progresses, we see that Eden has collapsed. The opening mood of the book reflects the absolute pointlessness of living when one can think of nothing to hope for. Despair prompts the liturgical addresses to the god (seven Matins by day in the first half of the sequence, ten Vespers by night in the second half). Most of the other titles in the sequence are names of flowers, beginning with the wild iris and ending with the silver lily, the gold lily and the white lilies.

Glück links herself in these flower-poems to her two chief predecessors in using flowers as images of the soul, George Herbert and Emily Dickinson. In spiritual deprivation, the soul is like a bulb hidden underground. In spring, it finds its season of flowering and renewal....

And how does the story end? It has several endings. One is the poet's; she blossoms in spite of herself (the last Vespers). Three are the god's: the tender "Sunset," the stern "Lullaby" and the pitiless "September Twilight," as the god erases his work. Two are poems spoken by a single flower: "The Silver Lily" reassures the poet about the end, while "The Gold Lily" is full of terror and abandonment. Finally "The White Lilies" offers a colloquy between two lovers, as one calms the fear of the other with the old paradox that temporal burial is the avenue to imaginative eternity....

These old reciprocals—burial and permanence, mortality and eternity—are lyric standbys. But Glück's white lily, unlike Dickinson's and Herbert's flowers, will not rise from its "mold-life" except on the page.

What a strange book *The Wild Iris* is, appearing in this fin-de-siècle, written in the language of flowers. It is a *lieder* cycle, with all the mournful cadences of that form. It wagers everything on the poetic energy remaining in the old troubadour image of the spring, the Biblical lilies of the field, natural resurrection. It depends, too, on old religious notions of spiritual discipline. It is pre-Raphaelite, theatrical, staged and posed. It is even affected. But then, poetry has a right to these postures. When someone asked Wallace Stevens's wife whether she liked his poems, she answered, "I like Mr. Stevens's poems when they are not affected. But they are so often affected." And so they were. The trouble lay, rather, in Elsie Stevens's mistrust of affectation. It is one of the indispensable gestures in the poet's repertory.

**Source:** Vendler, Helen, "Flower Power," in *New Republic,* May 24, 1993, pp. 35–8.

## Sources

Chevalier, Jean, and Alain Gheerbrant, *The Penguin Dictionary of Symbols,* London: Penguin, 1996.

Glück, Louise, *Proofs and Theories: Essays on Poetry,* Hopewell, NJ: The Ecco Press, 1994.

———, "Voices." *American Poetry Review,* May/June 1993, p. 19.

Kitchen, Judith, "The Woods Around It," *Georgia Review,* Spring 1993, pp. 145-59.

Muske, Carol, "*The Wild Iris,*" *The American Poetry Review,* January-February 1993, pp. 52-4.

Spellenberg, Richard, *The Audubon Society Field Guide to North American Wildflowers,* New York: Alfred A. Knopf, 1988.

Taylor, Henry, "Easy Listening (Part II)," *Poetry,* May 1993, pp. 96-110.

Vendler, Helen, "Flower Power," *The New Republic,* May 24, 1993, pp. 35-8.

## For Further Study

Bramwell, Anna, *Ecology in the 20th Century,* New Haven, CT: Yale University Press, 1989.
    Bramwell examines the origins of and ideas behind the growth of the ecological movement, from 1880 to the present day.

Merchant, Carolyn, *The Death of Nature: Women, Ecology and the Scientific Revolution,* San Francisco: Harper and Row, 1983.
    Women and nature have an age-old association. Common to both is an egalitarian perspective that Merchant explores in her history.

Rousseau, Jean-Jacques, *The Essential Rousseau,* New York: The New American Library, 1974.
    This book is a compendium of works by one the most prominent deists in history. The volume includes the following: *The Social Contract, Discourse on Inequality, Discourse on the Arts and Sciences.*

Shepard, Paul, *Man in the Landscape: A Historic View of the Esthetics of Nature,* College Station, TX: Texas A & M University Press, 1991.
    This is a pioneering exploration of the roots of human attitudes toward nature. This was among the first books (1967) of this new genre.

# I Heard a Fly Buzz—When I Died—

## Emily Dickinson
## 1896

Written in 1862, "I Heard a Fly Buzz—When I Died—" was first published in Emily Dickinson's third posthumous collection of poetry, *Poems by Emily Dickinson,* third series, 1896. The poem has been an object of much critical debate, for there is disagreement over the meaning of the fly as a symbol and its relationship to the death of the poem's speaker.

The poem's persona seems to be a person who is speaking from somewhere beyond death. The speaker tells the story of his/her own deathbed scene, describing the final experiences and sensations before the exact moment of death. This is a fascinating point of view, for although many people have claimed to return from near-death experiences with stories of life after death, no one has ever been able to describe the moment of death itself. Dickinson, who was both fascinated by the subject of death and skeptical about immortality, offers her own insight into what is both a common and indescribable mystery of human experience.

Why does the speaker pay attention to a fly in the room? One reason might be because it is a petty annoyance that is distracting the speaker from the important business of putting his or her affairs in order. The fact that a little fly takes on such importance in the midst of what could be a profound moment of spiritual revelation shows that the speaker is still firmly tied to the physical world. Another reason might be because the fly is a creature that eats carrion, or dead flesh, and so it is an ironic and cruel reminder of the fate of the dead

*Emily Dickinson*

her elder brother, Austin, and his wife, Susan, lived next door. She began writing verse at an early age, practicing her craft by rewriting poems she found in books, magazines, and newspapers. During a trip to Philadelphia in the early 1850s, Dickinson fell in love with a married minister, the Reverend Charles Wadsworth; her disappointment in love may have brought about her subsequent withdrawal from society. Dickinson experienced an emotional crisis of an undetermined nature in the early 1860s. Her traumatized state of mind is believed to have inspired her to write prolifically: in 1862 alone, she is thought to have composed more than three hundred poems. In that same year, Dickinson initiated a correspondence with Thomas Wentworth Higginson, the literary editor of the *Atlantic Monthly* magazine. Over the years, Dickinson sent nearly one hundred of her poems for his criticism, and he became a sympathetic adviser and confidant, but he never published any of her poems. Dickinson's isolation further increased when her father died unexpectedly in 1874 and her mother suffered a stroke that left her an invalid. Dickinson and her sister provided her constant care until her death in 1882. Dickinson was diagnosed in 1886 as having Bright's disease, a kidney dysfunction that resulted in her death in May of that year.

person's body after he or she is gone. A third reason might be that this experience of death is catalogued according to the loss of the senses. The sound of the fly is like a tether that connects the speaker to the world of the living. When the sound of the fly fades, the speaker also fades, until the poem's final moment of blindness and silence.

## Author Biography

Dickinson was born in Amherst, Massachusetts, in 1830 and lived there all her life. Her grandfather was the founder of Amherst College, and her father, Edward Dickinson, was a lawyer who served as the treasurer of the college. He also held various political offices. Her mother, Emily Norcross Dickinson, was a quiet and frail woman. Dickinson went to primary school for four years and then attended Amherst Academy from 1840 to 1847 before spending a year at Mount Holyoke Female Seminary. Her education was strongly influenced by Puritan religious beliefs, but Dickinson did not accept the teachings of the Unitarian church attended by her family, and she remained agnostic throughout her life. Following the completion of her education, Dickinson lived in the family home with her parents and younger sister, Lavinia, while

## Poem Text

I heard a Fly buzz—when I died—
The Stillness in the Room
Was like the Stillness in the Air—
Between the Heaves of Storm—

The Eyes around—had wrung them dry—          5
And Breaths were gathering firm
For that last Onset—when the King
Be witnessed—in the Room—

I willed my Keepsakes—Signed away
What portion of me be                        10
Assignable—and then it was
There interposed a Fly—

With Blue—uncertain stumbling Buzz—
Between the light—and me—
And then the Windows failed—and then         15
I could not see to see—

## Poem Summary

### Line 1:

The first line informs the reader that the experience in this poem is being described from a unique point of view. The persona of the poem is already dead and is looking back at the experience of dying. Oddly enough, the speaker focuses on the sound of a fly, something that most people would consider trivial during an incident of such monumental importance as one's own death. This opening leads the reader to wonder why the fly is significant enough to be the speaker's most immediate and enduring memory of the experience of death.

### Lines 2-4:

The speaker describes a stillness, or absence of movement and noise, in the room where the death scene takes place. The feeling in the room is compared to "the Stillness in the Air— / Between the Heaves of Storm." This is a comparison to what is known as the eye of a hurricane, or the circular area of relative calm that is found at the center of a cyclone. The poem's speaker suggests that there is a moment of absolute calm and quiet between the storms of life and death.

### Lines 5-6:

In these lines, Dickinson uses metonymy. "Eyes" represents the mourners themselves, who are observed standing around the bed of the dying person. Also, "Eyes" means, quite literally, the *eyes* of those same people who have been crying for the loved one who is dying. Their eyes "had wrung them dry," meaning that the people had cried all the tears that they could during this exhausting death ritual. "Breaths" is also an example of metonymy, for the word represents both the people themselves and their breathing. The people at the death bed are "gathering firm," meaning perhaps that they have gathered together to support each other in the fixed and unalterable understanding that the loved one will die, and they are waiting for the end to come. At the same time, their breathing has stopped shaking and trembling because they are calmly awaiting what is now inevitable.

### Lines 7-8:

In these lines, "that last Onset" probably means the final stage of the dying process. Because the mourners in the room were most likely to be nineteenth-century American Protestants, they would have been expecting some formal sign that their loved one had been welcomed into the Kingdom of God, or into the arms of Christ the "King." Perhaps the speaker recognizes the eagerness of his or her loved ones to "witness" Christ in the room. This expectation is quite ironic because the poem's speaker sees not Christ but a common blowfly.

## Media Adaptations

- *Into The Beautiful: Selected Poems of Emily Dickinson* is performed by Meryl Streep and is available from Time Warner Audiobooks.

- *Poems and Letters of Emily Dickinson* is available from Harper Collins Audiobooks.

- A 1998 film titled *Beauty Crowds Me,* directed by Julie Trimingham and starring Denise Clark, features the poetry of Emily Dickinson.

### Lines 9-12:

In this stanza, the speaker describes the completion of personal business as an important part of the dying process. He or she has made a last will and testament, giving "Keepsakes," or token possessions, away to relatives and friends. "Signed away / What portions of me be / Assignable" probably refers to the dying person's request for the memorial ceremony and disposal of the body. These acts have more to do with the needs of the living than the needs of the dead, and yet they are commonly accepted and widely expected rituals of death and dying in Western society. In the midst of all this business activity, "There interposed a Fly—." This could mean that the speaker is interrupted from the social ritual of death by the fly's presence.

### Lines 13-14:

The color blue is usually Dickinson's symbol for eternity. Here, perhaps it is used ironically because the fly, as a creature that lays its eggs in dead flesh, is usually symbolic of mortality. The fly's buzz is described as "uncertain" and "stumbling," perhaps indicating the way that the sound of a fly can move in and out of human consciousness. The fly comes between the speaker and the "light." Here, light can have two meanings. Literally, it describes the actual light of day and touches upon the fact that the speaker's sense of sight is failing at the moment of death. Figuratively, the "light" might mean the light of Christ, or the spiritual world. In any case, it is the *sound* of the fly that interrupts the speaker's experience.

### Lines 15-16:

The "Windows" can have two possible meanings in this line. Perhaps the speaker is transposing the experience of the light failing (blindness) to the windows, describing the loss of the sense of sight in terms of an external, inanimate object. On the other hand, perhaps "Windows" is a metaphor for the eyes, much in the sense that people call eyes the windows of the soul. The final line of the poem is a description of blindness. On one level, it is the loss of the physical sense of sight. On another level, it might be a spiritual blindness, indicating that there is no great spiritual vision after death but rather nothingness. This second explanation is in keeping with Dickinson's reputation as a skeptic, but it does not explain how the poem's persona could be describing this incident after extinction.

## Themes

### Death

Dickinson was fond of using oxymorons to assert the double truth of what was seemingly contradictory. She wrote of abstemious ecstacy, of hoary boys, and of piercing comfort. Likewise, death was, for Dickinson, the "enhancing shadow" of life—something that draws value to life even as it threatens it. In a dynamic similar to the Puritan ethic that views sorrow, trial, or threat as a necessary feature of a world finally defined by its participation in an unseen, divine justice, death is, for Dickinson, a true and serious sorrow that is necessary if we are to fully relish and appreciate our temporary freedom from its grasp.

In "I Heard a Fly Buzz—When I Died—," death has already taken the speaker; the poem both visits and revisits its coming. Yet, the poem is equally concerned with life: it is preoccupied with the "Stillness" that rests between life and death; it repeatedly draws our attention to sight and sound; it gives us a room, and windows in that room. If, in the end, it documents the failure of these features of life, the poem manages to dignify them at the same time. After all, the postmortem speaker is presumably in a position to narrate for us the features of the afterworld. Drawn instead to focus on eyes, ears, windows, and house, we are brought features of the world made precious and poignant by their dissolution. Whether or not a transcendent reality awaits us after death is never fully solved in the poem. The high value of the small features of this world are, however, fully confirmed. If death

is ushered in by a vivid fly and signaled by the disappearance of that fly with a dying person's failed vision, we can perhaps be encouraged to appreciate the abundance of sensory experience we enjoy while alive. The oxymoronic "I Heard a Fly Buzz—When I Died—" is in this sense a death poem about life.

### Public vs. Private Life

"Nature is a Haunted House—but Art—a House that tries to be Haunted," Dickinson once wrote in a letter. Psychoanalyst Sigmund Freud claimed that a house is the only consistent psychic symbol of the body. The household room in "I Heard a Fly Buzz—When I Died—" can be read as a symbol both of the body whose death is symbolized through "failed" windows, and of the haunted grasp of nature—and life—on the speaker.

Notorious for never marrying, for spending the majority of her time in the Amherst household where she grew up, and for composing her hundreds of poems in her own room there, Dickinson was perhaps the most domestic poet ever. She was, however, part of an unusually public household situated in the center of town near the parsonage, the town hall, and Grace Episcopal church, and one that frequently filled with the guests her socially active family entertained for teas, dinners, and parties. How isolating her life was has been a regular subject of debate, particularly among feminists seeking to understand Dickinson's position as a woman in a restrictively sexist world. Feminist literary historian Sandra Gilbert has claimed, in her *The Madwoman in the Attic,* that Dickinson was "a helpless agoraphobic trapped in a room in her father's house." Modern poet Adrienne Rich, on the other hand, has called Dickinson a private rebel and a psychic escapee who won autonomy and mastery of life without having to venture away from her home. The poet made, Rich claims, a virtue of necessity.

The room of "I Heard a Fly Buzz—When I Died—" certainly supports the claim that Dickinson was able to be private and public at the same time. If we take the poem's speaker to be Dickinson and if we take the group gathered in the death chamber as her public, we see a society composed of loved ones who enter into the home, rather than those whose place is beyond it. But even in the crowded room where the speaker dies, the speaker's prime experience in "I Heard a Fly Buzz—When I Died—" is impenetrable by the witnesses. Instead it is the personal perceptions and observations of a buzz and failed light that define the poem and the experience of death. Finally, life transpires and expires in a private zone of mind and sensation that goes unshared; it seems that those who have gathered to witness the speaker see nothing and gather nothing of what transpires. Whether this solitude is enforced or assumed, jailing or liberating, is an issue as binding to questions of the personal lifestyle of Dickinson as it is to the debate surrounding the final fate of the poem's speaker.

Additionally, in "I Heard a Fly Buzz—When I Died—," readers are addressed intimately in the confidence of the speaker and are privy to the private, mental events that characterize death. Our reading of this poem more than one hundred years after it was written confirms this private observation's grand and prolonged publicity. But did Dickinson have in mind the vast distribution and publication of her work? We cannot be sure. Dickinson herself published only ten or so poems during her lifetime. All her loved ones expressed great surprise upon her sister Lavinia's discovery of nearly 2,000 neatly bundled poems after Emily's death. Whether they were meant to become public, we do not know.

## *Topics for Further Study*

- What is the significance of the fly in this poem?

- If we conclude that the fly's significance is a riddle, what can we conclude about the effect on the reader of such a riddle? Must all riddles have solutions? What kind of riddles refuse solutions?

- Pay attention to the meter of "I Heard a Fly Buzz—When I Died—." What does that meter suggest about the rhythm of the speaker's last moments? What happens to time—as expressed in syllable, sound, and beat—as this speaker's lifetime ends?

## Style

"I Heard a Fly Buzz—When I Died—" is a lyric poem composed in four quatrains, or four-line stanzas. The lines of each stanza alternate regularly between eight and six syllables. The rhyme scheme, on the other hand, is much less conventional, with "was/buzz" and "me/be" the only true rhymes. Dickinson creates other tonal harmony, though, in her rich, highly original images: "Heaves of Storm," "Breaths … gathering firm," "Blue—uncertain stumbling Buzz," "Windows failed."

In the seventeenth and eighteenth centuries, common English nouns and other words were often capitalized. Dickinson adopted this out-of-fashion form in this poem, capitalizing "Fly," "Stillness," "Room," "Air," "Heaves," "Storm," "Eyes," Breaths," "Onset," "King," "Keepsakes," "Signed," "Blue," "Buzz," and "Windows." She does this, perhaps, because her poetry is a celebration of the exact, perfect word, and capitalization can be used to highlight the intensity of meaning.

Dickinson is also noted for her unusual handling of punctuation. In this poem, she uses dashes both at the ends of lines and between phrases. This peculiar technique has been the subject of much critical study, but it is generally believed that Dickinson, who did not typically follow the standard rules of grammar, used dashes to indicate how words, phrases and clauses should be interpreted. The dashes in line one, for instance, isolate and intensify the surprising revelation that the "I" in the opening clause is speaking from the grave."

## Historical Context

It seems as through the episode in "I Heard a Fly Buzz—When I Died—" could be described by anyone, anywhere. Indeed, since the poem's speaker is dead, we are given reason to believe that the message is timeless—that it concerns not just one person, but everyone who lives and dies. Nevertheless, the poem's reference to anticipated arrival of the King suggests a specifically Christian view of death and dying. Even more particularly, the death chamber ritual of people gathering to witness both their friend's death and the arrival of Christian salvation indicates that the episode is in keeping with religious and social rites of late nineteenth-century, Protestant New England.

A focus on immortal, general themes that yields, on closer reading, to an impression of culture and belief locked within strict Christian parameters is typical of Emily Dickinson's poetry.

# Compare & Contrast

- **Late nineteenth century:** The Civil War, as well as bacterial infection and widespread diseases such as consumption, made of death a familiar part of daily life in the United States.

  **Today:** Through live news reports from both network and cable television, Americans viewers are presented with images death and tragedy from around the world with an immediacy previously inconceivable.

- **Late nineteenth century:** New Englander death rituals took place in the home, with the dying being surrounded by friends and family in household rooms temporarily made into death chambers. There, the company awaited signs of the dying's heavenly salvation, received last requests and wills, and witnessed the repentance of sins during the last rites sacrament. The faithful dying sometimes gave witness to the approach, then presence of heavenly salvation. For the onlookers, contact with the dead and dying was considered an important part of living, in that it reminded them of the temporality of the body and the potential passage of the spirit into heavenly eternity.

  **Today:** In most cases, the dying are removed from their homes and cared for in specialized facilities such as hospitals, nursing homes, and hospices. In all cases—and by law—corpses are removed from houses and prepared for burial by mortuary specialists. Even in instances in which the dead are viewed postmortem, their bodies are carefully prepared and doctored. In the eyes of the general public, contact with the dead and dying is seen—both rationally and irrationally—as dangerous, harmful, and disturbing.

- **1830-1855:** Transcendentalism, an American philosophical and literary movement born in New England, is at its height. An outgrowth of Romanticism, the transcendentalist attitude opposed middle-class commercialism and looked for evidence of the divine in the world while conceiving very liberally of godliness. It gave priority to personal intuition, organized mysticism, and a broad optimism about human nature.

  **Today:** While many people espouse views of divinity and have faith in a transcendent motor of the world we see, the domain of the mysterious—concerning aspects of everything from causes of death to weather patterns to human behavior—in increasingly collapsed by advances in human sciences.

---

Granddaughter of one of the founders of Amherst College and daughter of a Congressman, prominent lawyer, and champion of railroad development, she lived in a socially connected, distinguished family during some of the most consequential and tumultuous years of American history—from 1830-1886. In the United States, these were years of rapid economic expansion which saw burgeoning cities and expanding technology such as railroads. In addition, American culture was increasingly being defined by development within its own borders rather than by British influence, and Puritan and Calvinist religious traditions intermixed with newly ardent demands for an economically potent nation.

These changes were brought to their most violent expression by the Civil War (1861-1865), which galvanized both northern and southern Americans with notions of nationhood forged through bloody battle, for the sake of economic and cultural prosperity, with the blessing of God. Though the North and the South subscribed to similar ideals, they did so in ways that pitted them against each other: it was, above all, a fraternal war—a smashing of brethren in the name of a differently imagined national fate. Dickinson, however, rarely mentions the war in either her poetry or the many letters she left. Therefore, her readers have often considered her connection to the Civil

War to be weak at best and have deemed her to be too interior a thinker, too private a person, to have been deeply affected by the war or greatly articulate on its effects.

This period was, however, Dickinson's most prolific: out of approximately 1,700 poems, she wrote 852 during the years of the Civil War. And though her explicit references to battle are few, there is much to suggest that her poetry is rooted in consciousness of the war. "Sorrow seems to me more general than it did, and not the estate of a few persons, since the war began," she wrote in one letter. Dickinson continued, "And if the anguish of others helped one with one's own, now would be many medicines. Tis dangerous to value, for only the precious can alarm." Her main literary correspondent, Thomas Wentworth Higginson, was a leading women's rights and antislavery activist as well as a colonel in the Union Army who helped lead its first black regiment. Certainly, then, Dickinson was aware of the war and its impact, but just as the historical circumstances that inform "I Heard a Fly Buzz—When I Died—" soak through a larger, more abstract set of observations, her views on the war emerge through her thick and abstract observations on sorrow and on human fate in the widest sense.

The Amherst religious orthodoxies of Calvinist Congregationalism, Puritanism, and Protestant Christianity also emerge in a general sense from Dickinson's contemplations on life, death, and afterlife; the nature of the sacred; and on the value of friendship. Champion of the sweetness to be found in bitter sadness, of the profound beauty of the austere everyday world, and of the nobility of those few truths that can withstand nature's erosion and transformations, Dickinson seems, in many ways, to preach a Puritanical appreciation of the world. Certainly her usage of hymnology as poetic meter and her frequent references to God tie her to a Christian perspective. Her invocations of religion are, however, often subversive—particularly given that she lived in a deeply religious town. As in "I Heard a Fly Buzz—When I Died—," the King is regularly invoked by Dickinson, but His presence is challenged.

The site of Dickinson's most constant engagement was, of course, not nation, town, or church, but household: following seminary studies at Mount Holyoke College, she returned to her childhood home in the town center of Amherst, Massachusetts, when she was nineteen. At home she remained, increasingly so as she aged. There she participated in womanly household duties—baking bread and pudding, sewing, playing piano, and tending the garden. Her extensive reading and writing, however, were extremely unusual for a woman of her era, and she took great pains within her household to earn the privilege to keep unusual hours and forego the extensive visiting, housekeeping, and hostessing that were asked of her. She made, finally, a telescope of her house and her placement there; the simplest of perspectives, the most austere surroundings, allowed her the broadest of views.

## Critical Overview

The omnipresent fly in "I Heard a Fly Buzz—When I Died—" has been a problem for critics since the poem's publication in 1896. Sharon Cameron, writing in her book *Lyric Time: Dickinson and the Limits of Genre*, believes that the fly plays an important role in the speaker's experience of death. According to Cameron, the poem is, in part, about "the conflict between preconception and perception." The person on his or her deathbed shifts perspective from "the ritual of dying" to "the fact of death." Cameron argues that the fly, by interrupting the dying speaker with its "Blue—uncertain stumbling Buzz—" obliterates his or her false notions of death. Cameron sees the fly's "stumbling" as evidence that it, too, is dying, and the speaker's "experience becomes one with the fly's."

Inder Nath Kher also discusses the symbolism of the fly in his book *The Landscape of Absence: Emily Dickinson's Poetry*. Kher believes that the sound of the fly represents "the last conscious link with reality." Kher points out that the poem lacks any hint of a life after death. The buzz of the fly is described as "Blue," and Kher, noting that blue is usually Dickinson's symbol for eternity, suggests that in this poem it becomes "the symbol of complete extinction."

## Criticism

### Jhan Hochman

*Jhan Hochman's articles appear in* Democracy and Nature, Genre, ISLE, *and* Mosaic. *He is the author of* Green Cultural Studies: Nature in Film, Novel, and Theory *(1998), and he holds a Ph.D in English and an M.A. in Cinema Studies. In the following essay, Hochman examines the motif of "I Heard a Fly Buzz—When I Died—" and examines the myth surrounding the fly.*

# *What Do I Read Next?*

- Three volumes of Emily Dickinson's *Letters* were edited by Thomas H. Johnson and published by Harvard University Press in 1958. In prose that is often as evocative as her poetry, these letters document Dickinson's friendships, preoccupations concerning writing (both hers and that of her contemporaries), and small or large loves.

- *The Essential Dickinson* is an excellent introductory volume of Dickinson's poetry, edited and with an introduction by Joyce Carol Oates, a modern American poet, novelist, playwright, and critic.

- Published in 1955, *The Poems of Emily Dickinson, Including Variant Readings Critically Compared with All Known Manuscripts* is the most complete edition of Dickinson's poetry.

- Elizabeth Barrett Browning's poetry, and the volume *Aurora Leigh* in particular, were named by Dickinson in a letter to Higginson as among her influences. Marian Erle's speech in Book VI, verses 1079-1087 may have specifically influenced "I Heard a Fly Buzz—When I Died—."

- Walt Whitman's *Leaves of Grass* includes poetry as lengthy as Dickinson's is brief and subject matter as public as Dickinson's is private. Whitman was a contemporary of Dickinson who, like her, worked to define a distinctly American poetic idiom.

---

Picture a vast desert, sun glaring. There, in the distance, a figure barely staggers across the arid landscape, then buckles, falls prone, and finally rolls over to await the onset of death. Staring into the sun, the man anticipates he will meet his maker. Instead, there is the onset of circling vultures who eventually descend to consume his corpse.

Emily Dickinson had never seen a Western, let alone any film. If she had, she might have noticed the similarity between "I Heard a Fly Buzz—When I Died—" and this motif in the Western film. Or perhaps similar images had already been described in the written and oral stories of America's invasion of the West—stories Dickinson might have read alone in her upstairs bedroom. Even in the enclosed space where the dying person lies in "I Heard a Fly Buzz—When I Died—," the out-of-doors does seep in, as when the "Stillness in the Room" is said to be like the stillness "Between the Heaves of storm." Dickinson's "stillness" might be comparable to the eye of the storm, or simply a lull between storms. Calling upon an outdoor occurrence, Dickinson is likely indicating the short stillnesses between the dying person's "storm" of heavy and troubled breathings—a storm that might be accompanied by the mourners tumultuous storm of mourning. The stillnesses between breaths are taut because each one might indicate death, at which time another storm of wailing might be taken up by the mourners. Or the stillness between storms might refer to the still moment of dying between the storm of life (earth) and the heaving storm of death (heaven). As the stormy breathings of the dying person were accompanied by the grievings of the onlookers, the stillness of the dying person is matched by the stillness of the mourners whose breath has been "gathering" up after the rain of tears and is now held "firm" like clouds regathering before the onset of another storm. Holding their breath, the mourners wait for the "Onset" of death and for the entrance of Christ the King to whisk the dying soul up to heaven. "Onset" has multiple applications to the dying scene. It can simultaneously mean an attack, a beginning (as of death), or the Advent, Christ's return as predicted by Seventh-Day Adventists. Perhaps Christ bears comparison to the cavalry, or hero, riding up at the last moment to save the desperate victim.

But King Jesus and his heavenly hosts fail to materialize, and instead of the legions of winged seraphim, all that appears—from what is probably an open window—is an ordinary fly. Who is this fly that has interposed itself upon the high drama of a dying scene? Several answers are possible. In

Dickinson's poem "Those Cattle Smaller than a Bee," though the fly is cited as an annoyance, Dickinson begs off pronouncing flies a scourge or a blessing and decides to leave the fly to nature's judgment. The fly of "Those Cattle Smaller than a Bee" could be similar to the fly of "I Heard a Fly Buzz—When I Died—," a creature that, while it might be annoying, is still not labelled as either repellant or evil. Perhaps this fly could be Beelzebub, or the Lord of the Flies, the winged but fallen angel sometimes conflated with Satan and sometimes known as one of Satan's officers—a fallen angel that has come to take the dead body to the Great Below. Beelzebub, as master of the Underworld, functions as an anti-Christ, as Death himself who, in Job 18:14, is called the "king of terrors." The fly is also that creature known to lay eggs in dead flesh, whereupon maggots are hatched and feed until they become flies. This is the fly as a kind of scavenger only mediated by maggots. Whether the fly is some of these or all of these, the insect would seem to represent a failure in comparison to the image of Christ descending in his chariot with his blinding ranks of winged angels that accompany him in taking the dead soul to heaven.

The dying person is herself uncertain as to who the fly is or what it represents. There is some blue on the fly, which may give the victim hope. Although the blue on the average housefly is usually darkly iridescent, blue is the color of a clear sky and, as such, is said to draw the individual toward the infinite and awaken a yearning for purity. Blue has a solemn supraterrestrial quality that the Egyptians considered to be the color of truth. This is why sky-blue is the color of the threshold that is considered to separate humanity from its rulers, from the Great Beyond, and from Fate. Blue and white are the colors worn by the Virgin Mary, and they express a detachment from the things of this world and the flight of the liberated soul toward God. So despite the fly's close association with fecal matter and decaying flesh, it is, nonetheless, a winged creature of the air. The dying person does not quite know what to make of the fly; this uncertainty is referred to in the poem as the fly's "uncertain stumbling Buzz." The uncertainty just might indicate that perhaps most of us have misunderstood flies. After all, are they not heavenly creatures? Some basis for this claim does exist, in that flies were sacred to the Ancient Greeks. Both Zeus and Apollo bear names that are related to flies. Some scholars theorize that flies were sacred to ancient Greeks because they evoked the turmoil of life on Olympus or the omnipresence of the gods.

> "*'I Heard a Fly Buzz—When I Died—' is a poem against the claim of knowing, against what it means to claim to know not only what will happen after death, but what a fly even is.*"

The fly of "I Heard a Fly Buzz—When I Died—" gets between the dying person and the light, and its buzz between the dying person and the stillness. Dickinson wrote that the "Windows failed," which may indicate that the victim's eyes (the windows to the soul) stopped seeing, not that the light from the sun stopped shining. Once the fly buzzes in, the speaker's experience of death becomes the experience of the fly. The fly not only blots out sound and light, but it obliterates all thought of anything else. The dying person is unable "to see to see"—to see in order to understand what is happening. Death is thus rendered unknowable. With no claim to knowledge of one's end, "I Heard a Fly Buzz—When I Died—" might be designated as agnostic, gently antireligious, irreverent, and even humorously sarcastic, considering the poem's unexpected visitation of the fly instead of Jesus who so many people, even today, claim to know so well. "I Heard a Fly Buzz—When I Died—" is a poem against the claim of knowing, against what it means to claim to know not only what will happen after death, but what a fly even is.

After a reading of Dickinson's poem, does it not seem right to fashion a newer, bolder myth for death and for flies? Why not a tale of the fly as the soul's liberator, a winged creature who hates seeing any winged thing trapped (and the soul is—according to a tradition beginning since at least Plato—winged). In this myth, which is, as a matter of fact, being hatched in the corpus of Dickinson's poem, the fly would save the soul by laying eggs in the corpse. The maggot offspring would then consume away the decaying flesh and thereby free the winged soul from the entrapping body. And then, in the company of the iridescently blue ranks of the omnipresent and heaven-sent fly, the soul is accompanied upward with its hosts. With a playful reading such as this, the fly might no longer be considered a mere "buzzard," a miniature buzzing vulture. Thus, the fly could be "re-mythed," not as the soul's tormentor, but as the soul's savior. We might even venture so far as to say that, after reading Emily Dickinson's, "I Heard a Fly Buzz—When I Died—," neither fly nor fly swatter will ever look quite the same.

**Source:** Jhan Hochman, in an essay for *Poetry for Students,* Gale, 1999.

## Michael Lake

*Michael Lake is a published poet who holds a M.A. in English from Eastern Illinois University. In the following essay, Lake examines how "I Heard a Fly Buzz—When I Died—" draws upon both Christian and Romantic sentiments in its examination of death.*

We who live at the end of the twentieth century in North America have a difficult time understanding the intimate familiarity our ancestors had with death. After antibiotics, disinfectants, and mass vaccinations, not to mention the delicate denial of death and decay fostered by the funeral and cosmetic industries, we often succeed in avoiding a direct confrontation with death until our own, final demise. Any discussion of the details of dying is now deemed "morbid," even antisocial, in a culture that chooses to ignore death and to focus instead upon staying "young" at any cost. This was certainly not the case in Emily Dickinson's America, however. Not only were mortality rates higher and life much less predictable, especially for the young, but the long Christian practice of contemplating death in order to stir up remorse for sin and contempt for the transitory life of this world had also not yet died from American popular culture.

In many ways, Emily Dickinson lived within the cusp of two worldviews. The Puritan perspective that had seen God's Providence in all life's situations, whether pleasant or painful, was already losing its grip upon popular consciousness in America, while a secular materialist view that refused to speculate beyond phenomenal surfaces was steadily usurping its place. For her own part, however, Dickinson was extremely uneasy with her ambivalent position. On one hand, her youthful rebellion against the mindless conformity demanded by bourgeois Christianity still raged within her. Moreover, she was curious about and very open to the many scientific discoveries that were overwhelming traditional beliefs during the nineteenth century. But on the other hand, she so greatly feared the extinction of the self and the loss of loved ones she observed in death that she desperately hoped for ultimate immortality. She had struggled hard to adopt Emerson's Romantic Transcendentalism in an attempt to reconcile a belief in a spiritual reality with scientific materialism, but she was too much the Puritan to settle for nice compromises. She opted instead to see the human condition with "double vision." This is why her poems about death (and they are many) seem to contradict one another when read together.

In her poem "I Heard a Fly Buzz—When I Died—," we have a wonderful meditation upon death set firmly within Dickinson's cusped point of view. This poem, dramatically exploring a subjective experience of dying, draws upon both orthodox Christian and more recent Romantic sentimentalist conventions of death poetry for its thematic presentation. But the poem's grisly irony exposes the utter estrangement a new "post-Christian" suffers at the prospect of a purely physical world that offers no transcendence or survival of consciousness beyond the grave.

The tradition of *memento mori,* a Latin phrase that literally means "remember you shall die," comes from the Christian Middle Ages. Hamlet's contemplation of death and mortality while peering into the sockets of "poor" Yorik's skull is a memorable example of this custom. But the poet who most closely resembles Emily Dickinson in his poetic obsession with death and loss is John Donne, a figure who also dwelt ambivalently within the cusp of two eras—the late medieval and the early modern. He went so far in stirring up the recollection of his own death as to sleep in a casket after his conversion in midlife to a deeper Christian commitment and his ordination into the Anglican priesthood. But where Donne's crisis of faith lay in whether he would personally find salvation at the end of a life that had so early turned toward "sin," Dickinson's lay much deeper. She doubted whether God and the human "soul" as an entity of continuing self-awareness really existed at all. Given the depth of her doubt, then, Dickinson's poetically representing death and the experience of dying could never accomplish what the tradition of *memento mori* was originally intended to do, that is, to bring the meditator to a change of perception and to an affirmation of divine transcendence. Her death poems could only present her most cherished wishes or her most dreaded fears.

In *The Long Shadow: Emily Dickinson's Tragic Poetry,* literary critic Clark Griffith noted that Dickinson's death poems always ask at least one of three questions: "What is death?"; "Why is death?"; and "What is it like to die?" As an answer to this last question, "I Heard a Fly Buzz—When I Died—" allows us to experience death vicariously through a first-person speaker's reminiscence about the sensations of a death yet to come, a rhetorical device called "prolepsis" (the representation of a future event as though it had already occurred). Of course, the appearance of a buzzing fly in its very first line signals the deep irony of the poem. In violation of the Romantic sentimentalist conventions exemplified in such works as those of the then-popular "death" poet Lydia Hunt Sigourney, "I Heard a Fly Buzz—When I Died—" actually desecrates the melodramatic sensibility prescribed by that currently popular genre with the intrusion of a buzzing fly into a perfectly composed tableau of the *moriens* or "dying one" and the assembled grieving loved ones. In fact, viewing the poem as a whole, we see that this "Fly" and its buzzing dominate three of the four stanzas. But Dickinson turns the poem's bitter irony to a more profound purpose than mere satire.

Accurately depicting the dimming consciousness and sensual distortions undergone by the dying in compressed and suggestive imagery, this poem is a gem among the many jewels among Dickinson's poetry because of its "slantness"—its oblique but "revelatory" language. From the first line, which presents us with the dramatic situation, to the twelfth, when "There interposed a Fly," the speaker sets the scene leading up to the dramatic event. But all the sensuous descriptions of the sounds in the room and the demeanor of its occupants act as counterpoint to the fly's insistent buzzing. For example, the "Stillness in the Room," the quiet of impending death, forms an island of silence like the quiet "Between the Heaves of Storm" (line 4). Moreover, the word "Heaves," meaning both lifting with an effort and rising and falling rhythmically, conjures up not only the deafening blasts of a violent storm, but also the rhythmic rattling and rasping after breath the dying often suffer during their "throes."

In the second stanza, the *moriens* distinguishes the mourners about her by their body parts and physical sounds, their "Eyes" and "Breaths." Also like the still point in the midst of a storm, the "Eyes around—had wrung them[selves] dry / And Breaths were gathering firm" (lines 5-6). Worn out with weeping, the mourners hold their breaths, both in

> *... [Dickinson] was too much the Puritan to settle for nice compromises."*

sympathy with the dying one's struggles and in anticipation of "that last Onset—when the King / Be witnessed—in the Room—" (lines 7-8). The word "Onset," by the way, can signify either a "beginning" of an action or an "attack" by an enemy. But whether the "beginning of the end" or the "final assault" of death, all in the room, in keeping with the conventions of nineteenth-century sentimentalist death lyrics, expect an "epiphany," a sign of the Divine presence, to signal the departure of the soul into glory.

In anticipation of this grand event, the fictive "I" "willed my Keepsakes—Signed away / What portions of me be / Assignable—" (lines 9-11). One must not fail to detect Dickinson's irony in this passage. Using the language of contract and common law (remember, her father was a lawyer), Dickinson describes the dying one's preparation for her approaching demise in terms of an exchange of property. In my opinion, Dickinson uses this language to ridicule bourgeois acquisitiveness as well as the smugly middle-class conventions of Sigourney's death poetry. A far more orthodox Christian presentation would have shown the *moriens* relinquishing her passion for "filthy lucre" and treasures that "pass away" rather than making sure that her "Assignable" "portions" are properly disposed of, especially when anticipating the advent of the "King." Nevertheless, no King shows up, for "then it was / There interposed a Fly—."

As mentioned above, this buzzing fly dominates the poem, and there has been much critical discussion about its import within the poem. Interestingly, Dickinson had previously used the image of flies buzzing at a window to signify a death. The poem "How Many Times These Low Feet Staggered—" sets the reader a riddle with its line "Buzz the dull flies—on the chamber window—" indicating the negligence of the "Indolent Housewife—in Daisies—lain!" In other words, the house is in disarray because the woman whose social responsibility it had been to "keep" the house has had the audacity to die. But in the poem at hand, the "disorder" the fly portends has meta-physical ramifications. For example, to "inter-pose" oneself doesn't just mean to "come between"; it also carries the added signification of to "get in the way." This interposing fly actually obstructs the light coming in from the window. Still, we would be overburdening the metaphor to note that Beelzebub, the "Lord of the Flies," would certainly delight in coming between a dy-ing soul and the "light." Our fly here is much less sinister. After all, its buzz is "uncertain—stum-bling" (line 13), paralleling the fragile mortality and failing consciousness of the poem's speaker herself. Besides, the fact that the buzz is "Blue" (an example of "synesthesia," that is, the melding of two sensations into one) usually indicates "eter-nity" in Dickinson's color palette, although in this case, "extinction" may be its symbolic value. No, the fly stands for the ultimate destiny of all cor-poreal existence: decay, disintegration, and noth-ingness.

When "the Windows failed—and then / I could not see to see—" (lines 15-16), the speaker leaves the buzzing and the mourners behind in the room and proceeds on to what? Dickinson, of course, leaves the question unanswered in this poem. But that buzzing fly discloses an abyss. If modern ma-terialism is right in its godlessness and the universe is subject to endless cycles of growth, death, and decay, then life has no ultimate transcendent mean-ing. As much as some critics extol Emily Dickin-son as some sort of "protoexistentialist," there is also much in her verse to argue that she was not at all comfortable with nihilism. Behind the irony in her apparent lampoon of the popular death poetry of her day lurks an agonized question. Is death an empty end to a life without metaphysical meaning? In the other poems she wrote about death, she asked different questions and came up with different an-swers.

**Source:** Michael Lake, in an essay for *Poetry for Students,* Gale, 1999.

## *Kristina Zarlengo*

*Kristina Zarlengo, who received her doctorate in English from Columbia University in 1997, taught literature and writing for five years at Co-lumbia University. A scholar of modern American literature, her articles have appeared in academic journals and various periodicals. In the following essay, Zarlengo analyzes Dickinson's use of the senses of sound and sight in "I Heard a Fly Buzz— When I Died—."*

The packed first line of "I Heard a Fly Buzz— When I Died—" is like an overture to an opera: it introduces us to the themes and sounds the larger piece will deliver in full. First, our attention is drawn to sound—we learn of a familiar, suggestive noise: a buzz. Then, even as "died" repeats the vowel sound of "Fly," we learn that the small and common noise of a buzz is a distinctive feature of dying. The association is surprising. It is hard to imagine a more quotidian or minute creature than a fly; how strange, then, that the mysterious, enor-mous passage from life to death should happen to the sound of its flight. Finally, we learn in the first line that the speaker has the authority of having al-ready trespassed the border between life and death. We are given to understand that we receive the poem's message from someplace beyond our world and our consciousness. The association of dying with the noise of a common insect is all the more jarring coming from such an unusual authority. The poem's sound, ironic mixture of the common and the grand, and transcendent wisdom are unpacked during the remainder of this remarkably dense, brief poem.

"I Heard a Fly Buzz—When I Died—" reads immediately as a hymn-like, firsthand description of a death scene; like much of Dickinson's poetry, it yields more and more information as it is re-peatedly read. Close reading rewards attention to the details of the poem with a surprising nest of in-sights as well as riddles, whose solutions are some-times suggested, sometimes evaded. The form of the poem is the common meter hymnal Dickinson preferred: each of the four stanzas is four lines—a quatrain; the lines alternate between eight and six syllables each; the dominant foot is the iamb, which is one unaccented syllable followed by one ac-cented syllable. Read aloud, the lines are alternately of three or four iambs, adding up to an easily mem-orable song-like rhythm of ta-TA, ta-TA, ta-TA, ta-TA; ta-TA, ta-TA, ta-TA (pause).

The form of most religious hymns, this lyric pattern usually has the lulling, regular beat of a metronome and can overwhelm the content of the words with their highly regular expression in sound. In "I Heard a Fly Buzz—When I Died—," however, Dickinson's pattern is broken visually (as read silently) by her use of dashes, which suggest pauses, and capital letters, which suggest uncom-mon emphasis. Audibly (as read aloud), the sound pattern is broken by sequences of unstressed sylla-bles, such as "in the Room" and "in the Air," and by another dimension of sound: the poem's rhymes. The poem's only traditional, full rhyme comes in the last stanza, with the words "see" and "me." But in the first and second stanzas, the second and fourth lines all end in "m" sounds—they rhyme a little, in end consonants only. These partial rhymes suggest unity among the stanzas' words—and by extension the ideas they express—but do not deliver it so perfectly that we are lulled to sleep by sets of overly parallel sounds. They also suggest imperfect pairings, and these sounds that are almost, but not quite, alike finally yield to the last stanza's perfect rhyme, delivering an impression of unity achieved at the moment of death.

Through these sounds, Dickinson also addresses sound as a subject of "I Heard a Fly Buzz— When I Died—." It is the sound of the buzz that brings us into this meditation on death; this sound is contrasted twice in the first stanza to "Stillness." Arriving in the midst of total silence, it is, ironically, a loud, large buzz. The second and third stanzas then address sight: eyes are dry, waiting to witness something as yet unseen; like the silence between "Heaves of Storm," eyes and vision are empty, waiting. Then, the speaker wills and signs away "What portion of me be / Assignable—": what can be written and recorded of the speaker's person has been divided out and left behind when, in the final stanza, we are brought back to the buzz. This time, however, the noise affects sight, blocking light; then, the windows fail; then, sight fails and the speaker is dead. The buzz, furthermore, is blue—sight and sound have mixed. Is this synaesthesia a self-referential echo of the capacity of the poem's language to be expressive visually on the page or to be audibly spoken, like a hymn? Or does a perfect combination of sight and sound always lead to a perspective beyond life? Is this synaesthesia a feature of death, or a feature of the life the speaker has just lost? Such questions are posed all the more poignantly in the disturbed, imperfect rhythm of Dickinson's hymn.

The imperfection of Dickinson's rhymes, her heavy use of dashes, and her ambiguous grammar and syntax were evidence to early readers of her poetry that she was a flawed poet. Though she was well enough supported by friends and family to warrant publication of several volumes of poetry shortly after her death, Dickinson's first reviews measured her work against an ideal of more perfectly rhymed, lengthy, strictly grammatical poetry. "Poetry has been defined as the best thought in the best words," wrote an anonymous British reviewer in an 1891 edition of the London *Daily News.* Dickinson's verses, he continued, "are conspicuously in the worst possible words, and the thought, as far as

> *It is hard to imagine a more quotidian or minute creature than a fly; how strange, then, that the mysterious, enormous passage from life to death should happen to the sound of its flight."*

any thought can be detected, is usually commonplace or absurd." Even Dickinson's early supporters—most were Americans—were frugal with their praise. Literary critic Maurice Thompson wrote in 1891: "In all my reading I have not found a more interesting book of verse; one with so many beauties almost buried by so many blemishes. The good things in it are like incomparable crystals set in ugly fragments of worthless stone." By 1924, she was taken more seriously, but even in the midst of praise of her work that did much to stimulate reconsideration of her achievement, fellow poet Conrad Aiken, in his introduction to the volume of her poetry he edited, called her "brilliant," yes, but also "erratic." Again, his distaste was for her form. "Her disregard for accepted forms or for regularities was incorrigible. Grammar, rhyme, metre—anything went by the board as it stood in the way of thought or freedom of utterance." Indeed, early editions of Dickinson's poems attempted to correct her imperfections: in one early printing of "I Heard a Fly Buzz—When I Died—," for instance, "in the room" was changed to "round my form" so that it would perfectly rhyme—rather than being merely consonant—with "storm."

It is the critical estimate of the twentieth century, and in particular the rise of "free verse"—the unrhymed, meter-free poetry that has gained respect, then predominance through the work of Walt Whitman, William Carlos Williams, Ezra Pound and others—that have both made Dickinson's verse seem to modern eyes highly patterned in some ways, deliciously irregular in others, and unambiguously brilliant. This estimate is highly informed by hindsight; in her own day, Dickinson was considered not only unpleasantly unusual inasmuch as she was a "poetess" (who, like her contemporaries Elizabeth Barrett Browning and Christina Rossetti, was tolerated as capable only of sentimental, small successes), but also insofar as her poetic form was, in the eyes of her peers, unpleasantly chaotic in its disregard (understood as incapacity) for traditional poetic form. Today, Dickinson's unique, brave tailoring of language to common but grand subject matter is widely hailed, even venerated. In her day, however, it signified nothing but mediocrity.

Even as Dickinson broke with the formal traditions that were upheld by her female poet contemporaries, she did not eschew them as her contemporary Whitman did. Where he did not begin to observe rhyme or meter—and indeed celebrated his disposal of them— Dickinson observed, yet then broke, her rhymes and meters. Thematically, too, she invokes the holiest themes of her day, only to break with them. Hymns, after all, were predominant in the New England of her day as liturgical forms—they were part of worshiping a glorious God. Is "I Heard a Fly Buzz—When I Died—" a celebration of a Protestant God? Yes and no. Our attention is brought to life after death—indeed we are confronted in the poem with a speaker whose very description of dying affirms that beyond life, one can still sing. More important, our attention is emphatically drawn to the moment when the divine—"the King"—is to appear in the silent, bright gulf between life and death to escort the speaker to the beyond. But does salvation occur? If so, it occurs somehow in conjunction with a fly and a mere buzz, of all things—associations that are already somewhat blasphemous. Perhaps we cannot be certain that salvation occurs at all. Perhaps the failing windows are not just those of the speaker, or those she sees in the room she is dying away from, but those between this world and the next. The poem is ambiguous, open to being read as testimony to the nothing that persists beyond our worldly sense perceptions of light and sound. This could be a larger blasphemy—a hymn that invokes the King only to then cast doubt upon his presence.

One popular hymn of Dickinson's era is, like many hymns, still familiar to us in tune, though less often in its content. The lyrics to "The Battle Hymn of the Republic" are, however, a valuable Civil War cultural artifact, particularly in their combined celebration of God, nation, and soldier: "I have read a fiery gospel writ in burnished rows of steel / As ye deal with my contemners, so you with my grace shall deal / Let the Hero, born of woman, crush the serpent with his heel / Since God

is marching on." God and human heroism were also Dickinson's perpetual themes; but her invocations are always also questions—she summons up such themes not for the sake of worship but for the sake of posing riddles. Whole revelation is refused; instead, she gives us ironic incompletion, quests without conclusions, doubt about the very sacredness of objects of worship. "I don't wonder that the good angels weep—and bad ones sing songs," she wrote. And, in a poem about the Civil War dead, "A bayonet's contrition / Is nothing to the dead." However wrong we may now consider the early opinion of Dickinson to have been, we can hardly be surprised at it. Deeply original, she trafficked in the most familiar and sacred subjects and forms of her day, only to trouble them, worry that they were inadequate, and question their value. Her originality was also reactionary and critical. What she perpetually delivers, however, is a somber delight in critical inquiry, in the importance of the details of the world. In the end, it is neither life nor death, but a stalled, bright moment between the two that we are vividly delivered with "I Heard a Fly Buzz—When I Died—." Delayed in riddle, wrapped up in suspense about assumptions Dickinson both asserts and refutes, we are, when contemplatively, attentively reading this poem, brought into confrontation not just with our world or the mystery of what lies beyond it, but with the mystery of our world.

**Source:** Kristina Zarlengo, in an essay for *Poetry for Students,* Gale, 1999.

## Sources

Anderson, Charles, R., *Emily Dickinson's Poetry,* New York: Holt, Rinehart and Winston, 1960.

Blake, Caesar R., and Carlton F. Wells, eds., *The Recognition of Emily Dickinson: Selected Criticism Since 1890,* Ann Arbor: The University of Michigan Press, 1964.

Cameron, Sharon, "Et in Arcadia Ego," in her *Lyric Time: Dickinson and the Limits of Genre,* John's Hopkins University Press, 1979, pp. 91–135.

Capps, Jack L., *Emily Dickinson's Reading,* Cambridge, MA: Harvard University Press, 1966.

Cody, John, *After Great Pain: The Inner Life of Emily Dickinson,* Cambridge, MA: Harvard University Press, 1971.

Dickinson, Emily, *The Essential Dickinson,* edited by Joyce Carol Oates, New Jersey: Ecco Press 1996.

———, *The Letters of Emily Dickinson,* 3 vols., edited by Thomas H. Johnson and Theodora Wald, Cambridge, MA: Harvard University Press, 1958.

————, *The Poems of Emily Dickinson, Including Variant Readings Critically Compared with All Known Manuscripts,* 3 vols., edited by Thomas H. Johnson, Cambridge, MA: Harvard University Press, 1963.

Dyer Lucas, Dolores, *Emily Dickinson and Riddle,* DeKalb: University of Illinois Press, 1969.

Filho, Blanca Lobo, *The Poetry of Emily Dickinson and Henriqueta Lisboa,* Norwood, PA: Norwood, 1978.

Hogue, Caroline, "Dickinson's 'I Heard A Fly Buzz When I Died,'" *The Explicator,* November 1961.

Kher, Inder Nath, "Death: The Cosmic Dance," in his *The Landscape of Absence: Emily Dickinson's Poetry,* Yale University Press, 1974. pp. 178–228.

Leyda, Jay, *The Years and Hours of Emily Dickinson,* New Haven, CT: Yale University Press, 1960.

Lindberg-Seyersted, Brita, *The Voice of the Poet: Aspects of Style in the Poetry of Emily Dickinson,* Cambridge, MA: Harvard University Press, 1968.

Martin, Wendy, *An American Triptych: Anne Bradstreet, Emily Dickinson, Adrienne Rich,* Chapel Hill: University of North Carolina Press, 1984.

Miller, Ruth, *The Poetry of Emily Dickinson,* Middletown, CT: Wesleyan University Press, 1968.

Mudge, Jean McClure, *Emily Dickinson and the Image of Home,* Amherst: University of Massachusetts Press, 1975.

Patterson, Rebecca, *The Riddle of Emily Dickinson,* New York: Cooper Square Publishers, Inc., 1973.

Taggard, Genevieve, *Life and Mind of Emily Dickinson,* New York: Alfred A Knopf, 1930.

Weisbuch, Robert, *Emily Dickinson's Poetry,* Chicago: University of Chicago Press, 1975.

Whicher, George Frisbie, *This Was a Poet: A Critical Biography of Emily Dickinson,* New York: Charles Scribner's Sons, 1938.

Wolosky, Shira, *Emily Dickinson: A Voice of War,* New Haven, CT: Yale University Press, 1984.

# In Flanders Fields

*John McCrae*

*1915*

One of Canada's best-known poems, "In Flanders Fields" was written on May 2, 1915, when Canadian serviceman John McCrae was stationed at an army hospital in Flanders, Belgium, during World War I. McCrae was not satisfied with the poem, and he threw it away, but another officer retrieved it and sent it to several publications in England. *Punch* magazine published the poem in December of that year.

"In Flanders Fields" was a huge success almost immediately, and it was reprinted in newspapers across the world, inspiring soldiers and touching the hearts of patriots at home. In 1917 the Canadian government used "In Flanders Fields" in its advertisements for Victory Loan Bonds, with unimaginable success: the bonds raised $400 million for the war effort. The poem was also credited with arousing American support for the war. The United States entered World War I in April of 1917, and by the end of 1918, the Central Powers were forced to admit defeat. Each year, countries across the globe use poppies—mentioned in the poem's first stanza—as a symbol to celebrate the armistice that ended World War I on November 11th, and "In Flanders Fields" is read at Remembrance Day celebrations each year on that day in countries across the British Commonwealth. Due to the impact of this poem, many veterans' groups sell poppies as a token of those who died in war.

## Author Biography

John McCrae was born in Guelph, Ontario, Canada, in 1872. He was talented in writing and art as a child, but when he was in school, he decided to study sciences. He earned a degree in biology from the University of Toronto in 1894 and then returned to the university for medical degrees in physiology and pathology in 1898. It was while he was in medical school that his first poems were published. After graduating, McCrae practiced medicine briefly at Toronto General Hospital and Johns Hopkins University in Boston. He then moved to Montreal to take up a fellowship in pathology at McGill University, which he was associated with the rest of his life: almost all of his poems that were published from then on were published in McGill's *University Magazine*. He was also a pathologist at Montreal General at the same time.

In 1900 McCrae joined a Canadian regiment that was helping the British fight the Boer War in South Africa. He returned home as a major in the Canadian Army and settled into a respected medical career, publishing thirty-three papers on medical topics and coauthoring a textbook on pathology. At the same time, he also kept active as a poet and was a member of Montreal's exclusive Pen and Pencil Club. He was highly cstccmcd as a physician and was elected to the Royal College of Physicians in London and to the Association of American Physicians.

In 1914, when World War I broke out, McCrae was on vacation in England, and he immediately volunteered as a medical officer in the Canadian Army. He was at a field hospital near Ypres, just outside of the Flanders section of Belgium, on May 1, 1915. Weeks before, at the infamous Second Battle of Ypres, the Germans had used chlorine gas for the first time in warfare and the Canadian troops had saved the day. On that day, McCrae watched a friend and former student, Lieutenant Alexis Helmer, die of shrapnel wounds. The death affected him more than others he had witnessed during the war. Helmer was buried in a small cemetery within clear sight of the field hospital, with McCrae performing the funeral ceremony because there was no chaplain available. The following day, he wrote "In Flanders Fields," scribbling the poem out in 20 minutes almost exactly as it was originally published. It was rejected by the British magazine *The Spectator* before being published, unsigned, in *Punch* on December 8, 1915. The poem became an international success, reprinted in newspapers throughout the world. After serving in Flanders, McCrae was promoted to lieutenant colonel and was appointed to run a military hospital in Boulogne, France. He contracted pneumonia, however, and after a prolonged battle with the disease, he died there on January 28, 1918.

## Poem Text

In Flanders fields the poppies blow
Between the crosses, row on row,
That mark our place; and in the sky
The larks, still bravely singing, fly
Scarce heard amid the guns below.          5
We are the Dead. Short days ago
We lived, felt dawn, saw sunset glow,
Loved and were loved, and now we lie
in Flanders fields.
Take up our quarrcl with thc foc:          10
To you from failing hands we throw
The torch; be yours to hold it high.
If ye break faith with us who die
We shall not sleep, though poppies grow
In Flanders fields.                        15

## Poem Summary

### Lines 1-5:

The first stanza of "In Flanders Fields" establishes the poem's setting and tone by presenting the contrasts of poppies growing among crosses (marking graves) and birds' songs drowned out by gunfire. The slight motion of the wind-blown poppies in the first line renders the crosses' stoic solidity fearsome; this effect is boosted by the somber gravity of the rows, implying that death is rigid and heartless. The use of poppies in this poem is significant in several ways. First, the poppy is a bright flower, which creates a striking visual image since the poppies are set against the presumably drab or white colors of the crosses. Second, poppies grow in freshly turned soil, implying that the cemetery has seen much activity recently. Also, the poppy is the source of narcotics, such as opium and heroin, that create a dream-like sense of unreality: death is often compared to sleeping and dreaming, an idea that the poem addresses in line 14. The shift from the ground to the sky in the last half of this stanza broaden the poem's visual range and adds sound to the sights that have been presented. This part of the stanza gives readers an oddly uneven perspective concerning the poem's speaker: the focus of the visual imagery is presented as if the speaker is "in the sky," away from the guns that are "down be-

## Media Adaptations

- An eight-part series titled *The Great War and the Shaping of the Twentieth Century* was produced by Carl Byker and is available on videocassette from Public Broadcasting System Home Video.

- James L. Stokesbury's *A Short History of World War I* was released on audio cassette by Recorded Books, Inc. in 1991.

- A television special titled *John McCrae's War: In Flanders Fields* was presented by the Canadian Broadcasting Corporation (CBC) on November 11, 1998. Written and directed by Robert Duncan, the film chronicles McCrae's life.

low." At the same time, however, the perspective is also on the ground, "amid the guns." This creates an unsettling effect, like a Cubist painting, with the reader being able to take in several points of view simultaneously. In an open space such as a battlefield or a cemetery, where one's attention would be drawn from one thing to another, this shift in perspective is hardly noticeable, but the impossibility of being in two places at the same time contributes to the poem's nightmarish quality.

### Lines 6-9:

Although the first-person, plural speaker of "In Flanders Fields" is alluded to in the third line, the reference is not very clear: the twisted syntax ("that" refers to "crosses," two phrases earlier) and the vagueness of what it means to have "our" places "marked" pushes the speakers' identity away from the reader. The second stanza, though, leaves no question about who is speaking. Not only is the poem spoken by the Dead—the word is capitalized to make them a specific group, not just a general category—, but the speakers are identified as recently slain soldiers. McCrae uses two ideas here to encompass all of the goodness of life and to, by contrast, emphasize the pathos of prematurely losing the gift of existence. Dawn and sunset repre-

sent all earthly experiences because they symbolize the full, circular span of a twenty-four hour day. In addition, the Dead did not just watch dawn happen, but the rising sun was "felt," indicating that not long ago, they were involved participants in the physical world. They experienced human emotions, too, which is summarized here by love. This leads readers to infer that their lives were full and complete, further signifying that their deaths were tragic, not a welcome release.

### Lines 10-15:

The last six lines of "In Flanders Fields" stand out as being very different from the rest of the poem. The first two stanzas are sad, while the third is defiant; the first two are physical, the third is mental; the first two are about the end of the speakers' lives, and the last is about those lives being carried on symbolically. Without a doubt, it is the last stanza's call to action that made "In Flanders Fields" hugely popular during the First World War and since that time. After first invoking the pity of death during wartime, the poem gives readers a chance to fight against that horror by catching and holding the "torch." This torch apparently stands for the ideals that the vanquished soldiers died for, but even without knowing the issues that propelled each side during World War I, whether the Dead supported good policies or bad, readers can sense that honor is involved, that honor is the torch, and that the torch can be extinguished without proper care. While the use of the first-person narrator makes the early part of the poem more touching by creating a degree of relationship with the reader that an anonymous narrator would lack, the same technique in the last stanza is vaguely threatening. Readers who are not stirred to action by the fear that honor will be extinguished are warned that if they "break faith" (their inaction is reversed to an action) the dead shall not sleep—a thought that should haunt the passive.

## Themes

### Death

McCrae frequently wrote about death, even in his many poems that were not about war. His fascination with the subject and the experience he had in exploring how death could be depicted in verse led to the ease with which he handled death in this poem; he used metaphor, imagery and personification so smoothly that it did not overshadow his other, complex ideas. The conceit of the deceased, especially the recently deceased, talking to us from the grave is not in itself unique. It is particularly fitting in a war poem, representing soldiers who have died struggling to achieve something and who have left their mission unfulfilled. In addition to giving us the plain, raw information about their deaths, McCrae presses readers into recognizing the fallen soldiers' place in the grand scheme of the universe by surrounding them with images from nature: the dawn and sunset, the larks, and the poppies. He intertwines these nature images with related images from the sphere of human interaction. Dawn and sunset are linked to loving and being loved, larks singing and flying are mirrored by the sound and flight of bullets and mortars, and the poppies, growing between the crosses, symbolize blood and perseverance almost as much as the crosses themselves. It is interesting that "In Flanders Fields" uses the first pairing of poppies and crosses to subtly bring to mind the contrast between death's stillness and life's activity: in an earlier version, McCrae used the static, inactive word "grow" in the first line, but "blow" gives readers a visual impression of motion, as opposed to the frozen stances of the rows of crosses. One advantage of this change is that the phrase "poppies grow" is not merely repetition when it appears in line 14. Another benefit is that it establishes a struggle between rest and motion early on in the poem, preparing the way for the final idea that the dead cannot peacefully rest in their graves.

### Honor

The "torch" tossed from the dead to the living is, of course, honor. It cannot represent a particular political ideology because the poem says nothing at all about right or wrong. The only way that the poem declares its loyalties is by mentioning the well-known battle site at Flanders. Even modern readers who are not familiar with World War I battles, who do not know the issues involved nor the dynamics of the struggle between the Triple Alliance and the Triple Entente, can appreciate the emotions that this speaker feels so strongly that he wants them carried on after his death. The important thing to this speaker is not the issues he stands for nor the policies that his enemy supports—he even uses the relatively mild word "quarrel" to refer to the conflict—but merely that his fighting spirit should continue. Losing the honorable spirit that the dead of this poem fought with would, in a sense, be mocking them, or "breaking faith" with them. Continuing their spirit, regardless of how one feels about their cause, is presented as a way to

## Topics for Further Study

- Poppies are still used to this day by veterans' groups around the world, signifying those who have died in wars. Research this flower's history: how it came to be associated with war and why it is an appropriate symbol for fallen soldiers.

- In a poem, respond for those who have had the torch passed to them.

- The Second Battles of Ypres was fought near Flanders, just months before this poem was published in 1915. It marked a turning point in modern warfare because it was the first time that chlorine gas was used against an enemy on the battlefield. Research the battle and explain how the Canadian Army, which McCrae belonged to, was able to save the day.

honor them as humans and grant their dead souls peace.

Since honor is an abstract emotion and not a specific course of action, this poem is adaptable to any number of circumstances beyond the occasion for which it was written. Anyone defeated in a struggle can relate to the speaker's desire that the "torch" will be carried on by someone else who finds the cause, or the defeated combatant, honorable. Anyone who cares about someone who has been defeated can relate to the hope that the defeat will not have been in vain. Anyone who knows someone who has been victorious, but who has eventually died anyway, can appreciate the nobility of honoring the dead. So inclusive are the emotions here that the lines about passing the torch are used for inspiration by a National Hockey League (NHL) team, inscribed both in English and French in the Montreal Canadiens' locker room. The Canadiens are the oldest team—being formed in 1917—and have won the most championships (Stanley Cups) of any NHL team. The lines "To you from failing hands we throw / The torch; be yours to hold it high" appear above pictures of the teams' former star players, reminding current team members that they have a long and glorious history to live up to and "honor." The "quarrel with our foe" in this case is a sporting challenge instead of a war, but "In Flanders Fields" stirs up the sense of honor so effectively that it works equally well.

### Revenge

This poem has been called an exquisitely effective piece of propaganda, and it was, in fact, used in its time to solicit contributions for the war fund in the McCrae's home country of Canada. Too often today we think of propaganda as a brainwashing tool, used to make evil look good, but it is actually not a good or bad thing: in this case, propaganda simply means that the poem is designed to stir up the greatest amount of empathy for the speaker and the greatest anger at his enemy. There is no doubt that, in the end, the poem encourages readers to take action against the foe. It influences readers by presenting death as a kind of peace in the first nine lines, but then, once that premise of peace is established, it threatens to deny peace to the dead soldiers if the enemy is not fought. The only mention of conflict in the first two stanzas is the vague mention of guns, and they are not even presented to readers directly, but are mentioned in context of the larks—noted as being somewhere below them. The poem's beginning emphasizes flowers, birds, and the setting and rising sun. It is in the tenth line, when the active command "Take" begins a call for fighting, that the initial serenity of "In Flanders Fields" is broken. If the poem had begun with a call to arms, it might have interested soldiers and those who are inclined to fight already, but in taking its time to establish readers' empathy with the poem's dead speaker, and then threatening the peace of the dead, it stirs readers to thoughts of vengeance.

## Style

This poem is a prime example of the highly stylized poetic form called the rondeau. Defining marks of the rondeau that are present here are that it is divided into three stanzas; that the stanzas have five, then four, then six lines; that the opening phrase of the first line is repeated in line 9 and again in line 15; and that, except for the repeated phrase, all of the lines have the same length (8 syllables). The rondeau is a French form and a member of what is sometimes referred to as the "rondeau family," which includes the triolet, the rondel, and the rondelet. Like many rondeaux, this poem is written in an iambic tetrameter rhythm. "Iambic" means that the even-numbered syllables are stressed, so that the general motion of the rhythm is from unstressed to stressed:

In **Flan**ders **field** the **pop**pies **blow**

"Tetrameter" means that there are four units per line (the units are called "feet," and in this case are two-syllable "iambs"). The rhyme scheme of "In Flanders Fields" is also typical of the rondeau, with only two sounds alternating at the ends of the lines: all of the lines here rhyme with "blow" or "sky," except for those which repeat the poem's initial phrase.

Most of the lines of this poem are *enjambed*— that is, they do not end with pauses for punctuation, but carry over into the lines that follow them. This gives it a sense of smooth continuity, making readers feel that one thought carries on from the last. The subject matter of the poem may command quiet concentration, but the structure of the poem is not broken down into units of thought, the way an intellectual inquiry can sometimes be. Instead, it is all run together smoothly, using the strong, clear repetition of the rhyming sounds to pace the rhythm.

## Historical Context

The emotions conveyed by "In Flanders Fields" are relevant to any war, but the poem was especially powerful during World War I, capturing the weariness and unflagging determination of its time so perfectly that it immediately became an international success, reprinted in newspapers throughout England, Canada, and countries allied with them. People needed the poem's encouragement at that particular time because the war had swelled to an immense scale that had never been seen before and the participants were faced with gruesome tools of mass destruction that had never been used in warfare before. As with any war, World War I (commonly referred to as "The Great War" by people of the time, who did not anticipate that a war of even greater proportions would come in the late 1930s) had numerous sociological and economical roots leading to its outbreak. Some historians believe that the accelerating factor was that Germany was looking for a reason to attack Russia; some believe that it was a last desperate attempt by the decrepit Austro-Hungarian Empire to hold onto its control of a sizable portion of Europe; but few ac-

# *Compare & Contrast*

- **1915:** The Great War in Europe was in its second year, although American troops did not join the battle until two years later.

**1990:** The United States, the world's only surviving superpower after the Soviet Union collapsed, led a coalition of countries in opposing Iraq's invasion of Kuwait. The war was over within a month of when the actual fighting began.

**Today:** The United States has had difficulty holding the coalition from the Gulf War in agreement, but most countries still seek international approval before taking military action.

- **1915:** The Ku Klux Klan was founded. Taking their name from a similar organization in the 1860s, the group's members hid their identities under sheets and, in the name of "white supremacy," committed terrorist attacks against blacks, Jews, and Roman Catholics.

**1989:** Former Klan grand wizard David Duke was elected to the Louisiana House of Representatives, shocking the rest of the nation.

**Today:** Although the Ku Klux Klan sometimes requests parade permits and presents itself as a legitimate political organization, most Americans reject it as a group based on hatred, violence, and bigotry.

- **1915:** The first experiments to cause cancer in laboratory animals were conducted in Japan, as chemists painted coal tar onto the ears of rabbits to examine the effects.

**Today:** Organizations that support animal rights advocate an end to laboratory testing, urging scientists to replace such tests with computer simulations.

---

cept the idea that the war was nothing but the result of a series of accidents, miscalculations, and personality conflicts, as the newspapers of the time presented it to be.

The direct cause of the war was the assassination of Archduke Franz Ferdinand, an heir to the Austro-Hungarian throne. On June 28, 1914, the archduke and his wife were shot while visiting the Bosnian capitol of Sarajevo. The man who killed them was a Serbian separatist who wanted Serbia to have independence from Austria-Hungary. He had gotten his gun from the separatist movement "The Black Hand," but it was never determined whether he was a member of the movement or if he just did business with them once. Also undetermined was whether the government of Serbia supported the Black Hand. The Austro-Hungarian government claimed that they did and that the Serbian government had helped and encouraged the assassination. The Serbians claimed that Austria-Hungary was inflating the importance of the incident in order to bully Serbia and to show all of the

countries in their confederation that they were still in control and could not be resisted.

On July 28, 1914, one month after the killing, Austria-Hungary issued a list of demands to Serbia. The Serbians agreed to all of the dictates except the most humiliating one: it stated that Austro-Hungarian troops should be allowed to search Serbian households for conspirators against the empire. The Serbs refused to allow foreign troops to come into their houses, and so on July 28, 1914, Austria-Hungary declared war against Serbia. Serbia had an agreement with Russia, though, requiring Russia to help defend Serbia in a war. Austria-Hungary was uncertain whether Russia was going to honor its part of the treaty, but they decided—partly due to Austro-Hungarian train schedules—to send troops to attack both Serbia and Russia at the same time. Germany was an ally of Austria-Hungary and had been anxious to break Russia's growing influence in Europe before it became too strong, so the Germans joined in the fighting immediately. The German Army was positioned for a fight with France, though, and since it was likely that France would eventually join the war, Germany attacked France. To get to France, Germany had to pass through Belgium (where Flanders is located). When Belgium's government did not grant permission to cut through their country, Germany attacked Belgium. England, which had a treaty to defend Belgium, joined the fight against Germany and Austria-Hungary. When England joined, Canada followed, and John McCrae joined up with the Canadian Army. Many Americans felt that the war was a European problem, and they did not want to spend money or lives on it, so the United States did not join the war until April of 1917. The infusion of American troops was critical to the Allied war effort, and World War I ended in November of 1918.

## Critical Overview

Few critics would be foolish enough to dispute the impact that "In Flanders Fields" had on the world when it was first published. Critical disagreements arise, however, regarding the question of how much craft was put into the poem and whether John McCrae earned the praise that was heaped on "In Flanders Fields" or if he was just lucky. Early on, when the world was still freshly enamored with the poem and its author, reviewers viewed the poem's achievement as the logical result of the poet's years of anonymous toil as a writer. H. E. Harmon wrote in 1920 that McCrae had earlier "written some verse, but nothing to indicate that he could ever be the author of 'In Flanders Fields.'" Harmon's focus was almost entirely on the poem's effect, how it stirred patriotism in England, Canada, and the United States to step up support for the war. Likewise, J. D. Logan and Donald G. Finch, in a 1924 essay titled "The War Poetry of Canada," speak of this poem as if it were valued only because of its popularity, and they use its acceptance across the world to compare Canadian verse to works from other countries, making "In Flanders Fields" their champion in some unnamed competition: "If the formal finish of Canadian poetry in the world was not always quite the equal of British and American poetry," they wrote, "still, the altogether most famous and most popular poem of the war ... is neither the English poet-soldier, Rupert Brooke, nor the American soldier-poet, Alan Seeger ... but the lyric of the Canadian soldier-poet John McCrae."

By 1926, critic Lewis Wharton was dredging the earlier works of McCrae for evidence that "In Flanders Fields" was the obvious and logical result of the poetic concerns that had interested the poet all along. He refers readers to "The Night Cometh," a McCrae poem published in 1913, calling it "every whit as beautiful and inspiring" as this poem. Whaton's praise of McCrae's poetry, however, is jumbled together with admiration for the poet's happy life. His comments about McCrae being "large of stature and still more large of heart" raise suspicions about whether he is judging the poetry objectively.

By the 1970s, critics were not as responsive to the mystique of either the poet or the poem, and so they could address its worth more clearly. A. H. Brodie's "John McCrae: A Centenary Reassessment," published in *The Humanities Association Bulletin* in 1972, also finds the roots of "In Flanders Fields" in the poet's earlier works. Brodie goes back to 1898 and cites themes, such as the melancholy that later developed into a fascination with death, and the evolution of the first-person speaker. One of the only critics willing to openly show dislike for this beloved poem is Paul Fussell, whose groundbreaking book *The Great War and Modern Memory* (1975) gives him a perspective that separates the poet's real skill from his ability to stir up emotions. Fussell calls "In Flanders Fields" "an interesting poem because it manages to accumulate the maximum number of well-known motifs and images, which it gathers under the aegis of a mellow, if automatic, pastoral." If that faint praise has a somewhat sarcastic tone, Fussell is openly hostile later in the piece: "[T]hings fall apart two-thirds of the way through as the vulgarities of 'Stand Up! Stand Up And Play The Game!' begin to make inroads into the pastoral, and we suddenly have a recruiting-poster rhetoric apparently applicable to any war." He finds the last stanza entirely inappropriate for what came before, and wonders "what the 'torch' is supposed to correspond to in trench life." Fussell adds, "words like *vicious* and *stupid* would not seem to go too far" to describe the final stanza.

## Criticism

### David Kelly

*David Kelly is an instructor of creative writing at several community colleges in Illinois, as well as a fiction writer and playwright. In the fol-*

*What Do I Read Next?*

- McCrae was a minor poet whose works are not often anthologized, nor is there a collection of his work in print. "In Flanders Fields" is, however, published by itself in a surprisingly informative children's book entitled *"In Flanders Fields": The Story of the Poem by John McCrae,* with background information by Linda Granfield and illustrations by Janet Wilson. This Doubleday Book for Young Readers, published in 1995, does a good job of relaying basic information without talking down to readers and can serve readers of any age for basic historical facts.

- Of all of the renowned British writers involved in World War I, one of the greatest was the poet Robert Graves, whose memoirs of his war experience, *Goodbye to All That,* was published in the 1920s when he was relatively young and was reissued in 1995, with notes by his nephew and biographer, Richard Perceval Graves. This is one of the best first hand accounts of life in the trenches.

- A scholarly review of the fiction that came out of the war is *The First World War in Fiction,* which contains essays by seventeen prominent scholars who explore common themes in the literature and discuss how the stories that were told helped shape the way we remember the war, thereby influencing world history. The collection was edited by the estimable Holger Klein and published by Harper and Row's Barnes and Noble imprint in 1976.

- McCrae's presence in anthologies of war poetry is always spotty: some compilers consider him a minor poet with only "In Flanders Fields" worth mentioning, while others regard any collection without him as incomplete. He does not appear in one of the best collections of poetry from World War I, Viking Compass Press' 1968 *Men Who Marched Away,* edited with an introduction by I. M. Parsons. All of the other significant poets are represented, though, and the book is divided into interesting categories ("The Bitter Truth," "No More Jokes," "The Wounded," etc.) that are a great help in finding a perspective.

---

*lowing essay, Kelly considers whether a poem written today could find the same success as did "In Flanders Fields."*

When a thing is wildly successful, it is not just our privilege but our responsibility to examine it and understand the secret of its success. Scientific knowledge is based on learning from either successes or failures, taking care, of course, not to damage the thing in the process of examination. Bad science, the type that people fear, holds study to be more important than life. A mad scientist might remove an athlete's leg muscles and examine them in separate laboratories, but no one would object to improving the jumping abilities of all humans by studying the tension points in the athlete's calves. Luckily, poems are made to be studied, and we cannot harm a poem by scrutinizing it and extracting any elements that can be useful to our own society.

John McCrae's poem "In Flanders Fields" fits perfectly into the category of phenomenal success. It is one of those achievements that could never have been anticipated. McCrae was, by all accounts, a decent and responsible man, a good and steady friend, a valuable citizen, doctor, and soldier, but the poetry he produced can generally be considered as a hobbyist's dabbling. Like most great inventors, his one outstanding success was a singular conflux of inspiration and its time (some critics consider McCrae's "The Anxious Dead" to be an equal achievement, but it's not the sort of success that anyone reprints any more). A large measure of the poem's achievement should be credited to McCrae, but much of it is also due to the society that read the poem and embraced it. The issues it addresses must have touched its audience. Could the same thing happen today? It would be useless, after all, to study McCrae's poem if it were

> *A large measure of the poem's achievement should be credited to McCrae, but much of it is also due to the society that read the poem and embraced it."*

irrelevant to the present or the future. Contemporary poets studying how to make a work as effective as "In Flanders Fields" could benefit terrifically if they could tap into the store of energy that this poem has displayed.

The first thing poets will consider is the optimistic side, the belief that any well-crafted poem speaks to all of us across the span of time, across cultures and generations. Of course, "In Flanders Fields" addresses a particular place mired within a particular conflict, but death is death and courage is courage, so the subject of the poem doesn't have to be foreign to readers who take the trouble to meet it halfway in trying to understand it. So long as death is a one-way experience—a mystery that we can count on continuing for the foreseeable future—the shocking contrast of someone watching the sun rise one day and being dead the next will continue to give readers a chill. One does not have to have experienced war to appreciate the juxtaposition of crosses and flowers and of singing larks and exploding bombs.

"In Flanders Fields" is also nonspecific enough to survive the treacherous journey from one social setting to another. It avoids mentioning who was fighting against who, or the principles for which they were fighting. One of the first mistakes made by beginning poets is in confusing vagueness with universality, thinking (or hoping) that a scene lacking details will invite readers to see their own lives in the poem, while such openness usually says no more than "Someone did something," leaving readers bored, confused, and uninvolved. That effect they are straining for is the one that "In Flanders Fields" accomplishes, making itself applicable to different situations while providing concrete imagery, such as the torch, that gives the poem bal-

last. The most obvious reuse of this eighty-plus-year-old war poem is its place on the wall of the locker room of hockey's Montreal Canadiens, where the last stanza's first three lines are painted in English and French. If the sentiments in the poem can apply this well to a new, unintended situation, then we should guess it would be possible that a war poem could be written today with equal longevity, if it could serve other purposes when there is no war going on. Even in times of peace, courage is always in fashion.

This raises the most compelling argument for believing that "In Flanders Fields" has something to offer the contemporary poet who is excavating for something to make her or his own: war is still with us, and there is no reason to believe that it is going away soon. As the example of the Canadiens' locker room reminds us, humans are likely to find war anywhere, in the smallest and most symbolic places: anyone can find some personal meaning in the words "our quarrel with our foe." Since this poem is openly about warfare, though, and only implies all other forms of human opposition, a modern equivalent of it would work only if the modern world could support a war poem. Can it? The answer should be obvious—a world that has a place for war should also have a place for war poetry—but the world we live in is actually a very different one than the one in which John McCrae saw battle. Clearly, people in 1915 needed this poem. They found themselves in its fear, hope, and stubbornness, and they counted on others to relate to it in the same way, which is why it has been often used for memorial ceremonies and was effective in fund-raising advertisements for war bonds. Now, at the end of the twentieth century, our relationship to both war and poetry has changed.

It is almost impossible to imagine a contemporary poem that could receive the widespread popularity accorded to "In Flanders Fields." People in the general population just do not know poems anymore, because poetry seldom makes its way into the lives of ordinary people. No one really knows why this is, although that of course doesn't keep all interested observers from voicing opinions about it. One of the most convincing arguments states that the increased availability of college education since the end of World War II has created a whole class of poetry "specialists," with the end result being that those who are not specifically trained to read and write poetry feel unqualified, and so they leave it alone. The field of poetry itself has helped alienate mass audiences by shunning exactly the elements that beginning readers feel most comfortable with: rhythm and rhyme and sentimentality. At the same time, other diversions have been actively inviting the attention of mass audiences. Readers frustrated with postmodern poetry's labyrinth of meanings started long ago to appreciate the process of having their minds massaged, not challenged, by radio and television, and now several generations have passed with each caring less and less about making poetry part of their lives. Millions of people study poetry and millions more faithfully read it for pleasure, but it would be difficult to identify a single poem from the past twenty years that has become a part of our culture. The most recent example to come to mind is Allen Ginsberg's book-length "Howl," from 1956. The role poetry used to play has been taken up, mostly by popular music and, to some degree, by advertising.

Even if we suppose that a poem could have a resounding impact today—if poetry made a widespread, lasting resurgence in public life (beyond even the trademarked "Poetry Slams" that have taken readings out of lecture halls and into bars) or if, like some anthologies do to court students, we counted song lyrics as poems—it is still unlikely that a poem like "In Flanders Fields" could rise up and gain recognition across the world, given its subject matter. It is true that during times of war patriotic feelings swell, but that is balanced against the fact that, since the social turmoil during the Vietnam conflict that gave pacifism a voice, politicians around the world are hesitant to commit to fighting without a clear, nearly objection-proof rationale. The world is a much more cynical place: we are no longer willing to fight wars because politicians tell us to, because we distrust their motives and judgement. It seems naive, then, to think we would be willing to engage in warfare just to avoid breaking faith with strangers who came before.

There is a sense of history and tradition in McCrae's poem: though not mentioned, it holds the poem together. It is missing from our experience. Some people consider this a good thing, and they have a point. It is a complex world, jam-packed with information—where a grammar school student in Bettendorf, Iowa, can sit at her desk and access designs for an office center in Katmandu, and where a simple discussion of the common cold leads to the double-helix DNA strand and which chromosome makes who susceptible. With the flood of data that washes across us each day, each piece which might be significant, our brains are filling to capacity, and people have been making the

decision to quit retaining ideas about others who have already passed from the earth. Each year newspapers have great fun printing examples of college students who think the Civil War was fought in the 1940s or that Shakespeare and Aristotle knew each other, but they do not offer any useful advice about how to remember the past when there is so much else to pay attention to. The problem is that ignoring history, like ignoring anything, becomes too easy. Forgetting the soldier who wants to pass on his torch has become as easy as forgetting the date of the Magna Carta. This, above all else, is why it is unlikely that a poet would be able to write some version of "In Flanders Fields" for today. The question of whether or not we are too peaceful today to take up the fight is debatable, but contemporary humans are just too busy with what comes next to hear a plea from the dying or the dead.

**Source:** David Kelly, in an essay for *Poetry for Students,* Gale, 1999.

### Bruce Meyer

*Bruce Meyer is the director of the creative writing program at the University of Toronto. He has taught at several Canadian universities and is the author of three collections of poetry. In the following essay, Meyer explores the reasons why an admittedly flawed poem caught the world's attention and has remained popular for more than 80 years.*

John McCrae's "In Flanders Fields" is, without a doubt, the best-known Canadian poem. Written in the trenches in 1915 during the Battle of Ypres when Canadian troops distinguished themselves as a "national" unit for the first time, the poem was published soon after in the British magazine *Punch*. Almost immediately, "In Flanders Fields" acquired a popular reputation in much the same way that "John Brown's Body" or Julia Ward Howe's "Battle Hymn of the Republic" became a public mantra epitomizing the raison d'être for the American Civil War. From the perspective of the troops, "In Flanders Fields" recognized their sacrifice and their suffering in the trenches. From the public's point-of-view, the poem was couched in a poetic language that made the experience of the war accessible to the general reader—it speaks little of the horrors and attaches symbolism to experiences that would be too painful to convey if expressed in realistic terms.

As Paul Fussell suggests in his famous study of World War I literature, *The Great War and Mod-*

*ern Memory,* "In Flanders Fields" won instant recognition on both the battle and home fronts because it "manages to accumulate the maximum number of well-known motifs and images, which it gathers under the aegis of a mellow, if automatic pastoralism." Fussell goes on to comment, however, that the poem "falls apart" two thirds of the way through with its "recruitment poster rhetoric" of "Take up our quarrel with the foe." Yet, since the First World War, McCrae's poem has not diminished in its significance or in its public reception. For all the mixed signals that the poem sends—the confusion of a Virgilian pastoral elegiac patriotism and self-sacrifice with an overt and seemingly clumsy call to arms—it has succeeded in permeating the cultural consciousness, not only of Canadians but of English-speakers worldwide as a testament to the grim horrors of war. It is to McCrae's poem that generations since the First World War can trace the source of the poppy as a symbol of the conflict and the waste of war. Unlike other World War I poems, such as Wilfred Owen's "Anthem for Doomed Youth" or Siegfried Sassoon's "Does It Matter," which warn against war and dismiss its horrors, "In Flanders Fields" offers a covenant between the dead and the living: future generations should not "break faith with us who die" and should value the peace that was won at such an enormous cost. The question that "In Flanders Fields" constantly raises is how did this particular poem, for all its flaws, become so universally accepted in both the public consciousness and the poetic canon of the twentieth century? The answer to this puzzle is composed of several pieces.

The first piece of the puzzle is its language. One of the greatest problems facing the trench poets of the First World War was the linguistic gap between the brutal actuality of the war and the public perception and acceptance of the horrors. To a reading public, especially Canadian readers, during the First World War, the public ear and imagination had not yet left the Romantic era. At the root of what readers believed to be "acceptable" poetry was a gentle and natural pastoralism, a bucolic quietude that embraced Pan pipes over the filth and violence of the trench experience. One contemporary of McCrae's, Canadian poet Bernard Freeman Trotter, went into the trenches as a Victorian poet whose chief perceptions were poetic renderings of sunsets and stately pines. In the course of the trench experience, as evidenced by his final and tellingly haunting poem, "Ici Repose," Trotter was using such phrases as "tainted effluvia" to describe not simply the trench experience at the front, but the

complacent peace that might come from the bitter sacrifice. In truth, the reality of the war could not be borne by the public's perception to the point that critics such as E. K. Brown, in his trend-setting study titled *On Canadian Poetry*, simply dismissed the entire body of Canadian writing from the war as unimportant. Where McCrae seems to have succeeded in overcoming the perceptual gap between the reality and the imagination of the reality is through a compromise between poetic language and horrific reality.

The "motifs and images" mentioned by Fussell are ideally poetic. Rather than reciting a litany of shocking images, McCrae chooses to convey his ideas through the use of gentle images. The "poppies" are not torn apart by bombardments; they are gently "blowing" between the crosses. The "larks" are still "bravely singing" as they "fly," a symbol of nature's resistance and defiance of the grim reality of the guns that are not heard far off, but "below" in a subtle suggestion of a netherworld or Plutonian hell that exists, not in this world, but in an alternative reality. The poem, therefore, is not addressing the realities of war as much as it is commenting upon the certainties and fixed visibilities of this world.

Where McCrae takes leave of perceivable realities is in his use of the "ghost voice" persona of the poem. The narrator, we discover, is not a single, detached voice, but a gathering of voices, a chorus in the Greek fashion, commenting on the tragedy and announcing themselves in a short, almost frank sentence: "We are the dead." As absurd as it may seem to animate the dead for the purpose of raising a call to arms in the second half of the poem, there are some subtle ramifications to this move. First, the reader is meant to see that death is not an end but a prevention from action. The dead can no longer fight and are removed from this world and all its sensual beauty and intricacy: "Short days ago / We lived, felt dawn, saw sunset glow, / Loved and were loved, and now we lie / In Flanders Fields." There is the logical implication of life after death, at least in a classical "Shade" mode that is so often associated with the Underworld or "Nekusis" scenes from epics such as *The Aeneid* or *The Odyssey.* What is struck is a plea: the dead demand from the living both action and faith. The entire poem is thus moved to the level of a matter of belief and dedication, and the war is elevated to that of a religious quest. It is no wonder the troops found this poem as moving as they did, and it is easy to see how a poetic-minded public readership could buy into the plethora of devices that McCrae implements because there has been a conscious attempt on the part of the poet to address, through the language of poetry, the concerns and perceptions of two very disparate readerships.

The second piece of the puzzle is the poem's prosody. Sir Andrew Macphail, who wrote the introductory essay to the first edition of *In Flanders Fields* in 1919, wrongly argues that the poem is a nonce form of a Petrarchan sonnet. Macphail explains that the additional fifteenth line is appended to the end of the poem as a reiteration of both the setting and as a link to the opening line of the poem where the symbolism of the "poppies," a device embodying martyrdom and almost religious sacrifice, is established.

What seems to have misled Macphail is the rhyme scheme. As a sonnet variation, the poem hovers between a lyric and a piece of persuasion or rhetoric. The poem works on a very limited rhyme scheme—the "ow" rhymes and the "ie" rhymes and the additional truncated ninth and fifteenth lines comprised of an iamb and a trochee that toll like a knell—yet it retains a mysterious lyricism that is simultaneously grave and melodious in tone. What is surprising about the lyricism of the rhyme scheme is that it is "pretty," a problem that seems to disconnect the poem from the elevated nature of its content. The rhyme scheme, however, for all of its lyricism, serves to support the essentially melodic and lyrical structure of a Petrarchan sonnet and couch the poem in the linguistic nuances of one of the sonnet's traditional applications—a love poem. It should be remembered that the sonnet had its origins in religious hymns of the early Middle Ages and in its earliest applications by poets such as Dante and Petrarch was intended to elevate the lover to almost beatific proportions. The religious quality of the poem's final lines, the call not merely to arms but to faith, is likely the intent that McCrae sought when he slipped into what Fussell reads as war rhetoric. In this respect, "In Flanders Fields" raises the war to an ecstatic matter and the annihilation of so many soldiers to the level of martyrdom. Macphail may have been eager to justify the poem in these formal terms because such a reading would have placed the poem at the center of the public perception of the war in the years immediately following the hostilities. Where "In Flanders Fields" most closely approaches the sonnet form is in its sense of rhetoric. Sonnets are by nature more rhetorical than lyrical, and after a reasonably lyrical opening in which the dead are given both voice and personification, the poem (in what could be

construed as a sestet) concludes with a call to arms and a plea for faith in the cause for which so many have died: "Take up our quarrel with the foe." As an extended sonnet, however, "In Flanders Fields" approaches more of a nonce form because it extends the sonnet form beyond reasonable capability by arguing not one issue, but several: sacrifice, the relationship between life and death, the problems of faith and belief, and the continued support of a cause that, like the First World War itself, is never made completely clear. Macphail's reading does not work for one particular reason: he was mistaken about the poem's form.

In reality, "In Flanders Fields" is neither a sonnet nor a nonce form, but a traditional rondeau. As a very stylized, artificial and dance-like French form, the fifteen-line rondeau is designed both to delight the reader with its lyricism while at the same time rhetorically persuading the reader to a definite perception by its insistence on the repetition of a truncation of the opening line in lines nine and fifteen. Hence, the reader is constantly reminded of what took place "In Flanders fields," so that the entire world of the poem is permeated with a didactic refrain. The choice of the rondeau form on McCrae's part is an excellent illustration of Matthew Arnold's dictum at work: that poetry should both teach and delight. In a war where the lessons may have seemed few and far between, this memorializing process and this insistence on "what happened here" ritualizes the sense of sacrifice and forms both a reminder and a monument to the fallen. The rhetorical or persuasive aspects of the poem are further underscored through McCrae's use of enjambment—of running his statements syntactically rather than linearly. This serves to turn the lyrical qualities of the limited rhyme scheme into a low rumination, much like the sound of the "scarce heard" ... "below." This is use of enjambment in what should, at first hearing, sound in the ear of the reader as a piece of lyricism, but is muted by the wrapped sentences, so that sonically, the poem is more a rhetorical structure than a lyric. This is, perhaps, why Fussell takes such an exception to the piece as a "call to arms." After all, McCrae is establishing a very distinct and artificial form for the poem; he then deliberately sets out to undercut it through every means available to him. Why should McCrae do this? Perhaps the answer lies in Addorno's famous statement, "After Auschwitz, no poetry," the prevailing sentiment among many twentieth-century artists that language and its artifice is incapable of directly expressing the horrors of the era.

The third piece of the puzzle, and one addressed by Fussell, is the claim that "In Flanders Fields" is an elegy in the traditional sense. The reader is reminded of Thomas Gray's "Elegy Written in a Country Churchyard" and its ominous yet incontrovertible claims that "the paths of glory lead but to the grave." McCrae's poem opens with a cemetery scene, a setting that is far removed from the fight—a place not of trenches or even suffering and violence but of "poppies" that "blow." The image of peacefulness is juxtaposed with the events of "Short days ago" which are, in themselves, associated not with war but of life, so that the dead "lived, felt dawn, saw sunset glow, / Loved and were loved." The idea here is that the dead gave their lives in the cause of life and that the reader should "Take up our quarrel with the foe" not as a matter of defending a specific political position, but as a matter of defending life. This contrast between life and death, between the living and the dead, is one of the repeated elements that can be seen in the elegiac form. The subtle pastoralism of the opening lines of the poem is founded solely on the image of the poppies; yet McCrae evolves the entire poem on this powerful image so that one imagines the sacrifice to have taken place on a grand scale where "row on row" of crosses now fill many "fields," as if all of nature has been consumed by the struggle. The quest or challenge that is issued in the final lines of the poem is, therefore, a quest for a redemption of nature and, by association, the entire world, and not just a mere call to arms. To this end, the "torch" in the final lines is not merely a baton in a relay race toward mass destruction but an eternal flame—a promise to life that must be maintained, whatever the cost. What should be remembered is that elegies, traditionally, not only lament a loss but seek to rectify the problems that have beset nature. McCrae, however, offers no solution to the war. This is a perceptual problem that seems to have been beyond reach for both the public and the political mentalities of the time, and it is the issue for which Siegfried Sassoon was deemed "insane" by a court-martial tribunal. What the reader is meant to see in this simple poem is not a rectification but a remembrance. The dead cannot be brought back, but they serve as a reminder to the living for the principles of duty, sacrifice, and faith.

The most surprising aspect of the elegiac properties of the poem, and one that goes against the grain of traditional elegy, is the vocality of the dead. The device, however, should not be construed literally, even in the sense of "poetic literalness."

What the reader is confronting in "In Flanders Fields" is the dead being given voice by the living—a gesture of poetic justice that sounds as a note of remembrance. So clearly has McCrae sounded this note through his use of language, form, and content that the poem has, in Canada, been the centerpiece of a solemn national holiday— Remembrance Day—held each year on the anniversary of the Armistice that ended World War I on November 11. The poem is memorized and recited by schoolchildren in their classrooms and at memorials and cenotaphs across the country. At precisely eleven o'clock, all businesses, transit operations, offices, and pedestrians pause for a moment of silence in memory of those who fell in the First World War (a conflict in which Canada suffered one of the highest per capita losses of any Allied nation) and in tribute to the fallen from other wars and those who serve overseas on peace-keeping missions. As a gesture of solidarity with "the Dead" who "lived, felt dawn, saw sunset glow, / Loved and were loved," Canadians wear a red poppy on their lapels, a symbol that was given to them, in memory and with a religious reverence, through the poem McCrae penned during the Battle of Ypres.

**Source:** Bruce Meyer, in an essay for *Poetry for Students,* Gale, 1999.

### Milton Acorn

*In the following excerpt, Acorn comments upon John McCrae and his most famous poem, "In Flanders Fields."*

"In Flanders Fields" [**IFF**] is a poem of such power that virtually every born or integrated Canadian can quote from it, when they can't quote the whole work by heart. As to the rest of McCrae's verse, it is probable that the greater part has never achieved print, let alone adequate distribution. Astounding as it may seem, the supplement to *THE GOLDEN TREASURY OF ENGLISH VERSE* collected by another famous war poet C. Day Lewis at a time when **IFF** was unquestionably the most popular poem in at least the English-speaking world, does not list it. Years ago at a Contact Poetry Reading I expressed the opinion that the reason Canadian poetry was not world famous was because Canada had only a small army. Ireland has suffered long from a similar difficulty, but has overcome it, so much so that today when we refer to English poetry we usually mean Irish.

I might add that to classify John McCrae as a war-poet does him an injustice. Much of his life was lived in the bloodiest century of all human history; as a Canadian, a member of the most formidable nation of all the British Empire's mercenary array. As a doctor—indeed a famous surgeon—he was bound to be involved....

As for classifying "In Flanders Fields" as a war poem (it certainly was no "Charge Of The Light Brigade") I ask you to consider the final verse:

> Take up the quarrel with the foe:
> To you with failing hands we throw
> The torch; be yours to hold it high.
> If ye break faith with us who die
> We shall not sleep, though poppies grow
> In Flanders fields.

This verse hangs permanently in the dressing room of the world champion Montreal Canadiens, who have won far more Stanley Cups than any other team, and is most appropriately there. For it can be easily interpreted as a call to celebrate the Olympic Games in 1916, after which there would have been no more war. The Olympic torch, used there as a symbol of continuing struggle, was a peace emblem. This is the only section of **IFF** which *might* be interpreted unambiguously as pro-war. Otherwise it is a poem of the pity and horror of war, and McCrae's other writings on the Second Battle of Ypres make this abundantly clear.

The fact is that **IFF** was a poem against fascism, whose existence McCrae was one of the first to detect....

[McCrae] was not a very professional poet but a doctor, in fact a famous one. His poems were very thorough, though not in the popular sense. Until "In Flanders Fields" he sent few out except by request. It is an easy guess that he assumed that popularization of his poetry, full in the Canadian democratic tradition, would detract from his income as a doctor. Then after the block-buster poem "In Flanders Fields" hit the world, before the war was over and his soldier's duty ended, he died. Probably an early victim of 'the spanish flu' or it could have been his role in combat. After his service at 2nd. Ypres, according to [Andrew] MacPhail's testimony, he was never healthy and could have perhaps obtained a discharge. But his rank became very high and he died as chief consultant of the British Medical Services. Besides his realization of the importance of the first of *The Wars* would have prevented his wangling a discharge anyhow.

He was, by the way, never optimistic about the result of the conflict in which he was involved. When he said *"failing hands"* he meant it.

In the end one more note about the remarkable qualities of "In Flanders Fields" (please still notice

> *'In Flanders Fields' is a poem of such power that virtually every born or integrated Canadian can quote from it, when they can't quote the whole work by heart."*

the acrosticism) it's ease of translation. Take note of these two lines traduced in English and French:

> *To you with failing hands we throw*
> *Le flambeau! Tenir-le en haut!*

My French is too spotty to carry on with this task, but it can easily be seen that it requires not even a translation, just transposition. So **IFF** spread through both the British and French armies in World War I. Since the Germans are indefatigable translators it is likely that many copies were spread among them as well ...

Is it possible that the Christmas Mutiny of 1916, which spread to both sides of the line and was finally broken up by artillery shells flung from both sides, was a consequence of this Canadian poem? Well what was the end of it? What did it all mean? One of the little-mentioned facts about the Second World War was that the Nazi U-boat fleet was present in full force in the Norwegian Campaign ... but the British didn't know it! Every torpedo thrown at the Brits turned out to be useless, certainly sabotaged by skilled workers, whose mental motto is "Run silent, Run deep".

Presuming that to be true never again call poetry a useless ornament to society.

**Source:** Acorn, Milton, "From Isandhlwawa to Flanders Fields: With John McCrae," in *Waves,* vol. 15, nos. 1 and 2, fall 1986, pp. 92–6.

### John F. Prescott

*In the following excerpt, Prescott discusses the publication and reception of "In Flanders Fields."*

On 8 Dec. 1915 *Punch* published *In Flanders Fields,* anonymously, though the index of that year attributed authorship to McCrae. This poem was the most popular English poem of the Great War. In 1915 there was intense hatred of Germany in England, fuelled by the *Lusitania* sinking, the Zeppelin raids, the use of poison gas, and the atrocity stories. People felt that a long suspected German barbarism had finally revealed itself. McCrae's immensely popular poem did much to encourage the British in the need to defeat the Germans and to avenge the increasing and staggering numbers of British war dead, soldiers and civilians alike. His poem made the poppy, the symbol of oblivion, inseparable from the experience of the First World War. The poem gave "expression to a mood which at the time was universal, and will remain as a permanent record when the mood is passed away."

The poem has McCrae's usual themes of death bringing peace after struggle, and of the voice from the grave; it echoes his 1906 poem *The unconquered dead.* It was the ferocious last third of the poem, so different from the rest, which was used extensively to further the war effort—for recruiting, raising money, attacking both pacifists and profiteers, and comforting the relatives of the dead. It also was a useful piece of propaganda in the Canadian general election of 1917. Together with Rupert Brooke's *The soldier* (1914), Julian Grenfell's *Into battle* (1915), and Laurence Binyoun's *For the fallen* (1914), it was one of the most quoted poems of the war, and of these poems it was the most popular. All were poems written before the monstrous slaughter of the war turned the poetry of the fighting soldiers to bitterness, disillusion, anger, pity, or escapism.

Everyone in the English-speaking world knew the poem. Canadians, especially McCrae's Montreal friends, were proud. Leacock wrote later that "to us in Canada it is a wonderful thought that Jack McCrae's verses and memory should now become part of the common heritage of the English people. These are works of Empire indeed." The poem was especially popular in the United States when she entered the war, and it made McCrae's a household name, albeit a frequently misspelt one....

McCrae received many requests to use *In Flanders Fields* for raising money for the cause. He was sent translations in many languages, including Latin *In agro belgico* ("it needs only Chinese now, surely," said McCrae.) He was modest about its success; his mother sent him clippings about its use and effect. "I return the clippings. I would like to believe them if I dared. I wish they would get to printing 'In F.F.' correctly: it never is nowadays." Apart from seeing his name misspelt, McCrae was surprised to discover the variety of his ranks. "I am promoted Captain this time (Lt. previously)." He was sometimes amused by the response, "Tom sent me some bunk from *The Herald* about me as a 'Guelph boy.' I would fain remind *The Herald* of one or two things in its history—not least the Guelph Junction Railway Bill."

The success of the poem, together with McCrae's early recruitment into the army and his courage at the battle of Ypres, made him a hero to his friends, to the Canadian army, and within the hospital. As for McCrae himself, he was satisfied if the poem enabled men to see where their duty lay....

Although John McCrae would have felt that he had broken faith had he lived while so many had died, the reaction of his friends and contemporaries to his death in France in 1918 was one of great grief. They wrote of his unswerving fidelity, his professional ability, his many talents, his wide knowledge, his kindliness, and his charm. McCrae was greatly loved by all who knew him, and his contemporaries felt that death had cheated them of the best which was to come. His brother tried to comfort the family by telling them that the bitter and disillusioned man who would have returned from the war was not the sparkling man who went to it.

Had McCrae lived, he would have been proud that the war had given a new pride to Canada and a new identity to her sons in the changed relation with the mother country. From a population of eight million, 620,000 Canadians fought in France, 61,326 were killed, and one-third were wounded —the colonial country rose to nationhood through the courage of her soldiers. McCrae would have been scathing of the Treaty of Versailles, in which the next war was implicit. He would have been pleased that, because of *In Flanders Fields,* the poppy was adopted to remember the war dead of the British empire, and is sold in millions every November 11 around the world. He would have remained grief-stricken by the deaths of so many of his friends and patients but pleased to know that his medical colleagues remembered him in a stained-glass window in Montreal which called him "Pathologist, Poet, Physician, Soldier, a Man among Men."

Before he died McCrae knew his poem to be the most popular of the English-language war verses. It had captured the mood of the British public in 1915. He was pleased by its effects in the empire and in the United States. Its impact was enormous. It was the poem of the British army. It was quoted everywhere—with frenzy in selling war bonds and encouraging recruiting, with conviction in harassing pacifists or pillorying profiteers, and with compassion in comforting the relatives of the myriad war dead. The poem was written by a man who had previously published little poetry and who wrote verse as a form of relaxation. But *In Flanders Fields* has the hallmarks of his other poems—the preoccupation with death, the desire for oblivion, and the voice from the grave.

Modern critics, favouring poets more gifted and more critical of the slaughter have placed McCrae's poem in a quiet corner. The British world was changed irrevocably by the Great War, and *In Flanders Fields* is now an anachronism, to be dusted off for lip-service to dead heroes, or to be learned as an exercise by school children. To understand the poem, the poet, and the circumstances of the writing is to enter a lost world, a world unscarred by the futility of the trenches. It is to know how men felt who volunteered for the War, men who believed that they were fighting evil for the future of mankind. But reality was Passchendaele, Arras, Hill 70, Verdun, Vimy Ridge, The Somme, and other killing grounds. Soldiers do not die without wounds, and McCrae saw it all, from the cheering crowds to the obscenity of corrupted flesh. The War broke his heart.

**Source:** Prescott, John F., *In Flanders Fields: The Story of John McCrae,* Erin, Ontario: The Boston Mills Press, 1985.

## Sources

Brodie, A. H., "John McCrae: A Centenary Reassessment," *The Humanities Association Bulletin,* Vol. 23, No. 1, winter 1972, pp 12-22.

Fleming, D. F., *The Origins and Legacies of World War I,* Garden City, NY: Doubleday and Co., 1968.

Fussell, Paul, *The Great War and Modern Memory,* New York: Oxford University Press, 1975.

Gilbert, Martin, *The First World War: A Complete History,* New York: Henry Holt, 1994.

Harmon, H. E., "Two Famous Poems of the World War," *South Atlantic Quarterly,* Vol. 19, No. 1, January 1920, pp. 9-17.

Haythornthwaite, Philip J., *The World War I Source Book,* London: Arms and Armour Press, 1992.

Lamb, W. Kaye, *The History of Canada: From Discovery to Present,* New York: American Heritage Press, 1971.

Logan, J. D., and Donald G. French, "The War Poetry of Canada," *Highways of Canadian Literature: A Synoptic Introduction to the Literary History of Canada (English) from 1760 to 1924,* Toronto: McClelland and Stewart Ltd., 1924.

Stokesbury, James L., *A Short History of World War I,* New York: William Morrow and Co., 1981.

Wharton, Lewis, "Who's Who in Canadian Literature: John McCrae," *The Canadian Bookman,* Vol. 8, No. 8, August 1926, pp. 237-40.

## For Further Study

Bergonzi, Bernard, *Heroes' Twilight: A Study of the Literature of the Great War,* New York: Coward-McCann Co., 1965.

> The one mention of McCrae in this text comes up during a discussion the use of "poppies" as symbols in World War I poetry. The book does, though, offer a sharp and comprehensive overview of the poets it does discuss.

Fussell, Paul, *The Great War and Modern Memory,* New York: Oxford University Press, 1975.

> Fussell examines the ways in which literature has depicted the events of World War I and the effect of these portrayals on how we view the war today. He deems "In Flanders Fields" inferior to other poems written at the time, categorizing it as a piece of inconsistency that works as pro-war propaganda.

Quinn, Tom, *Tales of the Old Soldiers,* Dover, NH: Alan Sutton Publishing Inc., 1993.

> This book compiles the reminiscences of ten British soldiers who were involved in World War I. Most of the interviewees were in their nineties and one was a hundred years old. The subjects are thus able to put their youthful experiences into the perspective of their full lives.

Winter, Jay, and Blaine Baggett, *The Great War and the Shaping of the 20th Century,* New York: Penguin Studio, 1996.

> This book is the companion piece for the Public Broadcasting Service (PBS) television series of the same name. Meticulously researched and designed to make the pictures and text relevant to the modern young reader, it can be used either for a general overview of the war or for in-depth details.

# Kubla Khan

## Samuel Taylor Coleridge
## 1816

Although Samuel Taylor Coleridge is one of the major literary figures of the Romantic movement in England, as a poet his reputation stands on primarily just three works, "The Rime of the Ancient Mariner," "Christabel," and "Kubla Khan." All three were written between 1797 and 1800; however, "Kubla Khan" was not published until 1816. At that time, Coleridge subtitled it "A Vision in a Dream: A Fragment" and added a prefatory note explaining the unusual origin of the poem. This preface describes how Coleridge, after taking some opium as medication, grew drowsy while reading a passage about the court of Kubla Khan in Samuel Purchas's *Pilgrimage,* a seventeenth-century travel book recounting the adventures of early explorers. Soon he fell into a deep sleep which lasted about three hours. During this period, he composed from 200 to 300 lines of poetry based on the vivid images in his dream. When he woke, he remembered the entire poem and immediately began to write it down. Unfortunately, however, a visitor interrupted him, distracting him for about an hour. When Coleridge returned to his writing, the vivid images had fled, leaving him with only vague recollections and the fifty-four lines of this poetic fragment.

Many critics challenge the truthfulness of Coleridge's version of this story, feeling that the poem is complete as it stands and much too carefully crafted to be solely the result of a dream. However, whether whole or fragment, dream or not, the poem examines issues of vital importance to Coleridge: creativity and the function of the imagination. The poem, including his prefatory comment, focuses on the process by which art is developed and how it may be lost or destroyed. When the poem begins, Kubla Khan orders the construction of an architectural marvel, his pleasure-dome; he locates his grand palace by a sacred river, one of nature's wonders. The poem continues by contrasting human creativity with the power of the natural world. The final stanza provides still another illustration of the process of creation, as the poet struggles to revive his poetic vision.

## Author Biography

Coleridge was born in 1772 in the town of Ottery St. Mary, Devon, England. He was the tenth child of John Coleridge, a minister and schoolmaster, and his wife, Ann Bowdon Coleridge. Coleridge was a dreamy, isolative child who read constantly. His father died when he was ten, and he was sent to Christ's Hospital, a boarding school in London. There he was befriended by fellow student Charles Lamb. In 1791 he entered Cambridge University, showing promise as a gifted writer and brilliant conversationalist. He studied to become a minister but, in 1794, before completing his degree, Coleridge left Cambridge. He went on a walking tour to Oxford, where he became friends with poet Robert Southey. Inspired by the initial events of the French Revolution, Coleridge and Southey collaborated on *The Fall of Robespierre. An Historic Drama* (1794). As an outgrowth of their shared belief in liberty and equality for everyone, they developed a plan for "pantisocracy," an egalitarian and self-sufficient agricultural system to be built in Pennsylvania. The pantisocratic philosophy required every member to be married, and at Southey's urging, Coleridge wed Sarah Fricker, the sister of Southey's fiancee. However, the match proved disastrous, and Coleridge's unhappy marriage was a source of grief to him throughout his life. To compound these difficulties, Southey later lost interest in the scheme, abandoning it in 1795.

Coleridge then moved to Nether Stowey in England's West Country. Lamb, William Hazlitt, and other writers visted him there, making up an informal literary community. In 1796 William Wordsworth, with whom Coleridge had exchanged letters for some years, moved into the area. The two poets became instant friends, and they began a literary collaboration. Around this time Coleridge composed "Kubla Khan" and the first version of

*Samuel Taylor Coleridge*

"Rime of the Ancient Mariner"; the latter work was included as the opening poem in Coleridge and Wordsworth's joint effort, *Lyrical Ballads, with a few Other Poems,* which was published in 1798. That same year, Coleridge traveled to Germany where he developed an interest in the German philosophers Immanuel Kant, Friedrich von Schelling, and the brothers Friedrich and August Wilhelm von Schlegel; he later introduced German aesthetic theory in England through his critical writing. Soon after his return in 1799, Coleridge settled in Keswick near the Lake District, which now gained for him—together with Wordsworth and Southey who had also moved to the area—the title "Lake Poet." During this period, Coleridge suffered poor health and personal strife; his marriage was failing, and he had fallen in love with Wordsworth's sister-in-law, Sarah Hutchinson—a love that was unrequited and a source of great pain. He began taking opium as a remedy for his poor health.

Seeking a more temperate climate and to improve his morale, Coleridge began a two-year trip to Italy, Sicily, and Malta in 1804. Upon his return to England, Coleridge began a series of lectures on poetry and Shakespeare, which are now considered the basis of his reputation as a literary critic. Because of Coleridge's abuse of opium and alcohol, his erratic behavior caused him to quarrel with

Wordsworth, and he left Keswick to return to London. In the last years of his life, Coleridge wrote political and philosophical works and his *Biographia Literaria,* considered his greatest critical writing, in which he developed artistic theories that were intended to be the introduction to a great philosophical work. Coleridge died in 1834 of complications stemming from his dependence on opium.

## Poem Text

In Xanadu did Kubla Khan
A stately pleasure-dome decree:
Where Alph, the sacred river, ran
Through caverns measureless to man
   Down to a sunless sea.                                   5
   So twice five miles of fertile ground
   With walls and towers were girdled round:
And there were gardens bright with sinuous rills,
Where blossomed many an incense-bearing tree;
And here were forests ancient as the hills,          10
Enfolding sunny spots of greenery.

But oh! that deep romantic chasm which slanted
Down the green hill athwart a cedarn cover!
A savage place! as holy and enchanted
As e'er beneath a waning moon was haunted           15
By woman wailing for her demon-lover!
And from this chasm, with ceaseless turmoil
    seething,
As if this earth in fast thick pants were breathing,
A mighty fountain momently was forced;
Amid whose swift half-intermitted burst             20
Huge fragments vaulted like rebounding hail,
Or chaffy grain beneath the thresher's flail:
And 'mid these dancing rocks at once and ever
It flung up momently the sacred river.
Five miles meandering with a mazy motion            25
Through wood and dale the sacred river ran,
Then reached the caverns measureless to man,
And sank in tumult to a lifeless ocean:
And 'mid this tumult Kubla heard from far
Ancestral voices prophesying war!                   30
   The shadow of the dome of pleasure
   Floated midway on the waves;
   Where was heard the mingled measure
   From the fountain and the caves.
It was a miracle of rare device,                     35
A sunny pleasure-dome with caves of ice!

   A damsel with a dulcimer
   In a vision once I saw:
   It was an Abyssinian maid,
   And on her dulcimer she play'd,                  40
   Singing of Mount Abora.
   Could I revive within me
   Her symphony and song,
To such a deep delight 'twould win me,
That with music loud and long,                       45
I would build that dome in air,

That sunny dome! those caves of ice!
And all who heard should see them there,
And all should cry, Beware! Beware!
His flashing eyes, his floating hair!                50
Weave a circle round him thrice,
And close your eyes with holy dread,
For he on honey-dew hath fed,
And drunk the milk of Paradise.

## Poem Summary

### Lines 1-2:

In these lines, Coleridge introduces Kubla Khan, ruler of the Mongol Empire in China during the thirteenth century A.D. His kingdom symbolized wealth and mystery to Europeans ever since Marco Polo first wrote about his travels there; throughout the poem, Coleridge builds a sense of the exotic and mysterious. The second line emphasizes Kubla Khan's power as he orders a fitting palace for himself. It also hints at one of the many contrasts that will appear in the poem as the word "stately" conveying the grandeur and majesty of Kubla Khan's creation, is paired with the idea of a pleasure dome, a place of luxury and leisure.

The opening images of the poem bear striking similarities to the following quotation from Purchas's *Pilgrimage,* which Coleridge said he was reading immediately before he drifted into his deep sleep:

> "In Xamdu did Cublai Can builde a *stately* Palace, encompassing sixteene *miles* of plaine *ground* with a *wall,* wherein are *fertile* Meddowes, pleasant springs, delightful Streames, and all sorts of beasts of chase and game, and in the middest thereof a suptuous house of *pleasure.*"

As you look through the first eight lines, notice the words that Coleridge has borrowed. It is also interesting to notice the changes which he made. For example, Xanadu fits the poem's iambic tetrameter, where Xamdu would not.

### Line 3:

Khan chooses to build this dome on the site of a sacred river, which Coleridge calls the Alph. Although no river with this name exists, the name itself suggests or has the connotation of a beginning. This is because Alph is so similar to Alpha, the first letter of the Greek alphabet, which has as an alternate meaning, beginning. Coleridge, like many poets, likes to experiment with language and invent words to provide added guides to meaning. Critics have also identified the Alph with such different rivers as the Nile, the Alpheus river in Greece, and the fourth river to flow out of the Garden of Eden. Note that the word river is always accompanied by the adjective "sacred." Since rivers and water are life-giving, the sacred river may be seen as a symbol of life.

### Lines 4-5:

A second contrast is introduced with these lines. After the river leaves the area where Kubla Khan creates his kingdom, it flows beyond man's reach into a series of underground caverns. "Measureless to man" conveys not only caverns that man cannot physically map, but areas that are beyond the reach of his full comprehension. The river has as its ultimate destination the sunless sea, a place without light and life and a complete contrast to the earlier impression of the river.

### Lines 6-7:

In these lines, Coleridge returns to the construction of Khan's kingdom. Ten miles of land, which are exceptionally rich, are enclosed behind a wall with towers to protect it. The pleasure dome is not a public sight available to anyone who wishes to visit. It is a private domain. This makes it quite different from the poet's creation that will be discussed later in the poem.

### Lines 8-11:

Here another contrast is introduced. The gardens, planted or cultivated areas designed by humans, fill part of the area with brightly colored flowers and sweet smelling trees, watered by numerous winding brooks that branch off from the sacred river. These gardens are set among ancient forests, which have been there as long as the land itself. The river and forests provide an ageless backdrop for Khan's dream. Although Coleridge notes the differences between Khan's planned estate and nature's realm, both seem to exist in a harmonious balance. The kingdom described in lines 6 to 11 is created by using an evocative series of images of an earthly paradise, perhaps even a type of Eden.

### Lines 12-13:

Line 12 begins by signaling new and even greater contrasts that the following lines will develop as they describe the deep crack in the earth hidden under the grove of cedar trees.

### Line 14:

This is no artificial or manmade place. It is unreached by cultivation and civilization, a magic and even blessed spot that exists outside of man's understanding. The calm and balance of lines 8 through 11 are missing in this primitive, wild place. When holy and enchanted are joined together in this description, they convey a sense of the pagan and the supernatural.

### Lines 15-16:

Coleridge uses a simile to show the distance of this site from Khan's imposing gardens. The waning moon describes that period as the moon decreases from full, so less and less of it is visible. Thus, this mysterious chasm is compared to a spot haunted by a woman crying in anguish, as the moon's light diminishes, for her demon lover. Any relationship between a human and the supernatural would be impossible in the balanced garden of Khan. It could only exist in the passionate upheaval of the chasm.

### Lines 17-19:

This mysterious chasm is pictured in constant turbulence, very different from the garden's calm. Symbolist critics point out sexual and birth imagery in these lines. The language makes it easy to picture the earth in labor, giving birth to the fountain.

### Lines 20-22:

The power of the fountain that pours forth the river is apparent as huge boulders are tossed up with the water. Two similes are used to illustrate this force. In the first, the huge boulders are compared to hail. The second makes them seem even lighter. A thresher is a person or machine who separates the useful, heavier part of a kernel of grain from its lighter, useless shell or chaff. When the grain is hit with a flail, the kernel drops down immediately into a container; the chaff is blown away by the wind.

### Lines 23-28:

The next lines reveal all the contradictions in the river's path. Along with the boulders, the river emerges. The previous similes describing the boulders both use images involving striking: hail hits the earth; the thresher hits the grain. The mood of lines 12-22 is of turmoil and upheaval. After the rocks leave the chasm, they are described again, using a gentler metaphor, as "dancing rocks." This phrase is also an example of personification, where inanimate objects are given human characteristics. After its tumultuous beginning, the river slowly takes a wandering path through the gardens. The poet uses alliteration in line 25 to add a slow, hum-

## Media Adaptations

- A video by Bayley Silleck entitled *Coleridge: The Fountain and the Cave* is available from Pyramid Media.

- An audio cassette of readings by Christopher Plummer entitled *The Rime of the Ancient Mariner and Other Great Poems* is available from Listening Library.

ming sound, with the words "miles," "meandering," "mazy," and "motion." The repetition of lines 3 to 5 in 26 to 28 slows the pace as well.

### Lines 29-30:

Although Khan's gardens initially seem a place of peace and balance, Khan himself hears a different message coming from the distant rumbles of the chasm and the cave. The tumult of the river issues a warning that human creations are not permanent. The voices of his ancestors provide testimony to the fact that the greatest creations of the world eventually come to ruin. Thus, too, the elegant dome is threatened with the destruction of war.

### Lines 31-34:

The various contrasts Coleridge has described in the poem so far come together in these lines. The poem returns to that part of this earthly paradise which Kubla Khan has constructed, the pleasure-dome; however, in these lines, it is not seen directly, merely as a shadow. Now the contrasting element, the turmoil of the fountain and the message of the caverns, seems to overshadow the dome's image, warning that man's creation is transitory; nature endures.

### Lines 35-36:

In these lines, Coleridge ends the first part of the poem, describing Kubla Khan and his world. The meter returns to iambic pentameter here, giving the lines a slower, measured quality. This meter helps to emphasize the mood of regret and loss in these lines as they summarize Kubla Khan's cre-

ative achievement. He harmonized opposing forces, sun and ice, in his miraculous dome, which has since vanished without trace.

### Lines 37-38:

The poet himself becomes the subject as the poem moves from Kubla Khan's physical creation to the poet's vision as he recounts seeing a young girl playing a stringed musical instrument in a dream. The poem shifts from third person to the first person, I. Note that the meter also changes again and becomes even more regular as the poem returns to the light, upbeat tempo of iambic tetrameter throughout much of this stanza.

### Lines 39-41:

Coleridge again invents or adapts names to conjure a sense of mystery or the exotic. The maid in the vision, like Kubla Khan, is from a foreign place. Abyssinia is another name for Ethiopia. Mount Abora, like Alph, is a name that Coleridge created. However, several critics note its similarity to Mount Amara in Milton's *Paradise Lost*. The reader is not given any details of the vision; no images are provided. The reader may assume that Mount Abora is similar to Khan's paradise only because the poet says that it creates such deep delight.

### Lines 42-45:

This phrasing of these lines is unusual. Could is used as a conditional verb here, and the entire sentence becomes a speculation. If the poet can recover the dream, he will create a vision of Paradise; the beauty of the vision will transform the poet and enable him to use the music of his poetry to build with words what Kubla Khan had built in his kingdom. The poem leaves unanswered whether or not the poet will be able to capture that dream.

### Lines 46-48:

Here, the poet describes the power of successful poetic vision; not only can he renew his vision, but he has the power to convey it to all who hear or who read his words. This serves as a contrast to the Khan's pleasure-dome, bound by walls and not meant for all to use.

### Lines 49-52:

All of those around the poet are wary of him because he is caught up in a kind of enchantment or madness during his vision. His eyes glitter in a frenzy of creativity. This creativity, like that of the sacred river, comes from tumult. He is viewed with "holy dread" because he has drawn his vision from a place similar to the chasm described earlier, a place sacred and enchanted, pagan yet blessed. The idea of the poet being "possessed" by his vision is not new with Coleridge. The Greeks believed that creativity was often a type of momentary madness.

### Lines 53-54:

Honey-dew refers to the sweet honey-like substance that certain flowers, such as honeysuckle, produce in the summer. Another word for this liquid is nectar, known as the food of the gods. With his words, the poet, when he achieves his dream, can combine the chasm and the gardens, thus tasting Paradise.

## Themes

### Nature and its Meaning

The opening lines of "Kubla Khan" immediately thrust us into a strange world where the remarkable is commonplace. Kubla Khan orders a "pleasure-dome" to be built next to a sacred river that erupts from a chasm, flows in "sinuous rills" through gardens, then descends "in tumult" into "caverns measureless to man." Encircling the centrally placed dome, walls and towers inscribe a defining limit around "forests ancient as the hills." These elegant and civilized structures actually enclose a "deep romantic chasm … A savage place" that spurts life-giving waters to the gardens like a spouting heart or a birthing mother. In other words, despite human artifice, nature vivifies the whole and gives it meaning. So Kubla Khan, the prototypical Romantic artist, in order to create his masterpiece, merely defines a limit with his art around the uncontrollable magic of untrammeled nature and allows it to feed and inform his art work. And this, in fact, was the aesthetic Coleridge and other Romantic poets practiced. For them, poetry, as an "imitation of nature," merely delimits in image and form the divine beauty of raw nature.

But in "Kubla Khan," as Coleridge informs us in the preface to the 1816 edition of the poem, the wild nature of the gardens, the fountain "with ceaseless turmoil seething," and "Alph, the sacred river," actually emerge from the poet's dream consciousness. The Romantics believed that, at its core, the self is one with nature. Childhood and dreams fascinated them thematically in their poetry because both, like nature, were simple, raw, and unrestrainable. They recognized that in all of its forms, nature yearns with omnidirected desire. Just like a "woman wailing for her demon-lover," nature is, in William Blake's words, "Energy." And what Blake says in *The Marriage of Heaven and Hell* of this "Energy" also applies here in "Kubla Khan": "Energy is the only life, and is from the Body; and Reason is the bound or outward circumference of Energy…. Energy is Eternal Delight." The "outward circumference" of the Khan's towers and walls circumscribes the "Eternal Delight" of untamed nature, which is both "holy and enchanted" and certainly beyond human control.

### Consciousness

Read as the beginning of a longer poem, Coleridge's poetic "fragment" sets forth a fantastic world, set both in the "mysterious" Orient and in the "magical" Middle Ages. But read as a whole complete unto itself, "Kubla Khan" evokes the fleeting images of a waking dream that speak not in words but in symbols. And although many critics point to the Crewe manuscript version of "Kubla Khan" found in 1934 as proof that Coleridge "consciously" revised the text, the poem as it stands successfully replicates the dream state and unveils a genuine glimpse into an archetypal world, a world Carl Jung, a Swiss psychoanalyst, called the "collective unconscious." The first thirty-six lines of the poem imagistically present a symbolic diagram of the "self," in which consciousness strives to find integration with the incalculably greater depth of the unconscious mind, while the last eighteen lines reflect upon the power of the unconscious mind when Coleridge finally realized that the full recollection of his dream work was impossible.

By demarcating a circular space from the "forests ancient as the hills" with protective walls and towers, Kubla Khan creates a kind of "mandala" whose circumference is described by the "stately pleasure-dome" at its center. A Sanskrit technical term from Tantric Buddhism for a circular "cosmogram" used for "centering" and meditation, the mandala is a map of the inner world (the microcosm) that mirrors the outer world (the macrocosm). According to Jung, the mandala serves to define and protect the self as it seeks to integrate with the unruly forces of the unconscious mind. But in "Kubla Khan," the "sunny spots of greenery" and the bright "sinuous rills" within the conscious world of the self appear tenuous, fragile, and minuscule in comparison to the cavernous deeps of the "sunless sea." In fact, all of the paired opposites that appear within the poem (sun and moon, light and dark, male and female, movement

# Topics for Further Study

- Reread the poem's description of the Khan's "girdled" gardens, pleasure-dome, chasm, etc. Now use your own powers of imagination to visualize details to supplement the poem's rather broad descriptions: colors, shapes, textures, sounds, and so forth. Now write, draw, or graphically represent your version of the Khan's earthly paradise. Members of the class should share their personal visions with each other for an interesting class discussion about the universal and the personal in the creative imagination.

- Research information on the historical Kublai or Kubilai Khan and compare what you have learned with Coleridge's dream-figure. In the poem, ancestral voices prophesy war. What was the political situation in the Eurasian land mass during the Khan's reign? What was the political, technological, and economic "balance of power" between Europe and Asia at the time?

- Examine the female figures and images in Coleridge's poem. Some feminist critics applaud Coleridge's sharing his "feminine side" in this poem while others reject the way women are portrayed (especially the "woman wailing for her demon-lover"). What is your opinion in this regard? Are women portrayed positively or negatively (or both) in this poem? Follow the text of the poem closely, and use good critical sources to defend your position.

---

and rest, and good and evil) struggle without success to find balance within this delicate world fed by the waters of the collective unconscious.

### Creativity and Imagination

As mentioned previously, "Alph, the sacred river," suffuses consciousness with creative "Energy." This overwhelming creativity fecundates the conscious mind ("twice five miles of fertile ground") via the spouting chasm that flings up water and "dancing rocks" from the underworld. This birth-giving chasm, clearly associated with the "woman wailing for her demon-lover," charges the visionary with almost frenzied inspiration.

In the last eighteen lines, the speaker recalls yet another female figure he had once seen in vision, the "damsel with a dulcimer." Her strange song, if he could but "revive [it] within" himself, would so permeate him with numinous powers that he would be able to recreate the Khan's dome and the "caves of ice" in the air itself. Such magical powers, the fruit of a kind of possession, would then make the speaker into an object of taboo, both holy and dangerous to the common sort of humanity. Like the chasm, both "holy and enchanted," the inspired poet becomes an ambivalent figure "beyond good and evil," for "he on honey-dew hath fed, / And drunk the milk of Paradise." Not surprisingly, many critics have commented that this "milk of Paradise" might be nothing more than laudanum, a solution of opium in alcohol, to which Coleridge was addicted most of his life. Unfortunately, Coleridge's dependence on drugs cut short his poetically most productive period.

### Style

"Kubla Khan" is an intricately structured poem, using a amazing variety of metric and rhythmic devices. Lines 1 to 7 and 37 to 54 are written primarily in iambic tetrameter.

In order to analyze the rhythm or meter of a line of poetry, the line is divided into syllables. Iambs are units of two syllables, where the first syllable is unstressed, or not emphasized, and the second syllable is stressed. Notice the syllables in the first line of "Kubla Khan":

In **Xa** / na **du** / did **Ku** / bla **Khan**

When the line is read aloud, the emphasis falls on every second syllable. The meter is iambic tetrameter because there are four of these units in each line (a total of eight syllables). Between lines 8 and 53, the meter shifts to other meters, primarily iambic pentameter.

The poem uses an equally elaborate rhyme scheme. Lines 1, 3, and 4 rhyme, as do lines 2 and 5. The next two lines, 6 and 7, are a couplet. In the following four lines, an alternating rhyme pattern is used: rills, tree, hills, greenery. This variety continues throughout the poem.

The complicated use of rhyme is not limited to the last words in each line. A close examination of the first line provides examples of the intricate rhyme within a line. Each of the eight syllables is involved some type of internal rhyme: *xa / na / bla; / du / ku*. Note also the syllabic alliteration of do and did. The only syllables left, in and Khan, contain a half rhyme. The elaborate rhyme continues throughout the poem. For example, each of the first five lines ends with alliteration: Kubla Khan, dome decree, river ran, measureless man, sunless sea. These shifts in meter, along with clever word play, help to reinforce the poem's theme of creativity and poetic vision.

## Historical Context

Born a little less than four years before the signing of the Declaration of Independence, Coleridge came of age during the French Revolution. Like most of his generation, he was indelibly marked by the Revolution for the rest of his life, even though in his maturity he came to reject its fundamental premises. Even as he was turning away from political radicalism, however, Coleridge came to embrace German philosophical idealism, itself an intellectual result of the Revolution. For its own part, the French Revolution, child of the Enlightenment, had also outgrown the rational and empirical restraints of the Enlightenment's Cartesian and Newtonian world view. What had been declared "self-evident" and a matter of reason and natural law by the proponents of the American Revolution very easily and rapidly evolved into ideological articles of faith for the zealots of the new religion of "Man." This "sea change" was made manifest when a Jacobin-led mob took over Notre Dame Cathedral, renamed it the "Temple of Reason," and then enthroned a naked prostitute on the high altar to worship her as the "Goddess of Reason." These events seem bizarre enough in themselves, and yet the roots of this revolt against reason in the name

of reason ironically lie within the rationalism of the Enlightenment's scientific culture.

The scientific revolutions of the sixteenth, seventeenth, and eighteenth centuries precipitated not only technological, economic, and social revolutions that continue to escalate to this day but also a spiritual and intellectual crisis that has only deepened over time. When René Descartes' radical skepticism could find no firm foothold upon which to stand to ascertain the truth about reality, the philosopher and mathematician clutched on to his ego's own ability to think in order to affirm his own existence: "I think, therefore I am" (*cogito ergo sum*). By substituting epistemology, the philosophy of knowing and apprehension, for metaphysics, the philosophy of being, Descartes put the self with its reasoning faculties at the center of his search for scientific certitude. In other words, the Enlightenment thinkers who followed Descartes came to focus on the "knower" as much as (if not more than) on the "known." This began the so-called "epistemological crisis" of Western thought, a crisis that finds echoes even today in Heisenberg's uncertainty principle in quantum mechanics.

The scientific discoveries of Sir Isaac Newton, on the other hand, tended to substantiate a mechanistic view of the physical universe. Deists, unwilling to relinquish completely the idea of God, proposed a deity that was a master "clock maker" who had put together the universe only to "wind it up" and watch it go from a distance. More consistent thinkers suggested, however, that the machine of the universe had no real need a maker because the Deists' God was already so completely absent from the physical phenomena of his "clock works" as not to exist. The combined effect of Descartes' speculations and Newton's discoveries not only eroded traditional faith in the Christian God, but also reinforced two major streams of philosophical thinking that had already been growing within Western civilization. Cartesian doubt regarding sense perception combined with Francis Bacon's scientific methods to beget empiricism, the philosophical basis of scientific method even to this day. But by focusing on the ego's powers of reason in order to affirm objective reality, Descartes was also responsible for the development of philosophical idealism that countered empirical skepticism by studying the inner workings of the self.

But the thinker who provided the ultimate philosophical and ideological justification for the Revolution's revolt against reason was Jean-Jacques Rousseau. While not an idealist in the philosophical sense of the word, Rousseau rejected

# *Compare & Contrast*

- **1789-1815:** The French Revolution, starting with the storming of the Bastille in July of 1789, takes on a life of its own and quickly becomes increasingly more radical until Robespierre and the Committee of Safety perpetrate the "Reign of Terror" on Paris from October of 1793 until July of 1794. Because the Revolution seeks to spread its ideology by military means to other countries in Europe, the people's army and its leaders become increasingly more powerful until Napoleon takes dictatorial control in a coup d'état, eventually crowning himself Emperor in 1804. Only at the Battle of Waterloo is allied Europe freed from the "specter of revolution" they saw exemplified in the person of Napoleon himself. Despite the reactionary politics in Europe after the Napoleonic wars, however, revolutionary cadres continue their work underground.

  **1917-1989:** The November Revolution of the Bolsheviks leads to a "reign of terror" for more than seventy years as Marx and Engels' conception of the "Dictatorship of the Prolertariat" (the working class) over the bourgeoisie (the middle class) is put into practice by Lenin as a dictatorship of the Communist Party over everybody. After Lenin's death, internal power struggles within the Party results in Stalin's becoming dictator. Furthermore, before his death in 1953, Stalin's campaigns of terror cause the death of more than 25 million people, more than those killed in Hitler's concentration camps. Only Mikhail Gorbachev's policy of "glasnost" in 1985 ends rule by terror in the Soviet Union, but soon afterward, Communism's political control of Eastern Europe "withers away."

- **1839-1842:** Because of China's economic self-sufficiency, British merchants begin trading opium from India to China in the late eighteenth century in order to siphon off Chinese reserves of gold. When Lin Tse-hsu, an imperial agent, dumps more than 20,000 chests of opium into Canton's harbor in 1839, the British respond with war. As one of the spoils of their victory in the Opium War, the British take Hong Kong as a colonial port.

  **1997:** Hong Kong returns to Chinese political control.

  **Today:** Since it was formed twenty-five years ago, the Drug Enforcement Administration (DEA) has been waging an ongoing war in Latin America and the United States against the illegal importation of cocaine. Produced primarily in Colombia, Bolivia, and Peru, cocaine is Latin America's second-most important export after petroleum and yields annual revenues estimated at $9 to 10 billion. Americans spend more on cocaine than on airline tickets, gas utilities, and periodicals.

- **1938-1943:** In 1938 while searching for a circulatory stimulant, Dr. Albert Hoffman, a research chemist for Sandoz pharmaceutical laboratories in Basel, Switzerland, first synthesizes lysergic acid diethylamide (abbreviated as LSD from its name in German). When no medicinal properties are observed in laboratory animals, the chemical is dropped from further study. But Hoffman, acting on a hunch, synthesizes LSD once again in 1943 and accidentally ingests some during the process. Hoffman's "acid trip" leads to modern research on the class of drugs now known as *psychedelica.*

  **1960-1963:** Harvard University research psychologists Timothy Leary, Dick Alpert, and Ralph Metzner, begin to experiment with psychedelics as therapeutic tools to help patients and prisoners deal with a wide variety of problems. After parents and university officials become alarmed at the effects of their research, the three professors are summarily fired. Leary and Alpert continue their work illegally until personal disagreements and Alpert's conversion to yogic Hinduism separate them. Leary goes on to wage war in what he terms the "politics of consciousness." His slogan of "turn on, tune in, and drop out" becomes a revolutionary mantra as the right of "self-determination" over one's individual consciousness joins racial equality and the war in Vietnam as issues of the "cultural revolution" of the 1960s and early 1970s.

  **Today:** LSD and other psychedelics are again growing in popularity with young people, although not in the numbers of the later 1960s. For many, however, computer-generated "virtual reality" legally replicates the altered states of consciousness found in psychedelics.

the artificiality of the arts and sciences and said that human authenticity could only be found within the self restored to its original, natural goodness. He believed that as humans "return to Nature," their proclivity toward evil withers away. In his opinion, since civilization as a whole had alienated people from their original simplicity, formal intellectual inquiry could only further estrange them from their true selves. Because of his faith in humanity's "natural goodness," Rousseau advocated direct democracy and an end to all hierarchical classes. Needless to say, with these premises the Revolution could justify any barbarous act as an expedient for humanity's return to "Nature."

Rousseau, of course, has been hailed as the "first Romantic." By rejecting reason and championing individual, emotional response over the mores of civil society, Rousseau provided artists and revolutionaries alike with a ready-made warrant to act upon their inner promptings without reference to "objective" standards of behavior. But Enlightenment science had already cleaved an unbridgeable gap between the knower and the known. If the truth of beings cannot be safely apprehended through sense perception, then how can any "natural law" of proper human conduct be objectively predicated? Coleridge, like many of his era, sought desperately to close this gap. Turning away from his youthful radicalism, he long tried to reestablish the moral primacy of the old order of society. Significantly, however, he did not choose the metaphysics of classical realism to defend his "neo-conservatism" but the relatively new philosophy of German idealism that undertook to ascertain the nature of reality by studying human consciousness, not the essence of being as such.

## Critical Overview

John Livingston Lowes, in *The Road to Xanadu,* produced the first extensive analysis of Coleridge's poetry. His primary interest was tracing Coleridge's sources. Lowes was convinced that "Kubla Khan" had indeed been conjured up in a dream, inspired not only by Purchas' *Pilgrimage,* but by several other works that Coleridge had read. He traces influences in such varied sources as Plato, Milton, and several early travel books, particularly John Bruce's *Travels to Discover the Source of the Nile.* His work provides an excellent background on which many other critics build their analyses. In *Coleridge, Opium and "Kubla Khan,"* Elizabeth Schneider provides a detailed analysis of the poem.

Unlike Lowes, Schneider feels that "not only do the first thirty-six lines of the poem refuse to sound as if they had been dreamed, they sound more than anything else like a fine opening for a romantic narrative of some magnitude." The final lines are then added to explain the artist's loss or dimming of vision. She stresses the careful construction of the poem, in its use of rhyme and meter, in its use of parallel development, and in its contrasts. Schneider also analyzes the tone of the poem, describing it as ambivalent, moving from one position to another. In spite of the fact that several characters are named in the poem, not one is totally present: Kubla Khan represents the past; the wailing woman exists in a simile; the Abyssinian maid is part of a vision which may or may not be recalled. Even the poet himself is shrouded by his floating hair.

Both J. B. Beer, in *Coleridge the Visionary,* and Max Shultz in *The Poetic Voices of Coleridge,* discuss the two distinct sections of "Kubla Khan." Beer feels that the poem has two main themes, creativity and the loss of Paradise. As the poem opens, Kubla Khan struggles to rebuild a paradisiacal garden, while the forces of nature threaten to reassert themselves and overwhelm his creation. In the last stanza, the poet, too, attempts to use his vision to regain paradise. Schulz notes the contrasting points of view and the two climaxes. He believes that the poem is typical of Coleridge's search for balance, finding "a reconciliation of opposites, particularly of nature and art, is a ruling tenet of his thought."

Humphry House, in *Coleridge: The Clark Lectures,* maintains that "Kubla Khan" "is a triumphant positive statement of the potentialities of poetry." To prove this, he discusses different critical views of line 41, in which the poet wonders, "Could I revive within me / Her symphony and song." While some critics assert that this line describes the poet's grief for the beauty that he has lost and is unable to recover, House sees it in a more positive light—as a query. In this case, "Could I?" might easily be answered, "Yes!" He supports his views by discussing the lighter, faster meter in this section. In his opinion, the entire poem is a celebration of the marvelous power of poetry.

## Criticism

### Mary Mahony

*Mary Mahony is an instructor of English at Wayne County Community College in Detroit, Michigan. In the following essay, Mahony argues that "Kubla Khan" is not a poetic fragment re-*

# *What Do I Read Next?*

- William Blake's *The Marriage of Heaven and Hell* explicitly explores overcoming the opposing duality of the conscious (Heaven) and unconscious (Hell) minds just as Coleridge's "Kubla Khan" does symbolically. The two works share many ideas about the importance of the imagination as a conduit of prophetic inspiration. Interestingly enough, both poets were strongly influenced in their thinking by Jacob Boehme, a sixteenth-century Lutheran mystic who described his experiences and his theology with alchemical symbolism.

- Johann Wolfgang von Goethe's tragedy *Faust* provides yet another artistic expression of Jacob Boehme's ideas during the Romantic period. In the traditional Faust myth, Faust is punished for selling his soul to the devil to gain secret knowledge and magical powers (see also Christopher Marlow's *Doctor Faustus*). But in Goethe's play, Faust is redeemed at the end of part two by the "Eternal Feminine" because his universal desire for consciousness and experience places him "beyond good and evil."

- Carl Gustav Jung's two books, *Psychology and Alchemy* and *Archetypes of the Collective Unconscious,* although somewhat difficult to read, provide excellent examples of Jacob Boehme's influence in modern depth psychology. Freud's most favored pupil who was destined to take over as leader of the psychoanalytic movement upon the "master's" death, Jung came to reject Freud's preoccupation with sexuality as the chief cause of psychopathological states. Jung noticed that his patients' dreams or hallucinations more often resembled mythological or religious symbolism. Eventually Jung founded his own school of psychoanalysis based upon a theory of genetic as well as personal memories to explain recurring motifs in all states of altered consciousness.

- Richard Haven has written an excellent book called *Patterns of Consciousness: An Essay on Coleridge.* This work draws upon all of Coleridge's writings to explore his personal and philosophical struggles to understand the nature of consciousness and the unconscious.

---

*sulting from a dream, but a complex and carefully organized work that illustrates Coleridge's poetic principles.*

Samuel Taylor Coleridge is regarded as one of the great English Romantic poets. Many critics consider *Lyrical Ballads,* published by Coleridge and William Wordsworth in 1798, the first expression of the Romantic movement in English poetry. This collection explored new directions in poetic language and style while breaking away from the formal and highly stylized poetry of the eighteenth century. Coleridge was also a brilliant literary critic. His literary analysis, particularly in *Biographia Literaria,* attempted to define both the nature of poetry and the poet. These definitions, as well as Coleridge's philosophical theories about creativity and the imagination, greatly influenced

writers who followed. Unfortunately, however, he was frequently attacked on both a personal and literary level. Many of his friends felt that he had betrayed his initial promise. His life, plagued by ill health and drug use, was often moralistically presented as a cautionary tale. In the third chapter of *Biographia Literaria,* Coleridge compared this persecution by fellow critics to being dragged for seventeen years through a "literary gauntlet."

This same negative attitude often extended to Coleridge's poetry. "Kubla Khan" is an excellent example. Nineteenth-century critics tended to dismiss it as a rather inconsequential or meaningless triviality. In large part, this was due to Coleridge's own introduction to the poem. When it was first published in 1816, he subtitled it "A Vision in a Dream: A Fragment." The preface went on to note that it was only being "published at the request of a poet of great and deserved celebrity [Lord Byron], and, as far as the Author's own opinions are concerned, rather as a psychological curiosity, than on the ground of any supposed poetic merit." Coleridge was taken at his word, and for nearly a century the poem was dismissed. After its publication, poet and critic Thomas Moore included the previous quote in his critique in *The Edinburgh Review,* adding that he totally agreed with Coleridge's evaluation of its merit. That same year another critic, Josiah Condor, voiced a similar opinion in *The Eclectic Review,* expressing regret that Coleridge had even bothered to have the poem published and comparing it to a "mutilated statue."

Those poets and critics who admired "Kubla Khan," such as Algernon Charles Swinburne and Leigh Hunt, did so for its marvelous melodic quality. In an article about Coleridge in *International Quarterly,* critic Arthur Symons called "Kubla Khan" one of the finest examples of lyric poetry. However, he added that it had "just enough meaning to give it bodily existence, otherwise it would be disembodied music." Even John Livingston Lowes, who produced some of the first detailed analytic studies of Coleridge in *The Road to Xanadu,* tended to see the poem as nothing more substantial than a marvelous dream.

Not until the mid-twentieth century did critics start to explore the poem's meaning, finding that it presented a remarkably coherent picture. Although critical interpretations of key images and phrases often vary, more and more scholars believe that the main reason, perhaps the only reason, that the poem has been considered incomplete for all these years is because Coleridge said so in his preface. "Kubla Khan" is complex and, at times, ambiguous; the variety of critical interpretations demonstrates this. However, instead of being inexplicable because of its incomplete state, it has some very specific and unambiguous themes, including creation, inspiration, and the loss of that inspiration.

Briefly review what happens in the poem. The opening stanza describes a marvelous earthly paradise that Kubla Khan has created. The second stanza introduces a chasm, a place of passionate nature that cannot be controlled by any of man's decrees. This section also presents the lifeless ocean. These areas are bound together by the sacred river, which connects the uncontrolled chasm and stagnant ocean with the ordered world of Kubla Khan. The river travels symbolically from passion through order to chaos, from birth through life to death. As the river sinks into the realm of death, it is possible to hear in the tumult the prophecies of war. The stanza ends by mourning the loss of this wondrous pleasure dome where art and nature had briefly been blended together.

The third stanza seems to switch subjects abruptly, opening with a vision of a damsel. Yet it contains the same theme of creativity and loss that was presented in the first two stanzas. The poet, like Kubla Khan, has a creative vision. If he can recall it—a point that Coleridge leaves undetermined in the poem—, he will be able to recreate a vision of Khan's paradise/pleasure dome. However, both the stanza and the poet fail to do so. The reader sees only the shadow of the pleasure dome at the end of stanza two and is left with the tantalizing promise of what might have been in stanza three.

A careful reading of the prefatory note provides another illustration of the same theme. It is written in the third person. Instead of using the pronoun I, Coleridge refers to "the Author," almost as if he is a distinct persona. Although Coleridge uses both first and third person in prefatory notes to other poems, this has the effect of distancing him from the preface. The author composes a wondrous poem during a drug-induced sleep. Upon awakening, he rushes to record it, only to be distracted by the alliterative "person on business from Porlock." When he dismisses the visitor more than an hour later, he can only remember a few lines: "all the rest had passed away like the images on a stream into which a stone has been cast." This occurrence parallels the two experiences described in the poem. The author, like Kubla Khan and the poet in the last stanza, creates and then loses a vision of paradise. The description of the "images on a stream" bears a striking similarity to the shadow of the dome floating on the water. The entire incident is a counterpart to the vision of the damsel that the poet longs to recreate.

A detailed reading of "Kubla Khan" indicates that the miraculous musical quality of the poem is produced by an amazingly intricate structure of metric and poetic devices. For Coleridge, such a complex tapestry of language is an integral part of his view on poetics. In chapter XIV of his *Biographia Literaria,* he explains his philosophical and poetic principles, providing a multifaceted definition of poetry. Coleridge allows that any work having rhyme and rhythm may be described as a poem at the lowest level, simply because there is a pleasure derived from hearing recurring sounds and rhythms. However, he continues, for a poem to be "legitimate," the parts must "mutually support and explain each other; all in their proportion harmonizing with and supporting the purpose and known

*A detailed reading of 'Kubla Khan' indicates that the miraculous musical quality of the poem is produced by an amazingly intricate structure of metric and poetic devices. "*

influences of metrical arrangement." True poetry must be a harmonious entity that "brings the whole soul of man into activity." The meaning or truth of the poem is revealed through this harmony. For Coleridge, all of this should blend together in organic unity.

Coleridge's elegant rhyme in "Kubla Khan" helps to create this unity. The very first line, in which every syllable is connected by some form of rhyme, is just a beginning example. Almost every line includes some form of alliteration. The second stanza, which is less metrically regular than the first, is equally filled with alliteration: "cedarn cover," "mighty fountain momently was forced," "woman wailing."

The unpredictable end-rhyme scheme forces the reader or listener to focus on the words of the poem. At the same time, it reinforces the poem's themes. While the opening seven lines of the first two stanzas follow the same pattern, the third stanza breaks the rule. The subsequent rhyme scheme is different in each stanza. Throughout the poem, the end rhyme is quite elaborate, including some feminine rhymes, in which the rhyme extends for two or more syllables, such as in seething and breathing. Establishing a rhyme scheme and then breaking or embellishing that pattern provides yet another example of creation that initially stays within formal limits, but eventually surpasses its boundaries. It mirrors the difference between Kubla Khan's formal garden and the sumptuous realm of nature, between the calm of the damsel and the frenzy of the poet.

Coleridge's use of meter and rhythm is also carefully organized to support the poem's themes. Clearly, a blend of form and meaning takes place in "Kubla Khan." The first four lines of the poem,

written in perfect iambic tetrameter, describe Kubla Khan's carefully ordered paradise, which has been built to his specifications. Ultimately, however, he cannot control the nature around him, specifically the caverns that are described in the fourth line as "measureless to man." Those words at the end of the line remind the reader that there are things that man cannot control. The fifth line reinforces this with its abrupt change in meter and syllable count. The next two lines, a couplet, return to iambic tetrameter. Once again the poem describes Kubla Khan's attempts to impose his will on nature. However, the poetic lines themselves break free, and the meter starts to shift in lines eight through eleven. Kubla Khan may be able to impose his authority by building walls and towers to keep outsiders out of his pleasure gardens, but he cannot exercise these rigid rules on the ancient forests. The meter itself helps to indicate man's tenuous ability to bend nature to his will.

In the second stanza describing the savage chasm, the shifts in meter become even more apparent. The lines are longer, usually varying between ten and twelve syllables. Once again, the meter itself supports the meaning. For example, in line eighteen the poem describes the earth breathing in "fast thick pants." The meter reinforces this image by using three stressed words together. In the following line, the fountain erupts almost as if the earth has given birth to it. This image is suggested in large part by the heavily accented labor of line eighteen. Lines thirty-one through thirty-four, still metrically varied, signal another shift in subject. These lines are shorter, less substantial, as they describe the shadow of the dome that "floated midway on the waves." The final two lines in the second stanza are written in iambic pentameter, the most common metrical form. They provide a formal ending to the entire first part of the poem. The metric structure helps serve as an epitaph for Kubla Khan's amazing accomplishment. The formal tone of regret is clear, reinforcing the theme of the poem: a glorious vision has disappeared.

Initially, the third section, in which the poet describes his vision, may seem to be totally, even confusingly, separate from Kubla Khan and his pleasure dome. However, Coleridge uses meter as a connecting element. Thus, the first seven lines of this stanza mirror the rhythm of the first seven lines of the poem. The very flow of the lines encourages the reader to recognize the relationship between the poet's vision and Kubla Khan's paradise. Line forty-four deliberately breaks the rhythm just as line eight did. Again the meter reinforces the poem's theme. It is not certain that the poet will be able to recreate his dream; that "deep delight" may vanish as completely as Kubla Khan's world did. Some critics, however, contend that the poem does indicate that the poet will succeed. They use the existence of heavy stresses on "I would build" at the beginning of line forty-six as evidence to help support their theory. The fact that the lines that follow return to the iambic tetrameter of the poem's opening also helps to connect the poem's end to the description of Kubla Khan's paradise in the beginning of the poem.

An additional element indicating the poem's careful construction involves the use of contrast to develop the theme (which is in itself a contrast) of creativity and loss. For Coleridge, the use of contrast was a key element in poetry. In chapter XIV of *Biographia Literaria,* he states that the poet must exercise control by balancing discordant elements in order to create poetic harmony. In "Kubla Khan," the contrasts can be placed into broad categories.

One group deals with images relating to life and death, the ultimate expression of creation and loss. Thus, these opposing forces are central to developing Coleridge's theme. The fertility of both nature and the garden is juxtaposed with the barren desolation of the measureless caverns. Pictures of light, "sunny greenery" and dark, "the sunless sea" further reinforce this point. The voices of war and death spring from the furor produced as the river plunges from Kubla Khan's gardens into this nether world, suggesting both paradise and paradise lost. A second category centers on the two types of creation in the poem—the natural and the artificial. The cultivated world holds quiet and order, while nature's realm is unbridled and uncontrollable, a savage and enchanted place. The two women who appear in the poem represent these polarities. The damsel quietly playing on a musical instrument creates a very different image than the sexual passion of the wailing woman. Many other individual contrasts appear throughout the poem: reality and shadow, calm and frenzy, day and night, sacred and profane. All add to the complexity and texture of "Kubla Khan."

This complexity makes it difficult to fully believe that "Kubla Khan" is nothing more than the remnant of a half-remembered dream. The thematic repetition, intricacy of rhyme and metrical schemes, as well as the carefully juxtaposed images beautifully "harmonize and support" the poem's purpose and theme. In "Kubla Khan," Coleridge has created more than simple lyric poetry.

He has fulfilled his poetic ideal of a harmonious blend of meaning and form, which results in a "graceful and intelligent whole."

**Source:** Mary Mahony, in an essay for *Poetry for Students,* Gale, 1999.

### *Regina Hewitt*

*In the following excerpt, Hewitt uses a sampling of Coleridge's own criticism on the subject of poetry to analyze the two poet figures in "Kubla Khan."*

"Kubla Khan" consists of two successive sections that parallel each other in subject matter. The first part (1–36) deals with the manufacture of poetry through skilled, rational craftsmanship; the second (37–54), with the generation of poetry through artless, irrational inspiration. Each section contains a problem that shows its approach to poetry to be inadequate, its poet figure false. Hence, the poem as a whole displays a dilemma: it shows that the two extant theories accounting for poetic composition fail to provide a sufficient explanation of that phenomenon. By implication, it calls for a new theory of poetic creation. Although it does not suggest what that theory should be and does not present a figure of a true poet, it contributes to the formulation of new theories and new symbols by pointing out the pitfalls fresh thought must avoid. In essence, "Kubla Khan" shows Coleridge weighing the merits of inherited ideas of poetic creation, finding them wanting, and leaving a space for a new idea to fill. A closer look at "Kubla Khan" may make this reading of the poem more readily apparent.

As [George] Watson notes [in his article on "Kubla Khan" in *A Review of English Literature*], the first thirty-six lines of "Kubla Khan" may be assigned a historical referent. They are emblematic of Neo-classical or Augustan poetic theory with its prescriptions and proscriptions. The Khan, as Neo-classical poet, brings his work into existence by "decree" and refines it by system and measure ("So twice five miles of fertile ground / With walls and towers were girdled round"). The architectural metaphor reduces the poem to the status of any ordinary object put together piece-by-piece according to an exact blueprint. The Khan's plans, however, cannot account for all aspects of the natural environment in which his construction occurs. The "twice five miles" fail to incorporate the chasm and the river, which violate the enclosure....

The river escapes the Khan's confines, reaching the caverns—themselves measureless—and the ocean—obviously illimitable, especially within "twice five miles," no matter how one construes the geometry of that figure.

The Khan's method results in an illusory order, a shaky structure on the brink of overthrow by the elements it could momentarily ignore but not permanently exclude. The first section draws to a close by adumbrating the destruction of the Khan's little world: it addresses "ancestral voices prophesying war," and it shifts its focus from the pleasure-dome to the *shadow* of the pleasure-dome appearing on waves, waves to which the excluded river and fountain have contributed and which can, by a bit of agitation, break up the mere illusion reflected on them. Following from the architectural vehicle, the tenor of the metaphor indicates the unstable and incomplete nature of a Neo-classicism that tries to exclude structural and thematic elements inconvenient to its limited design. It implies that the poet must take into account all parts of the organic, natural order, for these elements belong in poetry and will surface there despite all rules to the contrary.

Juxtaposed to the flawed Neoclassical view of poetic creation is a second different but still flawed view—the ancient fury of the poet shown in the last eighteen lines of "Kubla Khan." This poet, with his "flashing eyes" and "floating hair," portrays — possibly even parodies—the "enthused" poet that Plato condemned. This poet's own mind and judgment have been usurped by some spirit. The poet becomes the passive instrument through which the spirit expresses itself in a way that may or may not be intelligible. Watson notes the analogue, of course. But he privileges it as if it were the view of the poet that Coleridge prefers, whereas "Kubla Khan" makes this figure suspect. He believes himself to have received some extraordinary vision ("A damsel with a dulcimer / In a vision once I saw"). He was passive at the time and continues passive to the extent that he cannot recollect the experience sufficiently to write anything about it....

His is "the poem that does not exist" because it cannot and should not. His is a private ecstasy. It results from an esoteric fantasy and not from an insight into nature. Failing at poetic creation, this poet falls back on the exaggerated affectations of "irritable" genius, relishing his ability to mystify others ("And all should cry, Beware! Beware!") instead of welcoming a chance to convey his insight to them (as a true poet would).

It seems, perhaps, odd to reject both figures of the poet in "Kubla Khan." After all, finding a "Romantic" poet critical of Neoclassicism constitutes almost a stock response, but finding him critical of inspiration disturbs some standard assumptions. A glance at Coleridge's attitude toward the figure of the poet as he expresses it in some of his prose works may help to justify the second rejection. The bulk of his writings show an unqualifiedly positive valuation of the possessed poet to be inconsistent with his statements about the nature of poetic genius.

Most of Coleridge's reflections on this matter occur in works of a later date than the time at which "Kubla Khan" is alleged to have been written. *The Watchman,* however, provides at least one example from the later 1790s of what Coleridge then considered an acceptable figure of a poet. Of Louis de Boissy, Coleridge writes in his essay for Thursday, May 5, 1796:

> Boissy, the author of several dramatic pieces, that were acted with applause, met with the usual fate of those men, whom the very genius, that fits them to be authors, incapacitates for successful authorship. — Their productions are too refined for the lower classes, and too sincere for the wealthier ranks of Society. Boissy in addition to great intellectual ability, possessed the virtues of Industry and Temperance; yet his works produced him fame only. He laboured incessantly for uncertain bread.

Hence, Coleridge ranks the poet among men of genius and characterizes those as intelligent, industrious, temperate, and hard-working. Instances of failure are really triumphs, for they stem from an inability to pander to popular taste. While this early essay neither provides a definitive anatomy of genius nor purports to explain how works of genius come into being, it does allow certain attributes to the genius that could not be imputed to a manic bard. Anyone adhering to the Platonic notion of frenzied inspiration would have had a different explanation of Boissy's talents and fate.

Since "Kubla Kahn" returned to Coleridge's thoughts at least once later in his career—when he published it, for whatever reason, in 1816—it may not be inappropriate to examine Coleridge's statements in later prose on this question. Coleridge's early description of Boissy as a "man of genius" suggests that further information be sought in the second chapter of *Biographia Literaria,* the chapter on "irritable" genius. With Chaucer, Shakespeare, and Spenser as examples, Coleridge finds that "men of the greatest genius ... appear to have been of calm and tranquil temper," whereas the "counterfeit" genius is characterized by irritability, fanaticism, and morbid sensibility. In the former, passion serves insight; in the latter, "passion [is] in inverse proportion to ... insight." Persons of true genius build on and sustain themselves by a "foundation within their own minds." They control and are not controlled by their insights so that they are characterized above all by their "creative and self-sufficing power."

In "Shakespeare's Judgment Equal to His Genius," Coleridge singles out the Bard as the epitome of true poetic genius and carefully defends him from the Neoclassicists' charges that he was

> a delightful monster, wild, indeed, and without taste or judgment, but like the inspired idiot so much venerated in the East, uttering, amid the strangest follies, the sublimest truths.

Had Coleridge subscribed to the "inspired idiot" theory of poetic genius, he would not have found the Neoclassical view of Shakespeare objectionable. He would have endorsed it, holding it up as the proper model for the poet, for it describes someone who creates by the caprice of nature and not by the engagement of his mind. It describes someone in whom passion ranges far from any mental foundation or genuine insight. Coleridge, however, does not welcome such a view. He rejects it as a "dangerous falsehood," and opposes to it his argument that "the judgment of Shakespeare is commensurate with his genius, nay that his genius reveals itself in his judgment, as in its most exalted form"; his essay pleads for the critical discovery of the organization inherent in Shakespeare's works, an organization that takes its pattern from nature (and not from artificial Neoclassical rules) in which every "living body is of necessity an organized one ... [evidencing] the connection of parts in and for a whole, so that each part is at once an end and a means."

It is Shakespeare's ability to make these organic, natural connections that Coleridge most often praises and most often cites to approximate how the imagination works. In "Shakspeare [sic], a Poet Generally," Coleridge argues that Shakespeare's imagination was greatest because it succeeded in "produc[ing] that ultimate end of all human thought and human feeling, unity." Coleridge acknowledges the rarity of such achievement, but never suggests that it is not fully human. In fact, he often repeats "human" and "humanizing" throughout the essay in connection with the operation of Shakespeare's imagination. His emphasis in no way contradicts his famous statement on imagination in Chapter 13 of the *Biographia,* the statement in which he establishes a link between the creative ac-

tivity of the imagination and the creative activity of God. That statement identifies the authority and precedent for the function of the imagination. Far from suggesting that the operation is aberrent from human activity, it reinforces its appropriateness to it. The appropriateness obtains likewise in the operation of the more specialized secondary imagination, for Coleridge sees the poet's imagination as "co-existing with [his] conscious will," a condition that shows Coleridge to be opposed to the idea of a poet inspired irrespective of his volition.

Coleridge again addresses the "human" aspects of poetry in "On Poesy or Art," writing: "Poetry also is purely human; for all its materials are from the mind ... and all its products are for the mind." His emphasis surely precludes manic "enthusiasm," but perhaps his most definitive rejection of it is to be found in *Anima Poetae:*

> Idly talk they who speak of poets as mere indulgers of fancy, imagination, superstition, etc. They are the bridlers by delight, the purifiers; they that combine all these with reason and order—the true protoplasts—Gods of Love who tame chaos.

Even such a fitful perusal of Coleridge's criticism as is represented above suffices to show that neither figure in "Kubla Khan" possesses the attributes of a true poet. One is a Urizenic type, capable only of weighing and measuring and desirous of forcing his control upon all things; the other is an "indulger of fancy," who can achieve no order at all and who has given up even his self-control to the sway of his visions. Neither is a "bridler by delight." What, then, is the function of the false poets in "Kubla Khan"?

The answer to that question may draw on [Anthony John] Harding's recent exploration [titled "Inspiration and the Historical Sense in 'Kubla Khan'"] of inspiration and "Kubla Khan" in which he posits that "tension itself [between two views of inspiration] was Coleridge's real subject in 'Kubla Khan.'" On the one hand, "Kubla Khan" contains the ancient "belief in the possibility that divine truth may be imparted to human minds," as evidenced by the success (albeit temporary) of the Khan's creation; on the other hand, it accomodates the modern "historicist outlook ... that the normative tradition must be the judge of any inspired or oracular utterance," as evidenced by the concluding reflections "of the bard who knows what it is to be possessed, and knows too that this inspired state has escaped him."

Harding's explanation poses a problem similar to Watson's insofar as it makes the will-usurped condition of the inspired poet seem attractive, while Coleridge takes a less wistful attitude toward the manic bard. One may, however, borrow from Harding the key idea of tension and posit a different development. The tension in "Kubla Khan" may be seen as a tension between the extant theories of poetic creation—represented by the false poets—which Coleridge rejects and the new theory of imaginative creation that Coleridge embraces but cannot quite completely work out.

Coleridge turned to the imagination to find the alternative to the theories of poetic creation he had inherited from previous generations and found unsatisfactory. "The poem that does not exist"—but should—is the poem of imaginative creation. To finish that poem, Coleridge would also have to finish the thirteenth chapter of his *Biographia Literaria.* He would have to pronounce how, specifically, the imagination operates so he could display it emblematically and set it forth as the true alternative to the faulty theories of creation. This Coleridge did not do. His insights into the flaws suggested by "Kubla Khan" nevertheless remain with his other monumental contributions to the development of Romantic theories of imaginative poetic creation.

**Source:** Hewitt, Regina, "The False Poets in 'Kubla Khan,'" in *English Language Notes,* Vol. 26, No. 2, December 1988, pp. 48–54.

## John Spencer Hill

*In the following excerpt, Hill comments on Coleridge's use of opium and its role in the creation of "Kubla Khan."*

Coleridge's use of opium has long been a topic of fascination, and the grouping of Coleridge, opium and *Kubla Khan* formed an inevitable triad long before Elisabeth Schneider combined them in the title of her book. It is tempting on a subject of such instrinsic interest to say more than is necessary for the purpose in hand, and I shall do my best to resist temptation by exploring only four of the most obvious and essential aspects of it: (1) the contemporary view of opium in the late eighteenth century; (2) the extent of Coleridge's use and reliance on opiates in the late 1790s; (3) myths and medical evidence about the relationship between opium and the poetic imagination; and (4) *Kubla Khan* as an "opium dream".

The most striking features about opium in the eighteenth and early nineteenth centuries are the contradictory facts that, while it was widely used and easily available, almost nothing was known about it. Medical knowledge of the drug's properties was scanty and unreliable: few people realised, for example, that opium was addictive, and no one understood that withdrawal symptoms were the result of discontinuation or diminished dosages. Indeed, everything that was known about it seemed positive and beneficial. Laudanum (i.e. the simple alcoholic tincture of opium) was freely dispensed to relieve pain in cases as different as toothache and cholera; similarly, opium was used as a "cure" for a host of emotional and psychological disorders; and, in such seemingly innocent patent-medicines as Godfrey's Cordial, it served as a soothing syrup to quieten restless babies, often permanently. In Coleridge's day, as Alethea Hayter has pointed out [in *Opium and the Romantic Imagination*], "most doctors and patients still thought of opium not as a dangerous addictive drug but mainly as a useful analgesic and tranquilliser of which every household should have a supply, for minor ailments and nervous crises of all kinds, much as aspirin is used today".

Since the medicinal use of opium was so common and wide-spread, it is not surprising to learn that its use involved neither legal penalties nor public stigma. All of the Romantic poets (except Wordsworth) are known to have used it, as did many other prominent contemporaries. Supplies were readily available: in 1830, for instance, Britain imported 22,000 pounds of raw opium. Many Englishmen, like the eminently respectable poet-parson George Crabbe, who took opium in regular but moderate quantity for nearly forty years, were addicts in ignorance, and led stable and productive lives despite their habit. By and large, opium was taken for granted; and it was only the terrible experiences of such articulate addicts as Coleridge and DeQuincey that eventually began to bring the horrors of the drug to public attention.

Coleridge's case is a particularly sad and instructive one. He had used opium as early as 1791 and continued to use it occasionally, on medical advice, to alleviate pain from a series of physical and nervous ailments. "I am seriously ill", he wrote to Joseph Cottle in November 1796; "The complaint, my medical attendant says, is nervous—and originating in *mental* causes. I have a Blister under my right-ear—& I take Laudanum every four hours, 25 drops each dose." The evidence of Coleridge's letters argues that during the period 1791–1800 he used opium only occasionally and almost always for medical reasons. The turning-point, as E. L. Griggs has shown [in his essay titled "Samuel Taylor Coleridge and Opium" in *Huntington Library Quarterly*], may be traced to the winter and spring of Coleridge's first year at Greta Hall, Keswick, in 1800–1. During this period a prolonged and debilitating succession of illnesses, which Coleridge blamed on the raw, wet climate of the Lake District, caused him to use regular and increasingly larger doses of laudanum in an effort to assuage the torments of what he described as an "irregular Gout combined with frequent nephritic attacks". But the opium cure proved ultimately to be more devastating in its effects than the troubles it was intended to treat, for such large quantities taken over so many months seduced him unwittingly into slavery to the drug. And his life between 1801 and 1806 (when he returned from Malta) is a sombre illustration of a growing and, finally, a hopeless bondage to opium.

By the time he realised he was addicted, however, it was too late. He consulted a variety of physicians; he attempted more than once (with nearly fatal results) to break off his use of opium all at once; and, at last, in 1816, when he submitted his case to James Gillman (in whose house he was to spend the rest of his life), he was able to control his habit and reduce his doses, although he was never able to emancipate himself entirely. Contemporary medical science, it must be remembered, concerned itself largely with opium as a panacea and was almost powerless (owing to ignorance) to provide meaningful assistance to those who became victims of its prescriptions. In this light, Coleridge's struggle with his addiction must be seen as heroic and experimental; and it should be added that his experience of addiction led not only (as is sometimes asserted) to sloth and self-pity, but more characteristically to a dearly purchased and altruistic desire to keep others out of the black pit into which he had fallen....

But to return to the 1790s: what can we say about Coleridge's experience of opium at the time of composing *Kubla Khan?* Despite some dissent, the majority of recent scholars agree with E.L. Griggs that, until 1800–1, Coleridge was an occasional user of opium (usually for medicinable purposes, but sometimes for the pleasurable sensations which the drug induced) and that he was not, in any proper sense of the term, an opium-addict before this time. It is not surprising to find, then, that in the late 1790s Coleridge's opium experiences were essentially pleasurable; it was only in later years, when his slavery was firmly rooted, that the evil of

> *By and large, opium was taken for granted [in the late eighteenth and early nineteenth centuries]; and it was only the terrible experiences of such articulate addicts as Coleridge ... that eventually began to bring the horrors of the drug to public attention."*

opium manifested itself in the corrosive nightmares described in *The Pains of Sleep* (1803)....

As we know from the Crewe endnote, Coleridge took "two grains of Opium" before he wrote *Kubla Khan;* and this fact naturally raises the issue of the drug's effect on the poet's creative imagination. Early critics, guided by Coleridge's statements in the 1816 Preface, assumed that there was a direct and immediate correlation between opium and imagination. In 1897 [in *New Essays towards a Critical Method*] J.M. Robertson could not bring himself to doubt that "the special quality of this felicitous work [*Kubla Khan*] is to be attributed to its being all conceived and composed under the influence of opium"; and in 1934 M.H. Abrams declared [in *The Milk of Paradise*] that the "great gift of opium" to men like Coleridge and DeQuincey "was access to a new world as different from this as Mars may be; and one which ordinary mortals, hindered by terrestrial conceptions, can never, from mere description, quite comprehend". More recent criticism, however, grounded on modern medical studies, controverts such conclusions decisively. According to Elisabeth Schneider [in *Coleridge, Opium and "Kubla Khan"*], "it is widely agreed now that persons of unstable psychological makeup are much more likely to become addicted to opiates than are normal ones" and that, among such neurotic users of opium, "the intensity of the pleasure" produced by the drug seems (on the evidence of medical case-studies) "to be in direct proportion to the degree of instability". The explanation ... of the supposed creative powers of opium lies in the euphoria that it produces....

Alethea Hayter, although she wishes to avoid the "extremes" of the positions of Abrams and Schneider, nevertheless comes much closer in her conclusions to the latter than to the former. Opium, she argues [in *Opium and the Romantic Imagination*], can only work "On what is already there in a man's mind and memory", and, "if he already has a creative imagination and a tendency to rêverie, dreams and hypnagogic visions", then opium may intensify and focus his perceptions. Her final verdict—which "can be no more than a hypothesis"—is that "the action of opium, though it can never be a substitute for innate imagination, can uncover that imagination while it is at work in a way which might enable an exceptionally gifted and self-aware writer to observe and learn from his own mental processes". The most reasonable conclusion to be drawn from these various explorations of the relationship between opium and the operation of the creative imagination is that, while *Kubla Khan* might well not have been produced without opium, it most assuredly would never have been born except for the powerfully and innately imaginative mind of Samuel Taylor Coleridge.

**Source:** Hill, John Spencer, *A Coleridge Companion: An Introduction to the Major Poems and the Biographia Literaria,* London: Macmillan, 1983, pp. 73–8.

## Sources

Abrams, M. H., *The Mirror and the Lamp,* Oxford University Press, 1953.

Adair, Patricia M., *The Waking Dream: A Study of Coleridge's Poetry,* Edward Arnold, 1967.

Baker, James Volant, *The Sacred River: Coleridge's Theory of the Imagination,* Louisiana State University, 1957.

Beer, J. B., in *Coleridge the Visionary,* Chatto & Windus, 1959, 367 p.

Coleridge, Samuel Taylor, *Biographia Literaria,* Oxford: Clarendon Press, 1907.

Condor, Joseph, "Christabel, Kubla Khan, a Vision. The Pains of Sleep," in *The Eclectic Review,* Vol. 5, June 1816, pp. 565-72.

Fruman, Norman, *Coleridge, the Damaged Archangel,* George Braziller, 1971.

Heninger, S. K., Jr., "A Jungian Reading of 'Kubla Khan,'" in *Journal of Aesthetics and Art Criticism,* Vol. 18, 1960, pp. 358-67.

House, Humphry, in *Coleridge: The Clark Lectures, 1951-52,* Rupert Hart-Davis, 1953, 167 p.

Lowes, John Livingston, in *The Road to Xanadu: A Study in the Ways of the Imagination,* Houghton-Mifflin Company, 1927, 639 p.

Moore, Thomas, "Christabel, Kubla Khan, a Vision. The Pains of Sleep," in *The Edinburgh Review,* Vol. 28, September 1816, pp. 58-67.

Schneider, Elizabeth, in *Coleridge, Opium and "Kubla Khan,"* University of Chicago Press, 1953, 378 p.

Shultz, Max F., in *The Poetic Voices of Coleridge: A Study for Spontaneity and a Passion for Order,* Wayne State University Press, 1963, 233 p.

Symons, Arthur, "Coleridge," in *International Quarterly,* Vol. 9, No. 11, June-September 1904, pp. 317-34.

## For Further Study

Lowes, John Livingston, *The Road to Xanadu: A Study in the Way of the Imagination,* Princeton University Press, 1986.

> First published in 1928, Lowes's work is now considered a classic in Coleridgian criticism. Although somewhat dated by the fact that it was written before the discovery of the Crewe manuscript, Lowes's monograph does an incredible job of detailing many of Coleridge's sources. Even if you don't accept the dream theory of the poem's origin, Lowe makes a compelling case for the recreative power of the unconscious.

Williams, Anne, "Coleridge and the Mysterious (M)other," in *Approaches to Teaching Coleridge's Poetry and Prose,* edited by Richard E. Matlak, 1991, pp. 147-57.

> There are four excellent essays about "Kubla Khan" in Matlak's collection, but this particular one brings a fascinating feminist perspective to the subject. Citing French theorists of *l'écriture féminine,* Williams notes that Coleridge, much like a woman, writes "the body" and describes hysteria imagistically. Using a feminist interpretation of Freud, Williams arrives at conclusions surprisingly similar to Jungian criticism.

# Lament for the Dorsets

## Al Purdy
## 1968

"Lament for the Dorsets," from Al Purdy's 1968 collection, *Wild Grape Wine,* is a quintessentially Canadian poem from Canada's superstar-poet of the 1960s. "Lament for the Dorsets" appeared at a stage in Purdy's career in which he had matured in both vision and technique. The poem is informed by Purdy's experience during the summer of 1965, during which he wrote poems in a tent in an Inuit village on Baffin Island, located in Canada's Northwest Territories. The Dorsets of the poem's title are a people who are distant ancestors of contemporary Inuits. The name derives from Cape Dorset, situated on the southwest coast of Baffin Island. Dorset civilization was spread over an extensive area of northern Canada and is thought to have existed for approximately two thousand years. While the Dorset people became extinct in the fourteenth century, a remnant of their culture has been preserved in the tiny tools and artifacts they left behind.

Although Purdy is a prolific poet who has published more than 600 poems, "Lament for the Dorsets" is one of the few known to Americans—if indeed Purdy is known at all to Americans—because it was included in *The Norton Anthology of Modern Poetry* (1986). "Lament for the Dorsets" is an elegy for a unique civilization that died out because it was unable to survive in changing conditions or because it was pushed out by a more technologically sophisticated people (the Thule). The poem, however, is not just a lament. It is also a paean to the permanence of art and the impor-

*Al Purdy*

tance of the artist to the life of a people. Purdy shows that a tiny carving of an ivory swan is what enables the Dorsets to live beyond their graves until their civilization is discovered some 600 years later.

## Author Biography

One would be hard put to find a more prolific poet than Al Purdy. As of 1989, Purdy had thirty-seven books of verse, one novel, an autobiography, a memoir, several edited collections, and two books of correspondence—one with critic and scholar George Woodcock and the other with barfly-poet Charles Bukowski. Purdy is also one of Canada's most eminent poets: his numerous awards and prizes include the Order of Canada (1987). Though hardly known in the United States, four of his poems are included in the *Norton Anthology of Modern Poetry*.

Born December 30, 1918, Purdy was raised by his mother, his father having died when Alfred was two. Purdy went to college and served as a noncombatant in the air force during World War II. His many jobs and avocations include riding the rails, running a taxi business, and five years making mat-

tresses. At age thirteen, he began writing poetry and published his first poems in *The Enchanted Echo* (1944), a volume he paid for and later referred to as "crap." By the 1960s, with the help of the Canadian government's support for artists, Purdy began writing full time, supplementing his income with reading, speaking, and teaching engagements. Up until 1962, Purdy said his style was derivative, but he asserts that with *Poems for All the Annettes* he had abandoned traditional rhythm and stanza forms for ones demanded by the poem being written. Other critics have disagreed as to when Purdy broke through to his own style: some say it was with *The Crafte So Longe to Lerne* (1959). Others say it was *The Cariboo Horses* (1965), for which he won the Governor-General's award.

Purdy's style is singular: "I believe that when a poet fixes on one style or method he severely limits his present and future development. By the same token I dislike the traditional forms. But I use rhyme, metre, and (occasionally) standard forms when a poem seems to call for it." In subject matter, Purdy is firmly Canadian and also a poet of underdogs—be they workers, prisoners, or Eskimos. He is also a poet more of the immanent than the transcendental, of earthly more than fantastic worlds. Finally, in reception, Purdy's independence has made him one of Canada's most respected and most popular poets: a nonacademic respected by the academy and a popular poet whose poetry shuns pop. Purdy is the consummate autodidact and individual, and in this sense is a poet not only of and for Canada but for the United States.

## Poem Text

### (Eskimos extinct in the 14th century A.D.)

> Animal bones and some mossy tent rings
> scrapers and spearheads
>     carved ivory swans
> all that remains of the Dorset giants
> who drove the Vikings back to their long ships
> talked to spirits of earth and water          5
> —a picture of terrifying old men
> so large they broke the backs of bears
> so small they lurk behind bone rafters
> in the brain of modern hunters
> among good thoughts and warm things
> and come out at night          10
> to spit on the stars

The big men with clever fingers
who had no dogs and hauled their sleds
over the frozen northern oceans
awkward giants                                          15

    killers of seals
they couldn't compete with little men
who came from the west with dogs
Or else in a warm climatic cycle                        20
the seals went back to cold waters
and the puzzled Dorsets scratched their heads
with hairy thumbs around 1350 A.D.
—couldn't figure it out
went around saying to each other                        25
plaintively
    'What's wrong? What happened?
    Where are the seals gone?'
And died

Twentieth century people                                30
apartment dwellers
executives of neon death
warmakers with things that explode
—they have never imagined us in their future
how could we imagine them in the past                   35
squatting among the moving glaciers
six hundred years ago
with glowing lamps?
As remote or nearly
as the trilobites and swamps                            40
when coal became
or the last great reptile hissed
at a mammal the size of a mouse
that squeaked and fled

Did they ever realize at all                            45
what was happening to them?
Some old hunter with one lame leg
a bear had chewed
sitting in a caribou skin tent
—the last Dorset?                                       50
Let's say his name was Kudluk
carving 2-inch ivory swans
for a dead grand-daughter
taking them out of his mind
the places in his mind                                  55
where pictures are
He selects a sharp stone tool
to gouge a parallel pattern of lines
on both sides of the swan
holding it with his left hand                           60
bearing down and transmitting
his body's weight
from brain to arm and right hand
and one of his thoughts
turns to ivory                                          65
The carving is laid aside
in beginning darkness
at the end of hunger
after a while wind
blows down the tent and snow                            70
begins to cover him
After 600 years
the ivory thought
is still warm

### *Lines 1-12:*

    The first stanza, or section, is actually one sentence describing what the Dorsets have left behind. Purdy first refers to traces of the civilization discovered by archaeologists. In several sites in Greenland, Baffin Island, Newfoundland, and the extreme north of Quebec, digs have uncovered bones, carvings, and small tools of the people now known as the Dorsets, a group that lived from around 1000 B.C.E. to 1350 C.E. Tent rings, a fairly common sight in Canada's Arctic north, are circles of stones that once weighted down the sides of tents. Next, the poet refers to Inuit stories about the Dorset culture that have been passed down through generations. The "long ships" Purdy mentions were the warships of the feared Scandinavian warriors who attacked the coasts of Europe and the British Isles, who were known for their cruelty, and who often settled in the areas they conquered. According to legend, when the Vikings attempted to invade Greenland in the tenth century, they were driven back to their ships by Dorset ferocity. In addition to exalting their ancestors' courage, Inuit stories describe the Dorsets as hunters who were unusually strong and gigantic enough to kill bears. Purdy also poeticizes that the Dorsets were "small enough" to hide in (or influence) the thoughts of present-day Inuit hunters. Purdy compares these minds to rooms with bone rafters.

### *Lines 13-29:*

    One of the distinguishing characteristics of the Dorsets was that they pulled their own sleds instead of using dogs to perform the task. The "little men who came from the west" were the Thule (pronounced *two*-le), a later Inuit group that used dogs and a possessed a higher level of technology than did the Dorsets. While it might have been the Thule who forced the extinction of the Dorsets, it could have also been that the Dorsets starved because of climate conditions that forced a change in seal migration.

### *Lines 30-38:*

    Purdy believes that Dorsets could scarcely have imagined inhabitants of the twentieth century: people who kill not with harpoon or spear, but with high-tech armaments; and a culture whose urban lifestyle and tenets of mass production and consumption (advertised in neon by corporate executives) results in the death of nature. Purdy also points out that modern people would have had sim-

## Media Adaptation

- A recording titled *Al Purdy* was released in 1971 by the Ontario Institute for Studies in Education.

ilar trouble fathoming Dorset culture if not for the presence of artifacts. "Glowing lamps" refers to small blubber lamps found at Dorset digs that, by Inuit accounts, hunters kept under their clothing to keep them warm while they waited at breathing holes for seals.

### Lines 39-44:

Here, Purdy is simply remarking that although Dorset civilization vanished 600 years ago, it might as well have become extinct millions of years earlier like the dinosaurs and the small sea creatures known as trilobites. In a sense, then, the past is a single time—a time of loss. The dinosaur and small mammal confrontation thus resembles the showdown between the Dorsets and Vikings described earlier.

### Lines 45-50:

The poet now speculates on the causes behind the Dorsets' extinction, and he questions whether they were cognizant of their impending demise. Purdy imagines the last Dorset as a hunter handicapped with a lame leg after being mauled by a bear.

### Lines 50-56:

In his imagination, Purdy is now shooting a close-up of this last Dorset, deciding even to name him, probably to make the image more vivid. Kudluk is carving an ivory swan, a symbol of rebirth, for his dead granddaughter. Purdy compares the mind to a room from which the artist pulls out pictures to use as the guide for his sculpture.

### Lines 57-65:

Purdy describes Kudluk carving and transforming the thought of a swan into an ivory figure. The pattern of parallel lines, a kind of exoskeleton, is a common feature of Dorset sculpture. Purdy

hints at the mystery of how images in the mind become objects in space with his description of the carving and his phrase "one of his thoughts turns to ivory."

### Lines 66-74:

This last section of the poem describes Kudluk's death after he finishes his sculptures. The lines "in beginning darkness / at the end of hunger" could refer to the time of day after the evening meal, but they could also signify the onset of death, with its freedom from everyday drives such as hunger. Kudluk likely froze to death, as he was unable to escape the snowstorm because of his lame leg. Purdy contrasts this image with his portrayal of the sculpture, or "ivory thought," as "still warm." Six hundred years after it was created, the ivory swan is, in a sense, still alive because it can be seen. And although he has died, a piece of Kudluk lives on in his sculpture. That a dying man was sculpting a symbol of rebirth seems sadly ironic, yet it has its intended effect on a larger scale than Kudluk could have ever imagined: the discovery of the sculpture helps bring the entire Dorset culture back to life.

## Themes

### Alienation and Loneliness

Kudluk is isolated from the rest of his culture, because all of the other Dorsets are either dead or have left in search of seals. He is also alienated from his environment; due to his lame leg, he can no longer hunt or escape from the ravages of weather. People would say that Kudluk's is a hostile, or unfriendly, environment or an indifferent nature. Both of these descriptions personify nature as a being with emotional responses. With the mention of Kudluk's granddaughter, Purdy points out a more personal instance of loss. This makes Kudluk thrice alienated and lonely: from society, from nature, and from family. Furthermore, Kudluk is waiting for death, which some think of as ultimate alienation and loneliness.

So why write about the loneliness of a Dorset? For one, it is a superhuman exercise in memory, far more difficult than an attempt to remember someone recently dead, whether stranger, friend, or family member. But there is something else as well. Perhaps if Purdy can empathize, or at least sympathize, with Kudluk, then he might better understand his own loneliness or that of present-day society. It's possible to imagine Purdy sitting alone in a tent—as was the case in 1965—on Baffin Island in Canada's Northwest Territories, unable to speak the native language of the Inuit around him and in an environment where food and companions were less than bountiful. And this isolation might only be an extreme form of that which Purdy feels regularly—as a poet, a traveler to unknown places, and as a resident of a rather isolated part of Ontario. Perhaps this was how Purdy came to think about Kudluk and empathize with him. It could also be that Purdy thinks Kudluk's situation bears resemblance to the isolation of contemporary apartment dwellers who barely know their neighbors. Purdy might be making the point that loneliness and alienation are nothing new; they are widespread conditions that once haunted the tenth-century Dorset and now afflict contemporary urbanites.

### Symbolism

Although Dorset carvings of various types of animals have been recovered from archeological digs, the swan is special because of the amount of symbolism surrounding it. Among some peoples, perhaps even the forebears of Dorsets, the swan was the virgin female impregnated by a hunter represented by earth or water who gave birth to the human race. Hence, the swan is a birth symbol—one that might be employed to bring a dead person back to life. Another story explains that babies were born from the marriage of earth and water and were brought to their care givers by swans. Conversely, the figure of the swan also pertains to death, most notably in the well-known expression "swan song," which means the end or last appearance of something. This expression derives from the baseless notion that swans sing before they die. The idea of singing swans and the legend that the birth of Apollo, the Greek god of poetry, was heralded by flying swans seem to have led to swans representing poets and poetry. Thus, Shakespeare was called the Swan of Avon; Homer, the Swan of Meander; and Virgil, the Swan of Mantua. Kudluk carving a swan (to help him stay alive while attempting to bring his granddaughter back to life) is analogous to Purdy writing, or "giving birth" to, a poem that helps keep the Dorsets alive in contemporary memory. Kudluk's final act of carving a swan also serves as the swan song of the Dorset people.

### Artists and Society

Artists keep themselves "alive" through art, while also keeping society "alive" by stimulating

## Topics for Further Study

- Do a research project on the Dorsets using both visual and textual elements. Include maps on migrations and settlements and describe objects they made.

- Compile separate lists of possible reasons for the extinction of plants, animals, and people. Correlate similarities and differences between the lists.

- In a research report, explain how Dorset art differs from later Eskimo art of the Thule and Inuit.

it to think new thoughts and reexamine old ones. One of the artist's roles is to refresh society. Paradoxically, a predominant way an artist does this is through examination of death, a major theme in all of the arts. Purdy appears to say that artists—those who keep people "alive" by speaking about death—are to be contrasted with "executives of neon death" and "warmakers with things that explode." And as art makes the Dorsets "live" even after the artists have died, the desire for raw materials and weapons results in the death of people and nature even as neon executives and arms dealers live comfortably from the profits of death and destruction.

### Style

In 1969, a year after the publication of *Wild Grape Wine,* which contained "Lament for the Dorsets," Purdy described his writing methods this way: "My technique, I suppose, takes a bit from [William Carlos] Williams, a bit from [Charles] Olson; for instance, I agree for the most part with using the contemporary, the modern, idiom. On the other hand, if I were writing a certain kind of poem I might avoid colloquialisms, idiosyncrasies, slang, and so on. It just depends; it all has to do with the poem. No, I pay no attention to the breathing bit; and I never compose on a typewriter, as Olson is supposed to do. Most of the time when I'm writing I don't think of how to write the thing at all, consciously; sometimes I do. When I wrote a poem about hockey players, I deliberately put in swift rhythms to simulate the players going down the ice. And there are times, whatever rhythm you get in there seem accidental; though I don't suppose it is, because a poet writes a lot of poems. I'm concerned with techniques, yes, but I don't consciously spend so much time thinking of them as Williams and Olson do." While Purdy does not use the term "free verse" to describe his poetry, the label has been applied to his work. Free verse is really not verse at all, because verse is metrical. Nor is free verse usually rhymed or arranged in regular stanzas. But while Purdy's poem eschews meter, rhyme, and regular stanzas, line breaks become a preoccupation. Purdy banishes commas and periods, and instead uses line breaks to signal pauses and capital letters to indicate new sentences. Only in two places does Purdy make use of run-on lines where, for example, the end of a sentence is ignored, or the subjects of sentences appear early, that is, in the sentence before. Thus, in the following lines, "The carving is laid aside / in beginning darkness / at the end of hunger / after a while wind / blows down the tent and snow / begins to cover him," Purdy's arrangement hurries the sentence to convey the speed of death and extinction.

To signal the beginning of a sentence, Purdy uses capital letters, but to make clear to the reader that this is not prose, he flushes all but a few lines at the left margin. So why the tension between prose and poetry? Perhaps to show that despite the absence of the traditional (outdated) signs of poetry, this piece of writing is still a highly wrought object, perhaps as complex in formation as Kudluk's two-inch ivory swan.

## Historical Context

Against a background of increasing tension between French Quebec and the rest of mostly English Canada, Al Purdy penned "Lament of the Dorsets" (1968). This poem can be said to lament a time when Inuits flourished throughout Canada, a time when neither France nor England—nor their Québécois and Canadian offspring—had any knowledge or claim to what they both, in the 1960s, thought of as their land. In June of 1960 Jean Lesage became the Liberal Party's premier of Quebec, a primarily French province within the domi-

nant English nation of Canada. Under the motto, *"If faut que ça change!"* ("Things must change!"), the Quebec Liberal party began to bring their various factions together into a united province. Meanwhile, Quebec's newfound urban prosperity created a high-salaried, secular bureaucracy that undermined the dominance of Catholicism's advocacy of nonmaterialist values—arguments that many Québécois began to see as an endorsement of poverty for the poor and riches for the rich. Catholicism came under attack especially in education. By 1964, Quebec had newly created a centralized provincial, nonreligious education system with secondary schools and a network of junior colleges (a system that, by 1966, led the other provinces to also take charge of their province's education). Not only was education nationalized, but the provincial government also nationalized, or, more accurately, provincialized, Quebec's formerly private hydroelectric industry. Voters showed their overwhelming acceptance. Quebec's "Quiet Revolution" was approved by the rest of Canada as well, since, it seemed, Quebec was becoming a "real" province like all of the other already consolidated provinces of Canada. But what the rest of Canada thought was modernization and Canadianization, was predominately Quebec's growing nationalism, a prelude to what would become calls for separation from its adopted English parent, the rest of Canada.

By 1963, one Québécois in six believed in separation. Some were even willing to use bombs in the name of *"Québec libre"* ("Independent Quebec"). The new Quebec would be symbolized by a world's fair, Montreal's Expo '67, a show that seemed as if it would never make the stage. When it did, Quebec became Canada's star province, an entity to be reckoned with. After France's President Charles de Gaulle proclaimed, *"Vive Montréal! Vive le Québec! Vive le Québec libre!"* Quebec would soon become emboldened enough to claim that henceforth the State of Quebec would be an equal to the rest of Canada. By the end of 1967, a movement to unite the separatist factions into a single independence movement, a Mouvement Souveraineté-Association, would be undertaken.

At the same time Quebec was consolidating itself in terms of Canada, the nation of Canada, with its twenty-year, postwar prosperity, was consolidating itself in terms of other nations, especially the United States. Federal income doubled between 1957 and 1967. Thousands of artists and actors, playwrights and poets lived off the bounty

# Compare & Contrast

- **1961:** 22,998 people are living in the Northwest Territories of Canada, home to the Inuit Eskimos.

  **1996:** 64,402 people living in the Northwest Territories of Canada.

- **1968:** The Parti Québécois for an independent Quebec is founded with René Lévesque as its leader.

  **1995:** A referendum held in the province of Quebec concerning independence is defeated by one percentage point.

- **1968:** The Inuit Eskimos live scattered across the Northwest Territories of Canada.

  **April, 1999:** The Inuits begin living in and mostly governing the new Canadian Territory of Nunavut ("Our Land"). The Territory, the result of an agreement signed in 1993 between Inuits and the Canadian government, designates 2.2 million square miles of what was mostly the Keewatin District as Inuit land, with its capital to be established at Iqaluit (formerly Frobisher Bay) on Baffin Island.

---

of the state. Universities were the beneficiaries of government monies. National health insurance became a reality. Personal income also soared, enabling Canadians to vacation around the world. Youth proclaimed national pride and their distinction from the youth of the United States by the very visible maple-leaf patch—a replica of Canada's new national flag—sewn to their backpacks. Cities that during the early postwar years had pushed ever-higher with the international style of concrete and steel, and suburbs that had sprawled ever farther with asphalt and cement, began to conserve older Canadian styles, sites, and structures. Dominated groups like native peoples and women also increasingly demanded, and got some share of, inclusion into Canadian prosperity. Student and worker demands even met with sympathy. Universities included student input in management and in creation of academic programs. Between 1964 and 1968, virtually all provincial and federal employees won rights to bargain and strike. Not only did human groups become forces to be reckoned with in an increasingly multicultural Canada, but so too the "rights" of nature in an increasingly environmentally conscious Canada. Native peoples found themselves in the difficult position of being embraced by the new forces of inclusion and environmentalism and, at the same time, attacked for their traditional livelihoods of hunting and trapping.

While the demands of women, native peoples, blacks, and nature were voiced, and to some extent met, Quebec's voice for nationhood was still the loudest and rowdiest, a voice that in 1970 would be put down by Canadian martial law. The rest of Canada could not ignore Quebec. Perhaps the greatest symbol of Quebec's rising power in Canadian politics was the election of bilingual prime minister Pierre Trudeau in 1968. Trudeau attempted to get the Québécois to help rule Canada rather than separate from it. The cornerstone of his administration was the Official Languages Act, which established the equality of French and English and encouraged a move to make the officials and agencies of the central government bilingual. Canada would become one of the few prosperous countries of the West that would think of itself as a bilingual, multicultural society, even if Quebec did not cease from its demands to be independent.

## Critical Overview

George Woodcock, scholar and poet of Canadian letters, classifies Purdy under the category "Canadian Modernist" and goes on to call him "the most vigorous of all traveller poets, who has given us Canada in verse, from east to west, from the Great Lakes to the Arctic, and not content with that, has added Europe and Asia and Africa." Woodcock classes *Poems for All the Annettes* (1962), *The Cariboo Horses* (1965), and *Wild Grape Wine* (1968) as Purdy's most important collections. In the 1960s, Purdy was also one of Canada's most popular readers on college campuses and one of the country's best-known poets. But despite this popularity, Woodcock goes on to describe him as "one of the most fluent and idiosyncratic of Canadian poets, extraordinarily open to impressions, and perhaps more able than any of his contemporaries to set into verse the historical and geographical complexities that make Canada."

In a review of *Wild Grape Wine* in *Poetry,* the dean of Canadian literature, Margaret Atwood, called the volume a "satisfying" book and adds: "These poems go beyond Purdy's interest in people and incidents to the process of human life within the larger process of nature; they create, not a personality and a speaking voice ... but a landscape with figures, both alive and dead. It's this Purdy ... a lonely, defiant, almost anonymous man, dwarfed by rocks, trees, and time but making a commitment, finally, to his own place ... where grim ancestors reach up from the ground to claim him."

In an article in *Canadian Literature,* George Bowering describes *Wild Grape Wine* as having smaller "'books' of poems wherein the poet may be seen alighting in some corner of the land or elsewhere, and joining detailed observations to lyrical reflections in order to provide longer looks at the places and people that make up our land and imaginations." If this is generally true of *Wild Grape Wine,* it is exactly fitting for "Lament for the Dorsets," which displays most eloquently, Woodcock's description of Purdy's voice as "idiosyncratic," Atwood's description as "anonymous," and Bowering's as "detailed and "lyrical."

## Criticism

### Jhan Hochman

*Jhan Hochman's articles appear in* Democracy and Nature, Genre, ISLE, *and* Mosaic. *He is the author of* Green Cultural Studies: Nature in Film, Novel, and Theory *(1998), and he holds a Ph.D in English and an M.A. in Cinema Studies. In the following essay, Hochman discusses ancient Dorset culture and finds a corollary with the contemporary separatist movement in the Canadian province of Quebec.*

Purdy is a poet of place. Most often that place is Canada—Canada as a separate entity, one with its own particularities and heritage. As former colonies of England and France have broken away from the "mother country," they have attempted to find their own voice in the language of the country that once utterly dominated them. If Hawthorne, Melville, Poe, and Whitman, were voices of a distinctly American literature, Purdy is one of the voices of a specifically Canadian literature, one that has taken longer to find its proper key. Dennis Lee, the critic who wrote about Purdy's poetry in the afterword to *The Collected Poems of Al Purdy* (1986) characterizes Purdy this way:

> He has been one of the giants of the recurrent process in which, language by language and country by country over the last sixty years, the hinterlands of empire have broken through to universal resonance by learning to speak locally. Purdy has claimed, and in many ways created, an indigenous imaginative patrimony in English Canada. There have been many Canadian writers whose excellence is unmistakable, but in his rootedness, his largeness, and his impulse to forge a native idiom for the imagination, Purdy is one of a distinct breed: the heroic founders, who give their people a voice as they go about their own necessities.

Before Lee, George Bowering called Purdy "the world's most Canadian poet." It is from these remarks and my own experience reading Purdy that I developed a thesis about "Lament for the Dorsets," a poem included in the volume, *Wild Grape Wine* (1968). My thesis is that whatever else can be said about "Lament," (for instance, that it is an impassioned call for the preservation of Inuit people and their culture), the poem serves as a political poem to keep the province of mostly French Quebec from separating from the rest of mostly English Canada. At the same time "Lament for the Dorsets" served as a national agglutinative, it also worked as an international wedge asserting Canadian individuality as it acted more and more on the world stage, a wedge especially intent on prying a space between Canada and its southern neighbor, the United States, the country whose shadow it no longer wanted to be. These two movements, the uniting of Canada and the assertion of Canadian individuality, happened at about the same time, the mid-1960s. During this same time, Purdy summered on Baffin Island, one of the lands of the Dorsets, and important finds of artifacts from Dorset archaeological sites had recently been discovered.

But how could a poem about Dorsets both bind and delineate Canada? To answer this is to begin

*What Do I Read Next?*

- During the 1970s, Purdy wrote idiosyncratic, impressionistic travel essays and anecdotal portraits of people and places that were published in *Maclean's* and *Weekend* and were eventually collected in *No Other Country,* (1977).

- In 1968 Purdy wrote *The New Romans: Candid Canadian Opinions of the U.S.,* a polemical anthology written as a critique of the United States and in support of Canadian nationalism which Purdy supported in the 1960s.

- A seminal work in African-American literature is W. E. B. Dubois's *The Souls of Black Folk* (1969), a series of essays on what it means to be a black American.

- A cross-cultural narrative anthropology, T. C. McLuhan's *The Way of the Earth* (1994) explores the ancient beliefs and narratives of the native peoples of Australia, Japan, Greece, Africa, South America, and North America.

- Rudolph Arnheim's *Visual Thinking* (1969) investigates the interaction between the senses and thought, a text that therefore must deal with the connection between psychology, philosophy, the arts, and the sciences.

with what is known about the Dorsets. These Paleo-Eskimos named after Cape Dorset on the southern coast of Baffin Island might just be the people most likely to be called the original Canadians. As Pre-Dorset peoples moved for thousands of years across Alaska and the Yukon of Arctic Canada, a distinctive culture began to congeal somewhere near eastern Victoria Island, above Alberta and Saskatchewan. Classical Dorset culture is thought to have flourished from about 1000 B.C.E. to 1300 C.E. in a vast area as far west as the west side of Victoria Island, as far north as Parry Channel and Greenland, as far east as Labrador and Newfoundland, and as far south as Payne Lake on the Ungava Peninsula of northern Quebec. Dorset sites have been discovered nowhere else but in areas between these mostly Canadian locales and were especially prevalent in the heart of the Canadian Northwest Territories, in the Foxe Basin, bordered on the north by Baffin Island. Not only were Dorsets spread out throughout most of Arctic Canada, but their culture was remarkably similar from site to site, indicating a great deal of travel and commerce among different bands or large family groups. And while Indians were spread all over North America, Eskimos, of which Dorsets are surely members, inhabited only the Arctic regions, and especially the Northwest Territories of Canada. This would make the Inuit the native people, and the Dorsets the paleo-natives of Canada, a once "united" Canada unbroken by province borders and linguistic barriers.

Another reason for calling the Dorsets the "first Canadians" is that Dorset civilization is the earliest civilization for which there is a well-preserved fossil record. While Dorset skeletons have been found on Mansel Island off the west coast of Quebec and in Northern Quebec near Sugluk on the Hudson Strait, no skeletons have been found for Pre-Dorsets, thought to have lived from around 4000 to 2000 B.C.E. Dorset skeletons show them not only to be the first skeletons of Quebec, but the first of Canada, near-contemporaries of Ancient Egyptians and Greeks. The point to be extracted here is that Quebec is not only part of Canada, but a crucial part.

Egyptian civilization is known for its mummies and monumental constructions, and Greece for its monuments and literature, but Dorsets are known by their miniature objects, tiny precision tools, and magical art objects. So tiny were the metal and ivory tools and household objects of Dorset households, that all could be easily packed into a small backpack when pulling up stakes to move to new hunting grounds. And this despite the legends of Dorsets being that race of giants spoken of in Inuit legend and in Purdy's "Lament." In these miniatures—that are visible outside the museums

> *... Canada likes to think of itself as a country that does not flourish by conquering peoples and nature but by living small in a large land."*

of Canada in the color plates of Robert McGhee's *Ancient People of the Arctic*—can be seen Canada's retort to monumental cultures and civilizations that lived large, such as Greece, Rome, Britain, and the United States. Unlike these, Canada likes to think of itself as a country that does not flourish by conquering peoples and nature but by living small in a large land. Legend even has it that not only did Dorsets spread out without conquering other peoples, but that they also successfully defended their homelands on the southeast coast of Greenland from invading Norseman. This would make them not only the first Greenlanders and Canadians, but brave defenders of their culture and homeland—a Canada that could have become Scandinavian instead of French and British.

Another characteristic of Dorset culture is its remarkable ability to have survived for so long in such a frozen area without certain tools used by peoples that lived even before Dorsets. While most Eskimos used dogs to pull their sleds, Dorsets pulled the sleds themselves. They also appear not to have used bows and arrows, hand-drills, or kayaks—devices that predated them and would probably have allowed them to kill more animals. No one knows why, nor whether it was by choice or ignorance. This, then, is another way Dorsets lived small: using simple technology that exploited nature to a lesser degree. While small artifacts and simple technology do not distinguish Canada from other nations, Canada does have one of the best environmental records of modern societies.

Despite two thousand years of Dorset civilization, it eventually disappeared from a change of climate, in turn leading to the disappearance, as Purdy suggests, of their food supply and/or from being overpowered by the Thule, the immediate Eskimo ancestors of the Inuit who had the bows and arrows, kayaks, drills, and dog-pulled sleds that the

Dorsets lacked or renounced, and that, archaeologists believe, led to the Thule takeover of northern areas of Canada. While this might be a lesson for Canadians wanting to live small, it is not so much what the Dorsets did not have as what they did—that culture of miniatures—that has made such a lasting impression on Canadians, especially Purdy. The most Canadian of poets laments the loss of the Dorsets for they seem like just the symbol that could heal the split between Quebec and Canada and distinguish Canada as a country with a unique heritage, ethnic make-up, and way of life. Purdy unearths the Dorsets in his own swan song, one less to do with swans singing about death and extinction than about the swan as a symbol of rebirth, not just in terms of Kudluk's dead granddaughter, but of Canada. Dorset magical art objects can speak to Canadians about the value of living small, staying together, and using art to spread its ideas and vision well beyond the grave. And "Lament for the Dorsets" is itself a kind of Dorset miniature, a small sculpture in language functioning to return the Dorsets to memory, and, by so doing, return Canada to unity.

**Source:** Jhan Hochman, in an essay for *Poetry for Students*, Gale, 1999.

### Bruce Meyer

*Bruce Meyer is the director of the creative writing program at the University of Toronto. He has taught at several Canadian universities and is the author of three collections of poetry. In the following essay, Meyer explains how, in "Lament for the Dorsets," Purdy "seeks to connect past to present through both artifact and imagination."*

The poetry of Al Purdy can easily be compared to the records of an archaeologist who is in search of a past. Many of his finest poems, such as those written about his home in the small hamlet of Ameliasburgh, Ontario, examine the ways in which the past is buried beneath the layers of living. By digging down, by examining artifacts, shards, and pieces of the puzzle that are left to the present, Purdy is able to construct, at least imaginatively, an experience that connects the past to the present. This may not seem to be such an important matter. After all, few poets would deny that one of his or her key roles is that of chronicler or historiographer—either of the past or of the present time. But given the context of his poetry, that of both map-maker and myth-maker within the Canadian imagination, Purdy's works are a fundamental means by which the past can be connected to the present, a creative ideal designed to counteract any claim that Canada is a place without a history or a broad context of time. "Lament for the Dorsets," a poem that examines the anomaly of presence within absence, is key to Purdy's canon because it seeks to connect past to present through both artifact and imagination.

Like the majority of Purdy's poems, "Lament for the Dorsets" is written in free verse in a voice that at times sounds broad and ambling. In much of his poetry, Purdy appears as a storyteller/observer and as a guide who is sifting through the remains of past worlds or through the observations of this world and who attempts to use storytelling as a means of threading his way through a labyrinth of images and suppositions. For Purdy, the story is what breathes life into inanimate objects such as the "animal bones" and "mossy tent rings," the garbage and remnants that bespeak life and vitality, even in the face of extinction, time, and entropy. What makes these shards—these remains—human is that they are, poetically, connected to real or imagined human beings. For Purdy, the signs of life are proof not only of the presence of past lives that continue to articulate their hopes, dreams, and visions, but of the presence of a vitality with which the reader can identify.

The imagining of "Kudluk," the carver and last of the Dorsets, operates on several levels. On the first level, Kudluk is an attempt by the poem's persona, the storyteller of the present, to put a human face on the inanimate "ivory swans," the artifacts that are all that remain of the Dorsets. What Purdy is doing is creating a subtle parallel between himself, the modern storyteller, and the ancient sculptor of the "ivory swans": both are creating not only artifacts of thought, perception, and belief, but also testaments of how time is borne by human beings and how life is contained in objects of memory such as carvings or poems. When Kudluk carves the "ivory swans" "for a dead grand-daughter," he is himself filling the absence and the grief with the power of his imagination. Like his imaginary predecessor, Purdy is filling a perceived void with an act of the imagination that reminds us of a human presence, so that the carving and the poem "Lament for the Dorsets" are literally identical objects as records of life. In this regard, Purdy seems to be saying that the power of the human imagination not only serves to remedy grief and loss but to fill voids, so that the carver and the poet/storyteller both serve the same function: "taking them out of his mind / where pictures are" so that "After 600 years / the ivory thought / is still warm." Here, Purdy is raising one of the great, continual claims

> *'Lament for the Dorsets,' a poem that examines the anomaly of presence within absence, is key to Purdy's canon because it seeks to connect past to present through both artifact and imagination."*

for poetry, a claim made by such poets as Shakespeare (in "Sonnet 18"): that poetry can animate the inanimate and provide a bridge between presence and absence and life and death. In a literature where such notable Canadian critics as Northrop Frye have charged poets with the responsibility of creating not only a poetry but a living mythology, Purdy seems to have made an important contribution, because one of the key purposes of mythology is to make us believe that life continues even in death.

"Lament for the Dorsets" also makes an important, yet equally subtle, comment on the nature of mythology, not just as a vehicle for life and consciousness, but as a structure in itself. Like such mythographers as Ovid in *The Metamorphoses,* Homer in *The Iliad* or *The Odyssey,* or Virgil in *The Aeneid,* Purdy enlists the assistance of factual history that he links with his powers of the imagination to give the imaginary aspects of the poem, especially the character of Kudluk, more credence and plausibility. Hence, "Lament for the Dorsets" opens with a history lesson. Purdy explains that these "Dorset giants" "drove the Vikings back to their long ships," and then, "around 1350 A.D.," suddenly vanished "And died." The suggestion is that either climatic changes that drove off the seals or the invasion of smaller, much more adaptable "little men" who "came from the west with dogs" caused the downfall of the Dorsets. What Purdy is establishing with this information is a "set-up" for a parallel structure where he links the plight of the Dorsets to the predicament of modern man in the twentieth century. One must remember that mythologies are never written for the past; they are directed at the readers of the present, and Purdy sounds a warning to "Twentieth century people" that they must stop destroying their environment and stop warring with their neighbors if they are to survive. As World War I poet Wilfred Owen suggested in his famous statement about war poetry, "the poetry is in the pity," likewise Purdy has created a situation in "Lament for the Dorsets" that raises, in a rather rhetorical fashion, pity by comparison. In this case, the factual history of the Dorsets and even the touchingly pitiable tale of the imaginary Kudluk are serving only as exemplum in the argument. Rather than attack the issue of modern man's indifference to their own situation, Purdy has created a parallel example in the form of a story that distracts the reader from any direct charges that the poet is leveling against contemporary society and habits. But the lines "Did they ever realize at all / what was happening to them?" are not addressed to the Dorsets (after all, they are dead) as much as they are to the modern reader. What the reader is supposed to perceive in the poem is the concept that our world is just as fragile and perishable as that of those swan carvers, and that our size, our power, and our importance are little more than hubris toward our own tragedy if we fail to recognize our own situation.

In a final note of reversal, Purdy wonders aloud if the Dorsets ever imagined us in their future, the "apartment dwellers / executives of neon death / warmakers with things that explode / —they have never imagined us in their future / how could we imagine them in the past / squatting among the moving glaciers / six hundred years ago / with glowing lamps?" For Purdy, one of the challenges of "Lament of the Dorsets," a challenge that he confronts time and time again in his canon, is the difficulty of making the past aware of the present and the present aware of the past. Like his Canadian contemporary, poet Eli Mandel, who declared that "the future is foretold in the past," Purdy has taken up the theme of not only bridging time but of acting as a translator and mediator who enables worlds to communicate and who conveys a kind of wisdom from one era to another. The question then remains, what is the past? This is a central question in Canadian poetry and Canadian literature, especially in the writings of Purdy's close contemporaries, such as novelists Margaret Laurence and Timothy Findley and poets such as Milton Acorn, Eli Mandel, George Bowering, and James Reaney. For those who emerged with Purdy as significant voices in Canadian literature during the second half of the twentieth century, the past is something we reconstruct from what is left behind—shards that are quite often indistinguishable from rubbish. What connects these pieces of a grand puzzle together is the imagination. Novelist Timothy Findley, in his brilliant work *The Wars*, tells his readers that the past is not simply a collection of photographs but the way we animate those still images through the power of our own imaginations. Likewise, in "Lament for the Dorsets," Purdy seems to be telling his readers that the past is as much a creation of our ability to read our own lives and our own feelings into shards and remnants as it is the shards and remnants themselves, so that history is not only a creation of the past but a product of the present.

For Canadians living in the latter half of the twentieth century, the past is largely accessible only through the power of the imagination. Canada, it should be remembered, was not historically a result of great bloody battles or grandiose speeches, but a manifestation of gradual processes, bureaucratic documents, and unspeakably boring transformations that are hardly of note or interest. For Canadians to embrace their past, however, they must first grapple with a kind of absence where the time scale is more geological than recent and where the recognition of emptiness is an invitation to the imagination to find something living and breathing in a very large and seemingly empty terrain. "Lament for the Dorsets," therefore, is a classic example of the Canadian imagination both at work and at play. Here the possibility of absence, extinction, and lonely death calls into question the contemporary situation in life. The message is that what can happen to the Dorsets can happen to those in the contemporary world; yet the poem is not a cry of despair or even a dismal resignation to doom. On the contrary, "Lament for the Dorsets" is a celebration of what is continuous in life, the "pictures" of our "minds," the reality of experience that is fundamentally dear to us, and a record of the desire to shape it into a chronicle that will not only outlast us but speak for us and about us. After all, Purdy says, imagination is, at best, a two-way street, and in that respect, it is the avenue that eludes time, just as all good mythologies outlast their storytellers.

**Source:** Bruce Meyer, in an essay for *Poetry for Students,* Gale, 1999.

## Sources

Atwood, Margaret, review of *Wild Grape Wine, Poetry,* June 1969, pp. 202-07.

Bowering, George, "Purdy: Man and Poet," *Canadian Literature,* winter 1978, pp. 24-35.

Geddes, Gary, "A. W. Purdy: An Interview," *Canadian Literature,* summer 1969, pp. 66-72.

Giddings, J. Louis, *Ancient Men of the Arctic,* New York: Alfred A Knopf, 1967.

Klinck, Carl F., ed., *Literary History of Canada: Canadian Literature in English,* 3 volumes, Toronto: University of Toronto Press, 1976.

McGhee, Robert, *Ancient People of the Arctic,* Vancouver: UBC Press, 1996.

Purdy, Al, *Collected Poems of Al Purdy,* edited by Russell Brown, Toronto: McClelland and Stewart, 1986.

## *For Further Study*

Bandi, Hans-Georg, *Eskimo Prehistory,* University of Alaska Press, 1969.
Bandi begins with the first discoverers of America and discusses sites in Alaska, Canada, and Greenland. There is a great deal of information on the Dorsets.

Brown, Craig, ed., *The Illustrated History of Canada,* Toronto: Lester & Orpen Dennys Ltd., 1987.
Beginning with the meeting of Cartier with native peoples in Canada, the book proceeds with politics, society, and culture until 1987.

Ellman, Richard, and Robert O'Clair, eds., *The Norton Anthology of Modern Poetry,* second edition, New York: W.W. Norton, 1988.
This massive anthology begins with Walt Whitman and ends with Cathy Song (who was born in 1955). Short critical biographies precede every poet.

Maxwell, Moreau S., *Prehistory of the Eastern Arctic,* Orlando: Academic Press, 1985.
This volume describes the Arctic climate and topography and goes on to detail what is known about the people who once inhabited it, including the Dorset and Thule cultures.

# Leviathan

## W. S. Merwin
## 1956

"Leviathan" is the first poem in W. S. Merwin's third volume of poetry, *Green with Beasts* (1956), and is one of the best of his earlier works. It has been praised for its mastery of both of sound and style, which is based upon an early and influential type of English poetry called Anglo-Saxon verse. Using the Anglo-Saxon line of four heavy beats marked and emphasized by alliterating three of the four accents, Merwin builds endless variations. At the same time, his frequent use of compound words and altered word order generates a poem laden with sound, begging to be juggled in the mouth as much as in the head.

Perhaps the chief influence on "Leviathan" is "The Whale," a tenth-century, Anglo-Saxon poem in a book of verse titled *The Exeter Book*. But there are other influences as well: the Old Testament books of Genesis, Job, Isaiah, and Jonah, and Herman Melville's classic whaling epic, *Moby Dick* (1851). While these influences and allusions make "Leviathan" enjoyable for the scholar and researcher, the reader need not know these texts to enjoy or think about the poem. "Leviathan" is divided into four parts, each with a different trajectory. The first part describes the whale plowing through the open sea. The second section repeats the *Exeter* legend of the whale as a piece of land that fools sailors looking to moor their boats. The third and shortest part is a series of allusions to the whale in history, and the fourth part describes the whale at rest. Taken together, Merwin's well-muscled lines portray a sense of the great power of the sea, the whale, nature, and God. Some critics have read these forces as apocalyptic—those that will someday rise to the surface and overwhelm all of creation, including that other "leviathan," humanity.

## Author Biography

W. S. (William Stanley) Merwin was born on September 30, 1927, in New York City and was raised in Union City, New Jersey, and Scranton, Pennsylvania. Merwin's father was a Presbyterian minister who Merwin said had a rather narrow view of life. Despite this, Merwin did begin his career in letters by writing hymns for his father. From 1944 to 1948, Merwin attended Princeton University, but he took a year-long recess to serve in the armed forces. He graduated with a degree in Romance Languages and studied with poet John Berryman and critic R. P. Blackmur (to whom Merwin's fifth book of verse, *The Moving Target* [1963] was dedicated). Several times during the late 1940s, he visited Ezra Pound—one of the most esteemed and controversial of modern poets—at a sanitarium where Pound had been confined after being labelled "criminally insane." Pound told Merwin to write all he could and to "read seeds not twigs," meaning that Merwin should go to the sources of poetry, the origins of verse, not its offshoots. After finishing his undergraduate degree in 1947, Merwin conducted one year of graduate work at Princeton, where he studied modern languages and translated French and Spanish literature. The next year found him starting what would become a seven-year sojourn in Europe.

Merwin's first job in Europe was tutoring in France and Portugal and then in Majorca for the son of poet-scholar Robert Graves. From 1951 to 1954, Merwin supported himself in London doing translations from French and Spanish for the British Broadcasting Corporation (BBC). At the same time, his first two books of poetry were published in the United States. In 1954 Merwin married. During 1956 and 1957, Merwin wrote a play in verse, *Darkling Child,* that was performed in London; he also returned to America to write plays for the Poets' Theatre in Cambridge. In 1956 he received a Rockefeller Playwriting Fellowship and published *Green with Beasts,* in which "Leviathan" appeared. In 1962 Merwin was named poetry editor of *The Nation.* The next year he married for a second time and divided his life between New York

*W. S. Merwin*

City and Lot, France. Through 1971, Merwin published and won numerous awards, the most prestigious being the Pulitzer Prize for his seventh book of verse, *The Carrier of Ladders* (1970). At this time, Merwin divided his time between France and Chiapas, Mexico, where he refurbished his own home. Continuing with his translation and writing, Merwin moved to Haiku, Hawaii. While he was letting his abandoned pineapple plantation revert back to rainforest, Merwin traveled frequently, doing readings across the United States. In 1979 Merwin won the Bollingen Prize for *Feathers from the Hills.* He received the Lenore Marshall/ *Nation* Poetry Prize in 1993 and the Tanning Poetry Prize in 1994.

## Poem Text

This is the black sea-brute bulling through wave-
    wrack,
Ancient as ocean's shifting hills, who in sea-toils
Travelling, who furrowing the salt acres
Heavily, his wake hoary behind him,
Shoulders spouting, the fist of his forehead          5
Over wastes gray-green crashing, among horses
    unbroken
From bellowing fields, past bone-wreck of vessels,

Tide-ruin, wash of lost bodies bobbing
No longer sought for, and islands of ice gleaming
Who ravening the rank flood, wave-marshalling,          10
Overmastering the dark sea-marches, finds home
And harvest. Frightening to foolhardiest
Mariners, his size were difficult to describe:
The hulk of him is like hills heaving,
Dark, yet as crags of drift-ice, crowns cracking in      15
      thunder,
Like land's self by night black-looming, surf
      churning and trailing
Along his shores' rushing, shoal-water boding
About the dark of his jaws; and who should moor
      at his edge
And far on afoot would find gates of no gardens,
But the hill of dark underfoot diving,                   20
Closing overhead, the cold deep, and drowning.
He is called Leviathan, and named for rolling,
First created he was of all creatures,
He has held Jonah three days and nights,
He is that curling serpent that in ocean is,             25
Sea-fright he is, and the shadow under the earth.
Days there are, nonetheless, when he lies
Like an angel, although a lost angel
On the waste's unease, no eye of man moving
Bird hovering, fish flashing, creature whatever          30
Who after him came to herit earth's emptiness
Froth at flanks seething soothes to stillness,
Waits; with one eye he watches
Dark of night sinking last, with one eye dayrise
As at first over foaming pastures. He makes no cry       35
Though that light is a breath. The sea curling,
Star-climbed, wind-combed, cumbered with itself
      still
As at first it was, is the hand not yet contented
Of the Creator. And he waits for the world to
      begin.

## Poem Summary

### Lines 1-12:

The word "leviathan" is mentioned repeatedly in the Bible's Old Testament—for example, in Job 3:8 and 41:1, Psalms 74:14, and Isaiah 27:1. A contemporary definition, according to *The American Heritage Dictionary of the English Language,* is a "large sea creature" or "anything unusually large for its kind." Traditionally, however, the leviathan has been associated with a whale, due to the word's derivation from the Hebrew term for "great water animal." Though the 39 lines of "Leviathan" are not divided into stanzas, the poem can be subdivided into four parts. The first section runs from lines 1 to 12, ending with "And harvest"; it describes a wild whale swimming at sea. This rather long section might be read more easily if the entire part is seen as a prosaic, two-part sentence with a beginning, main clause, "This is

the black sea-brute bulling through wave-wrack, ancient as ocean's shifting hills," and a much longer, dependent clause attached at the end of the independent clause: "who in sea-toils travelling, who furrowing the salt acres heavily, ... finds home and harvest." Line 4, "his wake hoary behind him," comes from a description of a whale in Job 41:32: "Behind him he leaves a shining wake; one would think the deep to be hoary." In this first part of "Leviathan," Merwin twice uses a literary device called metonymy, whereby characteristics are transferred from thing to another because they are near. For example, in "sea-toils" and "sea-marches," the "toilsome" swimming or "marching" of the whale through water is transferred to the sea which toils and marches; in "bellowing fields" the bellowing of horses becomes that of the fields; and in "wastes" and "tide-ruin," the corpses of men and horses, and the wreckage of ships, become the ocean itself. Merwin also uses metaphor, where one thing is substituted for another, as in "bone-wreck," where a wrecked futtock (the curved beams of a ship's hull) resemble the bony ribs of a floating creature, especially a whale. Through metaphor, the ocean becomes like a field ("salt-acres") and the whale like a plow ("furrowing") that collects a "harvest" from the ocean-field. This image somewhat complements the idea of the whale as an ox or bull pulling a plow, or, as Merwin says, "bulling" through the field. Lastly, lines 10 through 12 contain language that is somewhat militaristic: "ravening," "wave-marshalling," "overmastering," and "sea-marches." Here the whale is a kind of weapon or one-animal army marching over fields that present no obstacle to its powerful forward progress. All in all, the ocean is a field (see also "foaming pastures," line 35) across which the whale moves like a plow or army.

### Lines 12-21:

These lines are, in spirit, taken from *The Exeter Book,* a tenth-century Anglo-Saxon manuscript that includes a bestiary, a compendium of descriptions of animals through which morals are taught. For example, the poem "The Whale" describes how a whale is mistaken for land to such an extent that men will moor their boats to it, climb on top, and build a fire. Then, suddenly, the whale will dive and drown the men. In this respect, the whale is a kind of demon or devil that fools people and drowns them. In "Leviathan," the dark whale is also compared to land—an island to be exact—with waves slapping at its shores.

### *Lines 22-26:*

In these lines, Merwin gives us an abridged history of the whale in story and myth. "Named for rolling" comes from an etymology at the beginning of *Moby Dick,* in which Melville quotes *Webster's Dictionary:* "This animal is named from roundness or rolling for in Danish, *hvalt* is arched or vaulted." According to Genesis 1:21, the whale was the first of the animals created by God. And also in the Old Testament, the short book of Jonah tells the tale of a whale who swallowed Jonah in the sea and vomited him up on land three days later. Line 25 likely refers to the apocalyptic passage of Isaiah 27:1: "In that day the Lord, with his hard and great and strong sword, shall punish Leviathan the fleeing serpent, Leviathan the twisting serpent; and he will slay the dragon that is in the sea." Line 26 harkens back to *The Exeter Book,* with the word "shadow" referring to the whale's blackness mentioned in the previous section and to death, as in the word "shade"—the term for a dead person, specter, or ghost. Together, these descriptions promote the idea that the whale is deadly and, thus, an animal to be feared.

### *Lines 27-39:*

The theme of these lines is the whale as a symbol of rebirth, not of death as in the previous two sections. For example, when a repentant Jonah is vomited onto dry land, he is resurrected because he pledged his devotion to God. Resurrection also complements the whale as an "angel," even if a "lost angel." Some have interpreted the words "lost angel" to imply the whale's relation to Satan or the devils mentioned in *The Exeter Book.* What seems more fitting—since Merwin did note use the more common tag line given to the devil, "fallen angel"—is that "lost angel" merely refers to a whale alone, as if lost upon the vast sea. The whale alone, but not necessarily lonely, is reinforced by the image of the original whale that existed for a time before the rest of the animals were created. In this section of stillness, the whale waits quietly and alone for the unfinished world—symbolized by the restless, churning sea—to be reborn. It has one eye focused on the sunrise (birth) and the other on the sunset (death). The earth's oldest animal—according to biblical legend—cannot die and will continue to live as long as does the world. The whale is that a creature so large it spans the time from the world's beginning through its myriad deaths and rebirths. This master of the sea and angel of God, this whale that stands for the first whale and all whales that ever lived, cannot be made extinct, but is as immortal as God's power manifested in nature.

# *Media Adaptations*

- Merwin's poems have been recorded for the Archive of Recorded Poetry and Literature.

- Merwin's animal poems, including "Leviathan," were recorded in May and June of 1954 on the BBC Third Programme under the title *"Physiologus.*

## Themes

### *Nature and its Meaning*

W. S. Merwin's "Leviathan" (1956) concerns time and nature through the specific example of the whale as narrated in myth, legend, and observation. The two major elements to "Leviathan," are the whale and the sea. In the first eleven and a half lincs, thc sca is dcscribed almost as much as the whale, and the sea, overwhelmingly, appears as a place of death. The ocean is littered with animal corpses and ship wreckage and, for this reason, is referred to as "wastes," "tide-ruin," "rank flood," and "dark." There is some ambiguity, however, about whether the sea—apart from containing the wreckage of ships and bodies—is simply a place of death, since, for the whale, the ocean is a field it furrows and harvests, and, in addition, a home in which it dwells. It might be best to say that for creatures of land, the ocean is overwhelmingly deathly—a watery grave. But for whales, the sea is life-giving. This establishes the relationship between whale and ocean. The next lines (12-26) recount the relationship of whales to humans, especially in legend. Here, as in the ancient Anglo-Saxon poem "The Whale" in *The Exeter Book,* the whale is compared to an island dangerous or false to the man attempting to land on it. The whale, then, is treacherous and deadly for humans. If the whale is thought to represent the awesome power of nature, then nature as a whole becomes treacherous and deadly and, further, the measure of God's utter mastery. For a characteristic of the Old-Testament God was Him dishing out death and destruction, especially to those taken in by false

## Topics for Further Study

- Go through part or the whole of "Leviathan," and with each half-line and line explain the variation on the classic form of the Anglo-Saxon line as explained in the style section. For assistance, the student might first want to look at an excellent example of an almost exact imitation of the classic Anglo-Saxon form in Richard Wilbur's poem "Junk" (1961).

- Do a presentation on either the mythology or the biology of whales. As a class try to make comparisons between legend and research.

- Whaling is an internationally disputed practice. Collect articles from newspapers and the Internet about such disputes and then craft a presentation explaining the debate about the hunting and killing of whales.

idols—such as the false land represented by the whale in *The Exeter Book*. By the end of the poem, the sea is revisited, and its constant churning reveals that creation was not finished in seven days. Similar to the whale's mastery of the unmasterable sea at the beginning of the poem, the whale at the end of "Leviathan" waits calmly—perhaps even curiously—for what the sea, through the hand of God, will do next. One senses an awful power about to be born (perhaps worth comparing with the "rough beast" at the end of Yeats's "The Second Coming"). This is nature as all-powerful and something to fear—a potential candidate for ascriptions of both respect and evil.

### Permanence

Both the whale and the sea are symbols of permanence. Although the whale was, according to Genesis, the first animal created, the sea preceded it. Both, however, are still very much a part of this world. This long life might itself be a symbol of the changelessness of the "wind-combed" and "star-climbed" sea, of the "ancient" whale and, by inference, of all of nature. Merwin draws attention

to several viewpoints about the status of the natural world: the nature existing long before and during the "reign of humanity"; the nature, based on a rather early idea of a resource that cannot be exhausted or defeated, that will probably outlast people; and the nature presently emphasized in environmental rhetoric and imagery that is threatened and victimized by an upstart humanity. Merwin's poem was written before the birth of modern environmentalism in America, beginning either in 1962, the publication date of Rachel Carson's *The Silent Spring,* or in 1970, which featured the first Earth Day. To Merwin in 1956, earthly nature might have indeed seemed inexhaustible. This would have put him behind his time. Or, on the other hand, nature could have seemed to him exhaustible, and so he could have felt the need to write this poem and get people to once again revere nature. In this case, Merwin would be ahead of the downward curve of nature's decimation and the upward curve of environmental awareness.

### Strength and Weakness

In this poem it is nature, represented by sea and whale, that is strong. Conversely, humanity is weak. While the sea might symbolize or indicate a place of plenty for human nourishment, Merwin shows it, instead, to be a place of home and harvest for the whale and, oppositely, a grave for humankind. The ocean is littered with the wrecks of ships and corpses of animals—especially humans—that, it might seem, the ocean has swallowed. And the whale can wreak havoc too. Did it not swallow Jonah, and can it not drag foolish mariners who would mistake it for land to their doom? Is the whale not called a "serpent," a "curling serpent" in a "sea curling." Is he not "seafright" "and the shadow under the earth"? Merwin partially catalogs a list of terrible legends about the strength of a deadly sea and a treacherous whale that can tame the sea in the way it easily swims it. The message here is that nature is not to be taken lightly; it is a force full of threatening power like that of the Old Testament God who created it. The lesson of this poem, then, is beware the whale and ocean, beware nature, for it always was, is, and will be—though the world may begin again and again. "Leviathan" is a celebration of, or claim for, nature's power or strength, to which man's supposed power pales in comparison. This is quite a different impression about nature than that depicted at the end of the twentieth century, in which nature has become weakened, threatened, and destroyed.

## Style

Three style characteristics mark "Leviathan": altered syntax, compound word formations, and alliteration. First, altered syntax means that Merwin has changed standard prose word order. This, at least initially, makes the poem a bit difficult to comprehend, but readers can mentally rearrange the word order to make sense of it. For example, lines 2 and 3 read, "who in sea-toils / Travelling," but can be better understood by rearranging the syntax to "who travels in sea-toils." Likewise, lines 5 and 6, "the fist of his forehead / Over wastes gray-green crashing" can be read as "the fist of his forehead [moves] over crashing, gray-green wastes." The effect of such lines is to make them seem age-old, like the whale itself. The seeming archaism of such lines also ties the style to the ancient Anglo-Saxon poem "The Whale" from *The Exeter Book* (c. 940) that informed, if not inspired, "Leviathan."

Another feature of "Leviathan" is compound words, which are sometimes called "blends." These words can function as nouns, adjectives, or verbs. Examples from this poem include bone-wreck (n.), tide-ruin (n.), black-looming (adj.), star-climbed (adj.), and wave-marshalling (v.)—to name just a few. Use of compound words weds the poem to the ancient Greek poems attributed to Homer, *The Iliad* and *The Odyssey*. These classics featured heavy use of compound words, known as *epithets,* such as "rosy-fingered dawn," "many-minded Odysseus" and "earth-shaker." There is also an economy, or efficiency, in epithets that lends a concentrated intensity lost in more usual constructions.

The last major hallmark of "Leviathan" is alliteration, the repetition of sounds at the beginning of words. For example, in line 37—"Star-climbed, wind-combed, cumbered with itself still"—the sounds repeated are a hard "c" and the hissing "s" sound of the last two words. The alliteration helps tie the lines and poem together in a unified whole. But the alliteration also serves a more sophisticated purpose; it refers readers back to the "strong stress rhythm" of Anglo-Saxon accentual verse illustrated in "The Whale," part of *The Exeter Book* mentioned above. Merwin's poem plays with the form of Anglo-Saxon verse, a prosody characterized by lines divided in half, with two strong and any number of weak stresses per half-line, or hemistich. In the Anglo-Saxon line, three of the four strong accents are alliterated with the same sound. Merwin almost never follows this exact pattern, but instead utilizes variations. Here is one example:

This is the **b**lack **s**ea-brute / **bull**ing through **wave**-
 wrack

In this line, as in Anglo-Saxon verse, there are three alliterations of "b," but this sound is not always accented, as is the case with the work "brute." Furthermore, Merwin adds the near-alliteration of "w" and "r" at the end of the line. Here is another variation on the standard Anglo-Saxon line:

**Shoul**ders **spout**ing, / the **fist** of his **fore**head

This time Merwin employs two separate alliterations on accented syllables. These initial repetitions of sound not only serve to wed "Leviathan" to an older tradition, but to make meaning out of the materiality of sound. For example, in the first line, the repeated explosive sound of the "b" more or less fits the explosiveness of a whale spouting, swimming, and diving. Or see line 32 ("seething soothes to stillness"), in which the repeated alveolar sound of the whispering "s" helps the reader envision or hear the quietness of the waiting whale. Lastly, if the poem in divided into four sections (lines 1 to 12, 12 to 21, 22 to 26, and 27 to 39), one discovers that the first section reads faster to mimic the whale pounding through seawater, while the last section reads with numerous pauses to complement the whale almost slowing to stillness.

## Historical Context

The America of the 1950s was the setting for "Leviathan," a poem suffused with the power of nature. Perhaps the need for such a poem is no wonder. The status of nature hardly concerned anyone living in cities and suburbs; Americans were more interested in acquiring the new consumer products that had not been available or considered necessary during the years the United States was involved in World War II. If the war years yielded a frugal and less-procreative American, the postwar boom years introduced the extravagant consumer with children (what would be known as "the baby boom generation"), a consumer bombarded by television and magazine advertising promising a life made perfect by accumulation of homes, appliances, furniture, and automobiles. While war has always had a devastating effect on a more localized humanity and nature, peacetime, with its drive to re-create and consume, has its ruinous consequences as well—however slow, ignored, or unseen.

The pattern running through the fabric of the postwar years was that of great expectations in terms of both personal and national success. The

# *Compare & Contrast*

- **1956:** The United States deploys the first "tactical" nuclear weapons in Europe. Fired by artillery guns, the eight-inch-wide projectiles are capable of travelling more than eleven miles to battlefield targets and exploding with a force almost as great as the Hiroshima bomb.

  **1998:** The United States is predicted to spend $4.5 billion on nuclear weapons through 2008, whereas the country spent $3.7 billion on nuclear weapons during the Cold War

- **1950-60:** The Nature Conservancy is formed in 1951, the Clean Air Act becomes law in 1955, and the Clean Water Act becomes law in 1960—all of which indicate an incipient knowledge that humanity can destroy parts of nature and make it unfit to support animal, plant, or human life.

  **1998:** From January to September, each month has broken a record for the highest average global heat. Some point to this fact as evidence of global warming, a condition that, if left unchecked, could lead to negative effects—including changes in sea level—on the earth's natural environment

- **1950s:** The Aral Sea in south-central Asia is the fourth-largest sea in the world. The Soviet Union begins damming the rivers flowing into it for crop irrigation. At the same time, chemical fertilizers used on fields wash into rivers that feed the Aral Sea. The receding waters expose soil that dries out, becomes air-borne dust, and, along with the contaminated waters, result in birth abnormalities, liver cancer, and blood disease in some areas.

  **1990s:** The Aral Sea ranks as the world's sixth-largest sea; its meager fishing is confined to small, contaminated ponds.

---

economy, which had been at full tilt for the war effort, continued to run like a leviathan for the consumption effort. In order to keep factories bustling with laborers producing profits for business, Americans were called upon to consume as if they themselves were fighting a war against nature, whose plants, animals, seas, and land were—if not actually, then potentially—to be conquered. But the war waged against a defenseless nature was undeclared, unconscious, even unknown, since Americans were too busy "getting theirs" as factory production increased, personal income continued rising, the gap between rich and poor narrowed, and inflation was kept in check. But problems did surface, although not so much with nature.

The main problem is best summed up as America's preoccupation with the political ideology of communism. While it is debatable whether the fear of communism was cooked up and inflated or whether it was a very real danger, the Cold War cast a pall over Americans' pursuit of pleasure in the 1950s. Initially, America, with its can-do attitude, thought it could counter any Soviet threat with its nuclear stockpile. And so a nuclear subculture burgeoned around hopes for thermonuclear defense, a subculture illustrated in the documentary film *The Atomic Cafe* (1982). But when the Soviet Union also got the bomb and was gathering Eastern Europe and China within its sphere of control or influence, America, in 1950, went to war in Korea. The U.S. government claimed it was trying to stop communism from spreading throughout the world by means of the hypothetical "domino effect," whereby one country's transformation to communism meant that neighboring countries would "fall" too. The Korean war, however, changed nothing in terms of borderlines but everything in terms of American defense: it was the Korean War—far more than World War II—that established America's system of military bases around the world and quadrupled its defense budget. Although four million Koreans died in the war—three-quarters of them civilians—the border between communist North Korea and capitalist South Korea remained and, to this day, is heavily armed on both sides. America's inflated defense budget remains, and China, who fought the United States to a stalemate in the Korean War, is a major power in terms of its military and its markets.

The other known flaw in the hubris of 1950s America was what the rise of prosperity meant for African Americans. For it was white, not black, America that reaped the harvest of America's postwar boom. As "white flight" into the suburbs became as important a social event as transformation of the rural into an urban populace, the cities and its poor suffered, especially the African-American poor. The decay of the cities and the continued injustices blacks suffered led to what came to be known as the Civil Rights years (1954-1965), a time when Dr. Martin Luther King became a household name. And by the late-1960s, African Americans had conquered state-sanctioned, or obvious, segregation and had created a black middle class, even if a small one.

Postwar America created a huge network of global interests fueled by its fierce desire to possess and consume products extracted from what was once considered an inexhaustible nature. No longer. America, with its boundless desires that came to full fruition in the postwar years and continue unabated, is rapidly reducing leviathan—that is, nature—to a corpse. Merwin's poem might then be viewed as a last-ditch attempt to make nature matter—for something other than mere matter—and to reaffirm the awesome power of nature in a world where that new cultural leviathan, America, was wresting it away for the sake of its massive appetite for newer and better products.

## Critical Overview

"Leviathan," a selection from W. S. Merwin's third book of poems, *Green with Beasts* (1956), is one of the best-known poems from one of the poet's most-respected books. Paul H. Wild compares "Leviathan" to Yeats's "The Second Coming" in its theme of a powerful, primitive nature waiting to be born. But the theme, Wild believes, is insignificant beside the poem's "achievement of the language." Wild goes on to write in detail about the sound of the poem: its reversal of word order and its alliteration, as in "the black sea-brute bulling." Vernon Young (1978) asserts, without presenting any evidence, that "Leviathan" is about "the beast under the waters of consciousness." Cheri Davis, writing in *W. S. Merwin* (1981), notices that "Leviathan" was selected as the first poem in *Green*

*with Beasts* because the whale—called "sea monster" in Genesis—was the first of the animals created. But Davis, like Wild, is also taken with the sound of the poem. She writes: "An ebullient exaltation in the abilities of language to invoke the metaphysical reality of the serpent carries the poem forth simply on its own momentum. The rolling, choppy rhythms capture the rolling and wet slapping of the creature." In *W.S. Merwin the Mythmaker,* Mark Christhilf is interested less in the language than the meaning of "Leviathan." He says it and the majority of the poems in *Green with Beasts* are about celebration, about telling "the story of love's influence in the world," and he claims that Merwin's desire is "to become a vessel for this song," "the music of cosmic unity, arising from the harmony of all created things." When specifically addressing the poem "Leviathan," Christhilf does not talk about the whale, but the sea: " ... the sea obviously embodies the Creation's principle of love and renewal." In *W. S. Merwin: Essays on the Poetry,* Cary Nelson writes little about language or meaning, but pulls back to examine style: "Poems like 'Leviathan' seem designed ... to exhaust their subject matter through continual variation and reiteration of the same terms and images." Opposite to Cary Nelson, the comments of Edward Brunner (1991) pull in for a close-up. Brunner comments on how the poem begins one way—both in style and meaning—but ends another: "As 'Leviathan' deftly modulates from one perception to its opposite, inverting the terms with which it began, what we had once dismissed now appears, from a further perspective, as decidedly attractive." In other words, the whale that was "sea-fright" becomes an "angel," who is stilled because soothed by the rolling sea. This might remind one of a newborn lulled by being rocked, an image almost meshing with the whale waiting "for the world to begin."

## Criticism

### Jhan Hochman

*Jhan Hochman's articles appear in* Democracy and Nature, Genre, ISLE, *and* Mosaic. *He is the author of* Green Cultural Studies: Nature in Film, Novel, and Theory *(1998), and he holds a Ph.D in English and an M.A. in Cinema Studies. In the following essay, Hochman deems Merwin's motive in "Leviathan" as an attempt to inspire reverence for nature but argues that the poet might have unwittingly succeeded in reinforcing the idea of the whale as a creature to be feared and, thus, destroyed.*

Let me begin my essay with a minor inference: the overarching point to W. S. Merwin's "Leviathan" is to reinvigorate nature with what Edmund Burke (1729-97) called the sublime, a feeling of awe before the unlimited power of nature, a nature that might be represented in "Leviathan" as sea, whales, nature, or God. Here is some evidence (though I doubt the view is worthy of controversy). Right away, the sinews of this poem are pulled tight with the repetition of the initial explosive "b" and the close-knit similarity between the semi-vowel "w" and the liquid "r." The alliteration keeps up its powerful concatenation of sounds as is the way with the Anglo-Saxon verse that inspired this poem. In a line such as "The hulk of him is like hills heaving," it is not only basic alliteration made even more powerful by the alliteration of a glottal "h" that sounds like heavy breathing, but also the large meaning of "hulk," "hills," and "heaving" that give this poem its forward thrust.

While the poem's sound is there on the surface for any reader to see and feel, the poem's meaning might demand more in-depth study. The first set of lines describes the power of the whale in a medium—the ocean—that hampers the movement of and easily destroys powerful land animals, horses and humans. The "wave-wrack," "sea-toils," "tide-ruin," and "sea marches" do not hamper or hurt the whale; instead, the whale "overmasters" the sea. The second part of "Leviathan," inspired by *The Exeter Book,* shows the whale as huge as an island, a kind of trap for foolhardy mariners. Hugeness is almost always part of the sublime—a characteristic of mountains, vast spaces, and explosive occurrences.

The third section is a short summary of the whale in legend and story, a mostly biblical compendium presenting the whale as the oldest animal in creation—oldness often being an adjunct to a feeling of awe. And again, the Old-Testament whale is so powerful and large as to swallow a person whole and inspire the fear attending that other fearsome animal, the serpent, who, like the whale, has been associated with evil, with the devil himself. The last section of the poem shows a lone whale whose past not only extends back to the beginnings of the world, but extends indefinitely into the future. Here, then, is an animal so old, powerful, and large as to be everlasting; it is like a god or a representative of the inexhaustibility of nature, a nature humanity will never destroy or overpower.

Merwin's "Leviathan" ably qualifies to be called sublime.

Most critics have agreed that the style of the poem—especially its agglutination of sound thick with alliteration, consonance, and assonance—is a resounding success in terms of portraying the power of nature or creation. However, Merwin's descriptions of the whale and the allusions to the whale in Western narrative, while meant to inspire a reverential awe proper to the sublime, also have the potential to inspire an awe-ful fear, or, by this point in the late twentieth century, a mere smirk. First, take the awe-ful fear. With the sublime, one can be driven to fear as much as reverence. Sometimes these are complementary; often they are not. The sublime can make one fear and avoid nature as much it can as make one visit or revere it. This, of course, will depend upon the reader, whether he or she, after reading "Leviathan" will be inspired to go whale watching and act in some way to protect whales, or whether he or she will avoid or ignore the whale, as a creature or as an issue. So, in attempting to inspire reverence for nature, Merwin's strategy regarding description and allusion could backfire.

Another possible response to this poem's buildup of the whale is a smirk. Why? Because whales have long been utterly dominated by human hunters. Some species have been decimated to the point of potential extinction, a trend that was reversed only with intervention and regulations from the International Whaling Commission. Not only has the whale been dominated, but so has the sea, which is falling prey to pollution from human society. Almost since the atomic bombs were dropped on Hiroshima and Nagasaki, humanity has had the potential to not only destroy itself, but to bring down nature with it. What I am saying is that, in a time when humanity can easily demolish the planet or simply convert it into a nature park for human amusement, the scheme to evoke awe in nature just might be dated, perhaps was even wrongheaded at the time Merwin decided upon the strategy. Or perhaps what was ill-conceived was using the Bible to inspire awe. For who but a minority are inspired by the rather tired biblical stories of Jonah swallowed by a whale and later disgorged and of the tale of all animal species being created at the beginning of time? Or who now, in the time of the over-hunted whale and of *Free Willy,* starring the victimized killer whale, Keiko, will be inclined toward a view of whales as deceitful, luring mariners to their death by posing as land? The stories of the Bible and *The Exeter Book* are no longer capable

## *What Do I Read Next?*

- Steve Baker's *Picturing the Beast,* published in 1993, argues that representations of animals shape our understanding of both animal and human identity. Baker's examples range from Disney to zoos to political cartoons.

- Clarence Glacken's *Traces on the Rhodian Shore: Nature and Culture in Western Thought from Ancient Times to the End of the Eighteenth Century* is one of the best and most important books published on the history of nature. It is an invaluable reference book for anyone thinking about how the meaning of nature has changed through history.

- Stephen J. Gould's *Dinosaur in a Haystack: Reflections on Natural History* is a collection of thirty-four essays, originally published in the journal *Natural History,* that bring together different manifestations of culture and establish their roots in nature.

- Merwin's *The Lost Upland* (1992) is a semi-autobiographical short-story collection set in southwestern France. Its theme is the way gradual modernization replaces the ancient way of life in rural France.

- Merwin's *Regions of Memory: Uncollected Prose, 1949-82* (1987) includes fiction, autobiography, memoirs, and essays and statements regarding translation and a public conscience, especially in terms of ecology.

- Keith Thomas's *Man and the Natural World: A History of the Modern Sensibility* is a virtuoso study of Britain's regard for and treatment of nature, especially as it progresses from a nature that should be exploited to a nature deserving of care and preservation.

---

of provoking belief, let alone awe—manifested as fear or reverence—except perhaps in children.

Merwin is a bit more successful when not dishing out allusions. Perhaps he knew this, since the section of allusions is the shortest in the poem. But even in describing whale and ocean there are problems. The sea is largely described as a violent stretch of mostly human wreckage (corpse and shipwreck) through which (only?) the whale can make his way, even "overmastering" it. And the whale is described as a "brute," his forehead a fist, a creature who ravens the ocean. This, it seems to me, is the description of a violent creature, not a large but gentle creature. Even in the last section of poem, the whale's waiting "for the world to begin" can seem insidious, as if the whale was a stealthy submarine waiting to destroy the world. It is said that while finding fault is easy, it is more difficult to suggest alternatives. So, in place of depicting the whale as a powerful animal of doom in a sea of death within a nature that is likely to manifest God's Old Testament wrath bent on destroying human civilization, what could Merwin have done?

He could have called upon an array of other stories about the whale—those, by the way, usually not part of the Western cultural tradition. First, he could have marshalled the legends of Viet Nam. The fishermen of Viet Nam believe that whales are messengers from the god of the waters to protect sailors, and that a whale will carry shipwrecked sailors, and their boat as well, on its back to safety. Sometimes when fishermen find a dead whale or dolphin, they haul it to shore and bury it and declare its finder the "eldest son" of the animal. For three months and six days, the eldest son wears a mourning turban, after which the buried animal is dug up and deposited in a sanctuary bearing a name only given to the tombs of royalty or high public officials. The turban is then burned. Such a sanctuary is yearly paid obeisance to assure a bountiful fishing harvest. Some Vietnamese also believe that every time it rains for long periods, a whale or dolphin has died, and that in order to stop the rain, the mammal must be given a respectful burial.

The whale also occupies an important place in Islamic tradition. Here, once the earth was created, it floated on the waters. God then sent down an angel who took up the world on his shoulders, then God sent down a green rock to give the angel a safe place to stand, then a bull to hold the rock with the horns on its forty-thousand heads and its back resting on legs with forty-thousand hooves, and then all of this resting on a whale which floated on the waters. The cosmic whale is so huge that if all the waters of all the seas were collected in one of the whale's nostrils, it would be the size of a mustard seed in the desert. Earthquakes, then, are the result of the cosmic whale's wiggling. Not only does the whale carry the world, but, according to another Islamic legend, the whale that swallowed Jonah is one of only ten animals that were allowed to enter paradise

While more stories of "the good whale" exist, these should suffice to show that such tales are out there, that the whale is not only a creature associated with death, deception, and evil but with cosmic centrality and kindness as well—at least outside of Western cultures. It is not that Westerners need believe such tales as much as be exposed to them to counter their own tradition in which the whale is largely demonized. It is curious that Merwin did not seek to directly counter the tradition of the Bible and *The Exeter Book* or utilize already existing counter-stories of the whale that would have had a greater chance of making a difference in terms of our regard of the whale. For it has long been a Western tradition, or urge, to destroy what we fear. This, in part, is what the Western tradition is known for: an utter domination of nature to overcome our fear and prove our superiority. Not that Merwin should have tried to create a cuddly leviathan to be kept as a pet, like *Free Willy*'s Keiko, the killer whale that is unable to kill. Still, the problems with making Keiko a poster whale—an emasculation of wildness and a simultaneous virilization of humanity, or, on the other hand, a construal of humanity as saintly—might now be fewer and less serious than creating yet another text about a whale to be feared. Fear (as well as the desire for whale-related products) has got the whale nowhere but disregarded or slaughtered.

**Source:** Jhan Hochman, in an essay for *Poetry for Students*, Gale, 1999.

### Chris Semansky

*Chris Semansky is a published poet who regularly writes essays and reviews of modern and contemporary poetry. In the following essay Semansky explores how "Leviathan" describes a creature that human beings have historically imbued with meaning that inevitably have more to do with themselves than the whale.*

When people pledge allegiance to the American flag, they are not pledging fidelity to a piece of cloth with red and white stripes and a flock of stars in the left-hand corner; they are pledging allegiance to the abstract ideas the flag represents. These ideas include not only the country of the United States but also the values and ideas conventionally associated with the country—values such as freedom, democracy, and even capitalism. In this way, the flag can be said to be a symbol, because it stands for something. Poets often use words and phrases to signify a thing or event, which itself signifies yet something else. Because the "something else" frequently ranges widely, symbols can be notoriously difficult to interpret. In his poem "Leviathan," W. S. Merwin describes the multiple ways in which the whale has historically served as a symbol to human culture and the ways in which the image of the whale has served as a receptacle for human hopes and fears.

Merwin begins the poem by calling the animal "the black sea-brute bulling through wave-wrack, / Ancient as ocean's shifting hills." These lines couple the whale's symbolic importance as both an object of male sexual might and as an object representing the oldness of the physical world itself. In the eighteenth century, whales were often hunted for their ambergris, a gray waxy substance found in the sperm whale's intestine, because it was thought to be an aphrodisiac. Merwin underscores the sexual prowess and might of the whale in describing the animal's violent forays through the sea, itself long a symbol of the sexual. The image of the whale "furrowing the salt acres" of the ocean suggests a farmer ploughing his fields and preparing them for seed. Merwin's comparison of the ocean to land throughout the poem also highlights the whale's own evolutionary history. Scientists believe that the whale originated from land mammals, whose structure became adapted to living in the sea.

By describing the whale as a creature that exists almost outside of time, Merwin emphasizes the animal's place in myth. Myths are stories that cultures use to explain the natural world's behavior, and whales themselves have had, and continue to have, mythic importance for people. Arabians believed that the earth rested upon a whale named Bahamut and that when Bahamut moved, he caused earthquakes. The association of the whale with both good and evil is also evident in literary works such as *Moby Dick,* where the animal is variously described as a quasi-malevolent force of nature indifferent to the concerns of human beings and as a retributive response of a Christian God intent on sending humanity a signal not to mess with nature. The whale's meanings have multiplied over the years because so little has been known about it. As Merwin makes clear, both its elusiveness and sheer bulk make it a difficult creature to depict: "to foolhardiest / Mariners, his size were difficult to describe." In *Among Whales,* Roger Payne claims that the word "whale" derives from the Old-English word wheel, "the idea being that when viewed from a boat or from shore, a whale breathing at the surface, looked like a wheel revolving slowly in the sea." Wheels themselves are symbols of eternity—the yoking together of past, present, and future, the heavens and the earth. Merwin's descriptions themselves never show us the whale as it appears; rather they underscore the impossibility of words to render a complete visual image of the mysterious behemoth. It is significant that "Leviathan" was first published in 1956, for it wasn't until the 1960s, in fact, that marine biologists began to compile substantive factual information about whale habitats and behavior. The whale, then, has shifted from being an object of superstition, legend, and myth to a scientific object of critical inquiry. Or has it?

Ever since the environmental activist group Greenpeace began lobbying for the animal's protection, the whale has emerged in popular culture as an underdog, symbolically representing those parts of the natural world that are being hunted or harvested into extinction. Nowhere has this symbolism been more tangibly demonstrated than in the public's response to Keiko, an *Orcinus orca,* or "killer whale," that has spent almost its entire life in captivity. First caught—allegedly accidentally—off the shores of Iceland, the whale was sold to an aquarium in that country, then sold to Marineland in Ontario, Canada, which then sold it to Reino Aventura, an amusement park in Mexico City which, after an article in *Life* magazine detailing Keiko's living conditions instigated a public outcry, donated the whale to the Oregon Coast Aquarium in Newport, Oregon. Keiko's international popularity began in Mexico and derived in large part from his appearance in the film *Free Willy* that, ironically enough, told the story of a captured Orca whale helped to freedom by a young boy. After two years of "rehabilitation," in Newport, Keiko was sent back to Iceland in September of 1998, where he is now relearning to live in the ocean, albeit in a man-made bay pen. His handlers plan to release him after—and if—he can demonstrate that he can

> *By describing the whale as a creature that exists almost outside of time, Merwin emphasizes the animal's place in myth."*

hunt for himself and gain acceptance by other whales. International media coverage attended Keiko's preparation for his trip to Iceland; reports about what Keiko was experiencing, and speculation about his future, made news programs daily. Donations continued to pour in. Contributors to the Free Willy-Keiko Foundation inscribed these messages on the "Whaling Wall" located on the building that housed the aquarium were Keiko was kept in Oregon: "From another male Keiko" (Christopher Keiko Kaplan); "Swim Free Keiko. Love you." (Lokotah and Mischa); "Being Free is Living." (Lily 96); "The sea is cold. Yet you are warm." (The Abrahams); "Keiko / Warmth, Tenderness, Beauty, Trust. / It's all you." (Mac Technology Inc.)

These messages attest to the continuing symbology of the whale in popular culture. As Merwin suggests in "Leviathan," what is truly prodigious about the whale is more than simply its physical size; rather, it is its capacity to contain so much *human* meaning. These epigraphs not only imbue Keiko with human emotion, desire, and even identity, but they also participate in the ongoing commodification of the nonhuman world. Where formerly the whale was seen as a prime mover, emblematic of the inherent mystery and inscrutability of the uncharted earth, today it is seen as a pop icon, one more celebrity in an already crowded sea of celebrity. The epigraphs—some directly addressed to Keiko, some in memoriam of a loved one—are rooted in the kind of vapid sentimentality most commonly found in greeting cards and on bumper stickers. Their (quite literally) surface quality mimics the world of late-twentieth-century America, where the production and media manipulation of images helps to constitute a new world, one that cultural theorist Jean Baudrillard has aptly named the simulacra, where the "real" is no longer distinguishable from the world of representations. Though initially formed by his appearance in *Free*

*Willy,* Keiko's subsequent runaway celebrity was, in effect, choreographed by Warner Bros. and New Regency Productions, who provided the Free Willy-Keiko Foundation with some four million dollars in seed money. The return on this small investment has been astronomical, as the constant and widespread publicity the Foundation has generated for Keiko's story made these entertainment giants many millions more on *Free Willy 2: The Adventure Home* and merchandising tie-ins. The home video of this movie—some six million copies of which were released—also carry an emotional appeal by the movie's cast members to help Keiko. Never, in my opinion, has a private company so ruthlessly exploited a public issue for financial gain as Warner Bros. has with the story of Keiko.

Merwin's "Leviathan" describes a world in which the whale has seen everything: the "cold deep," shipwrecks, "lost bodies bobbing." The animal's symbolic status is that of a demigod who has both preceded and survived humanity. However, leviathan could never have known that the world he waited for to begin at the end of Merwin's poem would be one in which his own significance would be trivialized, his image hijacked by the anti-poets of the West, the media moguls whose primary concern wasn't educating the public about the whale's sacred, timeless character or its mythic and religious meanings, but squeezing as much profit as possible from the fifteen minutes of limelight this New Age hero was allotted.

**Source:** Chris Semansky, in an essay for *Poetry for Students,* Gale, 1999.

## Sources

Bradley, S. A. J., *Anglo-Saxon Poetry,* London: Dent, 1982.

Brunner, Edward J., *Poetry as Labor and Privilege: The Writings of W. S. Merwin,* Urbana: University of Illinois Press, 1991.

Christhilf, Mark, *W. S. Merwin the Mythmaker,* Columbia: University of Missouri Press, 1986.

Davis, Cheri, *W. S. Merwin,* Boston: Twayne, 1981.

Donaldson, Gary, *Abundance and Anxiety: America, 1945-1960,* Westport, CT: Praeger, 1997.

Morris, William, ed., *The American Heritage Dictionary of the English Language,* Boston, MA: Houghton Mifflin Co., 1976.

Nelson, Cary, and Ed Folsom, eds., *W. S. Merwin: Essays on the Poetry,* Urbana: University of Illinois Press, 1987.

Nelson, Cary, and Ed Folsom, " 'Fact Has Two Faces': An Interview with W. S. Merwin," *Iowa Review,* Winter 1982, pp. 30-66.

Payne, Roger, *Among Whales,* New York: Delta, 1995.

*The Whale* New York: Simon and Schuster, 1968.

## For Further Study

Albert, Judith Clavir, and Stewart Edward Albert, eds., *The Sixties Papers: Documents of a Rebellious Decade,* New York: Praeger, 1984.

  This anthology consists of essays by the leading lights (Mills, Ginsberg, Malcolm X, etc.,) and on the leading struggles (antiwar, counterculture, feminist) of the 1960s. The volume is introduced by an overview of the 1950s.

Burk, Robert Fredrick, *The Eisenhower Administration and Black Civil Rights,* Knoxville: University of Tennessee Press, 1984.

  Burk exposes the government's failures regarding civil rights.

Goldman, Eric F., *The Crucial Decade: America, 1945-55,* New York: Alfred A. Knopf, 1956.

  Goldman's history includes material on Truman's Presidency, the end of World War II, the onset of the Cold War, the Korean War, and the Eisenhower "Era of Equilibrium."

Williams, Juan, *Eyes on the Prize: America's Civil Rights Years, 1954-65,* New York: Penguin, 1987.

  For a history heavily informed by those who participated in the civil rights struggle, this anthology is excellent. The volume includes time lines, myriad quotes and photos, and there is the excellent PBS companion video series.

# Lost Sister

## Cathy Song
## 1983

"Lost Sister" was published in 1983 in Cathy Song's first volume of poems, *Picture Bride*. Her book earned the Yale Younger Poets Award for 1983, as well as a nomination for a National Book Critics Circle Award. Poet Richard Hugo, the Yale Award judge, praised *Picture Bride* for its "candor and generosity," and he specifically cited "Lost Sister" as an example of the way "Song does not shrink from the hard realities of the societal and familial traps set for women." In this poem, neither the daughter who stays home in China, nor the sister who leaves for the United States has found freedom. By employing images of movement and stasis, and by exploring the customs of naming and foot binding, Song attends to the Chinese woman's struggle for identity, whether at home or on "another shore." The poem is a cameo of the struggles women in many parts of the world face in negotiating freedom and power.

Born and raised in Hawaii, Cathy Song has returned there as an adult to live and write. Thus, most of the poems in *Picture Bride* tell family stories that grow out of the islands' rich soil. Some, such as "Lost Sister," reach back and across to more distant, but no less powerful stories about Song's Chinese and Korean ancestors. Because of this, the textures and tales of the book reach far beyond family history and beyond Hawaii. In choosing Song's book, Richard Hugo recognized its ability to express, through Hawaii's many cultures, the stories of anyone who has struggled to survive and adapt in a new land. *Picture Bride* is a polyphony of

*Cathy Song*

voices—Korean, Chinese, Japanese—that might otherwise be silent. In particular, "Lost Sister" tells the story of women who, like Cathy Song's Chinese grandmother, face the paradoxes of freedom and belonging.

## Author Biography

Cathy Song was born on August 20, 1955, in Honolulu, Oahu, Hawaii, to a Chinese-American mother and a Korean–American father. Song spent her early childhood in the small town of Wahiawa, which, like many other rural Hawaiian communities, made its livelihood raising sugar and pineapples for export. The title poem of *Picture Bride* speculates what the experience of immigrating to Hawaii must have been like for Song's Korean grandmother. It imagines her feelings upon first looking into "the face of the stranger / who was her husband," the man who had been waiting for her, picture in hand, "in the camp outside / Waialua Sugar Mill." In "Easter: Wahiawa, 1959," Song connects her memory of gathering Easter eggs as a four-year-old with the image of her Korean grandfather's hard-earned find of "a quail egg or two" along the riverbank as a young child, eggs

that "would gleam from the mud / like gigantic pearls."

Song began the writing life as a young student in the middle-class suburbs of Honolulu and continued at the University of Hawaii at Manoa, where she was mentored by poet John Unterecker. She finished her undergraduate studies at Wellesley College in 1977 and went on to earn an M.F.A. in creative writing in 1981 from Boston University. In 1987 she and her husband, Douglas Davenport, moved back to Honolulu, where they and their three children now live. Her second volume, *Frameless Windows, Squares of Light,* was published in 1988, and her most recent volume, *School Figures,* appeared in 1994. Besides winning the prestigious Yale Younger Poets Award, Song has also won the Shelley Memorial Award and, in 1994, the Hawaii Award for Literature.

In recent years, Song has taught creative writing for the Poets in the Schools program in Hawaii and at several universities. Since the publication of *School Figures,* Song has been concentrating on her own writing, supported in part by an NEA Poetry Fellowship, and has a manuscript for another volume of poetry forthcoming. She is a member of Bamboo Ridge, a group of Hawaiian poets and fiction writers. In 1991, the Bamboo Ridge Press published *Sister Stew,* an anthology edited by Song and Juliet Kono featuring the fiction and poetry of contemporary Hawaiian women.

## Poem Text

### 1

In China,
even the peasants
named their first daughters
Jade—
the stone that in the far fields          5
could moisten the dry season,
could make men move mountains
for the healing green of the inner hills
glistening like slices of winter melon.

And the daughters were grateful:          10
They never left home.
To move freely was a luxury
stolen from them at birth.
Instead, they gathered patience,
learning to walk in shoes          15
the size of teacups,
without breaking—
the arc of their movements
as dormant as the rooted willow,
as redundant as the farmyard hens.          20

But they traveled far
in surviving,
learning to stretch the family rice,
to quiet the demons,
the noisy stomachs.                                              25

## 2

There is a sister
across the ocean,
who relinquished her name,
diluting jade green
with the blue of the Pacific.                                    30
Rising with a tide of locusts,
she swarmed with others
to inundate another shore.
In America,
There are many roads                                             35
and women can stride along with men.

But in another wilderness,
the possibilities,
the loneliness,
can strangulate like jungle vines,                               40
The meager provisions and sentiments
of once belonging—
fermented roots, Mah-Jong tiles and firecrackers—
    set but
a flimsy household
in a forest of nightless cities.                                 45
A giant snake rattles above,
spewing black clouds into your kitchen.
Dough-faced landlords
slip in and out of your keyholes,
making claims you don't understand,                              50
tapping into your communication systems
of laundry lines and restaurant chains.

You find you need China:
your one fragile identification,
a jade link                                                      55
handcuffed to your wrist.
You remember your mother
who walked for centuries,
footless—
and like her,                                                    60
you have left no footprints,
but only because
there is an ocean in between,
the unremitting space of your rebellion.

## Poem Summary

### Lines 1-4:

In the first lines of part one, the speaker of the poem takes the reader immediately to the homeland of Song's maternal grandmother and introduces a Chinese naming custom that will be reflected and refracted throughout the poem. First daughters throughout China, "even the peasants," are often named "Jade," a precious stone recog-

nized not only for its beauty but for its magical healing powers.

### Lines 5-9:

Here the speaker describes the powers of jade, using rural, natural, and agricultural images that will be contrasted in part two with menacing images of urban life. The jade stones and, by association, the young women so named are believed to bring life and healing to their homeland. Song's skillful use of color imagery can be seen here in the juxtaposition of the luminous green jade with the daughter-blessed, greening landscape of China, those "inner hills / glistening like slices of winter melon." Song's musical repetition of sounds and words in the lines "could moisten the dry season / could make men move mountains" also implies a kind of pastoral grace and power in the lives of these daughters. The image of "far fields" where the stones work their magic suggests not only the vast stretches of farmland in the China of Song's ancestry, but also begins the poem's melancholy play upon traveling "far," whether at home or abroad. It is a theme established in earlier poems in *Picture Bride*—in images of long walks, long bus rides, journeys into the forests of lilikoi vines, and journeys across the ocean.

### Lines 10-20:

The speaker next tells us "the daughters were grateful," ostensibly to have such a beautiful name and to occupy such an important place in the family. Consequentially, "they never left home." But there are other reasons for their stasis that cast an ironic light on such gratitude. Subtly but suddenly, the reader discovers in the next lines that the freedom to leave home was "stolen" from the beginning. The harsh reality Song introduces in these lines is the centuries-old custom of foot binding.

From the end of the T'ang dynasty in the eleventh century A.D. until as recently as the 1920s, Chinese women, initially of the upper class, were required to begin binding their feet around five years of age in order to make them tiny and "feminine." Using three tightly wound yards of cloth, the binding procedure distorted the natural flexion and shape of the foot by forcibly bending the toes under the metatarsal area of the foot—sometimes even breaking the bones—and tightly drawing the entire upper foot toward the heel, leaving the big toe free to serve as the delicate point of the "lotus petal." The binding thus created a foot that would fit in a three-inch shoe the shape of a half moon or a flower petal. A woman's bound feet were called

## Media Adaptations

- An audio recording of a reading by Cathy Song at the Honolulu Academy of Art was made on April 2, 1983.

- *The Best of Bamboo Ridge* (audio recordings), Vols. 1 and 2, include Song reading several of her own poems.

- Poetry in Motion, a project designed to bring poetry into the daily life of the American public, has featured "Lost Sister" on posters installed in buses and subways in New York, Atlanta, Dallas, Los Angeles, and Washington, D.C.

her "golden lotuses," a euphemism for a crippling custom that effectively rendered all but the poorest laboring classes of Chinese women "footless" and immobile for centuries. As the poem says, these women had to learn to "travel far" in shoes "the size of teacups, / without breaking—." With this image, Song deftly renders a portrait of women forced to be quite delicate physically, but strong emotionally. They must be "rooted" like the willow tree, itself a symbol of both sadness (the weeping willow, which is native to China) and of inexhaustible life.

### Lines 21-25:

Hobbled in body, Chinese women faced another sort of journey: "surviving." The demons one might meet on the road, according to many Chinese folk tales, are met instead under these daughters' own roofs, incarnated as "the noisy stomachs" of hungry children, husbands, and in-laws. This startling new meaning for "travel" provides a pivot point in the poem. Against it, the "freedom" in part two will emerge with ambiguity.

### Lines 26-30:

Cathy Song's affinity for color and painting shapes this introduction to the "rebellious" daughter: jade's pure green is "diluted" by Pacific blue. This daughter left home, crossed the ocean for a

different life, and thereby "relinquished her name." Names are not bestowed lightly in Chinese culture; they hold sacred meanings and power. But instead of saying so outright, the speaker uses an image of color blending to keep alive in the poem the strength of jade as a symbol for Chinese beauty and loyalty and the blue of the Pacific as the vast threat to that cultural and familial purity.

### Lines 31-36:

The poem compares this daughter to the locust, an insect associated with plague, famine, and destruction. In so doing, it makes important metaphorical links that reach both back into part one, and further into part two. The locust image is a sharp contrast to the submissive daughter who nourishes her family in part one. As an image of famine and anonymity, this swarming "tide of locusts" reaches forward into the poem toward the disillusioning portrait of the United States as a place that starves both body and soul. With a line to itself, "In America" parallels the poem's opening lines, "In China," and prepares the reader for more deep contrasts. Rumor has it that across the ocean, women, footloose and free, "can stride along with men" on America's "many roads." Those tightly wrapped sisters who remain behind can only wear a "redundant" path between stove and farmyard with their tiny feet.

### Lines 37-52:

This stanza exposes the harsh reality behind the rumor. For the immigrant, the possibilities strangle rather than nourish. The poem lists artifacts of "once belonging," which are unmistakably Chinese in order to sharpen the tone of loneliness in the strange land. The Chinese use fermented roots of turnips, carrots, and other vegetables in soup and broth. Mah-Jong tiles are the pictorial pieces of a popular game usually played among four people, and often associated, like poker, with gambling. And firecrackers are a staple in Chinese celebrations, used for welcoming guests, chasing away evil, and attracting the gods' attention at festivals and holidays.

Yet, these things cannot really re-create home in an alien, urban landscape, devoid as it is not only of "jade" in its many meanings, but of all color except dismal shades of black and white. How could any sister be but "lost" in this nightmarish jungle of a place, an atmosphere the poem establishes by comparing landlords to pasty ghosts who "slip in and out of keyholes" and city subways to Jumanji-sized snakes. The inhospitable Americans in this portrait use language as a weapon against the immigrant—to confuse, cheat, and spy. Until now, the speaker has described and reported in the third person, but it is important to note that in this stanza, the address to this sister is in the second person, "you" and "your," and the poem thereby acquires a more intimate and urgent voice.

### Lines 53-64:

With complete candor, the speaker describes the lesson this sister presumably has learned, or at least needs to have articulated. "You find you need China," it declares, and that means recognizing the ways in which she is bound to the homeland. Here, jade returns, now "handcuffed to your wrist," an image of binding that makes the reader recall the constrictive shoes in part one. Whether a woman stays or goes, the poem seems to be saying, true freedom is won neither through submission nor rebellion. The poem offers no alternative explicitly, but hints at its possibility: "you have left no footprints," the speaker tells the lost sister, but "only because" of the rebellious path she has taken. There need not be this "unremitting space," the language implies. Behind "only because" lies another path, the possibility the poem holds out for a way of life in which a Chinese woman may be named Jade and also leave footprints.

## Themes

### Limitations and Opportunities

Together, the two parts of "Lost Sister" challenge conventional definitions of "limitation" and "opportunity." Which daughter is the limited one? Which one has opportunities? The second stanza casts doubt on the name "Jade," with all of its associations of power and healing influence that in most circumstances would create a better, more prosperous life. Yes, this precious green stone *could* do its work in "the far fields," but the fact is, this Jade-daughter cannot even leave her own house, bound as she is by both body and custom. The poem says she "traveled far" in a different way, however, in "learning to stretch the family rice." In casting survival as a kind of journey, the poem asks us to consider "opportunity" in ways quite foreign to the American dream, where mobility, acquisition, and advancement are taken for granted.

In contrast, the daughter in part two who travels far for the opportunities rumored as America's "many roads," finds herself instead lost in some "nightless" city, bound and hobbled by language, economics, and hostility. The fantasy of a life free from limiting roles and traditions becomes instead a "wilderness" of possibilities that strangle rather than liberate. While this woman does not suffer the limitations and pain of bound feet, she has not found the opportunity to "stride along with men," either. Metaphors of vines and handcuffs carry the image of binding from part one of "Lost Sister" to part two, defining freedom and its limits through figurative language. Both submission and rebellion create their own sets of limitations and opportunities, and the poem is unwilling, ultimately, to privilege one way of being over the other.

### Identity and Sex Roles

In a country in which infant girls are known to have been quietly smothered at birth, where older girls have been sold by their own families into slavery, or where "bad" daughters-in-law have reportedly been tortured, it is no wonder that Song can barely veil the bitter irony of naming first daughters after a precious stone. The value of jade, and the importance Song grants to the word "could," through its repetition and placement in lines 6 and 7—"could moisten the dry season, / could make men move mountains"—speaks volumes about the potential power of women to heal and transform. But the power is laid waste. The China portrayed in this poem considers mobility for women a "luxury" society cannot afford and thus steals such freedom from them "at birth." Yet, the same China that hobbles the feet of its women also, paradoxically, tells them tales of "the woman warrior," a phenomenon Maxine Hong Kingston explored in her 1976 novel by that name. Weapon in hand, feet shod for running, this "warrior woman" spirit anticipates striding alongside men on another shore in part two of "Lost Sister."

This poem makes it impossible to consider a Chinese woman's identity apart from her traditional sex role and its inherent set of paradoxes. In China, she is both victim and survivor of the culture that binds her feet and circumscribes her movement, not only physically, but morally and intellectually. In America, she is strong enough to have crossed the blue threshold to the West, only to find herself stereotyped as quiet, cute, and delicate. Song weights the acts of naming and binding with this heavy dilemma of identity, culminating in the last stanza: "your one fragile identification, / a jade link / handcuffed to your wrist." Jade, symbol of her identity as a Chinese woman, is at once essential and limiting—a blessing and a curse.

## Topics for Further Study

- Trace the rise and fall of a modern fashion that has been harmful to the body, male or female. What sorts of cultural forces brought the trend into being? Kept it there? What was responsible for its demise?

- Write an imaginary series of letters between the "jade" daughter who stays in China and the sister who leaves. Include not only the characters' thoughts and feelings about their respective situations, but also the social, political, and economic realities of their time and place.

- Write a poem about your own footprints. Where do you leave them? What is their shape? Who finds them? Where are they going?

- Investigate the lives of two or three Americans of Asian descent who have made notable contributions to science, law, education, business, or the arts.

### Wilderness

When most people think of wilderness, they think of those vast stretches of natural space that resist human habitation. Deserts, dense forests, glaciers, oceans—the perils and wastes of these spaces challenge human survival. T. S. Eliot's landmark 1922 poem "The Wasteland" helps define another sort of wilderness, one that has all the trappings of civilization, but which is inhospitable to the human soul. In Eliot's urban wilderness, that "Unreal City, / Under the brown fog of a winter dawn," the arc of vision is short, and breathing shallow: "Sighs, short and infrequent, were exhaled, / And each man fixed his eyes before his feet." The external landscape mirrors the human inner landscape in Eliot's modernist imagination, a phenomenon he called "objective correlative." With the twentieth century, therefore, came the possibility of defining wilderness as any space or state of being characterized by loneliness and threatened survival, menaced by the chaos of too much, or the barrenness of too little. In other words, any place or state of mind can be a wilderness.

There are two kinds of wildernesses in "Lost Sister." The obvious one, in part two, is an urban wilderness, portrayed as a jungle with its strangling vines, giant snakes, and ceaseless, predatorial night life. The immigrant is suffocated by loneliness in this place, despite the artifacts of "once belonging" which do little to assuage her displacement and disillusion, her dis-ease of not belonging. Nor are America's many Chinatowns places in which the immigrant can truly be at home, which suggests another poem in *Picture Bride*. They are look-alike wildernesses of "sleazy movie houses / & oily joints," where "Grandmother is gambling" with Mah-Jong tiles and "bamboo chopstick tenements / pile up like noodles."

Notice that Song calls the American scene "*another* wilderness" in part two, thus asking the reader to look back in part one at the China endured by the foot-bound daughter as "wilderness," also. This other wilderness in the poem is primarily an inner one. Despite the familiar clucking of farmyard hens, the poem implies that this woman is trapped in a landscape barren of choice and crippling in its expectations and assumptions. She is therefore alienated from herself and lost to a way of being that moving freely might reveal and nourish. On the other hand, the wilderness can also be a place of testing and transformation. Stripped of comfort—physical, psychological, or otherwise—the wilderness survivor must bring all his or her resources and strengths to bear. Both sisters have the opportunity to prove their inner strength against their particular wastelands and resident demons.

### Style

"Lost Sister" is a two-part poem of five stanzas. The two stanzas of part one describe the "jade" daughters of China who stayed home. Part two tells of the sister, presumably the "lost" one, who leaves for America. The final stanza judges them both to be "footless." "Lost Sister" is written in free verse, a poetic form that may appear to be without form, especially when compared to the metrical, rhymed patterns of formal verse patterns such as the sonnet. Instead of meter, free verse relies on the rhythms of word-sound combinations in ordinary speech. Instead of end-rhyme, it relies on patterns of images and metaphors throughout the poem as well as upon varieties of "internal" rhyme, within and among words in the line. You can find the internal rhyme devices of alliteration and assonance, for example, in the first stanza. Alliteration is the repetition of beginning consonants and can be heard in the repeated "m" sounds in line 7: "could make men move mountains." Assonance, or the repetition of vowel sounds, occurs in the short and long "i" sounds in "glistening like slices of winter melon." One can almost see and feel the image by listening to the sounds.

Line-length is variable, not prescribed, in free verse; therefore, the poet can break a line according to the sound and emphasis needed. This poem gives great importance, for example, to "Jade" by placing it on a line by itself in the first stanza of the poem; likewise, "footless" in the last stanza. The carefully constructed line breaks in "Lost Sister" frequently lead to a surprising reversal or expansion of meaning from one line to the next. For example, one might expect "But they traveled far" (line 21) to be followed by a distant place. But "In surviving" is no place at all, at least not externally. In giving this line the same grammatical form as other similar lines—"In China," "In America"—the reader is asked to think of "surviving" as a psychological space where one might carry on another sort of journey. Through this attention to the line, the poem challenges traditional meanings and ordinary expectations. The repetition of parallel phrases such as "In China," "In America," and then "in another wilderness" also helps unify the different parts of the poem and establishes the comparisons and contrasts essential to its themes.

## Historical Context

According to Howard Levy in his *Chinese Foot-binding,* the custom lamented in "Lost Sister" probably began with palace dancers in the late-tenth century, during the waning years of the T'ang dynasty. The ruler Li Yu is said to have constructed a six-foot-high lotus out of gold and ordered his favorite concubines to bind their feet into the shape of a "moon sickle" and dance upon its petals. Obviously, the bindings were not severe enough at first to hamper dancing. The tiny, graceful feet of the dancers pleased the men and were admired by the women. The practice caught on, and more and more upper-class women were required to bind their feet, not necessarily for dancing, but as a criterion of beauty and symbol of their class status.

The morally repressive Sung dynasty enthusiastically took foot binding another step further in the eleventh century. According to Levy, a proverb of the time best expresses it: "Why must the foot be bound? To prevent barbarous running around!" The more liberal marriage laws and sexual mores of the T'ang dynasty had yielded to the Sung's stringent moral codes for women, as well as a serious curbing of their intellectual freedom, viewing the education of women as a "disadvantage." This government took the "a woman's place is in the home" philosophy to a painful extreme, requiring that women bind their feet so excessively that every step required the support of a cane or another person. Thus, not only were women conveniently rendered incapable of infidelity, but also of hard work. Foot binding in its earliest centuries of practice remained associated with the aristocracy. Those with "golden lotus" feet could literally do nothing but lead a life of leisure and the sedentary arts. To use Song's words in a different context, the pleasures of physical labor were "stolen from them at birth."

The practice of foot binding spread during the Mongol rule of the twelfth century as well as in Yuan and Ming dynasties through the sixteenth century. Society considered women with unbound feet ugly and unfit for marriage. By this time, not only the aesthetic but the erotic merits of the custom were firmly established. Poetry and songs of those centuries glorified the tiny foot as a sexual object par excellence, despite its historical associations with moral repression. Chinese men reported that women swayed with an alluring gait on their "golden lotuses," and Chinese prostitutes attracted their customers with that "mincing step" that is now a cliche for promiscuous body language. The shoe itself was considered a work of art, and lovers devised erotic rituals of drinking from the shoe, and caressing and bathing the tiny foot.

Over the centuries, foot binding spread beyond the gentility and was adopted throughout China by women in most provinces and classes. Only the poorest laboring women remained "duck-footed." After conquering China in the seventeenth century, the Manchus attempted to abolish the practice by official decree and carried out serious punishments for disobedience. But foot binding cannot be considered distinct from the broader social patterns and ideologies that repress women to this degree. Levy suggests that the Manchus failed to eradicate the custom because they failed to liberate women more comprehensively.

The nearly thousand-year-old practice of foot binding continued into the earliest parts of the twentieth century, when it was abolished, slowly and erratically, by a combination of political and

# *Compare*
# *&*
# *Contrast*

- **1850:** The first national women's rights convention, in Worcester, Massachusetts, was attended by delegates from nine states.

  **1874:** The following was printed in a San Francisco real estate circular: "All comparisons between Irish and German immigration and that of the Chinese are unjust. The former make their homes here, buy farms and homesteads, are of the same general race, are buried here after death, and take an interest and aid in all things pertaining to the best interest of the country. The Chinese come for a season only; and, while they give their labor, they do not expend the proceeds of such labor in the country. They do not come to settle or make homes, and *not one in fifty of them is married.* Their women are all suffering slaves and prostitutes, for which possession, murderous feuds and high-handed cruelty are constantly occurring. To compare the Chinese with even the lowest white laborers is, therefore, absurd."

  **1875:** The Page Law was passed to prohibit the entry of Chinese prostitutes into the United States, but was enforced so broadly that it also excluded Chinese wives.

  **1908:** Through the "Gentleman's Agreement" with Japan, 60,000 women immigrated to the United States as "picture brides."

  **1920:** Women's suffrage is ratified in the United States via the 19th amendment. Women represent 46 percent of the Japanese population in Hawaii and 35 percent in California.

  **1966:** The National Organization for Women (NOW) is founded in the United States on behalf of the movement to gain equal social, political, and economic rights for women.

  **1997:** Thirty-six hundred children from China were adopted by families in the United States Ninety-five percent of them were girls.

  **Today:** Of China's 320 million families (1.2 billion population), only twenty percent have one child, despite the Beijing's official one-child-per-family planning policy instituted in the late 1970s. Western human rights groups say that the one-child policy has led to forced abortions and killings of baby girls by parents hoping for a son to carry the family line.

  **Today:** Amnesty International reports that the Chinese government "executed at least ten people in Beijing in its continuing crackdown to ensure 'public order' during the 4th United Nations Conference on Women."

---

social pressures both internal and external to China. Women in the large cities of Shanghai and Peking "let their feet out" long before those in rural villages who, well into the 1930s, resisted the "natural foot movement" in all its aesthetic, social, and political implications.

Meanwhile, nearly a century before foot binding began to wane, Chinese men were migrating to the West as laborers in the newly settled United States. They were virtually a "colony of bachelors," as Ronald Takaki puts it in *A Different Mirror: A History of Multicultural America.* Of the 12,000 Chinese in California in 1852, only seven were women, and that number grew to only five percent of the nearly 90,000 Chinese on the United States' mainland by 1900. In light of the gender roles in China, unchanged for hundreds of years, it is not hard to understand these statistics. Bound feet rendered the women of upper ranks incapable of making any physically demanding journey, and unbound peasant women were needed at home to perform work required by an agricultural economy. More than half of the Chinese women living in the United States in late 1860s were prostitutes, many of them having been sold as young girls by their fathers.

From the time they arrived on United States soil, the Chinese suffered virulent racial prejudice. Takaki points out that although the Chinese population in the United States "constituted a mere .002 percent," in 1880, President Rutherford Hayes resisted the "pernicious invasion" of yet another "weaker race," and grouped them along with "Negroes and Indians" as a national problem. Song's poem reflects this sense of invasion, albeit from another point of view, in the image of the Chinese as swarming locusts that "inundate another shore." The Chinese Exclusion Act, passed by Congress in 1882, closed all doors to Chinese immigration for the next twenty years and denied citizenship to those already living in the United States. Any "foreign" presence during those years was felt as a threat to a country suffering its first serious crises of unemployment, class conflicts, strikes, and riots. Prejudice dies hard, and even though part two of the poem likely "takes place" after the Exclusion Act was repealed, this Chinese daughter still experiences America as inhospitable and even threatening.

For a young woman to break out of her narrowly circumscribed roles and leave China would indeed be an act of great "rebellion" during the years in which foot binding was still a powerful cultural force and symbol. Thus, we can better understand the judgment in the last line of "Lost Sister" if we understand that the poem's speaker is probably a member of Song's maternal generation who see "rebellion" where Song's own contemporary sisters might see "liberation."

## Critical Overview

In his preface to *The Open Boat, Poems from Asian America,* editor Garrett Hongo cites the Yale Younger Poet's awarded to *Picture Bride* as good evidence that "there has been empowerment and a demonstrable rise in the recognition of works by Asian American poets," in part because of "the American voice that is great within us." Richard Hugo praised Song's ability to both express and transcend the specifics of her Asian-American background, a virtue that likely granted her inclusion in the popular Norton and Heath anthologies of American literature. Hugo called "Lost Sister," in particular, a tribute to one who paid an enormous "psychic price" for her independence, even though "the rebellion failed." Hugo's reading implies that such a tribute could be paid to anyone who, regardless of culture or gender, works to put "an ocean in between" themselves and their cultural traps, thereby creating "'an unremitting space' others can cross or fill."

Despite the early promises of a wider critical appraisal, however, most readings of Song's work seem to be confined to publications of multicultural, or specifically Asian-American interest. In her chapter on Korean-American literature in King-Kok Cheung's *An Interethnic Companion to Asian American Literature,* Elaine Kim noted Song's desire to be seen as foremost a poet "who happens to be Asian American" and recalled an interview in which Song said she doesn't want to be perceived as "leaning too heavily on the Asian-American theme," because "I write about other things, too." Those "other things"—childhood, motherhood, suburban life—emerge in her later volumes, where the ordinary details of contemporary life in Hawaii find a lyrical voice.

Kim herself leaned heavily on the images of "almost suffocating restriction" in *Picture Bride* in evaluating Cathy Song's place as an artist in America. The foot-binding image in "Lost Sister" is one of those powerful indications, in Kim's mind, that Song's Asian-American ancestry is central to her poetry, but that "she seems to feel restricted by them as an artist." Kim suggested that "to become an artist," Song, like the lost sister, "must leave home." Other critics perceive that Song has "left home" in important ways. Stephen Sumida noted that where other contemporary poets from Hawaii have used a local pidgin language for the voice in dramatic monologue, "Cathy Song ... writing in so-called standard English, may be said to demonstrate that poetic traditions of Hawai'i are by no means confined to Hawai'i Creole."

## Criticism

### Sean Robisch

*Sean Robisch teaches composition and literature at Purdue University and holds a Ph.D. in American literature. In the following essay, Robisch explores the influence of place, or physical environment, in "Lost Sister."*

The poet, maybe more so than any other kind of writer, must struggle with how to approach an image, receive it, and employ it with neither too much sentimentality nor too much bitterness. This is one of the things that makes good poetry diffi-

## What Do I Read Next?

- Maxine Hong Kingston's acclaimed 1976 novel, *The Woman Warrior, Memoirs of a Girlhood Among Ghosts,* has introduced an entire generation to the struggles of Chinese-American women to adapt to a culture of "ghosts," the term for anyone not Chinese. Through her Chinese mother's "talk-stories" and her own experience, a young girl growing up in California must sort through the conflicting expectations and perceptions of Asian women.

- Two volumes of poetry by Cathy Song have followed *Picture Bride.* While neither *Frameless Windows, Squares of Light* (1988), nor *School Figures* (1994) has received the same critical acclaim as her first book, they have helped establish Song as an artist capable of much more, says reviewer Pat Monaghan, than "second-person recitations of family history." These poems are concerned with the inner life of the poet and her family, Monaghan notes, a "complex terrain" Song explores "with delicate exactitude."

- In 1991, along with Juliet S. Kono, Cathy Song edited *Sister Stew,* Bamboo Ridge Press's anthology of fiction and poetry by Hawaiian women, including Morgan Blair (Fay Kicknosway), Marie Hara, and Lois-Ann Yamanaka. Bamboo Ridge, with whom Song has close association, continues to nurture and publish the work of Hawaiian writers. New titles such as *Growing Up Local* and a calendar of events sponsored by the Press can be found on the World Wide Web at www.bambooridge.com.

- Dorothy Blair Shimer has made a valuable contribution to our understanding of women from China and Japan with her collection of stories and memoirs that span a thousand years, from the T'ang dynasty in China and the Heian period in Japan to the present. *Rice Bowl Women,* a 1982 anthology of writings by and about Chinese and Japanese women, reflects "the changing status and ongoing struggle" of the Asian women to whom Song gives voice in her poems.

- Tayo, the main character of Leslie Marmon Silko's *Ceremony,* is a kind of "lost brother" at the beginning of Silko's novel, first published in 1977. The young Laguna Indian has returned from his nightmarish service in World War II alienated from himself and his tribal heritage. Like "Lost Sister," this is a story in part about the profound struggles both to make peace with tradition and bring it creatively into a new time and place.

- Judy Yung uses the foot-binding theme to explore the changing status of Chinese women in San Francisco, the nexus of Chinese immigration, from the years of the Exclusion Act, which started in 1882, through World War II. In addition to factual information, *Unbound Feet: A Social History of Chinese Women in San Francisco* (1995) traces the history of these women through case studies and oral histories. A valuable supplement to this reading would be Yung's 1986 *Chinese Women of America: A Pictorial History.*

- Those intrigued by medieval court life in the Far East will want to look at *The Tale of Genji,* the classic Japanese "novel" by Lady Murasaki Shikibu. This long romance, completed in the 1020s, weaves the textures of Heian court life into stories of the adventures and loves of the idealized nobleman "Genji." It was during this same period of time that the practice of foot binding began among the aristocracy in China.

---

cult to write. The poet also must balance experiences of the real and tangible world with that of imagination. Therefore, where the image resides, its place and the place where the poet lives and works, will inevitably influence her perception of it. If a poet lives in the mountains, the mountains will rise up in the work; if she lives in a forest, chances are that there will be some arboreal presence, even if it isn't always the direct mention of trees, in a book of her poems. The poet's residence is also the residence of the images she experiences and uses in her language. Finally, perhaps ultimately, the issue of the poet's ethnicity—that matter we often too easily think of in terms of skin color, language, or culture—will be settled to some degree by the way she collects the images of her place.

Cathy Song is a resident of Hawaii. She grew up there, learning the stories of her Korean grandparents and of the Chinese members of her family. These stories were set as much in Hawaii as in Korea. She drew upon many of these tales in her first collection of poetry, *Picture Bride,* which won the Yale Younger Poets prize in 1983. Many second- and third-generation artists have been faced with recognition as multiracial, or multi-ethnic, while living all of their lives in the United States. This presents those writers with the problems of establishing their own identities and deciding to what degree they wish to accept their ethnic backgrounds as important to their work as artists. Cathy Song has faced these problems both in her writing and in her public discussions.

Another poet from Hawaii, Garrett Hongo, has described a kind of separation between those who favor the personal experience within the American venue and those who favor writing the more polemical (that is, the more confrontational and often political), piece. Cathy Song sees herself as landing firmly in the first camp. In interviews, she has stated that she would rather be thought of as a poet who "happens to be Asian-American" than as an Asian-American or Hawaiian poet. This echoes the struggle of many other writers— Kim Ronyoung, Peter Hyun, and Margaret Pai, among others—to balance writing the biographies of their elders with the establishment of their own voices and between the vivid descriptions of their places and the drive to have their work accepted beyond the borders of those places.

Song's resistance to being labelled is understandable. Still, it is difficult to deny the obvious uses of names as well as the references jade and Mah-Jong, certain foods, the history of the Hawaiian cane plantations, picture brides, and immigration. Perhaps, in order to honor both Song's (and many other multiethnic poets') desire to be acknowledged as a poet, even while we recognize the importance of the Korean, Chinese, and Hawaiian influences on her work, we might consider her poems in terms of how their specifically regional

concerns actually contain more general truths that are applicable to those of us who are not from Hawaii or Korea. That way, the poem is given credit for all the things it does with the images that the poet has chosen and gathered, like shells on a beach or stones from a river. The poet may then be simultaneously a practitioner of the word and a subject of the stuff that determines her ethnicity. In other words, the role of poet and the role of ethnic, cultural, and political being do not have to be treated separately. This is a sound platform from which to read the work of Cathy Song.

"Lost Sister" gives us a great opportunity to apply the idea that a poet's place is vital to her role as poet. *Picture Bride* is divided into five sections, with each named for a flower. Its structure is inspired by the work of Georgia O'Keefe and the names of her paintings. The original title of the book was to be "From the White Place," a reference to a location in New Mexico, near Ghost Ranch, where O'Keefe lived and worked for many years. Song visited this place and was inspired both by what O'Keefe had done with it and by the land itself. In many ways it is a strict contrast to Hawaii—dry and carved with mesas and canyons, as opposed to water-locked and verdant—and it must have been inspiring to Song. But the title of her book was changed to emphasize the subject matter most pervasive in the collection, particularly her grandmother's immigration to the United States during the picture-bride era, when hundreds of Asian women were "sent for" by men working in America who had only seen them in photographs. Whether or not this was to "capitalize" on Song's ethnicity as a way of selling the book, as some have posited, it is the more appropriate title. "From the White Place" is not nearly as strong of a poem as "Lost Sister" or other poems that demonstrate how much more familiar Song is with the material of Hawaii and the material of her grandparents' stories than with the New Mexican desert.

*Picture Bride* is packed with blue images. John Unterecker, one of Song's mentors while she was a young poet, commented that hers were among the "bluest" poems he had read. Added to the many other images of Hawaii, this blueness appears as an obvious, and valuable, characteristic of island poetry—of the sensibilities and images that come from the poet being closely surrounded at all times by the ocean.

Other themes pervade the book, the stronger ones all appearing in "Lost Sister." Richard Hugo, who selected the book for the Yale Younger Poets

> *[Song's] choices of language are often quiet and tightly focused, like fine beams of light on single images."*

award, recognized "leaving and escaping" as common themes in the poems, and in "Lost Sister" we have a poem of the daughter/sister who leaves her family, crosses the ocean, and finds that her escape has not even left any footprints. Several critics have remarked on the "quietude" of the poetry, what Lorrie Goldensohn called "that exquisite, clarifying precision we recognize as Asian in feeling." That last comment might give the most weight to Song's argument against being labelled for her ethnicity before her poetry, because Goldensohn risks stereotyping "Asian" work. However, Song's poems, "Lost Sister" perhaps most obviously among them, do focus intensely on the experience of someone Asian—in this case Chinese—experiencing a change in culture. Her choices of language are often quiet and tightly focused, like fine beams of light on single images. This need not be particularly Asian; it is simply a trait of Song's work, that, as she might say, "happens to" focus on Asian-American experience.

This brings us back to the important influence of place on "Lost Sister" as a way of reading it to include the matters of ethnicity, poetic sensibility, the collection and use of image, and narrative without labelling the poem too narrowly as only regional. Hugo's use of the word "escape" might be changed to "mobility," a word several critics have used to talk about "Lost Sister." In the poem, China is cast as a place where "the daughters never left home" and where their freedom of movement was "stolen from them at birth." The metaphor of "shoes the size of teacups" and later of the mother as "footless" both invoke the ancient practice of foot binding, through which a woman's feet were kept small by tightly wrapping them for several years, beginning in infancy. The metaphor is beautifully wrought in Song's poem, as the small, quiet image is also a powerfully oppressive one. The limited mobility of the Chinese mother is contrasted with the daughter's freedom when she reaches America, where "There are many roads / and women can stride along with men." The word "stride," as well as the image to which it is attached, implies a liberty of movement. But just as the contrast looks simple and the United States seems to be held above China by the young "sister," a long stanza follows that complicates the poem. It is earlier foreshadowed by the sister's relinquishment of her name, and it acts as a kind of rebuke.

Many of us have heard the adages, "the grass is always greener on the other side of the fence" and "be careful what you wish for, for you may surely get it." The sister, now in "another wilderness," clings to her few provisions that remind her of home and realizes that American liberty does not keep her from being lonely or oppressed. The landlords where she lives let themselves into her life, metaphorically and literally. The cities are "nightless," and the urbanity is threatening, as found in the image of a defective pipe in the kitchen as a snake. The images of footprint and ocean come together at the end of the poem to remind the young, immigrant sister that one cannot leave footprints on water and that the ocean, which diluted her "jade green," separates her from a place she now needs to maintain her identity. She may now only imagine China.

The poem's title is interesting in that the sister is not given sisterhood to anyone in particular. The first stanza implies that she is a peasant, possibly a first daughter named Jade (who changes her name when she comes to America), and has other sisters she has left behind. But this is all implication, however strong. One critic has speculated that the sister of the poem is herself a picture bride, but there is no evidence in the poem to support this conclusion. Sisterhood may be a powerful metaphoric device, as it is used for nuns, female members of organizations, and women of the same race. "There is a sister" the poet writes in section two, but there is no other sister or brother mentioned. The Lost Sister may be as much as sibling of her place as sister to the family that disappears by the beginning of the second stanza in section one. She is caught between allegiance to them and allegiance to her independence. She seeks out sisterhood, now that she has, paradoxically, both lost her name and come into her own. Maybe this is sisterhood to China, maybe to her own mother, but in any case it is a lost sisterhood. So the title of the poem implies more than one layer of meaning, as titles of poems often do.

In some ways, Song addresses her own resistance to being strictly an Asian-American poet in "Lost Sister." Although we cannot reduce the work of an artist to mere biography, the issue of identity and its roots in place and ethnicity is at hand throughout the poem and the book in which it appears: the blue, the jade, the Mah-Jong tiles, and the fireworks. These may be a "jade link handcuffed to her wrist," but Cathy Song needs them. They supply those who are not Asian-American, Hawaiian, or female with information about those experiences and about the experiences (even the fictitious ones of a character in a poem) that will teach us to value what we learn from our own freedoms and rebellions and from the consequences of both.

**Source:** Sean Robisch, in an essay for *Poetry for Students,* Gale, 1999.

## Chris Semansky

*Chris Semansky teaches writing and literature at Portland Community College in Portland, Oregon, and is a frequent contributor of poems and essays to literary journals. In the following essay, Semansky focuses on the speaker of "Lost Sister" and her existence between two cultures.*

In cultural studies, the phenomenon where cultures with asymmetrical power relations meet and clash is called the "contact zone." In such spaces—which can be conceptual as well as physical—people's very sense of self-identity is altered, sometimes to such an extent that an individual caught between these cultures is emotionally and psychologically lost to herself. In her poem "Lost Sister," Cathy Song, the American-born daughter of a Korean father and a Chinese mother, examines the psychological space of the contact zone to examine her dilemma of being lost between two different cultures.

In the first half of the two-part poem, the speaker imagines the historical circumstances of first daughters in rural China. Song's comparison of first daughters to jade is significant once we understand its importance to Chinese culture, where the stone symbolizes nobility, perfection, constancy, and immortality. For millennia, jade has been an intimate part of the lives of Chinese of all ranks and classes, and it is viewed as the most valuable of all precious stones. The speaker underscores the stone's significance to an agricultural community and its reputation as an object that protects people from misfortune and brings good luck when she

says that it could "moisten the dry season" and "make men move mountains." By implication, the speaker suggests that Chinese daughters too had this power. More likely, and given what else she says about how the daughters were treated, she is being ironic. We should remember, however, that this is the *speaker's* representation of Chinese daughters as she imagines them to have been. The speaker's take on Chinese history has as much to do with her own need to see the past in a particular way as it does with any conventional history of the country.

The Chinese have a saying that goes, "If jade is not properly cut, it cannot be made into a useful utensil." This is also true, the speaker suggests, for Chinese women. Just as shaping or cutting jade is important in producing useful articles, so too is shaping the desires and lives of Chinese daughters important in producing dutiful women. Using the Chinese practice of foot binding as a metaphor for discipline, Song emphasizes the submission that daughters endured:

> They never left home.
> To move freely was a luxury
> stolen from them at birth.
> Instead, they gathered patience,
> learning to walk in shoes
> the size of teacups,
> without breaking—

"Shoes the size of teacups" refers to the tiny shoes many Chinese women wore a thousand years ago, when the curious custom of breaking and binding the feet into the shape of a pointed lotus bud began. Until the early twentieth century when foot binding was outlawed, generations of women and girls tottered through life on three-to four-inch "lotus" feet encased in exquisitely embroidered, excruciatingly tiny "lotus" shoes.

In an article about the practice, Marie Vento explains that "In a society with a cult of female chastity, one primary purpose of foot binding was to limit mobility, radically modifying the means by which females were permitted to become a part of the world at large. Painfully and forcibly reducing a little girl's foot at the precise point in her life when she was expected to begin understanding the Confucian discipline of maintaining a 'mindful body' reinforced her acceptance of the practice." This was a discipline the daughters grew up with, then, one which became inseparable from how they came to think of themselves.

Song effectively establishes an image of what her ancestor might have been like in the first section of the poem in order to contrast it with a con-

> *Though aware of the oppressive treatment of women in her country of birth and the lack of freedom and opportunity there, the speaker nonetheless finds that her cultural heritage is one source of emotional stability ...."*

temporary image of herself in the second half of the poem.

There is a sister
across the ocean,
who relinquished her name,
diluting jade green
with the blue of the Pacific.

Opportunities are available in the United States where, the speaker tells us, "there are many roads / and women can stride along with men." But freedom brings with it peril. America holds promise but also uncertainty, and the exotic images used in the second part of the poem underline the fear that this uncertainty begets. Assimilating oneself into a foreign culture "can strangulate like jungle vines." Though the contemporary daughter takes with her markers of her previous life—"fermented roots, Mah-Jong tiles and firecrackers"—they are not enough to fashion a new life in an unfamiliar and frequently hostile environment where "dough-faced landlords / slip in and out of your keyholes." This hostility presents itself most explicitly in the image of the giant snake that "rattles above, / spewing black clouds into your kitchen." This evil snake, in fact, signifies the flip side of the Chinese dragon, which in Chinese culture is the personification of the demiurge, the first cause of the world. In the East the power of the dragon is mysterious and suggests the resolution of opposites. In ritual celebrations the dragon dance enables supplicants to receive heaven's blessing in the form of rain; indeed, the dragon itself engenders both rain and thunder, which are themselves inseparable. Like jade itself, which was diluted in crossing the Pacific, so too has the Dragon been diluted in its crossing. In the West it is merely a "giant snake," suggesting the mythical Judeo-Christian embodiment of evil, appropriately enough. By locating it in the kitchen, where it wreaks havoc, the speaker underlines the diminished nature of the great dragon in the West. The "lost sister," who is neither fully Eastern nor fully Western, can no longer think of the Chinese dragon as the mythic creator of the universe, but instead focuses merely on its demonic associations, attributing her troubles assimilating to a new culture to this force.

The lines detailing the lost sister's uncomprehending position in the West mark the first time that the second person "you" is used in the poem. Poets frequently use the second person to refer to an image of themselves in the poem. In this case, we can infer that Cathy Song has set up an alter ego of herself that her speaker is in dialogue with; it is an alter ego, however, that simultaneously represents all Chinese daughters who have emigrated to the United States.

It is this representative figure that the speaker addresses in the final stanza (or, conversely, it is the alter ego that addresses the speaker). Though aware of the oppressive treatment of women in her country of birth and the lack of freedom and opportunity there, the speaker nonetheless finds that her cultural heritage is one source of emotional stability, "your one fragile identification." Song once again evokes the image of foot binding to suggest the historical cultural invisibility of women ("You remember your mother / who walked for centuries, / footless") that is also her heritage. But unlike her mother, the speaker's own invisibility also stems from her desire to leave her country of birth. The speaker literally leaves no footprints because she has traveled across the Pacific Ocean and figuratively leaves no footprints because of her need to distance herself from the past. This poetic move, to imaginatively reconstruct the lost or erased history of some ancestor in order to reconstruct her own identity, is a typical strategy in Song's poems, according to critic Masami Usui, and is one used by other Asian-American writers as well.

The "Lost Sister" in this poem is the speaker, who is lost between the old world and the new. Regardless of her desire to be free of her past and to forge a new identity she finds that she cannot; China is "a jade link / handcuffed to ... [her] wrist." This image echoes the image of foot binding earlier in the poem and reminds us that our histories act as much to constrain us as any physical device. The "lost sister" leaves no footprints because she has not been able to embrace any single identity. She compares "the unremitting space of ... [her] rebellion" to an ocean, emphasizing not only that she is emotionally and culturally lost but also that she has lost much. As Richard Hugo put it in his foreword to *Picture Bride*, "The psychic price of her rebellion was great."

**Source:** Chris Semansky, in an essay for *Poetry for Students*, Gale, 1999.

## Sources

Goldensohn, Lorrie, "Flights Home," *Poetry,* April 1984, pp. 40-47.

Hongo, Garrett, ed., *The Open Boat: Poems from Asian America,* New York: Anchor Books, Doubleday, 1993.

Kim, Elaine H., "Korean American Literature," in *An Interethnic Companion to Asian American Literature,* edited by King-Kok Cheung, Cambridge: Cambridge University Press, 1997, 172-73.

Lee, Kyhan, "Korean-American Literature: The Next Generation," *Korean Journal,* Spring 1994, pp. 20-35.

Levy, Howard S., *Chinese Footbinding: The History of a Curious Erotic Custom,* New York: Walton Rawls, 1966.

Schultz, Susan M., "Cathy Song," *Dictionary of Literary Biography* Vol. 169, *American Poets since World War II,* 5th series, Gale Research, 1996, pp. 267-74.

Song, Cathy, *Picture Bride,* New Haven: Yale University Press, 1983.

———, *Frameless Windows, Squares of Light,* New York: Norton, 1988.

———, *School Figures,* Pittsburgh: University of Pittsburgh Press, 1994.

Sumida, Stephen, "Asian/Pacific American Literature" in *An Interethnic Companion to Asian-American Literature,* edited by King-Kok Cheung, Cambridge: Cambridge University Press, 1997, 280-81.

Takaki, Ronald, *A Different Mirror: A History of Multicultural America,* Boston: Little, Brown and Company, 1993.

Usui, Masami, "Women Disclosed: Cathy Song's Poetry and Kitagawa Ukiyoe," in *Studies in Culture and the Humanities,* 1995, pp. 1-19.

Vento, Marie, "One Thousand Years of Chinese Footbinding: Its Origins, Popularity and Demise," March 7, 1998, http://academic.brooklyn.cuny.edu/core9/phalsall/vento.html (accessed November 10, 1998).

## For Further Study

Hongo, Garrett, introduction to *The Open Boat: Poems from Asian America,* New York: Anchor Books, Doubleday, 1993, pp. xvii-xlii.

> Besides the fact that Hawaiian-born Hongo has included several of Cathy Song's poems in this important anthology, his introduction vibrantly tells the story of the Asian-American writers' struggling emergence out of the caricatures of "bit players, extras with buck teeth and pigtails" and into a literature of identity. At times, Hongo's writing reads almost like an incantation, even while it chronicles the growing awareness that "slowly, an alternative truth was being made available to us," to writers and artists of Asian descent. Within the discussion, Hongo annotates a number of journals, books, and anthologies that would be invaluable to anyone interested in the evolution of contemporary Asian-American literature.

Kim, Elaine H., *Asian American Literature: An Introduction to the Writings and Their Social Context,* Philadelphia: Temple University Press, 1982.

> Now called a "classic" in its field, this book ambitiously and successfully attempts to survey the Asian-American "experience" as revealed in the writings (in English) of Americans of Asian descent, from the late-nineteenth century to the early 1980s. The book missed by one short year the publication of Cathy Song's first book, and the contribution it would have made to Kim's important survey and discussion.

Lu, Tonglin, ed., *Gender and Sexuality in Twentieth-Century Chinese Literature and Society,* New York: State University of New York Press, 1993.

> These essays, compiled from a symposium on gender and sexuality, provide a broad-ranging conversation on the historical, political, and cultural forces shaping women's lives and voices in China. Among other things, it helps us understand the tensions that give dimension to the portraits of women in "Lost Sister."

# Mending Wall

## Robert Frost

## 1914

First published in Robert Frost's second collection, *North of Boston*, in 1914, "Mending Wall" is a narrative poem that presents an encounter between two neighbors whose property line is marked by a stone fence. Each spring, they cooperate in repairing the damage the winter weather has caused to it. Although the speaker of the poem claims to believe the wall is unnecessary, he is clearly ambivalent about its presence, since he also initiates the repair. His neighbor, on the other hand, strongly asserts his desire to maintain the wall, repeating the line, "Good fences make good neighbors." Throughout the poem, the wall functions as a metaphor, indicating the necessity of simultaneous connection and separation between human beings. Although individuals long to connect with one another, a connection that is too close or boundaries that are indistinct can be dangerous. Yet, disruption of these boundaries is probably inevitable, since the "frozen-ground-swell" that damages the wall, though it occurs annually, is never observed. The neighbors can only maintain their relationship through conscious attention to the wall that separates them.

## Author Biography

Born in San Francisco, Frost was eleven years old when his father died and his family relocated to Lawrence, Massachusetts, where his paternal grandparents lived. In 1892, Frost graduated from

Lawrence High School and shared valedictorian honors with Elinor White, whom he married three years later. After graduation, Frost briefly attended Dartmouth College, taught at grammar schools, worked at a mill, and served as a newspaper reporter. He published a chapbook of poems at his own expense and contributed the poem "The Birds Do Thus" to the *Independent,* a New York magazine. In 1897 Frost entered Harvard University as a special student, but left before completing degree requirements because of a bout with tuberculosis and the birth of his second child. Three years later, the Frosts' eldest child died, an event that led to marital discord and that, some critics believe, Frost later addressed in his poem "Home Burial."

In 1912, having been unable to interest American publishers in his poems, Frost moved his family to a farm in Buckinghamshire, England, where he wrote prolifically, attempting to perfect his distinct poetic voice. During this time, he met such literary figures as Ezra Pound, an American expatriate poet and champion of innovative literary approaches, and Edward Thomas, a young English poet associated with the Georgian poetry movement then popular in Great Britain. Frost soon published his first book of poetry, *A Boy's Will* (1913), which received appreciative reviews. Following the success of the book, Frost relocated to Gloucestershire, England, and directed publication of a second collection, *North of Boston* (1914). This volume contains several of his most frequently anthologized pieces, including "Mending Wall," "The Death of the Hired Man," and "After Apple-Picking." Shortly after *North of Boston* was published in Great Britain, the Frost family returned to the United States, settling in Franconia, New Hampshire. The American editions of Frost's first two volumes won critical acclaim upon publication in the United States, and in 1917 Frost began his affiliations with several American universities as a professor of literature and poet-in-residence. Frost continued to write prolifically over the years and received numerous literary awards as well as honors from the U.S. government and American universities. He recited his work at the inauguration of President John F. Kennedy in 1961 and represented the United States on several official missions. Though he received great popular acclaim, his critical reputation waned during the latter part of his career. His final three collections received less enthusiastic reviews, yet they contain several pieces acknowledged as among his greatest achievements. He died in Boston in 1963.

*Robert Frost*

## Poem Text

Something there is that doesn't love a wall,
That sends the frozen-ground-swell under it,
And spills the upper boulders in the sun;
And makes gaps even two can pass abreast.
The work of hunters is another thing:     5
I have come after them and made repair
Where they have left not one stone on a stone,
But they would have the rabbit out of hiding,
To please the yelping dogs. The gaps I mean,
No one has seen them made or heard them made,     10
But at spring mending-time we find them there.
I let my neighbor know beyond the hill;
And on a day we meet to walk the line
And set the wall between us once again.
We keep the wall between us as we go.     15
To each the boulders that have fallen to each.
And some are loaves and some so nearly balls
We have to use a spell to make them balance:
"Stay where you are until our backs are turned!"
We wear our fingers rough with handling them.     20
Oh, just another kind of outdoor game,
One on a side. It comes to little more:
There where it is we do not need the wall:
He is all pine and I am apple orchard.
My apple trees will never get across     25
And eat the cones under his pines, I tell him.
He only says, "Good fences make good neighbors."
Spring is the mischief in me, and I wonder
If I could put a notion in his head:
"Why do they make good neighbors? Isn't it     30

Where there are cows? But here there are no cows.
Before I built a wall I'd ask to know
What I was walling in or walling out,
And to whom I was like to give offence.
Something there is that doesn't love a wall,          35
That wants it down." I could say "Elves" to him,
But it's not elves exactly, and I'd rather
He said it for himself. I see him there
Bringing a stone grasped firmly by the top
In each hand, like an old-stone savage armed.          40
He moves in darkness as it seems to me,
Not of woods only and the shade of trees.
He will not go behind his father's saying,
And he likes having thought of it so well
He says again, "Good fences make good                  45
    neighbors."

## Poem Summary

### Lines 1-4:

Here the wall is introduced as a primary symbol in the poem. Whatever it is that protests against it, however, is vague and perhaps unnameable. This something is powerful, though, since it can create "gaps even two can pass abreast." Presumably, the speaker and his neighbor could step together from one side of the fence to the other, but they don't consider doing that.

### Lines 5-9:

In these lines the speaker contrasts the natural, yet almost secret, destruction of the wall by a "ground-swell" with the intentional destruction created by hunters. The speaker recognizes and understands their motive.

### Lines 10-11:

The speaker reinforces the idea that these breaks created by nature are more mysterious than those made by the hunters. This action cannot be observed, though the effects are consistent year after year.

### Lines 12-16:

Here, the speaker's ambivalence becomes apparent. Although he will attempt to present the desire for walls as belonging solely to his neighbor, he is the one who arranges to repair the wall. The separation between the two is emphasized in these lines, as they walk on opposite sides of the wall and as they are each responsible for replacing the stones that have fallen on each one's side. While they are performing this act together, they do not actually assist each other.

### Lines 17-19:

The tone becomes a bit more playful in these lines, as the farmers attempt to cast a "spell" on the stones. This idea will be reinforced later when the speaker thinks about "elves."

### Lines 20-22:

Although the speaker wants to present this activity as insignificant, as "just another ... game," he also reveals that the task has its difficult physical aspects.

### Lines 23-26:

In this section, which occurs near the center of the poem and explicitly illustrates the poem's central tension, the speaker attempts to present himself as desiring a closer relationship with his neighbor. He does this with a joke that is founded on a practical observation. Because farmers often use fences to keep their livestock separated, this fence should be unnecessary—pine trees and apple trees will not become confused with each other, nor will one eat the fruit or seeds of the other.

### Line 27:

In this line, the neighbor speaks for himself; he presents himself directly rather than through the eyes of the speaker. His personality is conveyed in this one line, which will be repeated later, but which is the only thought we receive from the neighbor. Rather than respond to the speaker's practical observation, the neighbor responds more abstractly, with a metaphor. Sometimes, he seems to suggest, the characteristics of our physical relationships directly influence our emotional relationships. Although he never states what he believes constitutes a good neighbor, he implies that some clear separation is essential.

### Lines 28-31:

Again, the speaker considers trying to provoke his neighbor with practical objections, but he never makes this statement out loud.

### Lines 32-35:

In this section the speaker also begins to speculate abstractly, and the symbolic significance of the wall becomes apparent as he uses the phrase "walling in" and "walling out." The double function of a wall is addressed, for not only are outsiders prevented from entry, but insiders are trapped inside. The speaker considers the possibility that walls "give offence" as he himself seems to be slightly offended, but he never reaches a conclusion about what it is within himself that is either walled in or walled out. Nor does he say that he himself doesn't love a wall, only that "Something" doesn't. We are meant to assume that the "something" is internal to the speaker, but his refusal to clearly acknowledge this attitude conveys his own ambivalence.

### Lines 36-38:

In these lines, the speaker again reveals his ambivalent attitude. He thinks about being playful, suggesting that "Elves" destroyed their wall, but he also longs for the neighbor to be playful, and besides, the speaker can't be entirely playful himself; he knows "it's not elves exactly."

### Lines 39-42:

Here the speaker presents his neighbor as more mysterious and primitive than himself, relying on a simile to convey his observation: "like an old-stone savage armed." This simile is appropriate because the farmers are literally using stones as their tools, but stone tools have the connotation of "savage." He implies that the neighbor is also using the stones as weapons; he is "armed." In a sense, then, the fence becomes a weapon, even if its purpose is primarily defense. The speaker then moves from thoughts of the Stone Age to thoughts of the Dark Ages, where darkness functions as a symbol for a lack of insight that is understood as progress. His darkness is more than literal, more than the shade provided by the trees, but also emotional in his refusal to become connected.

### Lines 43-45:

In these lines, the speaker indicates that the neighbor will not take a risk, because he will not reveal the reasons for his attitude beyond the fact that it reflects his father's attitude. Because the line "Good fences make good neighbors" has been repeated, and because it forms the last line of the poem, it becomes highly significant. The reader will remember it as the speaker remembers it, and perhaps the reader will have to puzzle out its meaning as the speaker attempts to do.

## Themes

### Alienation and Loneliness

Using the poem's central image of the stone wall, the speaker explores the reasons why people create boundaries around themselves. He believes

## Media Adaptations

- Robert Frost reads 23 of his poems, including "Mending Wall," on the Caedmon recording *Robert Frost Reads His Poetry,* which was recorded in 1956 at Frost's home in Cambridge, Massachusetts.

- *Robert Frost Reads,* an audio tape of the same recording session at Frost's Cambridge home, is available from HarperAudio.

that building a wall can "give offense," or alienate one's neighbor. Frost portrays the speaker and his neighbor as friendly with each other and able to work together, but essentially alienated from one another. The speaker does not see the necessity of maintaining the wall, apart from the fun of getting together to fix it; his neighbor, however, insists upon repairing it, because the ritual of repair is a tradition. The poem's opening line—"Something there is that doesn't love a wall"—implies that walls are unnatural, and that the vague "Something" is a force of nature that destroys the walls people build. This force seems not to want people to be separated from one another and breaks apart the wall: it "sends the frozen-ground-swell under it / And spills the upper boulders in the sun." Going against this natural force, the speaker and his neighbor will never truly know each other: as the speaker says, "We keep the wall between us as we go." Even as the two men are separated by the physical presence of the wall, they also alienate each other with their contrasting attitudes toward the wall, which illustrate a difference in their views toward life in general. While the speaker is imaginative and able to play with the image of the wall, his neighbor is unoriginal and can only repeat his own father's words about the wall: "'Good fences make good neighbors.'" To the speaker, the neighbor seems "like an old-stone savage" who "moves in darkness"—a primitive man who does not think or question. Nevertheless, the joint activity of repairing the wall does "'make good neighbors'" in the sense that it brings them together in a shared activity.

# *Topics for Further Study*

- Investigate the status of family farms in the United States today. Where are family farmers concentrated geographically, and how large are their farms on average, in terms of acreage and income?

- Look at the work of other major poets who were Frost's contemporaries in 1914: Ezra Pound, W. B. Yeats, Carl Sandburg. How do their subject matters and styles compare with Frost's? Can you account for Frost's wider popularity with the reading audience?

- From 1912 to 1914, Frost took his family with him to live in England. It was during this time that he wrote the poems published in *North of Boston,* including "Mending Wall." What major social and political issues were being faced in England and Europe during these years that Americans did not have to confront?

- Consider the neighbor's repeated statement in "Mending Wall": "'Good fences make good neighbors.'" Why does the neighbor think good fences make good neighbors? How does the poem show us that good fences can make good neighbors in other ways?

## Custom and Tradition

The speaker and his neighbor have a custom "at spring mending-time" of meeting at the wall that divides their properties "to walk the line / And set the wall between us once again." The speaker initiates this activity each year and enjoys it in a playful way: the wall's restoration is "just another kind of outdoor game, / One on a side. It comes to little more" than this for him. Yet he questions the wall's usefulness, seeing no real need for it: "My apple trees will never get across / And eat the cones under his pines." Although the speaker is able to challenge tradition, his neighbor cannot break away from the custom of maintaining fences between properties. Cherishing a tradition his father once carried out, the neighbor will not question the need for the wall. Unoriginal and unthinking in the speaker's eyes, the neighbor "moves in darkness," the darkness of blindly following custom without considering why he does so. The speaker points out that his neighbor "will not go behind his father's saying ... 'Good fences make good neighbors.'" He tries to tease his neighbor into looking below the surface of his father's words to ask why good fences make good neighbors, but the neighbor prefers simply to follow tradition for its own sake.

## Creativity and Imagination

The speaker's spirited imagination enables him to animate the natural world and have fun with the tedious job of repairing a stone wall while his duller neighbor can only see that the wall needs repair. The neighbor is unimaginative: he does not think too deeply about why he is repairing the wall and is only able to repeat his father's words, "'Good fences make good neighbors.'" While the neighbor views walls as necessary dividers of property, the speaker questions the usefulness of walls and contemplates their various meanings. He presents the "Something ... that doesn't love a wall" as mysterious and whimsical: for instance, the "something" could be "'elves,'" but "it's not elves exactly." The speaker sees the stones from the wall as "loaves" and "balls," objects of domesticity and play, and he says that the ritual of fixing the wall is "just another kind of outdoor game, / One on a side." He does not take this job of mending the wall too seriously, claiming that he and his neighbor "have to use a spell to make [the stones] balance: 'Stay where you are until our backs are turned!'" Mischievously, the speaker tells his neighbor that "My apple trees will never get across / And eat the cones under his pines," but the neighbor does not appreciate the humor in this remark. The contrast between the speaker's imaginative view of the world and his neighbor's duty-bound view helps to build the poem's theme of alienation.

## Order and Disorder

The annual ritual of meeting to repair the stone wall dividing their properties represents the speaker and his neighbor's attempt to reestablish order in a disorderly world. The mildly named "Something ... that doesn't love a wall" is a powerful force of nature that is able to move boulders and destroy human handiwork. The fact that the wall-mending ritual is an annual event speaks of the futility of this activity: each spring, the two men fix the wall, and each winter "Something" breaks it apart again.

# Compare & Contrast

- **1913:** The International Exhibition of Modern Art, held at the Sixty-ninth Regiment Armory in New York City and known popularly as the Armory Show, shocked the art world with avant-garde works by Modern artists such as Pablo Picasso, Henri Matisse, Constantin Brancusi, and Marcel Duchamp. Conservatives who saw the Armory Show thought that the artists whose work was represented there were joking or were frauds.

  **1971:** Picasso was honored on his ninetieth birthday with an exhibition of his work at the Louvre in Paris. The presentation represented the first time that a living artist's work was shown at the Louvre.

  **1990s:** The work of once-avant-garde artists such as Picasso and Matisse is now so popular that it appears on such mass-produced items as wristwatches, T-shirts, and computer mouse pads.

- **1913:** Women in the United States did not have the right to vote. In May, a large parade of woman suffrage supporters, 10,000 strong, marched down Fifth Avenue in New York City, hoping to gain attention for their cause.

  **1996:** For the November elections, nearly 68 million American women were registered voters.

- **1913:** Henry Ford, founder of the Ford Motor Company, introduced into his factories the first assembly line for building automobiles, making production faster and more efficient.

  **1914:** More than half a million Ford Model T cars were being driven around the world.

  **1998:** In the months of July, August, and September alone, U.S. sales of Ford cars and trucks totaled 993,723.

- **1914:** World War I (known at the time as The Great War) began, resulting ultimately in the destruction of the great empires of Europe.

  **1990:** The Conference on Security and Co-operation in Europe— made up of 32 European countries, plus the United States and Canada— convened in Paris to create the Charter of Paris for a New Europe. The vision for this New Europe is based upon an agreement of mutual respect and cooperation among the participating countries.

Yet the speaker and his neighbor, needing to reestablish order, "set the wall between us once again," knowing that their order is fragile and will not last.

When such lines are read aloud, the rhythm can be clearly heard and the pattern recognized by the ear. The repetition of metrical verse is one of the qualities that make such poetry pleasurable.

## Style

"Mending Wall" is written in unrhymed iambic pentameter, or blank verse, a popular form in English. An iamb is a metrical foot containing two syllables, the first of which is unstressed and the second of which is stressed. In iambic pentameter, then, each line will consist of ten syllables. This is easiest seen if a line is diagrammed:

The **work** / of **hunt** / ers **is** / an **oth** / er **thing**.

## Historical Context

### Time of Transition

The years just prior to the Great War, now known as World War I (1914-1918), encompassed broad social and political change. Essentially, what is often referred to as "the old order"—imperialism, formality, rigid class boundaries—was dying away as a new order of society emerged. While aggressions among various European nations simmered and flared, anticipation of an all-out war grew. Under the threat of war, Europeans seemed to feel that old, long-held constrictions could be loosened; and while Americans did not feel the threat of war as immediately as the Europeans, by 1913 the world knew that everything familiar was about to change dramatically. In major cities around the world, suffragists campaigned for women's right to vote; a sensuous new dance known as the tango titillated and shocked polite society; women's fashions became more revealing and bold, with tight skirts and nearly transparent fabrics; and the art world presented wondrous new images that the average viewer could not understand. The middle class gained unprecedented mobility with Henry Ford's Model T automobile, and jazz and ragtime music were growing in popularity. The wealthy and powerful viewed the rise of Socialism as a threat. This proved to be a prophetic response to a political philosophy that would come to help shape the new, postwar Europe.

### Modernism in Art and Music

With the Armory Show in New York and the first performance of Igor Stravinsky's masterpiece *The Rite of Spring* in Paris, 1913 was a year in which Modernism in the arts announced itself to the world. Artistic originality and creativity defined the years just prior to the start of World War I. During the decade before the war, Cubism emerged in painting, expressing an abstract vision of the world. During this period, the arts in general—music, literature, architecture, fine arts—reflected a growing interest in technology. The Armory Show, first held in a New York armory and officially known as The International Exhibition of Modern Art, was a large-scale presentation of works by Modern European and American artists. The exhibition shocked its audience with paintings and sculpture that broke away from traditional, familiar Romantic forms. The work of Impressionists, Symbolists, Postimpressionists, Fauves, and Cubists was unlike any artwork people had ever seen. Cubist painter Marcel Duchamp's famed work *Nude Descending a Staircase, No. 2,* one of the more famous of the works exhibited in the Armory Show, has been described as looking like " 'an explosion in a shingle factory.' " The hugely influential Armory Show traveled around the United States and was viewed by close to 300,000 Americans.

Nineteen thirteen was also an explosive year musically. With the opening performance in Paris of the revolutionary ballet *The Rite of Spring,* scored by Russian composer Igor Stravinsky, choreo-graphed by Vaslav Nijinsky, and produced by Sergey Pavlovich Diaghilev, Modernism in music had arrived. The opening night audience, used to traditional ballets such as *Swan Lake* and *Giselle,* reacted with outrage to Stravinsky's work, so startling to them were the dissonances and violent rhythms. Stravinsky's composition, described by many as anarchic, intends to evoke the fervor of primitive human beings taking part in a pagan ritual.

## Critical Overview

Like many of Robert Frost's poems, "Mending Wall" has received significant attention from critics who refuse to agree with one another regarding its interpretation and meaning. Although most critics recognize the motif of separation and connection as typical of Frost, they disagree vehemently about the overall success of the poem. In his book *Robert Frost and New England: The Poet as Regionalist,* John C. Kemp claims that the speaker in this poem illustrates Frost's "characteristic role as an outsider who is both disturbed and fascinated by an environment he can neither change nor fully accept." A. Zverev, in an article published in *20th Century American Literature: A Soviet View,* describes the metaphor of the wall as "a rich image which serves to convey notions of true and false in the mind of the people." Zverev believes that the strength of the poem lies in its attention to exact detail and, especially, in its ability to convey the resistance many people feel to separation.

Critic Allen Tate, on the other hand, writing in *Robert Frost: Lectures on the Centennial of His Birth,* describes this poem in a tone that can only be described as bitingly sarcastic. "And now the famous wall that has a fine, domestic, and civic effect upon the people it divides," Tate begins, already indicating that his critique will be negative. Later in the article, he continues, "I hope my rather feckless paraphrase of this poem is at least as tiresome as the poem itself. I have a little more to say about it. Good neighbors are good to have, but good fences do not make them good neighbors. Here we have Frost's perilous teetering upon the brink of sentimentality." Tate is accusing Frost here of making an association that is too easy to be accurate. He suggests that though it may be tempting to believe that "Good fences make good neighbors" automatically, human relations are in fact much more complicated and cannot be reduced to such a pat phrase.

# What Do I Read Next?

- Frost said that "'Mending Wall' takes up the theme where 'A Tuft of Flowers' [sic] in *A Boy's Will* (1913) laid it down." "The Tuft of Flowers," deals with the theme of men working together, in spirit if not in actuality.

- "After Apple-Picking," another poem in *North of Boston*, like "Mending Wall," portrays working and thinking as united. The act of picking apples, a farm chore not unlike mending stone walls, leads the speaker in "After Apple-Picking" to think about the chore and what it means.

- One of the dramatic dialogues in *North of Boston*, "The Death of the Hired Man" explores the theme of home and human connection through the characters of a farmer, his wife, and their old hired hand. The poem is an excellent example of Frost's skill at capturing spoken voices.

- John Jerome's 1996 collection of essays, *Stone Work: Reflections on Serious Play and Other Aspects of Country Life*, is a thoughtful treatment of building a stone wall among other aspects of rural life.

- *Building Stone Walls* (1986) by John Vivian is a how-to guide to building several types of stone walls.

- *Rock Fences of the Bluegrass (Perspective on Kentucky's Past)*, by Carolyn Murray-Wooley, Karl Raitz (contributor), and Ron Garrison (photographer), is an historic exploration of the rock fences that run throughout Kentucky's Bluegrass country and the masons who built them. The book contains photographs, drawings, and lists of masons' names.

# Criticism

## Craig Dworkin

*Craig Douglas Dworkin is an assistant professor of English at Princeton University. In the following essay, Dworkin traces a series of encoded words through Robert Frost's "Mending Wall" in order to expose the complexity of language the poet's conversational and narrative style seems to belie.*

Robert Frost's "Mending Wall," like much of his poetry, invites a range of conventional interpretations; readers may be tempted to meet its homespun wisdom with moralizing humanist pieties, or to match its smug wit with equally condescending judgements about the two characters and their psychological portraits. Moreover, if the regionalist New-England setting suggests that we read "Mending Wall" as a realistic description of a rural landscape, the poems structured oppositions and the symbolic weight of the "wall" also encourages a host of allegorical readings. On any of these counts, however, the poem comes up short.

Despite its air of profound judgement, the poem never rises above platitudes and simple-minded ideas, and its language wavers between goofy faux-colloquialisms and stilted inversions. But that language, however poorly handled, demonstrates an infinite resourcefulness. The inventive play of language itself, in fact, restores "Mending Wall" to the status of poetry and saves it from becoming the doggerel to which Frost's poems seem to aspire.

Frost's wall requires attention because of "the gaps," and the gaps in his poem deserve attention as well. In his study the *Semiotics of Poetry*, theorist Michael Riffaterre argues that poetic texts are created when a gap opens between a word and a text. Poems, in his view, are constructed around absent centers (in the same way that a doughnut, say, takes shape around an empty hole). The absent center of the poem is a single unwritten word or phrase that does not actually appear in the poem, but around which the poem is written. Riffaterre calls that encoded, unwritten core the "matrix." Around this core, the rest of the poem presents variations of the matrix, offering equivalents to the key word or phrase but never mentioning the specific word

> *... [W]e must learn to read the letters and words that are absent from the page but ever-present in the logic of a poem's language. That language always says more than it seems, and its confessions are worth listening to."*

or phrase itself. Just as the wall in Frost's poem warps and strains and breaks because of the empty swell beneath it, the words that do appear in a poem—according to Riffaterre—deform themselves around the unspoken matrix. As the language of the poem avoids the matrix, detouring around it and rewriting it in other words, ungrammatical and awkward phrases result. Such grammatical disruptions, like the stilted phrases in "Mending Wall," are clues to the presence of the matrix. The poetic text thus "functions something like a neurosis," in Riffaterre's psychoanalytic terms: "as the matrix is repressed, the displacement produces variants all through the text, just as the repressed symptoms break out somewhere else in the body."

With an analogy to the way in which an anagram encodes a word by rearranging its letters, Riffaterre calls the encryption of the matrix a "hypogram" (*hypo* "under" + *gram* "writing"); the hypogram is quite literally the subtext of the poem, underwriting the text on the page without actually appearing as part of that text. The word "hypogram," moreover, derives directly from the Greek *hypographein,* which denotes a signature, and this etymology nicely underscores the fact that the hypogram in "Mending Wall" is indeed a signature. Another name for the opening image of "the frozen ground swell," of course, is a frost, and so even without an autograph or title page, (Robert) Frost has already signed the poem in its second line. Indeed, such signatures are common in Frost's oeuvre, in which references to snow and ice recur; the autumnal or winter landscapes that so often serve as the background for his poetry frequently provide an opportunity for explicit inscriptions of the au-

thor's name. Close textual analyses like Riffaterre's are usually seen as ways of avoiding the author; rather than concerning themselves with biographical information (whether Frost ever mended walls with his neighbor, for instance), close readings focus on the text itself and the relationship between the words on the page. In "Mending Wall," however, where the name of the poet is encoded into the machinery of textual production, such textual details turn out to be the very means of recovering the author's presence.

The speaker in "Mending Wall" is walking "the line" (line 13), both figuratively and literally in terms of lines of verse, between revealing and concealing the matrix. The phrase "the gaps I mean," isolated at the end of the ninth line, might be taken not as a corrective explanation but rather as an assertive confession; the speaker, if not the author himself, is acknowledging that his meaning is located in the gap between what is actually written ("frozen ground swell") and what is encoded (frost). That encoded inscription is still too near the surface, however, and we should not stop until we have reached the matrix's deeper level—akin to permafrost. The complete name for the type of frost that would swell the ground is "rime-frost." The pun is exact. In fact, although now chiefly archaic or poetic, "rime" is an alternate spelling for "rhyme." In Frost's first book of poetry, *A Boy's Will,* only one out of the thirty poems included failed to use a fixed pattern of end-rhymes. *When North of Boston*—the book that includes "Mending Wall"—was published one year later, in 1914, only three of the seventeen poems employed such rhyme schemes. Frost would return to end-rhymes throughout his career (indeed already by the time of his next book, *Mountain Interval,* published in 1916, Frost would revert to explicit rhyme schemes in more than three-quarters of poems included in the volume). With *North of Boston,* therefore, Frost was making a deliberate move away from rhyme, and so the placement of "Mending Wall" as the first poem in the volume makes perfect sense. Opening that largely unrhymed collection of verse, "Mending Wall" announces the book's stylistic change by not only suppressing the rhyme associated with Frost but also the rime associated with frost.

"Rime" points not only to the poem and its sounds, however, but also to the specifics of Frost's "Mending Wall." A rime is also a chink or cleft, and so the explicit references to "gaps" are one way that the poem rewrites the rime matrix. That matrix continues to be rewritten, in fact, not only with equivalents but also with a series of reversals that skirt the central hypogram like two poles of an electric motor. To "rim" means to wall, and to "wall," in turn, means to boil up—exactly the inverse of the frozen ground swell's "rime." The vocabulary of Frost's poem returns again and again, in various ways, to the matrix.

If such punning displacements around the matrix seems far-fetched, recall the more obvious shifts with which "Mending Wall" encodes key words. The speaker declares: "Before I built a wall I'd ask to know / What I was walling in or walling out, / And to whom I was like to give offence." With a slight shift across word boundaries (what linguists refer to as a transsegmental drift), "offence" contains the homophonic equivalent "a fence"—or, in other words, precisely what the persona would give if he were to build a wall. Such encoding may also be a clue to reading the cryptic and exceedingly bizarre statement: "I could say Elves to him, / But that's not it exactly, and I'd rather / He said it for himself." What could it mean to exclaim "Elves," and if the word he wants is not exactly "Elves," then what is it? The emphasized "himself" that concludes the sentence suggests one possibility: "[s]elves" is not exactly "elves," but it is very close, and the yearning for connection between isolated selves is precisely what "doesn't love a wall" and "wants it down." The matrix that structures the opening of the poem suggests another possibility, however; the word "delves" is also close to, but not exactly "elves," and delves are small cavities under the ground—or, in other words, exactly what the "frozen ground swell" would form once the rime-frost had melted "in the sun," leaving only empty cavities when the two neighbors find the swollen ground "at spring mending-time." Opening a hole with a swell might be graphically depicted by an open letter "o" gaping in the middle of the word itself to form "s[o]well," and ultimately—in the context of all of these encodings—one might even read "so well," the emphasized adverb of the penultimate line of the poem, as not just the destructive swell that threatens the wall but also the tool with which the neighbor makes the fences for which he is advocating and staking a claim; a "sowel" is the stake used in fence making.

If these examples are still not sufficiently obvious to prompt the readers' excavation of the matrix rime-frost, the text also gives two further hints to the reader to be on the lookout for such textual encodings. Those delves, the subterranean cavities left by the frozen ground swell, are crypts, and so

the rime-frost is quite literally encrypted. Moreover, the persona's invocation of a "spell" summons a similar reference to encryption. From the fourteenth century on, according to the *Oxford English Dictionary,* "to spell" originally meant "to read … letter by letter; to peruse, or make out, slowly or with difficulty." To spell, that is, originally meant not the correct formation of a word, but simply to read individual letters rather than entire words. To spell Frost's own poem, then, would be to puzzle over words like "elves" and "offence" and play with their individual letters. When Frost wrote "Mending Wall," the figurative use of "spell" would still have carried the meaning of guessing something secret or discovering something hidden, and the word would have explicitly denoted decipherment. Just as the speaker in "Mending Wall" has to use a spell to make the stones balance, "we have to use a spell" to make the poem balance with its matrix. Finally, the *Oxford English Dictionary* reminds us that as a noun, "spell" denotes not only a hint or intimation, but also "a splinter, chip, or fragment." So "spell," therefore, hints directly at the matrix, balancing the rime (in the sense of a chink) left by those fragments of stone broken off from the wall.

Having spelled out these transformations, it should be clear that the closest reading of the words themselves need not be an activity that disregards the thematic, referential content of a poem. In fact, we must undertake the effort of those letter-by-letter readings in order to better access the complexity of references woven into a poetic text; and to do so we must learn to read the letters and words that are absent from the page but ever-present in the logic of a poem's language. That language always says more than it seems, and its confessions are worth listening to. Indeed, as a way of [m]*ending* [w]*all,* a "frost," one should remember, is also a synonym for a literary failure. Whether Frost ultimately avoids that frost, as the poem avoids its matrix, depends on how carefully we mind the gaps he means but cannot mend.

**Source:** Craig Dworkin, in an essay for *Poetry for Students,* Gale, 1999.

### Bruce Meyer

*Bruce Meyer is the director of the creative writing program at the University of Toronto. He has taught at several Canadian universities and is the author of three collections of poetry. In the following essay, Meyer comments on the success of "Mending Wall" as an example of a narrative poem.*

In an essay for *The Reaper* magazine titled "How to Write Narrative Poetry," poets Robert Mc-Dowell and Mark Jarman suggest that there are ten considerations that must be addressed in a successful narrative poem. These ten points are: a beginning, a middle, and an end; observation; compression of time; containment; illumination of private gestures; understatement; humor; a distinct sense location or setting; memorable characters; and a compelling subject. As a narrative poem, Robert Frost's "Mending Wall" passes *The Reaper* test in several ways by presenting the reader with a situation of a man repairing a simple stone wall with his neighbor. What emerges from the poem is not simply a well-told story or even a detailed sense of the characters and their experiences, but a statement on the nature of human relations, boundaries, and individual identity.

The poem opens with a commonplace observation of how a wall winters and shifts as a result of freezing and thawing. Frost translates this observation into a universal truth so that the simple act of mending a wall becomes a gesture of supreme importance. The explicit quality of understatement is evident in this process. Frost sticks to his subject with an emphasis on direct speech—clear and unpoetic diction that adds a deceptive sense of the mundane to the action; yet the aphoristic structure of the opening line, "Something there is that doesn't love a wall," stays with the reader as a maxim that borders on an axiom. The sense of universal truth, or at least applicable observation that can be assumed into the shape of a law or saying, is an essential part of the poem's containment. The wall mending, the action between the neighbors, is all the world that Frost needs to portray in order to establish a philosophical statement on human relations. This containment, the unified limitation of both time and space and the focus on a very simple and uncomplicated action, is yet another means by which Frost uses understatement to his advantage.

The containment qualities of "Mending Wall," coupled with the sense of understatement and expression of a large truth in a very small way, is achieved through a very limited but well-defined setting. The delineated differences between the two fields, "He is all pine and I am apple orchard," is a modest yet distinctive expression of the setting. This is a world of boundaries where the setting is more than a backdrop to the meaning of the action and the poem—it is a metaphor for separateness, and the reason for the action is the maintenance of the distinction between two very unique worlds.

Frost strikes a note of wry and subtle humor when his wall mender observes, "My apple trees will never get across / And eat the cones under his pines." To this, the neighbor offers a rebuttal in the form of a proverb: "Good fences make good neighbors." The separation of the two farms and the two worlds within the poem is further enhanced by the strange quality of separation within the communication process between the two characters. One offers a joke. The other replies with a piece of unquestioned wisdom that he repeats, almost for rhetorical emphasis, at the conclusion of the poem. The communication between the two characters is understated, to say the least, but the message is conveyed elliptically that not only is this a poem about the separation of farms, but the separation of perspectives and modes of expression.

The differences between the two men, articulated in the act of possessing a wall and maintaining it for the sake of neighborliness, are a source of humor in the poem. Both men are focused on the same action and working toward the same end, yet their end is separateness: "To each the boulders that have fallen to each. / And some are loaves and some so nearly balls / We have to use a spell to make them balance." The irony of this situation is that they appear to be working not only against the destructive properties of climatic changes, but against unseen forces that they both acknowledge, a key element of the subtle humor that Frost builds into the poem. There appears to be an element of luck-of-the-draw involved in the work: "Something there is that doesn't love a wall, / That wants it down.' I could say 'Elves' to him / But that's not elves exactly, and I'd rather / He said it for himself." It appears that both men are thinking the same thing: that something in nature is working against them, that although they consciously and logically dismiss an animate presence in nature that destroys the wall, they both jokingly admit to its possible existence. Both utter "spells" to make the stones balance and stay in place once they have moved on to the next piece of the fallen barrier: "Stay where you are until our backs are turned!"

This reading of nature as containing animate possibilities suggests that for the narrator, at least, Frost has created a structure of an inner life, a psychology that is essential to creating a memorable character. The narrator muses to himself: "I wonder / If I could put a notion in his head: / 'Why do they make good neighbors? Isn't it / Where there are cows? But there are no cows." The sense of character that delineates each of the two men is established in different ways. For the narrator it is through this sense of the inner self observing and speculating on his opposite. For the neighbor, character is established by the process of understatement, so that he is composed with what he does not say and appears to the reader as a quiet individual of few words.

Characterization, in a process that is drawn more from the structures of fiction than from poetry, is further established through Frost's eye for minute detail and "illumination of private gestures." The gestures are not simply the details of the wall-mending process, although they contribute significantly to the characterizations Frost is trying to convey; they are the means by which the reader pictures and remembers the two individuals. The narrator focuses on his neighbor's gestures so that his character is created not through what he says but through what he does: "I see him there / Bringing a stone grasped firmly by the top / In each hand, like an old-stone savage armed. / He moves in darkness as it seems to me, / Not of woods only and the shade of trees." Here is a man of few words and many actions. The narrator, on the other hand, is a dreamer. His character is developed through what he thinks, rather than through what he says or does. He spends most of the poem watching the other man work, honoring his reticence, and imagining a number of speculative scenarios that he fails to implement either as conversation or observation. Frost, therefore, has not only created characterizations of two men in search of separateness; he has created two separate and fully fleshed entities that speak of both differences and of poles of human types, and it is for these reasons that they are memorable to the reader.

What is, perhaps, the most important aspect of "Mending Wall," and what categorizes it under McDowell and Jarman's classifications as a successful narrative poem, is the work's sense of drama. As in the case of classical theater, such as that identified by Aristotle in *The Poetics,* the drama of the poem is conveyed through a unity of time and place. "Mending Wall" focuses on a single time and a single place, and the actions could, plausibly, take place within the "real time" of the poem. This may appear to contradict the nature of narrative: after all, a narrative is, by definition, a sequence of connected events that form a single concept or story. In "Mending Wall," there is one event that is composed of small gestures. But what Frost is doing is making the gestures into events in themselves by focusing on the minute actions of the process, so that the narrative is a sequence of actions rather than a sequence of events. It is the

> *The wall mending, the action between the neighbors, is all the world that Frost needs to portray in order to establish a philosophical statement on human relations."*

enlargement of each minor action that contributes to the drama and to the success of the poem as a narrative. As a narrative poem in the McDowell and Jarman definition, "Mending Wall" does compress time, but only in a very minimal sense because the actions are so detailed and so precise.

The one outstanding question that remains to be answered is does "Mending Wall" have a compelling subject? Frost seems to be conscious of the need to make the action into an allegory, and he moves toward this through the uttering and repeating of maxims such as "Something there is that doesn't love a wall," and "Good fences make good neighbors." The point of the poem appears to be the demonstration of wisdom as a result of practice rather than the discovery of a truth through a process, a revelation, and a denouement. What the reader must remember is that wisdom, the central thrust of the poem, is a result of repeated processes and accumulated observations. The "spring mending-time" that Frost mentions is an annual necessity and part of regular farm maintenance—a calendar event that can be foreseen. The destructive forces of nature can also be foreseen. It should be remembered that the books of Wisdom in The Bible, such as Ecclesiastes, are not stories of individuals discovering the truth as much as they are acknowledgments of the way things work. The presence of wisdom rather than discovery is at the root of the neighbor's tenacious hold on his maxim, "Good fences make good neighbors." Wisdom is something to be accepted, not debated, and the narrator observes of his neighbor, "He will not go behind his father's saying, / And he likes the thought so well / He says it again."

What is compelling about "Mending Wall" is that it challenges the convention of the narrative

> *'Mending Wall'*
> *dramatizes the playfully*
> *imaginative man who has*
> *his world under full*
> *control . . . ."*

poem as a process (seen in fictional structures) of problem, struggle, climax, resolution, and denouement. Instead, Frost's poem presents the concept of two individuals confronting and accepting human truths. Their persistence, in both the action and the ideas that the action expresses, is in itself compelling and engaging.

**Source:** Bruce Meyer, in an essay for *Poetry for Students,* Gale, 1999.

### Frank Lentricchia

*In the following excerpt, Lentricchia compares the characters of the narrator and his neighbor in Frost's "Mending Wall."*

"Mending Wall" is the opening poem of Frost's second volume, *North of Boston.* One of the dominating moods of this volume, forcefully established in such important poems as "The Death of the Hired Man," "Home Burial," "The Black Cottage," and "A Servant to Servants," and carried through some of the minor pieces, flows from lives lived grimly, from the tension of having to maintain balance at the precipitous edge of hysteria. "Mending Wall" stands opposed to such visions of human existence—or, more precisely put, to existences that are fashioned by the neurotic visions of central characters like the wife in "Home Burial," the servant in "A Servant to Servants." "Mending Wall" dramatizes the playfully imaginative man who has his world under full control, who in his inner serenity is riding his realities, not being shocked by them into traumatic response.

The opening lines evoke the coy posture of the shrewed, imaginative man who understands the words of the farmer in "The Mountain": "All the fun's in how you say a thing."

> Something there is that doesn't love a wall,
> That sends a frozen-ground-swell under it,
> And spills the upper boulders in the sun,
> And makes gaps even two can pass abreast.

It does not take more than one reading of the poem to understand that the speaker is not a country primitive who is easily spooked by the normal processes of nature. He knows very well what it is "that doesn't love a wall." His fun lies in not naming it, and in not naming the scientific truth he is able to manipulate intransigent fact into the world of the mind where all things are pliable. The artful vagueness of the phrase "Something there is" is enchanting and magical, suggesting even the hushed tones of reverence before mystery in nature. And the speaker (who is not at all reverent toward nature) consciously works at deepening that sense of mystery:

> The work of hunters is another thing:
> I have come after them and made repair
> Where they would have left not one stone on a
>     stone,
> But they would have the rabbit out of hiding,
> To please the yelping dogs. The gaps I mean,
> No one has seen them made or heard them made,
> But at spring mending-time we find them there.

The play of the mature, imaginative man is grounded in ironic awareness, and must be, for even as he excludes verifiable realities from his fictive world the unmistakable tone of scorn for the hunters comes seeping through. He may step into a fictive world but not before glancing back briefly at the brutality that attends upon the play of others. Having paid for his imaginative excursions by establishing his ironic consciousness, he is free to close the magic circle cast out by his playful energies, and thereby close out the world reported by the senses ("No one has seen them made or heard them made"). In knowing how to say a thing in and through adroit linguistic manipulation, the fiction of the something that doesn't love a wall is created, the imaginative reality stands formed before him, ready to be entered.

But, like the selves dramatized in a number of other poems by Robert Frost, this persona would prefer not to be alone in his imaginative journey:

> I let my neighbor know beyond the hill;
> And on a day we meet to walk the line
> And set the wall between us once again.
> We keep the wall between us as we go.
> To each the boulders that have fallen to each.
> And some are loaves and some so nearly balls
> We have to use a spell to make them balance:
> "Stay where you are until our backs are turned!"
> We wear our fingers rough with handling them.
> Oh, just another kind of outdoor game,
> One on a side. It comes to little more:
> There where it is we do not need the wall:
> He is all pine and I am apple orchard.
> My apple trees will never get across

And eat the cones under his pines, I tell him.
He only says, "Good fences make good neighbors."

If the fact of a broken wall is excuse enough to make a fiction about why it got that way, then that same fact may be the occasion for two together to take a journey in the mind. For those who would like to read "Mending Wall" as political allegory (the narrator standing for a broad-minded liberal internationalism, the thick-headed second speaker representing a selfish super-patriotism) they must first face the line "I let my neighbor know beyond the hill." "Mending Wall" has nothing to do with one-world political ideals, good or bad neighbor policies: on this point the title of the poem is helpful. It is a poem that celebrates a process, not the thing itself. It is a poem, furthermore, that distinguishes between two kinds of people: one who seizes the particular occasion of mending as fuel for the imagination and therefore as a release from the dull ritual of work each spring and one who is trapped by work and by the past as it comes down to him in the form of his father's cliché. Tied as he is to his father's words that "Good fences make good neighbors," the neighbor beyond the hill is committed to an end, the fence's completion. His participation in the process of rebuilding is, for him, sheer work because he never really plays the outdoor game. The narrator, however, is not committed to ends, but to the process itself which he sees as having non-utilitarian value: "There where it is we do not need the wall." The process itself is the matrix of the play that redeems work by transforming it into the pleasure of an outdoor game in which you need to cast spells to make rocks balance. Overt magic-making is acceptable in the world of this poem because, governed as we are by the narrator's perspective, we are in the fictive world where all things are possible, where walls go tumbling for mysterious reasons. Kant's theory that work and the aesthetic activity are antagonistic, polar activities of man is, in effect, overturned, as the narrator makes work take on the aesthetic dimension. The real difference between the two people in the poem is that one moves in a world of freedom because, aware of the resources of the mind, he nurtures the latent imaginative power within himself and makes it a factor in every-day living, while the other, unaware of the value of imagination, must live his unliberated life without it. And this difference makes a difference in the quality of the life lived.

The narrator of "Mending Wall" does not give up so easily: he tries again to tempt his neighbor to enter into the fictive world with him and to share his experience of play:

Spring is the mischief in me, and I wonder
If I could put a notion in his head:
"*Why* do they make good neighbors? Isn't it
Where there are cows? But here there are no cows:
Before I built a wall I'd ask to know
What I was walling in or walling out,
And to whom I was like to give offence.
Something there is that doesn't love a wall,
That wants it down." I could say "Elves" to him,
But it's not elves exactly, and I'd rather
He said it for himself....

All to no avail, however: the outrageously appropriate pun on "offense" falls on deaf ears; he won't say "elves" (who may be defined as those little folk who don't love a wall); he will not enter the play world of imagination. The neighbor moves in "darkness," our narrator concludes, "like an old-stone savage armed." The characterization is philosophically precise in the logic of the tradition of post-Kantian aesthetics. For the recalcitrant and plodding neighbor is a slave to the rituals of the quotidian, a primitive whose spirit has not been freed by the artistic consciousness that lies dormant within. It is the play spirit of imagination, as Schiller suggests, which distinguishes the civilized man from his cave-dwelling ancestor—that "old-stone savage" who moved in "darkness."

**Source:** Lentricchia, Frank, "Experience as Meaning: Robert Frosts's 'Mending Wall,'" *The CEA Critic,* vol. 34, no. 4, May 1972, pp. 9–11.

## Sources

"Armory Show," from *Britannica Online,* http://www .eb.com:180/cgi-bin/g?DocF=micro/33/75.html, (Accessed October 12, 1998).

"Charter of Paris for a New Europe," from *Hellenic Resources Network,* http://www.hri.org/docs/Paris90.html, (Accessed October 16, 1998).

Cowles, Virginia, *1913: An End and a Beginning,* Harper & Row, 1968.

"Diaghilev, Sergey Pavlovich," from *Britannica Online,* http://www.eb.com:180/cgi-bin/g?DocF=micro/168/54.html, (Accessed October 15, 1998).

"European History and Culture: Revolution and the growth of industrial society, 1789-1914: MODERN CULTURE: The prewar period," from *Britannica Online,* http://www.eb.com:180/cgi-bin/g?DocF=macro/5002/20/205 .html, (Accessed October 15, 1998).

"Ford Motor Company," from *Britannica Online,* http://www.eb.com:180/cgi-bin/g?DocF=micro/214/80.html, (Accessed October 12, 1998).

Ford Motor Company Home Page at http://www.ford.com, (Accessed October 14, 1998).

Kemp, John C., *Robert Frost and New England: The Poet as Regionalist,* Princeton University Press, 1978, 273 p.

*The Oxford English Dictionary,* 2nd ed., prepared by J. A. Simpson and E. S. C. Weiner, Oxford: Clarendon Press; New York: Oxford University Press, 1989.

"Pablo Picasso on the WWW," at http://kultur-online .com/greatest/fr-picasso.htm, (Accessed October 16, 1998).

Riffaterre, Michael, *Semiotics of Poetry,* Bloomington: Indiana University Press, 1978.

"Stravinsky, Igor (Fyodorovich)," from *Britannica Online,* http://www.eb.com:180/cgi-bin/g?DocF=micro/569/4.html, (Accessed October 12, 1998).

Tate, Allen, " 'Inner Weather': Robert Frost as a Metaphysical Poet," in *Robert Frost: Lectures on the Centennial of His Birth,* edited by Helen Bacon et al., Library of Congress, 1975, pp. 57-68.

United States Bureau of Census, Table 23, Voting and Registration: November 1996, at http://www.census.gov/ population/socdemo/voting/history/vot23.txt, (Accessed October 14, 1998).

"Women Win the Vote," at http://www.inform.umd.edu: 8080/EdRes/Topic/WomensStudies/ReadingRoom/History/ Vote.html, (Accessed October 15, 1998).

Zverev, A., "A Lover's Quarrel with the World: Robert Frost," in *20th Century American Literature: A Soviet View,* translated by Ronald Vroon, Progress Publishers, 1976, pp. 241-60.

## For Further Study

Barry, Elaine, *Robert Frost on Writing,* New Brunswick, NJ: Rutgers University Press, 1973.
    A collection of letters, interviews, lectures, and other writings in which Frost explores his beliefs on writing and literature.

Poirier, Richard, *Robert Frost: The Work of Knowing,* New York: Oxford University Press, 1977.
    An excellent in-depth examination of Frost's poetry.

Pritchard, William H., *Frost: A Literary Life Reconsidered,* New York: Oxford University Press, 1984.
    A biography of Frost that explores the relationship between his work and his life.

Thompson, Lawrance, *Robert Frost: The Early Years,* New York: Holt, 1966.
    This is the first volume in Thompson's authoritative three-volume biography of Frost; this volume covers Frost's life from his birth in 1874 through his return to the United States after a two-year sojourn in England. When the biography was first published, it changed the way readers viewed Frost and his work, portraying him not as a simple, gentle-natured poet but as a powerful man with a potent dark side.

# Sonnet 55

## William Shakespeare
## 1609

Shakespeare wrote a total of 154 sonnets; the first 126 being addressed to a "Young Man" or "Friend" while sonnets 127 to 152 are addressed to a mysterious "Dark Lady," possibly the poet's mistress. In "Sonnet 55," addressed to the young friend, the speaker of the poem claims that his "powerful rhyme" will outlast "marble" and "gilded monuments," keeping the youth's memory alive until the Last Judgement. The poem makes a defiant statement about the power of poetry and love over death while, ironically, deriving much of its poetic interest through images of oblivion.

## Author Biography

Shakespeare was born in 1564 in Stratford-upon-Avon, a small market town in a rural region north of London, England. He had four sisters, only one of whom lived to adulthood, and three younger brothers, all of whom survived childhood, although none outlived Shakespeare himself. Shakespeare's father was a merchant who devoted himself to public service, attaining the position of bailiff and justice of the peace by 1568. Biographers have surmised that the elder Shakespeare's social standing and relative prosperity at this time would have enabled his son to attend the local grammar school in Stratford, where he would have received an education dominated by the study of Latin and the reading of such authors as Cicero, Ovid, Terence,

*William Shakespeare*

for the sonnets remains the subject of controversy and speculation.

In 1603 King James I granted the Lord Chamberlain's Men a royal patent, and the company's name was altered to the King's Men to reflect the king's direct patronage. Records indicate that Shakespeare's company remained the most favored acting company during the Jacobean era, averaging a dozen performances at the king's court each year. In addition to public performances at the Globe Theatre, the King's Men also played at the private Blackfriars Theatre, where many of Shakespeare's late plays were first staged. The playwright profited handsomely from his long career in the theater and invested in real estate, purchasing properties in both Stratford and London. As early as 1596 he had attained sufficient status to be granted a coat of arms and the accompanying right to call himself a gentleman. By 1610, with his reputation as the leading English dramatist unchallenged, Shakespeare is believed to have retired to Stratford, although business interests brought him to London on occasion. He died on April 23, 1616, and was buried in the chancel of Trinity Church in Stratford.

and Plautus, along with study of the Bible. At the age of eighteen, Shakespeare married Ann Hathaway, a woman eight years his senior. Their first child, Susanna, was born six months later, followed by twins, Hammet and Judith, in 1585. At an undetermined time following the birth of his twins, Shakespeare joined a professional acting company and traveled to London, where he began writing as well as acting. His first plays, three parts of the *Henry VI* history cycle, were presented in 1589-91. Shakespeare further established himself when he joined the Lord Chamberlain's Men, an acting company formed in 1594 under the patronage of Henry Carey, Lord Hunsdon. This group began performing at the playhouse known simply as the Theatre and at the Cross Keys Inn, moving to the Swan Theatre on Bankside in 1596 when municipal authorities banned the public presentation of plays within the limits of the city of London. Three years later, Shakespeare and other members of the company financed the building of the most famous of all Elizabethan playhouses, the Globe Theatre. By then the foremost London company, the Lord Chamberlain's Men also performed at the royal court on numerous occasions. It is widely believed that Shakespeare wrote many of his sonnets during the 1590s, although they were not published until 1609. The specific inspiration

## Poem Text

Not marble nor the gilded monuments
Of princes shall outlive this powerful rhyme;
But you shall shine more bright in these contents
Than upswept stone, besmeared with sluttish time.
When wasteful war shall statues overturn,                     5
And broils root out the work of masonry,
Nor Mars his sword nor war's quick fire shall burn
The living record of your memory.
'Gainst death and all oblivious enmity
Shall you pace forth; your praise shall still find          10
    room
Even in the eyes of all posterity
That wear this world out to the ending doom.
   So, till the Judgment that yourself arise,
    You live in this, and dwell in lovers' eyes.

## Poem Summary

### Lines 1-2:

References to "marble" and "gilded monuments / Of princes" combine images of lasting beauty with those of death. "Gilded monuments," for example, suggests the gilded tombs of English monarchs such as that of Henry V in Westminster Abbey.

### Lines 3-4:

Shakespeare states that the recipient of the poem—the "Young Man"—will receive more glory through his sonnet than the Princes who have mere "marble" or "unswept stone" to mark their graves. Whereas Shakespeare evokes beauty and grandeur in the opening two lines, he quickly turns to images of degradation, corruption, and decay with the phrase "besmeared with sluttish time." Here, time is personified as filthy and promiscuous, "besmearing" even the marble monuments that are supposed to remain untouched by the passage of time.

### Lines 5-6:

The motif of decay over time now becomes more violent and immediate; here Shakespeare evokes images of human destruction through "wasteful war" and "broils" (quarrels), which can easily "overturn" or ruin any statue, monument, or stone edifice created in an attempt to immortalize an individual.

### Lines 7-8:

Shakespeare heightens his use of war imagery with a reference to Mars, the ancient Roman god of war. These lines assert that not even fire and the god of war can erase the memory of the Young Man. The phrase "living record of your memory" is cryptic, as it either suggests that the poem is somehow a "living record" or points to other aspects of the Young Man's life as evidence of a "living record." For example, the poet's relationship with the Young Man may itself be a "living record" of the Young Man's memory—one more meaningful than a monument.

### Lines 9-10:

In the face of both death and a force of hatred that either wants the Young Man to be forgotten or is oblivious to life, the youth will still somehow be appreciated. The word "pace" suggests a calm steadiness that contrasts with the violence of preceding imagery while also creating alliteration and assonance with the word "praise."

### Lines 11-12:

The poet again evokes images of decay and decline with the notion that future generations will "wear this world out to the ending doom." "Ending doom" also suggests the Biblical idea of the Last Judgement—the end of the world and the end of time. Contrasting with this apocalyptic imagery is the idea that the youth will be remembered despite this inevitable "doom."

## Media Adaptations

- Audio recordings of Shakespeare's sonnets include *Living Literature: The Sonnets of Shakespeare,* by Crown Publishers, Inc.; *Sonnets of Shakespeare,* by Spoken Arts, Inc.; and *Shakespeare: The Sonnets,* by Argo Records.

- Video productions of Shakespeare's sonnets include *Selected Sonnets* (1988) by Films for the Humanities, in which critics including Stephen Spender and A. L. Rowse read and comment on Sonnets 65, 66, 94, and 127; *Shakespeare's Sonnets,* another Films for the Humanities production featuring recitation of selected sonnets by such actors as Ben Kingsley and Claire Bloom; and *The Sonnets of William Shakespeare* (1993) by Goldcrest Films for the Humanities, in which fifteen sonnets are performed and analyzed.

### Lines 13-14:

The phrase "till the judgement that yourself arise" extends the motif of the "Last Judgement," by imagining the youth "arising"—resurrected from the dead on judgement day. Until then, Shakespeare suggests, the youth will "live in this"—the poem—while also dwelling "in lovers' eyes." "Lovers' eyes" may either refer to the poet's affection for the young man, or to the public who will admire the image of the young man presented in the poem. It is interesting to note, however, that in Shakespeare's works such as *A Midsummer Night's Dream,* "lovers' eyes" are often portrayed as gullible and easily deluded.

## Themes

### Time

In "Sonnet 55," the speaker of the poem claims that his "powerful rhyme" will outlast "marble" and "gilded monuments," keeping the youth's memory alive until the Last Judgement. As in many of Shakespeare's sonnets, the passage of time is a major theme in "Sonnet 55." Time is portrayed predomi-

# *Topics for Further Study*

- Translate "Sonnet 55" into modern, casual speech. Is the poem now easier to understand? How, if at all, has the meaning or quality of the poem changed now that the language has changed?

- How would you characterize the poet's attitude toward life and death in "Sonnet 55?" What aspects of the language of the poem suggest this attitude or philosophy?

- Write a poem in free verse addressing someone you admire. How does your poem differ from sonnet form? Now attempt to restructure your poem into Shakespearean sonnet form, observing the techniques used in "Sonnet 55."

nantly as a negative force connected with death and decay. Line 3, for example, personifies time as a "sluttish" character who "besmears" human attempts to achieve immortality by building stone monuments. The poem reflects a common view during the Elizabethan age that the entire world was in a process of gradual decay and decline as humanity moved through time toward the Last Judgment—the Judeo-Christian idea of apocalypse and an end of time.

### *Death and Immortality*

"Sonnet 55" is predominantly concerned the human desire to be remembered and immortalized in an attempt to overcome death. The poem suggests a strong awareness of the inevitability of death; images of the aging effects of time and the destructive results of "wasteful war" are emphasized. Worse than death, suggests "Sonnet 55," are the forces that conspire to insure that an individual is forgotten, such as "war's quick fire" and the "all oblivious enmity" of other people. The anxiety running throughout the poem is not merely due to a fear of death, but the idea that all traces of the self might be completely erased from the earth. The poem rejects traditional human attempts at preserving the memory of an individual through the building of monuments, statues, or buildings as

doomed to either decay through the effects of time or to ruin through the violence of war. The sonnet itself ("this powerful rhyme"), however, is upheld as a vehicle of immortality that will not be destroyed. "You live in this," declares the poet in the last line of the sonnet, suggesting that the youth to which the poem is addressed can somehow be preserved through the poem, which is immune to physical destruction. The last line of the poem also connects love with eternity and immortality by asserting that despite death, the youth will always "dwell in lovers' eyes." This phrase suggests that while the body and self are lost and forgotten, love is eternal; the youth will somehow "live" in the eyes of all lovers who might read the poem throughout time. While "Sonnet 55" takes a defiant stand against oblivion, the speaker's attitude toward death can be seen as ultimately ambiguous. L. C. Knights in his 1934 essay on "Shakespeare's Sonnets" commented: "[I]n all the Sonnets [which promise some form of immortality], it is the contemplation of change, not the boasting and defiance, that produces the finest poetry; they draw their value entirely from the evocation of that which is said to be defied or triumphed over."

## *Style*

A sonnet is a fourteen-line poetic form originally developed by the Italian poet Petrarch. The rhyme scheme for a traditional Petrarchan sonnet is as follows: abba, abba, cdc, dcd. After sonnet form was adopted by the English during the mid-sixteenth century, variations in this rhyme scheme began to appear. Shakespeare in particular is noted for manipulating sonnet form in new ways that allow for greater flexibility, variety, and expressive power than that possible with Petrarchan sonnet form. Maintaining the basic fourteen-line sonnet structure, Shakespeare employed three quatrains followed by a rhyming couplet as follows: abab, cdcd, efef, gg. The variation in rhyme often mirrors the shifting thoughts and moods of the poet. In "Sonnet 55," for example, the initial concern with preserving the memory of the youth is gradually transformed into imagery that evokes his resurrection at the Last Judgement.

## *Historical Context*

Shakespeare lived during the Renaissance, an era regarded as an age of discovery and human en-

# *Compare & Contrast*

- **1587:** Excessive mortality occurs in Stratford, England due to an illness called "the burning ague." Some scholars have linked the "ague" with malnutrition, observing that the diet of poor people in England steadily deteriorated throughout the sixteenth century. By 1597 there were famine conditions in Stratford, England and burial rates had risen fifty-two percent.

  **1845-1849:** The great potato famines strike Ireland. A million die from starvation and disease. The famines were primarily caused by excessive reliance upon a single food crop.

  **Today:** North Korea is in the midst of a famine that started with a 1995 flood that ruined crops and killed livestock. Despite international relief efforts, in January of 1999, the United Nations reported that the country would need at least a million pounds of donated food.

- **Elizabethan Era:** For selling a volume of poetry to a printer or publisher, an author might receive only 2 pounds payment; alternatively, he might be forced to finance the printing on his own. The system of patronage—support from a wealthy individual—was essential for the economic survival of a writer or artist.

  **Today:** Capitalism, rather than patronage largely governs the publication of literature. With the exception of works financed by grants from government organizations such as the National Endowment for the Arts, writers must increasingly prove to publishers that their works will sell to a mass audience. Publishers pay authors a negotiable advance, after which the author is usually entitled to a royalty fee—a share of the profits. Few poets are able to support themselves solely through their art, although there are many outlets for the publication and distribution of poetry.

- **1588:** King Philip II of Spain sends the Spanish Armada, one of the largest naval fleets ever assembled, north to conquer England. Largely due to faulty equipment and stormy weather, Spain's conquest was defeated.

  **1981:** England engages in a military dispute with Argentina over the Falkland Islands. England is victorious due to superior military might.

- **1586:** Queen Elizabeth achieves something akin to celebrity status by distributing numerous miniature portraits of herself. Although aged at the time, the portraits portrayed the Queen as youthful and beautiful. A "cult" of veneration subsequently surrounded her name and image; some scholars have likened this adoration to the attitude of pre-Reformation Catholics toward images of the Virgin Mary.

  **1990s:** The media, rather than the portraits or statues of Shakespeare's age, is the source of fame in modern society. Politicians achieve fame and popularity largely through media images, although the deluge and range of information provided by the media, particularly in the United States, makes the maintenance of an image of perfection virtually impossible. Fame as it manifests itself in movie stars was largely an invention of the early silent film industry after it was discovered that people would flock to see films based on the appearance of a particular actor or actress. Fame became an increasingly important commodity as the "star system" replaced the "studio system" in Hollywood, with the most famous actors and actresses now often wielding immense power over which films get produced.

---

lightenment that ushered in the rise of modern science. While God, religion, and magic/superstition were at the center of human thought during the Middle Ages, humankind gradually became the focus of ideas during the Renaissance, with an increasing emphasis on man's ability to reason and to control his environment. The simultaneously magical and devout worldview of Medieval times, however, did not simply disappear all at once. The rise in witchcraft trials in England during the sixteenth and seventeenth centuries, for example, provides evidence of the overlapping of two different worldviews—one scientific, the other superstitious. Shakespeare's plays, for example, often suggest the presence of both medieval and modern/humanistic outlooks—a duality that characterized the Renaissance.

For many people, the Renaissance was also an era of suffering due to the spread of illness and economic hardship. For example, the bubonic plague spread through England several times during the sixteenth century, and mortality rates in England during the Elizabethan age indicate a life expectancy of about thirty-five to forty years. Although this life expectancy was considerably less than that of the modern era, it was, however, higher than that of most other countries in Europe during that time. Changing economic conditions as well as illness were a source of anxiety for the poor during the late sixteenth century. While members of the upper classes widely experienced the Renaissance as an age of opulence, with vast sums of money being spent on elaborate fashions, lavish entertainment, and the building of large manor houses, there was also an increasing divide between rich and poor and a rising population of homeless people, or "vagrants." New enclosure laws that prevented the use of land for "common grazing" (shared pasture) combined with higher rents and a sharp rise in prices during the sixteen century all added to the plight of many rural villagers.

## Critical Overview

Much critical controversy surrounding the Shakespeare Sonnets including "Sonnet 55" can be condensed into the following question: whom exactly is the poet addressing? The first 126 of Shakespeare's 154 sonnets are addressed to a "Young Man" or "Friend," while sonnets 127 to 152 are addressed to a mysterious "Dark Lady" who may have been the poet's mistress. Although the collection of sonnets published in 1609 was dedicated to "Mr. W. H.," critics such as A. L. Rowse have argued that this is in fact the publisher's dedication rather than Shakespeare's. The specific identity of Mr. W. H. remains the subject of debate along with the nature of his possible relationship with Shakespeare.

Arthur F. Marotti, in his essay "Love Is Not Love: Elizabethan Sonnet Sequences and the Social Order," detects the language of patronage in the sonnets. In other words, Shakespeare may have written "Sonnet 55" in order to flatter or serve the needs of a financial supporter. Some scholars argue that this theory does not fully account for language in some of the "Young Man" sonnets that suggest not only admiration but sexual infatuation. Critics such as Joseph Pequigney in his *Such Is My Love: A Study of Shakespeare's Sonnets* and Martin Seymour-Smith in his *Shakespeare's Sonnets* argue that this sequence of sonnets (including "Sonnet 55") suggests a homosexual love relationship. Other scholars, however, point out that our contemporary understanding of homosexuality does not necessarily apply to Renaissance times and offer a revised "homosocial" understanding of English society during the Renaissance. In a "homosocial" society, displays of affection or declarations of devotion between men or women are merely a common and widely acceptable indication of deep friendship, although the same behavior in today's society might be interpreted as evidence of a sexual relationship.

Helen Vendler in her *The Art of Shakespeare's Sonnets* argues that attempts to determine the social and psychological context of Shakespeare's sonnets may be ultimately missing the point of the poems. She notes that each sonnet is "intended to be voiceable by anyone reading it," and, therefore, the sex, class, and race and nature of the relationship between the poet and object of the poem are irrelevant. Vendler praises the structural coherence, logical development, unity, and, above all, the poetic language of Shakespeare's sonnets, arguing that their true value as poems is in their beauty rather than in their function as speculative social or psychological commentary.

## Criticism

### Jhan Hochman

*Jhan Hochman's articles appear in* Democracy and Nature, Genre, ISLE, *and* Mosaic. *He is the author of* Green Cultural Studies: Nature in Film, Novel, and Theory *(1998), and he holds a Ph.D in English and an M.A. in Cinema Studies. In the following essay, Hochman examines the universal conflicts referred to in "Sonnet 55" and discusses how poems are similar in some aspects to statues and buildings.*

Conflict is the foundation upon which Shakespeare builds "Sonnet 55." The conflicts are of three kinds: the war waged between time and art, the attack of political culture upon artistic culture, and the contest between the built world (primarily buildings and statuary) and poetry.

Time continually and everywhere is said to attack works of art, but especially those exposed to the elements. Culture defends its art by periodically sweeping clean, refurbishing, or reconstructing its monuments. In "Sonnet 55" time is called "sluttish"—meaning dirty—for "besmearing" buildings and statuary, "attacking" them with dirt, discoloration, and disfigurement. While Shakespeare's use of time might seem to belong to the realm of nature, time belongs, at least in this day, more properly or primarily to the realm of culture. It is the dirt produced by cities (airborne pollutants from cars, homes, and factories) which is now known to act most viciously on edifices, a problem now being confronted at the Acropolis in Greece and the pyramids in Egypt. The most dramatic subcategory of time is death, mentioned in line 9. When art of the commemorative kind—and virtually all art is commemorative, for if nothing else, the artisan or artist is commemorated—is attacked by time, the attack presents the threat of eventual death. Buildings and statuary are thus kept clean in order to keep away "the ending doom." In other words, cleaning prevents the destruction of things built, keeps away the "death" of those who built them or had them built, and, most obviously, postpones the "death" of those persons directly commemorated in buildings named for people and monumentalized in statuary of selected personages.

The second conflict of "Sonnet 55" is that attack of political or marshal culture upon artistic culture. I call this an attack, because art does not really fight back so much as supply an endless array of objects that wars seek to plunder, disfigure, or utterly "overturn" and "root out," as Shakespeare says. Why does one enemy or another seek out buildings and statuary to destroy? Not only to make it fearful and difficult for the other side to live, but to destroy the spirit of a people, its memories, its pride, its identity; the built world is personal identity exteriorized and rematerialized in stone and marble. The only greater insult than destruction of artistic and architectural culture is its replacement by those who destroyed it in the first place. This is the "enmity" Shakespeare mentions in line nine, an enmity of an enemy not just in war but in day-to-day living. Notice here that line 9 mentions both the war between art and time ("death") and the marshal (as in Mars, Roman god of war) attack of culture upon built and artistic culture ("enmity"). It might be helpful to note that while Shakespeare

## What Do I Read Next?

- Shakespeare's play *A Midsummer Night's Dream,* which was composed around the same period during which the sonnets are believed to have been written, explores the theme of reality and illusion seen through "lovers' eyes." The play offers a skeptical view of reality seen through the eyes of lovers.

- Shakespeare's play *Troilus and Cressida* explores themes of time, war, and decay.

- Published in 1633, John Donne's *Songs & Sonets* provides an example of the increasing flexibility of sonnet form. These acclaimed poems pose an interesting contrast with the sonnets of Shakespeare.

- The poems of the Italian poet Petrarch, an innovator of the sonnet form, are available in English translations such as Joseph A. Barber's *Rime Disperse* (1991).

only speaks of the attack of one culture upon another during war, the attack upon built culture also occurs internally, within a culture, as when buildings are inscribed with graffiti or torn apart by guerilla bombings, or art is officially censored or removed. This is the attack of one subculture upon another subculture or the larger culture. In the end, it is debatable whether the attacks of time (as in natural time) or the many and varied attacks of culture (pollution, war, attacks, eradication, censorship, etc.) pose the greatest threat to built culture.

Finally in "Sonnet 55," there is the contest between the built world (primarily buildings and statuary) and poetry. This is the most important conflict of the poem and, as such, is prominently introduced in the first two lines. Shakespeare's argument is that poetry is more "powerful" than the worlds created by art and architecture. Let us take his arguments one by one. First of all, it is commonly thought that the edifice and statue are more lasting monuments than a mere poem. Architecture and art may seem more lasting, but Shakespeare rightly remarks that art and architecture are subject to destruction by the armaments and fire of "broils." Poetry, on the other hand, while easily destroyed through burning and the tearing apart of books, is not as often sought out for destruction (nor the buildings that often house it). Unfortunately for the overall meaning of "Sonnet 55," seeking out buildings instead of books of verse indicates that poetry is usually far less important to a culture than are buildings and statuary. Despite this criticism, however, Shakespeare's point still stands.

Secondly, poetry is said to last through time better than buildings and statuary because poetry is not so exposed to the elements. Poetry does not get rained upon or blown upon, or get parched by the sun, nor is it used by various plants and animals as support or sanctuary. Poetry remains indoors and protected, subjected to the slower fluctuations of moisture, mildew, and dryness, and the repeated handling of its readers. Thus, while a building may become dirty and disfigured, the poem on the page remains in the same form it was always in. In addition, though Shakespeare does not say so, the poem, especially a short form like the sonnet, remains intact because it can be copied or mechanically reproduced numerous times very quickly. Thus the poem can exist in many locales whereas the building and statue exist in only one place.

In this competition between poetry and the world of built things, Shakespeare alludes to something without stating it: that poetry is itself like a building and a statue. Poetry is like a building in that it is constructed of parts built up into a structure. Letters are like the bricks or stones of a word, as words are like the building blocks of a line, as the poem's lines are the rows of bricks in the poem's "walls." And when a poem utilizes stanzas (which are implied in a sonnet), these are comparable to the walls or sides of a structure, a building whose title can be said to be a kind of roof. The poet is the mason who builds the poetic structure, holding together its lines with the mortar of sound and metrical similarities, and with punctuation. Or without this varied mortar between the words and lines of poetry, the poet carefully places lines one atop the other so as to be sound without the need for sonic and metrical similarities, so as to be meaningful without punctuation. One could even go so far as to say that the poem is a city: if you shift the whole of "Sonnet 55" forty-five degrees counterclockwise, the poem resembles the skyline of city packed with skyscrapers.

Poetry is also like statuary in that one does not often think of a poem as a series of separate bricks in a poetic edifice, but more as a series of moves congealing into a sculptured figure, that at its best is smooth and artless, a figure (poem) that seems to appear like a denizen of nature, one not showing in its structure how it was made. Furthermore, letters are themselves sculpted figures that can become sculptures in space (for example, Robert Indiana's LOVE sculpture from the 1960s). Finally, poetry is like building and statuary in that it is commemorative of a culture, a designer, maker, ruler, event, or a particular person or persons. And if Shakespeare is right, the edifice of poetry, especially of "Sonnet 55," commemorates even better than architecture and statuary for it can preserve and inspire love, love for the poem, the poet, and the commemorated. In the end, the only adversary that poetry—and all cultural artifacts for that matter—loses hands down to is time without end. Poetry is, as Shakespeare writes, only a temporary immortalization/commemoration in comparison to the eternality following Judgment Day, the time of real immortality (at least to Christians). "Powerful" poetry, even Shakespeare admits, is always and only a temporary heaven.

**Source:** Jhan Hochman, in an essay for *Poetry for Students,* Gale, 1999.

## Sean Robisch

*Sean Robisch teaches composition and literature at Purdue University and holds a Ph.D. in American literature. In the following essay, Robisch provides literary and historical context to consider when reading "Sonnet 55," as well as a brief overview of the poem.*

Whenever you are tempted to ask the question, "Why do we still study Shakespeare?" you will probably receive the best answer by seeing one of his plays or reading the sonnets. Some of his lines are so powerful that people occasionally mistake them for having appeared in the Bible, and we quote them regularly without even realizing it. Shakespeare's work is full of all the great things about literature, including the mysteries of how that work came to be written. Critics have speculated as to who wrote the plays, when the sonnets were composed, and how much of Shakespeare's life was written into his stories and poems. But finally, when the criticism is sifted through and the couplets and plot turns given the proper attention, the powerful rhyme is what we learn, and it strengthens our minds to have done so.

Shakespeare's sonnets were most likely written between 1592 and 1598, though the first publication of the collected 154 by Thomas Thorpe didn't happen until 1609. Thorpe established their order, based on clues in the writing, and it has been generally accepted that, while the order cannot be exactly determined, 126 of them were written to a young man of high rank, handsome looks, and questionable morals, who may be a "rival poet" of the narrator. "Sonnet 55," also known as "Not marble nor the gilded monuments" (they are sometimes called by first line), is one of these. It is also one of eight sonnets written about the poem as a monument to immortality, as a document that will outlast the life of its subject. This will be important when we look more closely at the poem itself. When Thorpe published the work, he included a cryptic dedication, which has been the subject of speculation by critics for centuries. The "W.H." to whom the volume is dedicated could be one of several men, but most likely either William Herbert, Earl of Pembroke, or Henry Wriothesley (with the letters transposed as part of the puzzle), Earl of Southampton. The relevance of this dedication, and to the attention it has received, is at least threefold: 1) It is of interest to scholars trying to solve the riddles of literature so that we may better understand it; 2) It introduces us to the idea of dedicating work, which is very important to sonnets in general and to Shakespeare's in particular; and 3) It reminds us to focus on the text in the midst of these interesting mysteries, and not to sacrifice the poem to the speculation about biographical information.

What we are able to see in the bulk of the sonnets is that Shakespeare wrote a great deal about dubious morality and unconventional subjects, even though he was using a very conventional form. The sonnet, an Italian formal poem initiated primarily by Dante and Petrarch, was well-worn in England by the time Shakespeare used it. Edmund Spenser, the Earl of Surrey, and Sir Philip Sidney, especially through his poem called *Astrophel and Stella,* had made the sonnet wildly popular throughout England, and Shakespeare knew this. But he took a certain form of sonnet enjoyed by these other poets, which uses three quatrains and a couplet, and made it do some new work.

First, the common subject of a sonnet during Shakespeare's time was a fair-skinned, blonde-haired, virtuous woman who represented the highest achievement of social acceptability. In addition to writing most of his sonnets about a man, Shakespeare chose for his other poems a "dark lady," a woman of dark hair and probably olive skin whose morals were also a bit "shady." Today, we see artists regularly attempt this accomplishment of challenging a conventional form often with little success. But Shakespeare went farther than simply breaking the rules. He also weaved a moral complexity into his work that addresses misogyny, superficial beauty versus depth of character, frustration with romantic love, celebration (in both reward and suffering), rivalry, and the moral role of the poem itself to express all these things. We may see this easily in "Sonnet 55," in such phrases as "sluttish time" or in the poem's attention to itself as a "powerful rhyme" that will outlive the monuments built to royalty. Many sonnets by Shakespeare's contemporaries preferred to demonstrate only the poet's wit, remaining lighthearted about their subjects without committing to the complexities of ethics or moral arguments. We still see this in the poetry and fiction that often reaches the best-seller list because it requires little work of the reader to sort out the most interesting material of our lives—that which cannot be easily said or judged.

The idea that the writer of "Sonnet 55" and the other 125 poems to a young man was attracted to that man has been debated extensively. Some critics argue that the poet's love for the man is purely platonic. In the first seventeen sonnets, the writer encourages the man to marry and have children. Also, in Shakepeare's era (as is often expressed in his plays), to express "love" often merely meant respect and admiration, deep friendship. However, all of these facts may easily be read as the necessary defenses of someone whose attractions might, if expressed directly, ruin him in his society. Other critics, such as Joseph Pequingney, argue forcefully that the group of 126 poems are certainly traditional love poems written from the nontraditional homoerotic perspective. Another way to read the poems is offered by a third set of critics and is also accepted as another element of the work by those speculating about the nature of the love expressed: many of them are written to a "rival poet." The man of "Sonnet 55," whom the writer wants to memorialize, has been, in other poems, the object of frustration for the writer. Their friendship is rocky, as the rival poet may be competing with the writer for the money of an art patron. So "Sonnet 55" would be a bright moment, a way of one poet burying the hatchet with his friend and rival. The final word should probably be, once again, that not enough information is available to guess at the precise relationship between writer and young man.

We must also be careful not to mix up Shakespeare himself with the narrator of the sonnets. We may consider Shakespeare's choices as the writer, but those choices may not be autobiographical. Even though Wordsworth believed that "with this key [the sonnet] Shakespeare unlocked his heart," Browning disagreed, and renowned critics such as Sir Sydney Lee have been quick to point out that they could just as easily been products of poetic convention that had nothing to do with Shakespeare. Certainly the man who could write such great fabrications as *Romeo and Juliet* could fabricate as well a narrator's persona and then let that persona "speak" these sonnets. Remember that Shakespeare was an actor, and he loved to write into his work the metaphor of the world as a stage. To assume that a work of literature is "about" the writer is called the *intentional fallacy,* and it takes away from that writer his or her ability to invent. So, in "Sonnet 55" we have a narrator writing a memorial to a friend—and this is all we know. Ironically, this sonnet, considered one of Shakespeare's best, has no mention of the sex of the subject. The hypothesis that it is a man, while having some evidence behind it, is based largely on context and conjecture, not on anything direct in this particular poem. You could consider the sonnet as though it were written to *you* and carried to you from the past over all this time on something as flimsy as a page.

What is apparent in the poem is Shakespeare's specific attention to the memorial and to the poem itself. I say Shakespeare now because we may see that Shakespeare wrote the poem, even while possibly inventing a narrator to deliver it. That is, Shakespeare himself chose to make his narrator talk about the poem outlasting marble and gilded monuments, about the subject to whom the poem is addressed—like a letter—passing from the Day of Judgment to the immortality of life in "lovers' eyes." It's a great way of saying that the best thing a writer may do to see some tangible possibility of immortality is to write down words that may outlast human life. And we have some proof that this works, though we certainly cannot say for how long (immortality is, after all, a permanent state). Sonnet "55" was written approximately 400 years ago, and here we are reading it, studying it, wondering about the person who wrote the poem and to whom he wrote it. So it is possible that not "Mars his sword nor war's quick fire shall burn the living record" written in the poetry's most powerful habitat—the human memory. This is an excellent reason, among others, to memorize the sonnet. When we commit poetry to memory and are able to speak it, as the sonnet was written partly to help us do,

we understand it better and may find it surprisingly useful one day.

You might wonder why, if Shakespeare figured his poems to be monuments to immortality, it took Thomas Thorpe several years to publish them. Actually, the subject was quite common. Many poets wrote their work at least pretending to have the sense that the words on the page were sufficient to last—that the act of writing, not publishing, was the creation of the monument. We might also remember that Shakespeare wrote all the sonnets while he was writing a number of plays that incorporated the sonnet form: *Venus and Adonis, Love's Labours Lost, Richard I,* and *Romeo and Juliet* (which had quite a bit to say about poetry and mortality). He knew the convention of the "immortal poem" and used it to his advantage.

Given all of this context and possibility in reading the poem, we might now look at it closely. The first quatrain concerns the poem as a more powerful form of monument than marble, gilded monuments to princes, or chiseled stone. The phrase "besmeared with sluttish time" personifies the passage of time as a lazy housemaid (the connotations of "sluttish" are a bit different today) who either fails to maintain the monument or who in fact wipes it away. The first sentence (two lines) is written in the third person about "this powerful rhyme," so the opening subject is the poem itself, not its recipient. This is important. What appears at the beginning and end of a piece is often most easily remembered; the beginning influences our attitude toward the rest of that piece, and the end leaves us with the final image or idea we will take with us after closing the book. Not until the second sentence (lines 3 and 4) does the narrator use the second person and address his object directly. Even then, where this person "shines" is in the poem in "these contents."

The second quatrain gives the poem epic scope, connects it to the immortal. It begins by switching the scale of the poem to something larger than one person: to war. War as "wasteful" means literally that it lays waste to things, that it is destructive (not simply careless, as "wasteful" has come to mean today). It overturns statues and smashes walls (a broil is a battle). Shakespeare then takes war to its epic persona, to the god Mars and the sword and fire of epic conflict. But the quatrain again turns the attention back to the poem and its object simultaneously. The recipient of the poem will outlive even the efforts of Mars through, once again, the "living record" of the sonnet.

The third quatrain takes the poem logically from monuments and wars to the subject of death, first of the person (the young man, let's say) who will "pace forth" even against death then to the end of the world. The "eyes of posterity" set us up for the poem's couplet, the rhymed, two-line ending by which we so often recognize Shakespeare. The Judgment follows death, and the young man—or lover, or rival poet, or reader—"arises" and is taken up in the rapture of humanity, to live "in this" (that is, the poem) and "in lovers' eyes." So the ending, that other powerful position in the sonnet, leaves us with lovers' eyes as the image that outlasts marble and gilded monuments. This is, in many respects, the perfect sonnet, in that its form is not just contrived to rhyme, but contributes to the subject matter. This is why we still read Shakespeare. His writing still works.

**Source:** Sean Robisch, in an essay for *Poetry for Students,* Gale, 1999.

## Katherine Duncan-Jones

*In the following excerpt, Duncan-Jones discusses Shakespeare's famous volume of sonnets and speculates about the identity of the young man that sonnets 1–126 reportedly address.*

Shakespeare's *Sonnets*—or, as they were called on the original title-page, SHAKE-SPEARES SONNETS—were first printed in 1609. During the seventeenth and eighteenth centuries they were not often discussed, or even mentioned. Eminent critics such as Doctor Johnson passed them by in silence. However, the admirable Edmond Malone included them in the Supplement to his edition of Shakespeare in 1780....

When the *Sonnets* began to receive more searching attention from critics and scholars during the nineteenth century, widespread embarrassment was felt that the majority of them—Sonnets 1–126—appeared to be addressed to a young male friend, not a female mistress. In Sonnets 1–17 this is quite clear. The poet amasses a succession of reasons why the young man—who seems *very* young, and perhaps a shade narcissistic —should, by marrying, fertilise one of the 'maiden gardens' eagerly awaiting him (16.6), and reproduce his beauty for future generations. This seems harmless enough, and can be linked with similar persuasions to marriage in classical literature and in a model closer to home, Sir Philip Sidney's *Arcadia* (published 1590). But Sonnet 20 has a distinctly 'naughty' flavour, with its stress on the young man's epicene beauty....

The poet declares himself the 'slave' or 'vassal' of the young man (57, 58), who appears to be of a superior social class; and though many sonnets, such as 18, 19, 38, 54, 55, 60 and 65, suggest that the speaker's chief aim is to conquer Time by immortalising his friend's beauty and worth in verse, others, such as some of those on absence, hint that physical proximity is what he most craves....

To many nineteenth-century biographers and critics, bent on making England's national poet approximate to the figure of a respectable Victorian man of letters, the implications of all this were intolerable....

Scholars dealt with this embarrassment in various ways. Perhaps, *pace* Wordsworth, the situation suggested in these sonnets was wholly fictional; or perhaps the sonnets themselves were not truly Shakespearian. Some scholars placed all their emphasis on the 'Dark Lady' sonnets, 127–52; some suggested that the addressee was, in fact, female almost throughout the sequence, but that the sonnets had been misleadingly or maliciously tampered with or rearranged. Editorial rearrangement to make the love-object female throughout began as early as 1640, with John Benson's edition. Other scholars, more plausibly, tried to draw the *Sonnets* within the conventions of Renaissance poetry addressed to patrons. What nearly all critics and editors, up to and including J. Dover Wilson in the New Cambridge edition of 1966, were agreed on was that Shakespeare could not possibly have intended his sonnets to see the light of day. Some developed elaborate conspiracy theories, with supposed enemies of Shakespeare banding together to steal his private poems and get them into print, and many, including the distinguished bibliographer Sir Sidney Lee, made out that the publisher, Thomas Thorpe, was the villain of the piece. By the early twentieth century belief that the 1609 quarto was an unauthorised publication had become standard, and a conjecture that it had been suppressed shortly after publication solidified into a received certainty, despite the absence of evidence. Shakespeare, despite his declaration in Sonnet 110 that he has 'made himself a motley to the view', must, it was supposed, have been ashamed of these poems, and taken steps to prevent them from reaching a wide audience.

There is, however, nothing manifestly irregular about the publication of SHAKE-SPEARES SONNETS, and some external evidence suggests that Shakespeare—whose name is proudly pro-

> *The 'sense of felt life'
> in many of [Shakespeare's
> Sonnets] is both
> overpowering, and
> overpoweringly
> idiosyncratic. They are
> almost too strong for their
> framework."*

claimed at the top of every page, as well as on the title-page—may, in fact, have authorised publication. The book was registered with the Stationers in the correct fashion on 20 May 1609. Although, as most critics broadly agree, some or all of the sonnets had probably been written well before this date, Shakespeare had a likely financial motive for taking them to a publisher in the spring of 1609, for a prolonged plague outbreak had led to an order closing the theatres. Shakespeare, who had been a shareholder of the Globe since 1599, stood to lose a great deal of money while the order was in force....

SHAKE-SPEARES SONNETS, with its final, sub-classical, playful sonnets on Diana's cooling fountain (153, 154), followed by *A Lover's Complaint,* approximates to the pattern established by [Samuel] Daniel [in his *Delia*] and copied by others. Many of the 'complaint' poems appended to sonnet sequences concerned unhappy women of history or legend who were seduced or betrayed by men of high rank. Shakespeare's *A Lover's Complaint* conforms to this general theme, but is unusual in its lack of mythological or historical reference. Like the chief characters in the *Sonnets,* the three main characters in the *Complaint,* old man, maiden, and charming seducer, have no names. But though the young(ish) woman in the *Complaint* does not seem like the 'Dark Lady' of Sonnets 127–52, the young man by whom she has been betrayed, charismatic, high-ranking, and unreliable, does sound distinctly like the young 'friend' celebrated in *Sonnets* 1–126. Possibly, as in other Elizabethan sonnet sequence volumes, some deliberate counterpointing of male and female viewpoints is intended in the juxtaposition of

*Sonnets* and *Complaint.* Both poet and maiden are painfully attached to a comparable—or identical?—young man.

That young man has provoked much debate. Is he the same as the 'Mr W.H.' described by Thorpe as the 'only begetter' of the *Sonnets?* And if so, can he, perhaps, be William Herbert, who became Third Earl of Pembroke in the spring of 1601? Herbert had the right initials, received dedications in books published subsequently by Thomas Thorpe, and was, along with his younger brother, dedicatee of the First Folio in 1623, where he is praised as one who favoured Shakespeare during his life. The allusion to 'thy mother's glass' in Sonnet 3 would in this case be a compliment to Sir Philip Sidney's sister, the celebrated patroness and poet Mary Herbert, Countess of Pembroke; and pervasive echoes of Sidney's poetry and *Arcadia* both in *Sonnets* and *Complaint* might be included by design, as graceful references to the young man's famous uncle. However, other claimants cannot be eliminated. Henry Wriothesley, Earl of Southampton, was undoubtedly the dedicatee of Shakespeare's narrative poems, and though his initials are in the wrong order, it is possible that T.T.'s dedication, enigmatic and riddling as it is, alludes to him. Other possibilities are Southampton's stepfather, Sir William Harvey; a young law student, William Hatcliffe; kinsmen of Shakespeare, William Hart or William Hathaway; a young actor imagined by Oscar Wilde, Willy Hughes; or a score of others, including 'William Himself'. The one name definitely referred to in the sequence is 'William', and whatever the young man's surname, it does seem likely that poet and friend shared a Christian name. To me, Pembroke seems by far the most plausible candidate, but conjecture must stop well short of certainty....

... To what extent the *Sonnets* grew out of real-life experiences—which could include the experience of reading other poets—we shall never know.

The ultimate interest and value of Shakespeare's *Sonnets* transcend their many problems—such questions as when they were written, to whom they allude, whether they are in the right order. Though some metaphors, like the reference to the world as a 'huge stage' in Sonnet 15, or to an 'unperfect actor' in Sonnet 23, remind us that these are the poems of an actor-dramatist, the *Sonnets* are for the most part profoundly unlike Shakespeare's plays. The 'sense of felt life' in many of them is both overpowering, and overpoweringly idiosyncratic. They are almost too strong for their frame-work. The richly inclusive vision of humanity that enabled Shakespeare to breathe life into such diverse dramatic characters —Richard III, Juliet, Falstaff, Lady Macbeth, Prospero, to name but a few—is surely at work here, but to totally different effect....

These sonnets are not mini-dramas, or fragments of dramatic speech, despite the fact that many closing couplets resemble 'exit lines'. They are intense poetic meditations, coloured throughout by all acute sense of the nearness of death and of the imperfection of all mortal things—love, beauty, friendship, even poetry itself. Shakespeare (or his persona) celebrates his friend's beauty, though he knows it will fade (18, 19); he affirms his integrity, though he knows he is unreliable (33–5); he praises the loyalty and beauty of a woman who is neither chaste nor fair (137, 138). More bleakly, the poet acknowledges his own divided, perhaps degraded, way of life (109–11) ; and though at some moments he claims immortality for the sonnets themselves, at others he apologises for them as monotonous and old-fashioned, of only 'sentimental value' (32, 76). At times, it seems, he can hardly write about his friend at all (100–103), and even has to confess to having given away a notebook given him by his friend (122). Despite all the poet's affirmation of the power of love and art, imperfection is everywhere.

What gives the *Sonnets* their lasting power and greatness has little to do with who Shakespeare's real-life friends or lovers may have been, though the inclusion of particularity within the universal contributes to their unique force. These are poems of search, not of statement, in which the speaker struggles repeatedly, as we all must, to find something lasting in a universe of decay. The immortalising thread that runs through the whole sequence, the *Complaint* included, is the theme of human love: an imaginative alchemy which assimilates and transfigures all the dross of sin and weakness. Shakespeare celebrated such transfiguring love quite often in his plays, as when Antonio gives and hazards all he has for his friend Bassanio in *The Merchant of Venice*; or when Desdemona forgives her murderer-husband in the words: 'Nobody, I myself. Farewell. Commend me to my kind lord': or when Cordelia says to Lear, 'No cause, no cause.' But only the *Sonnets* gave Shakespeare scope to explore this theme in all its depth and complexity. Like the nameless maid in the *Complaint*, the poet loves his friend not in spite of his imperfection, but in the very midst of his imper-

fection. Where human frailty is most apparent, love most abounds.

**Source:** Duncan-Jones, Katherine, introduction *to Shakespeares Sonnets and A Lover's Complaint,* London: Folio Society, 1989.

## Sources

Bergeron, David M., and Geraldo U. DeSousa, *Shakespeare: A Study and Research Guide,* third edition, revised, Lawrence, KS: University of Kansas Press, 1995.

Boyce, Charles, *Shakespeare A to Z,* NY: Bantam Doubleday Dell, 1990.

Bradby, G. F., *Short Studies in Shakespeare,* Brooklyn, NY: Haskell House Publishers, 1977.

Craig, Hardin, *Shakespeare: A Historical and Critical Study with Annotated Texts of 21 Plays,* Chicago: Scott, Foresman, & Co., 1931.

Duncan-Jones, Katherine, ed., *The Arden Shakespeare: Shakespeare's Sonnets,* Thomas Nelson and Sons Ltd., 1997.

Evans, G. Blakemore, ed., *The Riverside Shakespeare,* Boston: Houghton Mifflin Co., 1974.

Hubler, Edward, *The Sense of Shakespeare's Sonnets,* New York: Hill and Wang, 1952.

Jones, Peter, ed., *Shakespeare: The Sonnets, A Casebook,* London: The Macmillan Press Ltd., 1977.

Lever, J. W., ed. *Sonnets of the English Renaissance,* London: University of London, Athlone Press, 1974.

Marotti, Arthur F., "Love Is Not Love: Elizabethan Sonnet Sequences and the Social Order," *ELH,* Summer, 1982, pp. 396-428.

Martin, Philip, *Shakespeare's Sonnets: Self, Love and Art,* Cambridge: Cambridge University Press, 1972.

Pequigney, Joseph, *Such Is My Love: A Study of Shakespeare's Sonnets,* Chicago: University of Chicago Press, 1985.

Seymour-Smith, Martin, *Shakespeare's Sonnets,* Oxford: Heinemann Educational Books, Ltd., 1963.

Spurgeon, Caroline F. E., *Shakespeare's Imagery and What It Tells Us,* Cambridge: Cambridge University Press, 1935.

Willen, Gerald, and Victor B. Reed, *A Casebook on Shakespeare's Sonnets,* New York: Thomas Y. Crowell, 1964.

## For Further Study

Bradbrook, M. C., *Shakespeare and Elizabethan Poetry: A Study of his Earlier Work in Relation to the Poetry of the Time,* London: Chatto and Windus, 1965.
    Includes discussion of Shakespeare's works in the context of the changing medieval worldview during

the Renaissance. Also examines Elizabethan language, the Elizabethan stage, and character in Shakespeare's plays.

Guy, John, *Tudor England,* Oxford: Oxford University Press, 1988.
Covers English history from 1460 through the death of Elizabeth I. Includes chapters on the economics and political culture of Elizabethan government.

Levi, Peter, *The Life and Times of William Shakespeare,* London: Macmillan, 1988.
Discusses Shakespeare's entire career and argues that some of the Sonnets were written for the Earl of Southampton.

Strong, Roy, *The Cut of Elizabeth: Elizabethan Portraiture and Pageantry,* London: Thames and Hudson, 1977.
Examines images of Queen Elizabeth and her court and provides supplementary historical discussion.

Thomson, Peter, *Shakespeare's Professional Career,* Cambridge, England: Cambridge University Press, 1992.
Tells the story of Shakespeare's career, and describes "the accommodation of his remarkable talents to the circumstances of his time: the social, political and professional life of Jacobean England."

# A Supermarket in California

## Allen Ginsberg
## 1955

Written in 1955, "A Supermarket in California" appeared the next year in *Howl and Other Poems,* Allen Ginsberg's controversial and groundbreaking book of verse that is often credited with initiating the Beat movement. "Beat" is a term coined by writer Jack Kerouac to mean both "beat down" and "beatitude." It was meant to describe the dissatisfaction and spiritual exhaustion of a generation that came of age during the 1940s and 1950s.

A whimsical, almost comic poem, "A Supermarket in California" addresses, in a surrealistic fashion, Ginsberg's own relation to Walt Whitman, the nineteenth-century, American poet considered by many to be the father of modern poetry and one of Ginsberg's literary idols. As in most of Ginsberg's poems, the speaker is Ginsberg himself (rather than a poetic persona), and he uses the supermarket as a metaphoric setting for dreaming about the possibilities that America offers and lamenting the country it has instead become.

One of Ginsberg's most frequently anthologized shorter poems, "A Supermarket in California" not only acknowledges Ginsberg's debt to Whitman's vision of America as a place of possibility and abundance, but also allows Ginsberg to place himself (more explicitly) in a tradition of gay writers. When Ginsberg writes "I saw you, Walt Whitman, childless, lonely old grubber, poking among the meats in the refrigerator and eyeing the grocery boys," he alludes to the homoerotic desire so prevalent in Whitman's own work. This possibility of being openly gay in America is one of the

*Allen Ginsberg*

many opportunities that Whitman's poetry enabled for Ginsberg.

The primary theme of the poem, however, is the moral choice with which America is faced. Will it, as Ginsberg suggests in this and other poems, continue to be a place of acquisitiveness, empty material values, and alienated individuals? Or will America recognize its inherent spirituality and embrace the possibilities for living in a real human community? Ginsberg asks, "Where are we going, Walt Whitman? The doors close in an hour. Which way does your beard point tonight?" Ginsberg is troubled and looking to Whitman for answers at the end of this poem.

## Author Biography

A cultural icon of the 1950s and 1960s, as well as a leading Beat poet, Allen Ginsberg was born June 3, 1926, in Newark, New Jersey, the son of poet and high school teacher Louis Ginsberg and Russian immigrant Naomi Ginsberg. After being expelled from Columbia University in 1946, Ginsberg—like so many of his Beat contemporaries such as Jack Kerouac, William Burroughs, Neal Cassady, Gary Snyder, etc.—tried his hand at a

number of jobs, including dishwasher, welder, literary agent, night porter, and copy boy. He returned to Columbia in 1948, eventually graduating with a bachelor of arts degree. It was during this second tenure at Columbia that Ginsberg experienced the first of a series of mystic visions of eighteenth-century poet William Blake; these visions led to a reevaluation of his own relationship to reality, and he participated in psychoanalysis and various forms of therapy while spending eight months in 1949 at Rockland (New York) State Hospital. This time was instrumental in the development of Ginsberg's poetic voice, which was heavily influenced by Blake and Walt Whitman and attempted to break down the barriers between poetry and religion, religion and being.

In 1954 Ginsberg moved to San Francisco, where he published *Howl and Other Poems* (1956) with City Lights Books. Now considered the spark that ignited the San Francisco literary Renaissance, "Howl," the second section of which was written during a peyote vision, was part lament, part polemic, and all prophetic voice. More than any other single poem from the 1950s, "Howl" describes the disaffection and disillusionment so many young people of his generation had with American values. The language and subject matter of "Howl" hit such a raw nerve with the U.S. government that litigation over it led to an obscenity trial.

The success of "Howl" made Ginsberg an international figurehead for other Beat writers, and he traveled widely giving readings and speaking out against the empty material values of the West. Following "Howl," Ginsberg wrote a different kind of lament—"Kaddish" (1961)—that detailed the tortured (but loving) relationship he had with his mother, Naomi, herself a victim of mental illness and emotional torment. Poet Robert Lowell referred to this poem as Ginsberg's "terrible masterpiece."

Ginsberg solidified his status as a counterculture hero of the West during the 1960s in his next books *Reality Sandwiches* (1963) and *Planet News* (1969), which continued to question popular conceptions of reality. *The Fall of America,* which registers a sustained protest against the Vietnam War in particular and the spiritual emptiness of the West in general, received the National Book Award for 1972. Other books include *Collected Poems: 1947-1980,* the annotated *Howl, White Shroud: Poems 1980-1985,* and *Cosmopolitan Greetings: Poems 1986-1992.* Rhino records issued his compact disc set *Holy Soul Jelly Roll: Poems and Songs 1949-*

*1993.* Ginsberg was also a member of the American Academy of Arts and Letters and cofounder of the Jack Kerouac School of Disembodied Poetics at Naropa Institute in Boulder, Colorado, the Western world's first accredited Buddhist college.

Allen Ginsberg died on April 5th, 1997.

## Poem Text

What thoughts I have of you tonight, Walt
　　Whitman, for I walked down the sidestreets
　　under the trees with a headache self-
　　conscious looking at the full moon.
In my hungry fatigue, and shopping for images,
　　I went into the neon fruit supermarket,
　　dreaming of your enumerations!
What peaches and what penumbras! Whole
　　families shopping at night! Aisles full of
　　husbands! Wives in the avocados, babies in
　　the tomatoes!—and you, Garcia Lorca, what
　　were you doing down by the watermelons?

I saw you, Walt Whitman, childless, lonely old
　　grubber, poking among the meats in the
　　refrigerator and eyeing the grocery boys.
I heard you asking question of each: Who killed　5
　　the pork chops? What price bananas? Are
　　you my Angel?
I wandered in an out of the brilliant stacks of
　　cans following you, and followed in my
　　imagination by the store detective.
We strode down the open corridors together in
　　our solitary fancy tasting artichokes,
　　possessing every frozen delicacy, and never
　　passing the cashier.

Where are we going, Walt Whitman? The doors
　　close in an hour. Which way does you beard
　　point tonight?
(I touch your book and dream of our odyssey in
　　the supermarket and feel absurd.)
Will we walk all night through solitary streets?　10
　　The trees add shade to shade, lights out in
　　the houses, we'll both be lonely.
Will we stroll dreaming of the lost America of
　　love past blue automobiles in driveways,
　　home to out silent cottage?
Ah, dear father, graybeard, lonely old courage-
　　teacher, what America did you have when
　　Charon quit poling his ferry and you got out
　　on a smoking bank and stood watching the
　　boat disappear on the black waters of Lethe?

## Poem Summary

### Lines 1-3:

The first stanza introduces us to a speaker experiencing a vision of sorts. Although in most cases it is not fair to conflate the identity of the speaker of a poem with the poet, because of Ginsberg's own autobiographical approach toward poetry we can assume that the speaker is Ginsberg himself. Right away we know that he is in a state of exhaustion and not seeing the world in a conventional way, as he describes himself as having a headache and being in a "hungry fatigue." As well as being a possibly literal description of his feeling, these words also suggest that Ginsberg is world weary—that he suffers from a spiritual, as much as a physical exhaustion. While searching for something that will set him right, he dreams of Walt Whitman as a source of inspiration. Whitman is a literary and spiritual hero to Ginsberg and, in many ways, Ginsberg emulates Whitman's style and subject matter in his own poems.

Ginsberg is being ironic when he writes that he is "shopping for images" in a "neon fruit supermarket." One does not normally think about "buying" images, especially not in a supermarket. But by looking for his poetic inspiration in a commercial setting, Ginsberg underscores one of the themes of his poem: the reduction of every thing and thought in America to something that can be bought and sold. By saying that he is dreaming of Whitman's "enumerations," Ginsberg means the way in which Whitman in his own verse catalogued or counted (e.g., "enumerated") what he saw and thought. Ginsberg does this himself in the last sentence when he lists what he sees in the supermarket. The last image, that of Spanish poet Frederico Garcia Lorca, is surprising but significant when we understand that Lorca, like Ginsberg, was a heavily persecuted gay writer (poet and playwright). Lorca, also an admirer of Whitman (one of his well-known poems is called "Ode to Walt Whitman"), was executed by anti-republican rebels in Granada in 1936 at the beginning of the Spanish Civil War.

### Lines 4-7:

The speaker addresses Whitman directly here, but Ginsberg's vision of Whitman is not a romantic one, but rather a vision of a sad, old man who is poking around the meats looking for a bargain. This is how Ginsberg imagines Whitman might be had he lived in modern America. He calls him a "lonely old grubber," but means it as a term of affection rather than an insult. Ginsberg underscores his own sexual desires and his knowledge of Whitman's homoerotic impulses when he says that he sees him "eyeing the grocery boys." In actuality, Whitman was anything but a lecherous old man. Even his sexuality remains a mystery, though many critics theorize he had same-sex love affairs. The

## Media Adaptations

- Rhino Records released a boxed set of four compact discs of Ginsberg's poems and songs titled *Holy Soul Jelly Roll: Poems & Songs 1949-1993.*

- In 1993 Elektra Nonesuch released a libretto written by Allen Ginsberg (with music by Phillip Glass) called "Hydrogen Jukebox."

- In 1993 Fantasy Records released *Howls, Raps & Roars: Recordings from the San Francisco Poetry Renaissance,* which includes Ginsberg reading *Howl & Other Poems.*

- Jerry Aronson directed and produced the documentary *The Life and Times of Allen Ginsberg* in 1993 for the American Masters Series of the Public Broadcasting System. This documentary is available at many libraries, video stores, and at amazon.com.

- The Naropa Institute Tape Archive in Boulder, Colorado, has many tapes of Ginsberg both reading and playing music from 1974 to 1988.

kinds of questions that Whitman asks of the meat and boys suggest how Ginsberg himself sees Whitman: as someone who is ravenous of all kinds of knowledge, both practical and inspirational. In following Whitman, Ginsberg imagines that he himself is being followed by store detectives. This line and the one that follows speak to the influence that Whitman has had on Ginsberg and to the controversial reputation of both poets. The store detective can be seen as the controlling force of conventional morality, a force that poets have struggled against in all cultures. That both poets taste freely of the store's delicacies without having to pay highlights Ginsberg's own fantasy that he can be different (both poetically and socially) and not have to pay the consequences.

### Lines 8-12

The speaker opens the last stanza by asking Whitman where they are going, because "the doors close in an hour." Ginsberg does not mean that the doors literally close in an hour, but that America has very little time left to change itself and become an open, tolerant society that has a spiritual rather than a materialistic orientation to the world. Whitman's beard metaphorically functions as a moral compass, suggesting that America will or will not heed the imperative to change. The only line in parenthesis in the entire poem clues us in to the genesis of Ginsberg's vision: he has been reading Whitman's book *Leaves of Grass.* Whitman worked on *Leaves of Grass* almost his entire life, first publishing it in 1855, then putting out revised and expanded versions for the next thirty years. The poems in *Leaves of Grass* describe America and the diversity of individuals who make up the idea of America. Whitman's long, sprawling lines lament, celebrate, and explore the ways in which human beings are both solitary creatures and a part of something larger (hence the title), and the work is almost epic in scope. Ginsberg feels "absurd" about his supermarket fantasy because he feels he is trivializing Whitman's work.

Ginsberg is nostalgic about an America that has passed, no doubt the America described by Whitman himself in *Leaves of Grass.* The 1950s America that Ginsberg sees himself living in is a conformist one, where people work long hours at unfulfilling jobs to acquire their houses, cars, and families. This is summed up by the image "blue automobiles in driveways." Ginsberg ends his poem by invoking the spirit of Whitman and asking him what America was like when he died. He does this metaphorically, however, by placing Whitman literally at the gates of hell. Charon is the elderly boatman in Greek mythology who ferried the souls of the recently dead cross the river Lethe to the underworld. Since Lethe is the river of forgetting, Ginsberg seems to be asking if Whitman's America, the America of individuality and spirituality, has itself been forgotten. The last image of the poem—Whitman standing on the banks of the river watching the boat disappear—underscores Ginsberg's elegiac tone throughout the poem and questions as it complicates the bonds between the past and the present.

## Themes

### American Dream

Historically America has held the promise of freedom—freedom not only to worship one's own God, but freedom also to pursue material wealth.

"A Supermarket in California" asks the question what happens when the God that one worships is material wealth itself? The very setting of the poem emphasizes this dilemma. Supermarkets are places of abundance and choice and can be seen as metaphor for American-style capitalism. A "neon fruit supermarket" takes that metaphor over the top, as fruit suggests fecundity and neon the gaudy advertisement of it. Placing the supermarket in California, the largest of the United States and historically thought of as "a promised land" (think of the Gold Rush of 1849), further underscores the idea of material acquisition. The first stanza of the poem exaggerates the commodification of all things in America. Ginsberg's celebratory description suggests nothing so much as a place where people worship this abundance, where what they buy becomes interchangeable with who they are: "Aisles full of husbands! Wives in the avocados, babies in the tomatoes!" Ginsberg writes.

The second stanza places Walt Whitman, the nineteenth-century, American poet who celebrated America's spiritual unity, in modern America—in that same supermarket—to explore what has become of the American Dream in the twentieth century. What results is an image of a lecherous "old grubber" who cannot keep his hands off the merchandise. Ginsberg sees himself and Whitman as outlaws of sorts as they sample the market's delicacies but never pay for them. Such transgressions have their price, however, as Ginsberg imagines himself being followed by the store detective. This demonstrates how the laws of the market (buying and paying for food) become the laws of our conscience and determine not only how we think about the world outside of us, but how we think about ourselves as well.

Ginsberg shows nostalgia for a better, more spiritually cohesive America in the last stanza when he asks Whitman where the country is headed ("Which way does your beard point tonight?"). Whitman's America celebrated not so much the riches that made the United States, as the workers and common man and woman who made the riches possible. The last sentence of the poem suggests that the America that Whitman celebrated in *Leaves of Grass*—the America where the labor that went into products was as valuable as the products themselves, the America where each person was singularly creative and different—is a thing of the past.

### Artists and Society

"A Supermarket in California" investigates the historical relationship that poets have had to soci-

## Topics for Further Study

- For Ginsberg, the supermarket symbolized both the freedom of choice and the spiritual bankruptcy of America. Think of a place that holds conflicting feelings for you and write about the reasons you feel this way.

- Think about the relationship between your dreams and your waking life. Write a poem that explores what a dream has shown you about how you live.

- Interview a few people who are at least twenty years older than you and ask them how they felt about the future when they were your age. What are the similarities and differences between their memories about the future and your own attitude toward it?

ety, exploring Ezra Pound's claim that they are "the antennae of our race." In the opening stanza, as the speaker experiences the metaphysical exhaustion so common to artists, he begins to dream of poets Walt Whitman and Frederico Garcia Lorca, both of whom were chroniclers of their age and also social outcasts. Ginsberg the speaker finds solace in imagining how other poets would respond to the crass materialism of twentieth-century America. He does this by imagining both Whitman and Lorca in a California supermarket, literally a place of material abundance. Finding comfort and community with others who share your values remains a human activity not only for poets but for all of us. By imagining that Whitman himself is with Ginsberg as he travels through the material culture of modern America, Ginsberg echoes popular assumptions about poets as spiritual guides through confusing time and places. Just as Dante relied on Virgil to show him through the maze of hell, so too does Ginsberg rely on Whitman to show him the direction that America will take. That the poem ends with a question, not a statement, suggests that Ginsberg remains unsure about whether America can live up to its potential.

## Style

"A Supermarket in California" is written in an expansive, free-verse form. Free verse is an open form of writing in which the rhythmic pattern is not organized into meter—that is, into units of stressed and unstressed syllables—but rather follows more natural or organic patterns of composition. Ginsberg treats his lines as single breath units, foregrounding the fact that his verse is meant to be read aloud. In *A Short History of American Poetry,* Donald Barlow Stauffer observes that "This is oral poetry, and the printed page can only suggest the side range of devices Ginsberg uses in his public readings: the shouting, the whispering, the carefully timed *sotto voce* asides, the comic Jewish inflections, the gestures of hands, arms, and waggling beard, the pauses and crescendos, the chanting, are all devices that relate his poetry to music and dance and help to establish a new oral tradition."

Ginsberg organizes his sentences into three stanzas of increasing length (three, then four, then five sentences). The effect of this type of organization is one of building momentum. The additive nature of the stanzas also underscores one of the points of the poem: that America has become a bankrupt society based on material acquisitiveness.

The poem is part description, part meditation, and part lament, and its associative logic is more akin to a daydream. This is also borne out by the imagery, which is surreal or dream-like. When the speaker exclaims "What peaches and penumbras! Whole families shopping at night! … Wives in the avocados, babies in the tomatoes," we understand that this isn't an empirical, objective supermarket being described, but rather a vision of a supermarket filtered through a particular (daydreaming) consciousness. It is the experience of the vision that the poet attempts to communicate, as much as the vision itself. Dream visions were a poetic form widely employed by medieval poets. In the dream vision, the narrator falls asleep and—in his dream—meets a guide who teaches him things about the world. The narrator then wakes up and relates the content of his dream. Ginsberg's guide in this poem is Whitman, the "lonely old courage teacher," whom he follows through the supermarket and then "through solitary streets."

It is significant that although others have noticed techniques and poetic devices that Ginsberg uses, he himself has denied any conscious intention to use these techniques and devices. "Primary fact of my writing is that I don't have any craft and I don't know what I'm doing," Ginsberg said in an interview. "There is absolutely no art involved, in the context of the general use of the words 'art' and 'craft.' Such craft of art as there is, is in illuminating mental formations, and trying to observe the naked activity of my own mind. Then transcribing that activity down on paper."

## Historical Context

"A Supermarket in California" was written in 1955, in the midst of postwar economic expansion in the United States. America's move to the suburbs, which Ginsberg equated with a kind of spiritual death and diminished individuality, was literally underway. Fueled by a lack of housing for returning veterans of World War II, developers began building on the outskirts of large cities. War contractor William J. Levitt's developments epitomized what would come to define the suburban experience. Between 1947 and 1951, Levitt converted a potato field in Levittown, Long Island, into a development of 17,000 Cape Cod houses that housed 75,000 people. Using prefabricated materials and package deals that included everything (including the kitchen sink), Levitt was able to produce a four-and-a-half room house for $8,000. Levitt eventually perfected his system so that he could put up a house every sixteen minutes. Once in the house, you needed entertainment, and by 1957 Americans owned more than forty million television sets. Advertising—then as now—dictated programming and the broadcast schedule, and Americans were inundated with messages to buy home-care products for their new homes. Where else would they buy these products than at the supermarket? The supermarket itself was a relatively new entity in 1950s America, as mom-and-pop grocery stores and other small food stores closed because they were unable to compete with well-capitalized chain stores. Between 1948 and 1958, nearly 100,000 independent groceries went out of business. To get to the supermarkets, Americans relied increasingly on the automobile. The "blue automobiles" that the speaker and Whitman stroll past in "A Supermarket in California" were only a few of the millions being pumped out by Ford, General Motors, and Chrysler. Auto registration in the United States increased from forty million in 1950 to sixty-two million in 1960. In addition to all the consumer spending on televisions, automobiles, housing, and home appliances, Amer-

# *Compare & Contrast*

- **1948-55:** Although The Kinsey Report claims that 37 percent of the men and 13 percent of the women interviewed had post-adolescent homosexual experience, the federal government considered homosexual inclination a security risk during the Cold War.

  **1993:** The United States armed forces adopt a "Don't Ask, Don't Tell" policy toward gay men and women in the military, effectively keeping homosexuality a violation of army code and forcing gay individuals to conceal their sexuality.

- **1954-55:** Movies such as *The Wild One* and *Rebel Without a Cause* showed disillusioned youth questioning and rejecting the materialistic values of their parents.

  **1988:** Oliver Stone's film *Wall Street* detailed the relationship between a wealthy corporate takeover artist and a materialistic young stockbroker, both of whom are caught violating securities trading laws.

  **Today:** Movies such as Jean-Jacques Annaud's *Seven Years in Tibet* and Martin Scorcese's *Kundun* demonstrate the West's fascination with the spiritualism of the East.

- **1947:** There were ten major television broadcasting stations.

  **1951:** The first coaxial cable linked East Coast and West Coast, enabling all Americans to see the same television program at the same time.

  **Today:** Cable television has given Americans access to literally hundreds of television channels. In addition, the internet allows almost instantaneous transmission of data over phone lines and cable worldwide.

---

icans were also buying spirituality, as they returned to churches in record numbers, partly as an attempt to establish some sense of community or belonging that they had lost as they lived further and further away from centers of social activity. But the churches were not selling salvation as much as they were exhorting people to believe in themselves. The Reverend Norman Vincent Peale's best-seller, *The Power of Positive Thinking* (1952), exemplifies the kind of "new" evangelism that postwar affluence engendered. That Congress added the words "under God" to the Pledge of Allegiance in 1954 is significant as a response to the increasing anxiety Americans had about religion and the place (or lack of it) in their lives.

The 1950s in America also witnessed a growing movement against the conformity and oppressive sameness of daily life. Many young people opted to drop out and experience the world rather than get married, take a nine-to-five job, and pollute the air with gas-guzzling automobiles on their commute to and from work. The Beat movement, of which Allen Ginsberg was an integral part, was both a response to such oppression and an enabler of further rebellion. Jack Kerouac's hit novel *On the Road,* published in 1957, told the story of rebellious hipsters who lived spontaneously, crisscrossing the country while high on Benzedrine, marijuana, and alcohol and always ready for a sexual (mis)adventure. Kerouac's prose celebrated sexual freedom and the possibility to do what you wanted when you wanted. The Beats championed the bebop jazz of Dizzy Gillespie and Charlie Parker, whose improvisatory methods of composition they frequently followed in their own lives and art.

## *Critical Overview*

Published as part of *Howl and Other Poems,* "A Supermarket in California" piggybacked on the notoriety and success of that volume. After already selling out the first edition (printed by Villiers in

England), a portion of the second printing of *Howl* was stopped by United States Custom officials at San Francisco, who impounded it, claiming that the writing was obscene. After a series of hearings during which the book's social relevance was debated, charges were dropped and the book was released. "Howl" comprises the bulk of the book, and "A Supermarket in California" is one of the shorter "other" poems in the volume, which also includes "In the Baggage Room at Greyhound"; "Sunflower Sutra"; and "America." In *Allen Ginsberg,* Thomas Merrill asserts that "A Supermarket in California" mirrors Ginsberg's own bewilderment with America, as he attempts to balance his own hope for and despair about the country. It is difficult, if not impossible, for the poet not to be a shopper. "Here is poet as consumer filling his shopping cart for the ingredients of his art among 'Aisles full of husbands!'" Merrill writes.

In a mixed review written in 1957 and appearing in *Sewanee Review,* poet and critic James Dickey argues that Ginsberg lacks a sense of craft in "Howl," claiming that just about anybody can be a poet. "In each case the needed equipment is very simple," Dickey says, "a life, with its memories, frustrations, secret wishes ... an ability to write elementary prose and to supply it with rather more exclamation points than might normally be called for." Dickey goes on to question Ginsberg's approach toward poetry itself. "Confession is not enough," he remarks, "and neither is the assumption that the truth of one's experience will emerge if only one can keep talking long enough in a whipped-up state of excitement. It takes more than this to make poetry. It just does."

In his *The San Francisco Renaissance: Poetics and Community at Mid-century,* Michael Davidson focuses on the subtext of "A Supermarket in California," charging that Whitman functions as an alter ego for Ginsberg "who himself is 'self-conscious' and 'shopping for images.'" Viewing the poem as a statement on Ginsberg's own sexual alienation, Davidson writes that Ginsberg's evocation of Whitman "emphasizes that this loneliness is also the historical loneliness of the homosexual who is denied the opportunity to participate in the bounty of 'normal' American life."

A good part of the poem's popularity can be traced to its brevity and its themes. Unlike "Howl," "A Supermarket in California" can be printed on one page, and its royalties are considerably less than those of the longer work. "A Supermarket in California" also touches on many of the ideas that appear in Ginsberg's longer poems: the spiritual desolation of America; homoeroticism; the influence of the past (specifically Walt Whitman's influence); and the isolation of the modern individual. These factors, along with the attention garnered from Ginsberg's recent death, continue to make the poem attractive to anthologists.

## Criticism

### Tyrus Miller

*Tyrus Miller is an assistant professor of comparative literature and English at Yale University, where he teaches twentieth-century literature and visual arts. In the following essay, Miller compares Ginsberg's vision of America as presented in "A Supermarket in California with that of Whitman's in poems such as "Song of Myself."*

Allen Ginsberg's "A Supermarket in California," written in Berkeley, California, in 1955, mourns the recent fate of the great poetic vision Walt Whitman had pronounced one hundred years earlier in "Song of Myself." Whitman had put himself poetically at the center of the cosmos, as if he were a radiant node in which the smallest and humblest thing found equal place with the grandest stars the night sky. Employing a long, flexible, unrhymed line ultimately derived from the King James Bible, Whitman's poems often enumerate objects, people, places, and names in great lists. Along with his innovations in poetic form, he also included a much-expanded range of subject matter, some of which was thought poetically inappropriate at the time, such as matters of sex and the body, scenes of physical injury and death, and images of common labor and slavery. Whitman saw the American democracy of the mid-nineteenth century as the political corollary of his poetry. American poetry and American politics were to be open, democratic, tolerant, accepting, ever-questioning, and grand in scale. Whitman presented himself as communicating with every point in this cosmos, passing outward poetically through a series of widening concentric rings: the body, the city, the American nation, the world, and the universe. At the beginning of "A Supermarket in California," Ginsberg introduces himself as pondering this magnificent democratic vista of poetry and later as holding a volume of Whitman's poetry. Constantly alluding to various aspects of Whitman's poetry and life, Ginsberg ironically and humorously measures himself against Whitman's grandiose poetic self-depiction and compares

Whitman's ideal view of America with what it had actually become in the era of anti-Communist witch-hunts, preprocessed food, television advertising, and nuclear bombs.

Coming a hundred years after Whitman, Ginsberg is inspired by the bard's vision of a vigorously democratic America sung by a new, public poetry. But he is far less confident that this vision can actually be fulfilled, either by the American consumer society of the mid-twentieth century or by the young poet Allen Ginsberg. Ginsberg signals his worries in a number of ways. Most important, he employs the physical setting of his poem in a symbolically significant way. Whereas Whitman's best-known poetry takes place amidst the populous bustle of Manhattan, along the open road, or at the ocean side, Ginsberg's setting is far more humble, even suburban: the large-chain grocery store. Ginsberg has taken Whitman's spacious poetry of the outdoors and thrust it back indoors. What was once open space is now bounded and carefully policed. No longer can Ginsberg innocently "loiter "and "loaf" (two verbs Whitman uses to describe how he witnesses the American scene) in the claustrophobic space of the supermarket. Its stacks of cans and its aisles jammed with carts and shopping families are a poor substitute for the bustle of the city and the highways that Whitman celebrated, and there are suspicious employees watching the dreamy, aimless poet at every step to make sure he is not shoplifting. If in his poetic dream of comradeship with Whitman, Ginsberg can stride "down the open corridors" of the supermarket, tasting the fruit and frozen food and not paying, this only serves to remind his reader how much life in the America of the 1950s was hemmed in by disapproving "detectives" and "cashiers"—by the power of the law and the almighty dollar.

Ginsberg also shifts from Whitman's typical images of work and production to images of spending money and consuming. In section 12 of "Song of Myself," for example, Whitman presents a figure who might still be seen, in a different incarnation, in Ginsberg's supermarket: "The butcher-boy puts off his killing-clothes, or sharpens his knife at the stall in the market, / I loiter enjoying his repartee and his shuffle and break-down." The poet catches the working boy at a pause in his labor and listens to him bantering with his fellow workers. In Ginsberg's poem, in contrast, Whitman is presented as the lonely gay cruiser, surrounded mostly by products for sale and consumption rather than the activity of producing: "I saw you, Walt Whitman,

# What Do I Read Next?

- On April 21, 1967, Harvey Cox wrote "An Open Letter to Allen Ginsberg" in the Catholic weekly *Commonweal,* answering Ginsberg's question about what religion is doing to make itself relevant today.

- Tom Clarke's Spring, 1966 *Paris Review* interview of Ginsberg delves into Ginsberg's views on poetic technique and, especially, how his own technique embodies spirituality and what Ginsberg calls "emotional nakedness."

- *The Fall of America,* which Ginsberg dedicated to Walt Whitman and for which Ginsberg won the National Book Award in 1972, is a register of Ginsberg's political and personal consciousness from 1965-1971. These poems provide an unfiltered description of any and everything that passed before Ginsberg's eyes and through his mind during these years.

- In *The Dark Ages: Life in the United States, 1945-1960,* Mary Jezer provides a detailed social history of America, including the development of suburban culture. The study was published in 1982.

- The emergence of gay communities is detailed in John D'Emilio's *Sexual Politics, Sexual Communities: The Making of a Homosexual Minority in the United States, 1940-1970,* published in 1983.

childless, lonely old grubber, poking among the meats in the refrigerator and eyeing the grocery boys. / I heard you asking questions of each: Who killed the pork chops? What price bananas? Are you my Angel?" The marketplace labor of the butcher-boy in Whitman's earlier poem is nowhere to be seen in the modern supermarket, only the precut and packaged meat glowing unnaturally under the fluorescent lights. The bananas, from somewhere in Latin America, similarly conceal the labor of cultivating and picking them beneath an abstract price tag. Even the "Angel," as an image

> *Ginsberg finds himself a social splinter whose only true comrades are ghosts. He finds only solitary roles left to fill: the late-night shopper, ... the American poet without an audience. "*

of pure spirit without body, is a kind of false label put on a much earthier desire of the body. Each question Whitman poses here implies a form of absence and disembodied existence, ironically revealing the artificially lit "neon fruit supermarket" to be the exact opposite of that intensely present "body electric" praised in Whitman's poem "I Sing the Body Electric." Moreover, by implanting sly sexual puns in his imagery, Ginsberg's poem suggests that even the boys whom Whitman once poetically presented at work have become for him one more consumable item among the "meat" and "fruit." Playfully inviting obvious but silly Freudian interpretations of his poem, Ginsberg even has old queer Whitman inquire about the price of bananas!

This shift from production to consumption is also reflected in the way Ginsberg presents himself in the poem. He encounters the shade of Whitman in a state of physical and poetic vacancy: hungry and tired, he shops for food; poetically uninspired, he goes "shopping for images." Just as Whitman set himself among the working men of the marketplace to collect experience for his poetry, so too does Ginsberg go to the market for literary materials. Yet unlike Whitman's individuals, among these strangely glowing vegetables and pork chops there are only two individualized figures, and they both are the ghosts of dead gay poets: the Spanish poet Federico Garcia Lorca, killed by fascists during the Spanish Civil War in the late 1930s, and Walt Whitman. Whereas Lorca had been able to identify himself and his poetry with the aspirations of the whole Spanish people for freedom, and Whitman had been able to reflect back to his American readers an idealized image of their democratic life,

Ginsberg finds himself a social splinter whose only true comrades are ghosts. He finds only solitary roles left to fill: the late-night shopper, the lonely gay male without a lover, the American poet without an audience. Moreover, even the "representative" poets Whitman and Lorca are themselves now only ghosts, and their claim to be the voice of their people rests solely on the ability of their poetry to compel conviction in later readers and writers such as Ginsberg. No longer does their status depend on what they, as poets, produce, but rather on how their work, in their absence and under the sign of their signature, will be "consumed" by the generations that follow them.

The full impact of what has been lost in the century since Whitman pronounced his "America of love" comes home in the magnificent final stanza. Situating himself in a long tradition of visionary poetry, Ginsberg makes Whitman his guide into the spaces of the dead, just as centuries earlier Dante had taken the Latin poet Virgil as his guide through hell in the *Divine Comedy*. By evoking the supermarket's closing time, Ginsberg signals his awareness of his own mortality, hoping that his own poetry, guided by Whitman's, will help him in that time in which he will no longer have need to shop for either food or images: "Where are we going, Walt Whitman? The doors close in an hour. Which way does your beard point tonight?" Even as he raises this serious question, however, he doubts whether he can justifiably use the heightened poetic rhetoric of the visionary tradition. By comparison, for example, to the descent into the underworld that is a central episode in Homer's epic *Odyssey,* in Virgil's *Aeneid,* and again in Dante's *Inferno,* Ginsberg's small-case "odyssey" among ghosts in the supermarket seems both self-consciously literary ("I touch your book") and contrived ("and feel absurd").

These doubts, expressed parenthetically in the second line, get powerfully answered by the sheer elegiac force of the last three lines, in which Ginsberg struggles to convince himself and his readers of his right to put himself, even before death, in the visionary company of Whitman, thus anticipating his posthumous fame as the older poet's heir. The final lines combine two effects, which work together to give the poem's close its extraordinary resonance. Almost like a stage manager overseeing a fade-out, Ginsberg narrows the visual focus to the two poets, Whitman and Ginsberg, and concludes with their complete vanishing in blackness and smoke. At the same time, however, these final lines have a strong outward movement, as if we were watching them walk away from us until they disappeared from view altogether. The first of the three ultimate lines sets these effects side-by-side and thus allow us to see how Ginsberg, with great skill, makes them converge in the long concluding line. "Will we walk all night through solitary streets?" lends the line its outward sweep, while the sentence that follows drops the lights to a single focus: "The trees add shade to shade, lights out in the houses, we'll both be lonely." After this fall into near-blackness, the next line picks up the forward momentum again: "Will we stroll dreaming of the lost America of love past blue automobiles in driveways, home to our silent cottage?" Then, as if imitating the movement of the boat of Charon, ferryman into the underworld, over the river Lethe's water of forgetfulness, Ginsberg evokes four short dips of the oars and a long glide over three printed lines without a comma break up to the question mark that ends the poem: "Ah, dear father, graybeard, lonely old courage-teacher, what America did you have when Charon quit poling his ferry and you got out on a smoking bank and stood watching the boat disappear on the black waters of Lethe?"

This beautiful ending does not, however, ultimately dispel the doubts raised in the poem about the ability of poetry to connect with a larger community and thus overcome isolation, loneliness, and death. For though Ginsberg movingly evokes his bond of poetic son with father Whitman and his deep appreciation of his lonely old "courage-teacher," this personal and ghostly community of gay poets is no longer Whitman's idealized "America of love." In essence, Ginsberg suggests that time has revealed Whitman's amatory America to be a myth and no longer a credible source of inspiration for a poet with ambitions to walk in Whitman's footsteps. The poem ends on a profoundly unsettling and questioning note: What America, Ginsberg asks his great predecessor in the final line, was left to you to turn into poetic myth when the last spark of your consciousness was extinguished by death? Is there anything that remains of that past America for me, Allen Ginsberg, to preserve in your name? The answer remains open beyond the bounds of the final question mark. But Ginsberg's conclusion on the word "Lethe," connoting forgetfulness, suggests his pessimism: America, it seems, cannot be rendered eternal by poetry, even by the greatest poetry. It may be already that it has almost fallen into oblivion.

**Source:** Tyrus Miller, in an essay for *Poetry for Students,* Gale, 1999.

## Marisa Anne Pagnattaro

*Marisa Anne Pagnattaro, J.D., Ph.D. in English, is a freelance writer and a Robert E. West Teaching Fellow in the English Department at the University of Georgia. In the following essay, Pagnattaro explores Ginsberg's love for Walt Whitman and his sense of isolation from mainstream America in the 1950s.*

Nearly fifteen years before he wrote "A Supermarket in California," a high-school English teacher introduced Allen Ginsberg to the poetry of Walt Whitman (1819-1892). Barry Miles notes in *Ginsberg: A Biography* that Ginsberg "has described how one afternoon she 'read aloud verses from Whitman's Song of Myself in so enthusiastic and joyous a voice, so confident and lifted with laughter, that I immediately understood "I wear my hat indoors as well as out ... I find no fat sweeter than that which sticks to my bones" forever.'" Whitman's poetry did, indeed, stick to Ginsberg's bones. Throughout his life, Whitman's work formed an important basis for Ginsberg's individualism and his desire to write using clear language, thereby making poetry accessible to many people.

"A Supermarket in California" is a tribute to Whitman's legacy of writing about the world in which he lived and is an expression of Ginsberg's sense of isolation from the mainstream values of America in the 1950s. Ginsberg's world may have been far removed from Whitman's, yet the two shared the kind of poetic perspective necessary to comment on their time. Indeed, the mere title of the poem evokes a place that was unknown to the nineteenth-century poet; the word "supermarket" was not even in existence until the middle of the twentieth century. By 1955, however, when Ginsberg wrote the poem in Berkeley, California, the phenomenon of a chain of large self-service stores signaled progress and abundance for many Americans. For Ginsberg, this place prompts a sense of loneliness, as well as nostalgia, for Whitman's expansive and all-embracing vision of America.

In the first stanza, Ginsberg summons Whitman into his thoughts during a moonlit stroll to relieve the pain of self-reflection. As an artist who was at the forefront of a counterculture movement in opposition to the "Leave-it-to-Beaver" Eisenhower years, Ginsberg was an outsider on a suburban street. He had already written his controversial long poem "Howl," which was in the process of sparking what would later come to be known as the Beat Generation Movement. Ac-

> *As an artist who was at the forefront of a counterculture movement in opposition to the 'Leave-it-to-Beaver' Eisenhower years, Ginsberg was an outsider on a suburban street."*

knowledging the power of the poem in his introduction to "Howl," poet William Carlos Williams admonished readers: "Hold back the edges of your gowns, Ladies, we are going through hell." In contrast, the tone of "Supermarket" is quieter and more reflective, and yet it still bears all of Ginsberg's poetic self-consciousness.

Using the long verse line inspired by Whitman and English poet William Blake (1757-1827), Ginsberg shops "for images" in the "neon fruit supermarket, dreaming of your enumerations." Whitman is well known for the "enumerations" in his poems—lists or catalogs of people and images from the world he observed. Readers are meant to compare Whitman's vision of plenty in America with the much more contained and less natural world that Ginsberg now observes. Ginsberg also taps into the tradition of the Modernists he admired, Ezra Pound and William Carlos Williams, who advocated concrete expression of images to capture the moments of experience. Ginsberg then confronts his readers with a smattering of images. The exuberance of the following line momentarily creates an almost frantic mood: "What peaches and what penumbras! Whole families shopping at night! Aisles full of husbands! Wives in the avocados, babies in the tomatoes!—and you, Garcia Lorca, what were you doing down by the watermelons?" The introduction of the Spanish poet and dramatist Garcia Lorca (1899-1936) creates a surrealistic atmosphere, pulling a sense of the subconsciousness into the present. Similar to Lorca's work, which was characterized by the interconnectedness of dreams and reality in his characters' lives, the entire scene takes on a fantastic quality. This is significant in that Ginsberg stood completely apart from the 1950s conventional notion of "family," with its neat composition of a mother, father, and babies.

Ginsberg's affinity with Whitman is evident in the next stanza in which the old poet suddenly appears as an incongruous, yet welcome, element: "I saw you, Walt Whitman, childless, lonely old grubber, poking among the meats in the refrigerator and eyeing the grocery boys." Like Ginsberg, Whitman was also homosexual and would have felt equally out of place in the glare of the supermarket, a wholesome bastion where families feel free to shop at night. Even his questions underscore his discordant presence: "Who killed the pork chops? … Are you my Angel?" For Ginsberg, Whitman offers a kindred spirit, one who is unabashed by his difference in the glare of the supermarket. He offers a new perspective on the meat isle as he equates death with food and propositions a bag boy. In his imagination, Ginsberg follows Whitman and the two are trailed by "the store detective." It is as if both are suspect; they are illicit variables marring the respectable veneer of mainstream America. Leaving behind his self-consciousness, Ginsberg brazenly strolls with Whitman in "solitary fancy tasting artichokes, possessing every frozen delicacy, and never passing the cashier." They indulge in sensual, edible pleasures and are not held accountable to the "real world" in this fantasy.

The indulgence, however, will soon be over ("The doors close in an hour"), and the questions begin, signaling the return of Ginsberg's uncertainty about the world. He asks: "Where are we going Walt Whitman?" The overtones are also sexual: "Which way does your beard point tonight?" Ginsberg looks for a phallic indication of what is to come. In an erotic parenthetical Ginsberg professes "(I touch your book and dream of our odyssey in the supermarket and feel absurd)." Ginsberg is on an odyssey of sorts; like Odysseus in Homer's *Odyssey,* there is the sense that he is trying to get home. Although for Ginsberg, he cannot return to the "home" of Whitman's America and there is no clear sense of such a place in the poem. The pair is left with the option of walking "all night through solitary streets" on what appears to be a journey with no real place of belonging in the contemporary world. He laments that "the lights will be out in the houses, we'll both be lonely." The lively excursion into the supermarket is over, replaced by questions.

The final stanza begins with another somber question, which again underscores Ginsberg's sense of isolation from mainstream America: "Will we stroll dreaming of the lost America of love past blue automobiles in driveways, home to our silent cottage?" Whitman was a great believer in Thomas Jefferson's democratic ideals, which were continued at the beginning of the nineteenth century during Andrew Jackson's presidency. The America that Ginsberg bemoans lacks the spiritual fellowship once envisioned by Whitman. In its place is a world of personal identification through consumerism and conformity, of "blue automobiles in driveways." This complacent suburban ideal has little to offer a radical and highly individualistic thinker such as Ginsberg.

The last question and line of the poem, which directly addresses Whitman as a wise and aged figure, requires readers to take a deep breath and sigh along with Ginsberg: "Ah, dear father, graybeard, lonely old courage-teacher, what America did you have when Charon quit poling his ferry and you got out on a smoking bank and stood watching the boat disappear on the black waters of Lethe?" In Greek mythology, Charon was the aged boatman charged with the responsibility of ferrying the souls of the deceased to Hades, the god of death. By allowing Whitman to get out of Charon's boat, Ginsberg places him in an unresolved state. The boat disappears on the Lethe, the underworld's river of forgetfulness. Greek mythology provides that the spirits of the dead would drink from its waters to forget the sorrows of their earthly existence before entering Elysium, a land of perfect peace and happiness. Myth, however, also provides that when Aeneas, the Trojan prince, visited the underworld, he saw many such souls wandering on the banks of the Lethe because before the spirits could live in the world above, they must drink from the river to forget the happiness of Elysium. Whitman is left standing on the bank filled with the sorrow of the world and not yet partaking in the bliss of Elysium, which has long been regarded as the place where the souls of dead poets go to rest as a reward for their virtuousness in life. Readers are left with an impression of Whitman watching the world around him literally going to hell.

Ginsberg's admiration for Whitman continued throughout his life. Many years after writing "A Supermarket in California," Ginsberg reaffirmed his great respect for Whitman in his 1984 poem "I Love Old Whitman So." Written while Ginsberg was in Baoding, China, this effusive tribute recalls images from *Leaves of Grass* and Whitman's all-embracing sense of humanity. Ginsberg was still touched by what he deems Whitman's "desperado farewell": "Who touches this book touches a man."

Ginsberg lived in that grand humanistic tradition and expanded on Whitman's democratic vision.

Unlike Whitman, who never received the recognition he deserved during his lifetime, many contemporaries appreciated Ginsberg's "barbaric yawp." When he died in 1997, Ginsberg was praised by Charles McGrath in his article "Street Singer" because he "liberated poetry from the library and took it boldly into cafes and onto the street corner. He believed in poetry of the people, not the professoriate." Ginsberg was what Whitman always wanted to be—a poet of the people. In the eulogistic poem for himself, "Death & Fame," Ginsberg catalogs the eclectic assortment of people he envisioned attending his funeral. At the end of the poem he states: "Everyone knew they were part of 'History' except the deceased / who never knew exactly what was happening even when I was alive." Perhaps he did not know "exactly what was happening," but he certainly had the keen ability to comment on the times.

**Source:** Marisa Anne Pagnattaro, in an essay for *Poetry for Students*, Gale, 1999.

### Chris Semansky

*Chris Semansky is a published poet who regularly writes essays and reviews of modern and contemporary poetry. In the following essay, Semansky characterizes "A Supermarket in California" as a lament about the materialistic, spiritually vapid culture of mid-twentieth-century America that underscores the inherent conflict embodied in living in an advanced capitalist country and the emotional and psychologically devastating effects of such conflict.*

When we talk about tone in literature, we refer to the stance or attitude the speaker has toward his listener or audience and to the subject of the work. The audience for "A Supermarket in California" is complicated in that the speaker is addressing both Walt Whitman—or at least an idea of who Whitman was (his ghost)—and a public that is (ostensibly) sympathetic to the poet's feelings about America. The poet's own contradictory attitude toward Whitman mirrors his ambivalent attitude about America. On the one hand, he dreams of Whitman's poetry, his "enumerations," and allies with him in the poem, "[striding] down the open corridors together in our solitary fancy tasting artichokes, possessing every frozen delicacy." Conversely, however, he refers to Whitman as a "lonely old grubber" who talks to bananas and pork chops. Similarly, while praising the United States for its

> *... Ginsberg ... implicitly critiques the American Dream, suggesting that it has become a nightmare of conformism and emptiness.*

material abundance (after all, the poem is set in a supermarket) and choice, waxing ecstatic at "Whole families shopping at night!", Ginsberg also implicitly critiques the American Dream, suggesting that it has become a nightmare of conformism and emptiness. Whereas once the American Dream represented individuality, a strong sense of community, and freedom from tyrannical work conditions, it now means slavery to an eight-to-five job, a house like every other house in a suburb like every other suburb, and a gas-guzzling automobile to take us to and from the cities where we work. For many Americans, Ginsberg suggests, pursuit of the Dream has come at a high cost. We find ourselves working longer hours, commuting greater distances, and spending the remaining time recovering in front of the television. This attitude is most evident when he asks Whitman if they will "... stroll dreaming of the lost America of love past blue automobiles in driveways, home to our silent cottage?"

The imagery in "A Supermarket in California" is almost typically Romantic, highlighting the difficulty the speaker has in thinking any one way about America. As with Romantic lyric poetry, the natural world is used as a setting for the speaker's meditation on a weighty subject. In the opening stanza we see the speaker walking alone under trees, "looking at the full moon." This peace and solitude affords him the opportunity to dream, which he does, of "a neon fruit supermarket." By setting the poem in a supermarket, Ginsberg zeroes in on what is almost an embarrassment of riches and choice in the industrialized Western world; by using the adjectives "neon fruit," Ginsberg underscores the gaudy aspect of so much conspicuous consumption, perhaps even punning on his own sexuality ("fruit" being a derogatory term for a homosexual). These contradictions, while illustrating the speaker's conflict, are also a staple of surreal-

ist verse. As an aesthetic and social movement, Surrealism advocated unfettering the conscious mind and removing what it saw as barriers to creativity and true expression. The resultant reality would be a "surreality," the prefix "sur" meaning over or above. Many surrealist poets, such as André Breton and Louis Aragon, practiced what they called automatic writing, whose purpose is to explore the materials of the unconscious mind without any preconceptions about what might be found there. For Ginsberg and his Beat contemporaries, automatic writing became one of the primary means of composition, because they distrusted logical reason and the world of appearances, and because they believed it put them in touch with a deeper, more authentic, self—above the selves they presented to society.

The difficulty Ginsberg has in arriving at any resolution to what America is or can be also points to his own alienation, not only from the country, but also from the process of writing and owning his own poems. In Marxist theory alienation in capitalist societies occurs when human beings no longer recognize themselves in the objects that they produce; they feel separated both from the objects and from one another, as they now see others as merely cogs in the machine of capital. Put another way, social relations become market relations. It was common during the 1950s and especially the 1960s to hear about young people's alienation from society. Popular history has it that many felt that they no longer had control over their own lives or decision-making processes. Ginsberg himself even suggested that madness was the only sane response to a mad world. Making Whitman the conduit for Ginsberg's own vision of America demonstrates what little control the poet felt he had over his own writing. His dependence on the vision of others only highlights the paucity of his own; similarly, his poetic style, derivative of Whitman and Blake's, dramatically highlights the difficulty of making something original. By asking Whitman which way the country is headed, Ginsberg demonstrates his own confusion in reading present reality. Calling on Whitman as his muse shows the importance of the past in understanding the present. That Whitman himself offers no resolution to Ginsberg's questions suggests that the country is beyond logic and repair and has entered the very dreamworld to which Ginsberg has escaped.

The supermarket's significance as a meeting ground of influences, past and present, should not be taken lightly. As the physical church for the new American religion of shopping, the supermarket actually enables the difficulty the speaker of the poem has in reaching a decision about America. Do I love it? Do I hate it? Should I buy the Post-Toasties or the Cocoa Puffs? Ecovision toilet paper or Charmin? Two-ply or four? Pesticide-free, organically grown, lower-fat California avocadoes? Or the local variety? The abundance of choice invades the poetic process itself, as the poet goes "shopping for images." Inspiration has become commodity; individuality just another brand name to be packaged and marketed along with everything else. This is not necessarily a far cry from the America that Whitman described in *Leaves of Grass* where, though he championed humanity's (and his own) indomitable spirit and capacity to transcend circumstance, he also showed its seamy underside— its violence, cruelty, and weakness. What would Whitman have thought if he were alive in 1955 to witness what had transpired in the sixty years between his death and the birth of Ginsberg's poem? And what vision of America did he have in mind when he finally died in 1892? Would Whitman's answers have helped Ginsberg resolve his own spiritual confusion, or are the questions themselves merely rhetorical? That is, does Ginsberg merely ask them for effect, already knowing the answers? Or, like Whitman, is Ginsberg's asking of the questions just another instance of his own attempt to contain within himself all of the possibilities of the universe, both good and evil, question and answer? If we look at "A Supermarket in California" in relation to the other poems in *Howl*, we can see that Ginsberg's stance toward America is unequivocally bleak. In Part II of "Howl," Ginsberg presents Moloch, an Old Testament God of the Ammonites and Phoenicians to whom children were sacrificed, as a symbol of America's social ills: "Moloch whose factories dream and croak in the fog! / Moloch whose smokestacks and antennae crown the cities!" If Ginsberg were to incorporate "A Supermarket in California" into "Howl," perhaps he would have written, "Moloch whose eternal aisles of tangerines and kiwis lead us into hell." But bleak as Ginsberg's America appears, he still retains a smidgen of hope. Michael Davidson writes in *The San Francisco Renaissance: Poetics and Community at Mid-century* that if "Whitman is placed in Hell ... [it is] not by his disbelief but because of his extreme faith." This is the faith that Ginsberg, along with Whitman's mantle, has inherited. It is a roughed-up faith, but it is a faith that Ginsberg nonetheless desires his readers to buy.

**Source:** Chris Semansky, in an essay for *Poetry for Students*, Gale, 1999.

## Sources

Ammons, R. S., "Ginsberg's New Poems," *Poetry,* June 1964, pp. 186-87.

Breslin, James E., "Allen Ginsberg's 'Howl,' " *From Modern to Contemporary: American Poetry, 1945-1965,* Chicago, IL: University of Chicago Press, 1984, pp. 77-109.

Breslin, Paul, "Allen Ginsberg as Representative Man: The Road to Naropa," *The Psycho-Political Muse: American Poetry Since the Fifties,* Chicago, IL: University of Chicago Press, 1987, pp. 22-41.

Dickey, James, "From Babel to Byzantium," *Sewanee Review,* Summer 1957, pp. 509-10.

Ehrlich, J. W., ed., *Howl of the Censor,* San Carlos, CA: Nourse Publishing Co., 1961.

Ginsberg, Allen, "Death & Fame," *New Yorker,* April 21, 1997, pp. 80-81.

———, "I Love Old Whitman So," *White Shroud: Poems 1980-1985,* New York: Harper & Row, 1986.

———, *Selected Poems 1947-1995,* New York: Harper Collins, 1996.

Howard, Richard, "Allen Ginsberg," *Alone with America: Essays on the Art of Poetry in the United States Since 1950,* New York: Atheneum, 1980, pp. 176-183.

Hyde, Lewis, ed., *On the Poetry of Allen Ginsberg,* Ann Arbor: University of Michigan Press, 1984.

Kramer, Jane, *Allen Ginsberg in America,* New York: Paragon House, 1969.

Kraus, Michelle, *Allen Ginsberg: An Annotated Bibliography, 1969-1977,* Metuchen, NJ: Scarecrow Press, 1980.

McGrath, Charles, "Street Singer," *New York Times Book Review,* April 27, 1997, p. 43.

Merrill, Thomas F., *Allen Ginsberg,* Boston: Twayne, 1988.

Miles, Barry, *Ginsberg: A Biography,* New York: Simon and Schuster, 1989.

Molesworth, Charles, "Republican Objects and Utopian Moments: The Poetry of Robert Lowell and Allen Ginsberg," *The Fierce Embrace,* Columbia: University of Missouri Press, 1979, pp. 37-60.

Mottram, Eric, *Allen Ginsberg in the Sixties,* Brighton, England: Unicorn Bookshop, 1972.

*On the Edge: A New History of 20th-century America,* edited by David A. Horowitz, Peter N. Carroll, and David D. Lee, Los Angeles: West Publishing Co., 1990.

Perloff, Marjorie, "A Lion in Our Living Room: Reading Allen Ginsberg in the Eighties," *Poetic License: Essays on Modernist and Postmodernist Lyric,* Evanston, IL: Northwestern University Press, 1990, pp. 199-230.

Portuges, Paul Cornel, *The Visionary Poetics of Allen Ginsberg,* Santa Barbara, CA: Ross-Erickson, 1978.

Rosenthal, M. L., and Sally M. Gall, *The Modern Poetic Sequence: The Genius of Modern Poetry,* New York: Oxford University Press, 1983, pp. 422-28.

Schumacher, Michael, *Dharma Lion: A Biography of Allen Ginsberg,* New York: St. Martin's Press, 1992.

Stauffer, Donald Barlow, *A Short History of American Poetry,* New York: E. P. Dutton & Co., Inc., 1974.

Stepanchev, Stephen, *American Poetry Since 1945,* New York: Harper Colophon Books, 1967.

## For Further Study

Davidson, Michael, *The San Francisco Renaissance: Poetics and Community at Mid-century,* New York: Cambridge University Press, 1989.
> One of the most provocative and informative studies of the San Francisco Renaissance ever written. Davidson places Ginsberg squarely in the tradition of Romantic poets while exploring the myths surrounding modern Romantic poets.

Knight, Arthur and Kit, eds., *Kerouac and the Beats: A Primary Sourcebook,* New York: Paragon House, 1988.
> A collection of correspondence and interviews of Beat writers, including Jack Kerouac, Allen Ginsberg, Herbert Huncke, Philp Whalen, and William Burroughs.

Mersmann, James F., *Out of the Vietnam Vortex: A Study of Poets and Poetry against the War,* Lawrence: University Press of Kansas, 1974.
> A historical account of American poets who were actively opposing the war in Vietnam.

Parkinson, Thomas, ed., *A Casebook on the Beat,* New York: Thomas Y. Crowell, 1961.
> An intelligent assessment of Ginsberg's place among Beat writers and poets.

Podhoretz, Norman, "My War With Allen Ginsberg," in *Commentary,* August 1997, Vol. 104, No. 2, pp. 27-40.
> A first-person historical account of a conservative Jewish literary critic's fifty-year (mostly adversarial) relationship with Allen Ginsberg.

# To His Coy Mistress

## Andrew Marvell
## 1678

"To His Coy Mistress" by Andrew Marvell is a classic carpe diem poem in which a sophisticated and mature man, the speaker in the poem, attempts to persuade his young mistress to yield to his amorous advances. Marvell lived during the seventeenth century in England, a time of radical changes in politics and modes of literary expression. For a while during the Commonwealth Period (1649-1660), drama disappeared, public theaters closed because of fears of immoral influences, and incendiary political pamphlets circulated. The Latin phrase carpe diem or "seize the day" is a very common literary motif in poetry. This kind of poem usually emphasizes that life is short and time is fleeting as the speaker attempts to entice his listener, a young lady usually described as a virgin. Poets writing carpe diem lyrics frequently use the rose as a symbol of transient physical beauty and the finality of death. Examples include Robert Herrick's "To the Virgins, to Make Much of Time" and Edmund Waller's "Go, Lovely Rose." However, Marvell's poem is a more psychologically complicated and original treatment of this theme. The poem pretends to explore the dramatic argument situation between the man and his mistress when it really hides a concrete address to death; its gripping second section is filled with unusually bold images of sterility, rotting corpses, tombs, and a shocking denial of the procreative activity of sex. "To His Coy Mistress" does much more than simply celebrate youthful passion and the flesh the way many love poems do. Marvell confronts mortality

*Andrew Marvell*

until 1657, when Marvell was appointed Assistant Latin Secretary to the Council of State through the influence of his friend John Milton, who then held the post of Latin Secretary. After Marvell was elected to Parliament in 1659, he began to concentrate on political satire and polemics in prose and stopped writing poetry. A dedicated, conscientious statesman, Marvell focused on his political career, serving the middle-class constituency of Hull in Parliament until his death. Although it has often been rumored that he was poisoned by his political enemies, scholars generally attribute Marvell's death on August 16, 1678 to a fever (although some believe he died of an accidental overdose of medicinal opiates). Admittedly, little is known about much of Marvell's life. While he is not thought to have married, shortly after his death, a woman claiming to be his widow published a volume of his poetry; that Mary Marvell was truly Marvell's wife has yet to be either disproved or substantiated.

directly and develops a convincing psychological stance that argues one should capitalize on life's opportunities. The speaker concludes in a riotous charge to live and to love to the fullest.

## Author Biography

The son of an Anglican clergyman, Marvell was born on March 31, 1621, in Winestead-in-Holderness, Yorkshire, England. He received his early education at nearby Hull Grammar School and, at the age of twelve, entered Trinity College at Cambridge University, where he earned his bachelor's degree in 1638. Scholars believe that Marvell remained at Cambridge until 1641 pursuing a master's degree, but he left after his father died and did not return to finish his studies. During the next four years Marvell travelled in Europe, evidently employed as a tutor. By the early 1650s he was living at Nunappleton in Yorkshire, tutoring the daughter of Sir Thomas Fairfax, the retired commander-in-chief of the Commonwealth Army under Oliver Cromwell. During his stay at Nunappleton, Marvell wrote the majority of the lyric poems that now form the basis of his literary reputation. Cromwell's ward William Dutton was Marvell's next student

## Poem Text

Had we but world enough, and time,
This coyness, lady, were no crime.
We would sit down, and think which way
To walk, and pass our long love's day.
Thou by the Indian Ganges' side                5
Should'st rubies find: I by the tide
Of Humber would complain. I would
Love you ten years before the Flood,
And you should, if you please, refuse
Till the conversion of the Jews.               10
My vegetable love should grow
Vaster than empires, and more slow.
An hundred years should go to praise
Thine eyes, and on thy forehead gaze:
Two hundred to adore each breast:              15
But thirty thousand to the rest;
An age at least to every part,
And the last age should show your heart.
For, lady, you deserve this state,
Nor would I love at lower rate.                20
    But at my back I always hear
Time's wingéd chariot hurrying near:
And yonder all before us lie
Deserts of vast eternity.
Thy beauty shall no more be found;             25
Nor, in thy marble vault, shall sound
My echoing song: then worms shall try
That long-preserved virginity,
And your quaint honor turn to dust,
And into ashes all my lust.                    30
The grave's a fine and private place,
But none, I think, do there embrace.
    Now, therefore, while the youthful hue
Sits on thy skin like morning dew,

And while thy willing soul transpires     35
At every pore with instant fires,
Now let us sport us while we may;
And now, like amorous birds of prey,
Rather at once our Time devour,
Than languish in his slow-chapt power.     40
Let us roll all our strength and all
Our sweetness up into one ball,
And tear our pleasures with rough strife,
Through the iron gates of life.
Thus, though we cannot make our sun     45
Stand still, yet we will make him run.

## Poem Summary

### Lines 1-2:

The basic theme of the poem is announced from the beginning, that time lays waste to youth and life passes quickly, so people should enjoy youth now and "seize the day." In the first section of the poem (to line 20), the speaker uses subjunctive mood verbs such as "would" and "were" that give a delicacy and tentativeness to his style. The speaker presents his "argument" to a listener, a young woman who holds back from reciprocating with her expression of love. The speaker says that coyness would be acceptable if time were in endless supply and if the world was big enough to accommodate all of his admiration for her.

### Lines 3-4:

Assuming time continues forever, the poem describes the leisurely pace of life spent in courtship and praise of the beloved, silent mistress.

### Lines 5-7:

Beginning with line 7 and continuing to line 20, the speaker embarks on some remarkable hyperbole to describe the praise he wants to bestow upon his mistress. He selects two rivers, India's Ganges, which is sacred to the Hindu religion and thought of as the earthly embodiment of a goddess, and England's Humber, which flows past Marvell's hometown of Hull. The wide distance of two hemispheres separating the rivers compares with the time needed to spend adequately in courtship. That the mistress would find rubies in the Ganges underlines the exotic nature of a river in India. The Humber river in England, by comparison, is a slow-moving, dirty estuary where one is more likely to find old shoes than precious stones. The distance between the speaker (by the Humber river) and the mistress (by the Ganges river) is a metaphor for the luxurious, leisurely consumption of time spent in praise.

### Lines 8-10:

In these lines, the speaker describes the amount of time it would take to love his mistress and how much time she would be allowed to turn his love aside. The poem invokes eschatological or "end of the world" events to compare the allotted time—the great Flood by which God cleanses the earth in the Bible or the conversion of the Jews popularly thought to happen immediately prior to the Last Judgment. These excessive comparisons stress the unimaginably large amount of time it would take to adequately define the speaker's love for his mistress.

### Lines 11-12:

The speaker creates the metaphor of "vegetable love" that grows very slowly but amasses enough bulk to be larger than a great dynasty or colonial empire. Because of the depth of his love, the speaker's "vegetable love" covers much of the earth's surface, as did the British empire during its peak in the nineteenth century.

### Lines 13-18:

The speaker fills out the hyperbole begun in line 7. This catalogue of the amount of years devoted to worship of each of his mistress's physical attributes is outrageous; we find staggering overstatement in the 100 years for her face, 200 years for each breast, and 30,000 years devoted to the rest of her body—an exponential increase! The speaker devotes at least one generation to praise of each part of his mistress, especially to praise of her pure heart, which is saved for last because of its special place as the seat of amorous passion. This catalogue resembles and perhaps parodies the style of Petrarchan sonnet writers, who used standard metaphors to describe their mistresses. However, Marvell's comparisons are notable for their excessiveness and originality.

### Lines 19-20:

In this close of section I, the speaker introduces a monetary metaphor: loving at a certain "rate," like an interest rate charged by a bank for lending money. The speaker implies that the mistress deserves this "state" of lavish praise because of her beauty.

### Lines 21-22:

This is the logical turn of the poem, shifting from wild exaggeration to somber images of the grave. The subject of death intrudes into this love poem, turning the mood away from the subjunctive to focus on the limitation of time. Time is person-

## Media Adaptations

- *Milton and 17th Century Poetry* was released on video cassette by Films for the Humanities in 1988.

- An audio album by Sir Cedric Hardwicke, titled *Poetry of the XVII Century,* is available from Caedmon Records.

- An audio cassette titled *The English Poets, #6: Richard Lovelace; Charles Cotton; Andrew Marvell; Samuel Butler; John Wilmot, Earl of Rochester; and John Milton* was released by Longman Group in 1979.

- *Andrew Marvell,* an audio reel, is available from the University of Colorado.

---

ified as a driver in a chariot. In popular culture, Time is usually pictured as a robed old man holding a scythe—a sinister figure inspiring fear. The verb choice of "hurrying" introduces anxiety and darkness into a formerly light and extravagant, lyric poem.

### Lines 23-24:

The image of vast deserts begins a macabre list of comparisons having to do with sterility. Deserts are hot and barren, a denial of the life-giving processes of love and sexual activity. No wet, living "vegetable love" can be found in Marvell's desert.

### Lines 25-27:

These lines emphasize the loss of beauty that happens to all people over time, especially pertaining to the mistress. The "marble vault" is the resting place for the deceased mistress's corpse. The speaker's song of praise will go unheard and unsung when death levels them both; thus the implication is that death is a final stopping place beyond which no magnificent love can escape.

### Lines 28-30:

The speaker's grotesque image of the worm penetrating the virgin corpse as it consumes the rot-

ting flesh shocks many readers. The point is that such preserved virtues mean nothing when stretched over the expanse of time. Thus, the speaker offers another persuasive reason for the mistress to give in. "Quaint honor" reflects that fact that virginity will seem a quaint but useless treasure at the end of life. The speaker alludes to the Biblical phrase of "ashes to ashes, dust to dust" (commonly used at funerals) to emphasize his thriving, passionate lust being reduced to oblivion, just like the mistress's virginity.

### Lines 31-32:

With the close of section II, the poem uses understatement and irony, praising the grave as a "fine" and "private" place. This is a perfect transition to the carpe diem theme of section III. The speaker uses a grammatical pause to interrupt line 32, making him seem humble and modest. The speaker's charm and tactfulness are implied by the restraint he uses to punctuate line 32. (In poetry, taking a pause in the middle of a line is a called a caesura.)

### Lines 33-34:

Section III returns to the theme of youthful lust. The speaker uses imperative mood verbs that give commands, exhortation, and urgent directions to his mistress. While youth is present, the mistress's skin glows in vitality like the morning dew. This simile as originally published used the word "glew" instead of "dew." Some scholars suggested that "glew" was a dialectal form of "glow," as in "the skin's healthy glow." The alternative possibility that "glew" means "glue" is not attractive to the tone of the lover's argument. Probably the best choice in modernizing a seventeenth-century poem would be to substitute "dew" as in the present text.

### Lines 35-37:

The speaker says that the young soul of his mistress breathes out through her beautiful skin in "instant fires" of enthusiasm and passion for love. The speaker wants his mistress to yield to his lust now while she can still respond before time takes its toll.

### Lines 38-40:

The speaker makes use of a set of harsh images that lend intensity and force to his expression. The simile of "birds of prey" is an unexpected choice for a love poem; some might consider it bizarre for the poem to compare a lover and his mistress to birds of prey who want to eat, not be eaten by Time. The comparison says that the speaker wants to devour Time like a hawk devours a rabbit caught in the fields—rapidly, in the heat of the moment, unthinkingly and instinctively. Time with his "slow-chapt power" is imagined as slowly chewing up the world and its people; thus the speaker implies he and his mistress are in a desperate fight against Time.

### Lines 41-44:

In these lines, the poem uses the metaphor of a cannonball of "strength" and "sweetness" rolled into a concentrated package of energy that "tears" through the barriers of restraint. The juxtaposition of "strife" with "pleasures" indicates the ferocious breakthrough of the speaker's argument winning over his mistress.

### Lines 45-46:

In the concluding couplet, the speaker and his mistress triumphantly turn back the destructive forces of Time, avidly eating Time instead of being eaten by it. The speaker and his mistress force the sun to race them instead of passively begging the sun to stand still like Joshua did in the Bible, when he pleaded with God to make the sun stand still so the Israelites might defeat the Amorites in broad daylight.

## Themes

### Time

Time is clearly the most important issue bothering the speaker of "To His Coy Mistress"; the subject spans the entire length of the piece, from the first line to the forty-sixth. The most obvious relationship to time here is that this work is a traditional carpe diem poem, which means that it encourages the listener to "seize the day"—to make the most of today and not put off action until tomorrow. In this particular case, the speaker is addressing a woman with whom he wants to have sex. He uses the threat of what time will do to her "quaint honor" and "long-preserved virginity" to convince her to give both up to him before they decay. A psychological interpretation—looking beneath the surface of the speaker's claims to see intentions that he himself is not aware of—might find the situation to be the reverse of what it seems: instead of using the idea of time to get the sex he desires, he might be using sex to push away his own awareness of time's passing. The first section

of the poem, lines 1 through 20, describes an idyllic fantasy of how the speaker would behave if time had no effect, while the second part (lines 21-32) presents time's effects in the most gruesome terms conceivable. In the last section, the speaker concocts a scheme to battle time's passage with a cannonball made up of "our sweetness." This tactic hints at desperation. It may be that he is overly anxious to take the woman's virginity and will therefore spin any elaborate hoax for which she might fall. Modern psychology, though, particularly the work of Carl Jung, might say that the fear of death the speaker stirs up is not just a ruse to weaken her defenses, it is a real fear, his fear. The poem's last image, of making the sun (representing time) run, indicates a need for distraction that applies as easily to this speaker's forty-six-line plea as it does to the person he is trying to convince.

### Love and Passion

"To His Coy Mistress" begins as a declaration of the speaker's love, but, by its end, it makes the assumption that the woman being addressed is as passionate as the speaker. He declares his love in fantastic, larger-than-life terms in the first twenty lines, because he is describing an admittedly unreal situation: his love would grow to span continents and stretch from the beginning of time to the end, he tells her, *if only it could.* Readers can recognize a slight touch of irony in the way that he pretends to be frustrated with reality for not allowing his wildly elaborate "proof" of love. After frightening the woman in the middle section of the poem, with visions of what will happen that are much worse than what he would like to happen, the speaker presumes her to be as lustful as he is. There is a clear turning point in lines 31 and 32, where he presumes her agreement in his sarcasm of isolation—he could list any number of things that people do not do in the grave, but his use of the double meaning of "embrace" (none embrace the grave and none embrace each other in the grave) takes for granted that embracing is the thing to do. The last part of the poem speaks from a conspiratorial "we" stance about how they can, together, fight life's limits with sex, most overtly in the couplet "And tear our pleasures with rough strife / Through the iron gates of life."

### Beauty

The woman's concern for her beauty, her vanity, is the tool that the speaker of this poem tries to use to make time's passage a threat to her. His initial flattery of her beauty is abstract, with no men-

## Topics for Further Study

- Write a modern-day dialogue between Andrew Marvell and a girl who he is trying to pick up, including all of the arguments he uses in this poem and her counterarguments.

- Find one of the other poems written about the same time as this one that has the same theme, such as Christopher Marlowe's "The Passionate Shepherd to his Love," Ben Jonson's "Song: To Celia," or Robert Herrick's "To The Virgins, To Make the Most of Time." Describe your impression of each of the two poets. Who do you think would be more successful with his poem? Which one would you rather know? Why?

- This is a fairly long poem, especially for one that is about how little time we have on earth. Could the poet have made his point more quickly without losing anything crucial?

tion of her physical attributes at all, but only exaggerated, hyperbolic declarations of his love. In line 13, his admiration for the woman subtly shifts to praise for the parts of her he can see: her forehead, her eyes, both her breasts and "the rest." Before his inventory becomes too leering, though, he ends it with her heart, an unseen place where the physical and the spiritual come together. In line 25, he uses the impending loss of her beauty as something of a threat, as he reminds her of the ravages of death and decay and how they will destroy what she is trying to preserve by retaining her virginity.

### Death

The middle section of the poem, lines 21 to 32, applies the philosophical concept of time passing to the biological reality of life. Some of the imagery used to capture the idea of death is common and familiar—the marble vault, the grave, and the dust and ashes are all details that have been used before to represent the body's fate after death. The image of worms ravaging the corpse, however, is notably rough in this context; it is a little more vivid and disgusting than the speaker's thoughtful carpe

diem warning deserves. It is a tactile image, invoking the sense of touch, while the other images are visual, and, because it belongs to one of the less-used senses, it is more potent. At the same time that the poem is most graphic about death, it is also most direct about what the speaker's intent actually is: the sarcastic use of "quaint" and "long-preserved" within a context of absolute death makes it clear that honor and virginity are the central targets of his argument.

## Style

"To His Coy Mistress" is a poem of 46 lines that uses rhyming couplets and is divided into three verse-paragraphs. Marvell presents a rhetorical situation with a speaker addressing his mistress. The poem masquerades as a syllogism, a three-part argument with major premise, minor premise, and conclusion. A syllogism is used in formal logic, but the three-part structure of "To His Coy Mistress" is deceptively illogical. In part 1 (lines 1-20), the speaker says in hypothetical conjecture that if he had enough time, he would praise his beloved mistress forever. In part 2 (lines 21-32), the tone abruptly shifts as the rapid movement of time rushes past, threatening to waste the speaker's passion and the mistress's glorious physical beauty. In part 3 (lines 33-46), the speaker urges—in violent, forceful language—that they should enjoy each other's company and defeat "Time" at his own game. If a syllogism is properly constructed, the conclusion is irrefutable. However, the speaker's conclusion is illogical: the mistress's yielding cannot stop the progress of the sun and speed it away. Yet Marvell's poem is sophisticated, evocative, and emotionally moving, certainly among the best of seventeenth-century lyrics and one of the most artfully executed carpe diem poems of all time.

Marvell is sometimes described as a metaphysical poet, a trait seen in his style and choice of metaphors. Metaphysical poets were a group of seventeenth-century writers who attempted to reinvigorate the artificial, idealized views of human nature and sexual love common in poems of the previous century. The Petrarchan love poem, particularly, had become standardized and unimaginative, describing lovely women with cliched metaphors. For example, Petrarchan poets described cold and unreachable women being worshipped by distressed lovers from afar. These poets compared their mistress's eyes to the sun, their hair to golden grain, their white skin to snow, their red lips to roses, and so forth. Metaphysical poets such as Marvell tried to reanimate the poetic line to resemble more closely the actual verbal exchanges of people. They organized their poems in the form of heated arguments with a reluctant mistress, a friend, God, Death, or the poet himself. Metaphysical poets sometimes employed twisted, illogical turns of thought and spiced up their lines with witty metaphors and outrageous, shocking puns and paradoxes. Sometimes serious and sometimes playful, the metaphysical poets deliberately confused the language of erotic love with the language of intense religious experience. It was not until well into the twentieth century that the metaphysical poets were really appreciated for their originality.

## Historical Context

### The English Civil War

During Marvell's lifetime, the government of England underwent startling changes, including the overthrow of King Charles I, then his return from exile, his beheading, the establishment of a new government, and, finally, the restoration of the monarchy with Charles II on the throne. Causes for the troubles can be traced back throughout history, but a good place to start is in the early 1600s, during the reign of King James I, who was King of England from 1603 to 1625. James came from Scotland and was the cousin of the ruler he replaced, Queen Elizabeth I. Because James was from outside of England, his political base was weak. Instead of working with the established government, however, he supported the idea that the king held power by God's will and was responsible to nobody. While the monarchy and the parliament had worked together fairly well during Elizabeth's reign, James did not have the negotiating skill or the inclination to be cooperative. As a result, the loyalties of the English citizens were divided between the Monarchists, who supported the king, and the supporters of the parliament, who were called Roundheads. At the same time, the Puritans, who were members of the Church of England who supported stricter (purer) adherence to the Bible, felt that the monarchy opposed their religious beliefs: they built up hopes during the reign of Elizabeth that the next king would be more understanding, but the Hapton Court Conference soon after James's coronation made the government's intolerance perfectly clear. Some Puritans fled to the colonies in North America as a result, while others stayed in England and actively opposed the king.

The public's support of the monarchy was weakened during James's reign, but it became much worse after his son, Charles I, succeeded him in 1604, when Marvell was four years old. Charles was a morally decent man, unlike James, but he was not intelligent, and he was not up to maintaining the public's support. Historians still debate about the specific dynamics that brought the Civil War about—which political or religious groups had more influence in riling up change—but the bare fact is that by 1640 relationships were so strained between the king and the House of Commons that fighting was inevitable. By 1642, armed conflicts were common between supporters of each side. The king's forces fell in 1645 at the Battle of Naseby, and Charles left the country for Scotland. With him gone, the winning side divided within itself, with the army and the parliament disagreeing about how the country should be run. In 1648, Charles returned with an army of Scots, but the opponents of the monarchy were able to unite enough to defeat him, and he was beheaded at a public execution in 1649 (an event that Marvell depicted in his poem "An Horatian Ode upon Cromwell's Return from Ireland").

From this turmoil, it was Oliver Cromwell who emerged to head the revolutionary government. Cromwell had been a leader in parliament before the revolution, and he had sided with the army against the parliament after the king was chased away. Many hopes for the revolution were destroyed, however, when Cromwell, trying to restore order to a country that had fallen apart, became more of a dictator than the king had ever been. In 1653, he declared himself the Lord High Protector of the Commonwealth, and he dissolved the parliament. This move settled the power struggles between various political factions and did bring peace, but it also ruined Cromwell's hope of ever being considered a legitimate ruler. He promoted greater tolerance for religious beliefs, and he expanded the army and the navy, which enabled the British Empire to expand its influence throughout the world. When Oliver Cromwell died in 1658, his son Richard became Lord Protector, but he ruled for only approximately nine months before the monarchy took back its power. Charles II was made king in 1660. Cromwell's body was dug up and his head was removed, put on a pole, and mounted above Westminster Hall—a warning to all future rebels.

# *Compare & Contrast*

- **1678:** Twelve of the thirteen colonies that originally comprised the United States had been settled. The last, Pennsylvania, was settled in 1782.

  **1776:** The United States of America declared its independence from England and established itself as an independent country.

  **Today:** The United States quit expanding in 1959, when Alaska and Hawaii were admitted into the Union.

- **1678:** Dutch traders bought black slaves in Angola and sold them in the New England Colonies for ten times what they paid. 15,000 slaves per year were sold this way.

  **1863:** On January 1, the Emancipation Proclamation, signed by President Lincoln, went into effect, outlawing slavery in the United States. The states that had quit the United States to form the Confederacy did not honor President Lincoln's proclamation: they were in the middle of a Civil War to establish their independence from the United States government.

  **1865:** When the Civil War ended with the Confederacy's defeat, slavery became illegal in the United States.

  **Today:** The effects of the period of slavery can still be felt in the country's uneven race relations.

- **1678:** Almost half of England's population lived in the country. The population was approximately 5.5 million people.

  **Today:** The population of England, now referred to as Great Britain, is 58.5 million people, but this number is expected to drop in the next twenty years.

### The Metaphysical Poets

The term "Metaphysical Poets" is applied to poets of the seventeenth century who came after John Donne (1572-1631) and who wrote like him, showing his influence in their style and their themes. Donne's poetry was notable for the complexity of its imagery and the unevenness of its form, in contrast to the smooth elegance of the Elizabethan sonnets that writers before him were producing. Even when he was writing about uplifting subjects such as love, Donne's poetry displayed an intellectual, philosophical bent—an interest in metaphysics ran through everything he did. In the same way that Marvell was a favorite of Cromwell and was involved in the government of his day, Donne was a favorite of King James I and was appointed by him to be dean of St. Paul's Cathedral. The term Metaphysical Poets was not used by the poets of the 1600s to describe themselves: it was applied almost a hundred years later, by the famous Dr. Samuel Johnson, who said in *A Life in Cowley,* "About the beginning of the Seventeenth Century, appeared a race of writers, that may be termed metaphysical poets." Different critics have different ideas about who is included in this group, but most are certain to include Donne and Marvell, George Herbert, Henry Vaughan, and Richard Crenshaw. During the Restoration, after the monarchy of England was restored with the start of Charles II's reign in 1660, poets began to concentrate on outer, social concerns, rather than thoughts and emotions. This change is seen in Marvell's works, which developed from his earlier lyric poetry to social satires later in his life.

### Critical Overview

Marvell's reputation has risen spectacularly during this century; his poetry was dismissed as obscene and obscure by previous generations, who generally preferred the polished artificiality of Elizabethan love poetry and sonnet cycles. Earlier criticism tends to focus on reviving interest in metaphysical poets such as Marvell, John Donne, and George Herbert, while later criticism discusses the poem's rhetoric, persona, and implied audience. T. S. Eliot initiated the critical reevaluation of Marvell's work with his essay "Andrew Marvell" in his *Selected Essays,* originally published in 1921. Eliot argued that critics misunderstood "Puritan" writers and failed to see the wit beneath poems such as "To His Coy Mistress." Eliot viewed "To His Coy Mistress" as based on a great traditional theme of European literature, but he also noted the manner in which Marvell transformed this theme through wit and playfulness. Eliot argued that the poem's rapid lines, concentration of an astonishing variety of images, and surprising comparisons make it superior to John Milton's shorter poems. Eliot also found that Marvell's ability to navigate between levity of tone and seriousness of message gave the poem poise, inventiveness, clarity, and power unsurpassed by any seventeenth-century poet.

Joseph J. Moldenhauer, in *Texas Studies in Literature and Language,* wrote that although Marvell worked within the narrow range of traditional carpe diem lyrics, he had a superb appreciation for the poem as rhetorical discourse. Moldenhauer described the way that Marvell capitalized on the poem's hypothetical situation of speaker addressing a silent listener, inventing a distinct and dramatic rhetorical situation. The critic also argued that Marvell's persona is perfectly suited to his purpose; he is an urbane and sophisticated speaker, not the irrational and lust-driven youth we expect in a love poem. Moldenhauer believed that the mistress, however equal in social position, is probably younger and less sophisticated than the speaker. She expects to be praised but is surprised by the extent of the poet's charms.

Recent criticism focuses on gender issues and tensions between the sexes present in "To His Coy Mistress." Bernard Duyfhuizen, in *College English,* argues that a female reader of the poem might have difficulty appreciating the smooth strategic argument of the speaker and would instinctively identify more with the silent mistress. The female student reading the poem may recognize as familiar the passionate, masculine appeal to love. Duyfhuizen believes the female reader is likely to feel upset at the poet's display of egoism and his proud assault on her virginity. A female reader would see the movement of the poem's logic differently by contemporary standards, with the understood social and physical consequences of giving in to a lover's plea. He feels women are likely to be angered by the poem's marginalization of the mistress through the discrepancy in power inherent in the poem's argument.

## Criticism

### David Kelly

*David Kelly is an instructor of creative writing at several community colleges in Illinois, as well as a fiction writer and playwright. In the following essay, Kelly examines what makes Marvell's poetry particularly popular with poets, finding the answer in the connection between the wit of his imagery and the serious ideas he examines.*

Andrew Marvell is a poet's poet. Non-poets can see what is going on in his works and appreciate it, usually on a distant, intellectual level, but nobody gets quite the kick out of Marvell that other poets do. It is the same way that short story writers relate to Chekhov, that filmmakers watch John Ford, or how saxophonists, when they're home, spin Eric Dolphy records. When poets read Marvell, it is not a case of their "studying" an artist that they want to copy, any more than the process of growing up can properly be referred to as "studying" your parents. Marvell is studied and mentioned by historians of the seventeenth century because he was an active participant in the politics of the times, and because his work fits neatly into that pocket of post-Donnian writers we know as the Metaphysical Poets. It is not, however, just his style, but his thoughts that end up showing their influence in other poets' works. Archibald MacLeish's "You, Andrew Marvell" seems like something Marvell would appreciate, but it doesn't cling onto his style the way that creepier homages do; T. S. Eliot understands him so well that his use of Marvell's images in "The Love Song of J. Alfred Prufrock" is not even rightly called borrowing, since he has made them belong to the new poem.

And part of his being a poet's poet, just like being an anything's anything, is that the rest of us never really, truly get what the fuss is all about. Sure, we can go over "To His Coy Mistress" word by word, backward and forward, throwing strands of web to other poems of the carpe diem tradition and spinning theories about what is eternal and what is cultural and what is Western in sexual relations. In the end, though, most of us still leave the poem standing as an inanimate object: we leave it amicably, but still leave it, and it leaves us.

In his famous essay "Andrew Marvell," Eliot speaks with reverence about his subject's use of wit. He talks about how wit has meant different things in different generations, an observation that is more crucial for us today than it has been in the

# *What Do I Read Next?*

- A recent collection of Marvell's poetry is 1991's *The Essential Marvell,* from Ecco Press. The book is edited by poet Donald Hall, who also wrote a fascinating introduction that makes the material relevant to today's students.

- Robert H. Ray's *An Andrew Marvell Companion,* published in 1998 by Garland Publishers, offers students a wealth of information on the poet.

- Archibald MacLeish's poem "You, Andrew Marvell" is a main reason that some students develop an interest in Marvell. It is considered one of MacLeish's best works. This poem is often anthologized and can be found in *Collected Poems,* by Archibald MacLeish, published in 1985 by Houghton Mifflin.

- Students who are doing research on the seventeenth century are almost certain to come across the works of Christopher Hill, who is considered to be the most knowledgeable and prolific writer about England during that era. His works are as thorough as any historian's, yet they are written for the nonhistorian to understand. Among the numerous books Hill wrote are *Intellectual Origins of the English Revolution* (1965), *Change and Continuity in 17th-Century England* (1974), and *God's Englishman: Oliver Cromwell and the English Revolution* (1970).

- There is a clear connection between this poem and Christopher Marlowe's "The Passionate Shepherd to His Love" (1599), Sir Walter Raleigh's "The Nymph's Reply to the Shepherd" (1600), Robert Herrick's "To The Virgins, to Make Much of Time" (1648), and Ben Jonson's "Song: To Celia" (1606). Because these poems were published well before today's copyright laws were written, they are available in numerous poetry anthologies.

---

past. In our cynical world, it is hardly even a compliment to call a writer a wit anymore—the word, too often used by the half-intelligent to describe the fifty-five-percent intelligent, is used more often sarcastically, to capture a particularly pathetic strain of self-delusion, than it is used to identify mastery of words and ideas. But it is exactly in the field of words and ideas that Eliot tells us wit has skated around, from one generation to the next. Some wits are funny and others are nasty; some wise and some silly; and some witty poets are all about the ways in which their words intertwine with each other in their own pure space, away from the real world. Others—and this is where Eliot places Andrew Marvell—are wits because of the ways their words reflect an identifiable world, but do it in their own terms.

Every poet who has written throughout the ages has, of course, been moved by a unique inspiration, but all have had the same few tools to work with. The same essay by Eliot cites Samuel Taylor Coleridge on the varieties of balances, the sliding scales that, differently calibrated, all make up the thing we call imagination. We find it revealed in qualities

> of sameness, with difference; of the general, with the concrete; the idea with the image; the individual with the representative; the sense of novelty and freshness with old and familiar objects; a more than usual state of emotion with more than usual order; judgement ever awake and steady self-possession with enthusiasm with feeling profound or vehement....

In other words, the differences that we observe in poetic imaginations are the results of the almost infinite varieties of ways different poets resolve these differences. Poet A might lean closer toward sameness, concreteness, imagery, representation, etc., than Poet B, while Poet C's tastes could incline in the entirely opposite direction, and so on.

Marvell's poetry tends, in general, to draw upon the least expected sources for its images. The reason that poets use images at all is to make us see things differently than they appear to the naked eye. Similes and metaphors tell us that two things are like each other, and the less they have in common, the more readers have to think in order to realize the connection. For instance, "wispy clouds" might give a sense of what the clouds look like, but "clouds like an old man's beard" implies a whole new dimension of meaning. Marvell's comparisons are admired because they join things that the rest of us would not notice as having any common ground. Two lovers might get themselves jumbled in a ball, literally or symbolically, but not every poet could turn that ball into a cannonball and fire it at "the gates of life." Very few poets would think of comparing love and vegetation because vegetation just does not seem like a lovely thing, but the comparison works in "To His Coy Mistress" because of the way Marvell is able to focus his readers on the qualities that love and vegetation do share: slow growth and the ability to spread almost indefinitely.

Bringing unlike things together in this way takes the kind of cleverness that we usually associate with wit in its most unpleasant form: empty cleverness, or cleverness for its own sake. This is the kind of wit that we are amused with, but we usually can dismiss it easily enough, the way a good joke is put aside once it has been heard. Hollow wit, in fact, is often like a joke in that surprise is all that it has to offer. Marvell's comparisons, on the other hand, linger on well beyond the initial jolt of recognition. The ideas that he is explaining are important ideas, not throwaways. Superficial readers, who feel that all they need to see about "To His Coy Mistress" is that the speaker has an overactive libido, are missing a whole world of understanding that the poem presents. Whether you believe that his use of death imagery is sincere or just the speaker's trick on the girl, the fact remains that, using sex and love and wordplay, this poem can take readers closer to the truth about life and death than they would ordinarily choose to go. This is why Eliot describes the particular type of wit that Marvell displays as most often "... a structured decoration of a serious idea."

Everybody likes to be entertained. It is often a huge disappointment to students to find out that there is nothing about great ideas requiring them to be even the slightest bit entertaining: sometimes, it even seems that great thinkers are measured by how uninteresting they can be. On the other hand, nothing disgusts true artists more than someone using the tools of art to make themselves popular. Poetry is great thought made appealing: it is easy for poets

> *Marvell's comparisons ... linger on well beyond the initial jolt of recognition.*"

to veer too far to either side, to be too thoughtful or too clever, giving up too much of the side being neglected. If we go by what T. S. Eliot said in his essay about Andrew Marvell and by what we can see of Marvell on display in "To His Coy Mistress," the secret of his success appears to be that he struck the right balance. Maybe it isn't the right balance for most of us: average readers would like to be amused with more wit, and academics might find intellectual poetry more interesting, but then, poets, like any special group, tend to see things in their own way.

**Source:** David Kelly, in an essay for *Poetry for Students,* Gale, 1999.

### Bruce Meyer

*Bruce Meyer is the director of the creative writing program at the University of Toronto. He has taught at several Canadian universities and is the author of three collections of poetry. In the following essay, Meyer examines Marvell's use of rhetoric in "To His Coy Mistress."*

Andrew Marvell's "To His Coy Mistress" features one of the best-known opening lines in English poetry: "Had we but world enough, and time." What makes this poem both interesting and engagingly complex is Marvell's use of rhetoric, perhaps the most overlooked critical aspect in discussions of poetry. Put simply, rhetoric is the art of persuasion through language, where the speaker attempts to convince the listener to an action, a belief, or to an idea by presenting an argument in support of a particular position.

Throughout the course of "To His Coy Mistress," Marvell evolves an elaborate argument in which a man attempts to persuade a young woman to have sex with him. As pickup lines go, "To His Coy Mistress" ranks as one of the most memorable. The poem, as a rhetorical structure, is composed of five separate units, each with its own argument and subconclusion. The poem opens, lines 1-2, with a

> *As pickup lines go,
> 'To His Coy Mistress' ranks
> as one of the most
> memorable. "*

statement of expediency, the thesis of his discussion. The body of the discussion within the poem contains four sub-arguments on the topics of what he would do with eternity if he had all the time in the world to wait for the woman to make her decision about losing her virginity (lines 3-13); a flattering examination of her body in which he praises the parts of her physique (lines 14-20); a somber and solemn discussion on the nature of death and how it would affect their relationship (lines 21-32); and, finally, a concluding discussion that returns to the opening statement on the need for expediency. Although it is unknown whether the young woman in question found his arguments convincing enough to acquiesce to the persona's suggestions, the poem stands as one of the finest pieces of poetic persuasion.

As a poem about the need to love, "To His Coy Mistress" has little to do with love, yet it borrows quite substantially from the traditions of love lyrics. The sentiment expressed in the opening couplet, "Had we but world enough, and time, / This coyness, lady, were no crime" is a standard's lover's plea. The persona of the poem is suggesting to the "coy" young woman that time is of the essence, that if they had eternity, her "coyness" or reticence would not be a problem in their relationship, and the speaker surmises all the wondrous things they might do (other than sex) to fill their blissful eternity. Time, however, is not on their side. This awareness of time creates an urgency to the matter of their consummation in much the same way that Juliet decries the singing of the lark at daybreak in Romeo and Juliet or Donne offers mock disgust to the dawn in "The Sun Rising." Marvell, however, turns this prototypical lover's complaint into a playful series of exemplums for speculation at the opening of "To His Coy Mistress."

Lines 3 to 20 are a wonderful catalogue of exotic images that answer the question of what the persona would do if he had eternity to spend waiting. There is the suggestion echoed through lines

3 and 4 that the eternity shared by the two would-be lovers is an Edenic extemporality—a circumstance that is not only outside of time, but a single "long love's day." After all, hints Marvell, the extemporal condition is without the meaningful natural measure of the seasons so that time, or the absence of it, is perceived as a stretch of possibilities. In this imaginative expanse, the woman might walk "by the Indian Ganges' side" while the persona would strike a melancholy pose and "by the tide / Of Humber would complain." In effect, what the speaker is envisioning is an artificial, almost posed, set of circumstances that are both fanciful and exotic and that form a tableau where the woman journeys to the mysteries of the East while the persona waits at home and frets deeply and anxiously about his desires. His unquenched desires, however, are not without conviction, and he follows the tableau with a promise that future poets, such as Auden in "As I Walked Out One Evening" or Burns in "My Love is Like a Red, Red Rose" express: the concept of timeless devotion. Marvell writes, "I would / Love you ten years before the Flood, / And you should, if you please, refuse / Till the conversion of the Jews." Essentially, what emerges from the opening lines of the poem (3-10) is a portrait of two individuals with a great deal of time on their hands where the poet strikes a subtle allusion to a situation akin to Adam and Eve in a paradisal state of eternal timelessness. Like the Eden in Milton's Paradise Lost, this timeless state is a fecund place, if not for humans, at least for vegetables. In a splendid note of wry wit, the persona compares his love to a vast empire that is nothing more than an extensive vegetable garden: "My vegetable love should grow / Vaster than empires, and more slow." The suggestion here may be that although this love may be fertile, it is unharvested and slow-growing, and coupling this image with the previous discussion of time and expediency strikes a quiet though suggestive note of the presence of entropy in the world. The need to reap what has been sown while the "fresh" opportunity exists seems to be the implicit question that this odd couplet begs from the reader and presumably the "coy mistress" to whom the poem is addressed. After all, as Marvell perceives it, love has a short shelf life.

At line 13, however, the structure of the speculation of what to do with such timelessness shifts away from the exotic and the fanciful, and the poet falls back on an accepted poetic convention centered on the beloved, where the lover "studies" her from head to toe. What results is epideictic rhetoric, the rhetoric of praise and blame that is most often at the core of poems about love or desire, in which a lover is considering the beloved's physical attributes. Marvell plays the convention with gusto and emphasis.

In what amounts to pure flattery on the lover's part, "To His Coy Mistress" borrows a solemn convention that is used by other poets such as Shakespeare in "Sonnet 130" ("My mistress' eyes are nothing like the sun") or Chaucer in "Parliament of Fowles." This "top to bottom" process of examining each part of the beloved's anatomy and pausing at each aspect for an apt comparison has its origins in the love poetry of the Bible, "The Song of Solomon." As in "The Song of Solomon," "To His Coy Mistress" suggests, in a very flattering passage, that the best usage of time would be for the lover to contemplate his beloved, starting at her "eyes" and then moving on to her "forehead." The "forehead" is an important aspect of the female anatomy in any naming of a beloved's body parts because, at least in the conventions that arose from Medieval love poetry, the Virgin Mary was supposedly the owner of a high and very beautiful forehead. Also, the mention of the forehead (which by the seventeenth century was no longer considered a focal point for the female body) lends to the poem and the mistress an archaic, if not nostalgic note in much the same way that Spenser's *The Faerie Queene* borrowed heavily from the conventions of Medieval romance literature for an affected sense of archaism. What should be remembered is that archaism is, rhetorically and poetically, a form of elevation. If it is the poet's aim to elevate the "coy Mistress," then the standard application of naming body parts is an apt and recognizable place to start, and it is an action that charmingly locates the woman amongst a catalogue of the most praised women in literature.

After declaring that he would spend "thirty thousand years" to "adore each breast," the persona follows this hyperbolized statement by announcing that he would spend "An age at least to every part." What hyperbole does in a love poem is that it leads to more hyperbole, and the greater the pronouncement on the part of the poet, the wilder the assumption. As ridiculous as this may sound, it serves, rhetorically, as an elaborate and entertaining form of persuasion in which the poet is given the opportunity not only to describe and praise the beloved but to show the breadth and skill of his imagination in an effort to impress and flatter.

Marvell then assures the woman that she is worthy of such hyperbole when he notes that "lady, you deserve this state / Nor would I love at a lower rate." This reassurance of worthiness is the conclusion of his subtopic into flattery, for he suddenly returns to the theme of expediency and time with a bathetic introduction of the theme of death: "But at my back I always hear / Time's wingéd chariot hurrying near." The world beyond, he is sorry to say, is not paradise or even a broad range of extemporal activities and pleasures but "Deserts of vast eternity." The metrical truncation of line 24 sounds like a curfew bell on the pleasures of dreaming and, rhetorically, brings the argument back to the factuality of reality. What is really confronting them is the lack of time, the spectre of death, and the end to all earthly pleasures: "Thy beauty shall no more be found; / Nor, in thy marble vault, shall sound / My echoing song: then worms shall try / That long-preserved virginity, / And your quaint honor turn to dust, / And into ashes all my lust." Coyness, the persona concludes, serves no one after he or she is dead. "The grave's a fine and private place," he tells her as if to drive home the point in a conclusion to the sub-argument on death, but it is a place where no one loves and "none, I think, do there embrace." As a subsection to the poem, the introduction of the argument on death is intended partly as a shock to the listener after the pleasant earlier sections of the poem and as a memento mori, a reminder of the presence of death in the world and a sharpener of both the senses and the urgency underlying the need to love.

The final section of the poem, lines 33-44, returns to the opening theme of expediency in the face of fleeting time. The speaker pleads with the woman not to waste her youth, her beauty, and the moment itself by holding her virginity in reserve: "Now let us sport us while we may," he advises. Marvell borrows the concept of "devouring Time" from Shakespeare's "Sonnet 19," another allusion that is designed to reinforce the argument for expediency. The "amorous birds of prey" in line 38 is a perplexing image, perhaps suggesting a sense of carpe diem, of taking control of the situation and seizing the moment by rolling "all our strength and all / Our sweetness up into one ball" in an act of both spiritual and sexual union. This union of the two souls would then permit them the free reign of passion in defiance of the world and all of its hardships so that they would "tear our pleasures with rough strife / Thorough the iron gates of life."

The poem concludes, as a student's essay might conclude, with a passage beginning with the word "Thus." This "Thus" is an equal sign where all the elements in the rhetorical structure, like all the parts of a balanced equation, are put in sum with the suggestion that there can be no other possible conclusion to the situation than the one the persona reaches through his discourse. Although they "cannot make the sun / Stand still," effect a miracle, or stop time like a Biblical prophet, the persona assumes that together as a "we," rather than as separate entities, they can "yet make him run," suggesting that it is better to face time together than alone. As a rhetorical strategy, "To His Coy Mistress" is a frontal assault on a topic, a very blatant effort to address the delicate issue of seduction. What makes it interesting and enjoyable as a poem is not simply the ardor of the persona in his quest for the woman's virginity, but the various plays he pulls from his bag of persuasive tricks. It is this combination of energy and ingenuity as a "come-on" line that has kept this poem fascinating for generations of readers and would-be lovers.

**Source:** Bruce Meyer, in an essay for *Poetry for Students,* Gale, 1999.

## Sources

Aylmer, G. E., *The Interregnum: The Quest for Settlement, 1646-1660,* Hamden, CT: Archon Books, 1972.

Beer, Patricia, *An Introduction to the Metaphysical Poets,* Totowa, NJ: Rowman and Littlefield, 1972.

Duyfhuizen, Bernard, "Textual Harassment of Marvell's Coy Mistress: The Institutionalization of Masculine Criticism," *College English,* Vol. 50, April 1988, pp. 411-23.

Eliot, T. S., "Andrew Marvell," in his *Selected Essays,* Harcourt, Brace, Jovanovich, 1950, pp. 251-63.

Moldenhauer, Joseph J., "The Voices of Seduction in 'To His Coy Mistress': A Rhetorical Analysis," *Texas Studies in Literature and Language,* Vol. 10, No. 1, Spring 1968, pp. 189-206.

Untermeyer, Louis, "Puritans and Cavaliers," *Lives of the Poets: The Story of One Thousand Years of English and American Poetry,* New York: Simon and Schuster, 1959, pp. 152-169.

## For Further Study

Becker, Ernest, *The Denial of Death,* New York: The Free Press (Macmillan), 1973.

This innovative breaking book by one of the most introspective of recent psychologists looks at the ways in which humans turn to pursuits like sex in order to suppress their fear of dying. This is the same idea that Marvell was writing about three hundred years earlier.

Brett, R. L., ed., *Andrew Marvell: Essays on the Tercentenary of His Death,* London: Oxford University Press, 1979.

This collection analyzes how Marvell's reputation has grown over the 300 years since he died, giving a late-twentieth-century understanding of the poets that he has influenced.

Jones, Richard Foster, *The Seventeenth Century: Studies in the History of English Thought and Literature from Bacon to Pope,* Stanford, CA: Stanford University, 1969.

This groundbreaking work presents a collection of essays by Jones, one of the most respected scholars in the study of Marvell's time, and also includes more than a dozen essays by other thinkers and researchers who were influenced by Jones's writings.

Paglia, Camille, *Sexual Personae: Art and Decadence from Nefertiti to Emily Dickinson,* New York: Vintage Books, 1991.

As the title implies, Paglia's book examines the role of sex in literature and the roles that men and women have played in literary works throughout history.

Semler, L. E., *The English Mannerist Poets and the Visual Arts,* Madison, NJ: Fairleigh Dickinson Press/Associated University Presses, 1998.

Marvell does not play a large part in Semler's study, but students who are interested in seventeenth-century painting should appreciate the ideas this book has to offer.

Stephens, Dorothy, *The Limits of Eroticism in Post-Petrarchan Narrative: Conditional Pleasure From Spenser to Marvell,* New York: Cambridge University Press, 1998.

Although written at a complex level for the professional scholar, Stephens's work addresses a central question about Marvell. We study "To His Coy Mistress" today as much to find out about the sexual mores of his time as we do for his technique.

# Glossary of Literary Terms

## A

**Abstract:** Used as a noun, the term refers to a short summary or outline of a longer work. As an adjective applied to writing or literary works, abstract refers to words or phrases that name things not knowable through the five senses.

**Accent:** The emphasis or stress placed on a syllable in poetry. Traditional poetry commonly uses patterns of accented and unaccented syllables (known as feet) that create distinct rhythms. Much modern poetry uses less formal arrangements that create a sense of freedom and spontaneity.

**Aestheticism:** A literary and artistic movement of the nineteenth century. Followers of the movement believed that art should not be mixed with social, political, or moral teaching. The statement "art for art's sake" is a good summary of aestheticism. The movement had its roots in France, but it gained widespread importance in England in the last half of the nineteenth century, where it helped change the Victorian practice of including moral lessons in literature.

**Affective Fallacy:** An error in judging the merits or faults of a work of literature. The "error" results from stressing the importance of the work's effect upon the reader—that is, how it makes a reader "feel" emotionally, what it does as a literary work—instead of stressing its inner qualities as a created object, or what it "is."

**Age of Johnson:** The period in English literature between 1750 and 1798, named after the most prominent literary figure of the age, Samuel Johnson. Works written during this time are noted for their emphasis on "sensibility," or emotional quality. These works formed a transition between the rational works of the Age of Reason, or Neoclassical period, and the emphasis on individual feelings and responses of the Romantic period.

**Age of Reason:** See *Neoclassicism*

**Age of Sensibility:** See *Age of Johnson*

**Agrarians:** A group of Southern American writers of the 1930s and 1940s who fostered an economic and cultural program for the South based on agriculture, in opposition to the industrial society of the North. The term can refer to any group that promotes the value of farm life and agricultural society.

**Alexandrine Meter:** See *Meter*

**Allegory:** A narrative technique in which characters representing things or abstract ideas are used to convey a message or teach a lesson. Allegory is typically used to teach moral, ethical, or religious lessons but is sometimes used for satiric or political purposes.

**Alliteration:** A poetic device where the first consonant sounds or any vowel sounds in words or syllables are repeated.

**Allusion:** A reference to a familiar literary or historical person or event, used to make an idea more easily understood.

**Amerind Literature:** The writing and oral traditions of Native Americans. Native American literature was originally passed on by word of mouth, so it consisted largely of stories and events that were easily memorized. Amerind prose is often rhythmic like poetry because it was recited to the beat of a ceremonial drum.

**Analogy:** A comparison of two things made to explain something unfamiliar through its similarities to something familiar, or to prove one point based on the acceptedness of another. Similes and metaphors are types of analogies.

**Anapest:** See *Foot*

**Angry Young Men:** A group of British writers of the 1950s whose work expressed bitterness and disillusionment with society. Common to their work is an anti-hero who rebels against a corrupt social order and strives for personal integrity.

**Anthropomorphism:** The presentation of animals or objects in human shape or with human characteristics. The term is derived from the Greek word for "human form."

**Antimasque:** See *Masque*

**Antithesis:** The antithesis of something is its direct opposite. In literature, the use of antithesis as a figure of speech results in two statements that show a contrast through the balancing of two opposite ideas. Technically, it is the second portion of the statement that is defined as the "antithesis"; the first portion is the "thesis."

**Apocrypha:** Writings tentatively attributed to an author but not proven or universally accepted to be their works. The term was originally applied to certain books of the Bible that were not considered inspired and so were not included in the "sacred canon."

**Apollonian and Dionysian:** The two impulses believed to guide authors of dramatic tragedy. The Apollonian impulse is named after Apollo, the Greek god of light and beauty and the symbol of intellectual order. The Dionysian impulse is named after Dionysus, the Greek god of wine and the symbol of the unrestrained forces of nature. The Apollonian impulse is to create a rational, harmonious world, while the Dionysian is to express the irrational forces of personality.

**Apostrophe:** A statement, question, or request addressed to an inanimate object or concept or to a nonexistent or absent person.

**Archetype:** The word archetype is commonly used to describe an original pattern or model from which all other things of the same kind are made. This term was introduced to literary criticism from the psychology of Carl Jung. It expresses Jung's theory that behind every person's "unconscious," or repressed memories of the past, lies the "collective unconscious" of the human race: memories of the countless typical experiences of our ancestors. These memories are said to prompt illogical associations that trigger powerful emotions in the reader. Often, the emotional process is primitive, even primordial. Archetypes are the literary images that grow out of the "collective unconscious." They appear in literature as incidents and plots that repeat basic patterns of life. They may also appear as stereotyped characters.

**Argument:** The argument of a work is the author's subject matter or principal idea.

**Art for Art's Sake:** See *Aestheticism*

**Assonance:** The repetition of similar vowel sounds in poetry.

**Audience:** The people for whom a piece of literature is written. Authors usually write with a certain audience in mind, for example, children, members of a religious or ethnic group, or colleagues in a professional field. The term "audience" also applies to the people who gather to see or hear any performance, including plays, poetry readings, speeches, and concerts.

**Automatic Writing:** Writing carried out without a preconceived plan in an effort to capture every random thought. Authors who engage in automatic writing typically do not revise their work, preferring instead to preserve the revealed truth and beauty of spontaneous expression.

***Avant-garde:*** A French term meaning "vanguard." It is used in literary criticism to describe new writing that rejects traditional approaches to literature in favor of innovations in style or content.

# B

**Ballad:** A short poem that tells a simple story and has a repeated refrain. Ballads were originally intended to be sung. Early ballads, known as folk ballads, were passed down through generations, so their authors are often unknown. Later ballads composed by known authors are called literary ballads.

**Baroque:** A term used in literary criticism to describe literature that is complex or ornate in style or diction. Baroque works typically express tension, anxiety, and violent emotion. The term "Baroque Age" designates a period in Western European literature beginning in the late sixteenth century and ending about one hundred years later.

Works of this period often mirror the qualities of works more generally associated with the label "baroque" and sometimes feature elaborate conceits.

**Baroque Age:** See *Baroque*

**Baroque Period:** See *Baroque*

**Beat Generation:** See *Beat Movement*

**Beat Movement:** A period featuring a group of American poets and novelists of the 1950s and 1960s—including Jack Kerouac, Allen Ginsberg, Gregory Corso, William S. Burroughs, and Lawrence Ferlinghetti—who rejected established social and literary values. Using such techniques as stream of consciousness writing and jazz-influenced free verse and focusing on unusual or abnormal states of mind—generated by religious ecstasy or the use of drugs—the Beat writers aimed to create works that were unconventional in both form and subject matter.

**Beat Poets:** See *Beat Movement*

**Beats, The:** See *Beat Movement*

*Belles-lettres:* A French term meaning "fine letters" or "beautiful writing." It is often used as a synonym for literature, typically referring to imaginative and artistic rather than scientific or expository writing. Current usage sometimes restricts the meaning to light or humorous writing and appreciative essays about literature.

**Black Aesthetic Movement:** A period of artistic and literary development among African Americans in the 1960s and early 1970s. This was the first major African-American artistic movement since the Harlem Renaissance and was closely paralleled by the civil rights and black power movements. The black aesthetic writers attempted to produce works of art that would be meaningful to the black masses. Key figures in black aesthetics included one of its founders, poet and playwright Amiri Baraka, formerly known as LeRoi Jones; poet and essayist Haki R. Madhubuti, formerly Don L. Lee; poet and playwright Sonia Sanchez; and dramatist Ed Bullins.

**Black Arts Movement:** See *Black Aesthetic Movement*

**Black Comedy:** See *Black Humor*

**Black Humor:** Writing that places grotesque elements side by side with humorous ones in an attempt to shock the reader, forcing him or her to laugh at the horrifying reality of a disordered world.

**Black Mountain School:** Black Mountain College and three of its instructors—Robert Creeley, Robert Duncan, and Charles Olson— were all influential in projective verse, so poets working in projective verse are now referred to as members of the Black Mountain school.

**Blank Verse:** Loosely, any unrhymed poetry, but more generally, unrhymed iambic pentameter verse (composed of lines of five two-syllable feet with the first syllable accented, the second unaccented). Blank verse has been used by poets since the Renaissance for its flexibility and its graceful, dignified tone.

**Bloomsbury Group:** A group of English writers, artists, and intellectuals who held informal artistic and philosophical discussions in Bloomsbury, a district of London, from around 1907 to the early 1930s. The Bloomsbury Group held no uniform philosophical beliefs but did commonly express an aversion to moral prudery and a desire for greater social tolerance.

*Bon Mot:* A French term meaning "good word." A *bon mot* is a witty remark or clever observation.

**Breath Verse:** See *Projective Verse*

**Burlesque:** Any literary work that uses exaggeration to make its subject appear ridiculous, either by treating a trivial subject with profound seriousness or by treating a dignified subject frivolously. The word "burlesque" may also be used as an adjective, as in "burlesque show," to mean "striptease act."

# C

**Cadence:** The natural rhythm of language caused by the alternation of accented and unaccented syllables. Much modern poetry—notably free verse—deliberately manipulates cadence to create complex rhythmic effects.

**Caesura:** A pause in a line of poetry, usually occurring near the middle. It typically corresponds to a break in the natural rhythm or sense of the line but is sometimes shifted to create special meanings or rhythmic effects.

*Canzone:* A short Italian or Provencal lyric poem, commonly about love and often set to music. The *canzone* has no set form but typically contains five or six stanzas made up of seven to twenty lines of eleven syllables each. A shorter, five- to ten-line "envoy," or concluding stanza, completes the poem.

*Carpe Diem:* A Latin term meaning "seize the day." This is a traditional theme of poetry, especially lyrics. A *carpe diem* poem advises the reader or the person it addresses to live for today and enjoy the pleasures of the moment.

**Catharsis:** The release or purging of unwanted emotions—specifically fear and pity—brought about by exposure to art. The term was first used by the Greek philosopher Aristotle in his *Poetics* to refer to the desired effect of tragedy on spectators.

**Celtic Renaissance:** A period of Irish literary and cultural history at the end of the nineteenth century. Followers of the movement aimed to create a romantic vision of Celtic myth and legend. The most significant works of the Celtic Renaissance typically present a dreamy, unreal world, usually in reaction against the reality of contemporary problems.

**Celtic Twilight:** See *Celtic Renaissance*

**Character:** Broadly speaking, a person in a literary work. The actions of characters are what constitute the plot of a story, novel, or poem. There are numerous types of characters, ranging from simple, stereotypical figures to intricate, multifaceted ones. In the techniques of anthropomorphism and personification, animals—and even places or things—can assume aspects of character. "Characterization" is the process by which an author creates vivid, believable characters in a work of art. This may be done in a variety of ways, including (1) direct description of the character by the narrator; (2) the direct presentation of the speech, thoughts, or actions of the character; and (3) the responses of other characters to the character. The term "character" also refers to a form originated by the ancient Greek writer Theophrastus that later became popular in the seventeenth and eighteenth centuries. It is a short essay or sketch of a person who prominently displays a specific attribute or quality, such as miserliness or ambition.

**Characterization:** See *Character*

**Classical:** In its strictest definition in literary criticism, classicism refers to works of ancient Greek or Roman literature. The term may also be used to describe a literary work of recognized importance (a "classic") from any time period or literature that exhibits the traits of classicism.

**Classicism:** A term used in literary criticism to describe critical doctrines that have their roots in ancient Greek and Roman literature, philosophy, and art. Works associated with classicism typically exhibit restraint on the part of the author, unity of design and purpose, clarity, simplicity, logical organization, and respect for tradition.

**Colloquialism:** A word, phrase, or form of pronunciation that is acceptable in casual conversation but not in formal, written communication. It is considered more acceptable than slang.

**Complaint:** A lyric poem, popular in the Renaissance, in which the speaker expresses sorrow about his or her condition. Typically, the speaker's sadness is caused by an unresponsive lover, but some complaints cite other sources of unhappiness, such as poverty or fate.

**Conceit:** A clever and fanciful metaphor, usually expressed through elaborate and extended comparison, that presents a striking parallel between two seemingly dissimilar things—for example, elaborately comparing a beautiful woman to an object like a garden or the sun. The conceit was a popular device throughout the Elizabethan Age and Baroque Age and was the principal technique of the seventeenth-century English metaphysical poets. This usage of the word conceit is unrelated to the best-known definition of conceit as an arrogant attitude or behavior.

**Concrete:** Concrete is the opposite of abstract, and refers to a thing that actually exists or a description that allows the reader to experience an object or concept with the senses.

**Concrete Poetry:** Poetry in which visual elements play a large part in the poetic effect. Punctuation marks, letters, or words are arranged on a page to form a visual design: a cross, for example, or a bumblebee.

**Confessional Poetry:** A form of poetry in which the poet reveals very personal, intimate, sometimes shocking information about himself or herself.

**Connotation:** The impression that a word gives beyond its defined meaning. Connotations may be universally understood or may be significant only to a certain group.

**Consonance:** Consonance occurs in poetry when words appearing at the ends of two or more verses have similar final consonant sounds but have final vowel sounds that differ, as with "stuff" and "off."

**Convention:** Any widely accepted literary device, style, or form.

*Corrido:* A Mexican ballad.

**Couplet:** Two lines of poetry with the same rhyme and meter, often expressing a complete and self-contained thought.

**Criticism:** The systematic study and evaluation of literary works, usually based on a specific method or set of principles. An important part of literary studies since ancient times, the practice of criticism has given rise to numerous theories, methods, and "schools," sometimes producing conflicting, even contradictory, interpretations of literature in general as well as of individual works. Even such basic issues as what constitutes a poem or a novel have been the subject of much criticism over the centuries.

# D

**Dactyl:** See *Foot*

**Dadaism:** A protest movement in art and literature founded by Tristan Tzara in 1916. Followers of the movement expressed their outrage at the destruction brought about by World War I by revolting against numerous forms of social convention. The Dadaists presented works marked by calculated madness and flamboyant nonsense. They stressed total freedom of expression, commonly through primitive displays of emotion and illogical, often senseless, poetry. The movement ended shortly after the war, when it was replaced by surrealism.

**Decadent:** See *Decadents*

**Decadents:** The followers of a nineteenth-century literary movement that had its beginnings in French aestheticism. Decadent literature displays a fascination with perverse and morbid states; a search for novelty and sensation—the "new thrill"; a preoccupation with mysticism; and a belief in the senselessness of human existence. The movement is closely associated with the doctrine Art for Art's Sake. The term "decadence" is sometimes used to denote a decline in the quality of art or literature following a period of greatness.

**Deconstruction:** A method of literary criticism developed by Jacques Derrida and characterized by multiple conflicting interpretations of a given work. Deconstructionists consider the impact of the language of a work and suggest that the true meaning of the work is not necessarily the meaning that the author intended.

**Deduction:** The process of reaching a conclusion through reasoning from general premises to a specific premise.

**Denotation:** The definition of a word, apart from the impressions or feelings it creates in the reader.

**Diction:** The selection and arrangement of words in a literary work. Either or both may vary depending on the desired effect. There are four general types of diction: "formal," used in scholarly or lofty writing; "informal," used in relaxed but educated conversation; "colloquial," used in everyday speech; and "slang," containing newly coined words and other terms not accepted in formal usage.

**Didactic:** A term used to describe works of literature that aim to teach some moral, religious, political, or practical lesson. Although didactic elements are often found in artistically pleasing works, the term "didactic" usually refers to literature in which the message is more important than the form. The term may also be used to criticize a work that the critic finds "overly didactic," that is, heavy-handed in its delivery of a lesson.

**Dimeter:** See *Meter*

**Dionysian:** See *Apollonian and Dionysian*

***Discordia concours:*** A Latin phrase meaning "discord in harmony." The term was coined by the eighteenth-century English writer Samuel Johnson to describe "a combination of dissimilar images or discovery of occult resemblances in things apparently unlike." Johnson created the expression by reversing a phrase by the Latin poet Horace.

**Dissonance:** A combination of harsh or jarring sounds, especially in poetry. Although such combinations may be accidental, poets sometimes intentionally make them to achieve particular effects. Dissonance is also sometimes used to refer to close but not identical rhymes. When this is the case, the word functions as a synonym for consonance.

***Double Entendre:*** A corruption of a French phrase meaning "double meaning." The term is used to indicate a word or phrase that is deliberately ambiguous, especially when one of the meanings is risque or improper.

**Draft:** Any preliminary version of a written work. An author may write dozens of drafts which are revised to form the final work, or he or she may write only one, with few or no revisions.

**Dramatic Monologue:** See *Monologue*

**Dramatic Poetry:** Any lyric work that employs elements of drama such as dialogue, conflict, or characterization, but excluding works that are intended for stage presentation.

**Dream Allegory:** See *Dream Vision*

**Dream Vision:** A literary convention, chiefly of the Middle Ages. In a dream vision a story is presented as a literal dream of the narrator. This device was commonly used to teach moral and religious lessons.

# E

**Eclogue:** In classical literature, a poem featuring rural themes and structured as a dialogue among shepherds. Eclogues often took specific poetic forms, such as elegies or love poems. Some were written as the soliloquy of a shepherd. In later centuries, "eclogue" came to refer to any poem that was in the pastoral tradition or that had a dialogue or monologue structure.

**Edwardian:** Describes cultural conventions identified with the period of the reign of Edward VII of England (1901-1910). Writers of the Edwardian Age typically displayed a strong reaction against the propriety and conservatism of the Victorian Age. Their work often exhibits distrust of authority in religion, politics, and art and expresses strong doubts about the soundness of conventional values.

**Edwardian Age:** See *Edwardian*

**Electra Complex:** A daughter's amorous obsession with her father.

**Elegy:** A lyric poem that laments the death of a person or the eventual death of all people. In a conventional elegy, set in a classical world, the poet and subject are spoken of as shepherds. In modern criticism, the word elegy is often used to refer to a poem that is melancholy or mournfully contemplative.

**Elizabethan Age:** A period of great economic growth, religious controversy, and nationalism closely associated with the reign of Elizabeth I of England (1558-1603). The Elizabethan Age is considered a part of the general renaissance—that is, the flowering of arts and literature—that took place in Europe during the fourteenth through sixteenth centuries. The era is considered the golden age of English literature. The most important dramas in English and a great deal of lyric poetry were produced during this period, and modern English criticism began around this time.

**Empathy:** A sense of shared experience, including emotional and physical feelings, with someone or something other than oneself. Empathy is often used to describe the response of a reader to a literary character.

**English Sonnet:** See *Sonnet*

**Enjambment:** The running over of the sense and structure of a line of verse or a couplet into the following verse or couplet.

**Enlightenment, The:** An eighteenth-century philosophical movement. It began in France but had a wide impact throughout Europe and America. Thinkers of the Enlightenment valued reason and believed that both the individual and society could achieve a state of perfection. Corresponding to this essentially humanist vision was a resistance to religious authority.

**Epic:** A long narrative poem about the adventures of a hero of great historic or legendary importance. The setting is vast and the action is often given cosmic significance through the intervention of supernatural forces such as gods, angels, or demons. Epics are typically written in a classical style of grand simplicity with elaborate metaphors and allusions that enhance the symbolic importance of a hero's adventures.

**Epic Simile:** See *Homeric Simile*

**Epigram:** A saying that makes the speaker's point quickly and concisely.

**Epilogue:** A concluding statement or section of a literary work. In dramas, particularly those of the seventeenth and eighteenth centuries, the epilogue is a closing speech, often in verse, delivered by an actor at the end of a play and spoken directly to the audience.

**Epiphany:** A sudden revelation of truth inspired by a seemingly trivial incident.

**Epitaph:** An inscription on a tomb or tombstone, or a verse written on the occasion of a person's death. Epitaphs may be serious or humorous.

**Epithalamion:** A song or poem written to honor and commemorate a marriage ceremony.

**Epithalamium:** See *Epithalamion*

**Epithet:** A word or phrase, often disparaging or abusive, that expresses a character trait of someone or something.

***Erziehungsroman:*** See *Bildungsroman*

**Essay:** A prose composition with a focused subject of discussion. The term was coined by Michel de Montaigne to describe his 1580 collection of brief, informal reflections on himself and on various topics relating to human nature. An essay can also be a long, systematic discourse.

**Existentialism:** A predominantly twentieth-century philosophy concerned with the nature and perception of human existence. There are two major strains of existentialist thought: atheistic and Christian. Followers of atheistic existentialism believe that the individual is alone in a godless universe and that the basic human condition is one of suffering and loneliness. Nevertheless, because there are no fixed values, individuals can create their own characters—indeed, they can shape themselves—through the exercise of free will. The atheistic strain culminates in and is popularly associated with the works of Jean-Paul Sartre. The Christian existentialists, on the other hand, believe that only in God may people find freedom from life's anguish. The two strains hold certain beliefs in common: that existence cannot be fully understood or described through empirical effort; that anguish is a universal element of life; that individuals must bear responsibility for their actions; and that there is no common standard of behavior or perception for religious and ethical matters.

**Expatriates:** See *Expatriatism*

**Expatriatism:** The practice of leaving one's country to live for an extended period in another country.

**Exposition:** Writing intended to explain the nature of an idea, thing, or theme. Expository writing is often combined with description, narration, or argument. In dramatic writing, the exposition is the introductory material which presents the characters, setting, and tone of the play.

**Expressionism:** An indistinct literary term, originally used to describe an early twentieth-century school of German painting. The term applies to almost any mode of unconventional, highly subjective writing that distorts reality in some way.

**Extended Monologue:** See *Monologue*

# F

**Feet:** See *Foot*

**Feminine Rhyme:** See *Rhyme*

**Fiction:** Any story that is the product of imagination rather than a documentation of fact. characters and events in such narratives may be based in real life but their ultimate form and configuration is a creation of the author.

**Figurative Language:** A technique in writing in which the author temporarily interrupts the order, construction, or meaning of the writing for a particular effect. This interruption takes the form of one or more figures of speech such as hyperbole, irony, or simile. Figurative language is the opposite of literal language, in which every word is truthful, accurate, and free of exaggeration or embellishment.

**Figures of Speech:** Writing that differs from customary conventions for construction, meaning, order, or significance for the purpose of a special meaning or effect. There are two major types of figures of speech: rhetorical figures, which do not make changes in the meaning of the words, and tropes, which do.

*Fin de siecle*: A French term meaning "end of the century." The term is used to denote the last decade of the nineteenth century, a transition period when writers and other artists abandoned old conventions and looked for new techniques and objectives.

**First Person:** See *Point of View*

**Folk Ballad:** See *Ballad*

**Folklore:** Traditions and myths preserved in a culture or group of people. Typically, these are passed on by word of mouth in various forms—such as legends, songs, and proverbs—or preserved in customs and ceremonies. This term was first used by W. J. Thoms in 1846.

**Folktale:** A story originating in oral tradition. Folktales fall into a variety of categories, including legends, ghost stories, fairy tales, fables, and anecdotes based on historical figures and events.

**Foot:** The smallest unit of rhythm in a line of poetry. In English-language poetry, a foot is typically one accented syllable combined with one or two unaccented syllables.

**Form:** The pattern or construction of a work which identifies its genre and distinguishes it from other genres.

**Formalism:** In literary criticism, the belief that literature should follow prescribed rules of construction, such as those that govern the sonnet form.

**Fourteener Meter:** See *Meter*

**Free Verse:** Poetry that lacks regular metrical and rhyme patterns but that tries to capture the cadences of everyday speech. The form allows a poet to exploit a variety of rhythmical effects within a single poem.

**Futurism:** A flamboyant literary and artistic movement that developed in France, Italy, and Russia from 1908 through the 1920s. Futurist theater and poetry abandoned traditional literary forms. In their place, followers of the movement attempted to achieve total freedom of expression through bizarre imagery and deformed or newly invented words. The Futurists were self-consciously modern artists who attempted to incorporate the appearances and sounds of modern life into their work.

# G

**Genre:** A category of literary work. In critical theory, genre may refer to both the content of a given work—tragedy, comedy, pastoral—and to its form, such as poetry, novel, or drama.

**Genteel Tradition:** A term coined by critic George Santayana to describe the literary practice of certain late nineteenth-century American writers, especially New Englanders. Followers of the Genteel

Tradition emphasized conventionality in social, religious, moral, and literary standards.

**Georgian Age:** See *Georgian Poets*

**Georgian Period:** See *Georgian Poets*

**Georgian Poets:** A loose grouping of English poets during the years 1912-1922. The Georgians reacted against certain literary schools and practices, especially Victorian wordiness, turn-of-the-century aestheticism, and contemporary urban realism. In their place, the Georgians embraced the nineteenth-century poetic practices of William Wordsworth and the other Lake Poets.

**Georgic:** A poem about farming and the farmer's way of life, named from Virgil's *Georgics*.

**Gilded Age:** A period in American history during the 1870s characterized by political corruption and materialism. A number of important novels of social and political criticism were written during this time.

**Gothic:** See *Gothicism*

**Gothicism:** In literary criticism, works characterized by a taste for the medieval or morbidly attractive. A gothic novel prominently features elements of horror, the supernatural, gloom, and violence: clanking chains, terror, charnel houses, ghosts, medieval castles, and mysteriously slamming doors. The term "gothic novel" is also applied to novels that lack elements of the traditional Gothic setting but that create a similar atmosphere of terror or dread.

**Graveyard School:** A group of eighteenth-century English poets who wrote long, picturesque meditations on death. Their works were designed to cause the reader to ponder immortality.

**Great Chain of Being:** The belief that all things and creatures in nature are organized in a hierarchy from inanimate objects at the bottom to God at the top. This system of belief was popular in the seventeenth and eighteenth centuries.

**Grotesque:** In literary criticism, the subject matter of a work or a style of expression characterized by exaggeration, deformity, freakishness, and disorder. The grotesque often includes an element of comic absurdity.

# H

*Haiku*: The shortest form of Japanese poetry, constructed in three lines of five, seven, and five syllables respectively. The message of a *haiku* poem usually centers on some aspect of spirituality and provokes an emotional response in the reader.

**Half Rhyme:** See *Consonance*

**Harlem Renaissance:** The Harlem Renaissance of the 1920s is generally considered the first significant movement of black writers and artists in the United States. During this period, new and established black writers published more fiction and poetry than ever before, the first influential black literary journals were established, and black authors and artists received their first widespread recognition and serious critical appraisal. Among the major writers associated with this period are Claude McKay, Jean Toomer, Countee Cullen, Langston Hughes, Arna Bontemps, Nella Larsen, and Zora Neale Hurston.

**Hellenism:** Imitation of ancient Greek thought or styles. Also, an approach to life that focuses on the growth and development of the intellect. "Hellenism" is sometimes used to refer to the belief that reason can be applied to examine all human experience.

**Heptameter:** See *Meter*

**Hero/Heroine:** The principal sympathetic character (male or female) in a literary work. Heroes and heroines typically exhibit admirable traits: idealism, courage, and integrity, for example.

**Heroic Couplet:** A rhyming couplet written in iambic pentameter (a verse with five iambic feet).

**Heroic Line:** The meter and length of a line of verse in epic or heroic poetry. This varies by language and time period.

**Heroine:** See *Hero/Heroine*

**Hexameter:** See *Meter*

**Historical Criticism:** The study of a work based on its impact on the world of the time period in which it was written.

*Hokku*: See *Haiku*

**Holocaust:** See *Holocaust Literature*

**Holocaust Literature:** Literature influenced by or written about the Holocaust of World War II. Such literature includes true stories of survival in concentration camps, escape, and life after the war, as well as fictional works and poetry.

**Homeric Simile:** An elaborate, detailed comparison written as a simile many lines in length.

**Horatian Satire:** See *Satire*

**Humanism:** A philosophy that places faith in the dignity of humankind and rejects the medieval perception of the individual as a weak, fallen creature. "Humanists" typically believe in the perfectibility of human nature and view reason and education as the means to that end.

**Humors:** Mentions of the humors refer to the ancient Greek theory that a person's health and personality were determined by the balance of four basic fluids in the body: blood, phlegm, yellow bile, and black bile. A dominance of any fluid would cause extremes in behavior. An excess of blood created a sanguine person who was joyful, aggressive, and passionate; a phlegmatic person was shy, fearful, and sluggish; too much yellow bile led to a choleric temperament characterized by impatience, anger, bitterness, and stubbornness; and excessive black bile created melancholy, a state of laziness, gluttony, and lack of motivation.

**Humours:** See *Humors*

**Hyperbole:** In literary criticism, deliberate exaggeration used to achieve an effect.

# I

**Iamb:** See *Foot*

**Idiom:** A word construction or verbal expression closely associated with a given language.

**Image:** A concrete representation of an object or sensory experience. Typically, such a representation helps evoke the feelings associated with the object or experience itself. Images are either "literal" or "figurative." Literal images are especially concrete and involve little or no extension of the obvious meaning of the words used to express them. Figurative images do not follow the literal meaning of the words exactly. Images in literature are usually visual, but the term "image" can also refer to the representation of any sensory experience.

**Imagery:** The array of images in a literary work. Also, figurative language.

**Imagism:** An English and American poetry movement that flourished between 1908 and 1917. The Imagists used precise, clearly presented images in their works. They also used common, everyday speech and aimed for conciseness, concrete imagery, and the creation of new rhythms.

*In medias res*: A Latin term meaning "in the middle of things." It refers to the technique of beginning a story at its midpoint and then using various flashback devices to reveal previous action.

**Induction:** The process of reaching a conclusion by reasoning from specific premises to form a general premise. Also, an introductory portion of a work of literature, especially a play.

**Intentional Fallacy:** The belief that judgments of a literary work based solely on an author's stated or implied intentions are false and misleading. Critics who believe in the concept of the intentional fallacy typically argue that the work itself is sufficient matter for interpretation, even though they may concede that an author's statement of purpose can be useful.

**Interior Monologue:** A narrative technique in which characters' thoughts are revealed in a way that appears to be uncontrolled by the author. The interior monologue typically aims to reveal the inner self of a character. It portrays emotional experiences as they occur at both a conscious and unconscious level. images are often used to represent sensations or emotions.

**Internal Rhyme:** Rhyme that occurs within a single line of verse.

**Irish Literary Renaissance:** A late nineteenth- and early twentieth-century movement in Irish literature. Members of the movement aimed to reduce the influence of British culture in Ireland and create an Irish national literature.

**Irony:** In literary criticism, the effect of language in which the intended meaning is the opposite of what is stated.

**Italian Sonnet:** See *Sonnet*

# J

**Jacobean Age:** The period of the reign of James I of England (1603-1625). The early literature of this period reflected the worldview of the Elizabethan Age, but a darker, more cynical attitude steadily grew in the art and literature of the Jacobean Age. This was an important time for English drama and poetry.

**Jargon:** Language that is used or understood only by a select group of people. Jargon may refer to terminology used in a certain profession, such as computer jargon, or it may refer to any nonsensical language that is not understood by most people.

**Journalism:** Writing intended for publication in a newspaper or magazine, or for broadcast on a radio or television program featuring news, sports, entertainment, or other timely material.

# K

**Knickerbocker Group:** A somewhat indistinct group of New York writers of the first half of the nineteenth century. Members of the group were linked only by location and a common theme: New York life.

*Kunstlerroman*: See *Bildungsroman*

# L

*Lais*: See *Lay*

**Lake Poets:** See *Lake School*

**Lake School:** These poets all lived in the Lake District of England at the turn of the nineteenth century. As a group, they followed no single "school" of thought or literary practice, although their works were uniformly disparaged by the *Edinburgh Review.*

**Lay:** A song or simple narrative poem. The form originated in medieval France. Early French *lais* were often based on the Celtic legends and other tales sung by Breton minstrels—thus the name of the "Breton lay." In fourteenth-century England, the term "lay" was used to describe short narratives written in imitation of the Breton lays.

*Leitmotiv*: See *Motif*

**Literal Language:** An author uses literal language when he or she writes without exaggerating or embellishing the subject matter and without any tools of figurative language.

**Literary Ballad:** See *Ballad*

**Literature:** Literature is broadly defined as any written or spoken material, but the term most often refers to creative works.

**Lost Generation:** A term first used by Gertrude Stein to describe the post-World War I generation of American writers: men and women haunted by a sense of betrayal and emptiness brought about by the destructiveness of the war.

**Lyric Poetry:** A poem expressing the subjective feelings and personal emotions of the poet. Such poetry is melodic, since it was originally accompanied by a lyre in recitals. Most Western poetry in the twentieth century may be classified as lyrical.

# M

**Mannerism:** Exaggerated, artificial adherence to a literary manner or style. Also, a popular style of the visual arts of late sixteenth-century Europe that was marked by elongation of the human form and by intentional spatial distortion. Literary works that are self-consciously high-toned and artistic are often said to be "mannered."

**Masculine Rhyme:** See *Rhyme*

**Measure:** The foot, verse, or time sequence used in a literary work, especially a poem. Measure is often used somewhat incorrectly as a synonym for meter.

**Metaphor:** A figure of speech that expresses an idea through the image of another object. Metaphors suggest the essence of the first object by identifying it with certain qualities of the second object.

**Metaphysical Conceit:** See *Conceit*

**Metaphysical Poetry:** The body of poetry produced by a group of seventeenth-century English writers called the "Metaphysical Poets." The group includes John Donne and Andrew Marvell. The Metaphysical Poets made use of everyday speech, intellectual analysis, and unique imagery. They aimed to portray the ordinary conflicts and contradictions of life. Their poems often took the form of an argument, and many of them emphasize physical and religious love as well as the fleeting nature of life. Elaborate conceits are typical in metaphysical poetry.

**Metaphysical Poets:** See *Metaphysical Poetry*

**Meter:** In literary criticism, the repetition of sound patterns that creates a rhythm in poetry. The patterns are based on the number of syllables and the presence and absence of accents. The unit of rhythm in a line is called a foot. Types of meter are classified according to the number of feet in a line. These are the standard English lines: Monometer, one foot; Dimeter, two feet; Trimeter, three feet; Tetrameter, four feet; Pentameter, five feet; Hexameter, six feet (also called the Alexandrine); Heptameter, seven feet (also called the "Fourteener" when the feet are iambic).

**Modernism:** Modern literary practices. Also, the principles of a literary school that lasted from roughly the beginning of the twentieth century until the end of World War II. Modernism is defined by its rejection of the literary conventions of the nineteenth century and by its opposition to conventional morality, taste, traditions, and economic values.

**Monologue:** A composition, written or oral, by a single individual. More specifically, a speech given by a single individual in a drama or other public entertainment. It has no set length, although it is usually several or more lines long.

**Monometer:** See *Meter*

**Mood:** The prevailing emotions of a work or of the author in his or her creation of the work. The mood of a work is not always what might be expected based on its subject matter.

*Motif*: A theme, character type, image, metaphor, or other verbal element that recurs throughout a single work of literature or occurs in a number of different works over a period of time.

*Motiv*: See *Motif*

**Muckrakers:** An early twentieth-century group of American writers. Typically, their works exposed the wrongdoings of big business and government in the United States.

**Muses:** Nine Greek mythological goddesses, the daughters of Zeus and Mnemosyne (Memory). Each muse patronized a specific area of the liberal arts and sciences. Calliope presided over epic poetry, Clio over history, Erato over love poetry, Euterpe over music or lyric poetry, Melpomene over tragedy, Polyhymnia over hymns to the gods, Terpsichore over dance, Thalia over comedy, and Urania over astronomy. Poets and writers traditionally made appeals to the Muses for inspiration in their work.

**Myth:** An anonymous tale emerging from the traditional beliefs of a culture or social unit. Myths use supernatural explanations for natural phenomena. They may also explain cosmic issues like creation and death. Collections of myths, known as mythologies, are common to all cultures and nations, but the best-known myths belong to the Norse, Roman, and Greek mythologies.

# *N*

**Narration:** The telling of a series of events, real or invented. A narration may be either a simple narrative, in which the events are recounted chronologically, or a narrative with a plot, in which the account is given in a style reflecting the author's artistic concept of the story. Narration is sometimes used as a synonym for "storyline."

**Narrative:** A verse or prose accounting of an event or sequence of events, real or invented. The term is also used as an adjective in the sense "method of narration." For example, in literary criticism, the expression "narrative technique" usually refers to the way the author structures and presents his or her story.

**Narrative Poetry:** A nondramatic poem in which the author tells a story. Such poems may be of any length or level of complexity.

**Narrator:** The teller of a story. The narrator may be the author or a character in the story through whom the author speaks.

**Naturalism:** A literary movement of the late nineteenth and early twentieth centuries. The movement's major theorist, French novelist Emile Zola, envisioned a type of fiction that would examine human life with the objectivity of scientific inquiry. The Naturalists typically viewed human beings as either the products of "biological determinism," ruled by hereditary instincts and engaged in an endless struggle for survival, or as the products of "socioeconomic determinism," ruled by social and economic forces beyond their control. In their works, the Naturalists generally ignored the highest levels of society and focused on degradation: poverty, alcoholism, prostitution, insanity, and disease.

**Negritude:** A literary movement based on the concept of a shared cultural bond on the part of black Africans, wherever they may be in the world. It traces its origins to the former French colonies of Africa and the Caribbean. Negritude poets, novelists, and essayists generally stress four points in their writings: One, black alienation from traditional African culture can lead to feelings of inferiority. Two, European colonialism and Western education should be resisted. Three, black Africans should seek to affirm and define their own identity. Four, African culture can and should be reclaimed. Many Negritude writers also claim that blacks can make unique contributions to the world, based on a heightened appreciation of nature, rhythm, and human emotions—aspects of life they say are not so highly valued in the materialistic and rationalistic West.

**Negro Renaissance:** See *Harlem Renaissance*

**Neoclassical Period:** See *Neoclassicism*

**Neoclassicism:** In literary criticism, this term refers to the revival of the attitudes and styles of expression of classical literature. It is generally used to describe a period in European history beginning in the late seventeenth century and lasting until about 1800. In its purest form, Neoclassicism marked a return to order, proportion, restraint, logic, accuracy, and decorum. In England, where Neoclassicism perhaps was most popular, it reflected the influence of seventeenth-century French writers, especially dramatists. Neoclassical writers typically reacted against the intensity and enthusiasm of the Renaissance period. They wrote works that appealed to the intellect, using elevated language and classical literary forms such as satire and the ode. Neoclassical works were often governed by the classical goal of instruction.

**Neoclassicists:** See *Neoclassicism*

**New Criticism:** A movement in literary criticism, dating from the late 1920s, that stressed close textual analysis in the interpretation of works of literature. The New Critics saw little merit in historical and biographical analysis. Rather, they aimed to examine the text alone, free from the question of how external events—biographical or otherwise—may have helped shape it.

**New Journalism:** A type of writing in which the journalist presents factual information in a form usually used in fiction. New journalism emphasizes description, narration, and character development to bring readers closer to the human element of the story, and is often used in personality profiles and in-depth feature articles. It is not compatible with "straight" or "hard" newswriting, which is generally composed in a brief, fact-based style.

**New Journalists:** See *New Journalism*

**New Negro Movement:** See *Harlem Renaissance*

**Noble Savage:** The idea that primitive man is noble and good but becomes evil and corrupted as he becomes civilized. The concept of the noble savage originated in the Renaissance period but is more closely identified with such later writers as Jean-Jacques Rousseau and Aphra Behn.

# O

**Objective Correlative:** An outward set of objects, a situation, or a chain of events corresponding to an inward experience and evoking this experience in the reader. The term frequently appears in modern criticism in discussions of authors' intended effects on the emotional responses of readers.

**Objectivity:** A quality in writing characterized by the absence of the author's opinion or feeling about the subject matter. Objectivity is an important factor in criticism.

**Occasional Verse:** poetry written on the occasion of a significant historical or personal event. *Vers de societe* is sometimes called occasional verse although it is of a less serious nature.

**Octave:** A poem or stanza composed of eight lines. The term octave most often represents the first eight lines of a Petrarchan sonnet.

**Ode:** Name given to an extended lyric poem characterized by exalted emotion and dignified style. An ode usually concerns a single, serious theme. Most odes, but not all, are addressed to an object or individual. Odes are distinguished from other lyric-poetic forms by their complex rhythmic and stanzaic patterns.

**Oedipus Complex:** A son's amorous obsession with his mother. The phrase is derived from the story of the ancient Theban hero Oedipus, who un-

knowingly killed his father and married his mother.

**Omniscience:** See *Point of View*

**Onomatopoeia:** The use of words whose sounds express or suggest their meaning. In its simplest sense, onomatopoeia may be represented by words that mimic the sounds they denote such as "hiss" or "meow." At a more subtle level, the pattern and rhythm of sounds and rhymes of a line or poem may be onomatopoeic.

**Oral Tradition:** See *Oral Transmission*

**Oral Transmission:** A process by which songs, ballads, folklore, and other material are transmitted by word of mouth. The tradition of oral transmission predates the written record systems of literate society. Oral transmission preserves material sometimes over generations, although often with variations. Memory plays a large part in the recitation and preservation of orally transmitted material.

*Ottava Rima:* An eight-line stanza of poetry composed in iambic pentameter (a five-foot line in which each foot consists of an unaccented syllable followed by an accented syllable), following the abababcc rhyme scheme.

**Oxymoron:** A phrase combining two contradictory terms. Oxymorons may be intentional or unintentional.

# P

**Pantheism:** The idea that all things are both a manifestation or revelation of God and a part of God at the same time. Pantheism was a common attitude in the early societies of Egypt, India, and Greece—the term derives from the Greek *pan* meaning "all" and *theos* meaning "deity." It later became a significant part of the Christian faith.

**Parable:** A story intended to teach a moral lesson or answer an ethical question.

**Paradox:** A statement that appears illogical or contradictory at first, but may actually point to an underlying truth.

**Parallelism:** A method of comparison of two ideas in which each is developed in the same grammatical structure.

**Parnassianism:** A mid nineteenth-century movement in French literature. Followers of the movement stressed adherence to well-defined artistic forms as a reaction against the often chaotic expression of the artist's ego that dominated the work of the Romantics. The Parnassians also rejected the moral, ethical, and social themes exhibited in the works of French Romantics such as Victor Hugo. The aesthetic doctrines of the Parnassians strongly influenced the later symbolist and decadent movements.

**Parody:** In literary criticism, this term refers to an imitation of a serious literary work or the signature style of a particular author in a ridiculous manner. A typical parody adopts the style of the original and applies it to an inappropriate subject for humorous effect. Parody is a form of satire and could be considered the literary equivalent of a caricature or cartoon.

**Pastoral:** A term derived from the Latin word "pastor," meaning shepherd. A pastoral is a literary composition on a rural theme. The conventions of the pastoral were originated by the third-century Greek poet Theocritus, who wrote about the experiences, love affairs, and pastimes of Sicilian shepherds. In a pastoral, characters and language of a courtly nature are often placed in a simple setting. The term pastoral is also used to classify dramas, elegies, and lyrics that exhibit the use of country settings and shepherd characters.

**Pathetic Fallacy:** A term coined by English critic John Ruskin to identify writing that falsely endows nonhuman things with human intentions and feelings, such as "angry clouds" and "sad trees."

**Pen Name:** See *Pseudonym*

**Pentameter:** See *Meter*

*Persona*: A Latin term meaning "mask." *Personae* are the characters in a fictional work of literature. The *persona* generally functions as a mask through which the author tells a story in a voice other than his or her own. A *persona* is usually either a character in a story who acts as a narrator or an "implied author," a voice created by the author to act as the narrator for himself or herself.

*Personae*: See *Persona*

**Personal Point of View:** See *Point of View*

**Personification:** A figure of speech that gives human qualities to abstract ideas, animals, and inanimate objects.

**Petrarchan Sonnet:** See *Sonnet*

**Phenomenology:** A method of literary criticism based on the belief that things have no existence outside of human consciousness or awareness. Proponents of this theory believe that art is a process that takes place in the mind of the observer as he or she contemplates an object rather than a quality of the object itself.

**Plagiarism:** Claiming another person's written material as one's own. Plagiarism can take the form of direct, word-for-word copying or the theft of the substance or idea of the work.

**Platonic Criticism:** A form of criticism that stresses an artistic work's usefulness as an agent of social engineering rather than any quality or value of the work itself.

**Platonism:** The embracing of the doctrines of the philosopher Plato, popular among the poets of the Renaissance and the Romantic period. Platonism is more flexible than Aristotelian Criticism and places more emphasis on the supernatural and unknown aspects of life.

**Plot:** In literary criticism, this term refers to the pattern of events in a narrative or drama. In its simplest sense, the plot guides the author in composing the work and helps the reader follow the work. Typically, plots exhibit causality and unity and have a beginning, a middle, and an end. Sometimes, however, a plot may consist of a series of disconnected events, in which case it is known as an "episodic plot."

**Poem:** In its broadest sense, a composition utilizing rhyme, meter, concrete detail, and expressive language to create a literary experience with emotional and aesthetic appeal.

**Poet:** An author who writes poetry or verse. The term is also used to refer to an artist or writer who has an exceptional gift for expression, imagination, and energy in the making of art in any form.

**Poete maudit:** A term derived from Paul Verlaine's *Les poetes maudits* (*The Accursed Poets*), a collection of essays on the French symbolist writers Stephane Mallarme, Arthur Rimbaud, and Tristan Corbiere. In the sense intended by Verlaine, the poet is "accursed" for choosing to explore extremes of human experience outside of middle-class society.

**Poetic Fallacy:** See *Pathetic Fallacy*

**Poetic Justice:** An outcome in a literary work, not necessarily a poem, in which the good are rewarded and the evil are punished, especially in ways that particularly fit their virtues or crimes.

**Poetic License:** Distortions of fact and literary convention made by a writer—not always a poet—for the sake of the effect gained. Poetic license is closely related to the concept of "artistic freedom."

**Poetics:** This term has two closely related meanings. It denotes (1) an aesthetic theory in literary criticism about the essence of poetry or (2) rules prescribing the proper methods, content, style, or diction of poetry. The term poetics may also refer to theories about literature in general, not just poetry.

**Poetry:** In its broadest sense, writing that aims to present ideas and evoke an emotional experience in the reader through the use of meter, imagery, connotative and concrete words, and a carefully constructed structure based on rhythmic patterns. Poetry typically relies on words and expressions that have several layers of meaning. It also makes use of the effects of regular rhythm on the ear and may make a strong appeal to the senses through the use of imagery.

**Point of View:** The narrative perspective from which a literary work is presented to the reader. There are four traditional points of view. The "third person omniscient" gives the reader a "godlike" perspective, unrestricted by time or place, from which to see actions and look into the minds of characters. This allows the author to comment openly on characters and events in the work. The "third person" point of view presents the events of the story from outside of any single character's perception, much like the omniscient point of view, but the reader must understand the action as it takes place and without any special insight into characters' minds or motivations. The "first person" or "personal" point of view relates events as they are perceived by a single character. The main character "tells" the story and may offer opinions about the action and characters which differ from those of the author. Much less common than omniscient, third person, and first person is the "second person" point of view, wherein the author tells the story as if it is happening to the reader.

**Polemic:** A work in which the author takes a stand on a controversial subject, such as abortion or religion. Such works are often extremely argumentative or provocative.

**Pornography:** Writing intended to provoke feelings of lust in the reader. Such works are often condemned by critics and teachers, but those which can be shown to have literary value are viewed less harshly.

**Post-Aesthetic Movement:** An artistic response made by African Americans to the black aesthetic movement of the 1960s and early '70s. Writers since that time have adopted a somewhat different tone in their work, with less emphasis placed on the disparity between black and white in the United States. In the words of post-aesthetic authors such as Toni Morrison, John Edgar Wideman, and Kristin Hunter, African Americans are portrayed as looking inward for answers to their own questions, rather than always looking to the outside world.

**Postmodernism:** Writing from the 1960s forward characterized by experimentation and continuing to apply some of the fundamentals of modernism, which included existentialism and alienation. Postmodernists have gone a step further in the rejection of tradition begun with the modernists by also rejecting traditional forms, preferring the anti-novel over the novel and the anti-hero over the hero.

**Pre-Raphaelites:** A circle of writers and artists in mid nineteenth-century England. Valuing the pre-Renaissance artistic qualities of religious symbolism, lavish pictorialism, and natural sensuousness, the Pre-Raphaelites cultivated a sense of mystery and melancholy that influenced later writers associated with the Symbolist and Decadent movements.

**Primitivism:** The belief that primitive peoples were nobler and less flawed than civilized peoples because they had not been subjected to the tainting influence of society.

**Projective Verse:** A form of free verse in which the poet's breathing pattern determines the lines of the poem. Poets who advocate projective verse are against all formal structures in writing, including meter and form.

**Prologue:** An introductory section of a literary work. It often contains information establishing the situation of the characters or presents information about the setting, time period, or action. In drama, the prologue is spoken by a chorus or by one of the principal characters.

**Prose:** A literary medium that attempts to mirror the language of everyday speech. It is distinguished from poetry by its use of unmetered, unrhymed language consisting of logically related sentences. Prose is usually grouped into paragraphs that form a cohesive whole such as an essay or a novel.

***Prosopopoeia:*** See *Personification*

**Protagonist:** The central character of a story who serves as a focus for its themes and incidents and as the principal rationale for its development. The protagonist is sometimes referred to in discussions of modern literature as the hero or anti-hero.

**Proverb:** A brief, sage saying that expresses a truth about life in a striking manner.

**Pseudonym:** A name assumed by a writer, most often intended to prevent his or her identification as the author of a work. Two or more authors may work together under one pseudonym, or an author may use a different name for each genre he or she publishes in. Some publishing companies maintain "house pseudonyms," under which any number of authors may write installations in a series. Some authors also choose a pseudonym over their real names the way an actor may use a stage name.

**Pun:** A play on words that have similar sounds but different meanings.

**Pure Poetry:** poetry written without instructional intent or moral purpose that aims only to please a reader by its imagery or musical flow. The term pure poetry is used as the antonym of the term "didacticism."

# Q

**Quatrain:** A four-line stanza of a poem or an entire poem consisting of four lines.

# R

**Realism:** A nineteenth-century European literary movement that sought to portray familiar characters, situations, and settings in a realistic manner. This was done primarily by using an objective narrative point of view and through the buildup of accurate detail. The standard for success of any realistic work depends on how faithfully it transfers common experience into fictional forms. The realistic method may be altered or extended, as in stream of consciousness writing, to record highly subjective experience.

**Refrain:** A phrase repeated at intervals throughout a poem. A refrain may appear at the end of each stanza or at less regular intervals. It may be altered slightly at each appearance.

**Renaissance:** The period in European history that marked the end of the Middle Ages. It began in Italy in the late fourteenth century. In broad terms, it is usually seen as spanning the fourteenth, fifteenth, and sixteenth centuries, although it did not reach Great Britain, for example, until the 1480s or so. The Renaissance saw an awakening in almost every sphere of human activity, especially science, philosophy, and the arts. The period is best defined by the emergence of a general philosophy that emphasized the importance of the intellect, the individual, and world affairs. It contrasts strongly with the medieval worldview, characterized by the dominant concerns of faith, the social collective, and spiritual salvation.

*Repartee*: Conversation featuring snappy retorts and witticisms.

**Restoration:** See *Restoration Age*

**Restoration Age:** A period in English literature beginning with the crowning of Charles II in 1660 and running to about 1700. The era, which was characterized by a reaction against Puritanism, was the first great age of the comedy of manners. The finest literature of the era is typically witty and urbane, and often lewd.

**Rhetoric:** In literary criticism, this term denotes the art of ethical persuasion. In its strictest sense, rhetoric adheres to various principles developed since classical times for arranging facts and ideas in a clear, persuasive, appealing manner. The term is also used to refer to effective prose in general and theories of or methods for composing effective prose.

**Rhetorical Question:** A question intended to provoke thought, but not an expressed answer, in the reader. It is most commonly used in oratory and other persuasive genres.

**Rhyme:** When used as a noun in literary criticism, this term generally refers to a poem in which words sound identical or very similar and appear in parallel positions in two or more lines. Rhymes are classified into different types according to where they fall in a line or stanza or according to the degree of similarity they exhibit in their spellings and sounds. Some major types of rhyme are "masculine" rhyme, "feminine" rhyme, and "triple" rhyme. In a masculine rhyme, the rhyming sound falls in a single accented syllable, as with "heat" and "eat." Feminine rhyme is a rhyme of two syllables, one stressed and one unstressed, as with "merry" and "tarry." Triple rhyme matches the sound of the accented syllable and the two unaccented syllables that follow: "narrative" and "declarative."

**Rhyme Royal:** A stanza of seven lines composed in iambic pentameter and rhymed *ababbcc*. The name is said to be a tribute to King James I of Scotland, who made much use of the form in his poetry.

**Rhyme Scheme:** See *Rhyme*

**Rhythm:** A regular pattern of sound, time intervals, or events occurring in writing, most often and most discernably in poetry. Regular, reliable rhythm is known to be soothing to humans, while interrupted, unpredictable, or rapidly changing rhythm is disturbing. These effects are known to authors, who use them to produce a desired reaction in the reader.

*Rococo*: A style of European architecture that flourished in the eighteenth century, especially in

France. The most notable features of *rococo* are its extensive use of ornamentation and its themes of lightness, gaiety, and intimacy. In literary criticism, the term is often used disparagingly to refer to a decadent or over-ornamental style.

**Romance:**

**Romantic Age:** See *Romanticism*

**Romanticism:** This term has two widely accepted meanings. In historical criticism, it refers to a European intellectual and artistic movement of the late eighteenth and early nineteenth centuries that sought greater freedom of personal expression than that allowed by the strict rules of literary form and logic of the eighteenth-century neoclassicists. The Romantics preferred emotional and imaginative expression to rational analysis. They considered the individual to be at the center of all experience and so placed him or her at the center of their art. The Romantics believed that the creative imagination reveals nobler truths—unique feelings and attitudes—than those that could be discovered by logic or by scientific examination. Both the natural world and the state of childhood were important sources for revelations of "eternal truths." "Romanticism" is also used as a general term to refer to a type of sensibility found in all periods of literary history and usually considered to be in opposition to the principles of classicism. In this sense, Romanticism signifies any work or philosophy in which the exotic or dreamlike figure strongly, or that is devoted to individualistic expression, self-analysis, or a pursuit of a higher realm of knowledge than can be discovered by human reason.

**Romantics:** See *Romanticism*

**Russian Symbolism:** A Russian poetic movement, derived from French symbolism, that flourished between 1894 and 1910. While some Russian Symbolists continued in the French tradition, stressing aestheticism and the importance of suggestion above didactic intent, others saw their craft as a form of mystical worship, and themselves as mediators between the supernatural and the mundane.

# S

**Satire:** A work that uses ridicule, humor, and wit to criticize and provoke change in human nature and institutions. There are two major types of satire: "formal" or "direct" satire speaks directly to the reader or to a character in the work; "indirect" satire relies upon the ridiculous behavior of its characters to make its point. Formal satire is further divided into two manners: the "Horatian," which

ridicules gently, and the "Juvenalian," which derides its subjects harshly and bitterly.

**Scansion:** The analysis or "scanning" of a poem to determine its meter and often its rhyme scheme. The most common system of scansion uses accents (slanted lines drawn above syllables) to show stressed syllables, breves (curved lines drawn above syllables) to show unstressed syllables, and vertical lines to separate each foot.

**Second Person:** See *Point of View*

**Semiotics:** The study of how literary forms and conventions affect the meaning of language.

**Sestet:** Any six-line poem or stanza.

**Setting:** The time, place, and culture in which the action of a narrative takes place. The elements of setting may include geographic location, characters' physical and mental environments, prevailing cultural attitudes, or the historical time in which the action takes place.

**Shakespearean Sonnet:** See *Sonnet*

**Signifying Monkey:** A popular trickster figure in black folklore, with hundreds of tales about this character documented since the 19th century.

**Simile:** A comparison, usually using "like" or "as", of two essentially dissimilar things, as in "coffee as cold as ice" or "He sounded like a broken record."

**Slang:** A type of informal verbal communication that is generally unacceptable for formal writing. Slang words and phrases are often colorful exaggerations used to emphasize the speaker's point; they may also be shortened versions of an often-used word or phrase.

**Slant Rhyme:** See *Consonance*

**Slave Narrative:** Autobiographical accounts of American slave life as told by escaped slaves. These works first appeared during the abolition movement of the 1830s through the 1850s.

**Social Realism:** See *Socialist Realism*

**Socialist Realism:** The Socialist Realism school of literary theory was proposed by Maxim Gorky and established as a dogma by the first Soviet Congress of Writers. It demanded adherence to a communist worldview in works of literature. Its doctrines required an objective viewpoint comprehensible to the working classes and themes of social struggle featuring strong proletarian heroes.

**Soliloquy:** A monologue in a drama used to give the audience information and to develop the speaker's character. It is typically a projection of the speaker's innermost thoughts. Usually delivered while the speaker is alone on stage, a soliloquy is intended to present an illusion of unspoken reflection.

**Sonnet:** A fourteen-line poem, usually composed in iambic pentameter, employing one of several rhyme schemes. There are three major types of sonnets, upon which all other variations of the form are based: the "Petrarchan" or "Italian" sonnet, the "Shakespearean" or "English" sonnet, and the "Spenserian" sonnet. A Petrarchan sonnet consists of an octave rhymed *abbaabba* and a "sestet" rhymed either *cdecde, cdccdc,* or *cdedce.* The octave poses a question or problem, relates a narrative, or puts forth a proposition; the sestet presents a solution to the problem, comments upon the narrative, or applies the proposition put forth in the octave. The Shakespearean sonnet is divided into three quatrains and a couplet rhymed *abab cdcd efef gg.* The couplet provides an epigrammatic comment on the narrative or problem put forth in the quatrains. The Spenserian sonnet uses three quatrains and a couplet like the Shakespearean, but links their three rhyme schemes in this way: *abab bcbc cdcd ee.* The Spenserian sonnet develops its theme in two parts like the Petrarchan, its final six lines resolving a problem, analyzing a narrative, or applying a proposition put forth in its first eight lines.

**Spenserian Sonnet:** See *Sonnet*

**Spenserian Stanza:** A nine-line stanza having eight verses in iambic pentameter, its ninth verse in iambic hexameter, and the rhyme scheme ababbcbcc.

**Spondee:** In poetry meter, a foot consisting of two long or stressed syllables occurring together. This form is quite rare in English verse, and is usually composed of two monosyllabic words.

**Sprung Rhythm:** Versification using a specific number of accented syllables per line but disregarding the number of unaccented syllables that fall in each line, producing an irregular rhythm in the poem.

**Stanza:** A subdivision of a poem consisting of lines grouped together, often in recurring patterns of rhyme, line length, and meter. Stanzas may also serve as units of thought in a poem much like paragraphs in prose.

**Stereotype:** A stereotype was originally the name for a duplication made during the printing process; this led to its modern definition as a person or thing that is (or is assumed to be) the same as all others of its type.

**Stream of Consciousness:** A narrative technique for rendering the inward experience of a character. This technique is designed to give the impression of an ever-changing series of thoughts, emotions, images, and memories in the spontaneous and seemingly illogical order that they occur in life.

**Structuralism:** A twentieth-century movement in literary criticism that examines how literary texts arrive at their meanings, rather than the meanings themselves. There are two major types of structuralist analysis: one examines the way patterns of linguistic structures unify a specific text and emphasize certain elements of that text, and the other interprets the way literary forms and conventions affect the meaning of language itself.

**Structure:** The form taken by a piece of literature. The structure may be made obvious for ease of understanding, as in nonfiction works, or may be obscured for artistic purposes, as in some poetry or seemingly "unstructured" prose.

***Sturm und Drang:*** A German term meaning "storm and stress." It refers to a German literary movement of the 1770s and 1780s that reacted against the order and rationalism of the enlightenment, focusing instead on the intense experience of extraordinary individuals.

**Style:** A writer's distinctive manner of arranging words to suit his or her ideas and purpose in writing. The unique imprint of the author's personality upon his or her writing, style is the product of an author's way of arranging ideas and his or her use of diction, different sentence structures, rhythm, figures of speech, rhetorical principles, and other elements of composition.

**Subject:** The person, event, or theme at the center of a work of literature. A work may have one or more subjects of each type, with shorter works tending to have fewer and longer works tending to have more.

**Subjectivity:** Writing that expresses the author's personal feelings about his subject, and which may or may not include factual information about the subject.

**Surrealism:** A term introduced to criticism by Guillaume Apollinaire and later adopted by Andre Breton. It refers to a French literary and artistic movement founded in the 1920s. The Surrealists sought to express unconscious thoughts and feelings in their works. The best-known technique used for achieving this aim was automatic writing—transcriptions of spontaneous outpourings from the unconscious. The Surrealists proposed to unify the contrary levels of conscious and unconscious, dream and reality, objectivity and subjectivity into a new level of "super-realism."

**Suspense:** A literary device in which the author maintains the audience's attention through the buildup of events, the outcome of which will soon be revealed.

**Syllogism:** A method of presenting a logical argument. In its most basic form, the syllogism consists of a major premise, a minor premise, and a conclusion.

**Symbol:** Something that suggests or stands for something else without losing its original identity. In literature, symbols combine their literal meaning with the suggestion of an abstract concept. Literary symbols are of two types: those that carry complex associations of meaning no matter what their contexts, and those that derive their suggestive meaning from their functions in specific literary works.

**Symbolism:** This term has two widely accepted meanings. In historical criticism, it denotes an early modernist literary movement initiated in France during the nineteenth century that reacted against the prevailing standards of realism. Writers in this movement aimed to evoke, indirectly and symbolically, an order of being beyond the material world of the five senses. Poetic expression of personal emotion figured strongly in the movement, typically by means of a private set of symbols uniquely identifiable with the individual poet. The principal aim of the Symbolists was to express in words the highly complex feelings that grew out of everyday contact with the world. In a broader sense, the term "symbolism" refers to the use of one object to represent another.

**Symbolist:** See *Symbolism*

**Symbolist Movement:** See *Symbolism*

**Sympathetic Fallacy:** See *Affective Fallacy*

# *T*

***Tanka:*** A form of Japanese poetry similar to *haiku*. A *tanka* is five lines long, with the lines containing five, seven, five, seven, and seven syllables respectively.

***Terza Rima:*** A three-line stanza form in poetry in which the rhymes are made on the last word of each line in the following manner: the first and third lines of the first stanza, then the second line of the first stanza and the first and third lines of the second stanza, and so on with the middle line of any

stanza rhyming with the first and third lines of the following stanza.

**Tetrameter:** See *Meter*

**Textual Criticism:** A branch of literary criticism that seeks to establish the authoritative text of a literary work. Textual critics typically compare all known manuscripts or printings of a single work in order to assess the meanings of differences and revisions. This procedure allows them to arrive at a definitive version that (supposedly) corresponds to the author's original intention.

**Theme:** The main point of a work of literature. The term is used interchangeably with thesis.

**Thesis:** A thesis is both an essay and the point argued in the essay. Thesis novels and thesis plays share the quality of containing a thesis which is supported through the action of the story.

**Third Person:** See *Point of View*

**Tone:** The author's attitude toward his or her audience may be deduced from the tone of the work. A formal tone may create distance or convey politeness, while an informal tone may encourage a friendly, intimate, or intrusive feeling in the reader. The author's attitude toward his or her subject matter may also be deduced from the tone of the words he or she uses in discussing it.

**Tragedy:** A drama in prose or poetry about a noble, courageous hero of excellent character who, because of some tragic character flaw or *hamartia*, brings ruin upon him- or herself. Tragedy treats its subjects in a dignified and serious manner, using poetic language to help evoke pity and fear and bring about catharsis, a purging of these emotions. The tragic form was practiced extensively by the ancient Greeks. In the Middle Ages, when classical works were virtually unknown, tragedy came to denote any works about the fall of persons from exalted to low conditions due to any reason: fate, vice, weakness, etc. According to the classical definition of tragedy, such works present the "pathetic"—that which evokes pity—rather than the tragic. The classical form of tragedy was revived in the sixteenth century; it flourished especially on the Elizabethan stage. In modern times, dramatists have attempted to adapt the form to the needs of modern society by drawing their heroes from the ranks of ordinary men and women and defining the nobility of these heroes in terms of spirit rather than exalted social standing.

**Tragic Flaw:** In a tragedy, the quality within the hero or heroine which leads to his or her downfall.

**Transcendentalism:** An American philosophical and religious movement, based in New England from around 1835 until the Civil War. Transcendentalism was a form of American romanticism that had its roots abroad in the works of Thomas Carlyle, Samuel Coleridge, and Johann Wolfgang von Goethe. The Transcendentalists stressed the importance of intuition and subjective experience in communication with God. They rejected religious dogma and texts in favor of mysticism and scientific naturalism. They pursued truths that lie beyond the "colorless" realms perceived by reason and the senses and were active social reformers in public education, women's rights, and the abolition of slavery.

**Trickster:** A character or figure common in Native American and African literature who uses his ingenuity to defeat enemies and escape difficult situations. Tricksters are most often animals, such as the spider, hare, or coyote, although they may take the form of humans as well.

**Trimeter:** See *Meter*

**Triple Rhyme:** See *Rhyme*

**Trochee:** See *Foot*

# U

**Understatement:** See *Irony*

**Unities:** Strict rules of dramatic structure, formulated by Italian and French critics of the Renaissance and based loosely on the principles of drama discussed by Aristotle in his *Poetics*. Foremost among these rules were the three unities of action, time, and place that compelled a dramatist to: (1) construct a single plot with a beginning, middle, and end that details the causal relationships of action and character; (2) restrict the action to the events of a single day; and (3) limit the scene to a single place or city. The unities were observed faithfully by continental European writers until the Romantic Age, but they were never regularly observed in English drama. Modern dramatists are typically more concerned with a unity of impression or emotional effect than with any of the classical unities.

**Urban Realism:** A branch of realist writing that attempts to accurately reflect the often harsh facts of modern urban existence.

**Utopia:** A fictional perfect place, such as "paradise" or "heaven."

**Utopian:** See *Utopia*

**Utopianism:** See *Utopia*

# V

**Verisimilitude:** Literally, the appearance of truth. In literary criticism, the term refers to aspects of a work of literature that seem true to the reader.

*Vers de societe:* See *Occasional Verse*

*Vers libre:* See *Free Verse*

**Verse:** A line of metered language, a line of a poem, or any work written in verse.

**Versification:** The writing of verse. Versification may also refer to the meter, rhyme, and other mechanical components of a poem.

**Victorian:** Refers broadly to the reign of Queen Victoria of England (1837-1901) and to anything with qualities typical of that era. For example, the qualities of smug narrowmindedness, bourgeois materialism, faith in social progress, and priggish morality are often considered Victorian. This stereotype is contradicted by such dramatic intellectual developments as the theories of Charles Darwin, Karl Marx, and Sigmund Freud (which stirred strong debates in England) and the critical attitudes of serious Victorian writers like Charles Dickens and George Eliot. In literature, the Victorian Period was the great age of the English novel, and the latter part of the era saw the rise of movements such as decadence and symbolism.

**Victorian Age:** See *Victorian*

**Victorian Period:** See *Victorian*

# W

*Weltanschauung:* A German term referring to a person's worldview or philosophy.

*Weltschmerz:* A German term meaning "world pain." It describes a sense of anguish about the nature of existence, usually associated with a melancholy, pessimistic attitude.

# Z

*Zarzuela:* A type of Spanish operetta.

*Zeitgeist:* A German term meaning "spirit of the time." It refers to the moral and intellectual trends of a given era.

# Cumulative
# Author/Title Index

Cumulative Author/Title Index

# Cumulative
# Nationality/Ethnicity Index

# Subject/Theme Index